WEBSTER'S
SPANISH
dictionary

Published 2005 by Geddes & Grosset,
David Dale House, New Lanark, ML11 9DJ, Scotland
First published in this edition 2005, reprinted 2006

ISBN 10: 1 84205 500 3
ISBN 13: 978 1 84205 500 7

Printed and bound in China

Contents

Abbreviations / Abreviaturas

abrev	abbreviation	abreviatura
adj	adjective	adjectivo
adv	adverb	adverbio
art	article	artículo
auto	automobile	automóvil
aux	auxiliary	auxiliar
bot	botany	botánica
chem	chemistry	química
col	colloquial term	lengua familiar
com	commerce	comercio
compd	in compounds	usada en palabras compuestas
comput	computers	informática
conj	conjunction	conjunción
dep	sport	deporte
excl	exclamation	exclamación
f	feminine noun	sustantivo femenino
fam	colloquial term	lengua familiar
ferro	railway	ferrocarrilero
fig	figurative use	uso figurado
gr	grammar	gramática
imp	impersonal	impersonal
inform	computers	informática
interj	interjection	interjección
invar	invariable	invariable
irr	irregular	irregular
jur	law term	jurisprudencia
law	law term	jurisprudencia
ling	linguistics	lingüística
m	masculine noun	sustantivo masculino
mar	marine term	vocablo marítimo
mat, math	mathematics	matemáticas
med	medicine	medicina
mil	military term	lo militar
mus	music	música
n	noun	sustantivo
pej	pejorative	peyorativo
pl	plural	plural
pn	pronoun	pronombre
poet	poetical term	vocablo poético

prep	preposition	preposición
quím	chemistry	química
rad	radio	radio
rail	railway	ferrocarilero
sl	slang	argot
teat	theatre	teatro
tec	technology	téchnica, tecnologia
TV	television	televisión
vb	verb	verbo
vi	intransitive verb	verbo intransitivo
vr	reflexive verb	verbo reflexivo
vt	transitive verb	verbo transitivo

Spanish–English
Dictionary

A

a *prep* to; in; at; according to; on; by; for; of.
abacería *f* grocery.
abacero *m* grocer.
ábaco *m* abacus.
abad *m* abbot.
abadejo *m* cod.
abadesa *f* abbess.
abadía *f* abbey.
abajo *adv* under; underneath; below; ~ **de** *prep* under, below.
abalanzarse *vr* to rush forward.
abalorio *m* glass bead.
abanderado *m* (*mil*) ensign; standard bearer.
abandonado/da *adj* derelict; abandoned; neglected.
abandonar *vt* to abandon; to leave; ~**se** *vr* ~ **a** to give oneself up to.
abandono *m* desertion; neglect; retirement.
abanicar *vt* to fan.
abanico *m* fan.
abaratar *vt* to lower the price of.
abarca *f* sandal.
abarcar *vt* to include.
abarrancarse *vr* to get into difficulties.
abarrotado/da *adj* packed.
abarrotar *vt* to tie down.
abastecedor/ra *m/f* supplier, purveyor.
abastecer *vt* to supply, provide.
abastecimiento *m* supplying; provisions.
abasto *m* supply of provisions.
abate *m* abbé, French abbot.
abatido/da *adj* dejected, low-spirited.
abatimiento *m* low spirits *pl*; depression.

abatir *vt* to knock down; to humble.
abdicación *f* abdication.
abdicar *vt* to abdicate.
abdomen *m* abdomen.
abdominal *adj* abdominal.
abecé *m* alphabet.
abecedario *m* alphabet; spelling book, primer.
abedul *m* birch tree.
abeja *f* bee; ~ **reina** queen bee.
abejar *m* beehive.
abejarrón *m* bumblebee.
abejón *m* drone; hornet.
abejorro *m* bumblebee.
aberración *f* aberration.
abertura *f* aperture, chink, opening.
abeto *m* fir tree.
abetunado/da *adj* dark-skinned.
abierto/ta *adj* open; sincere; frank.
abigarrado/da *adj* multicoloured.
ab intestato *adj* intestate.
abismal *adj* abysmal.
abismo *m* abyss; gulf; hell.
abjuración *f* abjuration.
abjurar *vt* to abjure, to recant; *vi*: ~ **de** to abjure, to recant.
ablandamiento *m* softening.
ablandar *vt, vi* to soften.
ablativo *m* (*gr*) ablative.
ablución *f* ablution.
abnegación *f* self-denial.
abnegado/da *adj* selfless.
abnegar *vt* to renounce.
abobado/da *adj* silly.
abobamiento *m* stupefaction.
abobar *vt* to stupefy.
abocado/da *adj* light (wine).
abocar *vt* to seize with the mouth; ~**se** *vr* to meet by agreement.

11

abochornar vt to swelter; **~se** vr to shame.

abofetear vt to slap.

abogacía f legal profession.

abogado/a m/f lawyer; barrister.

abogar vi to intercede; **~ por** to advocate.

abolengo m ancestry; inheritance from ancestors.

abolición f abolition, abrogation.

abolir vt to abolish.

abolladura f dent.

abollar vt to dent.

abominable adj abominable, cursed.

abominación f abomination.

abominar vt to detest.

abonado/da adj ready; prepared; * m/f subscriber; season ticket holder.

abonar vt to settle; to fertilize; to endorse; **~se** vr to subscribe; * vi to clear up.

abono m payment; subscription; dung, manure.

abordaje m boarding.

abordar vt (mar) to board; to broach.

aborigen m aborigine.

aborrecer vt to hate, to abhor.

aborrecible adj hateful, detestable.

aborrecimiento m abhorrence, hatred.

abortar vi to miscarry; to have an abortion.

abortivo/va adj abortive.

aborto m abortion; monster.

abortón m abortion.

abotagado/da adj swollen.

abotinado/da adj tied up.

abotonar vt to button.

abovedado/da adj vaulted.

abrasar vt to burn; to parch; **~se** vr to burn oneself.

abrazadera f bracket; clasp.

abrazar vt to embrace; to surround.

abrazo m embrace.

abrebotellas m invar bottle opener.

abrecartas m invar letter opener.

abrelatas m invar can opener.

abrevadero m watering place.

abrevar vt to water (cattle).

abreviación f abbreviation, abridgement; shortening.

abreviar vt to abridge, to cut short.

abreviatura f abbreviation.

abridor m opener.

abrigar vt to shelter; to protect; **~se** vr to take shelter.

abrigo m coat; shelter; protection; aid.

abril m April.

abrillantar vt to polish.

abrir vt to open; to unlock; **~se** vr to open up; to clear the way; to be open.

abrochador m buttonhook.

abrochar vt to button; to do up.

abrogar vt to abrogate.

abrumador/ra adj overwhelming; annoying.

abrumar vt to overwhelm.

abrupto/ta adj abrupt; steep.

absceso m abscess.

absentismo m absenteeism.

absolución f forgiveness, absolution.

absoluto/ta adj absolute.

absolutorio/a adj absolutory.

absolver vt to absolve.

absorbente adj absorbent.

absorber vt to absorb.

absorción f absorption; takeover.

absorto/a adj engrossed.

abstemio adj teetotal.

abstención f abstention.

abstenerse vr to abstain.

abstinencia f abstinence.

abstinente *adj* abstinent, abstemious.

abstracción *f* abstraction.

abstracto/ta *adj* abstract.

abstraer *vt* to abstract; ~**se** *vr* to be absorbed.

abstraído *adj* absent-minded.

absuelto/ta *adj* absolved.

absurdidad *f*, **absurdo** *m* absurdity.

absurdo *adj* absurd.

abuela *f* grandmother.

abuelo *m* grandfather.

abulia *f* lethargy.

abultado/da *adj* bulky, large, massive.

abultar *vt* to increase, to enlarge; * *vi* to be bulky.

abundancia *f* abundance.

abundante *adj* abundant, copious.

abundar *vi* to abound.

aburrido/da *adj* boring, dull.

aburrimiento *m* boredom.

aburrir *vt* to bore.

abusar *vt* to abuse.

abusivo/va *adj* abusive.

abuso *m* abuse.

abyección *f* abjectness.

abyecto/ta *adj* abject, wretched.

acá *adv* here.

acabado/da *adj* perfect, accomplished.

acabar *vt* to finish, to complete; to achieve; ~**se** *vr* to finish; to be over; to run out; * *vi* to finish; to die, to expire.

acabose *m*: **el** ~ the last straw.

acacia *f* acacia.

academia *f* academy.

académico/ca *m/f* academician; * *adj* academic.

acaecer *vi* to happen.

acallar *vt* to quiet, to hush; to soften, to appease.

acalorado/da *adj* heated.

acalorarse *vr* to become heated.

acampar *vt* to camp.

acanalado/da *adj* grooved; fluted.

acanalar *vt* to corrugate.

acanto *m* acanthus.

acantonamiento *m* cantonment.

acantonar *vt* to billet.

acaparar *vt* to monopolize; to hoard.

acariciar *vt* to fondle, to caress.

acarrear *vt* to transport; to occasion.

acarreo *m* carriage, transportation.

acaso *m* chance; * *adv* perhaps.

acatarrarse *vr* to catch (a) cold.

acaudalado/da *adj* rich, wealthy.

acaudalar *vt* to hoard.

acaudillar *vt* to command.

acceder *vi* to agree; ~ **a** to have access to.

accesible *adj* attainable; accessible.

acceso *m* access; fit.

accesorio/ria *adj*, *m* accessory.

accidentado/da *adj* uneven; hilly; eventful.

accidental *adj* accidental; casual.

accidentarse *vr* to have an accident.

accidente *m* accident.

acción *f* action, operation; share.

accionar *vt* to work.

accionista *m* shareholder.

acebo *m* holly tree.

acebuche *m* wild olive tree.

acechador/ra *m/f* spy, observer.

acechar *vt* to lie in wait for; to spy on, observe.

acecho *m* spying, watching; ambush.

aceitar *vt* to oil.

aceite *m* oil.

aceitera *f* oilcan.

aceitoso/sa *adj* oily.

aceituna *f* olive.

aceitunado/da *adj* olive-green.

aceitunero *m* olive seller.

aceituno *m* olive tree.

aceleración f acceleration.

aceleradamente adv swiftly, hastily.

acelerador m accelerator.

acelerar vt to accelerate; to hurry.

acelga f (bot) chard (a variety of beet).

acento m accent.

acentuación f accentuation.

acentuar vt to accentuate.

aceña f water mill.

acepción f acceptation.

aceptable adj acceptable.

aceptación f acceptance; approval.

aceptar vt to accept, to admit.

acequia f canal, channel; drain.

acera f pavement.

acerado/da adj steel compd, made of steel; sharp; steely.

acerbo/ba adj rigorous, harsh; cruel.

acerca prep about, relating to.

acercar vt to move nearer; ~se vr ~ a to approach.

acerico m pincushion.

acero m steel.

acérrimo/ma adj staunch; bitter.

acertado/da adj correct, proper; prudent.

acertar vt to hit; to guess right; * vi to get it right; to turn out true.

acertijo m riddle.

acervo m heap, pile.

acetato m (quim) acetate.

achacar vt to impute.

achacoso/sa adj sickly, unhealthy.

achantar vt (fam) to scare; ~se vr to back down.

achaparrado/da adj stunted; stocky.

achaque m ailment; excuse; subject, matter.

achicar vt to diminish; to humiliate; to bale (out).

achicharrar vt to scorch; to overheat.

achicoria f (bot) chicory.

achisparse vr to get tipsy.

aciago/ga adj unlucky; ominous.

acíbar m aloes; (fig) bitterness; displeasure.

acicalar vt to polish; ~se vr to dress in style.

acicate m spur.

acidez f acidity.

ácido m acid; * ~/da adj acid, sour.

acierto m success; solution; dexterity.

aclamación f acclamation.

aclamar vt to applaud, to acclaim.

aclaración f clarification.

aclarar vt to clear; to brighten; to explain; to clarify; ~se vr to understand; * vi to clear up.

aclimatar vt to acclimatize; ~se vr to become acclimatized.

acne m acne.

acobardar vt to intimidate.

acodarse vr to lean.

acogedor/ra adj welcoming.

acoger vt to receive; to welcome; to harbour; ~se vr to take refuge.

acogida f reception; asylum.

acolchar vt to quilt; to cushion.

acólito m acolyte; assistant.

acometer vt to attack; to undertake.

acometida f attack, assault.

acomodadizo adj accommodating.

acomodado/da adj suitable, convenient, fit; wealthy.

acomodador/ra m/f usher, usherette.

acomodar vt to accommodate, to arrange; ~se vr to comply.

acomodaticio/cia adj accomodating; pliable.

acompañamiento m (mus) accompaniment.

acompañar vt to accompany; to join; (mus) to accompany.

acompasado/da *adj* measured; well proportioned.

acondicionado/da *adj* conditioned.

acondicionar *vt* to arrange; to condition.

acongojar *vt* to distress.

aconsejable *adj* advisable.

aconsejar *vt* to advise; **~se** *vr* to take advice.

acontecer *vi* to happen.

acontecimiento *m* event, incident.

acopio *m* gathering, storing.

acopiar *vt* to gather, to store up.

acoplamiento *m* coupling.

acoplar *vt* to couple; to fit; to connect.

acorazado/da *adj* armoured; * *m* battleship.

acordado/da *adj* agreed.

acordar *vt* to agree; to remind; **~se** *vr* to agree; to remember.

acorde *adj* harmonious; * *m* chord.

acordeón *m* accordion.

acordonado/da *adj* cordoned-off.

acordonar *vt* to tie up; to cordon off.

acorralar *vt* to round up, corral; corner.

acortar *vt* to abridge, to shorten; **~se** *vr* to become shorter.

acosar *vt* to pursue closely; to pester.

acostado/da *adj* in bed; lying down.

acostar *vt* to put to bed; to lay down; **~se** *vr* to go to bed; to lie down.

acostumbrado/da *adj* usual.

acostumbrar *vi* to be used to; **~se ~ a** to get used to; * *vt* to accustom.

acotación *f* boundary mark; quotation in the margin; stage direction.

acotar *vt* to set bounds to; to annotate.

ácrata *m/f* anarchist.

acre *adj* acid; sharp; * *m* acre.

acrecentamiento *m* increase.

acrecentar *vt* to increase, to augment.

acreditar *vt* to guarantee; to assure, to affirm; to authorize; to credit; **~se** *vr* to become famous.

acreedor *m* creditor.

acribillar *vt* to riddle with bullets; to molest, to torment.

acriminar *vt* to incriminate; to accuse.

acrimonia *f* acrimony.

acrisolar *vt* to refine, to purify.

acritud *f* acrimony.

acróbata *m/f* acrobat.

acta *f* act; **~s** *fpl* records *pl*.

actitud *f* attitude; posture.

activar *vt* to activate; to speed up.

actividad *f* activity; liveliness.

activo/va *adj* active; diligent.

acto *m* act, action; act of a play; ceremony.

actor *m* actor; plaintiff.

actriz *f* actress.

actuación *f* action; behaviour; proceedings *pl*.

actual *adj* actual, present.

actualidad *f* present time; **~es** *fpl* current events *pl*.

actualizar *vt* to update.

actualmente *adv* at present.

actuar *vt* to work; to operate; * *vi* to work; to act.

acuarela *f* watercolour.

acuario *m* tank.

Acuario *m* Aquarius (sign of the zodiac).

acuartelamiento *m* quartering of troops.

acuartelar *vt* (*mil*) to quarter (troops).

acuático/ca *adj* aquatic.

acuchillar *vt* to cut; to plane.

acuciar vt to urge on.

acuclillarse vr to crouch.

acudir vi to go to; to attend; to assist.

acueducto m aqueduct.

acuerdo m agreement; **de ~** fam OK, all right.

acumular vt to accumulate, to collect.

acuñación f coining.

acuñar vt to coin, to mint; to wedge in.

acuoso/sa adj watery.

acupuntura f acupuncture.

acurrucarse vr to squat; to huddle up.

acusación f accusation.

acusador/ra m/f accuser; * adj accusing.

acusar vt to accuse; to reveal; to denounce; **~se** vr to confess.

acusativo m (gr) accusative.

acuse m: **~ de recibo** acknowledgement of receipt.

acústica f acoustics pl.

acústico/ca adj acoustic.

adagio m adage, proverb; (mus) adagio.

adalid m chief, commander.

adamascado/da adj damask.

adaptable adj adaptable.

adaptación f adaptation.

adaptador m adapter.

adaptar vt to adapt.

adecuado/da adj adequate, fit; appropriate.

adecuar vt to fit/to accommodate/to proportion.

adefesio m folly/nonsense.

adelantado/da adj advanced; fast.

adelantamiento m progress/improvement/advancement; overtaking.

adelantar vt, vi to advance, to accelerate; to pass; to ameliorate; to improve; **~se** vr to advance; to outdo.

adelante adv forward(s); **de hoy en ~** from now on; **más ~** later on; further on; * excl come in!

adelanto m advance; progress; improvement.

adelfa f (bot) rosebay.

adelgazar vt to make thin or slender; * vi to lose weight.

ademán m gesture; attitude.

además adv moreover, besides; **~ de** besides.

adentrarse vr to get inside; to penetrate.

adentro adv in; inside.

adepto/ta m/f supporter.

aderezar vt to dress, to adorn; to prepare; to season.

aderezo m adorning; seasoning; arrangement.

adeudado adj in debt.

adeudar vt to owe; **~se** vr to run into debt.

adherencia f adhesion, cohesion; alliance.

adherente adj adhering to, cohesive.

adherir vi: **~ a** to adhere to; to espouse.

adhesión f adhesion; cohesion.

adición f addition.

adicionar vt to add.

adicto/ta adj: **~ a** addicted to; devoted to; * m supporter; addict.

adiestrar vt to guide; to teach, to instruct; **~se** vr to practise.

adinerado/da adj wealthy, rich.

adiós excl goodbye; hello.

aditivo m additive.

adivinanza f enigma; riddle.

adivinar vt to foretell; to guess.

adivino/na m/f fortune-teller.

adjetivo m adjective.

adjudicación f adjudication.

adjudicar vt to adjudge; **~se** vr to appropriate.

adjuntar vt to endorse.

adjunto/ta adj united, joined, annexed; * m/f assistant.

administración f administration.

administrador/a m/f administrator.

administrar vt to administer.

administrativo/va adj administrative.

admirable adj admirable, marvellous.

admiración f admiration; wonder; (gr) exclamation mark.

admirar vt to admire; to surprise; **~se** vr to be surprised.

admisible adj admissible.

admisión f admission, acceptance.

admitir vt to admit; to let in; to concede; to permit.

admonición f warning.

adobado m pickled pork.

adobar vt to dress; to season.

adobe m adobe, sun-dried brick.

adobo m dressing; pickle sauce.

adoctrinar vt to indoctrinate; to teach.

adolecer vi to suffer from.

adolescencia f adolescence.

adolescente adj, m/f adolescent.

adonde adv (to) where.

adónde adv where.

adopción f adoption.

adoptar vt to adopt.

adoptivo/va adj adoptive; adopted.

adoquín m paving stone.

adoración f adoration, worship.

adorar vt to adore; to love.

adormecer vt to put to sleep; **~se** vr to fall asleep.

adormidera f (bot) poppy.

adornar vt to embellish, to adorn.

adorno m adornment; ornament; decoration.

adosado/da adj semidetached.

adquirir vt to acquire.

adquisición f acquisition.

adrede adv on purpose.

adscribir vt to appoint.

aduana f customs pl.

aduanero m customs officer; **~/ra** adj customs compd.

aducir vt to adduce.

adueñarse vr: **~ de** to take possession of.

adulación f adulation.

adulador/ra m/f flatterer.

adular vt to flatter.

adulterar vt to adulterate; * vi to commit adultery.

adulterio m adultery.

adúltero/ra m/f adulterer, adulteress.

adulto/ta adj, m/f adult, grown-up.

adusto/ta adj gloomy; stern.

advenedizo m upstart.

advenimiento m arrival; accession.

adverbio m adverb.

adversario m adversary; antagonist.

adversidad f adversity; setback.

adverso/sa adj adverse.

advertencia f warning, foreword.

advertido/da adj sharp.

advertir vt to notice; to warn.

Adviento m Advent.

adyacente adj adjacent.

aéreo/rea adj aerial.

aerobic m aerobics pl.

aerodeslizador m hovercraft.

aerodeslizante m hovercraft.

aerogenerador m wind turbine.

aeromozo/za m/f air steward/ess.

aeronauta m aeronaut.

aeronáutica f aeronautics.

aeronave f spaceship.

aeroplano m aeroplane.

aeropuerto m airport.

aerosol m aerosol.

aerostática f aerostatics.

afabilidad f affability.

afable adj affable.

afán m hard work; desire.

afanar vt to harass; (col) to pinch; **~se** vr to strive.

afanoso/sa adj hard, industrious.

afear vt to deform, to misshape.

afección f affection; fondness, attachment; disease.

afectación f affectation.

afectadamente adv affectedly.

afectado/da adj affected.

afectar vt to affect, to feign.

afectísimo/ma adj affectionate; ~ suyo yours truly.

afectivo/va adj fond, tender.

afecto m affection; passion; ~/ta adj affectionate; disposed; reserved.

afectuoso/sa adj affectionate; moving; tender.

afeitar vt, **~se** vr to shave.

afeite m make-up, rouge.

afeminado/da adj effeminate.

afeminar vt to make effeminate.

aferrado/da adj stubborn.

aferrar vt to grapple, to grasp, to seize.

afianzamiento m strengthening.

afianzar vt to strengthen; to prop up; **~se** vr to become established.

afiche m poster.

afición f affection; hobby; fans pl.

aficionado/da adj keen; * m/f lover, fan; amateur.

aficionar vt to inspire affection; **~se** vr ~ a to grow fond of.

afiladera f grindstone.

afilado adj sharp.

afilar vt to sharpen, to grind.

afín m related; similar.

afinar vt to tune; to refine.

afincarse vr to settle.

afinidad f affinity; analogy; relationship.

afirmación f affirmation.

afirmado m road surface.

afirmar vt to secure, to fasten; to affirm, to assure.

afirmativo/va adj affirmative.

aflicción f affliction, grief.

aflictivo/va adj distressing.

afligir vt to afflict, to torment.

aflojar vt to loosen, to slacken; to relax; * vi to grow weak; to abate; to relent; **~se** vr to relax.

aflorar vi to emerge.

afluente adj flowing; * m tributary.

afluir vi to flow.

afónico/ca adj hoarse; voiceless.

aforismo m aphorism.

afortunado/da adj fortunate, lucky.

afrancesado/da adj Frenchified.

afrenta f outrage; insult.

afrentar vt to affront; to insult.

afrontar vt to confront; to bring face to face.

afuera adv out, outside.

afueras fpl outskirts pl.

agacharse vr to stoop, to squat.

agalla f gill; ~s pl pluck, guts; tonsils pl; tonsillitis.

agarradero m handle.

agarrado/da adj miserly, stingy.

agarrar vt to grasp, to seize; **~se** vr to hold on tightly.

agarrotar vt to tie down; to squeeze tightly; to garrotte.

agasajar vt to receive and treat kindly; to regale.

agasajo m graceful reception; kindness.

ágata f agate.

agazaparse vr to crouch.

agencia f agency.

agenciarse vr to obtain.

agenda f diary.

agente m agent; policeman.

ágil adj agile.

agilidad f agility, nimbleness.

agitación f shaking; stirring; agitation.

agitar vt to wave; to move; ~se vr to become excited; to become worried.

aglomeración f crowd; ~ de tráfico traffic jam.

aglomerar vt, ~se vr to crowd together.

agnóstico/ca adj, m/f agnostic.

agobiar vt to weigh down; to oppress; to burden.

agolparse vr to assemble in crowds.

agonía f death throes pl.

agonizante adj dying.

agonizar vi to be dying.

agorar vt to predict.

agostar vt to parch.

agosto m August.

agotado/da adj exhausted; finished; sold out.

agotador/ra adj exhausting.

agotamiento m exhaustion.

agotar vt to exhaust; to drain; to misspend.

agraciado/da adj attractive; lucky.

agraciar vt to pardon; to reward.

agradable adj pleasant; lovely.

agradar vt to please; to gratify.

agradecer vt to be grateful for; to thank.

agradecido/da adj thankful.

agradecimiento m gratitude, gratefulness, thanks pl.

agrado m agreeableness, courteousness; will, pleasure; liking.

agrandar vt to enlarge; to exaggerate; to aggrandize; ~se vr to get bigger.

agrario/ria adj agrarian; agricultural.

agravante f further difficulty.

agravar vt to oppress; to aggrieve; to aggravate; to exaggerate; ~se vr to get worse.

agraviar vt to wrong; to offend; ~se vr to be aggrieved; to be piqued.

agravio m offence; grievance.

agredir vt to attack.

agregado m aggregate; attaché.

agregar vt to aggregate, to heap together; to collate; to appoint.

agresión f aggression, attack.

agresivo/va adj aggressive.

agresor m aggressor, assaulter.

agreste adj rustic, rural.

agriar vt to sour; to exasperate.

agrícola adj farming compd.

agricultor/ra m/f farmer.

agricultura f agriculture; ~ biológica organic farming.

agridulce adj sweet and sour.

agrietarse vr to crack.

agrimensor z surveyor.

agrimensura f surveying.

agrio adj sour, acrid; rough, sharp, rude, unpleasant.

agronomía f agronomy.

agropecuario/ria adj farming compd.

agrupación f group(ing).

agrupar vt to group, to cluster; to crowd.

agua f water; slope of a roof; ~ fuerte etching; ~ bendita holy water; ~s pl waters pl.

aguacate m avocado pear.

aguacero m short, heavy shower of rain.

aguachirle f slops pl.

aguado/da adj watery.

aguador m water carrier.

aguafuerte m etching.

aguamarina f aquamarine (precious stone).

aguanieve f sleet.

aguantar vt to bear, to suffer; to hold up.

aguante m firmness; patience.

aguar vt to water down.

aguardar vt to wait for.

aguardiente m brandy.

aguarrás f turpentine.

agudeza f keenness, sharpness; acuteness; acidity; smartness.

agudizar vt to make worse; ~**se** vr to get worse.

agudo/da adj sharp; keen-edged; smart; fine; acute; witty; brisk.

aguero m: **buen/mal ~** good/bad omen.

aguijar vt to prick, to spur, to goad; to stimulate.

aguijón m sting of a bee, wasp etc; stimulation.

aguijonear vt to prick; to spur; to stimulate.

águila f eagle; genius.

aguileño/ña adj aquiline; sharp-featured.

aguilucho m eaglet.

aguinaldo m Christmas box.

aguja f needle; spire; hand; magnetic needle; (ferro) points pl.

agujerear vt to pierce, to bore.

agujero m hole.

agujetas fpl stitch; stiffness; pains pl from fatigue.

agustino m monk of the order of St Augustine.

aguzar vt to whet, to sharpen; to stimulate.

ahí adv there.

ahijada f goddaughter.

ahijado m godson.

ahijar vt to adopt (as one's own child).

ahínco m earnestness; eagerness.

ahogar vt to smother; to drown; to suffocate; to oppress; to quench; ~**se** vr to drown; to suffocate.

ahogo m breathlessness; financial difficulty.

ahondar vt to deepen; to study deeply; * vi: ~ **en** to penetrate into.

ahora adv now, at present; just now.

ahorcar vt to hang; ~**se** vr to hang oneself.

ahorrar vt to save; to avoid.

ahorrativo/va adj thrifty, careful with money.

ahorro m saving; thrift.

ahuecar vt to hollow, to scoop out; ~**se** vr to get pig-headed.

ahumar vt to smoke, to cure (in smoke); ~**se** vr to fill with smoke.

ahuyentar vt to drive off; to dispel.

airado/da adj angry.

airarse vr to get angry.

airbag m airbag.

aire m air; wind; aspect; musical composition.

airearse vr to take the air.

airoso/sa adj airy; windy; graceful; successful.

aislado/da adj insulated; isolated.

aislar vt to insulate; to isolate.

ajar vt to spoil; to abuse.

ajardinado/da adj landscaped.

ajedrez m chess.

ajedrezado/da adj chequered.

ajenjo m wormwood, absinth.

ajeno/na adj someone else's; foreign; ignorant; improper.

ajetrearse vr to exert oneself; to bustle; to toil; to fidget.

ajetreo *m* activity; bustling.
ají *m* red pepper.
ajo *m* garlic.
ajorca *f* bracelet.
ajuar *m* household furniture; trousseau.
ajustado/da *adj* tight; right; close.
ajustar *vt* to regulate, to adjust; to settle (a balance); to fit; to agree on; * *vi* to fit.
ajuste *m* agreement; accommodation; settlement; fitting.
ajusticiar *vt* to execute.
al = a el.
ala *f* wing; aisle; row, file; brim; winger.
alabanza *f* praise; applause.
alabar *vt* to praise; to applaud.
alabastro *m* alabaster.
alacena *f* cupboard, closet.
alacrán *m* scorpion.
alado/da *adj* winged.
alambique *m* still.
alambrada *f* wire fence; wire netting.
alambrado *m* wire fence; wire netting.
alambre *m* wire.
alambrista *m/f* tightrope walker.
alameda *f* avenue; poplar grove.
álamo *m* poplar.
alano *m* mastiff.
alarde *m* show.
alargador *m* extension lead.
alargar *vt* to lengthen; to extend; to hasten; to stretch out; to spin out; ~**se** *vr* to get longer; to drag on.
alarido *m* outcry, shout; **dar** ~**s** to howl.
alarma *f* alarm.
alarmante *adj* alarming.
alarmar *vt* to alarm.
alarmista *m* alarmist.
alazán *m* sorrel.

alba *f* dawn.
albacea *m* executor.
albahaca *f* (*bot*) basil.
albañil *m* bricklayer.
albañilería *f* bricklaying.
albarán *m* invoice.
albarda *f* saddle.
albaricoque *m* apricot.
albedrío *m* free will.
alberca *f* reservoir; swimming pool.
albergar *vt* to lodge, to harbour; ~**se** to shelter.
albergue *m* shelter; ~ **de juventud** youth hostel.
albóndiga *f* meatball.
albor *m* dawn; whiteness.
alborada *f* dawn; reveille.
alborear *vi* to dawn.
albornoz *m* bath robe.
alborotado/da *adj* restless, turbulent.
alborotar *vi* to make a row; * *vt* to stir up; ~**se** to get excited; to get rough.
alboroto *m* noise; disturbance, riot.
alborozar *vt* to exhilarate; ~**se** *vr* to rejoice.
alborozo *m* joy.
albricias *fpl* good news *pl.*
albufera *f* lagoon.
álbum *m* album.
albumen *m* egg white.
alcachofa *f* artichoke.
alcahuete/ta *m/f* pimp, bawd.
alcalde *m* mayor.
alcaldesa *f* mayoress.
alcaldía *f* office and jurisdiction of a mayor; mayor's office.
alcalino/na *adj* alkaline.
alcance *m* reach; bad balance.
alcancía *f* money box.
alcanfor *m* camphor.
alcantarilla *m* sewer; gutter.

alcanzar vt to reach; to get, to obtain; to hit; * vi to suffice; to reach.

alcaparra f caper.

alcatraz m gannet.

alcayata f hook.

alcázar m castle, fortress.

alcoba f bedroom.

alcohol m alcohol.

alcohólico/ca adj, m/f alcoholic.

alcoholismo m alcoholism.

alcornoque m cork tree.

aldaba f knocker.

aldea f village.

aldeano/na m/f villager; * adj rustic.

ale excl come on!

aleación f alloy.

aleatorio/ria adj random.

aleccionar vt to instruct; to train.

alegación f allegation.

alegar vt to allege; to quote.

alegato m allegation; argument.

alegoria f allegory.

alegórico/ca adj allegorical.

alegrar vt to cheer; to poke; to liven up; ~**se** vr to get merry.

alegre adj happy; merry, joyful; content.

alegría f happiness; merriment.

alegrón m sudden joy; flicker.

alejamiento m remoteness; removal.

alejar vt to remove; to estrange; ~**se** vr to go away.

aleluya f hallelujah.

alemán/ana adj, m/f German; * m German language.

alentador/ra adj encouraging.

alentar vt to encourage.

alergia f allergy.

alero m gable-end; eaves pl.

alerta adj, f alert.

alertar vt to alert.

aleta f fin; wing; flipper; fender.

aletargarse vr to get drowsy.

aletazo m flap.

aletear vi to flutter.

aleteo m fluttering.

alevosía f treachery.

alevoso/sa adj treacherous.

alfabéticamente adv alphabetically.

alfabético/ca adj alphabetical.

alfabeto m alphabet.

alfalfa f (bot) lucerne.

alfarería f pottery.

alfarero m potter.

alféizar m window sill.

alférez m second lieutenant; (US navy) ensign.

alfil m bishop (at chess).

alfiler m pin; clip; clothes peg.

alfiletero m pincushion.

alfombra f carpet; rug.

alfombrar vt to carpet.

alfombrilla f mouse mat.

alforja f saddlebag; knapsack.

alga f (bot) seaweed.

algarabía f gabble, gibberish.

algarroba f (bot) carob.

algarrobo m (bot) carob tree.

algazara f din.

álgebra f algebra.

álgido/da adj chilly; crucial.

algo pn something; anything; * adv somewhat.

algodón m cotton; cotton plant; cotton wool.

algodón azucarado m candyfloss.

algodonero m cotton plant; dealer in cotton.

alguacil m bailiff; mounted official.

alguien pn someone, somebody; anyone, anybody.

alguno/na adj some; any; no; * pn someone, somebody.

alhaja f jewel.

alhelí m wallflower.

aliado/da adj allied.

alianza *f* alliance, league; wedding ring.

aliar *vt* to ally; **~se** *vr* to form an alliance.

alias *adv* alias.

alicaído/da *adj* weak; downcast.

alicates *mpl* pincers *pl*, nippers *pl*.

aliciente *m* attraction; incitement.

alienación *f* alienation.

aliento *m* breath; respiration.

aligerar *vt* to lighten; to alleviate; to hasten; to ease.

alijo *m* lightening of a ship; alleviation; cache.

alimaña *f* pest.

alimentación *f* nourishment; food; grocery.

alimentar *vt* to feed, to nourish; **~se** *vr* to feed.

alimenticio/cia *adj* food *compd*; nutritious.

alimento *m* food; **~s** *mpl* alimony.

alineación *m* alignment; line-up.

alinear *vt* to arrange in line; **~se** *vr* to line up.

aliñar *vt* to adorn; to season.

aliño *m* dressing; ornament, decoration.

alisar *vt* to plane; to polish; to smooth.

alistarse *vr* to enlist, to enrol.

aliviar *vt* to lighten; to ease; to relieve, to mollify.

alivio *m* alleviation; mitigation; relief; comfort.

aljibe *m* cistern.

allá *adv* there; over there; then.

allanamiento *m*: **~ de morada** burglary.

allanar *vt* to level, to flatten; to overcome difficulties; to pacify; to subdue; to burgle; **~se** *vr* to submit; to tumble down.

allegado/da *adj* near; * *m/f* follower.

allí *adv* there, in that place.

alma *f* soul; human being.

almacén *m* warehouse, store; magazine.

almacenaje *m* storage.

almacenar *vt* to store (up).

almanaque *m* almanac.

almeja *f* clam.

almena *f* battlement.

almendra *f* almond.

almendrado/da *adj* almond-shaped; * *m* macaroon.

almendro *m* almond tree.

almiar *m* haystack.

almíbar *m* syrup.

almidón *m* starch.

almidonado/da *adj* starched; affected; spruce.

almidonar *vt* to starch.

almirantazgo *m* admiralty.

almirante *m* admiral.

almirez *m* mortar.

almizcle *m* musk.

almohada *f* pillow; cushion.

almohadilla *f* small pillow; pad; pincushion.

almohadón *m* large cushion.

almorranas *fpl* haemorrhoids *pl*.

almorzar *vt* to have for lunch; * *vi* to have lunch.

almuerzo *m* lunch.

alocado/da *adj* crazy; foolish; inconsiderate.

alocución *f* allocution.

áloe *m* (*bot*) aloes.

alojamiento *m* lodging; housing.

alojar *vt* to lodge; **~se** *vr* to stay.

alondra *f* lark.

alpargata *f* rope-soled shoe.

alpinismo *m* mountaineering.

alpinista *m/f* mountaineer.

alpiste *m* canary seed.

alquería f farmhouse.

alquilar vt to let, to rent; to hire.

alquiler m renting, letting; hiring; rent; hire.

alquimia f alchemy.

alquimista m alchemist.

alquitrán m tar, liquid pitch.

alquitranado/da adj tarred.

alrededor adv around.

alrededores mpl surroundings pl.

alta f discharge from hospital.

altanería f haughtiness.

altanero/ra adj haughty, arrogant, vain, proud.

altar m altar; ~ **mayor** high altar.

altavoz m loudspeaker.

alterable adj changeable.

alteración f alteration; disturbance, tumult.

alterar vt to alter, to change; to disturb; ~**se** vr to get upset.

altercado m altercation, controversy; quarrel.

alternar vt, vi to alternate.

alternativa f alternative.

alternativo/va adj alternate.

alterno/na adj alternate; alternating.

Alteza f Highness (title).

altibajos mpl ups and downs pl.

altillo m hillock.

altiplanicie f high plateau.

altísimo/ma adj extremely high, most high; * m **el A~** the Most High, God.

altisonante, altísono/na adj high-sounding, pompous.

altitud f height; altitude.

altivez f haughtiness.

altivo/va adj haughty, proud, high-flown.

alto/ta adj high; elevated; tall; sharp; arduous, difficult; eminent; enormous; * m height; story; highland;

(mil) halt; (mus) alto; i~!, i~ ahí! interj stop!

altramuz m (bot) lupin.

altura f height; depth; mountain summit; altitude; ~**s** pl: **las ~s** the heavens.

alubia f bean.

alucinación f hallucination.

alucinar vt to blind, to deceive; * vi to hallucinate; ~**se** vr to deceive oneself, to labour under a delusion.

aludir vi to allude.

alumbrado m lighting; illumination.

alumbramiento m lighting; illumination; childbirth.

alumbrar vt to light; * vi to give birth.

aluminio m aluminium.

alumno/na m/f student, pupil.

alunizar vi to land on the moon.

alusión f allusion; hint.

alusivo/va adj allusive.

aluvión f alluvium; flood.

alvéolo m socket; cell of a honeycomb.

alza f rise; sight.

alzacuello m dog collar.

alzada f height; appeal.

alzamiento m rise; elevation; higher bid; uprising.

alzar vt to raise, to lift up; to construct, to build; to gather (in); ~**se** vr to get up; to rise in rebellion; ~**se con algo** vr to make off with something.

ama f mistress, owner; housewife; foster mother; ~ **de llaves** housekeeper; ~ **de leche** nurse.

amabilidad f kindness, niceness.

amable adj kind, nice.

amaestrado/da adj performing.

amaestrar vt to teach; to instruct; to train.

amagar vt to threaten; to shake one's fist at; * vi to feint.

amago m threat; indication; symptom.

amalgama f amalgam.

amalgamar vt to amalgamate.

amamantar vt to suckle.

amanecer vi to dawn; **al ~** at day-break.

amanerado/da adj affected.

amansar vt to tame; to soften; to subdue; **~se** vr to calm down.

amante m/f lover.

amanuense m amanuensis, clerk, copyist.

amapola f (bot) poppy.

amar vt to love.

amargar vt to make bitter; to exasperate; **~se** vr to be bitter.

amargo/ga adj bitter, acrid; painful; * m bitterness.

amargor m bitterness; sorrow, distress.

amargura f bitterness; sorrow.

amarillear vi to turn yellow.

amarillento/ta adj yellowish.

amarillo/lla adj yellow; * m yellow.

amarra f mooring rope.

amarrar vt to moor; to tie, to fasten.

amartelar vt to court, to woo; **~se** vr to fall in love with.

amartillar vt to hammer; to cock (a gun or pistol).

amasar vt to knead; (fig) to arrange, to settle; to prepare.

amasijo m dough; mixed mortar; medley.

amateur m/f amateur.

amatista f amethyst.

amatorio/ria adj relating to love.

amazona f amazon; masculine woman.

ambages mpl: **sin ~** in plain language.

ámbar m amber.

ambición f ambition.

ambicionar vt to crave, to covet.

ambicioso/sa adj ambitious.

ambidextro/tra adj ambidextrous.

ambientación f setting; sound effects pl.

ambiente m atmosphere; environment.

ambigüedad f ambiguity.

ambiguo/gua adj ambiguous; doubtful, equivocal.

ámbito m circuit, circumference; field; scope.

ambos/bas adj, pn both.

ambrosía f ambrosia.

ambulancia f ambulance.

ambulante adj travelling.

ambulatorio m state-run clinic.

ameba f amoeba.

amedrentar vt to frighten, to terrify; to intimidate.

amén m amen; so be it; **~ de** besides; except.

amenaza f threat.

amenazar vt to threaten.

amenizar vt to make pleasant.

ameno/na adj pleasant; delicious; flowery (of language).

América f America; **~ del Norte/del Sur** North/South America.

americano/na adj, m/f (Latin) American.

ametralladora f machine gun.

amianto m asbestos.

amiga f (female) friend.

amigable adj amicable, friendly; suitable.

amigo m friend; comrade; lover; **~/ga** adj friendly.

amilanar vt to frighten, to terrify; **~se** vr to get scared.

aminorar vt to diminish; to reduce.

amistad f friendship.

amistoso/sa adj friendly, cordial.

amnesia f amnesia.

amnistía f amnesty.

amo m owner; boss.

amodorrarse vr to grow sleepy.

amohinar vt to annoy; **~se** vr to sulk.

amoldar vt to mould; to adapt; **~se** vr to adapt oneself.

amonestación f advice; admonition; **~ones** fpl publication of marriage banns.

amonestar vt to advise; to admonish; to publish banns of marriage of.

amoníaco m ammoniac.

amor m love; fancy; lover; **~ mío** my love; **por ~ de Dios** for God's sake; **~ propio** self-love.

amoratado adj livid.

amordazar vt to muzzle; to gag.

amorfo/fa adj shapeless.

amorío m love affair.

amoroso/sa adj affectionate, loving; lovely.

amortajar vt to shroud.

amortiguador m shock absorber.

amortiguadores mpl suspension.

amortiguar vt to mortify; to deaden; to temper; to muffle.

amortización f repayment; redemption.

amortizar vt to entail (an estate), to render inalienable; to pay, to liquidate, to discharge (a debt).

amotinamiento m mutiny.

amotinar vt to incite rebellion; **~se** vr to mutiny.

amparar vt to shelter, to protect; to favour; **~se** vr to claim protection.

amparo m protection, support; help; refuge, asylum.

amperio m amp.

ampliación f amplification, enlargement.

ampliar vt to amplify, to enlarge; to extend; to expand.

amplificación f enlargement.

amplificador m amplifier.

amplificar vt to amplify.

amplio/lia adj ample, extensive.

amplitud f amplitude, extension, largeness.

ampolla f blister; ampoule.

ampuloso/sa adj pompous.

amputación f amputation.

amputar vt to amputate.

amueblar vt to furnish.

amuleto m amulet.

amurallar vt to surround with walls.

anacoreta m anchorite, hermit.

anacronismo m anachronism.

ánade m/f duck.

anadear vi to waddle.

anagrama f anagram.

anales mpl annals pl.

analfabetismo m illiteracy.

analfabeto/ta adj illiterate.

analgésico m painkiller.

análisis m analysis.

analista m/f analyst.

analítico/ca adj analytical.

analizar vt to analyze.

analogía f analogy.

analógico/ca, análogo/ga adj analogous.

ananá m pineapple.

anaquel m shelf (in a bookcase).

anaranjado/da adj orange-coloured.

anarquía f anarchy.

anárquico/ca adj anarchic, chaotic.

anarquismo m anarchism.

anarquista m/f anarchist.

anatema f anathema.

anatomía f anatomy.

anatómico/ca adj anatomical.

anca f rump.
ancho/cha adj broad, wide, large; * m breadth, width.
anchoa f anchovy.
anchura f width, breadth.
anciano/na adj old; * m/f old man/ woman.
ancla f anchor.
ancladero m anchorage.
anclaje m anchorage.
anclar vi to anchor.
andaderas fpl baby walker.
andadura f walk; pace; amble.
andamio m scaffold.
andamiaje m scaffolding.
andanada f (mar) broadside.
andar vi to go, to walk; to fare; to act, to proceed, to work; to behave; to elapse; to move; * vt to go, to travel; * m walk, pace.
andariego/ga adj wandering.
andarín m fast walker.
andas fpl stretcher.
andén m pavement, sidewalk; (ferro) platform; quayside.
andrajo m rag.
andrajoso/sa adj ragged.
andurriales mpl byways pl.
anécdota f anecdote.
anegar vt to inundate, to submerge; ~se vr to drown; to sink.
anejo/ja adj attached.
anemia f anaemia.
anestésico m anaesthetic.
anexar vt to annex; to join.
anexión f annexation.
anexionamiento m annexation.
anexo/xa adj annexed.
anfibio/bia adj amphibious.
anfiteatro m amphitheatre.
anfitrión/ona m/f host/ess.
ángel m angel.
angelical adj angelic, heaven-born.

angélico/ca adj angelic.
angina f angina.
anglicano/na adj, m/f Anglican.
anglicismo m anglicism.
angosto/ta adj narrow, close.
angula f elver.
angular adj angular; piedra ~ f cornerstone.
ángulo m angle, corner.
anguloso/sa adj angled, cornered.
angustia f anguish; heartache.
angustiar vt to cause anguish.
anhelante adj eager; longing.
anhelar vi to gasp; * vt to long for.
anhelo m desire, longing.
anidar vi to nestle, to make a nest; to dwell, to inhabit.
anillo m ring.
ánima f soul.
animación f liveliness; activity.
animado/da adj lively.
animador/ora m/f host(ess).
animadversión f ill-will.
animal adj, m animal.
animar vt to animate, to liven up; to comfort; to revive; ~se vr to cheer up.
ánimo m soul; courage; mind; intention, meaning; will; thought; * excl come on!
animosidad f valour, courage; boldness.
animoso/sa adj courageous, spirited.
aniñarse vr to act in a childish manner.
aniquilar vt to annihilate, to destroy; ~se vr to decline, to decay.
anís m aniseed; anisette.
aniversario/ria adj annual; * m anniversary.
ano m anus.
anoche adv last night.

anochecer vi to grow dark; * m nightfall.

anodino/na adj (med) anodyne.

anomalía f anomaly.

anómalo/la adj anomalous.

anonadar vt to annihilate; to lessen; ~**se** vr to humble oneself.

anonimato m anonymity.

anónimo/ma adj anonymous.

anormal adj abnormal.

anotación f annotation, note.

anotar vt to comment, to note.

anquilosamiento m paralysis.

ánsar m goose.

ansia f anxiety, eagerness, hankering.

ansiar vt to desire.

ansiedad f anxiety.

ansioso/sa adj anxious, eager.

antagónico/ca adj antagonistic; opposed.

antagonista m antagonist.

antaño adv formerly.

antártico/ca adj antarctic; * m: el A~ the Antarctic.

ante m suede; * prep before; in the presence of; faced with.

anteanoche adv the night before last.

anteayer adv the day before yesterday.

antebrazo m forearm.

antecámara f antechamber.

antecedente adj, m antecedent.

anteceder vt to precede.

antecesor/ra m/f predecessor; * m forefather.

antedicho/cha adj aforesaid.

antelación f; con ~ in advance.

antemano adv: de ~ beforehand.

antena f feeler, antenna; aerial; ~ parabólica satellite dish.

anteojo m eyeglass; ~ de larga vista telescope; ~s mpl glasses pl.

antepasado/da adj passed, elapsed; ~s mpl ancestors pl.

antepecho m (mil) parapet; ledge.

anteponer vt to place in front; to prefer.

anteproyecto m sketch; blueprint.

anterior adj preceding; former.

anterioridad f priority; preference.

antes prep, adv before; * conj before.

antesala f antechamber.

antiaéreo/rea adj anti-aircraft.

antibalas adj bullet-proof.

antibiótico m antibiotic.

anticición m anticyclone.

anticipación f anticipation.

anticipado/da adj advance.

anticipar vt to anticipate; to forestall; to advance.

anticipo m advance.

anticonceptivo m contraceptive.

anticongelante m antifreeze.

anticuado/da adj antiquated.

anticuario m antiquary, antiquarian.

anticuerpo m antibody.

antídoto m antidote.

antífona f antiphony; anthem.

antiestético/ca adj unsightly.

antifaz m mask.

antigualla f monument of antiquity; antique.

antiguamente adv in ancient times, of old.

antigüedad f antiquity, oldness.

antiguo/gua adj antique, old, ancient; * m senior; ~s mpl: los ~s the ancients.

antílope m antelope.

antinatural adj unnatural.

antimonio m antimony.

antipatía f antipathy.

antipático/ca adj unpleasant.

antípodas mpl antipodes.

antirrobo adj anti-theft.

antisemita adj anti-Semitic.

antiséptico/ca adj antiseptic.

antítesis f (gr) antithesis.

antojadizo/za adj capricious, fanciful.

antojarse vr to long, to desire; to itch.

antojo m whim, fancy; longing.

antología f anthology.

antorcha f torch; taper.

antro m (poet) cavern, den, grotto.

antropófago m cannibal.

antropología f anthropology.

antropólogo/ga m/f anthropologist.

anual adj annual.

anualidad f annuity.

anublar vt to cloud, to obscure; ~se vr to become clouded.

anudar vt to knot; to join; ~se vr to get into knots.

anulación f annulment; cancellation.

anular vt to annul; to revoke; to cancel; * adj annular.

anunciación f announcement.

anunciante m/f advertiser.

anunciar vt to announce; to advertise.

anuncio m advertisement.

anverso m obverse.

anzuelo m hook; allurement.

añadidura f addition.

añadir vt to add.

añejo/ja adj old; stale, musty.

añicos mpl bits pl, small pieces pl; hacer ~ to shatter.

añil m indigo plant; indigo.

año m year.

añojo m yearling calf.

añoranza f longing.

aorta f aorta.

aovar vi to lay eggs.

apabullar vt to squash.

apacentar vt to graze.

apacible adj affable; gentle; placid, quiet.

apaciguar vt to appease; to pacify, to calm.

apadrinar vt to support, to favour; to be godfather to.

apagado/da adj dull; quiet; muted; listless.

apagar vt to put out; to turn off; to quench, to extinguish; to damp; to destroy; to soften.

apagón m power cut, outage.

apalabrar vt to agree to; to engage.

apalancar vt to lever.

apalear vt to cane, to drub; to winnow.

apañado/da adj skilful; suitable.

apañar vt to grasp; to pick up; to patch; ~se vr to manage.

aparador m sideboard; store window.

aparato m apparatus; machine; ostentation, show.

aparatoso/sa adj showy; spectacular.

aparcamiento m car park.

aparcar vt, vi to park.

aparcería f partnership in a farm (or other business).

aparcero/ra m/f partner; associate.

aparecer vi to appear; ~se vr to appear.

aparecido/da m/f ghost.

aparejar vt to prepare; to harness (horses); to rig (a ship).

aparejo m preparation; harness, gear; (mar) tackle, rigging; ~s mpl tools pl, implements pl.

aparentar vt to look; to pretend; to deceive.

aparente adj apparent; convenient.

aparición f apparition; appearance.

apariencia f outward appearance.

apartadero m (ferro) siding.

apartado m paragraph; ~ **de correos** o **postal** PO Box.

apartamento m flat, apartment.

apartamiento m isolation; separation; flat, apartment.

apartar vt to separate, to divide; to remove; to sort; ~**se** vr to go away; to be divorced; to desist.

aparte m aside; new paragraph; * adv apart, separately; besides; aside.

apasionado/da adj passionate; devoted; fond; biased.

apasionar vt to excite; ~**se** vr to get excited.

apatía f apathy.

apático/ca adj apathetic, indifferent.

apeadero m halt, stopping place; station.

apearse vr to dismount; to get down/out/off.

apechugar vt to face up to.

apedrear vt to stone; * vi to hail.

apegarse vr: ~ **a** to become fond of.

apego m attachment, fondness.

apelación f (jur) appeal.

apelar vi (jur) to appeal; ~ **a** to have recourse to.

apelativo adj (gr): **nombre** ~ m generic name.

apellidar vt to call by name; to proclaim; ~**se** vr to be called.

apellido m surname; family name; epithet.

apelmazar vt to compress.

apenar vt to grieve; to embarrass; ~**se** vr to grieve; to be embarrassed.

apenas adv scarcely, hardly; * conj as soon as.

apéndice m appendix, supplement.

apendicitis f appendicitis.

apercibido/da adj provided; ready.

apercibirse vr to notice.

aperitivo m aperitif; appetizer.

apero m agricultural implement.

apertura f aperture, opening, chink; cleft.

apesadumbrar vt to sadden.

apestar vt to infect; * vi: ~ **a** to stink of.

apetecer vt to fancy.

apetecible adj desirable; appetizing.

apetito m appetite.

apetitoso/sa adj pleasing to the taste, appetizing; tempting.

apiadarse vr to take pity.

ápice m summit, point; smallest part of a thing.

apilar vt to pile up; ~**se** vr to pile up.

apiñado/da adj crowded; pyramidal; pine-shaped.

apiñarse vr to clog, to crowd.

apio m (bot) celery.

apisonadora f steamroller.

apisonar vt to ram down.

aplacar vt to appease, to pacify; ~**se** vr to calm down.

aplanar vt to level, to flatten.

aplastar vt to flatten, to crush.

aplatanarse vr to get weary.

aplaudir vt to applaud; to extol.

aplauso m applause; approbation, praise.

aplazamiento m postponement.

aplazar vt to postpone.

aplicable adj applicable.

aplicación f application; effort.

aplicado/da adj studious; industrious.

aplicar vt to apply; to clasp; to attribute; ~**se** vr: ~ **a** to devote oneself to.

aplique m wall light.

aplomo m self-assurance.

apocado/da adj timid.

Apocalipsis m Apocalypse.

apocamiento m timidity; depression.

apocar vt to lessen, to diminish; to contract; **~se** vr to feel humiliated.

apócrifo/fa adj apocryphal; fabulous.

apodar vt to nickname.

apoderado/da m/f proxy, attorney; agent.

apoderar vt to authorize; to give the power of attorney to; **~se** vr: **~ de** to take possession of.

apodo m nickname, sobriquet.

apogeo m peak.

apolillar vt to gnaw or eat (clothes); **~se** vr to be moth-eaten.

apología f eulogy; defence.

apoltronarse vr to grow lazy; to loiter.

apoplejía f apoplexy.

apoplético/ca adj apoplectic.

apoquinar vt (fam) to fork out.

aporrear vt to beat up.

aportar vi to arrive at a port; to arrive; * vt to contribute.

aposentar vt to harbour; to put up.

aposento m room.

aposición f (gr) apposition.

apósito m (med) external dressing.

aposta adv on purpose.

apostar vt to bet, to wager; to post soldiers; * vi to bet.

apostasía f apostasy.

apóstata m apostate.

apostatar vi to apostatize.

apostilla f marginal note; postscript.

apóstol m apostle.

apostolado m apostleship.

apostólico/ca adj apostolical.

apostrofar vt to apostrophize.

apóstrofe m apostrophe.

apóstrofo m (gr) apostrophe.

apostura f neatness.

apoteosis f apotheosis.

apoyar vt to rest; to favour, to patronize, to support; **~se** vr to lean.

apoyo m support; protection.

apreciable adj appreciable; valuable; respectable.

apreciar vt to appreciate; to estimate, to value.

aprecio m appreciation; esteem.

aprehender vt to apprehend, to seize.

aprehensión f apprehension, seizure.

apremiante adj urgent.

apremiar vt to press; to compel.

apremio m pressure, constriction; judicial compulsion.

aprender vt to learn; **~ de memoria** to learn by heart.

aprendiz/za m/f apprentice.

aprendizaje m apprenticeship.

aprensión f apprehension.

aprensivo/va adj apprehensive.

apresar vt to seize, to grasp.

apresurado/da adj hasty.

apresuramiento m hurry.

apresurar vt to accelerate, to hasten, to expedite; **~se** vr to hurry.

apretado/da adj tight; cramped;, difficult.

apretar vt to compress, to tighten; to constrain; to distress; to urge earnestly; * vi to be too tight.

apretón m squeeze.

apretura f squeeze.

aprieto m conflict; tight spot.

aprisa adv quickly, swiftly; promptly.

aprisco m sheepfold.

aprisionar vt to imprison.

aprobación f approbation, approval.

aprobar vt to approve; to pass; * vi to pass.

apropiación f appropriation, assumption.

apropiado/da adj appropriate.

apropiarse vr to appropriate.

aprovechable adj profitable.

aprovechado/da adj industrious; thrifty; selfish.

aprovechamiento m use; exploitation.

aprovechar vt to use; to exploit; to profit from; to take advantage of; * vi to be useful; to progress; ~se vr: ~ de to use; to take advantage of.

aproximación f approximation; closeness.

aproximado/da adj approximate.

aproximar vt to approach; ~se vr to approach.

aptitud f aptitude, fitness, ability.

apto/ta adj apt; fit; able; clever.

apuesta f bet, wager.

apuesto/ta adj neat.

apuntado/da adj pointed.

apuntador m prompter.

apuntalar vt to prop up.

apuntar vt to aim; to level, to point at; to mark; * vi to begin to appear or show itself; to prompt (theatre); ~se vr to score; to enrol.

apunte m annotation; prompting (theatre).

apuñalar vt to stab.

apurado/da adj poor, destitute of means; exhausted; hurried.

apurar vt to purify; to clear up, to verify; to exhaust; to tease and perplex; ~se vr to worry; to hurry.

apuro m want; pain, affliction; haste; jam.

aquejado/da adj afflicted.

aquel/~la adj that; ~los/~las pl those.

aquél/~la pn that (one); ~los/~las pl those (ones).

aquello pn that.

aquí adv here; now.

aquietar vt to quiet, to appease.

aquilino adj aquiline.

aquilón m north wind.

ara f altar.

árabe adj, m/f, m (ling) Arabic.

arabesco m arabesque.

arado m plough.

arancel m tariff.

arándano m bilberry; blueberry.

arandela f washer.

araña f spider; chandelier.

arañar vt to scratch; to scrape; to corrode.

arar vt to plough.

arbitraje m arbitration.

arbitrar vt, vi to arbitrate; to referee.

arbitrariedad f arbitrariness.

arbitrario/ria adj arbitrary.

arbitrativo/va adj arbitrary.

arbitrio m free will; arbitration.

árbitro m arbitrator; referee; umpire.

árbol m tree; (mar) mast; shaft.

arbolado/da adj forested; wooded; * m woodland.

arboladura f rigging; masts pl.

arbolar vt to hoist, to set upright.

arboleda f grove.

arbusto m shrub.

arca f chest, wooden box.

arcada f arch; arcade; ~s fpl retching.

arcaico/ca adj archaic.

arcaísmo m archaism.

arcángel m archangel.

arce m maple tree.

archipiélago m archipelago.

archivador *m* filing cabinet.

archivar *vt* to file.

archivero, archivista *m* keeper of records, archivist.

archivo *m* file(s) (*pl*); archives *pl*.

arcilla *f* clay.

arcilloso/sa *adj* clayey.

arcipreste *m* archpriest.

arco *m* arc; arch; fiddle bow; hoop; ~ **iris** rainbow.

arder *vi* to burn, to blaze.

ardid *m* stratagem, artifice; cunning.

ardiente *adj* burning; ardent, passionate; active; fiery.

ardilla *f* squirrel.

ardor *m* heat; valour; vivacity; fieriness, fervour.

ardoroso/sa *adj* fiery; restless.

arduo/dua *adj* arduous, difficult; high.

área *f* area.

arena *f* sand; grit; arena.

arenal *m* sandy ground.

arenga *f* harangue; speech.

arengar *vi* to harangue.

arenisca *f* sandstone; grit.

arenoso/sa *adj* sandy.

arenque *m* herring; ~ **ahumado** smoked herring, kipper.

argamasa *f* mortar.

argamasar *vi* to mix mortar.

argolla *f* large ring.

argot *m* slang.

argucia *f* subtlety.

argüir *vi* to argue, to dispute; * *vt* to deduce; to argue; to imply.

argumentación *f* argumentation.

argumentar *vt, vi* to argue, to dispute; to conclude.

argumento *m* argument.

aria *f* (*mus*) aria; tune, air.

aridez *f* drought, want of rain.

árido/da *adj* dry; barren.

Aries *m* Aries (sign of the zodiac).

ariete *m* battering ram.

ario/a *adj* Aryan.

arisco/ca *adj* fierce; rude; intractable.

aristocracia *f* aristocracy.

aristócrata *m* aristocrat.

aristocrático/ca *adj* aristocratic.

aritmética *f* arithmetic.

arlequín *m* harlequin, buffoon.

arma *f* weapon, arm.

armada *f* fleet, armada.

armadillo *m* armadillo.

armado/da *adj* armed; reinforced.

armador *m* ship owner; privateer; jacket, jerkin.

armadura *f* armour; framework; skeleton; armature.

armamento *m* armament.

armar *vt* to man; to arm; to fit; ~**la** to kick up a fuss.

armario *m* wardrobe; cupboard.

armatoste *m* hulk; contraption.

armazón *f* chassis; skeleton; frame.

armería *f* arsenal; heraldry; gunsmith's.

armero *m* gunsmith.

armiño *m* ermine.

armisticio *m* armistice.

armonía *f* harmony.

armonioso/sa *adj* harmonious.

armonizar *vt* to harmonize; to reconcile.

arnés *m* harness; ~**eses** *mpl* gear, trappings *pl*.

aro *m* ring; earring.

aroma *m* aroma, fragrance.

aromaterapia *f* aromatherapy.

aromático/ca *adj* aromatic.

arpa *f* harp.

arpegio *m* (*mus*) arpeggio.

arpía *f* (*poet*) shrew.

arpillera *f* sackcloth.

arpón *m* harpoon.

arqueado/da *adj* arched, vaulted.

arquear *vt* to arch; to bend.

arqueo *m* arching; gauging (of a ship).

arqueología *f* archaeology.

arqueólogo/ga *m/f* archaeologist.

arquero *m* archer.

arqueta *f* small trunk.

arquetipo *m* archetype.

arquitecto *m* architect.

arquitectónico/ca *adj* architectural.

arquitectura *f* architecture.

arrabal *m* suburb; slum.

arrabalero *m* suburbanite.

arraigado *adj* deep-rooted.

arraigar *vt* to root; to establish; * *vi* to establish; ~**se** *vr* to take root; to settle.

arrancar *vt* to pull up by the roots; to pull out; to wrest; to extract; * *vi* to start; to move.

arranque *m* sudden start; start; outburst.

arras *fpl* security.

arrasar *vt* to demolish, to destroy.

arrastrado/da *adj* miserable; painstaking; servile.

arrastrar *vt* to drag; * *vi* to creep, to crawl; to lead a trump at cards; ~**se** *vr* to crawl; to grovel.

arrastre *m* dragging.

¡arre! *excl* gee!, go on!

arrear *vt* to drive on; * *vi* to hurry along.

arrebañar *vt* to scrape together; to pick up.

arrebatado/da *adj* rapid; violent, impetuous; rash, inconsiderate.

arrebatar *vt* to carry off; to snatch; to enrapture.

arrebato *m* fury; rapture.

arrebol *m* rouge.

arrebujar *vt* to crumple; to wrap up.

arrecife *m* reef.

arrecirse *vr* to grow stiff with cold.

arreglado *adj* neat; regular, moderate.

arreglar *vt* to regulate; to tidy; to adjust; ~**se** *vr* to come to an understanding.

arreglo *m* rule, order; agreement; arrangement.

arrellanarse *vr* to sit at ease; to make oneself comfortable.

arremangar *vt* to roll up; ~**se** *vr* to roll up one's sleeves.

arremeter *vt* to attack; to seize suddenly.

arremetida *f* attack, assault.

arrendador *m* landlord.

arrendamiento *m* leasing; hire; lease.

arrendar *vt* to rent, to let out, to lease.

arrendatario/ria *m/f* tenant.

arreo *m* dress, ornament; ~**s** *mpl* harness.

arrepentido/da *adj* repentant.

arrepentimiento *m* repentance, penitence.

arrepentirse *vr* to repent.

arrestar *vt* to arrest; to imprison.

arresto *m* boldness; prison; arrest.

arriada *f* flood, overflowing.

arriar *vt* (*mar*) to lower; to strike; to pay out.

arriate *m* bed; causeway.

arriba *adv* above, over, up; high, on high, overhead; aloft.

arribada *f* (*mar*) arrival (of a vessel) in port.

arribar *vi* (*mar*) to put into harbour.

arribista *m/f* upstart.

arriendo *m* lease; farm rent.

arriero *m* muleteer.

arriesgado/da *adj* risky; daring.

arriesgar *vt* to risk, to hazard; to expose to danger; **~se** *vr* to take a chance.

arrimar *vt* to approach, to draw near; (*mar*) to stow (cargo); **~se** *vr* to side up; to lean.

arrinconar *vt* to put in a corner; to lay aside.

arrobado/da *adj* enchanted.

arrobamiento *m* rapture; amazement.

arrobarse *vr* to be totally amazed; to be out of one's senses.

arrocero/ra *adj* rice-producing.

arrodillarse *vr* to kneel down.

arrogancia *f* arrogance, haughtiness.

arrogante *adj* arrogant; haughty, proud; stout.

arrojadizo/za *adj* easily thrown.

arrojar *vt* to throw, to fling; to dash; to emit; to shoot, to sprout; **~se** *vr* to hurl oneself.

arrojo *m* boldness, fearlessness.

arrollador/ra *adj* overwhelming.

arrollar *vt* to run over; to defeat heavily.

arropar *vt* to clothe, to dress; **~se** *vr* to wrap up.

arrostrar *vt* to face (up to).

arroyo *m* stream; gutter.

arroz *m* rice.

arrozal *m* rice field.

arruga *f* wrinkle; rumple.

arrugar *vt* to wrinkle; to rumple; to fold; **~ la frente** to frown; **~se** *vr* to shrivel.

arruinar *vt* to demolish; to ruin; **~se** *vr* to go bankrupt.

arrullador/ra *adj* flattering, cajoling.

arrullar *vt* to lull; * *vi* to coo.

arrullo *m* cooing (of pigeons); lullaby.

arrumaco *m* caress.

arsenal *m* arsenal; dockyard.

arsénico *m* arsenic.

arte *m/f* art; skill; artfulness.

artefacto *m* appliance.

arteria *f* artery.

artero/ra *adj* dexterous, cunning, artful.

artesa *f* kneading trough.

artesanía *f* craftsmanship.

artesano *m* artisan, workman.

ártico/ca *adj* arctic; * *m*: **el A~** the Arctic.

articulación *f* articulation; joint.

articulado/da *adj* articulated; jointed.

articular *vt* to articulate; to joint.

artículo *m* article; clause; point; (*gr*) article; condition.

artífice *m* artisan; artist.

artificial *adj* artificial.

artificio *m* workmanship, craft; artifice, cunning trick.

artificioso/sa *adj* skilful, ingenious; artful, cunning.

artillería *f* gunnery; artillery.

artillero *m* artillery man.

artimaña *f* trap; cunning.

artista *m* artist; craftsman.

artístico/ca *adj* artistic.

artritis *f* arthritis.

arzobispado *m* archbishopric.

arzobispo *m* archbishop.

as *m* ace.

asa *f* handle; lever.

asado *m* roast meat; barbecue.

asador *m* spit.

asadura *f* offal.

asalariado/da *adj* salaried.

asaltador/a *m/f* assailant.

asaltante *m/f* assailant.

asaltar *vt* to assault; to storm (a position); to assail.

asalto *m* assault, attack.

asamblea f assembly, meeting.

asar vt to roast.

asbesto m asbestos.

ascendencia f ascendancy; ancestry.

ascendente adj ascending; (ferro) tren ~ m up train.

ascender vi to be promoted; to rise; * vt to promote.

ascendiente m forefather; influence.

Ascensión f feast of the Ascension.

ascenso m promotion; ascent.

ascensor m elevator.

asceta m ascetic.

ascético/ca adj ascetic.

asco m nausea; loathing.

ascua f red-hot coal.

aseado/da adj clean; elegant; neat.

asear vt to clean; to tidy.

asediar vt to besiege; to chase.

asedio m siege.

asegurado/da adj insured.

asegurador m insurer.

asegurar vt to secure; to insure; to affirm; to bail; ~se vr to make sure.

asemejarse vr to be like, to resemble.

asentado/da adj established.

asentar vt to sit down; to affirm, to assure; to note; * vi to suit.

asentir vi to acquiesce, to concede.

aseo m cleanliness; neatness; ~s mpl toilets pl.

aséptico/ca adj germ-free.

asequible adj attainable; obtainable.

aserción f assertion, affirmation.

aserradero m sawmill.

aserrar vt to saw.

aserrín m sawdust.

asertivo/va adj affirmative.

asesinar vt to assassinate; to murder.

asesinato m assassination; murder.

asesino m assassin; murderer.

asesor m counsellor, adviser, consultant.

asesorar vt to advise; to act as consultant to; ~se vr to consult.

asestar vt to aim, to point; to strike.

aseverar vt to affirm.

asfalto m asphalt.

asfixia f suffocation.

asfixiar vt to suffocate; ~se vr to suffocate.

así adv so, thus, in this manner; like this; therefore; so that; also; ~ que so that; therefore; **así, así** so-so; middling.

asidero m handle.

asiduidad f assiduousness.

asiduo/dua adj assiduous.

asiento m chair; bench, stool; seat; contract; entry; residence.

asignación f assignation; destination.

asignar vt to assign, to attribute.

asignatura f subject; course.

asilado/da m/f inmate; refugee.

asilo m asylum, refuge; ~ politico political asylum.

asimilación f assimilation.

asimilar vt to assimilate.

asimismo adv similarly, in the same manner.

asir vt to grasp, to seize; to hold; to grip; * vi to take root.

asistencia f audience; presence; assistance, help.

asistente m assistant, helper.

asistir vi to be present; to assist; * vt to help.

asma f asthma.

asmático/ca adj asthmatic.

asno m ass.

asociación f association; partnership.

asociado m associate.

asociar vt to associate; ~**se** vr to associate.

asolar vt to destroy; to devastate.

asolear vt to expose to the sun; ~**se** vr to sunbathe.

asomar vi to appear; ~**se** vr to appear, to show up.

asombrar vt to amaze; to astonish; ~**se** vr to be amazed; to get a fright.

asombro m dread, terror; astonishment.

asombroso/sa adj astonishing, marvellous.

asomo m mark, token, indication; conjecture.

asonancia f assonance; harmony.

aspa f cross; sail.

aspaviento m astonishment; fuss.

aspecto m appearance; aspect.

aspereza f roughness; surliness.

áspero/ra adj rough, rugged; craggy, knotty; horrid; harsh, hard; severe, austere; gruff.

asperón m grindstone.

aspersión f sprinkling; aspersion.

áspid m asp.

aspiración f breath; pause.

aspirante m aspirant, aspirer.

aspirar vt to breathe; to aspire; (gr) to aspirate.

aspirina f aspirin.

asquear vt to sicken; * vi be sickening; ~**se** vr to feel disgusted.

asqueroso/sa adj disgusting.

asta f lance; horn; handle.

astado/da adj horned.

asterisco m asterisk.

astilla f chip (of wood), splinter.

astillero m dockyard.

astral adj astral.

astringente adj astringent.

astro m star.

astrología m astrology.

astrológico/ca adj astrological.

astrólogo/ga m/f astrologer.

astronauta f/m astronaut.

astronave f spaceship.

astronomía f astronomy.

astronómico/ca adj astronomical.

astrónomo/ma m/f astronomer.

astucia f cunning, slyness.

astuto/ta adj cunning, sly; astute.

asueto m time off; holiday, vacation.

asumir vt to assume.

Asunción f Assumption.

asunto m subject, matter; affair, business.

asustar vt to frighten; ~**se** vr to be frightened.

atacar vt to attack.

atajo m short cut.

atalaya f watchtower.

atañer vi: ~ a to concern.

ataque m attack.

atar vt to tie; to fasten.

atardecer vi to get dark; * m dusk; evening.

atareado/da adj busy.

atascar vt to jam; to hinder; ~**se** vr to become bogged down.

atasco m traffic jam.

ataúd m coffin.

ataviar vt to dress up, to trim, to adorn.

atavío m dress; ornament; ~**s** mpl finery.

ateísmo m atheism.

atemorizar vt to frighten; ~**se** vr to get scared.

atenazar vt to grip; to torment.

atención f attention, heedfulness; civility; observance, consideration.

atender vt to be attentive; * vt to attend to; to heed, to expect, to wait for; to look at.

atenerse *vr*: ~ **a** to adhere to.

atentado *m* terrorist attack; transgression, offence.

atentamente *adv* observantly; **le saluda** ~ yours faithfully.

atentar *vt* to attempt; to commit.

atento/ta *adj* attentive; heedful; observing; mindful; polite, courteous, mannerly.

atenuante *adj* extenuating.

atenuar *vt* to diminish; to lessen.

ateo/a *adj*, *m/f* atheist.

aterciopelado/da *adj* velvety.

aterido/da *adj* frozen stiff.

aterirse *vr* to grow stiff with cold.

aterrador/a *adj* frightening.

aterrar *vt* to terrify; ~**se** *vr* to be terrified.

aterrizaje *m* landing.

aterrizar *vt* to land.

aterrorizar *vt* to frighten, to terrify.

atesorar *vt* to treasure *or* hoard up (riches).

atestación *f* testimony, evidence.

atestado/da *adj* packed; * *m* affidavit.

atestar *vt* to cram, to stuff; to attest, to witness.

atestiguar *vt* to witness, to attest.

atiborrar *vt* to stuff; ~**se** *vr* to stuff oneself.

ático *m* attic.

atildar *vt* to punctuate with a tilde; to censure.

atinado/da *adj* wise; correct.

atisbar *vt* to pry into; to examine closely.

atizar *vt* to stir (the fire) with a poker; to stir up.

atlántico/ca *adj* atlantic; * *m*: **el A~** the Atlantic.

atlas *m* atlas.

atleta *m/f* athlete.

atlético/ca *adj* athletic.

atletismo *m* athletics.

atmósfera *f* atmosphere.

atmosférico/ca *adj* atmospheric.

atolladero *m* bog; obstacle; impediment.

atollar *vt* to stick; ~**se** *vr* to get stuck.

atolondramiento *m* stupefaction, consternation.

atolondrar *vt* to stun, to stupefy; ~**se** *vr* to be stupefied.

atómico/ca *adj* atomic.

atomizador *m* spray.

átomo *m* atom.

atónito/ta *adj* astonished, amazed.

atontado/da *adj* stunned; silly.

atontar *vt* to stun, to stupefy; ~**se** *vr* to grow stupid.

atormentar *vt* to torture; to harass; to torment.

atornillar *vt* to screw on; to screw down.

atosigar *vt* to poison; to harass; to oppress.

atracadero *m* landing-place.

atracador/a *m/f* robber.

atracar *vt* to moor; to rob; ~**se** *vr*: ~ **(de)** to stuff oneself (with).

atracción *f* attraction.

atractivo/va *adj* attractive; magnetic; * *m* charm.

atraer *vt* to attract, to allure.

atragantarse *vr* to stick in the throat, to choke.

atrancar *vt* to bar (a door).

atrapar *vt* to trap; to nab; to deceive.

atrás *adv* backward(s); behind; previously, **hacia** ~ backward(s).

atrasado/da *adj* slow; backward; in arrears.

atrasar *vi* to be slow; * *vt* to postpone; ~ **el reloj** to put back a watch; ~**se** *vr* to stay behind; to be late.

atraso m backwardness; slowness; delay.

atravesado/da adj oblique; cross; perverse; mongrel; degenerate.

atravesar vt to cross; to pass over; to pierce; to go through; ~**se** vr to get in the way; to meddle.

atrayente adj attractive.

atreverse vr to dare, to venture.

atrevido/da adj bold, audacious, daring.

atrevimiento m boldness, audacity.

atribución f attribution, imputation.

atribuir vt to attribute, to ascribe; to impute.

atribular vt to vex, to afflict.

atributivo/va adj attributive.

atributo m attribute.

atrición f attrition.

atril m lectern; music stand.

atrio m porch; portico.

atrocidad f atrocity.

atrochar vi to take a short cut.

atropellado/da adj hasty, precipitate.

atropellar vt to trample; to run down; to hurry; to insult; ~**se** vr to hurry.

atropello m accident; push; outrage.

atuendo m attire.

atroz adj atrocious, heinous; cruel.

atufar vt to vex, to plague; ~**se** vr turn sour; to get mad.

atún m tuna (fish).

aturdido/da adj hare-brained.

aturdimiento m stupefaction; astonishment; dullness.

aturdir vt to stun, to confuse; to stupefy.

atusar vt to smooth.

audacia f audacity, boldness.

audaz adj audacious, bold.

audible adj audible.

audiencia f audience.

auditivo/va adj auditory.

auditor m auditor.

auditoría f audit.

auditorio m audience; auditorium.

auge m boom; climax.

augurar vt to predict.

augurio m omen.

aula f lecture room.

aullar vi to howl.

aullido/aúllo m howling.

aumentar vt to augment, to increase; to magnify; to put up; * vi to increase; to grow larger.

aumento m increase; promotion, advancement.

aún adv even; ~ **así** even so.

aun adv still; yet.

aunar vt to unite, to assemble.

aunque adv though, although.

¡aúpa! excl come on!

áureo/rea adj golden, gilt compd.

aureola f glory; nimbus.

auricular m receiver; ~**es** mpl headphones pl.

aurora f dawn.

auscultar vt to sound.

ausencia f absence.

ausentarse vr to go out.

ausente adj absent.

auspicio m auspice; prediction; protection.

austeridad f austerity.

austero/ra adj austere, severe.

austral adj southern.

autenticar vt to authenticate.

autenticidad f authenticity.

auténtico/ca adj authentic.

autillo m brown owl.

auto m judicial sentence; car; edict, ordinance; ~ **de fe** auto-da-fe.

autoadhesivo/va adj self-adhesive.

autobiografía f autobiography.

autobús m bus.
autocar m bus.
autocracia f autocracy.
autócrata m autocrat.
autóctono/na adj native.
autodefensa f self defence.
autodeterminación f self-determination.
autoedición f desktop publishing.
autoescuela f driving school.
autoestop f hitchhiking; **hacer ~** to hitchhike.
autoestopista, autostopista m/f hitchhiker.
autógrafo m autograph.
autómata m automaton.
automático/ca adj automatic.
automatización f automation.
automedicación f self-medication.
automotor m diesel train.
automóvil m automobile.
automovilismo m motoring; motor racing.
automovilista m/f motorist, driver.
automovilístico/ca adj car compd.
autonomía f autonomy.
autónomo/ma adj autonomous.
autonómico/ca adj autonomous.
autopista f motorway; **~ de la información** information superhighway.
autopsia f post mortem, autopsy.
autor/ra m/f author; maker; writer.
autoridad f authority.
autorización f authorization.
autorizar vt to authorize.
autorradio m car radio.
autorretrato m self-portrait.
autoservicio m self-service store; restaurant.
autosuficiencia f self-sufficiency.
autovía f state highway.
auxiliar vt to aid, to help, to assist; to attend; * adj auxiliary.

auxilio m aid, help, assistance.
aval m guarantee; guarantor.
avalancha f avalanche.
avance m advance; attack; trailer (for a film).
avanzada f (mil) vanguard.
avanzar vt, vi to advance.
avaricia f avarice.
avaricioso/sa adj avaricious, covetous.
avaro/ra adj miserly; * m/f miser.
avasallar vt to subdue; to enslave.
ave f bird; fowl.
avecinarse vr to be on the way.
avellana f hazelnut.
avellano m hazelnut tree.
ave maría f Hail Mary.
avena f oats pl.
avenencia f agreement, bargain; union.
avenida f avenue.
avenido/da adj agreed.
avenir vt to reconcile; **~se** vr to reach a compromise.
aventajado/da adj advantageous, profitable; beautiful; excellent.
aventajar vt to surpass, to excel.
aventar vt to fan; to expel.
aventura f adventure; event, incident.
aventurado/da adj risky.
aventurar vt to venture, to risk.
aventurero/ra adj adventurous.
avergonzar vt to shame, to abash; **~se** vr to be ashamed.
avería f breakdown.
averiado/da adj broken down; out of order.
averiarse vr to break down.
averiguación f discovery; investigation.
averiguar vt to inquire into; to investigate, to explore.

aversión f aversion, dislike; abhorrence.

avestruz m ostrich.

aviación f aviation; air force.

aviador/a m/f aviator.

avicultura f poultry farming.

avidez f covetousness.

ávido/da adj (poet) greedy, covetous.

avieso/sa adj irregular, out of the way; mischievous, perverse.

avinagrado/da adj sour.

avinagrarse vr to go sour.

avio m preparation, provision.

avión m aeroplane.

avioneta f light aircraft.

avisado/da adj prudent, cautious; **mal ~** ill-advised.

avisar vt to inform; to warn; to advise.

aviso m notice; warning; hint.

avispa f wasp.

avispado/da adj lively, brisk; vivacious.

avisperarse vr to worry.

avispero m wasp's nest.

avispón m hornet.

avistar vt to sight.

avituallar vt (mil) to supply (with food).

avivar vt to quicken, to enliven; to encourage.

avutarda f bustard.

axioma m axiom, maxim.

¡ay! excl ouch!; ow! **i~ de mí!** alas! poor me!

aya f governess, instructress.

ayer adv yesterday.

ayuda f help, aid; support; * m deputy, assistant.

ayudante m (mil) adjutant; assistant.

ayudar vt to help, to assist; to further.

ayunar vi to fast, to abstain from food.

ayuno m fasting, abstinence from food.

ayuntamiento m town/city hall.

azabache m jet.

azada f spade; hoe.

azafata f air hostess.

azafrán m saffron.

azahar m orange or lemon blossom.

azar m unforeseen disaster; unexpected accident; fate; **por ~** by chance; **al ~** at random.

azaroso/sa adj unlucky, ominous; risky.

azogue m mercury.

azor m goshawk.

azorar vt to frighten, to terrify.

azotaina f drubbing, sound flogging.

azotar vt to whip, to lash.

azote m whip.

azotea f flat roof of a house.

azteca m/f Aztec.

azúcar m/f sugar.

azucarado/da adj sugared; sugary.

azucarar vt to sugar, to sweeten.

azucarero m sugar bowl.

azucena f white lily.

azufre m sulphur, brimstone.

azul adj blue; **~ celeste** sky blue.

azulado/da adj azure, bluish.

azulejo m tile.

azuzar vt to irritate, to stir up.

B

baba f dribble, spittle.
babear vi to dribble, to drool.
babel m bedlam.
babero m bib.
babia f: **estar en ~** to be absent-minded or dreaming.
baboso/sa adj dribbling, drooling.
babucha f slipper.
baca f (auto) roof rack.
bacalao m cod.
bache m pothole.
bachillerato m baccalaureate.
báculo m stick.
bagaje m baggage.
bagatela f trifle.
bahía f bay.
bailador/ra m/f dancer.
bailar vi to dance.
bailarín/ina m/f dancer.
baile m dance, ball; **~ de disfraces** fancy-dress ball.
baja f fall; casualty.
bajada f descent; inclination; slope; ebb.
bajamar f low tide, low water.
bajar vt to lower, to let down; to lessen; to humble; to go/come down; to bend downward(s); * vi to descend; to go/come down; to grow less; **~se** vr to crouch; to lessen.
bajeza f meanness; lowliness.
bajío m shoal, sandbank; lowlands pl.
bajo/ja adj low; abject, despicable; common; dull (of colours); deep; humble; * prep under, underneath, below; * adv softly; quietly; * m (mus) bass; low place.
bajón m fall.
bakalao m (fam) rave music.

bala f bullet.
baladronada f boast, brag; bravado.
balance m hesitation; balance sheet; balance; rolling (of a ship).
balancear vt, vi to balance; to roll; to waver; **~se** vr to swing.
balanceo m balance beam; rocker arm; seesaw; balancing pole.
balanza f scale; balance.
balar vi to bleat.
balaustrada f balustrade, banister.
balazo m shot.
balbucear vt, vi to stutter.
balbuciente adj stammering, stuttering.
balcón m balcony.
baldar vr to cripple.
balde m bucket; **de ~** adv gratis, for nothing; **en ~** in vain.
baldío/día adj waste; uncultivated.
baldosa f floor; tile; flagstone.
balido m bleating, bleat.
balín m buckshot.
balística f ballistics pl.
ballena f whale; whalebone.
ballenato m calf of a whale.
ballenero m (mar) whaler.
ballesta f crossbow; **a tiro de ~** at a great distance.
ballestero m archer; crossbow-maker.
ballet m ballet.
balneario m spa.
balón m ball.
baloncesto m basketball.
balonmano m handball.
balonvolea m volleyball.
balsa[1] f balsa wood; raft, float.
balsa[2] f pool, pond.
bálsamo m balsam, balm.
baluarte m bastion; bulwark.

bamba f fat; (bot) swelling; flabbiness.
bambolear vi to reel; ~**se** vr to sway.
bamboleo m reeling, staggering.
bambú m bamboo.
banana f banana; plantain.
banano m banana tree.
banasta f large basket.
banca f bench; banking; ~ **electrónica** electronic banking.
bancario/ria adj bank(ing) compd.
bancarrota f bankruptcy.
banco m bench; work bench; bank.
banda f band; sash; ribbon; troop; party; gang; touchline.
bandada f flock; shoal.
bandearse vr to move to and fro.
bandeja f tray, salver.
bandera f banner, standard; flag.
banderilla f small decorated dart used at a bullfight.
banderillear vt to plant banderillas in a bull's neck or shoulder.
banderillero m thrower of banderillas.
banderín m small flag, pennant.
bandido m bandit, outlaw.
bando m faction, party; edict.
bandolera f bandoleer.
bandolero m bandit.
bandurria f bandore (musical instrument resembling a lute).
banquero/ra m/f banker.
banqueta f three-legged stool; pavement, sidewalk.
banquete m banquet; formal dinner.
banquillo m dock; bench.
bañador m swimsuit.
bañar vt to bathe; to dip; to coat (with varnish); ~**se** vr to bathe; to swim.
bañera f bath (tub).
bañero m lifeguard.
bañista m/f bather.
baño m bath; dip; bathtub; varnish; coating.

baptista m/f Baptist.
bar m bar.
baraja f pack of cards.
barajar vt to shuffle (cards); to jumble up.
baranda f rail.
barandilla f small balustrade, small railing.
baratijas fpl trifles pl, toys pl; trash, junk.
baratillo m secondhand goods pl; junkshop; bargain sale.
barato/ta adj cheap; **de** ~ gratis; * m cheapness; bargain sale; money extracted from winning gamblers.
baraúnda f noise, hurly-burly.
barba f chin; beard; ~ **a** ~ face to face; * m actor who impersonates old men.
barbacoa f barbecue.
barbaridad f barbarity, barbarism; outrage.
barbarie f barbarism; savagery.
barbarismo m barbarism (form of speech).
bárbaro/ra adj barbarous; cruel; rude; rough.
barbecho m first ploughing, fallow land.
barbería f barber's shop.
barbero m barber.
barbilampiño/ña adj clean-shaven; (fig) inexperienced.
barbilla f (tip of the) chin.
barbo m barbel.
barbudo/da adj bearded.
barca f boat; ship.
barco m boat; ship.
barítono m (mus) baritone.
barman m barman.
barniz m varnish; glaze.
barnizar vt to varnish.
barómetro m barometer.

barón m baron.

baronesa f baroness.

barquero m boatman.

barquilla f (mar) log; basket (of an air balloon).

barquillo m wafer; cornet, cone.

barra m bar; rod; lever; French loaf; sandbank; **de ~ a ~** from place to place.

barrabasada f trick, plot.

barraca f hut.

barranco m gully, ravine; (fig) great difficulty.

barranquismo m canyoning.

barrena f drill, bit, auger.

barrenar vt to drill, to bore; (fig) to frustrate.

barrendero m sweeper.

barreno m large drill; borehole.

barreño m tub.

barrer vt to sweep; to overwhelm.

barrera f barrier; turnpike, claypit.

barriada f suburb, area of a city.

barricada f barricade.

barrido m sweep.

barriga f abdomen; belly.

barrigudo/da adj pot-bellied.

barril m barrel; cask.

barrio m area, district.

barrizal m claypit.

barro m clay, mud.

barroco/ca adj baroque.

barrote m ironwork (of doors, windows, tables); crosspiece.

barruntar vt to guess; to foresee; to conjecture.

barrunto m conjecture.

bártulos mpl gear, belongings pl.

barullo m uproar.

basamento m base.

basalto m basalt.

basar vt to base; **~se** vr **~ en** to be based on.

basca f squeamishness, nausea.

báscula f scales pl.

base f base, basis.

básico/ca adj basic.

basílica f basilica.

basilisco m basilisk.

bastante adj sufficient, enough; * adv quite.

bastar vi to be sufficient, to be enough.

bastardo/da adj, m/f bastard.

bastidor m embroidery frame; **~es** mpl scenery (on stage).

bastión m bastion.

basto/ta adj coarse, rude, unpolished.

bastón m cane, stick; truncheon; (fig) command.

bastonazo m beating.

bastos m clubs pl (one of the four suits at cards).

basura f rubbish, trash, refuse; dung.

basurero m refuse collector, dustman; dunghill.

bata f dressing gown; overall; laboratory coat.

batacazo m noise of a fall.

batalla f battle, combat; fight.

batallador/a adj battling.

batallar vi to battle, to fight; to fence with foils; to waver.

batallón m (mil) battalion.

batata f sweet potato.

bate m bat.

batería f battery; percussion.

batida f beating (of woodland/moorland); search; chase.

batido/da adj shot (of silk); welltrodden (of roads); * m batter; **~ de leche** milk shake.

batidora f food mixer; whisk.

batir vt to beat; to whisk; to dash; to demolish; to defeat.

batista f fine cotton cloth, cambric.
batuta f baton.
baúl m trunk; (fam) belly.
bautismal adj baptismal.
bautismo m baptism.
bautizar vt to baptize, to christen.
bautizo m baptism.
baya f berry.
bayeta f cloth.
bayo/ya adj bay (colour of a horse).
bayoneta f bayonet.
bayonetazo m thrust with a bayonet.
baza f card trick.
bazar m bazaar.
bazo m spleen.
bazofia f refuse; hogwash.
be m baa (cry of sheep).
beatificación f beatification.
beatificar vt to beatify; to hallow, to sanctify, to make blessed.
beato/ta adj happy; blessed; devout; * m lay brother; m/f pious person; beatified person.
bebé m/f baby.
bebedero m drinking trough.
bebedizo m (love) potion.
bebedor/ra m/f (hard) drinker.
beber vt, vi to drink.
bebida f drink, beverage.
beca f fellowship; grant, bursary, scholarship; sash; hood.
becada f woodcock.
becerro m yearling calf.
bedel m janitor; uniformed employee.
befa f jeer, taunt.
befarse vr: ~ de to mock, to ridicule.
beldad f beauty.
belén m nativity scene.
bélico/ca adj warlike, martial.
belicoso/sa adj warlike; aggressive.
beligerante adj belligerent.
bellaco/ca adj artful; cunning.

belladona f (bot) deadly nightshade.
belleza f beauty.
bello/lla adj beautiful; handsome; lovely; fine.
bellota f acorn; (med) Adam's apple; pomander.
bemol m (mus) flat.
bencina f benzine.
bendecir vt to bless; to consecrate; to praise.
bendición f blessing, benediction.
bendito/ta adj saintly; blessed; simple; happy.
benedictino/na/benito/ta adj, m/f Benedictine.
beneficiado m incumbent; beneficiary.
beneficiar vt to benefit; to be of benefit to.
beneficiario/ra m/f beneficiary.
beneficio m benefit, advantage; profit; benefit night.
beneficioso/sa adj beneficial.
benéfico/ca adj beneficent, kind.
benemérito/ta adj worthy, meritorious.
beneplácito m consent, approbation.
benevolencia f benevolence.
benévolo/la adj benevolent, kindhearted.
benigno/na adj benign; kind; mild.
beodo/da adj drunk, drunken.
berberecho m cockle.
berenjena f eggplant.
bergantín m (mar) brig.
bermejo/ja adj red.
berrear vi to low, to bellow.
berrido m bellowing (of a calf).
berrinche m anger, rage, tantrum (applied to children).
berro m watercress.
berza f cabbage.

besamanos *m invar* levee; royal audience.
besamel *f* white sauce.
besar *vt* to kiss; to graze; **~se** *vr* to kiss.
beso *m* kiss; collision of persons or things.
bestia *f* beast, animal; idiot.
bestial *adj* bestial; *(fam)* marvellous, great.
bestialidad *f* bestiality.
besugo *m* sea bream.
besuquear *vt* to cover with kisses.
besuqueo *m* repeated kisses *pl*.
betún *m* shoe polish.
bezo *m* thick lip; swollen tissue in a wound.
biberón *m* feeding bottle.
Biblia *f* Bible.
bíblico/ca *adj* biblical.
bibliófilo/la *m/f* book-lover, book-worm.
bibliografía *f* bibliography.
bibliográfico/ca *adj* bibliographical.
bibliógrafo/fa *m/f* bibliographer.
biblioteca *f* library.
bibliotecario/ria *m/f* librarian.
bicarbonato *m* bicarbonate.
bicho *m* small animal; bug; **mal ~** villain.
bici *f (fam)* bike.
bicicleta *f* bicycle; **~ de montaña** mountain bike.
bidé *m* bidet.
bielda *f* pitchfork.
bien *m* good, benefit; profit; **~es** *mpl* goods *pl*, property; wealth; * *adv* well, right; very; willingly; easily; **~ que** *conj* although; **está ~** he is well.
bienal *adj* biennial.
bienaventuranza *f* blessedness; bliss; happiness; prosperity; **~s** *fpl* the Beatitudes.

bienestar *m* well-being.
bienhablado/da *adj* well-spoken.
bienhecho/cha *adj* well-shaped.
bienhechor/ra *m/f* benefactor.
bienio *m* space of two years.
bienvenida *f* welcome.
bifurcación *f* fork.
bigamia *f* bigamy.
bígamo/ma *m/f* bigamist.
bigote *m* moustache; whiskers *pl*.
bigotudo/da *adj* with a big moustache.
bikini *m* bikini.
bilingüe *adj* bilingual.
bilioso/sa *adj* bilious.
bilis *f* bile.
billar *m* billiards *pl*.
billete *m* note, banknote; ticket; *(ferro)* ticket; **~ sencillo** single ticket; **~ de ida y vuelta** return ticket.
billetero *m* wallet.
billón *m* trillion.
bimensual *adj* twice monthly.
bimotor *m* twin-engined plane.
binario *m* binary.
binoculares *mpl* binoculars *pl*; opera glasses *pl*.
biodegradable *adj* biodegradable.
biodiversity *f* biodiversity.
biografía *f* biography.
biógrafo/fa *m/f* biographer.
biología *f* biology.
biológico/ca *adj* biological.
biólogo/ga *m/f* biologist.
biombo *m* screen.
biopsia *f* biopsy.
bípedo *m* biped.
birlar *vt* to knock down at one blow; to pinch *(fam)*.
birreta *f* biretta.
bis *excl* encore.
bisabuela *f* great-grandmother.
bisabuelo *m* great-grandfather.
bisagra *f* hinge.

bisexual *adj* bisexual.

bisexualidad *f* bisexuality.

bisiesto *adj*: año ~ leap year.

bisnieto/ta *m/f* great-grand-son/daughter.

bisoño/na *adj* raw, inexperienced; novice.

bisonte *m* bison.

bistec *m* steak.

bisturí *m* scalpel.

bisutería *f* costume jewellery.

bizarro/rra *adj* brave, gallant; generous.

bizco/ca *adj* cross-eyed.

bizcocho *m* sponge cake; biscuit; ship's biscuit.

bizquear *vi* to squint.

blanco/ca *adj* white; blank; * *m* whiteness; white person; blank, blank space; target (to shoot at).

blancura *f* whiteness.

blandir *vt* to brandish a sword; ~se *vr* to swing.

blando/da *adj* soft, smooth; mild, gentle; (*fam*) cowardly.

blanducho/cha *adj* flabby.

blandura *f* softness; gentleness, mildness.

blanquear *vt* to bleach; to white-wash; to launder (money); * *vi* to show white.

blanquecino/na *adj* whitish.

blanqueo *m* laundering (of money).

blasfemador/ra *m/f* blasphemer.

blasfemar *vi* to blaspheme.

blasfemia *f* blasphemy; verbal insult.

blasfemo/ma *adj* blasphemous; * *m* blasphemer.

blasón *m* heraldry, honour, glory.

blasonar *vt* to emblazon; to praise highly.

bledo *m*: me importa un ~ I don't give a damn (*sl*).

blindado/da *adj* armour-plated; bullet-proof.

bloc *m* writing pad.

bloque *m* block.

bloquear *vt* to block; to blockade.

bloqueo *m* blockade.

blusa *f* blouse.

boato *m* ostentation, pompous show.

bobada *f* folly, foolishness.

bobear *vi* to act or talk in a stupid manner.

bobería *f* silliness, foolishness.

bobina *f* bobbin.

bobo/ba *m/f* idiot, fool; clown, funny man; * *adj* stupid, silly.

boca *f* mouth; entrance, opening; mouth of a river; ~ en ~ *adv* by word of mouth; a pedir de ~ to one's heart's content.

bocacalle *f* entrance to a street.

bocadillo *m* sandwich, roll.

bocado *m* mouthful.

bocal *m* pitcher; mouthpiece of a trumpet.

bocamanga *f* cuff.

bocanada *f* mouthful (of liquor); gust.

bocazas *m/f invar* loudmouth.

boceto *m* sketch.

bochorno *m* sultry weather, scorching heat; blush.

bochornoso/sa *adj* sultry; shameful.

bocina *f* trumpet; megaphone; horn (of a car).

boda *f* wedding.

bodega *f* wine cellar; warehouse; bar.

bodegón *m* cheap restaurant; still life (in art).

bodoque *m* pellet; lump; (*fam*) idiot.

bodorrio *m* quiet wedding.

bofes *mpl* lungs; lights.

bofetada *f* slap (in the face).

bofetón m hard slap.

boga f fashion; (ferro) bogey; rower; rowing; **estar en ~ to** be fashionable.

bogar vi to row, to paddle.

bohemio m/f Bohemian.

boicot m boycott.

boicotear vt to boycott.

boina f beret.

boj m box, box tree.

bola f ball; marble; globe; slam (in cards); shoe polish; (fam) lie, fib.

bolazo m blow with a ball.

bolchevique adj Bolshevik.

bolear vi to knock balls about (billiards); * vt to throw (a ball).

bolera f bowling alley.

bolero m bolero jacket; bolero dance.

boleta f entrance ticket; pass, permit.

boletín m bulletin; journal, review.

boleto m ticket.

boli m (fam) (ballpoint) pen.

boliche m jack (at bowls); bowls, bowling alley; dragnet.

bolígrafo m (ballpoint) pen.

bolillo m bobbin.

bollo m bread roll; lump.

bolo m ninepin; (large) pill.

bolsa f handbag; bag; pocket; sac; stock exchange.

bolsillo m pocket; purse.

bolsista m/f stockbroker.

bolso m purse.

bomba f pump; bomb; surprise; **dar a la ~ to** pump; **~ de gasolina** petrol pump.

bombardear vt to bombard.

bombardeo m bombardment.

bombardero m bomber.

bombazo m explosion; bombshell.

bombero m fireman.

bombilla f light bulb.

bombín m bowler hat.

bombo m large drum.

bombón m sweet; chocolate.

bonachón/ona adj good-natured.

bonanza f fair weather (at sea); prosperity; bonanza.

bondad f goodness, kindness; courtesy.

bondadoso/sa adj good, kind.

bonete m clerical hat; college cap.

bonito adj pretty, nice-looking; pretty good, passable; * m tuna (fish).

bono m (financial) bond.

boñiga f cow pat.

bonsái m bonsai.

boqueada f act of opening the mouth; **la última ~** the last gasp.

boquear vi to gape;, to gasp; to breathe one's last; * vt to pronounce, to utter (a word).

boquerón m anchovy; large hole.

boquete m gap, narrow entrance.

boquiabierto/ta adj open-mouthed; gaping.

boquilla f mouthpiece of a musical instrument; nozzle.

borbollón/borbotón m bubbling; **salir a borbollones** to gush forth.

borda f (mar) gunwale; hut.

bordado m embroidery.

bordadora f embroiderer.

bordar vt to embroider; to do anything very well.

borde m border; margin; (mar) board.

bordear vi (mar) to tack; * vt to go along the edge of; to flank.

bordillo m kerb.

bordo m (mar) board of a ship.

boreal adj boreal, northern.

borgoña m burgundy wine.

borla f tassel; tuft.

borona f millet; corn; corn bread.

borrachera f drunkenness; hard drinking; spree.

borracho/cha adj drunk, intoxicated; blind with passion; * m/f drunk, drunkard.

borrador m first draft; scribbling pad; eraser.

borraja f (bot) borage.

borrar vt to erase, to rub out; to blur; to obscure.

borrasca f storm; violent squall of wind; hazard; danger.

borrascoso/sa adj stormy.

borrego/ga m/f yearling lamb; simpleton, blockhead.

borrico/ca m/f donkey, ass; blockhead.

borrón m blot, blur; rough draft of a writing; first sketch of a painting; stain, blemish.

borronear vt to sketch.

boscaje m grove, small wood; landscape (in painting).

bosque m forest; wood.

bosquejar vt to make a sketch of (a painting); to make a rough model of (a figure).

bosquejo m sketch (of a painting); unfinished work.

bostezar vi to yawn; to gape.

bostezo m yawn; yawning.

bota f leather wine-bag; boot.

botánica f botany.

botánico/ca adj botanic; * m/f botanist.

botanista m/f botanist.

botar vt to cast, to fling; to launch.

bote m bounce; thrust; tin, can; boat.

botella f bottle.

botica f pharmacy.

boticario/ria m/f pharmacist.

botijo m earthenware jug.

botín m high boot, half-boot; gaiter; booty.

botiquín m medicine chest.

botón m button; knob (of a radio etc); (bot) bud.

botonadura f set of buttons.

botones m invar bellboy.

bóveda f arch; vault, crypt.

boxeador m boxer.

boxeo m boxing.

boya f (mar) buoy.

boyante adj buoyant, floating; (fig) fortunate, successful.

bozal m muzzle.

bozo m down (on the upper lip or chin); head collar (of a horse).

braceada f violent movement of the arms.

bracear vi to swing the arms.

bracero m day-labourer; farm-hand.

braga f sling, rope; nappy; ~s fpl panties pl.

bragazas m invar henpecked husband.

braguero m truss.

bragueta f fly, flies pl (of trousers).

braille m braille.

bramante m twine, string.

bramar vi to roar, to bellow; to storm, to bluster.

bramido m roar, bellow, howl.

brasa f live coal; **estar hecho una ~** to be very flushed.

brasero m brazier.

bravamente adv bravely, gallantly; fiercely; roughly; extremely well.

bravío/vía adj ferocious, savage, wild; coarse; * m fierceness, savageness.

bravo/va adj brave, valiant; bullying; savage, fierce; rough; sumptuous; excellent, fine; * excl well done!

bravura f ferocity; courage.

braza f fathom.

brazada f extension of the arms; armful.

brazado m armful.

brazal m armband; irrigation channel.

brazalete m bracelet.

brazo m arm; branch (of a tree); enterprise; courage; **luchar a ~** partido to fight hand to hand.

brea f pitch; tar.

brear vt to pitch; to tar; to abuse, to ill-treat; to play a joke on.

brebaje m potion.

brecha f (mil) breach; gap, opening; **batir en ~** (mil) to make a breach.

bregar vi to struggle; to quarrel; to slog away.

breva f early fig; early large acorn.

breve m papal brief; * f (mus) breve; * adj brief, short; **en ~** shortly.

brevedad f brevity, shortness, conciseness.

breviario m breviary; (fig) daily reading.

brezo m (bot) heather.

bribón/ona adj dishonest, rascally.

bribonear vi to be idle; to play dirty tricks.

bricolaje m do-it-yourself.

brida f bridle; clamp, flange.

bridge m bridge (cards).

brigada f brigade; squad, gang.

brigadier m brigadier.

brillante adj brilliant; bright, shining; * m diamond.

brillar vi to shine; to sparkle, to glisten; to shine, to be outstanding.

brillo m brilliance, brightness.

brincar vi to skip; to leap, to jump; to gambol; to fly into a passion.

brinco m leap, jump; bounce.

brindar vi : **~ a la salud de/~ por** to drink the health of, to toast; * vt to offer, to present.

brindis m invar toast.

brío m spirit, dash.

briosamente adv spiritedly, dashingly.

brioso/sa adj dashing, full of spirit; lively.

brisa f breeze.

brisca f card game.

broca f reel; drill; shoemaker's tack.

brocado m gold or silver brocade; **~/da** adj embroidered; like brocade.

brocal m rim, mouth; curb.

brocha f large brush; **~ de afeitar** shaving brush.

brochada f brushstroke.

broche m clasp; brooch; cufflink.

broma f joke.

bromear vi to joke.

bromista m/f joker.

bronca f row.

bronce m bronze.

bronceado/da adj tanned; * m bronzing, suntan.

broncearse vr to get a suntan.

bronco/ca adj rough, coarse; rude; harsh.

bronquitis f bronchitis.

broquel m shield.

brotar vi (bot) to bud, to germinate; to gush, to rush out; (med) to break out.

brote m (bot) shoot; (med) outbreak.

bruces adv: **de ~** face downward(s).

bruja f witch.

brujería f witchcraft.

brujo m sorcerer, magician, wizard.

brújula f compass.

bruma f mist; (mar) sea mist.

brumoso/sa *adj* misty.

bruñido *m* polish.

bruñir *vt* to polish; to put rouge on.

brusco/ca *adj* rude; sudden; brusque.

brutal *adj* brutal, brutish.

brutalidad *f* brutality; brutal action.

bruto *m* brute, beast; **~/ta** *adj* stupid; gross; brutish.

buba *f* tumour.

bucal *adj* oral.

bucear *vi* to dive.

buceo *m* diving.

bucle *m* curl.

bucólica *f* pastoral poetry; (*fam*) food.

buche *m* craw, maw; (*fam*) guts *pl*; mouthful; crease in clothes.

budismo *m* Buddhism.

buen *adj* (*before nouns*) good.

buenamente *adv* easily; willingly.

buenaventura *f* fortune, good luck.

bueno/na *adj* good, perfect; fair; fit, proper; good-looking; **¡buenos días!** good morning!; **¡buenas tardes!** good afternoon!; **¡buenas noches!** good night!; **¡~!** right!

buey *m* ox, bullock.

bufa *f* joke, mock.

búfalo *m* buffalo.

bufanda *f* scarf.

bufar *vi* to choke with anger; to snort.

bufete *m* desk, writing-table; lawyer's office.

bufido *m* snorting (of an animal).

bufo/fa *adj* comic; **ópera ~a** *f* comic opera.

bufón *m* buffoon; jester; **~/ona** *adj* funny, comical.

bufonada *f* buffoonery; joke.

buhardilla *f* attic.

búho *m* owl; unsocial person.

buhonero *m* pedlar, hawker.

buitre *m* vulture.

bujía *f* candle; spark plug.

bula *f* papal bull.

bulbo *m* (*bot*) bulb.

bulboso/sa *adj* bulbous.

bulevar *m* boulevard.

bulla *f* confused noise, clatter; crowd; **meter ~** to make a noise.

bullicio *m* bustle; uproar.

bullicioso/sa *adj* lively, restless, noisy, busy; turbulent; boisterous.

bulto *m* bulk; tumour, swelling; bust; baggage.

buñuelo *m* doughnut; fritter.

buque *m* vessel, ship, tonnage, capacity(of a ship); hull (of a ship).

burbuja *f* bubble.

burbujear *vi* to bubble.

burdel *m* brothel.

burdo/da *adj* coarse, rough.

burgués/sa *adj* bourgeois.

burguesía *f* bourgeoisie.

buril *m* engraver's chisel.

burla *f* trick; gibe; joke; **de ~s** in fun.

burlar *vt* to hoax; to defeat; to play tricks on, to deceive; to frustrate; **~se** *vr* to joke, to laugh at.

burlesco/ca *adj* burlesque; comical, funny.

burlón/ona *m/f* joker.

burocracia *f* bureaucracy.

burócrata *m/f* bureaucrat.

burrada *f* drove of asses; stupid action.

burro *m* ass, donkey; idiot; sawhorse.

bursátil *adj* stock exchange *compd*.

bus *m* bus.

busca *f* search, hunt; bleeper.

buscapiés *m invar* jumping jack (fireworks).

buscar vt to seek, to search for; to look for; to hunt after; * vi to look, to search, to seek.

buscavidas m prying person, busybody.

buscón m petty thief, small-time crook.

búsqueda f search.

busto m bust.

butaca f armchair; seat.

butano m butane.

butifarra f Catalan sausage.

buzo m diver.

buzón m letter box, postbox; conduit, canal; cover of a jar.

C

cabal adj just, exact; right; complete; accomplished.

cábalas fpl intrigue.

cabalgada f cavalcade; (mil) cavalry raid.

cabalgadura f mount horse, beast of burden.

cabalgar vi to ride, to go riding.

cabalgata f procession.

cabalístico/ca adj cabalistic.

caballa f mackerel.

caballar adj equine.

caballería f mount, steed; cavalry; cavalry horse; chivalry; knight-hood.

caballeriza f stable; stud; stable hands pl.

caballerizo m groom.

caballero m knight; gentleman; rider, horseman; horse soldier; ~ andante knight errant.

caballerosidad f chivalry.

caballeroso/sa adj noble; gentlemanlike.

caballete m ridge of a roof; painter's easel; trestle; bridge (of the nose).

caballo m horse; ~ de carreras racehorse; (at chess) knight; queen (in cards); a ~ on horseback.

cabaña f hut, cabin; hovel; livestock; balk (in billiards).

cabaré m cabaret.

cabecear vi to nod (with sleep); to shake one's head; (mar) to pitch.

cabeceo m nod; shaking (of the head).

cabecera f headboard; head; far end; pillow; headline; vignette.

cabecilla m ringleader.

cabellera f head of hair; wig; tail of a comet.

cabello m hair.

cabelludo/da adj hairy, shaggy.

caber vi to fit.

cabestrillo m sling.

cabestro m halter; bell-ox.

cabeza f head; chief, leader; main town, chief centre.

cabezada f butt; nod/shake of the head.

cabezal m pillow; compress.

cabezón m collar (of a shirt); opening in a garment for the head.

cabezudo/da adj big-headed; pig-headed.

cabida f room, capacity; tener ~ con una persona to have influence with someone.

cabildo m chapter (of a church); meeting of a chapter; corporation of a town.

cabina f cabin; telephone booth.

cabizbajo/ja, cabizcaído/da adj crestfallen; pensive, thoughtful.
cable m cable, lead, wire.
cabo m end, extremity; cape, headland; (mar) cable, rope.
cabra f goat.
cabrero m goatherd.
cabrío/a adj goatish.
cabriola f caper; gambol.
cabritilla f kidskin.
cabrito m kid.
cabrón m cuckold; i~! (fam) bastard! (sl).
cacahuete m peanut.
cacao m (bot) cacao tree; cocoa.
cacarear vi to crow; to brag, to boast.
cacareo m crowing of a cock, cackling of a hen; boast, brag.
cacería f hunting-party.
cacerola f pan, saucepan; casserole.
cachalote m sperm whale.
cacharro m pot; piece of junk.
cachear vt to frisk.
cachemir m cashmere.
cacheo m frisking.
cachete m cheek; slap in the face.
cachiporra f truncheon.
cachivache m pot; piece of junk.
cacho m slice, piece (of lemons, oranges, etc); horn.
cachondeo m (fam) farce.
cachondo/da adj randy; funny.
cachorro/ra m/f puppy; cub (of any animal).
cacique m chief; local party boss.
caco m pickpocket; coward.
cacofonía f cacophony.
cacto/cactus m cactus.
cada adj invar each; every.
cadalso m scaffold.
cadáver m corpse, cadaver.
cadavérico/ca adj cadaverous.

cadena f chain; series, link; radio or TV network.
cadencia f cadence.
cadente adj harmonious.
cadera f hip.
cadete m (mil) cadet.
caducar vi to become senile; to expire, to lapse; to deteriorate.
caducidad f expiry.
caduco/ca adj worn out; decrepit; perishable; expired, lapsed.
caer vi to fall; to tumble down; to lapse; to happen; to die; **~se** vr to fall down.
café m coffee; cafe, coffee house.
cafetera f coffee pot.
cafetería f cafe.
cafetero/ra m/f coffee merchant; cafe owner.
cafre adj savage, inhuman; rude.
cagar vi (fam) to have a shit (sl).
caída f fall, falling; slope, descent.
caimán m caiman, alligator.
caja f box, case; casket; cashbox; cash desk; check-out, till; **~ de ahorros** savings bank; **~ de cambios** gearbox; **~ negra** black box.
cajero/ra m/f cashier, teller; **~ automático** cash machine.
cajetilla f packet.
cajón m chest of drawers; locker.
cal f lime; **~ viva** quick lime.
cala f creek, small bay; small piece of melon, etc; (mar) hold; dipstick.
calabacín m small marrow, courgette.
calabaza f pumpkin, squash.
calabozo m prison; cell.
calada f soaking; lowering of nets; puff, drag; swoop.
calado m openwork in metal, wood or linen.
calafatear vt (mar) to calk.

calamar *m* squid.

calambre *m* cramp.

calamidad *f* calamity, disaster.

calamitoso/sa *adj* calamitous.

calaña *f* model; pattern.

calandria *f* calendra lark.

calar *vt* to soak, to drench; to penetrate, to pierce; to see through; to lower; ~se *vr* to stall (of a car).

calavera *f* skull; madcap.

calaverada *f* ridiculous or foolish action.

calcañar *m* heel.

calcar *vt* to trace, to copy.

calcáreo/rea *adj* calcareous.

calceta *f* (knee-length) stocking.

calcetín *m* sock.

calcinar *vt* to calcine.

calcio *m* calcium.

calco *m* tracing.

calcomanía *f* transfer.

calculable *adj* calculable.

calculadora *f* calculator.

calcular *vt* to calculate, to reckon; to compute.

cálculo *m* calculation, estimate; calculus; (*med*) gallstone.

caldear *vt* to weld; to warm, to heat up.

caldera *f* kettle, boiler; **las ~s de Pero Botero** (*fam*) hell.

calderada *f* stew.

calderilla *f* holy water fount; small change.

caldero *m* small boiler.

caldo *m* stock; broth.

caldoso/sa *adj* having too much broth or gravy.

calefacción *f* heating.

calendario *m* calendar.

calentador *m* heater.

calentamiento *m* ~ **global** global warming.

calentar *vt* to warm up, to heat up; ~se *vr* to grow hot; to dispute.

calentura *f* fever.

calenturiento/ta *adj* feverish.

calesa *f* calash, cab.

calibre *m* calibre; (*fig*) calibre.

calidad *f* grade, quality, condition; kind.

cálido/da *adj* hot; (*fig*) warm.

caliente *adj* hot; fiery; **en ~** in the heat of the moment.

califa *m* caliph.

califato *m* caliphate.

calificación *f* qualification; grade.

calificar *vt* to qualify; to assess, to mark; ~se *vr* to register as a voter.

caligrafía *f* calligraphy.

calistenia *f* callisthenics.

cáliz *m* chalice.

calizo/za *adj* calcareous.

callado/da *adj* silent, quiet.

callandico *adv* softly, silently.

callar *vi*, ~se *vr* to be silent, to keep quiet.

calle *f* street; road.

calleja *f* lane, narrow passage.

callejear *vi* to loiter about the streets.

callejero/ra *adj* loitering.

callejón *m* alley.

callejuela *f* lane, narrow passage; subterfuge.

callista *m/f* chiropodist.

callo *m* corn; callus; ~s *mpl* tripe.

callosidad *f* callosity.

calloso/sa *adj* callous; horny.

calma *f* calm, calmness.

calmante *m* (*med*) sedative.

calmar *vt* to calm, to quiet, to pacify. * *vi* to become calm.

calmoso/sa *adj* calm; tranquil.

calor *m* heat, warmth; ardour, passion.

caloría *f* calorie.

calumnia *f* calumny, slander.

calumniar *vt* to slander.

calumnioso/sa *adj* slanderous.

caluroso/sa *adj* warm; hot; lively.

calva *f* bald patch.

calvario *m* Calvary; (*fig*) debts *pl*.

calvicie *f* baldness.

calvinismo *m* Calvinism.

calvinista *m/f* Calvinist.

calvo/va *adj* bald; bare, barren.

calza *f* wedge.

calzado *m* footwear.

calzador *m* shoehorn.

calzar *vt* to put on (shoes); to wear (shoes); to stop (a wheel); ~**se** *vr* to put on one's shoes.

calzón *m* shorts *pl*; pants *pl*; panties *pl*.

calzonazos *m invar* stupid guy; **es un** ~ he is a weak-willed guy.

calzoncillos *mpl* underpants *pl*, shorts *pl*.

cama *f* bed; **hacer la** ~ to make the bed.

camada *f* litter (of animals); ~ **de ladrones** gang of thieves.

camafeo *m* cameo.

camaleón *m* chameleon.

camandulero/ra *adj* prudish; hypocritical; sly, tricky.

cámara *f* hall; chamber; room; camera; cine camera.

camarada *m/f* comrade, companion.

camarera *f* waitress; maid.

camarero *m* waiter.

camarilla *f* clique; lobby.

camarín *m* dressing room; lift car.

camarón *m* shrimp, prawn.

camarote *m* berth, cabin.

cambalache *m* exchange, swap.

cambalachear *vt* to exchange, to swap.

cambiable *adj* changeable, variable; interchangeable.

cambiar *vt* to exchange; to change. * *vi* to change, to alter; ~**se** *vr* to move house.

cambio *m* change, exchange; rate of exchange; bureau de change.

cambista *m/f* exchange broker.

camelar *vt* to flirt with.

camello *m* camel.

camilla *f* couch; cot; stretcher.

caminante *m/f* traveller, walker.

caminar *vi* to travel; to walk, to go.

caminata *f* long walk; hike.

camino *m* road; way.

camión *m* truck.

camioneta *f* van.

camisa *f* shirt; chemise.

camiseta *f* T-shirt; vest.

camisón *m* nightgown.

camorra *f* quarrel, dispute.

camorrista *m/f* quarrelsome person.

campamento *m* (*mil*) encampment, camp.

campana *f* bell.

campaña *f* countryside; level country, plain; (*mil*) campaign.

campanada *f* peal of a bell; (*fig*) scandal.

campanario *m* belfry.

campaneo *m* bellringing, chime.

campanero *m* bell founder; bellringer.

campanilla *f* handbell; (*med*) uvula.

campante *adj* excelling, outstanding; smug.

campánula *f* bellflower.

campear *vi* to go out to pasture; to work in the fields.

campechano/na *adj* open.

campeón/ona *m/f* champion.

campeonato *m* championship.

campesino/na, campestre *adj* rural.

campiña f flat tract of cultivated farmland.

camping m camping, campsite.

campista m/f camper.

campo m country; field; camp; ground; pitch; ~ **de refugiados** refugee camp.

campus m *invar* campus.

camuflaje m camouflage.

caña f cane, reed; stalk; shinbone; glass of beer; ~ **dulce** sugar cane.

canal m channel, canal.

canalizar vt to canalize.

canalla f mob, rabble.

canalón m large gutter.

cáñamo m hemp.

cañamón m hemp seed.

canana f cartridge belt.

canapé f couch, sofa.

canario m canary.

canas fpl grey hair; **peinar** ~ to grow old.

canasta f basket, hamper.

canastilla f small basket.

canasto m large basket.

cañaveral m reedbed.

cancel m storm door.

cancelación f cancellation.

cancelar vt to cancel; to write off.

Cáncer m Cancer (sign of the zodiac).

cáncer m cancer.

cancerígeno/na adj carcinogenic.

canceroso/sa adj cancerous.

cancha f (tennis) court.

canciller m chancellor; foreign minister.

canción f song.

cancionero m songbook.

candado m padlock.

candela f candle.

candelabro m candlestick.

candente adj red-hot.

candidato/ta m/f candidate.

cándido/da adj simple, naïve; white, snowy.

candil m oil lamp.

candilejas fpl footlights pl.

candor m candour; innocence.

canela f cinnamon.

canelón m icicle.

cañería f conduit of water, water pipe.

cangrejo m crab; crayfish.

canguro m kangaroo; * f baby-sitter.

caníbal m/f cannibal, man-eater.

canica f marble.

canícula f dog days pl.

canijo/ja adj weak, sickly.

canilla f shinbone; arm-bone; tap of a cask; spool.

canino/na adj canine; **hambre ~a** f ravenous hunger.

canje m exchange.

canjear vt to exchange.

caño m tube, pipe; sewer.

cano/na adj grey-haired; white-haired.

canoa f canoe.

canon m canon; tax; royalty; rent.

cañón m tube, pipe; barrel; gun; canyon.

cañonazo m gunshot; (fig) bombshell.

cañonear vt to shell, to bombard.

cañoneo m shelling, gunfire.

cañonera f gunboat.

canónico/ca adj canonical.

canónigo m canon, prebendary.

canonización f canonization.

canonizar vt to canonize.

canoso/sa adj grey-haired; white-haired.

cansado/da adj weary, tired; tedious, tiresome.

cansancio m tiredness, fatigue.

cansar vt to tire, to tire out; to bore; **~se** vr to get tired, to grow weary.

cantable adj suitable for singing.

cantante m/f singer.

cantar m song. * vt to sing; to chant. * vi to sing; to chirp.

cántara f pitcher.

cantarín/ina m/f someone who sings a lot.

cántaro m pitcher; jug; **llover a ~s** to rain heavily, to pour.

cantera f quarry.

cantero m quarryman.

cántico m canticle.

cantidad f quantity, amount; number.

cantimplora f water bottle; hip flask.

cantina f buffet, refreshment room; canteen; cellar; snack bar; bar.

cantinela f ballad, song.

canto m stone; singing; song; edge.

cantón m corner; canton.

cantonear vi to loaf around.

cantor/ra m/f singer.

canuto m (fam) joint (sl), marijuana cigarette.

caoba f mahogany.

caos m chaos; confusion.

capa f cloak; cape; layer, stratum; cover; pretext; **~ de ozono** ozone layer.

capacho m hamper; big basket.

capacidad f capacity; extent; talent.

capar vt to geld; to castrate; (fig) to curtail.

caparazón m caparison.

capataz m foreman, overseer.

capaz adj capable; capacious, spacious, roomy.

capazo m large basket; carrycot.

capcionar vt to seize, to arrest.

capcioso/sa adj wily, deceitful.

capear vt to flourish (one's cloak in

front of a bull); * vi (mar) to ride out or weather (a storm).

capellán m chaplain.

capeo m challenging of a bull with a cloak.

caperuza f hood.

capilar adj capillary.

capilla f hood, cowl; chapel.

capirote m hood.

capital m capital; capital sum; * f capital, capital city; * adj capital; principal.

capitalismo m capitalism.

capitalista m/f capitalist.

capitalizar vt to capitalize.

capitán m captain.

capitana f flagship; (woman) captain (in sport).

capitanear vt to captain; to command.

capitanía f captaincy.

capitel m capital (of a column).

capitolio m capitol.

capitulación f capitulation; agreement; **~ones** fpl marriage contract.

capitular vi to come to terms, to make an agreement.

capítulo m chapter of a cathedral; chapter (of a book).

capó m (auto) bonnet.

capón m capon.

caporal m chief, ringleader.

capota f hat, bonnet.

capote m greatcoat; bullfighter's cloak.

capricho m caprice, whim, fancy.

caprichoso/sa adj capricious, whimsical; obstinate.

Capricornio m Capricorn (sign of the zodiac).

cápsula f capsule.

captar vt to captivate; to understand; (rad) to tune in to, to receive.

captura f capture, arrest.

capturar vt to capture.

capucha f circumflex (accent); cap, cowl, hood of a cloak.

capuchino m Capuchin monk; **(café)** ~ cappuccino (coffee).

capullo m cocoon of a silkworm; rosebud; coarse cloth made of spun silk.

caqui m, adj khaki.

cara f face; appearance; ~ **a** ~ face to face.

carabina f carbine, rifle.

carabinero m carabineer.

caracol m snail; seashell; spiral.

caracola f shell.

caracolear vi to prance about (of a horse).

carácter m character; quality; condition; handwriting.

característico/ca adj characteristic.

caracterizar vt to characterize.

caradura m/f: **es un** ~ he's got a nerve.

caramba excl well!

carámbano m icicle.

carambola f cannon (at billiards); trick.

caramelo m candy.

caramente adv dearly.

caramillo m small flute; piece of gossip.

carantoña f hideous mask; dressed-up old woman; ~**s** fpl caresses pl.

carátula f pasteboard mask; **la** ~ the stage.

caravana f caravan; tailback (of traffic).

caray excl well!

carbón m coal; charcoal; carbon; carbon paper.

carbonada f grill; kind of pancake.

carboncillo m charcoal.

carbonera f coal tip; coal mine.

carbonería f coalyard.

carbonero m coal merchant; (mar) collier.

carbónico/ca adj carbonic.

carbonilla f coaldust.

carbonizar vt to carbonize.

carbono m (quím) carbon.

carbunclo/carbunco m carbuncle.

carburador m carburettor.

carcaj m quiver.

carcajada f (loud) laugh.

carcamal m nickname for an old person.

cárcel f prison; jail.

carcelero m warder, jailer.

carcoma f deathwatch beetle; woodworm; anxious concern.

carcomer vt to gnaw, to corrode; ~**se** vr to grow worm-eaten.

carcomido/da adj worm-eaten.

cardar vt to card (wool).

cardenal m cardinal; cardinal bird; (med) bruise, weal.

cardenalicio/cia adj belonging to a cardinal.

cárdeno/na adj purple; livid.

cardíaco/ca, cardiaco/ca adj cardiac; * heart compd.

cardinal adj cardinal, principal.

cardo m thistle.

carear vt to bring face to face; to compare; ~**se** vr to come face to face.

carecer vi: ~ **de** to want, to lack.

carencia f lack.

careo m confrontation.

carero/ra adj pricey.

carestía f scarcity, want; famine.

careta f pasteboard mask.

carga f load; freight, cargo; (mil) charge; duty, obligation; tax.

cargadero m loading place.

cargado/da adj loaded; (elec) live.

cargador m loader; carrier; long-shoreman.

cargamento m cargo.

cargar vt to load, to burden; to charge; * vi to charge; to load (up); to lean.

cargo m burden, loading; employment, post; office; charge, care; obligation; accusation.

carguero m freighter.

cariarse vr to decay.

caricatura f caricature.

caricia f caress.

caridad f charity.

caries f (med) tooth decay, caries.

carilargo/ga adj long-faced.

carilla f side (of paper); beekeeper's mask.

cariño m fondness, tenderness; love.

cariñoso/sa adj affectionate; loving.

caritativo/va adj charitable.

cariz m look.

carmelita adj, m/f Carmelite.

carmesí adj, m crimson.

carmín m carmine; rouge; lipstick.

carnada f bait, lure.

carnal adj carnal, of the flesh; **primo ~** first cousin.

carnaval m carnival.

carn f flesh; meat; pulp (of fruit).

carné, carnet m driving licence; **~ de identidad** identity card.

carnero m sheep; mutton.

carnicería f butcher's shop; carnage, slaughter.

carnicero/ra m/f butcher. * adj carnivorous.

carnívoro/ra adj carnivorous.

carnoso/sa, carnudo adj beefy, fleshy.

caro/ra adj dear; affectionate; dear, expensive; * adv dearly.

carótida f carotid artery.

carpa f carp (fish); tent.

carpeta f table cover; folder, file, portfolio.

carpintería f carpentry; carpenter's shop.

carpintero m carpenter.

carraca f carrack (ship); rattle.

carrasca f, **carrasco** m evergreen oak.

carraspera f hoarseness.

carrera f career; course; race; run, running; route; journey; **a ~ abierta** at full speed.

carreta f long narrow cart.

carrete m reel, spool, bobbin.

carretera f road.

carretero m carter, cartwright.

carretilla f carter; truck; trolley; go-cart; squib, cracker; wheel barrow.

carretón m small cart.

carril m lane (of highway); furrow; **~ bus** bus lane.

carrillo m cheek; pulley.

carro m cart; car.

carrocería f bodywork, coachwork.

carromato m covered wagon, (Gypsy) caravan.

carroña f carrion.

carroza f state coach; (mar) awning.

carruaje m carriage; vehicle.

carrusel m merry-go-round.

carta f letter; map; document; playing card; menu; **~ blanca** carte blanche; **~ bomba** letter-bomb; **~ credencial o de creencia** credentials pl; **~ certificada** registered letter.

cartabón m square (tool).

cartapacio m notebook; folder.

cártel m cartel.

cartel m placard; poster; wall chart; cartel.

cartera *f* satchel; handbag; briefcase; postwoman.

carterista *m/f* pickpocket.

cartero *m* postman.

cartilaginoso/sa *adj* cartilaginous.

cartílago *m* cartilage.

cartilla *f* first reading book, primer.

cartón *m* cardboard, pasteboard; cartoon.

cartuchera *f* (*mil*) cartridge belt.

cartucho *m* (*mil*) cartridge.

cartuja *f* Carthusian order.

cartujo *m* Carthusian monk.

cartulina *f* card, pass; thin cardboard.

casa *f* house; home; firm, company; ~ **de campo** country house; ~ **de moneda** mint; ~ **de huéspedes** boarding house.

casaca *f* coat.

casación *f* abrogation.

casadero/ra *adj* marriageable.

casado/da *adj* married.

casamentero/ra *m/f* marriage-maker, matchmaker.

casamiento *m* marriage, wedding.

casar *vt* to marry; to couple; to abrogate; to annul; ~**se** *vr* to marry, to get married.

cascabel *m* small bell; rattlesnake.

cascada *f* cascade, waterfall.

cascanueces *m invar* nutcracker.

cascar *vt* to crack, to break into pieces; (*fam*) to beat; ~**se** *vr* to be broken open.

cáscara *f* rind, peel; husk, shell; bark.

cascarón *m* eggshell.

casco *m* skull; helmet; fragment; shard; hulk (of a ship); crown (of a hat); hoof; empty bottle, returnable bottle; ~**s** *azules* blue berets.

cascote *m* rubble, fragment of material used in building.

casera *f* landlady.

caserío *m* country house; hamlet.

casero *m* landlord; janitor; * ~/**ra**, *adj* domestic; household *compd*; home-made.

caset(t)e *m* cassette; * *f* cassette-player.

casi *adv* almost, nearly; ~ **nada** next to nothing; ~ **nunca** hardly ever, almost never.

casilla *f* hut, cabin; box office; square (on a chess board); pigeon-hole, compartment.

casillero *m* (set of) pigeonholes *pl*; luggage locker.

casino *m* club, social club.

caso *m* case; occurrence, event; hap, casuality; occasion; (*gr*) case; **en ese** ~ in that case; **en todo** ~ in any case; ~ **que** in case.

casorio *m* unwise marriage.

caspa *f* dandruff; scurf.

casquete *m* helmet.

casquillo *m* bottle top; tip, cap; point.

casta *f* caste; race; lineage; breed; kind, quality.

castaña *f* chestnut; demijohn.

castañar *m* chestnut grove.

castañetear *vi* to play the castanets.

castaño *m* chestnut tree; ~/**ña** *adj* chestnut(-coloured), brown.

castañuela *f* castanet.

castellano/na *adj* Castilian, Spanish.

castidad *f* chastity.

castigar *vt* to castigate, to punish; to afflict.

castigo *m* punishment; correction; penalty.

castillo *m* castle.

castizo/za *adj* pure, thoroughbred.

casto/ta *adj* pure, chaste.

castor *m* beaver.

castrar vt to geld, to castrate; to prune; to cut the honeycombs out of (beehives).

casual adj casual, accidental.

casualidad f chance, accident.

casucha f hovel; slum.

casulla f chasuble.

cata f tasting.

catacumbas fpl catacombs pl.

catador/ra m/f wine tester.

catadura f looks pl, face.

catalejo m telescope.

catalizador m catalyst; catalytic converter.

catálogo m catalogue.

catamarán m catamaran.

cataplasma f poultice.

catapulta f catapult.

catar vt to taste; to inspect, to examine; to look at; to esteem.

catarata f (med) cataract; waterfall.

catarro m catarrh.

catarroso/sa adj catarrhal.

catástrofe f catastrophe.

catavino m small cup for tasting wine; ~s m/f invar wine-taster; tippler.

catecismo m catechism.

cátedra f professor's chair.

catedral f cathedral.

catedrático/ca m/f professor (of a university).

categoría f category; rank.

categórico/ca adj categorical, decisive.

catequismo m catechism.

caterva f mob.

catolicismo m catholicism.

católico/ca adj, m/f catholic.

catorce adj, m fourteen.

catre m cot.

cauce m riverbed; (fig) channel.

caucho m rubber; tyre.

caución f caution; (jur) security; bail.

caucionar vt to prevent, to guard against; (jur) to bail.

caudal m volume, flow; property, wealth; plenty.

caudaloso/sa adj carrying much water (of rivers); wealthy, rich.

caudillo m leader.

causa f cause; motive, reason; lawsuit; **a ~ de** considering, because of.

causal adj causal.

causante m/f originator; * adj causing, originating.

causar vt to cause; to produce; to occasion.

cáustico/ca adj caustic; ~/ca adj caustic.

cautela f caution, cautiousness.

cauteloso/sa adj cautious, wary.

cauterizar vt (med) to cauterize; to apply a drastic remedy to.

cautivar vt to take prisoner in war; to captivate, to charm.

cautiverio m captivity.

cautividad f captivity.

cautivo/va adj, m/f captive.

cauto/ta adj cautious, wary.

cava f digging and earthing of vines; wine cellar; sparkling wine.

cavar vt to dig up, to excavate; * vi to dig, to delve; to think profoundly.

caverna f cavern, cave.

cavernoso/sa adj cavernous.

cavidad f cavity, hollow.

cavilación f deep thought.

cavilar vt to ponder, to consider carefully.

caviloso/sa adj obsessed; suspicious.

cayada f, **cayado** m shepherd's crook.

caza f hunting; shooting; chase; game; * m fighter-plane.

cazador/ra m/f hunter; m huntsman; ~ **furtivo** poacher.

cazamoscas m invar flycatcher (bird).

cazar vt to chase, to hunt; to catch.

cazo m saucepan; ladle.

cazuela f casserole; pan.

cazurro/rra adj silent, taciturn.

cebada f barley.

cebar vt to feed (animals), to fatten.

cebo m feed, food; bait, lure; priming.

cebolla f onion; bulb.

cebolleta f spring onion, scallion.

cebollino m onion seed; chive.

cebón m fattened pig.

cebra f zebra.

cecear vt to pronounce s the same as c; to lisp.

cecina f dried meat; salt beef.

cedazo m sieve, strainer.

ceder vt to hand over; to transfer, to make over; to yield, to give up; * vi to submit, to comply, to give in; to diminish, to grow less.

cederrón m CD-ROM.

cedro m cedar.

cédula f certificate; document; slip of paper; bill; ~ **de cambio** bill of exchange.

cegar vi to grow blind; * vt to blind; to block up.

cegato/ta adj short-sighted.

ceguera f blindness.

ceja f eyebrow; edging of clothes; (mus) bridge of a stringed instrument; brow of a hill.

cejar vi to go backward(s); to slacken, to give in.

celada f helmet; ambush; trick.

celador m watchman.

celda f cell.

celdilla f cell; cavity.

celebración f celebration; praise.

celebrar vt to celebrate; to praise; ~ **misa** to say mass.

célebre adj famous, renowned; witty, funny.

celebridad f celebrity, fame.

celeridad f speed, velocity.

celeste adj heavenly; sky-blue.

celestial adj heavenly; delightful.

celibato m celibacy.

célibe m/f bachelor, spinster.

celo m zeal; rut (in animals); Sellotape™; ~**s** mpl jealousy.

celofán m cellophane.

celosía f lattice (of a window).

celoso/sa adj zealous; jealous.

célula f cell.

celular adj cellular.

celulitis f cellulitis.

celuloide m celluloid.

cementerio m graveyard.

cemento m cement.

cena f dinner, supper.

cenador m arbour.

cenagoso/sa adj miry, marshy.

cenagal m quagmire.

cenar vt to have for dinner; * vi to have supper, to have dinner.

cencerro m jangle, clatter.

cenicero m ashtray.

ceniciento/ta adj ash-coloured.

ceñido/da adj tight-fitting; sparing, frugal.

ceñir vt to surround, to circle; to abbreviate, to abridge; to fit tightly.

cenit m zenith.

ceniza f ashes pl; **miércoles de ~** Ash Wednesday.

ceño m frown.

censo m census; tax; ground rent; ~ **electoral** electoral roll.

censor/ra m/f censor; reviewer, critic.

censura f censorship; review; censure, blame.

censurar vt to review, to criticize; to censure, to blame.

centella f lightning; spark.

centellear vi to sparkle.

centena f hundred.

centenadas adv: a ~ by hundreds.

centenar m hundred.

centenario/ia adj centenary; * m centenary.

centeno m rye.

centésimo/ma adj hundredth; * m hundredth.

centigrado m centigrade.

centímetro m centimetre.

céntimo m cent.

centinela f sentry, guard; lookout.

central adj central; * f head office, headquarters; (telephone) exchange; ~ **nuclear** nuclear power station.

centralización m centralization.

centralizar vt to centralize.

céntrico adj central.

centrífugo/ga adj centrifugal.

centrista adj centrist.

centro m centre; ~ **comercial** shopping centre.

centuplicar vt to increase a hundredfold.

céntuplo/pla adj centuple, hundredfold.

ceñudo/da adj frowning, grim.

cepa f stock (of a vine); origin (of a family).

cepillar vt to brush.

cepillo m brush; plane (tool).

cepo m branch, bough; trap; snare; poor box.

cera f wax; ~**s** fpl honeycomb.

cerámica f pottery.

cerca f enclosure; fence; ~**s** mpl

objects pl in the foreground of a painting; * adv near, at hand, close by; ~ **de** close, near.

cercanías fpl outskirts.

cercano/na adj near, close by; neighbouring, adjoining.

cercar vt to enclose, to circle; to fence in.

cerciorar vt to assure, to ascertain, to affirm; ~**se** vr to find out.

cerco m enclosure; fence; (mil) siege.

cerdo m pig.

cereal m cereal.

cerebelo m cerebellum.

cerebro m brain.

ceremonia f ceremony.

ceremonial adj, m ceremonial.

ceremonioso/sa adj ceremonious.

cereza f cherry.

cerezo m cherry tree.

cerilla f wax taper; ear wax; match, safety match.

cerner vt to sift; * vi to bud, to blossom; to drizzle; ~**se** vr to hover; to swagger.

cernido m sifting.

cero m nothing, zero.

cerquita adv close by.

cerrado/da adj closed, shut; locked; overcast, cloudy; broad (of accent).

cerradura f locking-up; lock.

cerrajería f trade of a locksmith; locksmith's shop.

cerrajero m locksmith.

cerrar vt to close, to shut; to block up; to lock; ~ **una cuenta** to close an account; ~**se** vr to close; to heal; to cloud over; vi to close, to shut; to hoist.

cerril adj mountainous; rough, wild, untamed.

cerro *m* hill; neck (of an animal); backbone; combed flax or hemp; **en ~** bareback.

cerrojo *m* bolt (of a door).

certamen *m* competition, contest.

certero *adj* accurate; well-aimed.

certeza, certidumbre *f* certainty.

certificación *f* certificate.

certificado *m* certificate; **~/da** *adj* registered (of a letter).

certificar *vt* to certify, to affirm.

cervato *m* fawn.

cervecería *f* bar; brewery.

cervecero *m* brewer.

cerveza *m* beer.

cerviz *f* nape of the neck; cervix.

cesación *f* cessation, stoppage.

cesar *vt* to cease, to stop; to fire (*sl*); to remove from office; * *vi* to cease, to stop; to retire.

cese *m* suspension; dismissal.

cesión *f* cession; transfer.

césped *m* grass; lawn.

cesta *f* basket, pannier.

cestería *f* basket shop; basketwork.

cesto *m* (large) basket.

cetrino/na *adj* greenish-yellow; sallow; jaundiced, melancholic.

cetro *m* sceptre.

chabacano/na *adj* coarse, vulgar; shoddy.

chabola *f* shack.

cháchara *f* chitchat, chatter, idle talk.

chacolí *m* light white wine with a sharp taste.

chafar *vt* to crush; to ruin.

chal *m* shawl.

chalado/da *adj* crazy.

chale(t) *m* detached house.

chaleco *m* waistcoat.

chalupa *f* (*mar*) boat, launch.

chamarra *f* sheepskin jacket.

champán *m* champagne.

champiñón *m* mushroom.

champú *m* shampoo.

chamuscar *vt* to singe, to scorch.

chamusquina *f* scorching; (*fig*) row, quarrel.

chanchullo *m* (*fam*) fix, fiddle (*sl*).

chanciller *m* chancellor.

chancleta *f* slipper.

chanclo *m* clog; galosh.

chándal *m* tracksuit.

chanfaina *f* cheap stew.

chantaje *m* blackmail.

chanza *f* joke, jest; **~s** *fpl* fun.

chapa *f* metal plate; panel; (*auto*) numberplate.

chaparrón *m* heavy shower (of rain).

chapotear *vt* to wet with a sponge; * *vi* to paddle (in water).

chapucear *vt* to botch, to bungle.

chapucero *m* bungler; **~/ra** *adj* clumsy, crude.

chapurrar *vt* to speak (a language) badly; to mix (drinks).

chapuza *f* badly done job.

chapuzarse *vr* to duck; to dive.

chaqueta *f* jacket.

charca *f* pool.

charco *m* pool, puddle.

charcutería *f* shop selling pork meat products.

charla *f* chat, talk.

charlar *vi* to chat.

charlatán/ana *m/f* chatterbox.

charlatanería *f* talkativeness.

charol *m* varnish; patent leather.

charrada *f* coarse thing; bad breeding; bad taste.

charretera *f* shoulder pad.

charro *m* coarse individual; **~/rra** *adj* coarse; gaudy.

charter *m* charter flight.

chasco *m* disappointment; joke, jest.

chasis *m invar* (*auto*) chassis.
chasquear *vt* to crack (a whip); to disappoint.
chasquido *m* crack; click.
chatarra *f* scrap.
chato/ta *adj* flat, flattish; snub-nosed.
chaval/la *m/f* lad/lass.
cheque *m* cheque.
chequeo *m* check-up; service.
chequera *f* chequebook.
chicano/na *adj* Chicano.
chicha *f* corn liquor; meat.
chicharra *f* harvest fly.
chicharrón *m* (pork) crackling.
chichón *m* lump, bump.
chichonera *f* helmet.
chicle *m* chewing gum.
chico/ca *adj* little, small; * *m/f* boy/
    girl.
chifla *f* whistle; hiss.
chiflado/da *adj* crazy.
chiflar *vt* to boo.
chile *m* chilli pepper.
chillar *vi* to scream, to shriek; to
    howl; to creak.
chillido *m* squeak; shriek, howl.
chillón/ona *adj* loud, noisy; gaudy;
    * *m/f* whiner, moaner.
chimenea *f* chimney; fireplace.
china *f* pebble; porcelain, china-
    ware; China silk.
chinche *f* bug; drawing pin, thumb-
    tack; * *m* nuisance.
chincheta *f* drawing pin.
chinela *f* slipper.
chino/na *adj*, *m/f* Chinese; * *m* Chi-
    nese language.
chiquero *m* pig sty.
chiripa *f* fluke.
chirla *f* mussel.
chirriar *vi* to hiss; to creak; to chirp.
chirrido *m* chirping (of birds);
    squeaking.

chis *excl* sh!
chisgarabís *m* (*fam*) meddler.
chisme *m* tale; thingummyjig.
chismear *vi* to tell tales.
chismoso/sa *adj* gossiping; * *m/f*
    gossip.
chispa *f* spark; sparkle; wit; drop (of
    rain); drunkenness.
chispazo *m* spark.
chispeante *adj* sparkling.
chispear *vi* to sparkle; to drizzle.
chisporrotear *vi* to crackle; to spar-
    kle; to hiss (of liquids).
chistar *vi* to speak.
chiste *m* funny story, joke.
chistoso/sa *adj* witty; amusing,
    funny.
chivato *m* kid; child.
chivo/va *m/f* billy/nanny goat.
chocante *adj* startling; odd.
chocar *vi* to strike, to knock; to
    crash; * *vt* to shock.
chochear *vi* to dodder, to be senile;
    to dote.
chocho *adj* doddering; doting.
chocolate *m* chocolate.
chocolatera *f* chocolate pot.
chófer *m* driver.
chollo *m* bargain.
chopo *m* (*bot*) black poplar.
choque *m* shock; crash, collision;
    clash, conflict.
chorizo *m* pork sausage.
chorlito *m* plover.
chorrear *vi* to spout, to gush; to drip.
chorrera *f* channel; frill.
chorro *m* gush; jet; stream; **a ~s**
    abundantly.
choto *m* kid; calf.
choza *f* hut, shack.
chubasco *m* squall.
chuchería *f* trinket.
chucho *m* mongrel.

chufleta *f* joke; taunt, jeer.
chulada *f* funny speech or action.
chulear *vi* to brag.
chuleta *f* chop.
chulo *m* rascal; pimp.
chunga *f* fun, joke; **estar de ~** to be in good humour.
chunguearse *vr* to be in good humour.
chupado/da *adj* skinny; easy.
chupar *vt* to suck; to absorb.
chupete *m* dummy.
chupetear *vi* to suck gently.
chupón/ona *m/f* swindler, sponger (*sl*).
churro *m* fritter.
churruscarse *vr* to scorch.
churrusco *m* burnt toast.
chusco/ca *adj* pleasant; funny.
chusma *f* rabble, mob.
chuzo *m* little spear or spike; **llover a ~s** to pour heavily.
cianuro *m* cyanide.
ciática *f* sciatica.
ciático/ca *adj* sciatic.
cibercafé *m* Internet café.
ciberespacio *m* cyberspace.
cicatear *vi* to be mean.
cicatriz *f* scar.
cicatrizar *vt* to heal.
ciclismo *m* cycling.
ciclista *m/f* cyclist.
ciclo *m* cycle.
ciclón *m* cyclone.
cicloturismo *m* bicycle touriism.
cicuta *f* (*bot*) hemlock.
ciegamente *adv* blindly.
ciego/ga *adj* blind.
cielo *m* sky; heaven; atmosphere; climate.
cien *adj*, *m* a hundred.
ciénaga *f* swamp.
ciencia *f* science.

cieno *m* mud; mire.
cienpiés *m invar* centipede.
científico/ca *adj* scientific.
ciento *adj*, *m* a hundred.
cierne *m*: **en ~** in blossom; **estar en ~** to be in its infancy.
cierto/ta *adj* certain, sure; right, correct; **por ~** certainly.
cierva *f* hind.
ciervo *m* deer, hart, stag; **~ volante** stag beetle.
cierzo *m* cold northerly wind.
cifra *f* number, numeral; quantity; cipher; abbreviation.
cifrar *vt* to write in code; to abridge.
cigala *f* langoustine.
cigarra *f* cicada.
cigarrera *f* cigar case.
cigarrillo *m* cigarette.
cigarro *m* cigar; cigarette.
cigüeña *f* stork; crank (of a bell).
cilicio *m* hair shirt; spiked belt.
cilíndrico/ca *adj* cylindrical.
cilindro *m* cylinder.
cima *f* summit; peak; top.
címbalo *m* cymbal.
cimbor(r)io *m* cupola, dome.
cimbr(e)ar *vt* to shake, to swish, to swing; **~ a uno** to give one a clout (with a stick); **~se** *vr* to sway.
cimentado *m* refinement of gold.
cimentar *vt* to lay the foundation of (a building); to found; to refine (metals); to strengthen, to cement.
cimiento *m* foundation, groundwork; basis, origin.
cinc *m* zinc.
cincel *m* chisel.
cincelar *vt* to chisel, to engrave.
cincha *f* girth.
cinchar *vt* to girth.
cinco *adj*, *m* five.
cincuenta *adj*, *m* fifty.

cine *m* cinema.

cineasta *m/f* film maker.

cinematográfico/ca *adj* cinematographic.

cínico/ca *adj* cynical.

cinismo *m* cynicism.

cinta *f* band, ribbon; reel.

cinto *m* belt.

cintura *f* waist.

cinturón *m* belt, girdle; (*fig*) zone; ~ **de seguridad** seatbelt.

ciprés *m* cypress tree.

circo *m* circus.

circuito *m* circuit; circumference.

circulación *f* circulation; traffic.

circular *adj* circular; circulatory; * *vt* to circulate; * *vi* (*auto*) to drive.

círculo *m* circle; (*fig*) scope, compass.

circuncidar *vt* to circumcize.

circuncisión *f* circumcision.

circundar *vt* to surround, to encircle.

circunferencia *f* circumference.

circunflejo/ja *adj*: **acento** ~ *m* circumflex.

circunscribir *vt* to circumscribe.

circunscripción *f* division; electoral district.

circunspección *f* circumspection.

circunspecto/ta *adj* circumspect, cautious.

circunstancia *f* circumstance.

circunstante *m/f* bystander.

circunvalación *f*: **carretera de** ~ bypass.

cirio *m* wax candle.

ciruela *f* plum; ~ **pasa** prune.

ciruelo *m* plum tree.

cirugía *f* surgery.

cirujano *m* surgeon.

cisco *m* coaldust.

cisma *m* schism; discord.

cismático/ca *adj* schismatic.

cisne *m* swan.

cisterna *f* cistern.

cisura *f* incision.

cita *f* quotation; appointment, meeting.

citación *f* quotation; (*jur*) summons.

citar *vt* to make an appointment with; to quote; (*jur*) to summon.

cítrico/ca *adj* citric; ~**s** *mpl* citric fruits *pl*.

ciudad *f* city; town.

ciudadanía *f* citizenship.

ciudadano/na *m/f* citizen; * *adj* civic.

ciudadela *f* citadel.

cívico/ca *adj* civic.

civil *adj* civil; polite, courteous; * *m* Civil Guard; civilian.

civilización *f* civilization.

civilizar *vt* to civilize.

civismo *m* public spirit; patriotism.

cizaña *f* discord.

clamar *vt* to clamour for.

clamor *m* clamour, outcry; peal of bells.

clamoroso/sa *adj* noisy, loud.

clandestino/na *adj* clandestine, secret, concealed.

clara *f* egg-white.

claraboya *f* skylight.

clarear *vi* to dawn; ~**se** *vr* to be transparent.

clarete *adj*, *m* claret.

claridad *f* brightness, clearness.

clarificar *vt* to brighten; to clarify.

clarín *m* bugle; bugler.

clarinete *m* clarinet; * *m/f* clarinetist.

claro/ra *adj* clear, bright; evident, manifest; * *m* opening; clearing (in a wood); skylight.

claroscuro *m* chiaroscuro (in painting).

clase *f* class; rank; order.

clásico/ca *adj* classical.
clasificación *f* classification.
clasificar *vt* to classify.
claudicar *vi* to limp; to act deceitfully; to back down.
claustro *m* cloister; faculty (of a university); womb, uterus.
cláusula *f* clause.
clausura *f* closure, closing.
clavado/da *adj* tight-fitting; nailed.
clavar *vt* to nail; to fasten in, to force in; to drive in; (*fam*) to cheat, to deceive; **~se** *vr* to penetrate.
clave *f* key; (*mus*) clef; * *m* harpsichord.
clavel *m* (*bot*) carnation.
clavetear *vt* to decorate with studs.
clavicordio *m* clavichord.
clavícula *f* clavicle, collar bone.
clavija *f* pin, peg.
clavo *m* nail; corn (on the feet); clove.
claxon *m* horn.
clemencia *f* clemency.
clemente *adj* clement, merciful.
cleptómano/na *m/f* kleptomaniac.
clerecía *f* clergy.
clerical *adj* clerical.
clérigo *m* priest; clergyman.
clero *m* clergy.
clic, click *m* click.
cliché *m* cliché; negative (of a photo).
cliente *m/f* client.
clientela *f* clientele.
clima *m* climate.
climatizado/da *adj* air-conditioned.
clínica *f* clinic; private hospital.
clínico/ca *adj* clinical.
clip *m* paper clip.
cloaca *f* sewer.
cloquear *vi* to cluck.
clon *m* clone.

clonación *f* cloning.
clonar *vt* to clone.
clónico/ca *adj* cloned.
club *m* club.
clueca *f* broody hen.
coacción *f* coercion, compulsion.
coactivo/va *adj* coercive.
coadjutor/ra *m/f* coadjutor, assistant.
coagular *vt*, **~se** *vr* to coagulate; to curdle.
coágulo *m*: **~ sanguíneo** blood clot.
coalición *f* coalition.
coartada *f* (*jur*) alibi.
coartar *vt* to limit, to restrict, to restrain.
cobalto *m* cobalt.
cobarde *adj* cowardly, timid.
cobardía *f* cowardice.
cobaya *f* guinea pig.
cobertizo *m* small shed; shelter.
cobertura *f* cover; coverage; bedspread.
cobijar *vt* to cover; to shelter.
cobra *f* cobra.
cobrador/ra *m/f* conductor/conductress; collector.
cobrar *vt* to recover; **~se** *vr* (*med*) to come to.
cobre *m* copper; kitchen utensils *pl*; (*mus*) brass.
cobrizo/za *adj* coppery.
cobro *m* encashment; payment; recovery.
cocaína *f* cocaine.
cocción *f* cooking.
cocear *vt* to kick; (*fig*) to resist.
cocer *vt* to boil; to bake (bricks); * *vi* to boil; to ferment; **~se** *vr* to suffer intense pain.
cochambre *m* dirty, stinking object.
cochambroso/sa *a* nasty; filthy, stinking.

coche *m* car; coach, carriage; pram, baby carriage; ~ **bomba** car bomb; (ferro) ~ **cama** sleeping car; ~ **restaurante** restaurant car.

cochera *f* garage, lockup, carport, depot.

cochero *m* coachman.

cochinilla *f* woodlouse; cochineal.

cochino/na *adj* dirty, filthy; nasty; * *m* pig.

cochiquera *f* pigsty.

cocido/da *adj* boiled; (fig) skilled, experienced; * *m* stew.

cocina *f* kitchen; cooker; cookery.

cocinero/ra *m/f* cook.

coco *m* coconut; bogeyman.

cocodrilo *m* crocodile.

codazo *m* blow given with the elbow.

codear *vt, vi* to elbow; ~**se** *vr*: ~**se con** to rub shoulders with.

códice *m* codex, old manuscript.

codicia *m* covetousness, greediness.

codiciable *adj* covetable.

codiciar *vt* to covet, to desire.

codicilo *m* (jur) codicil.

codicioso/sa *adj* greedy, covetous.

código *m* law; set of rules; code; ~ **postal** post code.

codillo *m* knee of a four-legged animal; angle; (tec) elbow (joint).

codo *m* elbow.

codorniz *f* quail.

coerción *f* coercion; restraint.

coercitivo/va *adj* coercive.

coetáneo/nea *adj* contemporary.

coexistencia *f* coexistence.

coexistente *adj* coexistent.

coexistir *vi* to coexist.

cofia *f* (nurse's) cap.

cofrade *m* member (of a brotherhood).

cofradía *f* brotherhood, fraternity.

cofre *m* trunk.

cogedor *m* shovel; dustpan.

coger *vt* to catch, to take hold of; to occupy, to take up; ~**se** *vr* to catch.

cognitivo/va *adj* cognitive.

cogollo *m* heart of a lettuce or cabbage; shoot of a plant.

cogote *m* back of the neck.

cohabitar *vi* to cohabit, to live together.

cohechar *vt* to bribe, to suborn.

cohecho *m* bribery.

coherencia *f* coherence.

coherente *adj* coherent.

cohete *m* rocket.

cohibido/da *adj* shy.

cohibir *vt* to prohibit; to restrain.

cohorte *f* cohort.

coincidencia *f* coincidence.

coincidente *adj* coincidental.

coincidir *vi* to coincide.

coito *m* intercourse, coitus.

cojear *vi* to limp, to hobble; (fig) to go astray.

cojera *f* lameness; limp.

cojín *m* cushion.

cojo/ja *adj* lame, crippled.

col *f* cabbage.

cola^1 *f* tail; queue; last place.

cola^2 *f* glue.

colaborador/ra *m/f* collaborator; contributor.

colaborar *vi* to collaborate.

colación *f* collation, comparison; light meal.

colada *f* wash, washing; (quím) bleach; sheep run.

coladero *m* colander, strainer.

colador *m* sieve.

colapso *m* collapse.

colar *vt* to strain, to filter; * *vi* to ooze; ~**se en** to get into without paying.

colateral *adj* collateral.

colcha *f* bedspread, counterpane.
colchón *m* mattress.
colchoneta *f* mattress.
coleada *f* wagging (of an animal's tail).
colear *vi* to wag the tail.
colección *f* collection.
coleccionar *vt* to collect.
coleccionista *m/f* collector.
colecta *f* collection (for charity).
colectar *vt* to collect (taxes).
colectivo/va *adj* collective.
colector *m* collector; sewer.
colega *m/f* colleague.
colegial *m* schoolboy.
colegiala *f* schoolgirl.
colegiata *f* collegiate church.
colegio *m* college; school.
colegir *vt* to collect; to deduce, to infer.
cólera *f* bile; anger; fury, rage.
coléricamente *adv* in a rage.
colérico/ca *adj* angry; furious; bad-tempered.
colesterol *m* cholesterol.
coleta *f* pigtail.
colgadero *m* hook, hanger, peg.
colgadura *f* tapestry; hangings *pl*, drapery.
colgajo *m* tatter, rag.
colgante *adj* hanging; * *m* pendant.
colgar *vt* to hang; to suspend; to decorate with tapestry; * *vi* to be suspended.
colibrí *m* hummingbird.
cólico *m* colic.
coliflor *m* cauliflower.
colilla *f* end or butt of a cigarette.
colina *f* hill.
colindante *adj* neighbouring.
colindar *vi* to adjoin.
coliseo *m* coliseum; opera house; theatre.

colisión *f* collision; friction.
collar *m* necklace; (dog) collar.
colmar *vt* to heap up; * *vi* to fulfill, to realize.
colmena *f* hive, beehive.
colmenar *m* beehive stand; bee-house.
colmillo *m* eyetooth; tusk.
colmo *m* height, summit; extreme; **a ~** plentifully.
colocación *f* employment; placing; situation.
colocar *vt* to arrange; to place; to provide with a job; **~se** *vr* to get a job.
colon *m* (*med*) colon.
colonia *f* colony; silk ribbon.
colonial *adj* colonial.
colonización *f* colonization.
colonizador/a *m/f* settler; * *adj* colonizing.
colonizar *vt* to colonize.
colono *m* colonist; farmer.
coloquio *m* conversation; conference.
color *m* colour, hue; dye; rouge; suit (of cards).
coloración *f* colouring, coloration.
colorado/da *adj* ruddy; red.
colorar *vt* to colour; to dye.
colorear *vt* to colour; to excuse.
colorete *m* rouge.
colorido *m* colouring.
colosal *adj* colossal.
columna *f* column.
columnata *f* colonnade.
columpiar *vt*, **~se** *vr* to swing to and fro.
columpio *m* swing, seesaw.
colusión *f* collusion.
colza *f* (*bot*) rape; rape seed.
coma *f* (*gr*) comma; * *m* (*med*) coma.

comadre f midwife; godmother; neighbour.

comadreja f weasel.

comadrón/ona m/f midwife.

comandancia f command.

comandante m commander.

comandar vt to command.

comarca f territory, district.

comba f curve; warp (of timber); skipping rope.

combar vt to bend; ~se vr to warp.

combate m combat, conflict; fighting.

combatiente m combatant.

combatir vt to combat, to fight; to attack; * vi to fight.

combinación f combination; (quím) compound; cocktail; scheme.

combinar vi to combine.

combustible adj combustible; * m fuel.

combustión f combustion.

comedero m dining room; trough.

comedia f comedy; play, drama.

comediante m/f player, actor/actress.

comedido/da adj moderate, restrained.

comedirse vr to restrain oneself.

comedor/ra m/f glutton; * m dining room.

comendatorio/ria adj introductory (of letters).

comensal m/f fellow diner.

comentar vt to comment on, to expound.

comentario m comment, remark; commentary.

comentarista m/f commentator.

comenzar vi to commence, to begin.

comer vi to eat; to take (a piece at chess); * vi to have lunch.

comercial adj commercial.

comerciante m/f trader, merchant, dealer.

comerciar vi to trade, to do business.

comercio m trade, commerce; business; ~ electrónico e-commerce; ~ justo fair trade.

comestible adj eatable; * mpl ~s food, foodstuffs pl.

cometa m comet; * f kite.

cometer vt to commit, to charge; to entrust.

cometido m task.

comezón f itch; itching.

comicios mpl elections pl.

cómico/ca adj comic, comical.

comida f food; eating; meal; lunch; ~ basura junk food.

comienzo m beginning.

comillas fpl quotation marks pl.

comilón/ona m/f great eater, glutton; * f blow-out.

comino m cumin (plant or seed).

comisaría f police station; commissariat.

comisario/-a m/f commissioner.

comisión f commission; committee.

comisionado/da m/f; commissioner; committee member.

comisionar vt to commission.

comité m committee.

comitiva f suite, retinue, followers pl.

como adv as; like; such as.

cómo adv how?; why? * excl what?

cómoda f chest of drawers.

comodidad f comfort; convenience; ~es fpl wealth, comforts pl.

comodín m joker.

cómodo/da adj convenient; comfortable.

compact disc m compact disc.

compacto/ta adj compact; close, dense.

compadecer *vt* to pity; **~se** *vr* to agree with each other.

compadre *m* godfather; friend.

compaginar *vt* to arrange, to put in order; **~se** *vr* to tally.

compañero/va *m/f* companion, friend; comrade; partner.

compañía *f* company.

comparación *f* comparison.

comparar *vt* to compare.

comparativo/va *adj* comparative.

comparecer *vi* to appear in court.

comparsa *m/f* extra (in the theatre).

compartimento *m* compartment.

compartir *vt* to divide into equal parts.

compás *m* compass; pair of compasses; (*mus*) measure, beat.

compasión *f* compassion, commiseration.

compasivo/va *adj* compassionate.

compatibilidad *f* compatibility.

compatible *adj*: **~ con** compatible with, consistent with.

compatriota *m/f* countryman; countrywoman; fellow citizen.

compeler *vt* to compel, to constrain.

compendiar *vt* to abridge.

compendio *m* abridgment; summary.

compensación *f* compensation; recompense.

compensar *vt* to compensate; to recompense.

competencia *f* competition, rivalry; competence.

competente *adj* competent; adequate.

competer *vi* to be one's responsibility.

competición *f* competition.

competidor/ra *m/f* competitor, contestant; rival.

competir *vi* to vie; **~ con** to compete with, to rival.

compilación *f* compilation.

compilador *m* compiler.

compilar *vt* to compile.

compinche *m* pal, mate (*sl*).

complacencia *f* pleasure; indulgence.

complacer *vt* to please; **~se** *vr* to be pleased with.

complaciente *adj* pleasing.

complejo *m* complex; **~/ja** *adj* complex.

complementario/ria *adj* complementary.

complemento *m* complement.

completar *vt* to complete.

completo/ta *adj* complete; perfect.

complexión *f* constitution, temperament; build.

complicado/da *adj* complicated.

complicar *vt* to complicate.

cómplice *m/f* accomplice.

complicidad *f* complicity.

complot *m* plot.

componer *vt* to compose; to constitute; to mend, to repair; to strengthen, to restore; to adorn; to adjust; to reconcile; to compose, to calm; **~se** *vr*: **~se de** to consist of.

comportamiento *m* behaviour.

comportarse *vr* to behave.

composición *f* composition; composure, agreement; settlement.

compositor/ra *m/f* composer; compositor.

compostura *f* composition, composure; mending, repairing; discretion; modesty, demureness.

compota *f* stewed fruit.

compra *f* purchase; **~ a plazos** hire purchase.

comprador/ra *m/f* buyer; customer, shopper.

comprar *vt* to buy, to purchase.

comprender *vt* to include, to contain; to comprehend, to understand.

comprensible *adj* comprehensible.

comprensión *f* comprehension, understanding.

comprensivo/va *adj* comprehensive.

compresa *f* sanitary towel.

compresión *f* compression.

comprimido *m* pill.

comprimir *vt* to compress; to repress, to restrain.

comprobante *m* receipt; voucher.

comprobar *vt* to verify, to confirm; to prove.

comprometer *vt* to compromise; to embarrass; to implicate; to put in danger; ~**se** *vr* to compromise oneself.

compromiso *m* compromise.

compuerta *f* hatch; sluice.

compuesto *m* compound; ~/**ta** *adj* composed; made up of.

compulsar *vt* to collate, to compare; to make an authentic copy.

compulsivo/va *adj* compulsive.

compunción *f* compunction, regret.

compungirse *vr* to feel remorseful.

computador *m*, **computadora** *f* computer.

computar *vt* to calculate; to compute.

cómputo *m* computation; calculation.

comulgar *vt* to administer communion to; * *vi* to receive communion.

común *adj* common, usual, general; * *m* community; public; **en ~** in common.

comunal *adj* communal.

comunicación *f* communication; report.

comunicado *m* announcement.

comunicar *vt* to communicate; ~**se** *vr* to communicate (with each other).

comunicativo/va *adj* communicative.

comunidad *f* community; **Comunidad Europea** European Community.

comunión *f* communion.

comunismo *m* communism.

comunista *adj, m/f* communist.

comunitario/ria *adj* of the European Union.

con *prep* with; by; ~ **que** so then, providing that.

coñac *m* brandy, cognac.

conato *m* endeavour; effort; attempt.

concavidad *f* concavity.

cóncavo/va *adj* concave.

concebir *vt* to conceive; * *vi* to become pregnant.

conceder *vt* to give; to grant; to concede, to allow.

concejal/la *m/f* member of a council.

concejo *m* council.

concentración *f* concentration.

concentrar *vt*, ~**se** *vr* to concentrate.

concéntrico/ca *adj* concentric.

concepción *f* conception; idea.

concepto *m* conceit, thought; judgement, opinion.

concerniente *adj*: ~ **a** concerning, relating to.

concernir *v imp* to regard, to concern.

concertar *vt* to coordinate; to settle; to adjust; to agree; to arrange, to fix up; * *vi* (*mus*) to harmonize, to be in tune.

concesión *f* concession.

concesionario *m* agent.

concha f shell; tortoise-shell.

conchabar vt to mix, to blend; **~se** vr to plot, to conspire.

conciencia f conscience.

concienciar vt to make aware; **~se** vr to become aware.

concierto m concert; agreement; concerto; **de ~** in agreement, in concert.

conciliación f conciliation, reconciliation.

conciliar vt to reconcile; * adj council.

conciliatorio/ria adj conciliatory.

concilio m council.

concisión f conciseness.

conciso/sa adj concise, brief.

conciudadanía f joint-citizenship.

conciudadano/na m/f fellow citizen.

cónclave m conclave.

concluir vt to conclude, to end, to complete; to infer, to deduce; **~se** vr to conclude.

conclusión f conclusion.

concluyente adj conclusive.

concordancia f concordance, concord; harmony.

concordar vt to reconcile, to make agree; * vi to agree, to correspond.

concordato m concordat.

concordia f conformity, agreement.

concretar vt to make concrete; to specify.

concreto/ta adj concrete.

concubina f concubine.

concubinato m concubinage.

concupiscencia f lust.

concurrencia f concurrence; coincidence; competition; crowd, gathering.

concurrido/da adj busy.

concurrir vi to meet; to contribute; to coincide; to compete.

concursante m/f competitor.

concurso m crowd; competition; help, cooperation.

concusión f concussion.

condado m county.

conde m earl, count.

condecoración f medal.

condecorar vt to adorn; (mil) to decorate.

condena f condemnation.

condenable adj culpable.

condenar vt to condemn; to find guilty; **~se** vr to blame oneself; to confess (one's guilt).

condenatorio/ria adj condemnatory.

condensación f condensation.

condensar vt to condense.

condesa f countess.

condescendencia f helpfulness, willingness; acquiescence; compliance.

condescender vi to acquiesce, to comply.

condición f condition, state; quality; status; rank; stipulation.

condicionado/da adj conditioned.

condicional adj conditional.

condimentar vt to flavour, to season.

condimento m condiment, seasoning.

condiscípulo/la m/f fellow pupil; fellow student.

condolerse vr to sympathize.

condón m condom.

condonar vt to condone; to forgive.

conducción f conveyance; management; (auto) driving.

conducente adj: **~ a** a leading to.

conducir vt to convey, to conduct; to drive; to manage; * vi to drive; **~ (a)** to lead (to); **~se** vr to conduct oneself.

conducta f conduct, behaviour; management;

conducto *m* conduit, pipe; drain; (*fig*) channel.

conductor/ra *m/f* conductor, guide; (*ferro*) guard; driver.

conectado/da *adj* on-line.

conectar *vt* to connect.

conejera *f* warren, burrow.

conejo *m* rabbit.

conexión *f* connection; plug; relationship.

conexo/xa *adj* connected, related.

confabularse *vr* to conspire.

confección *f* preparation; clothing industry.

confeccionar *vt* to make up.

confederación *f* confederacy.

confederado/da *adj* confederate.

confederarse *vr* to confederate.

conferencia *f* conference; telephone call.

conferenciar *vi* to confer; to be in conference.

conferir *vt* to award; to compare.

confesar *vt* to confess; to admit.

confesión *f* confession.

confesionario *m* confessional.

confeso/sa *adj* (*jur*) self-confessed.

confesonario *m* confessional.

confesor *m* confessor.

confeti *m* confetti.

confiado/da *adj* trusting; confident; arrogant.

confianza *f* trust; confidence; conceit; familiarity; en ~ confidential.

confiar *vt* to confide, to entrust; * *vi* to trust.

confidencia *f* confidence.

confidencial *adj* confidential.

confidente *m/f* confidante; informer.

configurar *vt* to shape, to form.

confín *m* limit, boundary.

confinar *vt* to confine; * *vi*: ~ con to border upon.

confirmación *f* confirmation.

confirmar *vt* to confirm; to corroborate.

confiscación *f* confiscation.

confiscar *vt* to confiscate.

confite *m* candy.

confitería *f* sweet shop.

confitero/ra *m/f* confectioner.

confitura *f* preserve; jam.

conflagración *f* conflagration.

conflictivo/va *adj* controversial.

conflicto *m* conflict.

confluencia *f* confluence.

confluir *vi* to join (applied to rivers); to gather (applied to people).

conformar *vt* to shape; to adjust, to adapt; * *vi* to agree; ~se *vr* to conform; to resign oneself.

conforme *adj* alike, similar; agreed; * *prep* according to.

conformidad *f* similarity; agreement; resignation.

conformista *m/f* conformist.

confortable *adj* comfortable.

confortar *vt* to comfort; to strengthen; to console.

confortativo/va *adj* comforting.

confraternidad *f* fraternity.

confrontación *f* confrontation.

confrontar *vt* to confront.

confundir *vt* to confound, to jumble; to confuse; ~se *vr* to make a mistake.

confusamente *adv* confusedly.

confusión *f* confusion.

confuso/sa *adj* confused.

congelación *f* freezing.

congelado/da *adj* frozen; * *mpl*: ~s frozen food.

congelador *m* freezer.

congelar *vt* to freeze; ~se *vr* to congeal.

congeniar *vi* to get on well.

congestión f congestion.

congestionar vt to congest.

congoja f anguish, distress, grief.

congraciarse vr to ingratiate oneself.

congratulación f congratulation.

congratular vt to congratulate.

congregación f congregation, assembly.

congregar(se) f (vr) to assemble, to meet, to collect.

congresista m/f delegate.

congreso m congress.

cónico/ca adj conical.

conjetura f conjecture, guess.

conjeturar vt to conjecture, to guess.

conjugación f (gr) conjugation.

conjugar vt (gr) to conjugate; to combine.

conjunción f conjunction.

conjuntamente adv together.

conjunto/ta adj united, joint; * m whole; (mus) ensemble, band; team.

conjuración f conspiracy, plot.

conjurado/da m/f conspirator.

conjurar vt to exorcise; * vi to conspire, to plot.

conjuro m incantation, exorcism.

conmemoración f commemoration.

conmemorar vt to commemorate.

conmigo pn with me.

conminación f threat.

conminar vt to threaten.

conminatorio/ria adj threatening.

conmiseración f commiseration, pity, sympathy.

conmoción f shock; upheaval; commotion; (med) concussion.

conmovedor/ra adj touching.

conmover vt to move; to disturb.

conmutación f commutation, exchange.

conmutador m switch.

conmutar vt (jur) to commute; to exchange.

connotar vt to imply.

coño excl (fam) hell!, damn! (sl).

cono m cone.

conocedor/ra m/f connoisseur.

conocer vt to know, to understand; ~se vr to know one another.

conocido/da m/f acquaintance.

conocimiento m knowledge, understanding; (med) consciousness; acquaintance; (mar) bill of lading.

conque m condition.

conquista f conquest.

conquistador m conqueror; * adj ~/ra conquering.

conquistar vt to conquer.

consabido/da adj well known; above mentioned.

consagración f consecration.

consagrar vt to consecrate.

consanguíneo/nea adj related by blood.

consanguinidad f blood relationship.

consecución f acquisition; attainment.

consecuencia f consequence; conclusion; consistency; por ~ therefore.

consecuente adj consistent.

consecutivo/va adj consecutive.

conseguir vt to attain; to get, to obtain.

consejero/ra m/f adviser; councillor.

consejo m advice; council.

consenso m consensus.

consentido/da adj spoiled (of children).

consentimiento m consent.

consentir vt to consent to; to allow; to admit; to spoil (a child).

conserje *m/f* doorman, porter; caretaker; janitor.

conservación *f* conservation.

conservante *m* preservative.

conservar *vt* to conserve; to keep; to preserve (fruit).

conservas *fpl* canned food.

conservatorio *m* (*mus*) conservatoire.

considerable *adj* considerable.

consideración *f* consideration; respect.

consideradamente *adv* considerately.

considerado/da *adj* respected; considerate.

considerar *vt* to consider.

consigna *f* (*mil*) watchword; order, instruction; (*ferro*) left-luggage office.

consignación *f* consignment.

consignar *vt* to consign, to dispatch; to assign; to record, to register.

consignatario/ria *m/f* consignee.

consigo *pn* (*m*) with him; (*f*) with her; (*vd*) with you; (*reflexivo*) with oneself.

consiguiente *adj* consequent.

consistencia *f* consistence, consistency.

consistente *adj* consistent; firm, solid.

consistir *vi*: ~ en to consist of; to be due to.

consistorio *m* town council; town hall.

consocio/cia *m/f* fellow member; partner.

consola *f* control panel; console.

consolación *f* consolation.

consolador/ra *adj* consoling, comforting.

consolar *vt* to console, to comfort, to cheer.

consolidar *vt* to consolidate.

consomé *m* consommé.

consonancia *f* consonance.

consonante *m* rhyme; * *f* (*gr*) consonant; * *adj* consonant, harmonious.

consorcio *m* partnership.

consorte *m/f* consort, companion, partner; accomplice.

conspiración *f* conspiracy, plot.

conspirador/ra *m/f* conspirator, plotter.

conspirar *vi* to conspire, to plot.

constancia *f* constancy; steadiness.

constante *adj* constant; firm.

constar *vi* to be evident, to be certain; to be composed of, to consist of.

constatar *vt* to note; to check.

constelación *f* constellation.

consternación *f* consternation.

consternar *vt* to dismay; to shock.

constipado/da *adj*: **estar** ~ to have a cold.

constiparse *vr* to catch a cold.

constitución *f* constitution.

constitucional *adj* constitutional.

constituir *vt* to constitute; to establish; to appoint.

constitutivo/va *adj* constitutive; essential.

constituyente *adj* constituent.

constreñimiento *m* constraint.

constreñir *vt* to restrict; to force; (*med*) to constipate; to constrict.

constricción *f* constriction, contraction.

construcción *f* construction.

constructor/ra *m/f* builder.

construir *vt* to form; to build, to construct; to construe.

consuegro/gra *m/f* father-in-law/ mother-in-law of one's son or daughter.

consuelo m consolation, comfort.

cónsul m consul.

consulado m consulate.

consulta f consultation.

consultar vt to consult, to ask for advice.

consultivo/va adj consultative.

consultor/ra m/f adviser, consultant.

consultorio m (med) surgery.

consumación f consummation, finishing.

consumado/da adj consummate; complete; accomplished; perfect.

consumar vt to consummate, to finish; to carry out.

consumición f consumption; drink.

consumidor/ra m/f consumer.

consumir vt to contain, to burn; to use; to waste, to exhaust; ~**se** vr to waste away, to be consumed.

consumismo m consumerism.

consumo m consumption.

contabilidad f accounting; bookkeeping.

contable m/f accountant.

contacto m contact; (auto) ignition.

contado/da adj ~ scarce, few; * m: **pagar al** ~ to pay (in) cash.

contador m meter; counter in a cafe; ~/~a m/f accountant.

contaduría f accountancy; accountant's office.

contagiar vt to infect; ~**se** vr to get infected.

contagio m contagion.

contagioso/sa adj contagious.

contaminación f contamination; pollution.

contaminar vt to contaminate; to pollute; to corrupt.

contante m cash.

contar vt to count, to reckon; to tell; * vi to count; ~ **con** to rely upon.

contemplación f contemplation.

contemplar vt to look at; to contemplate; to consider; to meditate.

contemplativo/va adj contemplative.

contemporáneo/nea adj contemporary.

contemporizar vi to temporize.

contencioso/sa adj contentious; quarrelsome.

contender vi to contend, to compete.

contendiente m/f competitor.

contenedor m container.

contener vt to contain, to hold; to hold back; to repress; ~**se** vr to control oneself.

contenido/da adj moderate, restrained; * m contents pl.

contentar vt to content, to satisfy; to please; ~**se** vr to be pleased or satisfied.

contento/ta adj glad; pleased; content; * m contentment; (jur) release.

contestación f answer, reply.

contestador m: ~ **automático** answering machine.

contestar vt to answer, to reply; to prove, to corroborate.

contexto m context.

contienda f contest, dispute.

contigo pn with you.

contigüidad f contiguity.

contiguo/gua adj contiguous, close.

continencia f continence, abstinence, moderation.

continental adj continental.

continente m continent, mainland; * adj continent.

contingencia f risk; contingency.

contingente adj contingent, accidental; * m contingent.

continuación f continuation; sequel.

continuar vt, vi to continue.

continuidad f continuity.

continuo/nua adj continuous.

contonearse vr to walk affectedly.

contoneo m affected manner of walking.

contorno m environs pl; contour, outline; **en ~** round about.

contorsión f contortion.

contra prep against; contrary to; opposite.

contraataque m counter-attack.

contrabajo m (mus) double bass; bass guitar; low bass.

contrabandista m/f smuggler.

contrabando m contraband; smuggling.

contracción f contraction.

contrachapado m plywood.

contradecir vt to contradict.

contradicción f contradiction.

contradictorio/ria adj contradictory.

contraer vt to contract, to shrink; to make (a bargain); **~se** vr to shrink, to contract.

contrafuerte m buttress; foothill; heel-pad.

contragolpe m backlash.

contrahecho/cha adj deformed; hunchbacked; counterfeit, fake, false.

contralto m (mus) contralto.

contramaestre m (mar) boatswain; foreman.

contrapartida f (com) balancing entry.

contrapaso m back step.

contrapelo adv: **a ~** against the grain.

contrapesar vi to counterbalance.

contrapeso m counterpoise; counterweight.

contraponer vt to compare, to oppose.

contraposición f comparison; contrast.

contraproducente adj counterproductive.

contraprogramación f competitive scheduling.

contrapunto m (mus) counterpoint.

contrariar vt to contradict, to oppose; to vex.

contrariedad f opposition; setback; annoyance.

contrario/ria m/f opponent; * adj contrary, opposite; **por el ~** on the contrary.

contrarreloj f time trial.

contrarrestar vt to return a ball; (fig) to counteract.

contrarrevolución f counter-revolution.

contraseña f countersign; (mil) watchword.

contrasentido m contradiction.

contrastar vt to resist; to contradict; to assay (metals); to verify (measures and weights); * vi to contrast.

contraste m contrast.

contrata f contract.

contratación f signing-up, hiring.

contratar vt to contract; to hire, to engage.

contratiempo m setback; accident.

contratista m contractor.

contrato m contract, agreement.

contravención f contravention.

contraveneno m antidote.

contravenir vi to contravene, to transgress; to violate.

contraventana f shutter.

contribución f contribution; tax.

contribuir vt, vi to contribute.

contribuyente m/f contributor; taxpayer.

contrincante m competitor.

contrito/ta adj contrite, penitent.
controlador/ra m/f controller.
controlar vt to control; to check.
controversia f controversy, dispute.
contumacia f obstinacy, stubbornness; (jur) contempt of court.
contumaz adj obstinate, stubborn; (jur) guilty of contempt of court.
contundente adj overwhelming; blunt.
contusión f bruise.
convalecencia f convalescence.
convalecer vi to recover from sickness, to convalesce.
convaleciente m/f, adj convalescent.
convalidar vt to recognize.
convencer vt to convince.
convencimiento m conviction.
convención f convention, pact.
convencional adj conventional.
conveniencia f suitability; usefulness; agreement; ~s fpl property.
conveniente adj useful; suitable.
convenio m convention, agreement, treaty.
convenir vi to agree, to suit.
convento m convent, nunnery; monastery.
conventual adj monastic.
convergencia f convergence.
converger vi to converge.
conversación f conversation, talk; communication.
conversar vi to talk, to converse.
conversión f conversion, change.
converso/sa m/f convert.
convertir vt, ~se vr to convert.
convexo/xa adj convex.
convicción f conviction.
convicto/ta adj convicted (found guilty).
convidado/da m/f guest.
convidar vt to invite.

convincente adj convincing.
convite m invitation; banquet.
convivencia f living together.
convocar vt to convoke, to assemble.
convocatoria f summons; notice of a meeting.
convoy m convoy.
convulsión f convulsion.
convulsivo/va adj convulsive.
conyugal adj conjugal, married.
cónyuge m/f spouse.
cooperar vi to cooperate.
cooperativa f cooperative.
cooperativo/va adj cooperative.
coordinadora f coordinating committee.
coordinar vt to arrange, to coordinate.
copa f cup; glass; top of a tree; crown of a hat; ~s fpl hearts pl (at cards).
copete m quiff; pride.
copia f plenty, abundance; copy, duplicate.
copiador/ra m/f copyist; copier; **libro** ~ letter book.
copiar vt to copy; to imitate.
copioso/sa adj copious, abundant, plentiful.
copla f verse; (mus) popular song, folk song.
copo m small bundle; flake of snow.
copropietario/ria m/f joint owner.
cópula f copulation; conjunction; (gr) copula.
copulativo/va adj copulative.
coqueta f coquette, flirt.
coquetear vi to flirt.
coquetería f coquetry, flirtation.
coraje m courage; anger, passion.
coral m coral; choir; * adj choral.
coraza f cuirass; armour-plating.

corazón m heart; core; **de ~** willingly.

corazonada f feeling; inspiration; quick decision; presentiment.

corbata f tie.

corbeta f corvette.

corcel m steed, charger.

corchea f (mus) quaver.

corchete m clasp; hook and eye.

corcho m cork; float (for fishing); cork bark.

cordel m cord, rope; (mar) line.

cordero m lamb; lambskin; meek, gentle person.

cordial adj cordial, affectionate; * m cordial.

cordialidad f cordiality.

cordillera f range of mountains.

cordón m cord, string; lace; cordon.

cordura f prudence, good sense, wisdom.

corista m/f chorister.

cornada f thrust with a bull's horn.

cornadura f horns pl.

cornamenta f horns of an animal pl.

córnea f cornea.

cornear vt to gore.

córneo/ea adj horny, corneous.

corneta f bugle.

cornisa f cornice.

cornudo/da adj horned.

coro m choir; chorus.

corona f crown; coronet; top of the head; crown (of a tooth); tonsure; halo.

coronación f coronation.

coronar vt to crown; to complete, to perfect.

coronario/ria adj coronary.

coronel m (mil) colonel.

coronilla f crown of the head.

corpiño m bodice.

corporación f corporation.

corporal adj corporal.

corpóreo/rea adj corporeal.

corpulencia f corpulence.

corpulento/ta adj corpulent, bulky.

Corpus m Corpus Christi.

corral m yard; farmyard; corral; playpen.

correa f leather strap, thong; flexibility.

correaje m leather straps pl.

corrección f correction; reprehension; amendment.

correccional m reformatory.

correctivo/va adj corrective.

correcto/ta adj exact, correct.

corrector/ra m/f proof-reader.

corredizo/za adj sliding; easy to be untied.

corredor/ra adj running; * m/f broker, runner; m corridor.

corregir vt to correct, to amend; to reprehend; **~se** vr to reform.

correlación f correlation.

correo m post, mail; courier; postman; **~ electrónico** e-mail; **a vuelta de ~** by return of post; **~s** mpl post office.

correoso/sa adj flexible, leathery.

correr vt to run; to flow; to travel over; to pull (a drape); * vi to run, to rush; to flow; to blow (applied to the wind); **~se** vr to be ashamed; to slide, to move; to run (of colours).

correría f incursion.

correspondencia f correspondence; communication; agreement.

corresponder vi to correspond; to answer; to be suitable; to belong; to concern; **~se** vr to love one another.

correspondiente adj corresponding, suitable.

corresponsal *m/f* correspondent.

corretear *vi* to rush around; to hang about the streets.

corrida *f* run, dash; bullfight.

corrido/da *adj* expert; knowing; ashamed.

corriente *f* current; course, progression; (electric) current; * *adj* current; common, ordinary, general; fluent; flowing, running.

corrillo *m* circle of persons; clique.

corro *m* circle of people.

corroborar *vt* to corroborate.

corroer *vt* to corrode, to erode.

corromper *vt* to corrupt; to rot; to turn bad; to seduce; to bribe; **~se** *vr* to rot; to become corrupted; * *vi* to stink.

corrosión *f* corrosion.

corrosivo/va *adj* corrosive.

corrupción *f* corruption; rot, decay.

corruptible *adj* corruptible.

corrupto/ta *adj* corrupted, corrupt.

corruptor/ra *m/f* corruptor, perverter.

corrusco *m* broken bread.

corsé *f* corset.

cortacésped *m* lawn mower.

cortado *m* coffee with a little milk; **~/da** *adj* cut; sour; embarrassed.

cortadura *f* cut; cutting; incision; fissure; **~s** *fpl* shreds *pl*, cuttings *pl*, parings *pl*.

cortafuegos *m invar* fire lane, firebreak.

cortaplumas *m invar* penknife.

cortar *vt* to cut; to cut off, to curtail; to intersect; to carve; to chop; to cut (at cards); to interrupt; **~se** *vr* to be ashamed or embarrassed; to curdle.

cortauñas *m invar* nail clippers *pl*.

corte *m* cutting; cut; section; length

(of cloth); style; * *f* (royal) court; capital (city); **C~s** *fpl* Spanish Parliament.

cortedad *f* shortness, smallness; stupidity; bashfulness.

cortejar *vt* to court.

cortejo *m* entourage; courtship; procession; lover.

cortés/esa *adj* courteous, polite.

cortesana *f* courtesan.

cortesía *f* courtesy, good manners *pl*.

corteza *f* bark; peel; crust; (*fig*) outward appearance.

cortina *f* curtain.

cortinaje *m* set of curtains.

corto/ta *adj* short; scanty, small; stupid; bashful; **a la ~a o a la larga** sooner or later.

corvo/va *adj* bent, crooked.

corzo/za *m/f* roe deer, fallow deer.

cosa *f* thing; matter, affair; **¡no hay tal ~!** nothing of the sort!.

cosaco *m* cossack.

cosecha *f* harvest; harvest time; **de su ~** of one's own invention.

cosechar *vt* to harvest, to reap.

coser *vt* to sew; to join.

cosido *m* stitching, sewing.

cosmético/a *adj, m* cosmetic.

cosmopolita *adj, m* cosmopolitan.

cosquillas *fpl* tickling; (*fig*) agitation.

costa *f* cost, price; charge, expense; coast, shore; **a toda ~** at all events.

costado *m* side; (*mil*) flank; side of a ship.

costal *m* sack, large bag.

costalada *f* heavy fall.

costar *vt* to cost; to need.

coste *m* cost, expense.

costear *vt* to pay for.

costera *f* side; slope; coast.

costero/ra *adj* coastal; (*mar*) coasting.

costilla *f* rib; (*fig*) wife; cutlet; **~s** *fpl* back, shoulders *pl*.

costillar *m* human ribs *pl*.

costo *m* cost, price; expense.

costoso/sa *adj* costly, dear, expensive.

costra *f* crust; (*med*) scab.

costumbre *f* custom, habit.

costura *f* sewing; seam; needlework.

costurera *f* seamstress.

costurero *m* sewing box.

cotejar *vt* to compare.

cotejo *m* comparison, collation.

cotidiano/na *adj* daily.

cotilla *m/f* gossip.

cotización *f* quotation.

cotizar *vt* to quote; **~se** *vr*: **~ a** to sell at; to be quoted at.

coto *m* enclosure; reserve; boundary stone.

cotorra *f* magpie; small parrot; (*col*) chatterbox.

covacha *f* small cave, grotto.

coyote *m* coyote.

coyuntura *f* joint, articulation; juncture.

coz *f* kick; recoil (of a gun); ebbing (of a flood); (*fig*) insult.

cráneo *m* skull.

cráter *m* crater.

creación *f* creation.

creador/ra *adj* creative; * *m/f* creator.

crear *vt* to create, to make; to establish.

crecer *vi* to grow, to increase; to rise.

creces *fpl* increase.

crecida *f* swell (of rivers).

crecido/da *adj* full-grown (of a person); large; (*fig*) vain.

creciente *f* crescent (moon); (*mar*) flood tide; * *adj* growing; crescent.

crecimiento *m* increase; growth.

credenciales *fpl* credentials *pl*.

credibilidad *f* credibility.

crédito *m* credit; belief, faith; reputation.

credo *m* creed.

credulidad *f* credulity.

crédulo/la *adj* credulous.

creencia *f* credence, belief.

creer *vt, vi* to believe; to think; to consider.

crema *f* cream; custard.

cremallera *f* zipper.

crepúsculo *m* twilight.

crespo/pa *adj* curled; angry, displeased.

crespón *m* crepe.

cresta *f* crest (of birds).

creyente *m/f* believer.

cría *f* breeding; young.

criada *f* servant, maid.

criadero *m* (*bot*) nursery; breeding place.

criadilla *f* testicle; small loaf; truffle.

criado/da *m/f* servant; *adj* reared, brought up, bred.

criador *f* creator; breeder.

crianza *f* breeding, rearing.

criar *vt* to create, to produce; to breed; to nurse; to breast-feed; to bring up, to raise.

criatura *f* creature; child.

criba *f* sieve.

cribar *vt* to sift.

crimen *m* crime.

criminal *adj, m/f* criminal.

criminalista *m/f* criminologist; criminal lawyer.

crin *f* mane; horsehair.

crío/a *m/f* (*fam*) kid.

criollo/lla *adj, m/f* Creole.

cripta f crypt.

crisis f invar crisis.

crisma f chrism.

crisol m crucible; melting pot.

crispar vt to set on edge; to tense up.

cristal m crystal; glass; pane; lens.

cristalino/na adj crystalline.

cristalización f crystallization.

cristalizar vt to crystallize.

cristiandad f Christianity.

cristianismo m Christianity.

cristiano/na adj, m/f Christian.

Cristo m Christ.

criterio m criterion.

crítica f criticism.

criticar vt to criticize.

crítico/ca m/f critic; * adj critical.

croar vi to croak.

cromo m chrome.

crónica f chronicle; news report; feature.

crónico/ca adj chronic.

cronista m/f chronicler; reporter; columnist.

cronología f chronology.

cronológico/ca adj chronological.

cronómetro m stopwatch.

cruce m crossing; crossroads.

crucero m cruiser; cruise; transept; crossing; Southern Cross (constellation).

crucificar vt to crucify; to torment.

crucifijo m crucifix.

crucigrama m crossword.

crudeza f unripeness; crudeness; undigested food (in the stomach).

crudo/da adj raw; green, unripe; crude; cruel; hard to digest.

cruel adj cruel.

crueldad f cruelty.

cruento/ta adj bloody; cruel.

crujido m crack; creak; clash; crackling.

crujiente adj crunchy.

crujir vi to crackle; to rustle.

crustáceo m crustacean.

cruz f cross; tails (of a coin).

cruzada f crusade.

cruzado m crusader; ~/da adj crossed.

cruzar vt to cross; (mar) to cruise ~se vr to cross; to pass each other.

cuaderna f fourth part; timber; rib.

cuaderno m notebook; exercise book; logbook.

cuadra f block; stable.

cuadrado/da adj, m square.

cuadragenario/ria adj forty-year-old.

cuadragésimo/ma adj, m fortieth.

cuadrangular adj quadrangular, four-cornered.

cuadrángulo m quadrangle.

cuadrante m quadrant; dial.

cuadrar vt, vi to square; to fit, to suit, to correspond.

cuadricular adj squared.

cuadrilátero/ra adj, m quadrilateral.

cuadrilla f party, group; gang, crew.

cuadro m square; picture, painting; window frame; scene; chart; (dep) team; executive.

cuadrúpedo/da adj quadruped.

cuádruple adj quadruple.

cuádruplo/pla adj quadruple, fourfold.

cuajada f curd.

cuajar vt to coagulate; to thicken; to adorn; to set; ~se vr to coagulate, to curdle; to set; to fill up.

cuál pn which (one).

cual pn which; who; whom; * adv as; like; * adj such as.

cualidad f quality.

cualquier adj any.

cualquiera adj anyone, anybody;

someone, somebody; whoever; whichever.

cuándo *adv* when; ¿de ~ acá? since when?

cuando *adv* when; if; even; * *conj* since; **de ~ en ~** from time to time; **~ más, ~ mucho** at most, at best; **~ menos** at least.

cuantía *f* quantity, amount; importance.

cuantioso/sa *adj* numerous; substantial.

cuantitativo/va *adj* quantitative.

cuánto *adj* what a lot of; how much?; **¿~s?** how many?; * *pn, adv* how; how much; how many.

cuanto/ta *adj* as many as; as much as; all; whatever; * *adv* **en ~** as soon as; **en ~ a** as regards; **~ más** moreover, the more as.

cuarenta *adj, m* forty.

cuarentena *f* space of forty days; Lent; quarantine.

cuaresma *f* Lent.

cuarta *f* fourth; span; (*mar*) point (of the compass).

cuartear *vt* to quarter, to divide up; **~se** *vr* to split into pieces.

cuartel *m* quarter, district; barracks *pl*.

cuarteta *f* (*poet*) quatrain.

cuartilla *f* fourth part; sheet of paper.

cuarto *m* fourth part; quarter; room, apartment; span; **~s** *mpl* cash, money; **~/ta** *adj* fourth.

cuarzo *m* quartz.

cuatrero *m* horse thief.

cuatro *adj, m* four.

cuatrocientos/tas *adj* four hundred.

cuba *f* cask; tub; (*fig*) drunkard.

cubeta *f* small cask.

cúbico/ca *adj* cubic.

cubierta *f* cover; deck of a ship; (*auto*) bonnet; tyre; pretext.

cubierto *m* cover; shelter; place at table; meal at a fixed charge; **~s** *mpl* cutlery.

cubil *m* lair.

cubilete *m* tumbler; dice box.

cubo *m* cube; bucket.

cubo de la basura *m* dustbin.

cubrecama *m* bedspread.

cubrir *vt* to cover; to disguise; to protect; to roof a building; **~se** *vr* to become overcast.

cucaña *f* (*fam*) soft job (*sl*); bargain; cinch (*sl*).

cucaracha *f* cockroach.

cuchara *f* spoon.

cucharada *f* spoonful; ladleful.

cucharadita *f* teaspoonful.

cucharita *f* teaspoon.

cucharón *m* ladle; large spoon.

cuchichear *vi* to whisper.

cuchicheo *m* whispering.

cuchilla *f* large kitchen knife; chopping knife; blade.

cuchillada *f* cut; gash; **~s** *fpl* wrangles, quarrels.

cuchillo *m* knife.

cuchitril *m* pigsty.

cuclillas *adv*: **en ~** squatting.

cuclillo *m* cuckoo; (*fig*) cuckold.

cuco *m* cuckoo; **~/ca** *adj* sharp.

cucurucho *m* paper cornet.

cuello *m* neck; collar.

cuenca *f* bowl; deep valley; hollow; socket of the eye.

cuenco *m* earthenware bowl.

cuenta *f* calculation; account; bill (in a restaurant); count; counting; bead; importance.

cuentakilómetros *m invar* mileometer.

cuentarrevoluciones *m invar* rev counter.

cuentista *m/f* storyteller.

cuento *m* tale, story, narrative.

cuerda *f* rope; string; spring.

cuerdo/da *adj* sane; prudent, judicious, canny.

cuerno *m* horn.

cuero *m* hide, skin, leather.

cuerpo *m* body; cadaver, corpse.

cuervo *m* raven.

cuesta *f* slope, hill; incline; ir ~ abajo to go downhill; ~ arriba uphill.

cuestión *f* question, matter; dispute; quarrel; problem.

cuestionable *adj* questionable, problematic.

cuestionar *vt* to question, to dispute.

cueva *f* cave; cellar.

cuidado *m* care, worry, concern; charge.

cuidadosamente *adv* observantly.

cuidadoso/sa *adj* careful; anxious.

cuidar *vt* to care for; to mind, to look after.

culata *f* butt; breech (of a gun); hindquarters *pl* (of an animal); rear of a horse.

culebra *f* snake.

culinario/ria *adj* culinary.

culminación *f* culmination.

culo *m* backside; bum (*sl*); bottom.

culpa *f* fault, blame; guilt.

culpabilidad *f* guilt.

culpable *adj* culpable; guilty; * *m/f* culprit.

culpar *vt* to accuse, to blame.

cultivación *f* cultivation, culture.

cultivar *vt* to cultivate.

cultivo *m* cultivation; crop.

culto/ta *adj* cultured; refined, civilized; * *m* culture; worship.

cultura *f* culture.

cumbre *f* top, summit.

cumpleaños *m invar* birthday.

cumplido/da *adj* large, plentiful; complete, perfect, courteous; * *m* compliment.

cumplidor/ora *adj* reliable.

cumplimentar *vt* to compliment.

cumplimiento *m* fulfilment; accomplishment; completion.

cumplir *vt* to carry out, to fulfil; to serve (a prison sentence); to carry out (death penalty); to attain, to reach (a certain age); ~se *vr* to be fulfilled; to expire, to be up.

cúmulo *m* heap, pile.

comunicado *m* communiqué.

cuna *f* cradle.

cuña *f* wedge.

cuñado/da *m/f* brother/sister-in-law.

cundir *vi* to spread; to grow, to increase.

cuneta *f* ditch.

cuota *f* quota; fee.

cupé *m* (auto) coupé.

cupo *m* share.

cupón *m* coupon.

cúpula *f* cupola, dome.

cura *m* priest; * *f* cure; treatment.

curable *adj* curable.

curación *f* cure; curing.

curandero *m* quack (doctor).

curar *vt* to cure; to treat, to dress (a wound); to salt; to dress; to tan.

curativo/va *adj* curative, healing.

curia *f* ecclesiastical court.

curiosear *vt* to glance at; * *vi* to look round.

curiosidad *f* curiosity.

curioso/sa *adj* curious; * *m/f* bystander.

currante *m/f* (*fam*) worker.

currar *vi* (*fam*) to work.

currículum *m* curriculum vitae.

cursado/da *adj* skilled; versed.

cursar *vt* to frequent a place; to send, to dispatch; to study.

cursillo m short course of lectures (in a university).
cursivo/va adj italic (type).
curso m course, direction; year (at university); subject.
cursor m cursor.
curtidor m tanner.
curtidos mpl tanned leather.
curtir vt to tan leather; ~se to become sunburned; to become inured.
curva f curve, bend.
curvatura f curvature.
curvilíneo/nea adj curvilinear.

curvo/va adj curved, bent.
cuscurro m little crust of bread.
cúspide f summit, peak; apex.
custodia f custody, safekeeping, care; monstrance.
custodio m guard, keeper; watchman.
cutáneo/nea adj cutaneous.
cutícula f cuticle.
cutis m skin.
cutre adj (fam) mean, grotty (sl).
cuyo/ya pn whose, of which, of whom.

D

dactilógrafo/fa m/f typist.
dádiva f gift, present; donation.
dadivoso/sa adj generous, open-handed.
dado m die; ~s dice.
daga f dagger.
dale excl come on!
daltónico/ca adj colour-blind.
dama f lady, gentlewoman; mistress; queen; actress who performs principal parts.
damasco m damask (fabric); damson (plum).
damasquino/na adj damask.
damero m checkers board.
damnificar vt to hurt, to injure, to damage.
danza f dance.
danzar vi to dance; to meddle.
danzarín m fine dancer; meddler.
dañar vt to hurt, to injure; to damage.
dañino/na adj harmful; noxious; mischievous.
daño m harm, damage; prejudice; loss.
dar vt to give; to supply, to

administer, to afford; to deliver; to bestow; to strike, to beat, to knock; to communicate; ~se vr to conform (to the will of another); to give oneself up; ~se prisa to hurry.
dardo m dart.
datar vt to date.
dátil m (bot) date.
dativo m (gr) dative.
dato m fact.
de prep of; from; for; by; on; to; with.
deambular vi to stroll.
deán m dean.
debajo adv under, underneath, below.
debate m debate, discussion; contest; altercation.
debatir vt to debate, to argue, to discuss.
debe m (com) debit; ~ y haber debit and credit.
deber m obligation, duty; debt; * vt to owe; to be obliged to; * vi: **debe (de)** it must, it should.
debidamente adv justly, duly; exactly, perfectly.

débil *adj* feeble, weak; sickly; frail.

debilidad *f* dimness; weakness.

debilitar *vt* to debilitate, to weaken.

débito *m* debt; duty.

debutar *vi* to make one's debut.

década *f* decade.

decadencia *f* decay, decline.

decaer *vi* to decay, to moulder; to decline, to fade.

decaimiento *m* decay, decline.

decálogo *m* decalogue.

decano *m* senior; dean.

decantar *vt* to decant.

decapitación *f* decapitation, beheading.

decapitar *vt* to behead.

decena *f* ten.

decencia *f* decency.

decente *adj* decent; honest.

decepción *f* disappointment.

decidir *vt* to decide, to determine.

decimal *adj* decimal.

décimo/ma *adj*, *m* tenth.

decir *vt* to say; to tell; to speak; to name.

decisión *f* decision; determination; resolution; sentence.

decisivo/va *adj* decisive; final.

declamación *f* declamation, discourse, oration.

declamar *vi* to declaim; to harangue.

declaración *f* declaration; explanation, interpretation; (*jur*) deposition.

declarar *vt* to declare; to manifest; to expound; to explain; (*jur*) to decide; **~se** *vr* to declare one's opinion; * *vi* to testify.

declinación *f* declination, descent; decline.

declinar *vi* to decline; to decay, to degenerate; * *vt* (*gr*) to decline.

declive *m* slope; decline.

decolorarse *vr* to become discoloured.

decomiso *m* confiscation.

decoración *f* decoration.

decorado *m* scenery.

decorar *vt* to decorate, to adorn; to illustrate.

decorativo/va *adj* decorative.

decoro *m* honour, respect; circumspection; honesty; decency.

decoroso/sa *adj* decorous, decent.

decrecer *vi* to decrease.

decrépito/ta *adj* decrepit, worn out with age.

decrepitud *f* decrepitude.

decretar *vt* to decree, to determine.

decreto *m* decree; decision; judicial decree.

dechado *m*: **~ de virtudes** model of virtue and perfection.

dedal *m* thimble; very small drinking glass.

dedicación *f* dedication; consecration.

dedicar *vt* to dedicate, to devote; to consecrate; **~se** *vr* to apply oneself to.

dedicatoria *f* dedication.

dedo *m* finger; toe; small bit; **~ meñique** little finger; **~ pulgar** thumb; **~ índice** index finger; **~ corazón** middle finger; **~ anular** ring finger.

deducción *f* deduction, inference; derivation.

deducir *vt* to deduce, to infer; to allege in pleading; to subtract.

defección *f* defection; apostasy.

defectivo/va *adj* defective.

defecto *m* defect; defectiveness.

defectuoso/sa *adj* defective, imperfect, faulty.

defender *vt* to defend, to protect; to

justify, to assert, to maintain; to prohibit, to forbid; to resist, to oppose.

defensa f defence, justification, apology; guard, shelter, protection, fence.

defensiva f defensive.

defensivo m defence, safeguard; ~/va adj defensive.

defensor/ra m/f defender, protector; lawyer, defence counsel.

deferente adj pliant, docile, yielding.

deferir vi to defer; to yield (to another's opinion); * vt to communicate.

deficiencia f deficiency.

deficiente adj defective.

déficit m deficit.

definición f definition; decision.

definir vt to define, to describe, to explain; to decide.

definitivo/va adj definitive; positive.

deformar vt to deform; ~se vr to become deformed.

deforme adj deformed; ugly.

deformidad f deformity; ugliness; gross error.

defraudación f fraud; usurpation.

defraudar vt to defraud, to cheat; to usurp; to disturb.

defunción f death; funeral.

degeneración f degeneration; degeneracy.

degenerar vi to degenerate.

degollación f beheading.

degollar vt to behead; to destroy, to ruin.

degradación f degradation.

degradar vt to degrade; ~se vr to degrade or demean oneself.

degustar vt to taste.

dehesa f pasture.

deidad f deity, divinity; goddess.

dejadez f slovenliness, neglect.

dejado/da adj slovenly, idle, indolent; dejected.

dejar vt to leave, to quit; to omit; to let; to permit, to allow; to leave, to forsake; to bequeath; to pardon; ~ de to stop; to fail to; ~se vr to abandon oneself.

dejo m accent; aftertaste, tang.

del adj of the (contraction of de and el).

delantal m apron.

delante adv in front; opposite; ahead; ~ de in front of; before.

delantera f front, forepart (of something); advantage; forward line.

delantero/ra adj front; * m/f forward.

delatar vt to accuse; to denounce.

delator m accuser; informer, denouncer.

delegación f delegation; substitution.

delegado/da m/f delegate; deputy.

delegar vt to delegate; to substitute.

deleitar vt to delight.

deletrear vt to spell; to examine; to conjecture.

delfín m dolphin; dauphin.

delgadez f thinness.

delgado/da adj thin; delicate, fine; light; slender, lean; acute; ingenious; little, scanty.

deliberación f deliberation; resolution.

deliberadamente adv deliberately.

deliberar vi to consider, to deliberate; * vt to debate; to consult.

delicadeza f tenderness, softness; delicacy, daintiness; subtlety.

delicado/da adj delicate, tender; faint; exquisite; delicious, dainty; slender, subtle.

delicia f delight, pleasure.

delicioso/sa adj delicious; delightful.

delincuencia f delinquency.

delincuente m delinquent.

delineante m/f draftsman/woman.

delinear vt to delineate, to sketch; to describe.

delinquir vi to offend.

delirante adj delirious.

delirar vi to rave; to talk nonsense.

delirio m delirium; dotage; nonsense.

delito m offence; crime.

demacrado/da adj pale and drawn.

demagogia f demagogy.

demagogo m demagogue.

demanda f demand, claim; pretension, complaint; challenge; request.

demandado/da m/f defendant.

demandante m/f claimant.

demandar vt to demand; to ask; to claim; to sue.

demarcación f demarcation; boundary line.

demarcar vt to mark out (limits).

demás adj other; remaining; * pn **los/las ~** the others, the rest; **estar ~** to be over and above; to be useless or superfluous; **por ~** in vain, to no purpose.

demasía f excess; arduous enterprise; rudeness; want of respect; abundance, plenty; **en ~** excessively.

demasiado/da adj too; excessive; * adv too, too much.

demencia f madness.

demente adj mad, insane.

democracia f democracy.

demócrata m/f democrat.

democrático/ca adj democratic.

demoler vt to demolish; to destroy.

demolición f demolition.

demonio m demon.

demora f delay; demurrage.

demorar vt to delay; **~se** vr to be delayed; * vi to linger.

demostrable adj demonstrable.

demostración f demonstration; manifestation.

demostrar vt to prove, to demonstrate; to manifest.

demostrativo/va adj demonstrative.

denegación f denial; refusal.

denegar vt to deny; to refuse.

dengue m prudery.

denigración f defamation; stigma, disgrace.

denigrar vt to blacken; to insult.

denominación f denomination.

denominar vt to name; to designate.

denotar vt to denote; to express.

densidad f density; obscurity.

denso/sa adj dense, thick; compact.

dentado/da adj jagged, toothed; perforated (of stamps).

dentadura f set of teeth.

dentellada f gnashing of the teeth; nip; pinch with the teeth; **a ~s** snappishly, peevishly.

dentera f (fig) the shivers pl.

dentición f dentition, teething.

dentífrico m toothpaste.

dentista m/f dentist.

dentro adv within; * pn: **~ de** in, inside.

denuncia f denunciation; accusation; report.

denunciar vt to advise; to denounce; to report.

deparar vt to offer, to present.

departamento m department; (ferro) compartment; apartment.

dependencia f dependency; relation,

affinity; dependence; office; business, affair.

depender vi: ~ **de** to depend on, to be dependent on.

dependienta f saleswoman.

dependiente m shop assistant; * adj dependent.

depilar vt to depilate, remove hair from.

depilatorio m hair remover.

deplorable adj deplorable, lamentable.

deplorar vt to deplore.

deponer vt to depose; to declare; to displace; to deposit.

deportación f deportation.

deportar vt to deport.

deporte m sport.

deportista m/f sportsman/woman.

deportivo/va adj sports compd.

deposición f deposition; assertion, affirmation; (jur) deposition upon oath.

depositar vt to deposit; to confide; to put away for safekeeping.

depósito m deposit; warehouse; tank.

depravación f depravity.

depravar vt to deprave, to corrupt.

depreciar vt to depreciate.

depredador/ra adj predatory; * m predator.

depresión f depression.

deprimido/da adj depressed.

deprimir vt to depress; ~**se** vr to become depressed.

deprisa adv quickly.

depuración f purification.

depuradora f purifier.

depurar vt to cleanse; to purify; to filter.

de quitapón adj detachable, removable.

derecha f right hand, right side; right.

derecho/cha adj right; straight; just; perfect; certain; * m right, justice; law; tax, duty; fee; * adv straight.

derivación f derivation; source; origin.

derivado/da adj derivative; * m derivative; by-product.

derivar vt, vi to derive; (mar) to drift.

dermatología f dermatology.

dermatólogo/ga m/f dermatologist.

derogar vt to derogate, to abolish; to reform.

derogatorio/ria adj derogatory.

derramamiento m effusion; waste; dispersion; ~ **de sangre** bloodshed.

derramar vt to drain off (water); to spread; to spill, to scatter; to waste, to shed; ~**se** vr to pour out.

derrame m spilling; overflow; discharge; leakage.

derredor m circumference, circuit; **al** ~, **en** ~ around, about.

derrengado/da adj bent, crooked.

derrengar vt to sprain.

derretir vt to melt; to consume; to thaw; ~**se** vr to melt.

derribar vt to demolish; to flatten.

derribo m demolition; ruins of a demolished building pl.

derrocar vt to pull down, to demolish.

derrochador m spendthrift.

derrochar vt to dissipate; to squander.

derroche m waste.

derrota f ship's course; road, path; defeat.

derrotar vt to destroy; to defeat.

derrotero m collection of sea charts; ship's course; (fig) course, way.

derruir vt to demolish.

derrumbar vt to throw down; **~se** vr to collapse.

desabastecer vt to cut off supplies from.

desabillé m deshabille.

desabollar vt to take bulges out of.

desabotonar vt to unbutton; **~se** vr to come undone.

desabrido/da adj tasteless, insipid; rude; unpleasant.

desabrigado/da adj uncovered; unsheltered.

desabrigar vt to uncover; to deprive of clothes or shelter.

desabrochar vt to undo; **~se** vr to come undone.

desacatar vt to treat in a disrespectful manner.

desacato m disrespect, incivility.

desacertado/da adj mistaken, unwise; inconsiderate.

desacierto m error, gross mistake, blunder.

desaconsejado/da adj inconsiderate; ill-advised.

desaconsejar vt to advise against.

desacorde adj discordant.

desacostumbrado/da adj unusual.

desacreditar vt to discredit.

desafiar vt to challenge; to defy.

desafilado/da adj blunt.

desafinado/da adj out of tune.

desafinar vi to be out of tune.

desafío m challenge; struggle; contest, combat.

desaforado/da adj huge; disorderly, lawless; impudent.

desafortunadamente adv unfortunately.

desafortunado/da adj unfortunate, unlucky.

desafuero m outrage; excess.

desagradable adj disagreeable, unpleasant.

desagradar vt to displease; to pester.

desagradecido/da adj ungrateful.

desagradecimiento m ingratitude.

desagrado m harshness; displeasure.

desagraviar vt to make amends for.

desagravio m amends pl; satisfaction.

desaguar vt to drain; * vi to drain off.

desagüe m channel, drain; drainpipe; drainage.

desaguisado m outrage.

desahogado/da adj comfortable; roomy.

desahogar vt to ease; to vent; **~se** vr to recover; to relax; to let off steam.

desahogo m ease, relief; freedom.

desahuciar vt to cause to despair; to give up; to evict.

desahucio m eviction.

desairado/da adj disregarded; slighted.

desairar vt to disregard, to take no notice of.

desaire m disdain, disrespect; unattractiveness.

desajustar vt to make uneven; to unbalance; **~se** vr to get out of order.

desajuste m disorder; imbalance.

desalentador/ra adj disheartening.

desalentar vt to put out of breath; to discourage.

desaliento m dismay.

desaliño m slovenliness; carelessness.

desalinizadora f desalination plant.

desalinizar vt to desalinate.

desalmado/da adj cruel, inhuman.

desalojar vt to eject; to move out; * vi to move out.

desamarrar vt to cast off (a ship); to untie; to remove.

desamor m indifference.

desamparado/da adj helpless.

desamparar vt to forsake, to abandon; to relinquish.

desamparo m abandonment; helplessness; dereliction.

desamueblar vt to remove the furniture from.

desandar vt to retrace; to go back the same road.

desangrar vt to bleed; to drain (a pond); (fig) to exhaust (one's means); ~se vr to lose a lot of blood.

desanimado/da adj downhearted.

desanimar vt to discourage; ~se vr to lose heart.

desapacible adj disagreeable; unpleasant, harsh.

desaparecer vi to disappear.

desaparecido/da adj missing; * mpl ~s missing people.

desaparejar vt to unharness, unhitch (beasts); (mar) to unrig (a ship).

desaparición f disappearance.

desapego m coolness; lack of interest.

desapercibido/da adj unnoticed.

desaplicado/da adj lazy; careless, neglectful.

desapolillar vt to free from moths; ~se vr (fig) to get rid of the cobwebs.

desaprensivo/va adj unscrupulous.

desaprobación f disapproval.

desaprobar vt to disapprove; to condemn; to reject.

desaprovechado/da adj useless; unprofitable; backward; slack.

desaprovechar vt to waste, to turn to a bad use.

desarmar vt to disarm; to disband (troops); to dismantle; (fig) to pacify.

desarme m disarmament.

desarraigar vt to uproot; to root out; to extirpate.

desarraigo m eradication.

desarrapado/da adj ragged.

desarreglado/da adj untidy.

desarreglar vt to disorder, to upset.

desarreglo m disorder; untidiness.

desarrollar vt to develop; to unroll; to unfold; ~se vr to develop; to be unfolded; to open.

desarrollo m development.

desarropar vt to undress.

desarticular vt to take apart.

desasir vt to loosen, to disentangle; ~se vr to extricate oneself.

desasosegar vt to disquiet, to disturb.

desasosiego m restlessness; anxiety.

desastrado/da adj wretched, miserable; ragged.

desastre m disaster; misfortune.

desastroso/sa adj disastrous.

desatado/da adj untied; wild.

desatar vt to untie, to loose; to separate; to solve; ~se vr to come undone; to break.

desatascar vt to unblock; to clear.

desatender vt to pay no attention to; to disregard.

desatinado/da adj foolish; extravagant; * m fool, madman.

desatinar vi to talk nonsense; to reel, to stagger.

desatino m blunder; nonsense.

desatornillar *vt* to unscrew.

desatrancar *vt* to unbar; to unblock.

desautorizado/da *adj* unauthorized.

desautorizar *vt* to deprive of authority; to deny.

desavenencia *f* discord, disagreement.

desavenido/da *adj* contrary, disagreeing.

desaventajado/da *adj* disadvantageous, unprofitable.

desayunar *vt* to have for breakfast; ~**se** *vr* to breakfast; * *vi* to have breakfast;

desayuno *m* breakfast.

desazón *f* disgust; uneasiness; annoyance.

desazonado/da *adj* ill-adapted; ill-humoured.

desazonar *vt* to annoy; ~**se** *vr* to be annoyed; to be anxious.

desbancar *vt* to break (the bank in gambling); (*fig*) to supplant.

desbandarse *vr* to disband; to go off in all directions.

desbarajuste *m* confusion.

desbaratar *vt* to destroy.

desbarrar *vi* to talk rubbish.

desbastar *vt* to smooth; to polish; to waste.

desbloquear *vt* to unblock.

desbocado/da *adj* open-mouthed; wild (applied to a horse); foul-mouthed; indecent.

desbocarse *vr* to bolt.

desbordar *vt* to exceed; ~**se** *vr* to overflow.

descabalgar *vi* to dismount.

descabellado/da *adj* dishevelled; disorderly; wild, unrestrained; disproportionate; violent.

descabellar *vt* to ruffle.

descafeinado/da *adj* decaffeinated.

descalabrado/da *adj* wounded on the head; imprudent.

descalabrar *vt* to wound on the head; to smash.

descalabro *m* blow; misfortune; considerable loss.

descalificar *vt* to disqualify; to discredit.

descalzar *vt*, ~**se** *vr* to take off one's shoes.

descalzo/za *adj* barefooted; (*fig*) destitute.

descambiar *vt* to exchange.

descaminado/da *adj* (*fig*) misguided.

descaminar *vt* to misguide, to lead astray.

descamisado/da *adj* shirtless.

descampado/da *adj* disengaged; free; open; * *m* open space.

descansado/da *adj* rested, refreshed; quiet.

descansar *vt* to rest; * *vi* to rest; to lie down.

descansillo *m* landing.

descanso *m* rest, repose; break; interval.

descapotable *m* convertible.

descarado/da *adj* cheeky, barefaced.

descararse *vr* to behave insolently.

descarga *f* unloading; volley, discharge.

descargar *vt* to unload, to discharge; ~**se** *vr* to unburden oneself.

descargo *m* discharge; evidence; receipt.

descarnado/da *adj* scrawny.

descarnar *vt* to strip the flesh from; to clean away the flesh from; to corrode; ~**se** *vr* to grow thin.

descarado/da *adj* cheeky.

descaro *m* nerve.

descarriar *vt* to lead astray; to misdirect; ~**se** *vr* to lose one's way; to stray; to err.

descarrilamiento *m* (*ferro*) derailment.

descarrilar *vi* (*ferro*) to leave or run off the rails.

descarrío *m* losing of one's way.

descartar *vt* to discard; to dismiss; to rule out; ~**se** *vr* to excuse oneself.

descascarillado/da *adj* peeling.

descastado *adj* degenerate; ungrateful.

descendencia *f* descent, offspring.

descendente *adj* descending; **tren ~** *m* (*ferro*) down train.

descender *vt* to take down; * *vi* to descend, to walk down; to flow; to fall; ~ **de** to be derived from.

descendiente *adj* descending; * *m/f* descendant.

descenso *m* descent; drop; relegation.

descerrajar *vt* to force the lock (of a door etc); to discharge firearms.

descifrar *vt* to decipher; to unravel.

desclavar *vt* to draw out nails (from).

descocado/da *adj* bold, impudent.

descodificador *m* decoder (for TV).

descolgar *vt* to take down; to pick up; ~**se** *vr* to let oneself down.

descollar *vi* to excel.

descolorido/da *adj* pale, colourless.

descomedido/da *adj* impudent, insolent; huge.

descompaginar *vt* to disarrange.

descomponer *vt* to discompose, to set at odds; to disconcert; (*quím*) to decompose.

descomposición *f* disagreement; discomposure; decomposition.

descompuesto/ta *adj* decomposed; broken.

descomunal *adj* uncommon; huge.

desconcertado/da *adj* disconcerted; bewildered.

desconcertar *vt* to disturb; to confound; to disconcert; ~**se** *vr* to be bewildered; to be upset.

desconchado/da *adj* peeling.

desconchar *vt* to peel off.

desconcierto *m* disorder, confusion; uncertainty.

desconectar *vt* to disconnect.

desconfiado/da *adj* mistrustful, distrustful.

desconfianza *f* distrust; jealousy.

desconfiar *vi*: ~ **de** to mistrust, to suspect.

descongelar *vt* to defrost.

descongestionar *vt* to clear.

desconocer *vt* to disown, to disavow; to be totally ignorant of (a thing); not to know (a person); not to acknowledge (a favour received).

desconocido/da *adj* unknown; disguised; * *m/f* stranger.

desconocimiento *m* ignorance.

desconsiderado/da *adj* inconsiderate; imprudent.

desconsolado/da *adj* disconsolate; painful; sad.

desconsolar *vt* to distress.

desconsuelo *m* distress; trouble; despair.

descontado *adj*: **por ~** of course; **dar por ~** to take for granted.

descontar *vt* to discount; to deduct.

descontento *m* dissatisfaction; disgust.

descorazonar *vt* to dishearten, to discourage.

descorchar *vt* to uncork.

descorrer vt to draw.

descortés/esa adj impolite, rude.

descortesía f rudeness.

descoser vt to undo, take apart; to separate; ~**se** vr to come apart at the seams.

descosido/da adj unstitched; disjointed.

descoyuntar vt to dislocate; to vex, to annoy.

descrédito m discredit.

descreído/da adj incredulous.

descremado/da adj skimmed.

describir vt to describe; to draw, to delineate.

descripción f description; delineation; inventory.

descriptivo/va adj descriptive.

descuartizar vt to quarter; to carve.

descubierto m deficit; overdraft; ~**/ta** adj uncovered.

descubrimiento m discovery; revelation.

descubrir vt to discover, to disclose; to uncover; to reveal; to show; ~**se** vr to reveal oneself; to take off one's hat; to confess.

descuento m discount; decrease.

descuida excl don't worry!

descuidado/da adj careless, negligent.

descuidar vt to neglect; * vi, ~**se** vr to be careless.

descuido m carelessness, negligence; forgetfulness; incivility; improper action.

desde prep since; after; from; ~ **luego** of course; ~ **entonces** since then.

desdecirse vr to retract one's words.

desdén m disdain, scorn.

desdentado/da adj toothless.

desdentar vt to draw out (teeth).

desdeñable adj contemptible, despicable.

desdeñar vt to disdain, to scorn; ~**se** vr to be disdainful.

desdeñoso/sa adj disdainful; contemptuous.

desdicha f misfortune, calamity; great poverty.

desdichado/da adj unfortunate; wretched, miserable.

desdoblar vt to unfold, to spread open.

desear vt to desire, to wish; to require, to demand.

desecación f desiccation.

desecar vt to dry up.

desechar vt to depreciate; to reject; to refuse; to throw away.

desecho m residue; ~**s** mpl rubbish.

desembalar vt to unpack.

desembarazado/da adj free.

desembarazar vt to free; to clear; ~**se** vr: ~ **de** to get rid of.

desembarcadero m landing stage.

desembarcar vt to unload, to disembark; * vi to disembark, to land.

desembarco m landing.

desembargo m (jur) raising an embargo.

desembarque m landing.

desembocadura f mouth.

desembocar vi: ~ **en** to flow into.

desembolsar vt to pay out.

desembolso m expenditure.

desembragar vt to declutch.

desembuchar vt to disgorge; to tell all.

desempaquetar vt to unpack.

desempatar vt to hold a play-off.

desempate m play-off.

desempeñar vt to redeem; to extricate from debt; to fulfil (any duty or promise); to acquit; ~**se** vr to get out of debt.

desempeño *m* redeeming a pledge; occupation.

desempleado/da *adj* unemployed; * *m/f* unemployed person.

desempleo *m* unemployment.

desempolvorar *vt* to dust.

desencadenar *vt* to unchain; ~**se** *vr* to break loose; to burst.

desencajar *vt* to disjoint; to dislocate; to disconnect.

desencallar *vt* to refloat.

desencanto *m* disenchantment.

desenchufar *vt* to unplug.

desenfadado/da *adj* free; unembarrassed.

desenfado *m* ease; facility; calmness, relaxation.

desenfocado/da *adj* out of focus.

desenfrenado/da *adj* outrageous; ungovernable.

desenfreno *m* wildness; lack of self-control.

desenganchar *vt* to unhook; to uncouple.

desengañado/da *adj* disillusioned.

desengañar *vt* to disillusion; ~**se** *vr* to become disillusioned.

desengaño *m* disillusionment; disappointment.

desengrasar *vt* to take the grease off.

desenhebrar *vt* to unthread; to unravel.

desenlace *m* climax; outcome.

desenmarañar *vt* to disentangle; to unravel.

desenmascarar *vt* to unmask.

desenredar *vt* to disentangle.

desenrollar *vt* to unroll.

desenroscar *vt* to untwist; to unroll.

desentenderse *vr* to feign not to understand; to pass by without noticing.

desenterrar *vt* to exhume; to dig up.

desentonar *vi* to be out of tune; to clash.

desentrañar *vt* to unravel.

desentumecer *vt* to stretch; to loosen up.

desenvainar *vt* to unsheath; to show.

desenvoltura *f* sprightliness; cheerfulness; impudence, boldness.

desenvolver *vt* to unfold; to unroll; to decipher, to unravel; to develop; ~**se** *vr* to develop; to cope.

desenvuelto/ta *adj* forward; natural.

deseo *m* desire, wish.

deseoso/sa *adj* anxious.

desequilibrado/da *adj* unbalanced.

deserción *f* desertion; defection.

desertar *vt* to desert; *(jur)* to abandon (a cause).

desertificación *f* desertification.

desertor *m* deserter; fugitive.

desesperación *f* despair, desperation; anger, fury.

desesperado/da *adj* desperate, hopeless.

desesperar *vi*, ~**se** *vr* to despair; * *vt* to make desperate.

desestabilizar *vt* to destabilize.

desestimar *vt* to disregard, to reject.

desfachatez *f* impudence.

desfalcar *vt* to embezzle.

desfalco *m* embezzlement.

desfallecer *vt* to get weak; to faint.

desfallecimiento *m* fainting.

desfasado/da *adj* old-fashioned.

desfase *m* gap.

desfavorable *adj* unfavorable.

desfigurar *vt* to disfigure, to deform; to disguise.

desfiladero *m* gorge.

desfilar *vi* (*mil*) to parade.

desfogarse *vr* to give vent to one's passion or anger.

desforestación *f* desforestation.

desgajar vt to tear off; to break in pieces; **~se** vr to be separated; to be torn to pieces.

desgana f disgust; loss of appetite; aversion, reluctance.

desganado/da adj not hungry; half-hearted; **estar ~** to lose all pleasure in doing a thing; to lose one's appetite.

desgañitarse vr to scream, to bawl.

desgarrador/a adj heartrending.

desgarrar vt to tear; to shatter.

desgarro m tear; grief; impudence.

desgarrón m large tear.

desgastar vt to waste; to corrode; **~se** vr to get worn out.

desgaste m wear (and tear).

desglosar vt to break down.

desgracia f misfortune; disgrace; accident; setback.

desgraciado/da adj unfortunate; unhappy, miserable; out of favour; disagreeable.

desgreñado/da adj dishevelled.

desgreñar vt to dishevel (the hair); to disorder.

desguarnecer vt to strip down; to dismantle.

deshabitado/da adj deserted, uninhabited; desolate.

deshacer vt to undo, to destroy; to cancel, to efface; to rout (an army); to solve; to melt; to break up, to divide; to dissolve in a liquid; to violate (a treaty); to diminish; to disband (troops); **~se** vr to melt; to come apart.

desharrapado/da adj shabby, ragged, in tatters.

deshecho/cha adj undone, destroyed; wasted; melted; in pieces.

deshelar vt to thaw; **~se** vr to thaw, to melt.

desheredar vt to disinherit.

deshidratado/da adj dehydrated.

deshidratar vt to dehydrate.

deshielo m thaw.

deshilachar vt to unravel.

deshilar vt to fray.

deshinchar vt to deflate; **~se** vr to go flat, to go down.

deshojar vt to strip the leaves off.

deshollinador m chimney sweep.

deshonesto/ta adj indecent.

deshonra f dishonour; shame.

deshonrar vt to affront, to insult, to defame; to dishonour.

deshonroso/sa adj dishonourable, indecent.

deshora f unseasonable time.

deshuesar vt to rid of bones; to stone.

desidia f idleness, indolence.

desierto/ta adj deserted; solitary; * m desert; wilderness.

designación f designation.

designar vt to design; to intend; to appoint; to express, to name.

designio m design, purpose; road, course.

desigual adj unequal, unlike; uneven, craggy.

desigualdad f inequality, dissimilitude; inconstancy; roughness, unevenness.

desilusión f disappointment.

desilusionar vt to disappoint; **~se** vr to become disillusioned.

desinfección f disinfection.

desinfectar vt to disinfect.

desinflar vt to deflate.

desintegración f disintegration.

desinterés m unselfishness; disinterestedness.

desinteresado/da adj disinterested; unselfish.

desistir vi to desist, to cease.

desleal adj disloyal; unfair.

deslealtad f disloyalty, breach of faith.

desleír vt to dilute; to dissolve.

deslenguado/da adj foul-mouthed.

desligar vt to separate; to loosen, to unbind; ~**se** vr to extricate oneself.

desliz m slip, sliding; lapse, weakness.

deslizadizo/za adj slippery, slippy; glib.

deslizar vt to slip, to slide; to let slip (a comment); ~**se** vr to slip; to skid; to flow softly; to creep in.

deslucido/da adj tarnished; dull; shabby.

deslucir vt to tarnish; to damage; to discredit.

deslumbramiento m glare; confusion.

deslumbrar vt to dazzle; to puzzle.

desmán m outrage; disaster; misconduct.

desmandarse vr to behave badly.

desmantelar vt to dismantle; to abandon, to forsake.

desmaquillador m make-up remover.

desmarañar vt to disentangle.

desmayado/da adj unconscious; dismayed; appalled; weak.

desmayar vi to be dispirited or fainthearted; ~**se** vr to faint.

desmayo m unconsciousness; faint, swoon; dismay.

desmedido/da adj disproportionate.

desmejorar vt to impair; to weaken.

desmembrar vt to dismember; to separate.

desmemoriado/da adj forgetful.

desmentir vt to give the lie to; ~**se** vr to contradict oneself.

desmenuzar vt to crumble; to chip at; to fritter away; to examine minutely.

desmerecer vt to be unworthy of; * vi to deteriorate.

desmesurado/da adj excessive; huge; immeasurable.

desmontar vt to level; to remove (a heap of rubbish); to dismantle; * vi to dismount.

desmoralización f demoralization.

desmoralizar vt to demoralize.

desmoronar vt to destroy little by little; ~**se** vr to fall into disrepair.

desnatado/da adj skimmed.

desnatar vt to skim (milk); to take the choicest part of.

desnaturalizar vt to divest of naturalization rights; ~**se** vr to forsake one's country.

desnivel m unevenness of the ground.

desnucar vt to break (one's neck).

desnudar vt to undress; to strip; to discover, to reveal; ~**se** vr to undress.

desnudez f nakedness.

desnudo/da adj naked; bare, uncovered; ill-clothed; (fig) plain, evident.

desnutrición f malnutrition.

desnutrido/da adj undernourished.

desobedecer vt, vi to disobey.

desobediencia f disobedience; insubordination.

desobediente adj disobedient.

desocupado/da adj empty; at leisure.

desocupar vt to vacate; to empty; ~**se** vr to retire from a business; to withdraw from an arrangement.

desodorante m deodorant.

desolación f destruction; affliction.

desolado/da *adj* desolate, disconsolate.

desolar *vt* to lay waste; to harass.

desollar *vt* to flay, to skin; (*fig*) to extort.

desorden *m* disorder, confusion.

desordenado/da *adj* disorderly; untidy.

desordenar *vt* to disorder; to untidy; ~**se** *vr* to get out of order.

desorganización *f* disorganization.

desorganizar *vt* to disorganize.

desorientar *vt* to mislead; to confuse; ~**se** *vr* to lose one's way.

desovar *vi* to spawn.

despabilado/da *adj* watchful, vigilant; wide-awake.

despabilar *vt* to snuff (a candle); (*fig*) to dispatch quickly; to sharpen; ~**se** *vr* to wake up.

despacio *adv* slowly, leisurely; little by little; *i*~! softly!, gently!

despachar *vt* to dispatch; to expedite; to sell; to send.

despacho *m* dispatch, expedition; cabinet; office; commission; warrant, patent; expedient; smart answer.

despachurrar *vt* to squash, to crush; to mangle.

desparejar *vt* to make unequal or uneven.

desparpajo *m* ease; savoir-faire.

desparramar *vt* to disseminate, to spread; to spill; to squander; to lavish; ~**se** *vr* to be dissipated.

despavorido *adj* frightened.

despectivo/va *adj* pejorative, derogatory.

despecho *m* indignation; displeasure; spite; dismay, despair; deceit; derision, scorn; **a ~ de** in spite of.

despedazar *vt* to tear into pieces; to mangle.

despedida *f* farewell; sacking.

despedir *vt* to discharge; to dismiss (from office); to see off; ~**se** *vr*: ~ **de** to say goodbye to.

despegado/da *adj* cold; detached.

despegar *vt* to unglue; to take off; ~**se** *vr* to come loose.

despego *m* detachment; coolness.

despegue *m* take-off.

despeinado/da *adj* dishevelled.

despeinar *vt* to ruffle.

despejado/da *adj* sprightly, quick; clear.

despejar *vt* to clear away; ~**se** *vr* to cheer up; to clear; * *vi* to clear.

despellejar *vt* to skin.

despensa *f* pantry, larder; provisions *pl*.

despeñadero *m* precipice.

despeñar *vt* to precipitate; ~**se** *vr* to throw oneself headlong.

despepitarse *vr* to bawl.

desperdiciar *vt* to squander.

desperdicio *m* waste; ~**s** *mpl* rubbish; waste.

desperdigar *vt* to separate; to scatter.

desperezarse *vr* to stretch oneself.

desperfecto *m* slight damage; flaw.

despertador *m* alarm clock.

despertar *vt* to wake up, to rouse from sleep; to excite; * *vi* to wake up; to grow lively or sprightly; ~**se** *vr* to wake up.

despiadado/da *adj* heartless, merciless.

despido *m* dismissal.

despierto/ta *adj* awake; vigilant; fierce; brisk, sprightly.

despilfarro *m* slovenliness; waste; mismanagement.

despintar vt to deface (a painting); to obscure (things); to mislead; ~se to lose its colour.

despistar vt to mislead; to throw off the track; ~se vr to take the wrong way; to become confused.

desplante m bold statement; wrong stance; insolence.

desplazamiento m displacement.

desplazar vt to move; to scroll; ~se vr to travel.

desplegar vt to unfold, to display; to explain, to elucidate; (mar) to unfurl; ~se vr to open out; to travel.

despliegue m display.

desplomarse vr to fall to the ground; to collapse.

desplumar vt to fleece; to pluck.

despoblado m desert.

despoblar vt to depopulate; to desolate; ~se vr to become depopulated.

despojar vt: ~ (de) to strip (of); to deprive (of); ~se vr to undress.

despojo m plunder; loot; ~s mpl giblets pl; remains pl; offal.

desposado/da adj newlywed.

desposar vt to marry, to betroth; ~se vr to be betrothed or married.

desposeer vt to dispossess.

desposeimiento m dispossession.

déspota m despot.

despótico/ca adj despotic.

despotismo m despotism.

despreciable adj contemptible, despicable.

despreciar vt to offend; to despise.

desprecio m scorn, contempt.

desprender vt to unfasten, to loosen; to separate; ~se vr to give way; to fall down; to extricate oneself.

desprendimiento m alienation, disinterestedness.

despreocupado/da adj careless; unworried.

despreocuparse vr to be carefree.

desprestigiar vt to run down.

desprevenido/da adj unawares, unprepared.

desproporción f disproportion.

desproporcionado/da adj disproportionate.

desproporcionar vt to disproportion.

despropósito m absurdity.

desprovisto/ta adj unprovided.

después adv after, afterwards; next.

despuntar vt to blunt; ~ vi to sprout; to dawn; al ~ del día at break of day.

desquiciar vt to upset; to discompose; to disorder.

desquitar vt to retrieve (a loss); ~se vr to win one's money back again; to return by giving like for like; to take revenge.

desquite m recovery of a loss; revenge, retaliation.

desrizar vt to uncurl.

destacamento m (mil) detachment.

destacar vt to emphasize; (mil) to detach (a body of troops); ~se vr to stand out.

destajo m piecework; trabajar a ~ to do piecework.

destapar vt to uncover; to open; ~se vr to be uncovered.

destartalado/da adj untidy.

destello m signal light; sparkle.

destemplado/da adj out of tune; incongruous (applied to paintings); intemperate.

desteñir vt to discolour; ~se vr to fade.

desternillarse vr: ~ de risa to roar with laughter.

desterrar vt to banish; to expel, to drive away.

destetar vt to wean.

destete m weaning.

destierro m exile, banishment.

destilación f distillation.

destilar vt, vi to distil.

destinar vt to destine for, to intend for.

destinatario/a m/f addressee.

destino m destiny; fate, doom; destination; office.

destitución f destitution, abandonment.

destituir vt to dismiss.

destornillador m screwdriver.

destornillar vt to unscrew.

destreza f dexterity, cleverness, cunning, expertness, skill.

destripar vt to disembowel; to trample.

destronar vt to dethrone.

destrozar vt to destroy, to break into pieces; (mil) to defeat.

destrozo m destruction; (mil) defeat, massacre.

destrucción f destruction, ruin.

destructivo/va adj destructive.

destruir vt to destroy.

desunir vt to separate, to disunite; to cause discord between.

desuso m disuse.

desvaído/da adj tall and graceless.

desvalido/da adj helpless; destitute.

desvalijar vt to rob; to burgle.

desván m garret.

desvanecer vt to dispel; ~se vr to grow vapid, to become insipid; to vanish; to be affected with giddiness.

desvanecimiento m pride, haughtiness; giddiness; swoon.

desvariar vi to be delirious.

desvarío m delirium; giddiness; inconstancy, caprice; extravagance.

desvelar vt to keep awake; ~se vr to stay awake.

desvelo m want of sleep; watchfulness.

desvencijado/da adj rickety.

desvencijar vt to disunite, to divide; to weaken; ~se vr to be ruptured; to come apart.

desventaja f disadvantage; damage.

desventura f misfortune; calamity.

desventurado/da adj unfortunate; calamitous.

desvergonzado/da adj impudent, shameless.

desvergonzarse vr to behave in an impudent manner.

desvergüenza f impudence; shamelessness.

desvestir vt, ~se vr to undress.

desviar vt to divert; to dissuade; to parry (at fencing); ~se vr to go off course.

desvío m turning away, going astray; aversion; disdain; indifference.

desvivirse vr: ~ por to long for.

detallar vt to detail, to relate minutely.

detalle m detail.

detallista m f retailer.

detención f detention; delay.

detener vt to stop, to detain; to arrest; to keep back; to reserve; to withhold; ~se vr to stop; to stay.

detenidamente adv carefully.

detenido/da adj detailed; sparing, niggardly; slow, inactive.

detergente m detergent.

deterioración f deterioration; damage.

deteriorar vt to damage.

deterioro m deterioration.

determinación f determination, resolution; boldness.
determinado/da adj determined; resolute.
determinar vt to determine; ~**se** vr to decide.
detestable adj detestable.
detestar vt to detest, to abhor.
detonación f detonation.
detonar vi to detonate.
detractar vt to denigrate, to defame, to slander.
detrás adv behind; at the back, in the back.
detrimento m detriment; damage; loss.
deuda f debt; fault; offence.
deudor/ra m/f debtor.
devaluación f devaluation.
devanar vt to reel; to wrap up.
devastación f devastation, desolation.
devastador/ra adj devastating.
devastar vt to devastate.
devengar vt to accrue.
devoción f devotion, piety; strong affection; ardent love.
devolución f return; (jur) devolution.
devolutivo/va adj (jur) transferable.
devolver vt to return; to send back; to refund; to throw up; * vi to be sick.
devorar vt to devour, to swallow up.
devoto/ta adj devout, pious; devotional; strongly attached.
día m day.
diablo m devil.
diablura f prank.
diabólico/ca adj diabolical; devilish.
diácono m deacon.
diadema m/f diadem; halo.
diafragma m diaphragm; midriff.

diagnosis f invar diagnosis.
diagnóstico m diagnosis.
diagonal adj diagonal.
diagrama m diagram.
dialecto m dialect.
diálisis f invar dialysis.
diálogo m dialogue.
diamante m diamond.
diámetro m diameter.
diana f (mil) reveille; bull's-eye.
diapasón m (mus) diapason, octave.
diapositiva f transparency, slide.
diario m journal, diary; daily newspaper; daily expenses pl; ~/**ria** adj daily.
diarrea f diarrhoea.
dibujar vt to draw, to design.
dibujo m drawing; sketch, draft; description.
dicción f diction; style; expression.
diccionario m dictionary.
diciembre m December.
dictado m dictation.
dictador m dictator.
dictadura f dictatorship.
dictamen m opinion, notion; suggestion, insinuation; judgement.
dictar vt to dictate.
dicha f happiness, good fortune; por ~ by chance.
dicho m saying; sentence; declaration; promise of marriage; ~/**cha** adj said.
dichoso/sa adj happy, prosperous.
diecinueve adj, m nineteen.
dieciocho adj, m eighteen.
dieciséis adj, m sixteen.
diecisiete adj, m seventeen.
diente m tooth; fang; tusk.
diestro/tra adj right; dexterous, skilful, clever; sagacious, prudent; sly, cunning; * m skilful fencer; halter; bridle.

diesel, diésel adj diesel compd.
dieta f diet, regimen; diet, assembly; daily salary of judges.
diez adj, m ten.
diezmar vt to decimate.
diezmo m tithe.
difamación f defamation.
difamar vt to defame, to libel.
difamatorio/ria adj defamatory, calumnious.
diferencia f difference.
diferencial adj differential.
diferenciar vt to differentiate, to distinguish; ~se vr to differ, to distinguish oneself.
diferente adj different, unlike.
diferido/da adj recorded.
diferir vt to defer, to put off; to differ.
difícil adj difficult.
dificultad f difficulty.
dificultar vt to put difficulties in the way of; to render difficult.
dificultoso/sa adj difficult; painful.
difundir vt to diffuse, to spread; to divulge; ~se vr to spread (out).
difunto/ta adj dead, deceased; late.
difusión f diffusion.
difuso/sa adj diffusive, copious; large; prolix; circumstantial.
digerir vt to digest; to bear with patience; to adjust, to arrange; (chem) to digest.
digestión f digestion; concoction.
digestivo/va adj digestive.
digital adj digital.
digitalizar vt to digitize.
dignarse vr to condescend, to deign.
dignidad f dignity, rank.
digno/na adj worthy; suitable.
dije m relic; trinket.
dilapidar vt to squander, to waste.
dilatación f dilation, extension; greatness of mind; calmness.

dilatado/da adj large; numerous; prolix; spacious, extensive.
dilatar vt to dilate, to expand; to spread out; to defer, to protract.
dilatorio/ria adj dilatory.
dilema m dilemma.
diligencia f diligence; affair, business; call of nature; stage coach.
diligente adj diligent, assiduous, prompt, swift.
dilucidar vt to elucidate, to explain.
diluir vt to dilute.
diluviar vi to rain in torrents.
diluvio m flood, deluge, inundation; abundance.
dimensión f dimension; extent; capacity, bulk.
diminutivo/va adj diminutive.
diminuto/ta adj defective, faulty; minute, small.
dimisión f resignation.
dimitir vt to give up, to abdicate; * vi to resign.
dinámica f dynamics.
dinámico/ca adj dynamic.
dinamita f dynamite.
dínamo, dinamo f dynamo.
dinastía f dynasty.
dineral m large sum of money.
dinero m money.
diocesano/na adj diocesan.
diócesis f diocese.
Dios m God.
diosa f goddess.
diploma m diploma, patent.
diplomacia, diplomática f diplomacy.
diplomado/da adj qualified.
diplomático/ca adj diplomatic; * m/f diplomat.
diptongo m diphthong.
diputación f deputation.
diputado m deputy.

diputar vt to depute.

dique m dike, dam.

dirección f direction, guidance; administration; steering.

directivo/va adj governing.

directo/ta adj direct, straight; apparent, evident; live.

director/ra m/f director; conductor; president; manager; headmaster.

dirigir vt to direct; to conduct; to regulate, to govern; ~se vr to go toward(s); to address oneself to.

discernimiento m discernment.

discernir vt to discern, to distinguish.

disciplina f discipline.

discípulo m disciple; scholar.

disco m disc; record; discus; light; face (of the sun or moon); lens (of a telescope) ; ~ compacto compact disc.

díscolo/la adj ungovernable; peevish.

disconforme adj differing.

discordancia f disagreement, discord.

discordante adj dissonant, discordant.

discordar vi to clash, to disagree.

discorde adj discordant; (mus) dissonant.

discordia f discord, disagreement.

discoteca m discotheque, disco.

discreción f discretion; acuteness of mind.

discrecional adj discretionary.

discrepancia f discrepancy.

discrepar vi to differ.

discreto/ta adj discreet; ingenious; witty, eloquent.

discriminación f discrimination.

disculpa f apology; excuse.

disculpar vt to exculpate, to excuse;

to acquit, to absolve; ~se vr to apologize; to excuse oneself.

discurrir vi to ramble about; to run to and fro; to discourse (upon a subject); * vt to invent, to contrive; to meditate.

discurso m speech; conversation; dissertation; space of time.

discusión f discussion.

discutir vt, vi to discuss.

disecar vt to dissect; to stuff.

disección f dissection.

diseminar vt to scatter; to disseminate, to propagate.

disentería f dysentery.

disentir vi to dissent, to disagree.

diseñador/ra m/f designer.

diseñar vt to draw; to design.

diseño m design; draft; description; picture.

disfraz m disguise; mask.

disfrazar vt to disguise, to conceal; to cloak, to dissemble; ~se vr to disguise oneself as.

disfrutar vt to enjoy; ~se vr to enjoy oneself.

disgustar vt to disgust; to offend; ~se vr to be displeased; to fall out.

disgusto m disgust, aversion; quarrel; annoyance; grief, sorrow.

disidente adj dissident; * m/f dissident, dissenter.

disimular vt to hide; to tolerate.

disimulo m dissimulation; tolerance.

disipado/da adj prodigal, lavish.

disipar vt to dissipate, to disperse, to scatter; to lavish.

dislocación f dislocation.

dislocarse vr to be dislocated or out of joint.

disminución f diminution.

disminuir vt to diminish; to decrease.

disolución f dissolution; liquidation.

disolver vt to loosen, to untie; to dissolve; to disunite; to melt, to liquefy; to interrupt.

disonancia f dissonance; disagreement, discord.

disparar vt to shoot, to discharge, to fire; to let off; to throw with violence; * vi to shoot, to fire.

disparatado/da adj inconsistent; absurd, extravagant.

disparate m nonsense, absurdity, extravagance.

disparo m shot; discharge; explosion.

dispensar vt to dispense; to excuse; to dispense with; to distribute.

displicencia f displeasure; dislike.

disponer vt to arrange, to prepare; to dispose.

disponible adj available; disposable.

disposición f disposition, order; resolution; command; power, authority.

dispositivo m device.

dispuesto/ta adj disposed; fit, ready.

disputa f dispute, controversy.

disputar vt to dispute, to controvert, to question; * vi to debate, to argue.

disquete m floppy disk.

distancia f distance; interval; difference.

distanciarse vr to become estranged.

distante adj distant, far off.

distinción f distinction; difference; prerogative.

distinguido/da adj distinguished, conspicuous.

distinguir vt to distinguish; to discern; ~se vr to distinguish oneself.

distintivo m distinctive mark; particular attribute.

distinto/ta adj distinct, different; clear.

distracción f distraction, want of attention.

distraer vt to distract; ~se vr to be absent-minded, to be inattentive.

distraído/da adj absent-minded, inattentive.

distribución f distribution; division, separation; arrangement.

distribuidor m distributor.

distribuir vt to distribute.

distrito m district; territory.

disturbar vt to disturb, to interrupt.

disturbio m riot; disturbance, interruption.

disuadir vt to dissuade.

disuasión f dissuasion.

diurno/na adj daily.

diva f prima donna.

divagar vi to digress.

diván m divan.

divergencia f divergence.

divergente adj divergent.

diversidad f diversity; variety of things.

diversificar vt to diversify; to vary.

diversión f diversion; sport; amusement; (mil) diversion.

diverso/sa adj diverse, different; several, sundry.

divertido/da adj amused; amusing.

divertir vt to divert (the attention); to amuse, to entertain; (mil) to draw off; ~se vr to amuse oneself.

dividir vt to divide; to disunite; to separate; to share out.

divieso m (med) boil.

divinidad f divinity.

divino/na adj divine, heavenly; excellent.

divisa f emblem.

divisar vt to perceive.

divisible *adj* divisible.

división *f* division; partition; separation; difference.

divorciar *vt* to divorce; to separate; ~**se** *vr* to get divorced.

divorcio *m* divorce; separation, disunion.

divulgación *f* publication; dissemination.

divulgar *vt* to publish, to divulge.

dobladillo *m* hem; turn-up.

dobladura *f* fold.

doblar *vt* to double; to fold; to bend; * *vi* to turn; to toll; ~**se** *vr* to bend, to bow, to submit.

doble *adj* double; dual; deceitful; **al ~** doubly; * *m* double.

doblegar *vt* to bend; ~**se** *vr* to yield.

doblez *m* crease; fold; turn-up; * *f* duplicity.

doce *adj*, *m* twelve.

docena *f* dozen.

docente *adj* teaching.

dócil *adj* docile, tractable.

docilidad *f* docility, gentleness; compliance.

doctor/ra *m/f* doctor.

doctorado *m* doctorate.

doctrina *f* doctrine, instruction; science.

doctrinal *m* catechism; * *adj* doctrinal.

documentación *f* documentation.

documento *m* document; record.

dogma *m* dogma.

dólar *m* dollar.

dolencia *f* disease; affliction.

doler *vi* to feel pain; to ache; ~**se** *vr* to feel for the sufferings of others; to complain.

dolor *m* pain; aching, ache; affliction.

doloroso/sa *adj* painful.

domador/ra *m/f* tamer.

domar *vt* to tame; to subdue, to master.

domesticar *vt* to domesticate.

domiciliarse *vr* to establish oneself in a residence.

domicilio *m* domicile; home, abode.

dominación *f* domination; dominion; authority, power.

dominante *adj* dominant; domineering.

dominar *vt* to dominate; to be fluent in; ~**se** *vr* to moderate one's passions.

domingo *m* Sunday; (Christian) Sabbath.

dominguero/ra *adj* done or worn on Sunday; * *m/f* Sunday driver.

dominical *adj* Sunday.

dominio *m* dominion; domination; power, authority; domain.

donación *f* donation; gift.

donar *vt* to donate; to bestow.

donativo *m* contribution.

doncella *f* virgin, maiden; lady's maid.

donde *adv* where.

dónde *adv* where; ¿**de dónde?** from where?; ¿**por dónde?** where?

dondequiera *adv* anywhere.

dorado/da *adj* gilt *compd*; golden; * *m* gilding.

dorar *vt* to gild; (*fig*) to palliate.

dormilón/ona *m/f* dull, sleepy person.

dormir *vi* to sleep; ~**se** *vr* to fall asleep.

dormitorio *m* dormitory.

dorsal *adj* dorsal.

dos *adj*, *m* two.

doscientos/tas *adj pl* two hundred.

dosis *f invar* dose.

dotado/da *adj* gifted.

dotar vt to endow.
dote f dowry; ~s fpl gifts pl of nature; endowments pl.
dragón m dragon; (mil) dragoon.
drama m drama.
dramático/ca adj dramatic.
dramatizar vt to dramatize.
dramaturgo/ga m/f dramatist.
droga f drug; stratagem; artifice, deceit.
drogadicción f drug addiction.
drogadicto/ta m/f drug addict.
droguería f hardware store.
dromedario m dromedary.
dubitativo/va adj doubtful, dubious; uncertain.
ducado m duchy; ducat.
ducha f shower; (med) douche.
ducharse vr to have a shower.
ducho/cha adj skilled, experienced.
duda f doubt; suspense; hesitation.
dudar vt to doubt.
dudoso/sa adj doubtful, dubious.
duelo m grief, affliction; mourning.
duende m elf, hobgoblin.
dueño/ña m/f owner; landlord/lady; employer.
dulce adj sweet; mild, gentle, meek; soft; * m sweet, candy.

dulcificar vt to sweeten.
dulzura f sweetness; gentleness; softness.
dúo m (mus) duo, duet.
duodécimo/ma adj twelfth.
duplicación f duplication.
duplicado m duplicate.
duplicar vt to duplicate, to double; to repeat.
duplicidad f duplicity; falseness.
duplo m double.
duque m duke.
duquesa f duchess.
duración f duration.
duradero/ra adj lasting, durable.
durante adv during.
durar vi to last, to continue.
durazno m peach; peach tree.
duraznero m peach tree.
dureza f hardness; harshness; ~ de oído hardness of hearing.
durmiente adj sleeping; * m (ferro) sleeper.
duro/ra adj hard; cruel; harsh, rough; * m five peseta coin; * adv hard.
duunviro m magistrate in ancient Rome.

E

e conj and (before words starting with i and h).
ea interj hey!, come on!; i~ pues! well then!, let's see!
ebanista m cabinet-maker, carpenter.
ébano m ebony.
ebrio/ia adj drunk.
ebullición f boiling.
eccema m eczema.

echar vt to throw; to add; to fire; to pour out; to mail; to give off; to bud; ~se vr to lie down; to rest; to stretch out.
eclesiástico/ca adj ecclesiastical.
eclipsar vt to eclipse; to outshine.
eclipse m eclipse.
eco m echo.
ecografía f ultrasound scan.
ecología f ecology.

ecologismo *m* green movement.
ecologista *m/f* ecologist, environmentalist.
economato *m* cut-price store.
economía *f* economy.
económico/ca *adj* economic; cheap; thrifty; financial; avaricious.
economista *m/f* economist.
ecosistema *m* ecosystem.
ecotasa *f* ecotax.
ecoturismo *m* ecotourism.
ecuación *f* equation.
ecuador *m* equator.
ecuánime *adj* level-headed.
ecuestre *adj* equestrian.
ecuménico/ca *adj* ecumenical; universal.
edad *f* age.
edecán *m* (*mil*) aide-de-camp.
edición *f* edition; publication.
edicto *m* edict.
edificación *f* construction.
edificante *adj* edifying, instructive.
edificar *vt* to build, to construct; to edify.
edificio *m* building; structure.
editar *vt* to edit; to publish.
editor/ra *m/f* editor; publisher.
educación *f* education; upbringing; (good) manners *pl*.
educador/ra *m/f* teacher, educator.
educando/da *m/f* pupil.
educar *vt* to educate, to instruct; to bring up.
efectivamente *adv* exactly; really; in fact.
efectivo/va *adj* effective; true; certain.
efecto *m* effect; consequence; purpose; ~ **invernadero** greenhouse effect ~**s** *mpl* effects *pl*, goods *pl*; **en** ~ in fact, really.
efectuar *vt* to effect, to carry out.

efeméride *f* event (remembered on its anniversary).
efervescencia *f* effervescence, fizziness.
eficacia *f* effectiveness, efficacy.
eficaz *adj* efficient; effective.
eficiente *adj* efficient.
efigie *f* effigy, image.
efímero/ra *adj* ephemeral.
efluvio *m* outflow.
efusión *f* effusion.
efusivo/va *adj* effusive.
égloga *f* (*poet*) eclogue.
egoísmo *m* selfishness.
egoísta *m/f* self-seeker; * *adj* selfish.
egregio/gia *adj* eminent, remarkable.
eje *m* axle; axis.
ejecución *f* execution.
ejecutar *vt* to execute, to carry out, to perform; to put to death; (*jur*) to attach, to seize.
ejecutivo/va *adj* executive; * *m/f* executive.
ejecutor/ra *m/f* executor; (*jur*) distrainer.
ejecutoria *f* (*jur*) writ of execution.
ejecutorio/ria *adj* (*jur*) executory.
ejemplar *m* specimen; copy; example; * *adj* exemplary.
ejemplificar *vt* to exemplify.
ejemplo *m* example; **por** ~ for example, for instance.
ejercer *vt* to exercise.
ejercicio *m* exercise.
ejercitación *f* exercise, practice.
ejercitar *vt* to exercise; ~**se** *vr* to train.
ejército *m* army.
ejote *m* green bean.
el *art*, *m* the.
él *pn* he, it.
elaboración *f* elaboration.

elaborado/da adj elaborate.
elaborar vt to elaborate.
elasticidad f elasticity.
elástico/ca adj elastic.
elección f election; choice.
elector/ra m/f elector.
electorado m electorate.
electoral adj electoral.
electricidad f electricity.
electricista m/f electrician.
eléctrico/ca adj electric, electrical.
electrización f electrification.
electrizar vt to electrify.
electrocardiograma m electrocardiogram.
electrocutar vt to electrocute.
electrodoméstico m (electrical) domestic appliance.
electrónico/ca adj electronic.
electrotecnia f electrical engineering.
elefante m elephant.
elegancia f elegance.
elegante adj elegant, fine.
elegía f elegy.
elegir vt to choose, to elect.
elemental adj elemental; elementary.
elemento m element; ~s mpl elements pl, rudiments pl, first principles pl.
elevación f elevation; highness; rise; haughtiness; pride; height; altitude.
elevar vt to raise; to elevate; ~se vr to rise; to be enraptured; to be conceited.
eliminar vt to eliminate, to remove.
eliminatoria f preliminary (round).
elipse f (geom) ellipse.
elipsis f (gr) ellipsis.
elite, élite f elite.
elixir m elixir.

ella pn she; it.
ello pn it.
elocución f elocution.
elocuencia f eloquence.
elocuente adj eloquent.
elogiar vt to praise, to eulogize.
elogio m eulogy, praise.
elote m corn on the cob.
elucidación f elucidation, explanation.
eludir vt to elude, to escape.
emanación f emanation.
emanar vi to emanate.
emancipación f emancipation.
emancipar vt to emancipate, to set free.
embadurnar vt to smear, to bedaub.
embajada f embassy.
embajador/ra m/f ambassador.
embalaje m packing, package.
embalar vt to bale, to pack in bales.
embaldosar vt to pave with tiles.
embalsamador m embalmer.
embalsamar vt to embalm.
embalse m reservoir.
embarazada f pregnant woman; * adj pregnant.
embarazar vt to embarrass; to make pregnant; ~se vr to become intricate.
embarazo m pregnancy; embarrassment; obstacle.
embarazoso/sa adj difficult; intricate, entangled.
embarcación f embarkation; any vessel or ship.
embarcadero m quay, wharf; port; harbour.
embarcar vt to embark; ~se vr to go on board; (fig) to get involved (in a matter).
embargar vt to lay on an embargo; to impede, to restrain.

embargo *m* embargo; **sin ~** still, however.

embarque *m* embarkation.

embastar *vt* to stitch, to tack.

embate *m* breakers *pl*, surf, surge; sudden attack.

embaucador/ra *m/f* swindler; impostor.

embaucar *vt* to deceive; to trick.

embebecer *vt* to fascinate; **~se** *vr* to be fascinated.

embebecimiento *m* amazement, astonishment; fascination.

embeber *vt* to soak; to saturate; * *vi* to shrink; **~se** *vr* to be enraptured; to be absorbed.

embelesamiento *m* rapture.

embelesar *vt* to amaze, to astonish.

embeleso *m* amazement, enchantment.

embellecer *vt* to embellish, to beautify.

emberrincharse *vr* to have a tantrum.

embestida *f* assault, violent attack.

embestir *vt* to assault, to attack.

emblanquecer *vt* to whiten; **~se** *vr* to grow white; to bleach.

emblema *m* emblem.

embobado/da *adj* amazed; fascinated.

embobamiento *m* astonishment; fascination.

embobar *vt* to amaze; to fascinate; **~se** *vr* to be amazed; to stand gaping.

embobecer *vt* to make silly; **~se** *vr* to get silly.

embobecimiento *m* silliness.

émbolo *m* plunger; piston.

embolsar *vt* to put money into (a purse); to pocket.

emborrachar *vt* to intoxicate, to inebriate; **~se** *vr* to get drunk.

emboscada *f* (*mil*) ambush.

emboscarse *vr* (*mil*) to lie in ambush.

embotar *vt* to blunt; **~se** *vr* to go numb.

embotellamiento *m* traffic jam.

embotellar *vt* to bottle (wine).

embozado/da *adj* covered; covert.

embozar *vt* to muffle (the face); (*fig*) to cloak, to conceal.

embozo *m* part of a cloak, veil or anything with which the face is muffled; covering of one's face.

embrague *m* clutch.

embrear *vt* to cover with tar or pitch.

embriagar *vt* to intoxicate, to inebriate; to transport, to enrapture.

embriaguez *f* intoxication, drunkenness; rapture, delight.

embrión *m* embryo.

embrollador/ra *m/f* troublemaker.

embrollar *vt* to muddle; to entangle, to embroil.

embrollo *m* muddle.

embromar *vt* to tease; to cajole; to wheedle.

embrujar *vt* to bewitch.

embrutecer *vt* to brutalize; **~se** *vr* to become depraved.

embudo *m* funnel.

embuste *m* fraud; lie, fib (*sl*).

embustero/ra *m/f* impostor, cheat; liar; * *adj* deceitful.

embutido *m* sausage; inlay.

embutir *vt* to insert; to stuff; to inlay; to cram, to scoff.

emergencia *f* emergency.

emerger *vi* to emerge, to appear.

emético/ca *adj* emetic.

emigración *f* emigration; migration.

emigrado/da *adj* emigrated; * *m/f* emigrant.

emigrante *m/f* emigrant.

emigrar *vi* to emigrate.

eminencia *f* eminence.

eminente *adj* eminent, high; excellent, conspicuous.

emisario *m* emissary.

emisión *f* emission; broadcasting; programme; issue.

emisora *f* broadcasting station.

emitir *vt* to emit, to send forth; to issue; to broadcast.

emoción *f* emotion; feeling; excitement.

emocionante *adj* exciting.

emocionar *vt* to excite; to move, to touch.

emoliente *adj* emollient, softening.

emolumento *m* emolument.

emotivo/va *adj* emotional.

empacar *vt* to pack; to crate.

empachar *vt* to give indigestion; ~**se** *vr* to have indigestion.

empacho *m* (*med*) indigestion.

empachoso/sa *adj* indigestible.

empadronamiento *m* register; census.

empadronarse *vr* to register.

empalagar *vt* to sicken; to disgust.

empalago *m* disgust; boredom.

empalagoso/sa *adj* cloying; tiresome.

empalizada *f* (*mil*) palisade.

empalmadura *f* join; weld; splice.

empalmar *vt* to join.

empalme *m* (*ferro*) junction; connection.

empanada *f* (meat) pie.

empanar *vt* to cover with breadcrumbs.

empantanarse *vr* to get swamped; to get bogged down.

empañar *vt* to put a nappy on; to mist; to steam up; ~**se** *vr* to steam up; to tarnish one's reputation.

empapar *vt* to soak; to soak up; ~**se** *vr* to soak.

empapelar *vt* to paper.

empaquetar *vt* to pack, to parcel up.

emparedado *m* sandwich.

emparejar *vt* to level; to match, to fit; to equalize.

emparentar *vi* to be related by marriage.

emparrado *m* vine arbor.

empastar *vt* to paste; (*med*) to fill (a tooth).

empaste *m* (*med*) filling.

empatar *vi* to draw.

empate *m* draw.

empedernido/da *adj* inveterate; heartless.

empedernir *vt* to harden; ~**se** to be inflexible.

empedrado *m* paving.

empedrador *m* paver.

empedrar *vt* to pave.

empeine *m* instep.

empellón *m* push; heavy blow.

empeñado/da *adj* determined; pawned.

empeñar *vt* to pawn, to pledge; ~**se** *vr* to pledge oneself to pay debts; to get into debt; ~**se en algo** to insist on something.

empeño *m* obligation; determination; perseverance.

empeorar *vt* to make worse; * *vi*, ~**se** *vr* to grow worse.

empequeñecer *vt* to dwarf; (*fig*) to belittle.

emperador *m* emperor.

emperatriz *f* empress.

emperifollarse *vr* to dress oneself up.

empero *conj* yet, however.

emperrarse *vr* to get stubborn; to be obstinate.

empezar *vt* to begin, to start.

empinado/da *adj* high; proud.

empinar *vt* to raise; to exalt; * *vi* to drink heavily; ~se *vr* to stand on tiptoe; to soar.

empírico/ca *adj* empirical.

empirismo *m* empiricism.

empizarrado *m* slate roofing.

empizarrar *vt* to slate, to roof with slate.

emplasto *m* plaster.

emplazamiento *m* summons; location.

emplazar *vt* to summon; to locate.

empleado/da *m/f* official; employee.

emplear *vt* to employ; to occupy; to commission.

empleo *m* employ, employment, occupation.

empobrecer *vt* to reduce to poverty; * *vi* to become poor.

empobrecimiento *m* impoverishment.

empollar *vt* to incubate; to hatch; (*fam*) to swot (up).

empolvar *vt* to powder; to sprinkle powder upon.

emponzoñador/ra *m/f* poisoner.

emponzoñamiento *m* poisoning.

emponzoñar *vt* to poison; to taint, to corrupt.

emporio *m* emporium.

empotrado/da *adj* built-in.

empotrar *vt* to embed; to build in.

emprendedor/ra *m/f* entrepreneur.

emprender *vt* to embark on; to tackle; to undertake.

empresa *f* (*com*) company; enterprise, undertaking.

empresario/ria *m/f* manager.

empréstito *m* loan.

empujar *vt* to push; to press forward.

empuje *m* thrust; pressure; (*fig*) drive.

empujón *m* push; impulse; a ~ones in fits and starts.

empuñadura *f* hilt (of a sword).

empuñar *vt* to clench, to grip with the fist; to clutch.

emulación *f* emulation.

emular *vt* to emulate, to rival.

emulsión *f* emulsion.

en *prep* in; for; on, upon.

enaguas *fpl* petticoat.

enajenación *f* alienation; absent-mindedness.

enajenamiento *m* alienation; absent-mindedness.

enajenar *vt* to alienate; ~se *vr* to fall out.

enamoradamente *adv* lovingly.

enamoradizo/za *adj* inclined to fall in love.

enamorado/da *adj* in love, lovesick.

enamoramiento *m* falling in love.

enamorar *vt* to inspire love in; ~se *vr* to fall in love.

enano/na *adj* dwarfish; * *m* dwarf.

enarbolar *vt* to hoist, to raise high.

enardecer *vt* to fire with passion, to inflame.

enarenar *vt* to fill with sand.

encabezamiento *m* heading; foreword.

encabezar *vt* to head; to put a heading to; to lead.

encabritarse *vr* to rear (of horses).

encadenamiento *m* linking together, chaining.

encadenar *vt* to chain, to link together; to connect, to unite.

encajadura *f* insertion; socket; groove.

encajar *vt* to insert; to drive in; to encase; to intrude; ~se *vr* to squeeze; to gatecrash; * *vi* to fit (well).

encaje *m* encasing; joining; socket; groove; inlaid work.

encajera *f* lacemaker.

encajonamiento *m* . packing into boxes, etc.

encajonar *vt* to pack up in a box.

encalabrinar *vt* to make confused; ~**se** *vr* to become obstinate.

encaladura *f* whitening, whitewash.

encalar *vt* to whitewash.

encallar *vi* (*mar*) to run aground.

encallecer *vi* to get corns.

encamarse *vr* to take to one's bed.

encaminar *vt* to guide, to show the way; ~**se** *vr*: ~ **a** to take the road to.

encandilar *vt* to dazzle.

encanecer *vi* to grow grey; to grow old.

encantado/da *adj* bewitched; delighted; pleased.

encantador/ra *adj* charming; *m/f* magician.

encantamiento *m* enchantment.

encantar *vt* to enchant, to charm; (*fig*) to delight.

encanto *m* enchantment; spell, charm.

encañonar *vt* to hold up; to point a gun at; *vi* to grow feathers.

encapotar *vt* to cover with a cloak; ~**se** *vr* to be cloudy.

encapricharse *vr* to become stubborn.

encapuchar *vt* to cover with a hood.

encaramar *vt* to raise; to extol.

encararse *vr*: ~ **a** to come face to face with.

encarcelación *f* incarceration.

encarcelar *vt* to imprison.

encarecer *vt* to raise the price of; ~**se** *vr* to get dearer.

encarecimiento *m* price increase; con ~ insistently.

encargado/da *adj* in charge; * *m/f* representative; person in charge.

encargar *vt* to charge; to commission.

encargo *m* charge; commission; job; order.

encariñarse *vr*: ~ **con** to grow fond of.

encarnación *f* incarnation, embodiment.

encarnado/da *adj* incarnate; flesh-coloured; * *m* flesh colour.

encarnar *vt* to embody, to personify.

encarnizado/da *adj* bloodshot, inflamed; bloody, fierce.

encarrilar *vt* to put back on the rails; to put on the right track.

encasillar *vt* to pigeonhole; to typecast.

encasquetar *vt* to pull on (a hat).

encastillarse *vr* to refuse to yield.

encauzar *vt* to channel.

encebollado *m* casserole of beef or lamb and onions, seasoned with spice.

encenagado/da *adj* muddy, mud-stained.

encenagamiento *m* wallowing in mud.

encenagarse *vr* to wallow in mud.

encendedor *m* lighter.

encender *vt* to kindle, to light, to set on fire; to inflame, to incite; to switch on, to turn on; ~**se** *vr* to catch fire; to flare up.

encendido/da *adj* inflamed; high-coloured; * *m* ignition (of car).

encerado *m* blackboard.

encerar *vt* to wax; to polish.

encerrar *vt* to shut up, to confine; to contain; ~**se** *vr* to withdraw from the world.

encespedar *vt* to turf.

enchapar vt to veneer.

encharcarse vr to be flooded.

enchufar vt to plug in; to connect.

enchufe m plug; socket; connection; (fam) contact, connection.

encía f gum (of the teeth).

encíclica f encyclical.

enciclopedia f encyclopedia.

enciclopédico/ca adj encyclopedic.

encierro m confinement; enclosure; prison; bull-pen; penning (of bulls).

encima adv above; over; at the top; besides; ~ **de** prep above; over; at the top of; besides.

encina f holm oak, evergreen oak.

encinar m oakwood; oak grove.

encinta adj pregnant.

enclaustrado/da adj cloistered; hidden away.

enclenque adj weak, sickly; * m weakling.

encoger vt to contract, to shorten; to shrink; to discourage; ~**se** vr to shrink; (fig) to cringe.

encogidamente adv shyly, timidly, bashfully.

encogido/da adj shy, timid, bashful.

encogimiento m contraction; shrinkage; shyness; timidness; bashfulness.

encoladura f gluing.

encolar vt to glue.

encolerizar vt to provoke, to irritate; ~**se** vr to get angry.

encomendar vt to recommend; to entrust; ~**se** vr: ~ **a** to entrust oneself to; to put one's trust in.

encomiar vt to praise.

encomienda f commission, charge; message; (mil) command; patronage, protection; parcel post.

encomio m eulogy; praise; commendation.

enconar vt to inflame; to irritate.

encono m ill-feeling, rancour.

enconoso/sa adj hurtful, prejudicial; malevolent.

encontrado/da adj conflicting; hostile.

encontrar vt to meet, to encounter; vr: ~**se con** to run into; * vi to assemble, to come together.

encopetado/da adj presumptuous, boastful.

encorvadura f curvature; crookedness.

encorvar vt to bend, to curve.

encrespar vt to curl, to frizzle (hair); (fig) to anger; ~**se** vr to get rough (of the sea); (fig) to get cross.

encrucijada f crossroads; junction.

encuadernación f binding.

encuadernador/ra m/f bookbinder.

encuadernar vt to bind (books).

encubiertamente adv secretly; deceitfully.

encubierto/ta adj hidden, concealed.

encubridor/ra m/f concealer, harbourer; receiver of stolen goods.

encubrimiento m concealment, hiding; receiving of stolen goods.

encubrir vt to hide, to conceal.

encuentro m meeting; collision, crash; match, game.

encuesta f inquiry; opinion poll.

encumbrado/da adj high; elevated.

encumbramiento m elevation; height.

encumbrar vt to raise, to elevate; ~**se** vr to be raised; (fig) to become conceited.

encurtir vt to pickle.

endeble adj feeble, weak.

endecasílabo/ba adj consisting of eleven syllables.

endecha f dirge, lament.

endemoniado/da adj possessed with the devil; devilish.

enderezamiento m guidance, direction.

enderezar vt to straighten out; to set right; ~se vr to stand upright.

endeudarse vr to get into debt.

endiablado/da adj devilish, diabolical; ugly.

endiosar vt to deify; ~se vr to be high and mighty.

endosar vt to endorse.

endoso m endorsement.

endrina f sloe.

endrino m blackthorn, sloe.

endulzar vt to sweeten; to soften.

endurecer vt to harden, to toughen; ~se vr to become cruel; to grow hard.

endurecidamente adv cruelly.

endurecimiento m hardness; obstinacy; hard-heartedness.

enebro m (bot) juniper.

enemigo/ga adj hostile; * m enemy.

enemistad f enmity.

enemistar vt to make an enemy; ~se vr to become enemies; to fall out.

energía f energy, power, drive; strength of will; ~ nuclear nuclear power; ~ solar solar energy; ~ renovables renewable forms of energy.

enérgico/ca adj energetic; forceful.

energúmeno/na m/f (fam) madman/woman.

enero m January.

enervar vt to enervate.

enfadadizo/za adj irritable, crotchety.

enfadar vt to anger, to irritate; to trouble; ~se vr to become angry.

enfado m trouble; anger.

enfadoso/sa adj annoying, troublesome.

énfasis m emphasis.

enfático/ca adj emphatic.

enfermar vi to fall ill; * vt to make sick; to weaken.

enfermedad f illness.

enfermería f infirmary; sick bay.

enfermero/ra m/f nurse.

enfermizo/za adj infirm, sickly.

enfermo/ma adj sick, ill; * m/f invalid, sick person; patient.

enfervorizar vt to arouse; to inflame, to incite.

enflaquecer vt to weaken; to make thin.

enflaquecimiento m loss of weight; (fig) weakening.

enfocar vt to focus; to consider (a problem).

enfoque m focus.

enfrascarse vr to be deeply embroiled.

enfrentar vt to confront; to put face to face; ~se vr to face each other; to meet (two teams).

enfrente adv over against, opposite; in front.

enfriamiento m refrigeration; (med) cold.

enfriar vt to cool; to refrigerate; ~se vr to cool down; (med) to catch a cold.

enfurecer vt to madden, to enrage; ~se vr to get rough (of the wind and sea); to become furious or enraged.

enfurruñarse vr to get sulky; to frown.

engalanar vt to adorn, to deck.

engallarse vr to be arrogant.

engañabobos m invar trickster; trick, trap.

engañadizo/za *adj* gullible, easily deceived.

engañador/ra *adj* cheating; deceptive; * *m/f* cheat, impostor, deceiver.

engañar *vt* to deceive, to cheat; ~**se** *vr* to be deceived; to make a mistake.

enganchar *vt* to hook, to hang up; to hitch up; to couple, to connect; to recruit into military service; ~**se** *vr* (*mil*) to enlist.

engañifa *f* deceit, trick.

engaño *m* mistake; misunderstanding; deceit, fraud.

engañoso/sa *adj* deceitful, artful, false.

engarzar *vt* to thread; to link; to curl.

engastar *vt* to set, to mount.

engaste *m* setting, mount.

engatusamiento *m* deception, coaxing.

engatusar *vt* to coax.

engendrar *vt* to beget, to engender; to produce.

engendro *m* foetus, embryo; (*fig*) monstrosity; brainchild.

englobar *vt* to include.

engolfarse *vr* (*mar*) to sail out to sea; ~ **en** to be deeply involved in.

engolosinar *vt* to entice; ~**se** *vr* to find delight in.

engomadura *f* gluing.

engomar *vt* to glue.

engordar *vt* to fatten; * *vi* to grow fat; to put on weight.

engorro *m* nuisance, bother.

engorroso/sa *adj* troublesome, cumbersome.

engranaje *m* gear; gearing.

engrandecer *vt* to augment; to magnify; to speak highly of; to exaggerate.

engrandecimiento *m* increase; aggrandizement; exaggeration.

engrasar *vt* to grease, to lubricate.

engreído/da *adj* conceited, vain.

engreimiento *m* presumption, vanity.

engreír *vt* to make proud; ~**se** *vr* to grow proud.

engrosar *vt* to enlarge; to increase.

engrudo *m* paste.

engullidor/ra *m/f* devourer; guzzler.

engullir *vt* to swallow; to gobble, to devour.

enharinar *vt* to cover or sprinkle with flour.

enhebrar *vt* to thread.

enhilar *vt* to thread.

enhorabuena *f* congratulations *pl*; * *interj* congratulations.

enhoramala *interj* good riddance.

enigma *m* enigma, riddle.

enigmático/ca *adj* enigmatic; dark, obscure.

enjabonar *vt* to soap; (*fam*) to tick off.

enjaezar *vt* to harness (a horse).

enjalbegar *vt* to whitewash.

enjambre *m* swarm (of bees); crowd, multitude.

enjaular *vt* to shut up in a cage; to imprison.

enjoyar *vt* to adorn with jewels.

enjuagar *vt* to rinse out; to wash out.

enjuague *m* (*med*) mouthwash; rinsing, rinse.

enjugar *vt* to dry (the tears); to wipe off.

enjuiciar *vt* to prosecute, to try; to pass judgement on, to judge.

enjuto/ta *adj* dried up; (*fig*) lean.

enlace *m* connection, link; relationship.

enladrillado *m* brick paving.

enladrillador *m* bricklayer.

enladrillar *vt* to pave with bricks.

enlazable *adj* able to be fastened together.

enlazar *vt* to join, to unite; to tie.

enlodar *vt* to cover in mud; (*fig*) to stain.

enloquecer *vt* to madden, to drive crazy; * *vi* to go mad.

enloquecimiento *m* madness.

enlosar *vt* to lay with flags.

enlutar *vt* to put into mourning; ~**se** *vr* to go into mourning.

enmaderar *vt* to roof with timber.

enmarañar *vt* to entangle; to complicate; to confuse; ~**se** *vr* to become entangled; to get confused.

enmascarar *vt* to mask; ~**se** *vr* to go in disguise, to masquerade.

enmendar *vt* to correct; to reform; to repair, to compensate for; to amend; ~**se** *vr* to mend one's ways.

enmienda *f* correction, amendment.

enmohecer *vt* to make mouldy; to rust; ~**se** *vr* to grow mouldy or musty; to rust.

enmohecido/da *adj* mouldy. **enmudecer(se)** *vt* to silence; ~**se** *vr* to grow dumb; to be silent.

ennegrecer *vt* to blacken; to darken; to obscure.

ennoblecer *vt* to ennoble.

ennoblecimiento *m* ennoblement.

enojadizo/za *adj* peevish; short-tempered, irritable.

enojar *vt* to irritate, to make angry; to annoy; to upset; to offend; ~**se** *vr* to get angry.

enojo *m* anger, annoyance.

enojoso/sa *adj* offensive, annoying.

enorgullecerse *vr*: ~ (**de**) to be proud (of).

enorme *adj* enormous, vast, huge; horrible.

enormidad *f* enormity; monstrousness.

enramar *vt* to cover with the branches of trees.

enranciarse *vr* to grow rancid.

enrarecer *vt* to thin, to rarefy.

enredadera *f* climbing plant; bindweed.

enredador/ra *m/f* gossip; troublemaker; busybody.

enredar *vt* to entangle, to ensnare, to confound, to perplex; to puzzle; to sow discord among; ~**se** *vr* to get entangled; to get complicated; to get embroiled.

enredo *m* entanglement; mischievous lie; plot of a play.

enredoso/sa *adj* complicated.

enrejado *m* trelliswork.

enrejar *vt* to fix a grating to (a window); to grate, to lattice.

enrevesado/da *adj* complicated.

enriquecer *vt* to enrich; to adorn; ~**se** *vr* to grow rich.

enristrar *vt* to string (garlic); to straighten out; to go straight to.

enrobustecer *vt* to strengthen.

enrojecer *vt* to redden; * *vi* to blush.

enrolar *vt* to recruit; ~**se** *vr* (*mil*) to join up.

enrollar *vt* to roll (up).

enronquecer *vt* to make hoarse; * *vi* to grow hoarse.

enroscadura *f* twist.

enroscar *vt* to twist; ~**se** *vr* to curl or roll up.

ensalada *f* salad.

ensaladera *f* salad bowl.

ensaladilla (rusa) *f* Russian salad.

ensalmar *vt* to set (dislocated bones); to heal by spells.

ensalmo *m* enchantment, spell.

ensalzar *vt* to exalt, to aggrandize; to exaggerate.

ensamblador/ra *m/f* joiner.

ensamblar *vt* to assemble.

ensanchar *vt* to widen; to extend; to enlarge; ~**se** *vr* to expand; to assume an air of importance.

ensanche *m* dilation, augmentation; widening; expansion.

ensangrentar *vt* to stain with blood.

ensañar *vt* to irritate, to enrage; ~**se con** *vr* to treat brutally.

ensartar *vt* to string (beads, etc).

ensayar *vt* to test; to rehearse.

ensayo *m* test, trial; rehearsal of a play; essay.

ensenada *f* creek.

enseña *f* colours *pl*, standard.

enseñanza *f* teaching, instruction; education.

enseñar *vt* to teach, to instruct; to show.

enseres *mpl* belongings *pl*.

ensillar *vt* to saddle.

ensimismarse *vr* to be or become lost in thought.

ensoberbecer *vt* to make proud; ~**se** *vr* to become proud; (*mar*) to get rough.

ensordecer *vt* to deafen; * *vi* to grow deaf.

ensordecimiento *m* deafness.

ensortijamiento *m* curling the hair.

ensortijar *vt* to fix a ring in; to curl.

ensuciar *vt* to stain, to soil; to defile; ~**se** *vr* to wet oneself; to dirty oneself.

ensueño *m* fantasy; daydream; illusion.

entablar *vt* to board (up); to strike up (conversation).

entablillar *vt* (*med*) to put in a splint.

entallar *vt* to tailor (a suit); * *vi* to fit.

ente *m* organization; entity, being; (*fam*) odd character.

entendederas *fpl* understanding; brains *pl*.

entender *vt*, *vi* to understand, to comprehend; to remark, to take notice (of); to reason, to think; **a mi** ~ in my opinion; ~**se** *vr* to understand each other.

entendido/da *adj* understood; wise; learned, knowing.

entendimiento *m* understanding; knowledge; judgement.

enteramente *adv* entirely, completely.

enterar *vt* to inform; to instruct; ~**se** *vr* to find out.

entereza *f* entireness, integrity; firmness of mind.

enternecer *vt* to soften; to move (to pity); ~**se** *vr* to be moved.

enternecimiento *m* compassion, pity.

entero/ra *adj* entire, complete; perfect; honest; resolute; **por** ~ entirely, completely.

enterrador *m* gravedigger.

enterrar *vt* to inter, to bury.

entibiar *vt* to cool.

entidad *f* entity; company; body; society.

entierro *m* burial; funeral.

entoldar *vt* to cover with an awning.

entomología *f* entomology.

entonación *f* intonation; modulation; (*fig*) presumption, pride.

entonar *vt* to tune, to intone; to tone; * *vi* to be in tune; ~**se** *vr* to give oneself airs.

entonces *adv* then, at that time.

entontecer *vt* to fool; * *vi*, ~**se** *vr* to get silly.

entontecimiento *m* silliness.
entornar *vt* to half close.
entorpecer *vt* to dull; to make lethargic; to hinder; to delay.
entorpecimiento *m* numbness; lethargy.
entrada *f* entrance, entry; (*com*) receipts *pl*; entree; ticket (for cinema, theatre, etc).
entrambos/bas *pn, pl* both.
entrampar *vt* to trap, to snare; to mess up; to burden with debts; ~**se** *vr* get into debt.
entrañable *adj* intimate; affectionate.
entrañas *fpl* entrails *pl*, intestines *pl*.
entrante *adj* coming, next.
entrar *vi* to enter, to go in; to commence.
entre *prep* between; among(st); in; ~ **manos** in hand.
entreabrir *vt* to half open (a door), to leave ajar.
entrecano/na *adj* grey-black, greyish.
entrecejo *m* space between the eyebrows; frown.
entrecortado/da *adj* faltering; difficult.
entredicho *m* (*jur*) injunction; **estar en** ~ to be banned; **poner en** ~ to cast doubt on.
entrega *f* delivery; instalment.
entregar *vt* to deliver; to hand over; ~**se** *vr* to surrender; to devote oneself.
entrelazar *vt* to interlace.
entremedias *adv* in the meantime.
entremeses *mpl* hors d'oeuvres.
entremeter *vt* to put (one thing) between (others); ~**se** *vr* to interfere, to meddle.
entremetido/da *m/f* meddler; * *adj* meddling.

entremetimiento *m* insertion; meddling.
entrenador/ra *m/f* trainer, coach.
entrenar *vt* to train; ~**se** *vr* to train.
entreoír *vt* to half hear.
entrepaño *m* panel.
entrepierna *f* crotch.
entresaca *f* thinning out (of trees).
entresacar *vt* to thin out; to sift, to separate.
entresuelo *m* entresol; mezzanine.
entretanto *adv* meanwhile.
entretejer *vt* to interweave.
entretela *f* interfacing, stiffening, interlining.
entretener *vt* to amuse; to entertain, to divert; to hold up; to maintain; ~**se** *vr* to amuse oneself; to linger.
entretenido/da *adj* pleasant; amusing; entertaining.
entretenimiento *m* amusement, entertainment.
entrever *vt* to have a glimpse of.
entreverado/da *adj* patchy; streaky.
entrevista *f* interview.
entrevistar *vt* to interview; ~**se** *vr* to have an interview.
entristecer *vt* to sadden.
entrometer *vt* to put (one thing) between (others); ~**se** *vr* to interfere, to meddle.
entrometido/da *m/f* meddler; * *adj* meddling.
entroncar *vi* to be related or connected.
entronización *f* enthronement.
entronizar *vt* to enthrone.
entumecer *vt* to swell; to numb; ~**se** *vr* to become numb.
entumecido/da *adj* numb, stiff.
entumecimiento *m* numbness.
enturbiar *vt* to make cloudy; to obscure, to confound; ~**se** *vr* to

become cloudy; (*fig*) to get confused.

entusiasmar *vt* to excite, to fill with enthusiasm; to delight.

entusiasmo *m* enthusiasm.

entusiasta *m/f* enthusiast.

enumeración *f* enumeration.

enumerar *vt* to enumerate.

enunciación *f*, **enunciado** *m* enunciation, declaration.

enunciar *vt* to enunciate, to declare.

envainar *vt* to sheathe, to sheath.

envalentonar *vt* to give courage to; ~**se** *vr* to boast.

envanecer *vt* to make vain; to swell with pride; ~**se** *vr* to become proud.

envaramiento *m* stiffness; numbness.

envarar *vt* to numb.

envasar *vt* to pack; to bottle; to can.

envase *m* packing; bottling; canning; container; package; bottle; can.

envejecer *vt* to make old; * *vi*, ~**se** *vr* to grow old.

envenenador/ra *m/f* poisoner.

envenenar *vt* to poison; to embitter.

envenenamiento *m* poisoning.

envergadura *f* (*fig*) scope.

envés *m* wrong side (of material).

enviado/da *m/f* envoy, messenger.

enviar *vt* to send, to transmit, to convey, to dispatch.

enviciar *vt* to vitiate, to corrupt; ~**se** *vr* to get corrupted.

envidia *f* envy; jealousy.

envidiable *adj* enviable.

envidiar *vt* to envy, to grudge; to be jealous of.

envidioso/sa *adj* envious; jealous.

envilecer *vt* to vilify, to debase; ~**se** *vr* to degrade oneself.

envío *m* (*com*) dispatch, remittance of goods; consignment.

enviudar *vi* to become a widower or widow.

envoltorio *m* bundle of clothes.

envoltura *f* cover; wrapping.

envolver *vt* to involve; to wrap up.

enyesar *vt* to plaster; (*med*) to put in a plaster cast.

enzarzarse *vr* to get involved in a dispute; to get oneself into trouble.

épico/ca *adj* epic.

epicúreo/rea *adj* epicurean.

epidemia *f* epidemic.

epidémico/ca *adj* epidemic.

epidermis *f* epidermis; cuticle.

Epifanía *f* Epiphany.

epígrafe *f* epigraph, inscription; motto; headline.

epigrama *m* epigram.

epilepsia *f* epilepsy.

epílogo *m* epilogue.

episcopado *m* episcopacy; bishopric.

episcopal *adj* episcopal.

episódico/ca *adj* episodic.

episodio *m* episode, instalment.

epístola *f* epistle, letter.

epistolar *adj* epistolary.

epistolario *m* collected letters *pl*.

epitafio *m* epitaph.

epíteto *m* epithet.

epítome *m* epitome; compendium.

época *f* epoch; period, time.

epopeya *f* epic.

equidad *f* equity, honesty; impartiality, justice.

equidistar *vi* to be equidistant.

equilátero/ra *adj* equilateral.

equilibrar *vt* to balance; to poise.

equilibrio *m* balance, equilibrium.

equinoccial *adj* equinoctial.

equinoccio *m* equinox.

equipaje *m* luggage; equipment.

equipar *vt* to fit out, to equip, to furnish.

equipararse *vr*: ~ **con** to be on a level with.

equipo *m* equipment; team; shift.

equitación *f* horsemanship; riding.

equitativo/va *adj* equitable; just.

equivalencia *f* equivalence.

equivalente *adj* equivalent.

equivaler *vi* to be of equal value.

equivocación *f* mistake, error; misunderstanding.

equivocado/da *adj* mistaken, wrong.

equivocar *vt* to mistake; **~se** *vr* to make a mistake, to be wrong.

equívoco/ca *adj* equivocal, ambiguous; * *m* equivocation; quibble.

era *f* era, age; threshing floor.

erario *m* treasury, public funds *pl*.

erección *f* foundation, establishment; erection, elevation.

erguir *vt* to erect, to raise up straight; **~se** *vr* to straighten up.

erial *m* fallow land.

erigir *vt* to erect, to raise, to build; to establish.

erizamiento *m* standing on end (of hair, etc).

erizarse *vr* to bristle; to stand on end.

erizo *m* hedgehog; ~ **de mar** sea urchin.

ermita *f* hermitage.

ermitaño *m* hermit.

erosionar *vt* to erode.

erótico/ca *adj* erotic.

erotismo *m* eroticism.

errante *adj* errant; stray; roving.

errar *vi* to be mistaken; to wander.

errata *f* misprint.

erre: ~ **que** ~ *adv* obstinately.

erróneo/nea *adj* erroneous.

error *m* error, mistake, fault.

eructar *vi* to belch, to burp.

eructo *m* belch, burp.

erudición *f* erudition, learning.

erudito/ta *adj* learned, erudite.

erupción *f* eruption, outbreak.

esa: *f* of **ése**.

ésa: *f* of **ése**.

esbelto/ta *adj* slim, slender.

esbirro *m* bailiff; henchman; killer.

esbozo *m* outline.

escabechar *vt* to marinate; to pickle.

escabeche *m* pickle; pickled fish.

escabel *m* footstool.

escabrosidad *f* unevenness, roughness; harshness.

escabroso/sa *adj* rough, uneven; craggy; rude, risqué, blue.

escabullirse *vr* to escape, to evade; to slip through one's fingers.

escafandra *f* diving suit; space suit.

escala *f* ladder; (*mus*) scale; stopover.

escalador/ra *m* climber.

escalar *vt* to climb.

escaldado/da *adj* cautious, suspicious, wary.

escaldar *vt* to scald.

escalera *f* staircase; ladder.

escalfar *vt* to poach (eggs).

escalofríos *mpl* shivers *pl*.

escalofriante *adj* chilling.

escalón *m* step of a stair; rung.

escama *f* (fish) scale.

escamado/da *adj* wary, cautious.

escamar *vt* to scale, to take off the scales; **~se** *vr* to flake off; to become suspicious.

escamoso/sa *adj* scaly.

escamotear *vt* to swipe; to make disappear.

escampar *vi* to stop raining.

escanciador *m* wine waiter; cupbearer.

escanciar *vt* to pour (wine).

escandalizar *vt* to scandalize; **~se** *vr* to be shocked.

escándalo *m* scandal; uproar.

escandaloso/sa *adj* scandalous; shocking.

escanear *vt* to scan.

escáner *m* scanner.

escaño *m* bench with a back; seat (parliament).

escapada *f* escape, flight.

escapar *vi* to escape; ~se *vr* to get away; to leak (water, etc).

escaparate *m* shop window; wardrobe.

escapatoria *f* escape, flight; excuse.

escape *m* escape, flight; leak; exhaust (of motor); **a todo** ~ at full speed.

escapulario *m* scapulary.

escarabajo *m* beetle.

escaramuza *f* skirmish; dispute, quarrel.

escaramuzar *vt* to skirmish.

escarbadura *f* act and effect of scratching.

escarbar *vt* to scratch (the earth as hens do); to inquire into.

escarcha *f* white frost.

escarchar *vi* to be frosty.

escardador *m* weeding hoe.

escardillo *m* small weeding hoe.

escarlata *adj* scarlet.

escarlatina *f* scarlet fever.

escarmentar *vi* to learn one's lesson; * *vt* to punish severely.

escarmiento *m* warning, caution; punishment.

escarnecer *vt* to mock, to ridicule.

escarnio *m* gibe, ridicule.

escarola *f* (bot) endive.

escarpa *f* slope; escarpment.

escarpado/da *adj* sloped; craggy.

escarpín *m* sock; pump (shoe).

escasear *vi* to be scarce.

escasez *f* shortage; poverty.

escaso/sa *adj* small, short, little; sparing; scarce; scanty.

escatimar *vt* to curtail, to lessen; to be scanty with.

escena *f* stage; scene.

escenario *m* stage; set.

escepticismo *m* scepticism.

escéptico/ca *adj* sceptic, sceptical.

esclarecer *vt* to lighten; to illuminate; to illustrate; to shed light on (problem, etc).

esclarecido/da *adj* illustrious, noble.

esclarecimiento *m* clarification; enlightenment.

esclavina *f* short cloak or cape.

esclavitud *f* slavery, servitude.

esclavizar *vt* to enslave.

esclavo/va *m/f* slave; captive.

esclusa *f* sluice, floodgate.

escoba *f* broom, brush.

escobazo *m* blow given with a broom.

escobilla *f* brush, small broom; blade.

escocer *vt* to sting; to burn; ~se *vr* to chafe.

escoger *vt* to choose, to select.

escolar *m/f* schoolboy/girl; * *adj* scholastic.

escolástico/ca *adj* scholastic; * *m* scholar.

escollo *m* reef, rock.

escolta *f* escort.

escoltar *vt* to escort.

escombros *mpl* rubbish; debris.

esconder *vt* to hide, to conceal; ~se *vr* to be hidden.

escondidas: a ~ *adv* in a secret manner.

escondite *m* hiding place; **juego del** ~ hide-and-seek.

escondrijo *m* hiding place.

escopeta f shotgun; **a tiro de ~** within gunshot.

escopetazo m gunshot; gunshot wound.

escopetero m gunsmith.

escoplo m chisel.

escorbuto m scurvy.

escoria f dross; scum; dregs pl.

Escorpio m Scorpio (sign of the zodiac).

escorpión m scorpion.

escotado/da adj low-cut.

escotadura f low neck(line).

escotar vt to cut low in front.

escote m low neck (of a dress).

escotilla f (mar) hatchway.

escozor m smart; burning pain; sting(ing).

escriba m scribe (of the Hebrews).

escribanía f clerk's office; writing desk.

escribano m court clerk; notary.

escribiente m copyist.

escribir vt to write; to spell; * vi to write.

escrito m document; manuscript, text.

escritor/ra m/f writer, author.

escritorio m writing desk; office, study.

escritura f writing; deed.

escrúpulo m doubt, scruple, scrupulousness.

escrupulosidad f scrupulousness.

escrupuloso/sa adj scrupulous; exact.

escrutar vt to examine; to count (ballot papers).

escrutinio m scrutiny, inquiry.

escrutiñador m scrutinizer, inquirer.

escuadra f square; squadron; squad.

escuadrar vt to square.

escuadrón m squadron.

escuálido/da adj skinny; squalid.

escucha f listening(-in); * m scout.

escuchar vt to listen to, to heed.

escudar vt to shield; to guard from danger; **~se** vr to protect oneself.

escudero m squire; page.

escudilla f bowl.

escudo m shield.

escudriñamiento m investigation, scrutiny.

escudriñar vt to search, to examine; to pry into.

escuela f school; **~ primaria** primary school; **~ secundaria** secondary school.

escueto/ta adj plain; simple.

esculpir vt to sculpt.

escultor/ra m/f sculptor.

escultura f sculpture.

escupidera f cuspidor.

escupidura f spit.

escupir vt to spit.

escurreplatos m invar plate rack.

escurridizo/za adj slippery.

escurrir vt to drain; to drip; **~se** vr to slip away; to slip, to slide; * vi to wring out.

ese/esa adj that; **esos/as** pl those.

ése/ésa pn that (one); **ésos/as** pl those (ones).

esencia f essence.

esencial adj essential; principal.

esfera f sphere; globe.

esférico/ca adj spherical.

esferoide f spheroid.

esfinge m sphinx.

esforzado/da adj strong, vigorous; valiant.

esforzarse vr to exert oneself, to make an effort.

esfuerzo m effort.

esfumarse vr to fade away.

esgrima f fencing.

esgrimidor *m* fencer.

esgrimir *vt* to fence.

esguince *m* (*med*) sprain.

eslabón *m* link of a chain; steel; shackle.

eslabonar *vt* to link; to unite.

esmaltador *m* enameller.

esmaltar *vt* to enamel.

esmalte *m* enamel.

esmerado/da *adj* careful, neat.

esmeralda *m* emerald.

esmerar *vt* to polish; **~se** *vr* to take great care; to work hard.

esmeril *m* emery.

esmerillar *vt* to polish with emery.

esmero *m* careful attention, great care.

esnob *adj* snobbish; posh; * *m/f* snob.

eso *pn* that.

esófago *m* oesophagus; throat.

esos, ésos *pl* of **ese, ése.**

espabilar *vt* to wake up; **~se** *vr* to wake up; (*fig*) to get a move on.

espacial *adj* space *compd.*

espaciar *vt* to spread out; to space (out).

espacio *m* space; (radio or TV) programme.

espaciosidad *f* spaciousness, capacity.

espacioso/sa *adj* spacious, roomy.

espada *f* sword; ace of spades.

espadachín *m* bully.

espadaña *f* (*bot*) bulrush.

espadín *m* small short sword.

espaguetis *mpl* spaghetti.

espalda *f* back, back-part; **~s** *fpl* shoulders *pl.*

espaldilla *f* shoulder blade.

espantadizo/za *adj* timid, easily frightened.

espantajo *m* scarecrow; bogeyman.

espantapájaros *m invar* scarecrow.

espantar *vt* to frighten; to chase or drive away.

espanto *m* fright; menace, threat; astonishment.

espantoso/sa *adj* frightful, dreadful; amazing.

español/la *adj* Spanish; * *m/f* Spaniard; * *m* Spanish (language).

esparadrapo *m* sticking plaster.

esparcir *vt* to scatter; to divulge; **~se** *vr* to amuse oneself.

espárrago *m* asparagus.

esparto *m* (*bot*) esparto.

espasmo *m* spasm.

espátula *f* spatula.

especia *f* spice.

especial *adj* special; particular; **en ~** especially.

especialidad *f* speciality.

especie *f* species; kind, sort; matter.

especificación *f* specification.

especificar *vt* to specify.

específico/ca *adj* specific.

espectáculo *m* spectacle; show.

espectador/ra *m/f* spectator.

espectro *m* spectre, phantom, ghost, apparition.

especulación *f* speculation; contemplation; venture.

especulador/ra *m/f* speculator.

especular *vt* to speculate.

especulativo/va *adj* speculative; thoughtful.

espejismo *m* mirage.

espejo *m* mirror.

espeluznante *adj* horrifying.

espera *f* stay, waiting; (*jur*) respite, adjournment, delay.

esperanza *f* hope.

esperanzar *vt* to give hope to.

esperar *vt* to hope; to expect, to wait for.

esperma f sperm.
espesar vt to thicken; to condense; **~se** vr to grow thick; to solidify.
espeso/sa adj thick, dense.
espesor m thickness.
espesura f thickness; density, solidity.
espía m/f spy.
espiar vt to spy.
espiga f ear (of corn).
espigón m ear of corn; sting; (mar) breakwater.
espina f thorn; fishbone.
espinaca f (bot) spinach.
espinazo m spine, backbone.
espinilla f shinbone.
espino m hawthorn.
espinoso/sa adj thorny; dangerous.
espionaje m spying, espionage.
espiral adj, f spiral.
espirar vt to exhale.
espíritu m spirit, soul; mind; intelligence; **el E~ Santo** the Holy Ghost; **~s** pl demons pl, hobgoblins pl.
espiritual adj spiritual; ghostly.
espiritualidad f spirituality.
espiritualizar vt to spiritualize.
esplendidez f splendour.
espléndido/da adj splendid.
esplendor m splendour.
espliego m (bot) lavender.
espolear vt to spur, to instigate, to incite.
espolón m spur (of a cock); spur (of a mountain range); sea wall; jetty; (mar) buttress.
espolvorear vt to sprinkle.
espondeo m (poet) spondee.
esponja f sponge.
esponjar vt to sponge; **~se** vr to be puffed up with pride.
esponjoso/sa adj spongy.

esponsales mpl betrothal.
espontaneidad f spontaneity.
espontáneo/nea adj spontaneous.
esposa f wife.
esposar vt to handcuff.
esposas fpl handcuffs pl.
esposo m husband.
espuela f spur; stimulus; (bot) larkspur.
espuerta f pannier, basket.
espulgar vt to delouse; to examine closely.
espuma f froth, foam.
espumadera f skimmer.
espumajear vi to foam at the mouth.
espumar vt to skim, to take the scum off.
espumarajo m foam, froth (from the mouth).
espumoso/sa adj frothy, foamy; sparkling (wine).
espurio/ria adj spurious; adulterated; illegitimate.
esputo m spit, saliva.
esqueje m cutting (of plant).
esquela f note, slip of paper.
esqueleto m skeleton.
esquema m scheme; diagram; plan.
esquí m ski; skiing.
esquiar vi to ski.
esquife m skiff, small boat.
esquilador m sheep-shearer.
esquilar vt to shear sheep.
esquina f corner, angle.
esquinado/da adj cornered, angled.
esquinar vt to form a corner with.
esquirol m blackleg.
esquivar vt to shun, to avoid, to evade.
esquivez f disdain; shyness.
esquivo/va adj scornful; shy, reserved.
esta: f of **este**.

ésta: f of **éste.**

estabilidad f stability.

estable adj stable.

establecer vt to establish.

establecimiento m establishment.

establo m stable.

estaca f stake; stick; post.

estacada f fence; fencing; stockade.

estacazo m blow with a stick.

estación f season (of the year); station; railroad station, terminus; ~ **de autobuses** bus station; ~ **de servicio** filling station.

estacional adj seasonal.

estacionamiento m parking; car park; (mil) stationing.

estacionar vt to park; (mil) to station.

estacionario/ria adj stationary.

estadio m phase; stadium.

estadista m statesman; statistician.

estadística f statistics pl.

estadístico/ca adj statistical.

estado m state, condition.

Estados Unidos mpl United States (of America).

estafa f trick, fraud.

estafador/ra m/f swindler, racketeer.

estafar vt to deceive, to defraud.

estafeta f post office.

estallar vi to crack; to burst; to break out.

estallido m explosion; (fig) outbreak.

estambre m stamen.

estamento m estate; body; layer; class.

estameña f serge.

estampa f print; engraving; appearance.

estampado/da adj printed; * m printing; print; stamping.

estampar vt to print.

estampida f stampede.

estampido m report (of a gun); crack.

estampilla f seal, stamp.

estancar vt to check (a current); to monopolize; to prohibit, to suspend; ~**se** vr to stagnate.

estancia f stay; bedroom; ranch; (poet) stanza.

estanco m tobacconist's (shop); ~/**ca** adj watertight.

estándar adj, m standard.

estandarizar vt to standardize.

estandarte m banner, standard.

estanque m pond, pool; reservoir.

estanquero/ra m/f tobacconist.

estante m shelf (for books).

estantería f shelves pl, shelving.

estaño m tin.

estar vi to be; to be (in a place).

estatal adj state compd.

estática f statics pl.

estático/ca adj static.

estatua f statue.

estatura f stature.

estatuto m statute, law.

este m east.

este/ta adj this; **estos/tas** pl these.

éste pn m this (one); **éstos/tas** pl these (ones).

estera f mat.

estercolar vt to manure.

estercolero m dunghill.

estéreo adj invar, m stereo.

estereotipar vt to stereotype.

estereotipo m stereotype.

estéril adj sterile, infertile.

esterilidad f sterility, infertility.

esterilla f mat.

esterlina adj: **libra** ~ pound sterling.

estético/ca adj aesthetic; * f aesthetics.

estiércol *m* dung; manure.

estilar(se) *vi* (*vr*) to be in fashion; to be used.

estilo *m* style; fashion; stroke (in swimming).

estima *f* esteem.

estimable *adj* estimable, worthy of esteem.

estimación *f* estimation, valuation.

estimar *vt* to estimate, to value; to esteem; to judge; to think.

estimulante *adj* stimulating; * *m* stimulant.

estimular *vt* to stimulate, to excite; to goad.

estímulo *m* stimulus.

estío *m* summer.

estipendiario *m* stipendiary.

estipulación *f* stipulation.

estipular *vt* to stipulate.

estirado/da *adj* stretched tight; (*fig*) pompous.

estirar *vt* to stretch out.

estirón *m* pulling; tugging; **dar un ~** to grow rapidly.

estirpe *f* race, origin, stock.

estival *adj* summer *compd*.

esto *pn* this.

estocada *f* stab.

estofa *f*: **de baja ~** poor quality.

estofado *m* stew.

estola *f* stole.

estolidez *f* stupidity.

estólido/da *adj* stupid.

estomacal *adj* stomach *compd*.

estómago *m* stomach.

estopa *f* tow.

estoque *m* rapier, sword.

estorbar *vt* to hinder; (*fig*) to bother; * *vi* to be in the way.

estorbo *m* obstacle, hindrance, impediment.

estornudar *vi* to sneeze.

estornudo *m* sneeze.

estos, éstos *pl* of **este, éste**.

estrada *f* highway.

estrado *m* drawing room; stage, platform.

estrafalario/ria *adj* slovenly; eccentric.

estrago *m* ruin, destruction; havoc.

estrambótico/ca *adj* eccentric, odd.

estrangulador/ra *m/f* strangler.

estrangulamiento *m* bottleneck.

estrangular *vt* to strangle; (*med*) to strangulate.

estraperlo *m* black market.

estratagema *f* stratagem, trick.

estrategia *f* strategy.

estratégico/ca *adj* strategic.

estrato *m* stratum, layer.

estraza *f* rag; **papel de ~** brown paper.

estrechar *vt* to tighten; to contract, to constrain; to compress; **~se** *vr* to grow narrow; to embrace; **~ la mano** to shake hands.

estrechez *f* strictness, narrowness; shortage of money.

estrecho *m* straits *pl*; **~/cha** *adj* narrow, close; tight; intimate; rigid, austere; short (of money).

estrella *f* star.

estrellado/da *adj* starry; **huevos ~s** fried eggs.

estrellar *vt* to dash to pieces; **~se** *vr* to smash; to crash; to fail.

estremecer *vt* to shake, to make tremble; **~se** *vr* to shake, to tremble.

estremecimiento *m* trembling, shaking.

estrenar *vt* to wear for the first time; to move into (a house); to show (a film) for the first time; **~se** *vr* to make one's debut.

estreñido/da *adj* constipated.

estreñimiento *m* constipation.

estrépito *m* noise, racket; fuss.

estrepitoso/sa *adj* noisy.

estribar *vi*: ~ en to be supported by; to be based on.

estribillo *m* chorus.

estribo *m* buttress; stirrup; running board; perder los ~s to fly off the handle (*fam*).

estribor *m* (*mar*) starboard.

estricto/ta *adj* strict; severe.

estrofa *f* (*poet*) verse, strophe.

estropajo *m* scourer.

estropajoso/sa *adj* tough, leathery; despicable; mean; stammering.

estropear *vt* to spoil; to damage; ~se *vr* to get damaged.

estructura *f* structure.

estruendo *m* clamour, noise; confusion, uproar; pomp, ostentation.

estrujar *vt* to press, to squeeze.

estrujón *m* pressing, squeezing.

estuario *m* estuary.

estuche *m* case (for scissors, etc); sheath.

estudiante *m/f* student.

estudiantil *adj* student *compd*.

estudiar *vt* to study.

estudio *m* study; studio; ~s *mpl* studies *pl*; learning.

estudioso/sa *adj* studious.

estufa *f* heater, fire.

estufilla *f* muff; small stove.

estupefacción *f* stupefaction.

estupefaciente *m* narcotic.

estupefacto *adj* speechless; thunderstruck.

estupendo/da *adj* terrific, marvellous.

estupidez *f* stupidity.

estúpido/da *adj* stupid.

estupor *m* stupor; astonishment.

estupro *m* rape.

etapa *f* stage; stopping place; (*fig*) phase.

etcétera *adv* etcetera, and so on.

éter *m* ether.

etéreo/rea *adj* ethereal.

eternidad *f* eternity.

eternizar *vt* to eternalize, to perpetuate.

eterno/na *adj* eternal.

ética *f* ethics.

ético/ca *adj* ethical, moral.

etimología *f* etymology.

etimológico/ca *adj* etymological.

etiqueta *f* etiquette; label.

Eucaristía *f* Eucharist.

eufemismo *m* euphemism.

euforia *f* euphoria.

euro *m* euro.

eurocámara *f* European Parliament.

euroconector *m* Euroconnector.

eurodiputado/da *m/f* Euro-MP.

euroescéptico/ca *m/f* Eurosceptic.

Europa *f* Europe.

eurotúnel *m* Eurotunnel, Channel tunnel.

evacuación *f* evacuation.

evacuar *vt* to evacuate, to empty.

evadir *vt* to evade, to escape.

evaluar *vt* to evaluate.

evangélico/ca *adj* evangelical.

evangelio *m* gospel.

evangelista *m* evangelist.

evangelizar *vt* to evangelize.

evaporar *vt* to evaporate; ~se *vr* to vanish.

evasión *f* evasion, escape.

evasivo/va *adj* evasive; * *f* excuse.

eventual *adj* possible; temporary, casual (worker).

evidencia *f* evidence, proof.

evidente *adj* evident, clear.

evitable *adj* avoidable.

evitar *vt* to avoid.

evocación *f* evocation; invocation.

evocar *vt* to call out; to invoke.

evolución *f* evolution, development; change; (*mil*) manoeuvre.

evolucionar *vi* to evolve.

ex *adj* ex.

exacción *f* exaction; extortion.

exacerbar *vt* to exacerbate; to irritate.

exactamente *adv* exactly.

exactitud *f* exactness.

exacto/ta *adj* exact; punctual; accurate.

exageración *f* exaggeration.

exagerar *vt* to exaggerate.

exaltación *f* exaltation, elation.

exaltar *vt* to exalt, to elevate; to praise, to extol; ~**se** *vr* to get excited.

examen *m* exam, examination, test, inquiry.

examinador *m* examiner.

examinar *vt* to examine.

exánime *adj* lifeless, weak.

exasperación *f* exasperation.

exasperar *vt* to exasperate, to irritate.

excavación *f* excavation.

excavadora *f* excavator; digger.

excavar *vt* to excavate, to dig out.

excedente *adj* excessive.

exceder *vt* to exceed, to surpass, to excel, to outdo.

excelencia *f* excellence.

Excelencia *f* Excellency (title).

excelente *adj* excellent.

excelso/sa *adj* elevated, sublime, lofty.

excentricidad *f* eccentricity.

excéntrico/ca *adj* eccentric.

excepción *f* exception.

excepto *adv* excepting, except (for).

exceptuar *vt* to except, to exempt.

excesivo/va *adj* excessive.

exceso *m* excess.

excitación *f* excitement; excitation.

excitar *vt* to excite; ~**se** *vr* to get excited.

exclamación *f* exclamation.

exclamar *vt* to exclaim, to cry out.

excluir *vt* to exclude.

exclusión *f* exclusion.

exclusiva *f* exclusive; (*com*) sole right.

exclusivamente, exclusive *adv* exclusively.

exclusivo/va *adj* exclusive.

excomulgar *vt* to excommunicate.

excomunión *f* excommunication.

excremento *m* excrement.

excursión *f* excursion, trip.

excusa *f* excuse, apology.

excusable *adj* excusable.

excusado *m* toilet.

excusar *vt* to excuse; to avoid; ~ **de** to exempt from; ~**se** *vr* to apologize.

execrable *adj* execrable, abhorrent.

execrar *vt* to execrate, to curse.

exención *f* exemption; immunity, privilege.

exento/ta *adj* exempt, free.

exequias *fpl* funeral rites *pl*, obsequies *pl*.

exhalación *f* exhalation; fumes *pl*, vapour.

exhalar *vt* to exhale; to give off; to heave (a sigh).

exhausto/ta *adj* exhausted.

exhibición *f* exhibition, display.

exhibir *vt* to exhibit.

exhortación *f* exhortation.

exhortar *vt* to exhort.

exhumación *f* exhumation.

exhumar *vt* to disinter, to exhume.

exigencia f demand, requirement.

exigir vt to demand, to require.

exiguo/gua adj meagre, small.

exiliado/da adj exiled; * m/f exile.

exilio m exile.

eximir vt to exempt, to free; to excuse.

existencia f existence, being.

existente adj existing, in existence.

existir vi to exist, to be.

éxito m outcome; success; (mus, etc) hit; **tener ~** to be successful.

exoneración f exoneration.

exonerar vt to exonerate.

exorbitante adj exhorbitant, excessive.

exorcismo m exorcism.

exorcista m exorcist.

exorcizar vt to exorcize.

exótico/ca adj exotic.

expandir vt to expand.

expansión f expansion; extension.

expansivo/va adj expansive.

expatriarse vr to emigrate; to go into exile.

expectativa f expectation; prospect.

expectoración f expectoration.

expectorar vt to expectorate.

expedición f expedition.

expedicionario/ria adj expeditionary.

expediente m expedient; means; (jur) proceedings pl; dossier, file.

expedir vt to send, to forward, to dispatch.

expeditivo/va adj expeditious.

expedito/ta adj speedy; clear, free.

expeler vt to expel.

expensas fpl: **a ~ de** at the expense of.

experiencia f experience; trial.

experimentado/da adj experienced; expert.

experimental adj experimental.

experimentar vt to experience; * vi: **~ con** to experiment with.

experimento m experiment, trial.

experto/ta adj expert; experienced.

expiación f expiation; purification.

expiar vt to atone for; to purify.

expiatorio/ria adj expiatory.

expirar vi to expire.

explanada f esplanade.

explayarse vr to speak at length.

explicación f explanation.

explicar vt to explain, to expound; **~se** vr to explain oneself.

explícito/ta adj explicit.

exploración f exploration.

explorador/ra m/f explorer.

explorar vt to explore.

explosión f explosion.

explotación f exploitation; running.

explotar vt to exploit; to run; * vi to explode.

exponente m (mat) exponent.

exponer vt to expose; to exhibit.

exportación f export; exports pl.

exportar vt to export.

exposición f exposure; exhibition; explanation; account.

expresar vt to express.

expresión f expression.

expresivo/va adj expressive; energetic.

expreso/sa adj express, clear, specific; fast (train).

express m (ferro) express train.

exprimidor m squeezer.

exprimir vt to squeeze out.

ex profeso adv on purpose.

expropiar vt to expropriate.

expuesto/ta adj exposed; on display.

expulsar vt to expel, to drive out.

expulsión f expulsion.

exquisito/ta adj exquisite; excellent.

éxtasis *m* ecstasy, enthusiasm.

extático/ca *adj* ecstatic.

extender *vt* to extend, to stretch out; ~**se** *vr* to extend; to spread.

extensión *f* extension; extent.

extensivo/va *adj* extensive.

extenso/sa *adj* extensive.

extenuación *f* emaciation; debility, exhaustion.

extenuar *vt* to exhaust, to debilitate.

exterior *adj* exterior, external; * *m* exterior, outward appearance.

exteriormente *adv* externally.

exterminador *m* exterminator.

exterminar *vt* to exterminate.

exterminio *m* extermination.

externo/na *adj* external, outer; * *m/f* day pupil.

extinción *f* extinction.

extinguir *vt* to wipe out; to extinguish.

extintor *m* (fire) extinguisher.

extirpación *f* extirpation, extermination.

extirpar *vt* to extirpate, to root out.

extorsión *f* extortion.

extra *adj invar* extra; good quality; * *m/f* extra; * *m* bonus.

extracción *f* extraction.

extracto *m* extract.

extradición *f* extradition.

extraditar *vt* to extradite.

extraer *vt* to extract.

extranjero/ra *m/f* stranger; foreigner; * *adj* foreign, alien.

extrañar *vt* to find strange; to miss; ~**se** *vr* to be surprised; to grow apart.

extrañeza *f* strangeness; surprise.

extraño/ña *adj* foreign; rare; singular, strange, odd.

extraordinario/ria *adj* extraordinary, uncommon, odd.

extravagancia *f* extravagance.

extravagante *adj* extravagant.

extraviado/da *adj* lost, missing.

extraviar *vt* to mislead; ~**se** *vr* to lose one's way.

extravío *m* deviation; loss.

extremado/da *adj* extreme; accomplished.

extremaunción *f* extreme unction.

extremidad *f* extremity; brim; tip; ~**es** *fpl* extremities *pl*.

extremo/ma *adj* extreme, last; * *m* extreme, highest degree; **en** ~ extremely.

extrínseco/ca *adj* extrinsic, external.

extrovertido/da *adj, m/f* extrovert.

exuberancia *f* exuberance; luxuriance.

F

fábrica *f* factory.

fabricación *f* manufacture, production.

fabricante *m/f* producer, manufacturer.

fabricar *vt* to build, to construct; to manufacture; (*fig*) to fabricate.

fabril *adj* manufacturing *compd*, industrial.

fábula *f* fable; fiction; rumour, common talk.

fabulista *m/f* writer of fables.

fabuloso/sa *adj* fabulous, fictitious.

facción *f* (political) faction; feature.

faccioso/sa *adj* factious, turbulent.

facha *f* appearance, look; face.

fachada *f* facade, face, front.

fácil *adj* facile, easy.

facilidad f facility, easiness; **con ~** adv cosily, easily.
facilitar vt to facilitate.
fácilmente adv easily.
facineroso adj wicked, criminal.
facsímil m facsimile, fax.
factible adj feasible, practicable.
factor m (mat) factor; (com) factor, agent.
factoría f agency; factory.
factura f invoice.
facultad f faculty.
facultativo/va adj optional; * m/f doctor, practitioner.
faena f task, job; hard work.
faisán m pheasant.
faja f band, sash; strip (of land); corset.
fajo m bundle; wad.
falacia f fallacy; fraud.
falange f phalanx.
falaz adj deceitful, fraudulent; fallacious.
falda f skirt; lap; flap; train; slope, hillside.
faldero/ra adj: **hombre ~** ladies' man; **perrito ~** lap-dog.
faldón m coat-tails pl; skirt.
falible adj fallible.
fallar vt (jur) to pronounce sentence on, to judge; * vi to fail.
fallecer vi to die.
fallecimiento m decease, death.
fallido/da adj unsuccessful, frustrated.
fallo m judgement, sentence; failure.
falsamente adv falsely.
falsario/ria adj falsifying, forging.
falsear vt to falsify, to counterfeit.
falsedad f falsehood; untruth, fib (sl); hypocrisy.
falsete m (tec) plug; bung; (mus) falsetto.

falsificación f falsification.
falsificador/ora m/f forger, counterfeiter.
falsificar vt to falsify, to forge, to counterfeit.
falso/sa adj false, untrue; deceitful; fake.
falta f fault, defect; want; flaw, mistake; (dep) foul.
faltar vi to be wanting; to fail; not to fulfil one's promise; to need; to be missing.
falto/ta adj wanting, deficient, lacking; miserable, wretched.
faltriquera f pocket.
fama f fame; reputation, name.
famélico/ca adj starving.
familia f family.
familiar adj familiar; homely, domestic; * m/f relative, relation.
familiaridad f familiarity.
familiarizarse vr: **~ con** to familiarize oneself with.
famoso/sa adj famous.
fan m/f fan.
fanático/ca adj fanatical; enthusiastic; * m/f fanatic; fan.
fandango m fandango.
fanfarrón/ona m/f bully, braggart.
fanfarronada f boast, brag.
fanfarronear vi to bully, to brag.
fanfarronería f boast, brag.
fango m mire, mud.
fangoso/sa adj muddy, miry.
fantasía f fancy; fantasy; caprice; presumption.
fantasma m phantom, ghost.
fantástico/ca adj fantastic, whimsical; presumptuous.
fardo m bale, parcel.
farfullar vi to talk with a stammer.
farisaico/ca adj pharisaical; hypocritical.

fariseo m Pharisee; hypocrite.
farmacéutico/ca adj pharmaceutical; * m/f pharmacist.
farmacia f pharmacy.
faro m (mar) lighthouse; (auto) headlamp; floodlight.
farol m lantern.
farola f street light.
farsa f farce.
farsante m/f fraud, fake.
fascículo m part, instalment.
fascinación f fascination.
fascinar vt to fascinate; to enchant.
fascismo m fascism.
fascista adj, m/f fascist.
fase f phase.
fastidiar vt to annoy; to offend; to spoil.
fastidio m annoyance; boredom; disgust.
fastidioso/sa adj annoying; tedious.
fatal adj fatal; mortal; awful.
fatalidad f fatality; mischance, ill-luck.
fatalismo m fatalism.
fatalista m/f fatalist.
fatiga f weariness, fatigue.
fatigar vt to fatigue, to tire; to harass.
fatigoso/sa adj tiresome, troublesome.
fatuidad f fatuity, foolishness, silliness.
fatuo/tua adj fatuous, stupid, foolish; conceited.
fauces fpl jaws pl, gullet.
fausto/ta adj happy, fortunate; * m splendour, pomp.
favor m favour; protection; good turn.
favorable adj favourable.
favorecer vt to favour, to protect.
favorito/ta adj favourite.
fax m fax.

faz f face.
fe f faith, belief.
fealdad f ugliness.
febrero m February.
febril adj feverish.
fecha f date (of a letter etc).
fechar vt to date.
fechoría f misdeed; exploit.
fecundar vt to fertilize.
fecundidad f fecundity, fertility.
fecundo/da adj fruitful, fertile.
federación f federation.
felicidad f happiness.
felicitar vt to congratulate.
feligrés/esa m/f parishioner.
feliz adj happy, fortunate.
felpa f plush; towelling.
felpudo m doormat.
femenil adj feminine, womanly.
femenino/na adj feminine; female.
feminismo m feminism.
feminista adj, m/f feminist.
fenómeno m phenomenon; (fig) freak, accident; * adj (fam) great (sl), marvellous.
feo/ea adj ugly; bad, nasty.
feracidad f productivity, fertility.
feraz adj fertile, fruitful.
féretro m bier, casket.
feria f fair, rest day; village market.
fermentación f fermentation.
fermentar vi to ferment.
fermento m ferment; leaven.
ferocidad f ferocity, wildness; cruelty.
feroz adj ferocious, savage; cruel.
ferretería f ironmonger's, hardware store.
ferrocarril m railway.
ferroviario/ria adj rail compd.
ferry m ferry.
fértil adj fertile, fruitful.
fertilidad f fertility, fruitfulness.

fertilización f fertilization.

fertilizar vt to fertilize.

férula f ferule; (med) splint.

ferviente adj fervent; ardent.

fervor m fervour, zeal; ardour.

fervoroso/sa adj fervent, ardent, passionate.

festejar vt to feast; to court, to woo.

festejo m courtship; feast.

festín m feast.

festividad f festivity.

festivo/va adj festive, merry; witty; **día ~** holiday.

festón m garland; festoon.

festonear vt to ornament with garlands.

fétido/da adj foetid, stinking.

feto m foetus.

feudal adj feudal.

fiable adj trustworthy; reliable.

fiador/ra m/f guarantor; (com) backer.

fiambre m cold meat.

fiambrera f dinner pail.

fianza f (jur) surety.

fiar vt to entrust, to confide; to bail; to sell on credit; to buy on credit; * vi to trust.

fibra f fibre.

fibroso/sa adj fibrous.

ficción f fiction.

ficha f token, counter (at games); (index) card.

ficticio/cia adj fictitious.

fidedigno/na adj reliable, trustworthy.

fideicomisario/ria m/f trustee.

fideicomiso f trust.

fidelidad f fidelity; loyalty.

fideos mpl vermicelli pl.

fiebre f fever.

fiel adj faithful, loyal; * mpl **los ~es** the faithful pl.

fieltro m felt.

fiera f wild beast.

fiereza f fierceness, ferocity; cruelty.

fiero/ra adj fierce, ferocious; cruel; rough, harsh.

fiesta f party; festivity; **~s** fpl holidays pl, vacations pl.

figura f figure, shape.

figurado/da adj figurative.

figurar vt to figure; **~se** vr to fancy, to imagine.

figurilla f ridiculous little figure.

fijador m fixative; gel (for the hair).

fijar vt to fix, to fasten; **~se** vr to become fixed; to establish oneself; **~se en** to notice.

fijo/ja adj fixed, firm; settled, permanent.

fila f row, line; (mil) rank; **en ~** in a line, in a row.

filamento m filament.

filantropía f philanthropy.

filántropo/pa m/f philanthropist.

filete m fillet; fillet steak.

filiación f lineage; personal description, particulars pl.

filial adj filial; * f (com) subsidiary.

filibustero m pirate.

filigrana f filigree.

filmar vt to film.

filo m edge, blade.

filología f philology.

filológico/ca adj philological.

filólogo/ga m/f philologist.

filosofar vt to philosophize.

filosofía f philosophy.

filosófico/ca adj philosophical.

filósofo/fa m/f philosopher.

filtración f filtration.

filtrar vt to filter, to strain.

filtro m filter.

fin m end; termination, conclusion; aim, purpose; **al ~** at last; **en ~** (fig) well then; **por ~** finally, lastly.

final *adj* final; * *m* end; termination, conclusion; * *f* (dep) final.

finalizar *vt* to finish, to conclude; * *vi* to be finished.

finalmente *adv* finally, at last.

financiar *vt* to finance.

finca *f* land, property, real estate; country house; farm.

fineza *f* fineness, perfection; elegance; courtesy; small gift.

fingido/da *adj* feigned, fake, sham.

fingimiento *m* simulation, pretence.

fingir *vt* to feign, to fake; to invent; to imitate; ~**se** *vr* to pretend to be; * *vi* to pretend.

finito/ta *adj* finite.

fino/na *adj* fine, pure; slender; polite; acute; dry (of sherry).

finura *f* fineness.

firma *f* signature; (com) company.

firmamento *m* firmament, sky, heaven.

firmar *vt* to sign.

firme *adj* firm, stable, strong, secure; constant; resolute; * *m* road surface.

firmeza *f* firmness, stability, constancy.

fiscal *adj* fiscal.

fiscalía *f* office and business of the district attorney.

fiscalizar *vt* to inspect; to criticize.

fisco *m* treasury, exchequer.

fisgar *vt* to pry into.

fisgón/ona *m/f* prying person, snooper (sl).

física *f* physics.

físico/ca *adj* physical; * *m/f* physicist; * *m* physique.

fisonomía *f* physiognomy.

fisonomista *m/f*: **ser buen** ~ to have a good memory for faces.

flaco/ca *adj* lean, skinny; feeble.

flagelación *f* flagellation.

flagrante *adj* flagrant.

flamante *adj* flaming, bright; brand-new.

flan *m* crème caramel.

flanco *m* flank.

flanquear *vt* (mil) to flank.

flaquear *vi* to flag; to weaken.

flaqueza *f* thinness, leanness; feebleness, weakness.

flash *m* flash.

flato *m* (med) flatulence; depression.

flatulento/ta *adj* flatulent.

flauta *f* (mus) flute.

flautista *m/f* flute player, flautist.

flecha *f* arrow.

fleco *m* fringe.

flema *f* phlegm.

flemático/ca *adj* phlegmatic.

flemón *m* ulcer in the gums.

flequillo *m* fringe (of hair); bangs *pl*.

fletar *vt* to freight (a ship).

flete *m* (mar) freight; charter.

flexibilidad *f* flexibility.

flexible *adj* flexible; compliant; docile.

flojedad *f* feebleness; laxity, laziness; negligence.

flojera *f*: **me da** ~ I can't be bothered.

flojo/ja *adj* loose; flexible; lax, slack; lazy.

flor *f* flower.

florecer *vi* to blossom.

florero *m* vase.

floresta *f* wood, grove; beauty spot.

florete *m* fencing foil.

florido/da *adj* full of flowers; in bloom; choice.

florista *m/f* florist.

flota *f* fleet.

flotador *m* float; rubber ring.

flotante *adj* floating.

flotar *vi* to float.

flote *m*: **a ~** afloat.

flotilla *f* small fleet, flotilla.

fluctuación *f* fluctuation; uncertainty.

fluctuar *vi* to fluctuate; to waver.

fluidez *f* fluidity; fluency.

fluido/da *adj* fluid; (*fig*) fluent; * *m* fluid.

fluir *vi* to flow.

flujo *m* flux; flow; **~ de sangre** (*med*) loss of blood.

fluvial *adj* fluvial, river *compd*.

foca *f* seal.

foco *m* focus; centre; source; floodlight; (light)bulb.

fofo/fa *adj* spongy; soft; bland.

fogata *f* blaze; bonfire.

fogón *m* stove; hearth.

fogonazo *m* flash; explosion.

fogosidad *f* dash, verve; fieriness.

fogoso/sa *adj* fiery; ardent, fervent; impetuous, boisterous.

folk *m* folk (music).

follaje *m* foliage.

folletista *m/f* pamphleteer.

folleto *m* pamphlet; folder, brochure.

follón *m* (*fam*) mess; fuss.

fomentar *vt* to encourage; to promote.

fomento *m* promotion.

fonda *f* hotel; inn; boarding house.

fondeadero *m* anchorage.

fondear *vi* to drop anchor.

fondista *m/f* innkeeper.

fondo *m* bottom; back; background; space; **~s** *mpl* stock, funds *pl*, capital; **a ~** perfectly, completely.

fontanería *f* plumbing.

fontanero/ra *m/f* plumber.

footing *m* jogging.

forajido *m* outlaw.

foral *adj* belonging to the statute law of a country.

forastero/ra *adj* strange, exotic; * *m/f* stranger.

forcejear *vi* to struggle.

forense *adj* forensic; * *m/f* forensic scientist.

forjador/ra *m/f* framer; forger.

forjadura *f* forging.

forjar *vt* to forge; to frame; to invent.

forma *f* form, shape; pattern; (*med*) fitness; (*dep*) form; means, method; **de ~ que** in such a manner that.

formación *f* formation; form, figure; education; training.

formal *adj* formal; proper, genuine; serious, grave.

formalidad *f* formality; gravity.

formalizar *vt* (*jur*) to formalize; to regularize; **~se** *vr* to be regularized.

formar *vt/vi* to form, to shape.

formidable *adj* formidable, dreadful; terrific (*sl*).

fórmula *f* formula.

formulario *m* formulary.

fornicación *f* fornication.

fornicador *m* fornicator.

fornicar *vi* to commit fornication.

fornido/da *adj* well-built.

foro *m* court of justice; forum.

forraje *m* forage.

forrajear *vt* to forage.

forrar *vt* to line; to face; to cover.

forro *m* lining; book jacket.

fortalecer *vt* to fortify, to strengthen.

fortaleza *f* courage; strength, vigour; (*mil*) fortress, stronghold.

fortificación *f* fortification.

fortificar *vt* to strengthen; to fortify (a place).

fortín *m* (*mil*) small fort.

fortuito/ta *adj* fortuitous.

fortuna *f* fortune; wealth.

forzar vt to force.

forzoso/sa adj indispensable, necessary.

forzudo/da adj strong, vigorous.

fosa f grave; pit.

fósforo m phosphorus; ~s mpl matches pl.

fósil adj, m fossil.

foso vt pit; moat, ditch, fosse.

foto f photo.

fotocopia f photocopy.

fotografía f photography; photograph.

fotógrafo/fa m/f photographer.

frac m evening coat, dress coat.

fracasar vi to fail.

fracaso m failure.

fracción f fraction.

fractura f fracture.

fracturar vt to break (a bone).

fragancia f fragrance, sweetness of smell.

fragante adj fragrant, scented.

fragata f (mar) frigate.

frágil adj fragile, frail.

fragilidad f fragility, brittleness; frailty.

fragmento m fragment.

fragosidad f roughness; denseness.

fragoso/sa adj craggy, rough, uneven.

fragua f forge.

fraguar vt to forge; to contrive; * vi to solidify, to harden.

fraile m friar, monk.

frambuesa f raspberry.

francés/sa adj French; * m French (language); * m/f Frenchman/woman.

franco/ca adj frank; candid; free, gratis.

franela f flannel; vest.

franja f fringe.

franquear vt to clear; to overcome; to stamp (letters); ~se to unbosom oneself.

franqueo m postage.

franqueza f frankness.

franquicia f immunity from taxes.

frasco m flask.

frase f phrase.

fraternal adj fraternal, brotherly.

fraternidad f fraternity, brotherhood.

fratricida m/f fratricide (person).

fratricidio m fratricide (murder).

fraude m fraud, deceit; cheat.

fraudulento/ta adj fraudulent, deceitful.

frazada f blanket.

frecuencia f frequency.

frecuentar vt to frequent.

frecuente adj frequent.

fregadero m (kitchen) sink.

fregado m scouring, scrubbing; (fig) intrigue; underhand work.

fregar vt to scrub; to wash up.

fregona f kitchen maid; (perj) skivvy.

freír vt to fry.

frenar vt to brake; (fig) to check.

frenesí m frenzy.

frenético/ca adj frantic; frenzied; wild.

frenillo m speech impediment.

freno m bit; brake; (fig) check.

frente f front; face; ~ a ~ face to face; en ~ opposite; (mil) front; * m forehead.

fresa f strawberry.

fresal m strawberry plant; ground bearing strawberry plants.

fresco/ca adj fresh; cool; new; ruddy; * m fresh air; * m/f (fam) shameless or impudent person.

frescura f freshness; frankness; cheek, nerve.

fresno m ash tree.

frialdad f coldness; indifference.

fricción f friction.

friega f rubbing; nuisance.

frígido/da adj frigid.

frigorífico m fridge.

frijol m bean.

frío/fría adj cold; indifferent; * m cold; indifference.

friolento/ta adj chilly.

friolera f trifle

friso m frieze; wainscot.

fritada f dish of fried meat or fish.

frito/ta adj fried.

frivolidad f frivolity.

frívolo/la adj frivolous.

frondosidad f foliage.

frondoso/sa adj leafy.

frontera f frontier.

fronterizo/za adj frontier compd; bordering.

frontón m (dep) pelota court; pelota.

frotación, frotadura f friction, rubbing.

frotar vt to rub.

fructífero/ra adj fruit-bearing, fruitful.

fructificar vi to bear fruit; to come to fruition.

fructuoso/sa adj fruitful.

frugal adj frugal, sparing.

frugalidad f frugality, parsimony.

fruncir vt to pleat; to knit; to contract; ~ **las cejas** to knit the eyebrows.

frustrar vt to frustrate.

fruta f fruit; ~ **del tiempo** seasonal fruit.

frutal m fruit tree.

frutera f fruit dish.

frutería f fruit shop, greengrocer's shop.

frutero/ra m/f fruiterer, fruit seller, greengrocer; * m fruit basket.

frutilla f strawberry.

fruto m fruit; benefit, profit.

fuego m fire.

fuelle m bellows pl.

fuente f fountain; spring; source; large dish.

fuera adv out(side); away; ~ **de** prep outside; ¡~! out of the way!

fueraborda m outboard motor.

fuero m statute law of a country; jurisdiction.

fuerte m (mil) fortification, fort; forte; * adj vigorous, tough; strong; loud; heavy; * adv strongly; hard.

fuerza f force, strength; (elec) power; violence; **a ~ de** by dint of; ~**s** mpl troops pl.

fuga f flight, escape; leak (of gas).

fugarse vr to escape, to flee.

fugaz adj fleeting.

fugitivo/va adj, m/f fugitive.

fulano/na m/f so-and-so, what's-his-name/what's-her-name.

fulgurar vi to flash.

fullería f cheating.

fullero m cardsharp, cheat.

fulminar vt to fulminate; * vi to explode.

fumador/ra m/f smoker.

fumar vt, vi to smoke.

fumigación f fumigation.

funambulista m/f tightrope walker.

función f function; duties pl; show, performance.

funcionar vi to function; to work (of a machine).

funcionario/ria m/f official; civil servant.

funda f case, sheath; ~ **de almohada** pillowcase.

fundación f foundation.

fundador/ra m/f founder.

fundamental *adj* fundamental.
fundamentalismo *m* fundamentalism.
fundamentalista *adj*, *m/f* fundamentalist.
fundamento *m* foundation; groundwork; reason, cause.
fundar *vt* to found; to establish; to ground.
fundición *f* fusion; foundry.
fundir *vt* to fuse; to melt; to smelt; (*com*) to merge; to bankrupt; (*elec*) to fuse, to blow.
fúnebre *adj* mournful, sad; funereal.
funeral *m* funeral; **~es** *mpl* funeral, obsequies *pl*.
funerario/ria *adj* funeral *compd*; funereal.
funesto/ta *adj* ill-fated, unfortunate; fatal.

furgón *m* wagon.
furgoneta *f* pick-up (truck).
furia *f* fury, rage.
furibundo/da *adj* furious; frenzied.
furioso/sa *adj* furious.
furor *m* fury, rage.
furtivamente *adv* furtively.
furtivo/va *adj* furtive.
furúnculo *m* (*med*) boil.
fusible *m* fuse.
fusil *m* rifle.
fusilar *vt* to shoot.
fusilero *m* rifleman.
fusión *f* fusion; (*com*) merger.
fusta *f* riding crop.
fútbol *m* football.
futbolista *m/f* footballer.
fútil *adj* futile; trifling.
futilidad *f* futility.
futuro/ra *adj*, *m* future.

G

gabán *m* overcoat.
gabardina *f* gabardine; raincoat.
gabarra *f* (*mar*) lighter (boat).
gabinete *m* (*pol*) cabinet, study; office (of solicitors, etc).
gaceta *f* gazette.
gachas *fpl* porridge, pap.
gacho/cha *adj* curved, bent downward.
gafas *fpl* glasses *pl*, spectacles *pl*.
gafe *m* jinx.
gaita *f* bagpipe; flageolet.
gaitero/ra *m/f* bagpiper, bagpipe player.
gaje *m*: **~s del oficio** occupational hazards *pl*.
gajo *m* segment (of orange).
gala *f* full dress; (*fig*) cream, flower; **~s** *fpl* finery; **hacer ~ de** to display, to show off.

galán *m* lover; handsome young man; (*teat*) male lead.
galante *adj* gallant.
galanteador *m* lover, suitor.
galantear *vt* to court, to woo.
galanteo *m* gallantry, courtship.
galantería *f* gallantry; politeness; compliment.
galápago *m* tortoise.
galardón *m* reward, prize.
galardonar *vt* to reward, to recompense.
galaxia *f* galaxy.
galbana *f* laziness, idleness.
galeón *m* (*mar*) galleon.
galera *f* (*mar*) galley; wagon; (type-)galley.
galería *f* gallery.
galgo *m* greyhound.

gallardete m (mar) pennant, streamer.

gallardía f fineness, elegance, gracefulness; dash.

gallardo/da adj graceful, elegant; brave, daring.

galleta f biscuit.

gallina f hen; * m/f (fig) coward; ~ **ciega** blindman's buff.

gallinero m henhouse, coop; poulterer; (teat) top gallery; hubbub.

gallineta f woodcock (bird).

gallo m cock.

galón m (mil) stripe; braid; gallon.

galopar vi to gallop.

galope m gallop.

galvánico/ca adj galvanic.

galvanismo m galvanism.

gama¹ f (mus) scale; (fig) range, gamut.

gama² f doe (of the fallow deer).

gamba f shrimp; prawn.

gamberro/rra m/f hooligan.

gamo m buck of the fallow deer.

gamuza f chamois.

gana f desire, wish; appetite; will, longing; **de buena ~** with pleasure, voluntarily; **de mala ~** unwillingly, with reluctance.

ganadería f cattle raising; cattle; livestock.

ganadero m rancher; cattle dealer.

ganado m livestock, cattle pl; ~ **mayor** horses and mules pl; ~ **menor** sheep, goats and pigs pl.

ganancia f gain, profit; increase.

ganancial adj lucrative.

ganar vt to gain; to win; to earn; * vi to win.

gancho m hook; crook.

gandul adj, m/f layabout.

ganga f bargain.

gangoso/sa adj nasal.

gangrena f gangrene.

gangrenarse vr to become gangrenous.

gangrenoso/sa adj gangrenous.

ganso/sa m/f gander; goose; (fam) idiot.

garabatear vi, vt to scrawl, to scribble.

garabatos mpl scrawling letters or characters pl.

garaje m garage.

garante m/f guarantor; * adj responsible.

garantía f warranty, guarantee.

garañón m jackass, male donkey.

garapatear vi, vt to scrawl, to scribble.

garapiñar vt to freeze; to ice.

garbanzo m chickpea.

garbo m gracefulness, elegance; stylishness; generosity.

garboso/sa adj graceful; elegant; stylish; generous.

garduña f marten.

gargajo m phlegm, spit.

garganta f throat, gullet; instep; neck (of a bottle); narrow pass between mountains or rivers.

gargantilla f necklace.

gárgara f noise made by gargling.

gargarismo m gargling, gargle.

gargarizar vi to gargle.

garita f (mil) sentry box; (ferro) signal box.

garra f claw; talon; paw.

garrafa f carafe; (gas) cylinder.

garrafal adj great, vast, huge.

garrapata f tick (insect).

garrotazo m blow with a stick or garrotte.

garrote m stick, club, cudgel; (jur) garrotte.

garrotillo m (med) croup.

garrucha f pulley.

garza f heron.

garzo/za adj blue-eyed.

gas m gas.

gasa f gauze.

gaseoso/sa adj fizzy; * f lemonade.

gasfitero/ra m/f plumber.

gasoil m diesel (oil).

gasolina f petrol.

gasolinera f filling station, petrol station.

gasómetro m gasometer.

gastador/ra m/f spendthrift.

gastar vt to spend; to expend; to waste; to wear away; to use up; ~se vr to wear out; to waste.

gasto m expense, expenditure; use.

gastronomía f gastronomy.

gata f she-cat; a ~s on all fours.

gatear vi to go on all fours.

gatera f cat hole.

gatillazo m click of the trigger in firing.

gatillo m trigger of a gun; (med) dental forceps.

gato m cat; jack.

gatuno/na adj catlike, feline.

gaveta f drawer of a desk, locker.

gavilán m sparrow hawk.

gavilla f sheaf of corn.

gaviota f seagull.

gay (fam) adj invar, m gay (sl), homosexual.

gazapo m young rabbit; lie.

gazmoñada, gazmoñería f prudery; hypocrisy.

gazmoñero/ra, gazmoño/ña adj hypocritical.

gaznate m throttle, wind pipe.

gazpacho m Spanish cold tomato soup.

gazuza f ravenous hunger.

gelatina f jelly; gelatine.

gemelo/la m/f twin.

gemido m groan, moan, howl.

Géminis m Gemini (sign of the zodiac).

gemir vi to groan, to moan.

genciana f (bot) gentian.

gendarme m policeman.

gendarmería f police.

genealogía f genealogy.

genealógico/ca adj genealogical.

generación f generation; progeny, race.

general m general; * adj general; en ~ generally, in general.

generalidad f generality.

generalizar vt to generalize.

generalmente adv generally.

genérico/ca adj generic.

género m genus; kind, type; gender; cloth, material; ~s mpl goods pl, commodities pl.

generosidad f generosity.

generoso/sa adj noble, generous.

Génesis f Genesis.

genial adj inspired, brilliant; genial.

genio m nature, character; genius.

genital adj genital; * mpl ~es genitals pl.

genitivo m (gr) genitive case.

gente f people; nation; family.

gentil m/f pagan, heathen; * adj elegant; graceful; charming.

gentileza f grace; charm; politeness.

gentilhombre m gentleman.

gentío m crowd, throng.

genuflexión f genuflection.

genuino/na adj genuine; pure.

geografía f geography.

geográfico/ca adj geographical.

geógrafo/fa m/f geographer.

geología f geology.

geólogo/ga m/f geologist.

geometría f geometry.

geométrico/ca adj geometrical, geometric.

geranio m (bot) geranium.
gerente m/f manager; director.
geriatría f (med) geriatrics.
germen m germ, bud; source, origin.
germinar vi to germinate, to bud.
gerundio m (gr) gerund.
gesticular vi to gesticulate.
gestión f management; negotiation.
gesto m face; grimace; gesture.
giganta f giantess.
gigante m giant; * adj gigantic.
gigantesco/ca adj gigantic, giant.
gilipollas adj invar (fam) stupid; * m/f invar wimp (sl).
gimnasia f gymnastics.
gimnasio m gymnasium.
gimnasta m/f gymnast.
gimnástico/ca adj gymnastic.
ginebra f gin.
ginecólogo/ga m/f gynaecologist.
gira f trip, tour.
girar vt to turn around; to swivel; (com) to draw, to issue; * vi to go round, to revolve; (com) to do business; to draw.
giratorio/ria adj revolving.
girasol m sunflower.
giro m turning round; tendency; change; (com) draft.
gitano/na m/f Gypsy.
glacial adj icy.
glaciar m glacier.
glándula f gland.
glandular adj glandular.
globalización f globalization.
globo m globe; sphere; orb; balloon; ~ aerostático air balloon.
glóbulo m globule; corpuscle.
gloria f glory.
gloriarse vr: ~ en to glory in, to take pride in; to take delight in.
glorieta f bower, arbour; roundabout.
glorificación f glorification; praise.

glorificar vt to glorify.
glorioso/sa adj glorious.
glosa f gloss; comment.
glosar vt to gloss; to comment on.
glotón/ona m/f glutton.
glotonería f gluttony.
gobernación f government.
gobernador/ra m/f governor.
gobernar vt to govern; to regulate; to direct.
gobierno m government.
goce m enjoyment.
gol m goal.
goleta f schooner.
golf m golf.
golfa f (fam) slut.
golfo[1] m gulf, bay.
golfo[2] m (fam) urchin; lout.
golondrina f swallow.
golosina f dainty, titbit; sweet.
goloso/sa adj sweet-toothed.
golpe m blow, stroke, hit; knock; clash; coup; **de** ~ suddenly.
golpear vt to beat, to knock; to punch.
goma f gum; rubber; elastic.
gomosidad f stickiness, viscosity.
gomoso/sa adj gummy, viscous.
góndola f gondola; (ferro) freight truck.
gondolero m gondolier.
gordinflón/ona m/f very fat person.
gordo/da adj fat, plump, big-bellied; first, main; (fam) enormous.
gordura f grease; fatness, corpulence, obesity.
gorgojo m grub, weevil.
gorgorito m trill, warble.
gorila m gorilla.
gorjear vi to twitter, to chirp.
gorjeo m chirping.
gorra f cap; bonnet; (mil) bearskin.
gorrión m sparrow.
gorro m cap; bonnet.

gorrón/ona *m/f* scrounger.
gota *f* drop; (*med*) gout.
gotear *vt* to drip; to drizzle.
gotera *f* leak.
gótico/ca *adj* Gothic.
gotoso/sa *adj* gouty.
gozar *vt* to enjoy, to have, to possess;
~se *vt* to enjoy oneself, to rejoice.
gozne *m* hinge.
gozo *m* joy, pleasure.
gozoso/sa *adj* joyful, cheerful; content, glad, pleased.
grabación *f* recording.
grabado *m* engraving.
grabador *m* engraver.
grabadora *f* tape recorder.
grabar *vt* to engrave; to record.
gracejo *m* wit;, charm; gracefulness.
gracia *f* grace, gracefulness; wit;
i(muchas) ~s! thanks (very much); tener ~ to be funny.
gracioso/sa *adj* graceful; beautiful;
funny; pleasing; * *m* comic character.
grada *f* step of a staircase; tier; row;
~s *fpl* seats *pl* of a stadium or theatre.
gradería *f* (flight of) steps *pl*; row of seats.
grado *m* step; degree; de buen ~ willingly.
graduación *f* graduation; (*mil*) rank.
gradual *adj* gradual.
graduar *vt* to graduate.
gráfico/ca *adj* graphic; * *m* diagram; * *f* graph.
graja *f* rook.
grajo *m* rook.
grama *f* grass.
gramática *f* grammar.
gramatical *adj* grammatical.
gramático/ca *m/f* grammarian.
gramo *m* gram(me).

gran *adj* = grande.
grana *f* grain; scarlet.
granada *f* (*mil*) grenade; pomegranate.
granadero *m* (*mil*) grenadier.
granadilla *f* passionflower; passion fruit.
granado *m* pomegranate tree.
granate *m* garnet (precious stone).
grande *adj* great; big; tall; grand;
* *m/f* adult.
grandeza *f* greatness; grandeur; size.
grandiosidad *f* greatness; grandeur, magnificence.
grandioso/sa *adj* grand, magnificent.
granel *adv*: a ~ in bulk.
granero *m* granary.
granito *m* granite.
granizada *f* hail; hailstorm; shower, volley.
granizado *m* iced drink.
granizar *vi* to hail.
granizo *m* hail.
granja *f* farm.
granjero/ra *m/f* farmer.
grano *m* grain.
granuja *m/f* rogue; urchin.
grapa *f* staple; clamp.
grasa *f* suet, fat; grease.
grasiento/ta *adj* greasy; rusty; filthy.
gratificación *f* gratification; recompense.
gratificar *vt* to gratify; to reward, to recompense.
gratis *adj* free; *adv* freely.
gratitud *f* gratitude, gratefulness.
grato/ta *adj* pleasant, agreeable.
gratuito/ta *adj* gratuitous; free.
gravamen *m* charge, obligation; nuisance; tax.
gravar *vt* to burden; (*com*) to tax.

grave adj weighty, heavy; grave, important; serious.

gravedad f gravity; graveness.

gravemente adv gravely, seriously.

gravilla f gravel.

gravitación f gravitation.

gravitar vt to gravitate; to weigh down on.

gravoso/sa adj onerous, burdensome; costly.

graznar vi to croak; to cackle; to quack.

graznido m croak; cackle; quack.

greda f clay.

gremio m union, guild; society; company, corporation.

greña f tangle; shock of hair.

greñudo/da adj dishevelled.

gresca f clatter; outcry; confusion; wrangle, quarrel.

grieta f crevice, crack, chink.

grifo m tap; petrol station.

grilletes mpl shackles pl; fetters pl.

grillo m cricket; bud, shoot; ~s mpl fetters pl, irons pl.

grima f disgust; annoyance.

gripe f flu, influenza.

gris adj grey.

gritar vi to cry out, to shout, to yell.

gritería f shouting, clamour, uproar.

grito m shout, cry, scream.

grosella f redcurrant; ~ negra blackcurrant.

grosellero m currant bush.

grosería f coarseness, rudeness; vulgar comment.

grosero/ra adj coarse; rude, bad-mannered.

grosor m thickness.

grotesco/ca adj grotesque.

grúa f crane (machine); derrick.

grueso/sa adj thick; bulky; large; coarse; * m bulk.

grulla f crane (bird).

grumo m clot; curd.

grumoso/sa adj clotted.

gruñido m grunt; growl.

gruñidor/ra m/f grunter, mumbler; (fig) grumbler.

gruñir vi to grunt; to grumble; to creak (of hinges etc).

grupa f rump.

grupo m group.

gruta f grotto.

guadaña f scythe.

guagua f baby; bus.

gualdrapa f trappings pl (of a horse); tatter, rag.

guantada f slap.

guante m glove.

guapo/pa adj good-looking; handsome; smart.

guarda m/f guard, keeper; * f custody, keeping.

guardaagujas m invar (ferro) switchman.

guardabosque m gamekeeper; ranger.

guardacostas m invar coastguard vessel.

guardaespaldas m/f invar bodyguard.

guardafuegos m invar fireguard, guard.

guardameta m/f goalkeeper.

guardapolvo m dust cover; overall.

guardar vt to keep, to preserve; to save (money); to guard; ~se vr to be on one's guard; ~se de vr to avoid, to abstain from.

guardarropa f wardrobe; cloakroom.

guardia f guard; (mar) watch; care, custody; * m/f guard; policeman/ woman; * m (mil) guardsman.

guardián/ana m/f keeper; guardian.

guardilla f garret, attic.

guarecer vt to protect; to shelter; **~se** vr to take refuge.

guarida f den, lair; shelter; hiding place.

guarismo m figure, numeral.

guarnecer vt to provide, to equip; to reinforce; to garnish, to set (in gold, etc); to adorn.

guarnición f trimming; gold setting; sword guard; garnish; (mil) garrison.

guasa f joke.

guasón/ona m/f joker, jester.

gubernativo/va adj governmental.

guedeja f lock of hair.

guerra f war; hostility.

guerrear vi to fight, to wage war.

guerrero/ra m/f warrior; * adj martial, warlike.

guerrilla f guerrilla warfare; guerrilla group.

gueto m ghetto.

guía m/f guide; * f guidebook.

guiar vt to guide; (auto) to steer.

guijarral m stony place.

guijarro m pebble.

guillotina f guillotine.

guillotinar vt to guillotine.

guinda f cherry.

guindal m cherry tree.

guindilla f chilli pepper.

guiñapo m tatter, rag; rogue.

guiñar vt to wink.

guión m hyphen (in writing); script (of film).

guirigay m gibberish, confused language.

guirnalda f garland, wreath.

guisado m stew.

guisante m (bot) pea.

guisar vt to cook.

guiso m cooked dish; stew; seasoning.

guisote m hash, poor quality stew.

guitarra f guitar.

guitarrista m/f guitar player.

gula f gluttony.

gusano m maggot, worm.

gustar vt to taste; to sample; * vi to please, to be pleasing; **me gusta . . .** I like . . . .

gusto m taste; pleasure, delight; liking.

gustosamente adv gladly, with pleasure.

gustoso/sa adj pleasant; tasty.

gutural adj guttural.

H

haba f (bot) broad bean.

haber vt to get, to lay hands on; to occur; * v imp: **hay** there is, there are; * v aux to have; **~se** vr: **habérselas con uno** to have it out with somebody; * m income, salary; assets pl; (com) credit.

habichuela f bean.

hábil adj able, clever, skilful, dexterous, apt.

habilidad f ability, ableness, dexterity, aptitude.

habilitación f entitlement, qualification.

habilitar vt to qualify, to enable; to finance.

habitable adj inhabitable.

habitación f habitation, abode, lodging, dwelling, residence; room.

habitante m/f inhabitant, occupant.

habitar vt to inhabit, to live in.

hábito m dress; habit, custom.

habitual adj habitual, customary.

habituar vt to accustom; **~se** vr to become accustomed to.

habla f speech; language; dialect.

hablador/ra m/f talkative person.

habladuría f rumour; **~s** fpl gossip.

hablante adj speaking; * m/f speaker.

hablar vt, vi to speak; to talk.

hacedor/ra m/f maker; author.

hacendado m landowner; rancher.

hacendoso/sa adj industrious.

hacer vt to make; to do; to put into practice; to perform; to effect; to prepare; to imagine; to force; (mat) to amount to, to make; * vi to act, to behave; **~se** vr to become.

hacha f torch; axe, hatchet.

hachazo m blow with an axe.

hacia adv toward(s); about; **~ arriba/abajo** up(wards)/down-(wards).

hacienda f property; large farm; ranch; **H~** Treasury.

hacinar vt to stack or pile up; to hoard.

hada f fairy.

hado m fate, destiny.

halagar vt to cajole, to flatter.

halago m cajolery; pleasure.

halagüeño adj attractive, flattering.

halcón m falcon.

halconero m falconer.

hálito m breath; gentle breeze.

hall m hall; foyer.

hallar vt to find; to meet with; to discover; **~se** vr to find oneself; to be.

hallazgo m finding, discovery.

hamaca f hammock.

hambre f hunger; famine; longing.

hambriento/ta adj hungry; starved.

hamburguesa f hamburger.

haragán/ana m/f idler, good-for-nothing.

haraganear vi to idle, to loiter.

haraganería f idleness, laziness.

harapo m rag, tatter.

haraposo adj ragged.

hardware m hardware.

harina f flour; **~ de maíz** cornflour.

harinoso/sa adj floury.

hartar vt to satiate; to glut; to tire, to sicken; **~se** vr to gorge oneself (with food); to get fed up.

harto/ta adj full; fed up; * adv enough.

hartura f surfeit; plenty, abundance.

hasta prep up to; down to; until, as far as; * adv even.

hastío m loathing; disgust; boredom.

hatajo m lot, collection.

hato m clothes pl; herd of cattle, flock of sheep; provisions pl; crowd, gang, collection.

haya f beech tree.

haz m bunch, bundle; beam (of light).

hazaña f exploit, achievement.

hazmerreír m invar ridiculous person, laughing stock.

hebilla f buckle.

hebra f thread; vein of minerals or metals; grain of wood.

hebraico/ca adj belonging to the Hebrews.

hebreo/ea m/f Hebrew; Israeli; * m Hebrew language; * adj Hebrew; Israeli.

hechicería f witchcraft; charm.

hechicero/ra adj charming, bewitching; * m/f sorcerer/ sorceress.

hechizar vt to bewitch, to enchant; to charm.

hechizo m bewitchment, enchantment.

hecho/cha adj made; done; mature; ready-to-wear; cooked; * m action; act; fact; matter; event.

hechura f form, shape; fashion; making; workmanship; creature.

hectárea f hectare.

heder vi to stink, to smell bad.

hediondez f strong stench.

hediondo/da adj foetid, stinking.

hedor m stench, stink.

helada f frost; freeze-up.

helado/da adj frozen; glacial, icy; astonished; astounded; * m ice cream.

helar vt to freeze; to congeal; to astonish, to amaze; ~**se** vr to be frozen; to turn into ice; to congeal; * vi to freeze; to congeal.

helecho m fern.

hélice f helix; propeller.

helicóptero m helicopter.

hembra f female.

hemisferio m hemisphere.

hemorragia f haemorrhage.

hemorroides fpl haemorrhoids pl, piles pl.

henchir vt to fill up; ~**se** vr to fill or stuff oneself.

hendedura f fissure, chink, crevice.

hender vt to crack, to split; to go through; to open a passage.

hendidura f = **hendedura**.

heno m hay.

heraldo m herald.

herborizar vi to pick herbs; to collect plants.

heredad f patrimony, inherited property; farm.

heredar vt to inherit.

heredera f heiress.

heredero m heir.

hereditario/ria adj hereditary.

hereje m/f heretic.

herejía f heresy.

herencia f inheritance, heritage, heredity.

herida f wound, injury.

herido/da adj wounded, hurt.

herir vt to wound, to hurt; to beat, to strike; to affect, to touch, to move; to offend.

hermafrodita m hermaphrodite.

hermana f sister.

hermanar vt to match, to suit, to harmonize.

hermanastra f step-sister, half-sister.

hermanastro m step-brother, half-brother.

hermandad f fraternity; brotherhood.

hermano m brother; ~/na adj matched; resembling.

hermético/ca adj hermetic, watertight.

hermoso/sa adj beautiful, handsome, lovely; large, robust.

hermosura f beauty.

hernia f hernia, rupture.

héroe m hero.

heroicidad f heroism; heroic deed.

heroico/ca adj heroic.

heroína[1] f heroine.

heroína[2] f heroin (drug).

heroísmo m heroism.

herpes m herpes; * fpl (med) shingles.

herrador m farrier, blacksmith.

herradura f horseshoe.

herramienta f tool.

herrar vt to shoe (horses).

herrería f ironworks; forge.

herrero m smith.

hervidero m boiling; unrest; swarm.

hervir vt to boil; to cook; * vi to boil; to bubble; to seethe.

hervor m boiling; fervour, passion.

heterogeneidad f heterogeneous-ness.

heterogéneo/nea adj heterogeneous.
heterosexual adj, m/f heterosexual.
heterosexualidad f heterosexuality.
hexámetro m hexameter.
hez f lees pl, dregs pl.
hidalgo m nobleman.
hidalguía f nobility.
hidra f hydra.
hidráulica f hydraulics.
hidráulico/ca adj hydraulic.
hidroavión m seaplane.
hidrofobia f hydrophobia.
hidrógeno m (quím) hydrogen.
hidromasaje m whirlpool bath.
hiedra f ivy.
hiel f gall, bile.
hielo m frost; ice.
hiena f hyena.
hierba f grass; herb.
hierro m iron.
hígado m liver; (fig) courage, pluck.
higiene f hygiene.
higiénico/ca adj hygienic.
higo m fig.
higuera f fig tree.
hijastro/tra m/f stepson/daughter.
hijo/ja m/f son/daughter; child; offspring.
hilandero/ra m/f spinner.
hilar vt to spin.
hilera f row, line, file.
hilo m thread; wire.
hilván m tacking.
hilvanar vt to tack; to perform in a hurry.
himno m hymn.
hincapié m: hacer ~ en to emphasize.
hincar vt to thrust in, to drive in.
hincha m/f (fam) fan.
hinchado/da adj swollen; vain, arrogant.
hinchar vt to swell; to inflate; (fig) to

exaggerate; ~se vr to swell; to become vain.
hinchazón f swelling, lump.
hinojo m (bot) fennel.
hipar vi to hiccup.
hipérbola f hyperbola, section of a cone.
hipérbole f hyperbole, exaggeration.
hiperbólico/ca adj hyperbolic, hyperbolical.
hipermercado, híper m hypermarket, superstore.
hípica f horseracing; showjumping.
hipnotismo m hypnotism.
hipo m hiccups pl.
hipocondria f hypochondria.
hipocondríaco/ca adj hypochondriac.
hipocresía f hypocrisy.
hipócrita adj hypocritical; * m/f hypocrite.
hipódromo m racetrack.
hipopótamo m hippopotamus.
hipoteca f mortgage.
hipotecar vt to mortgage.
hipotecario/ria adj belonging to a mortgage.
hipótesis f hypothesis.
hipotético/ca adj hypothetical.
hisopo m (bot) hyssop; water sprinkler; paintbrush.
hispano/na adj Hispanic.
Hispanoamérica f Spanish America.
hispanoamericano/na adj, n Spanish American.
histeria f hysteria.
histérico/ca adj hysterical.
historia f history; tale, story.
historiador/ra m/f historian.
histórico/ca adj historical; historic.
historieta f short story; short novel; comic strip.
hito m landmark; boundary post; target.

hocico *m* snout; **meter el ~ en todo** to meddle in everything.

hogar *m* hearth, fireplace; *(fig)* house, home; family life.

hogaza *f* large loaf of bread.

hoguera *f* bonfire; blaze.

hoja *f* leaf; petal; sheet of paper; blade.

hojalata *f* tin (plate).

hojaldre *f* puff pastry.

hojarasca *f* dead leaves *pl*; rubbish.

hojear *vt* to turn the pages of.

hola *excl* hello!

holgado/da *adj* loose, wide, baggy; at leisure; idle, unoccupied, well-to-do; well-off.

holgar *vi* to rest; to be out of work; to be superfluous.

holgazán/ana *m/f* idler, slacker.

holgazanear *vt* to idle, to loaf around, to lounge around.

holgazanería *f* idleness, laziness.

holgura *f* looseness, bagginess; leisure; comfort; enjoyment.

hollín *m* soot.

holocausto *m* holocaust.

hombre *m* man; human being.

hombrera *f* shoulder pad.

hombro *m* shoulder.

hombruno/na *adj* manlike; virile, manly.

homenaje *m* homage.

homicida *m/f* murderer; * *adj* murderous, homicidal.

homicidio *m* murder.

homilía *f* homily.

homogeneidad *f* homogeneity.

homogéneo/nea *adj* homogeneous.

homólogo/ga *adj* homologous; synonymous.

homosexual *adj*, *m/f* homosexual.

honda *f* sling, catapult.

hondazo *m* throw with a sling.

hondo/da *adj* deep; profound; intense.

hondonada *f* dale, hollow; ravine.

hondura *f* depth, profundity.

honestidad *f* honesty; modesty; decency.

honesto/ta *adj* honest; modest.

hongo *m* mushroom; fungus; bowler hat.

honor *m* honour.

honorable *adj* honourable.

honorario/ria *adj* honorary; ~s *mpl* fees *pl*.

honorífico/ca *adj* creditable, honourable.

honra *f* honour, reverence; self-esteem; reputation; integrity; ~s funebres *pl* funeral honours *pl*.

honradez *f* honesty, integrity.

honrado/da *adj* honest; honourable; reputable.

honrar *vt* to honour.

honroso/sa *adj* honourable; respectable; honest.

hora *f* hour; time.

horadar *vt* to drill, to bore.

horario/ria *adj* hourly, hour *compd*; * *m* timetable.

horca *f* gallows; pitchfork.

horcajadas *adv*: **a ~** astride.

horchata *f* tiger-nut milk.

horizontal *adj* horizontal.

horizonte *m* horizon.

horma *f* mould, form.

hormiga *f* ant.

hormigón *m* concrete.

hormiguear *vi* to itch; to swarm; to team.

hormiguero *m* anthill; place swarming with people.

hormona *f* hormone.

hornada *f* batch.

horno *m* oven; furnace.

horóscopo m horoscope.

horquilla f pitchfork; hairpin.

horrendo/da adj horrible; frightful.

hórreo m granary.

horrible adj horrid, horrible.

horripilante adj hair-raising.

horror m horror, fright; atrocity.

horrorizar vt to horrify; ~se vr to be terrified.

horroroso/sa adj horrid, hideous, frightful.

hortaliza f vegetable.

hortelano/na m/f gardener; market gardener.

hortera m shop assistant; (fig) coarse person.

hosco/ca adj sullen, gloomy.

hospedaje m board and lodging.

hospedar vt to put up, to lodge; to entertain.

hospedería f inn; guest room; hospice.

hospedero/ra m/f landlord/lady; host/hostess.

hospicio m orphanage; hospice.

hospital m hospital.

hospitalario/ria adj hospitable.

hospitalidad f hospitality.

hostal m small hotel.

hostelería f hotel business or trade.

hostería f inn, tavern, hostelry.

hostia f host; wafer; (fam) whack (sl), punch.

hostigar vt to lash, to whip; to trouble, to pester, to bore.

hostil adj hostile; adverse.

hostilidad f hostility.

hostilizar vt (mil) to harry, to harass.

hotel m hotel.

hoy adv today; now, nowadays; **de ~ en adelante** as from today.

hoya f hole, pit.

hoyo m hole, pit; excavation.

hoz f sickle; gorge.

hozar vi to grub (of pigs).

hucha f money-box.

hueco/ca adj hollow, concave; empty; vain, ostentatious; * m interval; gap, hole; vacancy.

huelga f strike.

huella f track, footstep.

huérfano/na adj, m/f orphan.

huero/ra adj empty; addled.

huerta f market garden; irrigated region.

huerto m orchard; kitchen garden; **~ de hortalizas** market garden.

hueso m bone; stone, core.

huésped/da m/f guest, lodger; innkeeper.

hueste f army; crowd.

huesudo/da adj bony.

huevera f eggcup.

huevo m egg.

huida f flight, escape.

huir vi to flee, to escape.

hule m oilcloth.

humanidad f humanity; corpulence; **~es** fpl humanities pl.

humano/na adj human; humane, kind.

humareda f cloud of smoke.

humeante adj smoking; steaming.

humear vi to smoke.

humedad f humidity, moisture; wetness.

humedecer vt to moisten; to wet; to soak.

húmedo/da adj humid; wet; moist, damp.

humildad f humility, humbleness; submission.

humilde adj humble.

humillación f humiliation, submission.

humillar vt to humble; to subdue; ~se vr to humble oneself.

humo m smoke; fumes pl.
humor m mood, temper; humour.
hundir vt to submerge; to sink; to ruin; **~se** vr to sink, to go to the bottom; to collapse; to be ruined.
huracán m hurricane.
huraño/ña adj shy; unsociable.
hurgar vt to stir; to poke.
hurón m ferret; (fig) shy person;

busybody.
huronear vt to ferret out.
hurtadillas adv: **a ~** by stealth.
hurtar vt to steal, to rob.
hurto m theft, robbery.
húsar m hussar.
husmear vt to scent; to pry into.
huso m spindle.

I

ictericia f jaundice.
ida f departure, going; **(viaje de) ~** outward journey; **~ y vuelta** round trip; **~s y venidas** comings and goings pl.
idea f idea; scheme.
ideal adj ideal.
idealmente adv ideally.
idear vt to conceive; to think, to contrive.
ídem pn ditto.
idéntico/ca adj identical.
identidad f identity.
identificar vt to identify.
ideología f ideology.
idilio m idyll.
idioma m language.
idiosincrasia f idiosyncrasy.
idiota m/f idiot.
idiotez f idiocy.
idólatra m/f idolater.
idolatrar vt to idolize; to worship.
idolatría f idolatry.
ídolo m idol.
idoneidad f aptitude, fitness.
idóneo/nea adj suitable, fit.
iglesia f church.
ignominia f ignominy; infamy.
ignominioso/sa adj ignominious.
ignorancia f ignorance.

ignorante adj ignorant, uninformed.
ignorar vt to be ignorant of, not to know.
igual adj equal; similar; the same; **al ~** equally.
igualar vt to equalize, to equal; to match; to level off; **~se** vr to be equal; to agree.
igualdad f equality.
igualmente adv equally.
ijar m flank.
ilegal adj illegal, unlawful.
ilegalidad f illegality.
ilegitimidad f illegitimacy.
ilegítimo/ma adj illegal; illegitimate.
ileso/sa adj unhurt.
ilícito/ta adj illicit, unlawful.
ilimitado/da adj unlimited.
ilustrar vt to illustrate; to instruct.
iluminación f illumination.
iluminar vt to illumine, to illuminate, to enlighten.
ilusión f illusion; hope; **hacerse ~ones** to build up one's hopes.
ilusionista m/f conjurer.
iluso/sa adj easily deceived.
ilusorio/ria adj illusory.
ilustración f illustration; enlightenment.
ilustre adj illustrious, famous.

imagen f image.
imaginable adj imaginable.
imaginación f imagination; fancy.
imaginar vt to begin; to think up; vi, **~se** vr to imagine.
imán m magnet.
imbécil m/f imbecile, idiot.
imbecilidad f imbecility.
imbuir vt to imbue; to infuse.
imitable adj imitable.
imitación f imitation; **a ~ de** in imitation of.
imitador/ra m/f imitator.
imitar vt to imitate, to copy; to counterfeit.
impaciencia f impatience.
impacientar vt to make impatient; to irritate.
impaciente adj impatient.
impacto m impact.
impar adj odd.
imparcial adj impartial.
imparcialidad f impartiality.
impasibilidad f impassivity.
impasible adj impassive.
impavidez f intrepidity; cheek(iness).
impávido/da adj dauntless, intrepid; cheeky.
impecable adj impeccable.
impedimento m impediment, obstacle.
impedir vt to impede, to hinder; to prevent.
impeler vt to drive, to propel; to impel; to incite, to stimulate.
impenetrable adj impenetrable, impervious; incomprehensible.
impenitente adj impenitent.
impensado/da adj impenitent.
imperativo/va adj, m imperative.
imperceptible adj imperceptible.
imperdible m safety pin.
imperdonable adj unforgivable.

imperfección f imperfection.
imperfecto/ta adj imperfect.
imperial adj imperial.
impericia f lack of experience.
imperio m empire.
imperioso/sa adj imperious; arrogant, haughty; urgent.
impermeable adj waterproof; * m raincoat.
impermutable adj immutable.
impersonal adj impersonal.
impertérrito/ta adj intrepid, fearless.
impertinencia f impertinence; irrelevance.
impertinente adj not pertinent; touchy; impertinent.
imperturbable adj imperturbable; unruffled.
ímpetu m impetus; impetuosity.
impetuoso/sa adj impetuous.
implacable adj implacable, inexorable.
implicación f implication.
implicar vt to implicate, to involve.
implícito/ta adj implicit.
implorar vt to beg, to implore.
imponderable adj imponderable; (fig) priceless.
imponer vt to impose; to command; **~se** vr to assert oneself; to prevail.
impopular adj unpopular.
importación f importing; imports pl.
importancia f importance; significance, weight; size.
importante adj important, considerable.
importar vi to be important, to matter; * vt to import; to be worth.
importe m amount, cost.
importunar vt to bother, to pester.
importunidad f pestering; annoyance.
importuno/na adj annoying; unreasonable.

imposibilidad f impossibility.

imposibilitar vt to make impossible.

imposible adj impossible; extremely difficult; slovenly.

imposición f imposition; tax; deposit.

impostor/ra m/f impostor, fraud.

impostura f imposture, deceit, cheat.

impotencia f impotence.

impotente adj impotent.

impracticable adj impracticable, unworkable.

imprecación f curse.

imprecar vt to curse.

imprecatorio/ria adj containing curses, full of evil wishes.

impreciso/sa adj imprecise, vague.

impregnarse vr to be impregnated.

imprenta f printing; press; printing office.

imprescindible adj essential.

impresión f impression; stamp; print; edition.

impresionante adj impressive; marvellous; tremendous.

impresionar vt to move; to impress; ~se vr to be impressed; to be moved.

impreso m printed paper; printed book.

impresor m printer.

impresora f printer; ~ láser laser printer.

imprevisto/ta adj unforeseen, unexpected.

imprimir vt to print; to imprint; to stamp.

improbable adj improbable, unlikely.

improperio m insult, taunt.

impropio/pia adj improper; unfit; unbecoming.

improvisar vt to extemporize; to improvize.

improviso/sa adj: de ~ unexpectedly.

imprudencia f imprudence; indiscretion; carelessness.

imprudente adj imprudent; indiscreet; unwise.

impudencia f shamelessness.

impudente adj shameless.

impúdico/ca adj shameless; lecherous.

impuesto/ta adj imposed; * m tax, duty.

impugnación f opposition, contradiction.

impugnar vt to oppose; challenge; impugn.

impulsivo/va adj impulsive.

impulso m impulse; thrust; (fig) impulse.

impune adj unpunished.

impunidad f impunity.

impureza f impurity.

impuro/ra adj impure;, foul.

imputable adj attributable, chargeable.

imputar vt to impute, to attribute.

inaccesible adj inaccessible.

inacción f inaction, inactivity.

inadmisible adj inadmissible.

inadvertencia f carelessness, inadvertence.

inadvertido/da adj unnoticed.

inagotable adj inexhaustible.

inaguantable adj unbearable, intolerable.

inalterable adj unalterable.

inapelable adj without appeal.

inapreciable adj imperceptible; invaluable.

inaudito/ta adj unheard-of.

inauguración f inauguration, opening.

inaugurar vt to inaugurate.

incalculable adj incalculable.

incandescente adj incandescent.

incansable adj untiring, tireless.

incapacidad f incapacity, inability.

incapaz adj incapable, unable.

incauto/ta adj incautious, unwary.

incendiar vt to kindle, to set on fire.

incendiario/ria adj incendiary; * m/f arsonist.

incendio m fire.

incentivo m incentive.

incertidumbre f doubt, uncertainty.

incesante adj incessant, continual.

incesto m incest.

incestuoso/sa adj incestuous.

incidencia f incidence; incident.

incidente m incident.

incidir vi: ~ **en** to fall upon; to influence; to affect.

incienso m incense.

incierto/ta adj uncertain, doubtful.

incineración f incineration; cremation.

incipiente adj incipient.

incisión f incision, cut.

incisivo/va adj incisive.

inciso m (gr) comma.

incitación f incitement.

incitar vt to incite, to excite.

incivil adj uncivil, rude.

inclemencia f inclemency, severity; inclemency (of the weather).

inclinación f inclination.

inclinar vt to incline; to nod, to bow (the head); ~**se** vr to bow; to stoop.

incluir vt to include, to comprise; to incorporate; to enclose.

inclusión f inclusion.

inclusive adv inclusive.

incluso/sa adj included; * adv inclusively; even.

incógnito/ta adj unknown; **de** ~ incognito.

incoherencia f incoherence.

incoherente adj incoherent.

incombustible adj incombustible, fireproof.

incomodar vt to inconvenience; to bother, to annoy.

incomodidad f inconvenience; annoyance; discomfort.

incómodo/da adj uncomfortable; annoying; inconvenient.

incomparable adj incomparable, matchless.

incompatibilidad f incompatibility.

incompatible adj incompatible.

incompetencia f incompetence.

incompetente adj incompetent.

incompleto/ta adj incomplete.

incomprensible adj incomprehensible.

incomunicación f isolation; lack of communication.

incomunicado/da adj isolated, cut off; in solitary confinement.

inconcebible adj inconceivable.

incondicional adj unconditional; wholehearted; staunch.

inconexo/xa adj unconnected, disconnected.

inconfundible adj unmistakable.

incongruencia f incongruity, incongruence.

incongruo/grua adj incongruous.

inconmensurable adj immeasurable.

inconsciencia f unconsciousness; thoughtlessness.

inconsciente adj unconscious; thoughtless.

inconsecuencia f inconsequence.

inconsiderado/da adj inconsiderate, thoughtless.

inconsolable *adj* inconsolable.

inconstancia *f* inconstancy, unsteadiness.

inconstante *adj* inconstant, variable, fickle.

incontestable *adj* indisputable, incontrovertible, undeniable.

incontinencia *f* incontinence.

incontinente *adj* incontinent.

inconveniencia *f* inconvenience; impoliteness; unsuitability.

inconveniente *adj* inconvenient, unsuitable; impolite.

incorporación *f* incorporation, involvement.

incorporar *vt* to incorporate; **~se** *vr* to sit up; to join (an organization), to become incorporated.

incorrecto/ta *adj* incorrect.

incorregible *adj* incorrigible.

incorruptible *adj* incorruptible.

incredulidad *f* incredulity.

incrédulo/la *adj* incredulous.

increíble *adj* incredible.

incremento *m* increment; increase; growth; rise.

increpar *vt* to reprehend, to reprimand.

incruento/ta *adj* bloodless.

inculcar *vt* to inculcate.

inculpar *vt* to accuse, to blame.

inculto/ta *adj* uncultivated; uneducated; uncouth.

incumbencia *f* obligation; duty.

incumbir *vi*: ~ **a uno** to be incumbent upon one.

incurable *adj* incurable; irremediable.

incurrir *vt*: ~ **en** to incur; to commit (a crime).

incursión *f* incursion, raid.

indagación *f* search, inquiry.

indagar *vt* to inquire into.

indebido/da *adj* undue; illegal, unlawful.

indecencia *f* indecency.

indecente *adj* indecent.

indecible *adj* unspeakable, unutterable.

indecisión *f* hesitation; indecision.

indeciso/sa *adj* hesitant; undecided.

indecoroso/sa *adj* unseemly, unbecoming.

indefectible *adj* infallible.

indefenso/sa *adj* defenceless.

indefinible *adj* indefinable.

indefinido/da *adj* indefinite.

indeleble *adj* indelible.

indemnización *f* indemnification, compensation.

indemnizar *vt* to indemnify, to compensate.

independencia *f* independence.

independiente *adj* independent.

indestructible *adj* indestructible.

indeterminado/da *adj* indeterminate; indefinite.

indicación *f* indication.

indicador *m* indicator; gauge.

indicar *vt* to indicate.

indicativo/va *adj*, *m* indicative.

índice *m* ratio, rate; hand (of a watch or clock); index, table of contents; catalogue; forefinger, index finger.

indicio *m* indication, mark; sign, token; clue.

indiferencia *f* indifference, apathy.

indiferente *adj* indifferent.

indígena *adj* indigenous, native; * *m/f* native.

indigencia *f* indigence, poverty, need.

indigente *adj* indigent, poor, destitute.

indigestión *f* indigestion.

indigesto/ta *adj* undigested; indigestible.

indignación *f* indignation, anger.

indignar *vt* to irritate; to provoke, to tease; ~**se** *vr*: ~ **por** to get indignant about.

indigno/na *adj* unworthy, contemptible, low.

indirecta *f* innuendo, hint.

indirecto/ta *adj* indirect.

indisciplinado/da *adj* undisciplined.

indiscreción *f* indiscretion, tactlessness; gaffe.

indiscreto/ta *adj* indiscreet, tactless.

indisoluble *adj* indissoluble.

indispensable *adj* indispensable.

indisponer *vt* to spoil, to upset; to make ill; ~**se** *vr* to fall ill.

indisposición *f* indisposition, slight illness.

indispuesto/ta *adj* indisposed.

indisputable *adj* indisputable, incontrovertible.

indistinto/ta *adj* indistinct.

individual *adj* individual; single (of a room); * *m* (*dep*) singles.

individualidad *f* individuality.

individualizar *vt* to specify individually.

individuo *m* individual.

indivisible *adj* indivisible.

indocilidad *f* disobedience.

índole *f* disposition, nature, character; soft, kind.

indolencia *f* indolence, laziness.

indolente *adj* indolent, lazy.

indómito/ta *adj* untamed, ungoverned.

inducción *f* induction, persuasion.

inducir *vt* to induce, to persuade.

inductivo/va *adj* inductive.

indudable *adj* undoubted; unquestionable.

indulgencia *f* indulgence.

indulgente *adj* indulgent.

indultar *vt* to pardon; to exempt.

indulto *m* pardon; exemption.

industria *f* industry; skill.

industrial *adj* industrial.

industrialización *f* industrialization.

inédito/ta *adj* unpublished; (*fig*) new.

inefable *adj* ineffable, unspeakable, indescribable.

ineficacia *f* inefficacy.

ineficaz *adj* ineffective; inefficient.

ineptitud *f* inability; unfitness, ineptitude.

inepto/ta *adj* inept, unfit, useless.

inercia *f* inertia, inactivity.

inerme *adj* unarmed; defenceless.

inerte *adj* inert; dull; sluggish, motionless.

inescrutable *adj* inscrutable.

inesperado/da *adj* unexpected, unforeseen.

inestable *adj* unstable.

inestimable *adj* inestimable.

inevitable *adj* unavoidable.

inexactitud *f* inaccuracy.

inexacto/ta *adj* inaccurate, untrue.

inexorable *adj* inexorable.

inexperto/ta *adj* inexperienced.

infalibilidad *f* infallibility.

infalible *adj* infallible.

infame *adj* infamous.

infancia *f* infancy, childhood.

infanta *f* infanta, princess.

infante *m* infante, prince; (*mil*) infantryman.

infantería *f* infantry.

infanticida *m/f* infanticide (person).

infanticidio *m* infanticide (murder).

infantil *adj* infantile; childlike; children's.

infarto *m* heart attack; ~ **de miocardio** heart attack.

infatigable adj tireless, untiring.
infección f infection.
infectar vt to infect.
infeliz adj unhappy, unfortunate.
inferior adj inferior.
inferioridad f inferiority.
inferir vt to infer.
infernal adj infernal, hellish.
infestar vt to harass; to infest.
infidelidad f infidelity, unfaithfulness.
infiel adj unfaithful; disloyal; inaccurate.
infierno m hell.
infiltración f infiltration.
infiltrarse vr to infiltrate.
ínfimo/ma adj lowest; of very poor quality.
infinidad f infinity; immensity.
infinitivo m (gr) infinitive.
infinito/ta adj infinite; immense.
inflación f inflation.
inflamable adj flammable.
inflamación f ignition; inflammation.
inflamar vt to inflame; to excite, to arouse; ~se vr to catch fire.
inflamatorio/ria adj inflammatory.
inflar vt to inflate, to blow up; (fig) to exaggerate.
inflexibilidad f inflexibility.
inflexible adj inflexible.
influencia f influence.
influir vt to influence.
influjo m influence.
infografía f computer graphics.
información f information; news; (mil) intelligence; investigation, judicial inquiry.
informal adj irregular, incorrect; untrustworthy; informal.
informalidad f irregularity; untrustworthiness; informality.

informar vt to inform; to reveal, to make known; ~se vr to find out; * vi to report; (jur) to plead; to inform.
informática f computer science, information technology.
informe m report, statement; piece of information, account; * adj shapeless, formless.
infortunio m misfortune, ill luck.
infracción f infraction; breach, infringement.
infractor/ra m/f offender.
infructuoso/sa adj fruitless, unproductive, unprofitable.
infundado/da adj groundless.
infundir vt to infuse, to instil.
infusión f infusion.
infuso/sa adj infused; introduced.
ingeniar vt to devise; ~se vr: ~ para to manage to.
ingeniería f engineering; ~ genética genetic engineering.
ingeniero/ra m/f engineer.
ingenio m talent; wit; ingenuity; engine; ~ de azúcar sugar mill.
ingenioso/sa adj ingenious, clever; witty.
ingenuidad f ingenuousness; candour, frankness.
ingenuo/nua adj ingenuous.
ingerir vt to ingest; to swallow; to consume.
ingle f groin.
inglés/esa adj English; * m English (language); * m/f Englishman/woman.
ingratitud f ingratitude, unthankfulness.
ingrato/ta adj ungrateful, thankless; disagreeable.
ingrediente m ingredient.
ingresar vt to deposit; * vi to come in.

ingreso m entry; admission; **~s** mpl income; takings pl.

inhabilitar vt to disqualify, to disable.

inhabitable adj uninhabitable.

inherente adj inherent.

inhibición f inhibition.

inhibir vt to inhibit; to restrain.

inhumano/na adj inhuman.

inicial adj, f initial.

iniciar vt to initiate; to begin.

iniciativa f initiative.

inimaginable adj unimaginable, inconceivable.

inimitable adj inimitable.

ininteligible adj unintelligible.

iniquidad f iniquity, injustice.

injertar vt to graft.

injerto m graft.

injuria f offence; insult.

injuriar vt to insult, to wrong.

injurioso/sa adj insulting; offensive.

injusticia f injustice.

injusto/ta adj unjust.

inmaculado/da adj immaculate.

inmadurez f immaturity.

inmediaciones fpl neighbourhood; surrounding area.

inmediatamente adv immediately, at once.

inmediato/ta adj immediate.

inmemorial adj immemorial.

inmensidad f immensity.

inmenso/sa adj immense.

inmensurable adj immeasurable.

inmigración f immigration.

inmigrante m/f immigrant.

inmigrar vi to immigrate.

inminente adj imminent.

inmobiliario/ria adj real-estate compd; * f estate agency.

inmoral adj immoral.

inmortal adj immortal.

inmortalidad f immortality.

inmortalizar vt to immortalize.

inmóvil adj immovable.

inmovilidad f immobility.

inmueble m property; * adj: **bienes ~s** real estate.

inmundicia f nastiness, filth.

inmundo/da adj filthy, dirty; nasty.

inmune adj (med) immune; free, exempt.

inmunidad f immunity; exemption.

inmutabilidad f immutability.

inmutable adj immutable.

inmutarse vr to turn pale.

innato/ta adj inborn, innate.

innecesario/ria adj unnecessary.

innegable adj undeniable.

innovación f innovation.

innovador/ra m/f innovator.

innovar vt to innovate.

innumerable adj innumerable, countless.

inocencia f innocence.

inocentada f practical joke.

inocente adj innocent.

inoculación f inoculation.

inocular vt to inoculate.

inodoro m toilet.

inofensivo/va adj harmless.

inolvidable adj unforgettable.

inopinado/da adj unexpected.

inoxidable adj: **acero ~** stainless steel.

inquietar vt to worry, to disturb; **~se** vr to worry, to get worried.

inquieto/ta adj anxious, worried.

inquietud f uneasiness, anxiety.

inquilino/na m/f tenant; lodger.

inquirir vt to inquire into, to investigate.

insaciable adj insatiable.

insalubre adj unhealthy.

insalubridad f unhealthiness.

insano/na *adj* insane, mad.

inscribir *vt* to inscribe; to list, to register.

inscripción *f* inscription; enrolment, registration.

insecticida *m* insecticide.

insecto *m* insect.

inseguridad *f* insecurity.

inseminación *f* insemination; ~ **artificial** artificial insemination.

insensatez *f* stupidity, folly.

insensato/ta *adj* senseless, stupid; mad.

insensibilidad *f* insensitivity; callousness.

insensible *adj* insensitive; imperceptible; numb.

insensiblemente *adv* insensitively; imperceptibly.

inseparable *adj* inseparable.

inserción *f* insertion.

insertar *vt* to insert.

inservible *adj* useless.

insidioso/sa *adj* insidious.

insigne *adj* notable.

insignificante *adj* insignificant.

insignia *f* badge; ~**s** *fpl* insignia *pl*.

insinuación *f* insinuation.

insinuar *vt* to insinuate; ~**se** *vr*: to make advances; ~ **en** to worm one's way into.

insipidez *f* insipidness.

insípido/da *adj* insipid.

insistencia *f* persistence; insistence.

insistir *vi* to insist.

insolación *f* (*med*) sunstroke.

insolencia *f* insolence, rudeness, effrontery.

insolente *adj* insolent, rude.

insólito/ta *adj* unusual.

insolvencia *f* insolvency.

insolvente *adj* insolvent.

insomnio *m* insomnia.

insondable *adj* unfathomable; inscrutable.

insoportable *adj* unbearable.

inspección *f* inspection, survey; check.

inspeccionar *vt* to inspect; to supervise.

inspector/ra *m/f* inspector; superintendent.

inspiración *f* inspiration.

inspirar *vt* to inspire; (*med*) to inhale.

instalación *f* installation.

instalar *vt* to install.

instancia *f* instance.

instantáneo/nea *adj* instantaneous; * *f* snap(shot); **café** ~ instant coffee.

instante *m* instant; **al** ~ immediately, instantly.

instar *vt* to press, to urge.

instigación *f* instigation.

instigar *vt* to instigate.

instinto *m* instinct.

institución *f* institution.

instituir *vt* to institute.

instituto *m* institute.

institutriz *f* governess.

instrucción *f* instruction.

instructivo/va *adj* instructive; educational.

instructor/ra *m/f* instructor, teacher.

instruir *vt* to instruct, to teach.

instrumento *m* instrument; tool, implement.

insuficiencia *f* lack, inadequacy.

insuficiente *adj* insufficient, inadequate.

insufrible *adj* insufferable, insupportable.

insulina *f* insulin.

insulso/sa *adj* insipid; dull.

insultar *vt* to insult.

insulto *m* insult.

insuperable *adj* insuperable, insurmountable.

insurgente *m/f* insurgent.

insurrección *f* insurrection.

intacto/ta *adj* untouched; entire; intact.

integral *adj* integral, whole; **pan ~** wholewheat bread.

integrar *vt* to make up; to integrate.

integridad *f* integrity; completeness.

íntegro/gra *adj* integral, entire.

intelectual *adj, m/f* intellectual.

inteligencia *f* intelligence; understanding.

inteligente *adj* intelligent.

inteligible *adj* intelligible.

intemperie f: a la ~ out in the open.

intempestivo/va *adj* untimely.

intención *f* intention, purpose; plan.

intencionado/da *adj* meaningful; deliberate.

intendencia *f* administration, management.

intendente *m* manager.

intensidad *f* intensity; strength.

intenso/sa *adj* intense, strong; deep.

intentar *vt* to try, to attempt.

intento *m* intent, purpose; attempt.

intercalación *f* insertion.

intercalar *vt* to insert.

intercambio *m* exchange, swap.

interceder *vi* to intercede.

interceptar *vt* to intercept.

intercesión *f* intercession, mediation.

intercesor/ra *m/f* intercessor, mediator.

interés *m* interest; share, part; concern, advantage; profit.

interesado/da *adj* interested; prejudiced; mercenary.

interesante *adj* interesting; useful, convenient.

interesar *vt* to be of interest to, to interest; **~se** *vr:* **~ en, por** to take an interest in; * *vi* to be of interest.

interfaz, interface *f* interface.

interferir *vt* to interfere with; to jam (a telephone); * *vi* to interfere.

interfono *m* intercom.

interinidad *f* temporary holding of office.

interino/na *adj* provisional, temporary; * *m/f* temporary holder of a post; stand-in.

interior *adj* interior, internal; * *m* interior, inside.

interioridad *f* inwardness.

interiorismo *m* interior design.

interiorista *m/f* interior designer.

interjección *f* (*gr*) interjection.

interlocutor/ra *m/f* speaker.

intermediar *vt* to interpose.

intermedio/dia *adj* intermediate; * *m* interval.

interminable *adj* interminable, endless.

intermitente *adj* intermittent; *m* (*auto*) indicator.

internacional *adj* international.

internado *m* boarding school.

internar *vt* to intern; to commit; **~se** *vr* to penetrate.

interno/na *adj* interior, internal; * *m/f* boarder.

interpelación *f* interpellation, appeal, plea.

interpelar *vt* to appeal to.

interpolar *vt* to interpolate; to interrupt.

interponer *vt* to interpose, to put in.

interposición *f* insertion; interjection.

interpretación *f* interpretation.

interpretar *vt* to interpret, to explain; (*teat*) to perform; to translate.

intérprete *m/f* interpreter; translator; (*teat*) performer.
interracial *adj* interracial.
interrogación *f* interrogation; question mark.
interrogante *adj* questioning.
interrogar *vt* to interrogate.
interrogatorio *m* questioning; (*jur*) examination; questionnaire.
interrumpir *vt* to interrupt.
interrupción *f* interruption.
interruptor *m* switch.
intervalo *m* interval.
intervención *f* supervision, control; (*com*) auditing; (*med*) operation; intervention.
intervenir *vt* to control, to supervise; (*com*) to audit; (*med*) to operate on; * *vi* to participate; to intervene.
interventor/ra *m/f* inspector; (*com*) auditor.
interviú *f* interview.
intestino/na *adj* internal, interior; * *m* intestine.
intimar *vt* to intimate; * *vi* to become friendly.
intimidad *f* intimacy; private life.
intimidar *vt* intimidate.
íntimo/ma *adj* internal, innermost; intimate, private.
intolerable *adj* intolerable, insufferable.
intolerancia *f* intolerance.
intolerante *adj* intolerant.
intranquilizarse *vr* to get anxious or worried.
intranquilo/la *adj* worried.
intransigente *adj* intransigent.
intransitable *adj* impassable.
intransitivo/va *adj* (*gr*) intransitive.
intratable *adj* intractable, difficult.
intrepidez *f* intrepidity; fearlessness.
intrépido/da *adj* intrepid, daring.

intriga *f* intrigue.
intrigante *m/f* intriguer.
intrigar *vt, vi* to intrigue.
intrínseco/ca *adj* intrinsic.
introducción *f* introduction.
introducir *vt* to introduce; to insert.
introductor *m* introducer.
introvertido/da *adj, m/f* introvert.
intrusión *f* intrusion.
intruso/sa *adj* intrusive; * *m/f* intruder.
intuición *f* intuition.
intuitivo/va *adj* intuitive.
inundación *f* inundation, flood(ing).
inundar *vt* to inundate, to overflow; to flood.
inusitado/da *adj* unusual.
inútil *adj* useless.
inutilidad *f* uselessness.
inutilizar *vt* to render useless.
invadir *vt* (*mil*) to invade; to overrun.
invalidar *vt* to invalidate, to render null and void.
inválido/da *adj* invalid, null and void; * *m/f* invalid.
invariable *adj* invariable.
invasión *f* invasion.
invasor/ra *adj* invading; * *m/f* invader.
invencible *adj* invincible.
invención *f* invention.
inventar *vt* to invent.
inventario *m* inventory.
invento *m* invention.
inventor/ra *m/f* inventor.
invernadero *m* greenhouse.
invernar *vi* to pass the winter.
inverosímil *adj* unlikely, improbable.
inverosimilitud *f* unlikeliness, improbability.
inversión *f* (*com*) investment; inversion.

inverso/sa *adj* inverse; inverted; contrary.
invertir *vt (com)* to invest; to invert.
investidura *f* investiture.
investigación *f* investigation, research.
investigar *vt* to investigate; to do research into.
investir *vt* to confer.
invicto/ta *adj* unconquerable.
invierno *m* winter.
inviolabilidad *f* inviolability.
inviolable *adj* inviolable.
invisible *adj* invisible.
invitado/da *m/f* guest.
invitar *vt* to invite; to entice; to pay for.
invocación *f* invocation.
invocar *vt* to invoke.
involuntario/ria *adj* involuntary.
invulnerable *adj* invulnerable.
inyección *f* injection.
ir *vi* to go; to walk; to travel; ~**se** *vr* to go away, to depart.
ira *f* anger, wrath.
iracundo/da *adj* irate; irascible.
iris *m* iris (eye); **arco ~** rainbow.
ironía *f* irony.
irónico/ca *adj* ironic(al).
irracional *adj* irrational.
irradiación *f* irradiation.
irrazonable *adj* unreasonable.
irreal *adj* unreal.
irreconciliable *adj* irreconcilable.

irreflexión *f* rashness, thoughtlessness.
irregular *adj* irregular; abnormal.
irregularidad *f* irregularity; abnormality.
irremediable *adj* irremediable; incurable.
irremisible *adj* irretrievable; unpardonable.
irreparable *adj* irreparable.
irresistible *adj* irresistible.
irresoluto/ta *adj* irresolute; hesitant.
irreverencia *f* irreverence; disrespect.
irreverente *adj* irreverent; disrespectful.
irrevocable *adj* irrevocable.
irrisorio/ria *adj* derisory, ridiculous.
irritación *f* irritation.
irritar *vt* to irritate, to exasperate; to stir up; to inflame.
irrupción *f* irruption; invasion.
isla *f* island, isle.
Islam *m* Islam.
islámico/ca *adj* Islamic.
islote *m* small island.
istmo *m* isthmus.
italiano/na *adj* Italian; * *m* Italian (language); * *m/f* Italian man/woman.
ítem *m* item.
itinerario *m* itinerary.
izar *vt (mar)* to hoist.
izquierdo/da *adj* left; left-handed; * *f* left; left(-wing).

J

jabalí *m* wild boar.
jabalina *f* wild sow; *(dep)* javelin.
jabón *m* soap.
jabonar *vt* to soap.
jaca *f* pony.

jacinto *m* hyacinth.
jacuzzi *m* jacuzzi.
jactancia *f* boasting.
jactancioso/sa *adj* boastful.
jactarse *vr* to boast.

jadear vi to pant.

jaguar m jaguar.

jalea f jelly.

jaleo m racket, uproar.

jalón m pull, tug.

jamás adv never; **~ de siempre ~** for ever.

jamón m ham; **~ de York** (cooked) ham; **~ serrano** cured ham.

jaque m check (at game of chess); **~ mate** checkmate.

jaqueca f migraine.

jarabe m syrup.

jarcia f (mar) ropes pl, rigging.

jardín m garden.

jardinería f gardening.

jardinero/ra m/f gardener.

jarra f jug, jar, pitcher; **en ~s, de ~s** with arms akimbo; with hands to the sides.

jarro m jug.

jarrón m vase.

jaspe m jasper.

jaspear vt to marble; to speckle.

jaula f cage; cell for mad people.

jauría f pack of hounds.

jazmín m jasmin.

jazz m jazz.

jefatura f: **~ de policía** police headquarters.

jefe m chief, head, leader; (ferro) **~ de tren** guard, conductor.

jengibre m ginger.

jerarquía f hierarchy.

jerárquico/ca adj hierarchical.

jerga f coarse cloth; jargon.

jergón m coarse mattress.

jerigonza f jargon, gibberish.

jeringa f syringe.

jeroglífico/ca adj hieroglyphic; * m hieroglyph, hieroglyphic.

jersey m sweater, pullover.

Jesucristo m Jesus Christ.

jesuita m Jesuit.

jesuítico/ca adj jesuitical.

jibia f cuttlefish.

jícara f small cup (for chocolate).

jilguero m goldfinch.

jinete/ta m/f horseman/woman, rider.

jipijapa f straw hat.

jirafa f giraffe.

jirón m rag, shred.

jocosidad f humour, jocularity.

jocoso/sa adj good-humoured.

jornada f journey; day's journey; working day.

jornal m day's wage.

jornalero/ra m (day) labourer.

joroba f hump; * m/f hunchback.

jorobado/da adj hunchbacked.

jorobar vt to pester, to annoy.

jota f jot, iota; Spanish dance.

joven adj young; * m/f youth; young woman.

jovial adj jovial, cheerful.

jovialidad f joviality, cheerfulness.

joya f jewel; **~s** fpl jewellery.

joyería f jewellery; jeweller's shop.

joyero/ra m/f jeweller.

juanete m (med) bunion.

jubilación f retirement.

jubilado/da adj retired; * m/f senior citizen.

jubilar vt to pension off; to superannuate; to discard; **~se** vr to retire.

jubileo m jubilee.

júbilo m joy, rejoicing.

judaico/ca adj Judaic, Jewish.

judaísmo m Judaism.

judía f bean; **~ verde** green bean, French bean.

judicatura f judicature; office of a judge.

judicial adj judicial.

judío/día adj Jewish; * m/f Jewish man/woman.

juego *m* play; amusement; sport; game; gambling; **~s Olímpicos** Olympic Games.

juerga *f* binge; party.

jueves *m invar* Thursday.

juez *m/f* judge.

jugada *f* playing of a card; stroke, shot.

jugador/ra *m/f* player; gambler.

jugar *vt, vi* to play, to sport, to gamble.

jugarreta *f* bad play, unskilful play.

jugo *m* sap, juice.

jugoso/sa *adj* juicy, succulent.

juguete *m* toy, plaything.

juguetear *vi* to play.

juguetón/ona *adj* playful.

juicio *m* judgement, reason; sanity; opinion.

juicioso/sa *adj* judicious, prudent.

julio *m* July.

junco *m* (*bot*) rush; junk (small Chinese ship).

jungla *f* jungle.

junio *m* June.

junta *f* meeting; assembly; congress; council.

juntamente *adv* jointly; at the same time.

juntar *vt* to join; to unite; **~se** *vr* to meet, to assemble; to draw closer.

junto/ta *adj* joined; united; near; adjacent; **~s** together; * *adv:* **todo ~** all at once.

juntura *f* junction; joint.

Júpiter *m* Jupiter (planet).

jurado *m* jury; juror; member of a panel.

juramento *m* oath; curse.

jurar *vt, vi* to swear.

jurídico/ca *adj* lawful, legal; juridical.

jurisdicción *f* jurisdiction; district.

jurisprudencia *f* jurisprudence.

jurista *m/f* jurist.

justa *f* joust, tournament.

justamente *adv* justly; just.

justicia *f* justice; equity.

justificación *f* justification.

justificante *m* voucher; receipt.

justificar *vt* to justify.

justo/ta *adj* just; fair, right; exact, correct; tight; * *adv* exactly, precisely; just in time.

juvenil *adj* youthful.

juventud *f* youthfulness, youth; young people *pl*.

juzgado *m* tribunal; court.

juzgar *vt, vi* to judge.

K

karaoke *m* karaoke.

ketchup *m* ketchup.

kilogramo *m* kilogram.

kilometraje *m* distance in kilometres.

kilómetro *m* kilometre.

kilovatio *m* kilowatt.

kiosco *m* kiosk.

L

la *art f* the; * *pn* her; you; it.

laberinto *m* labyrinth.

labia *f* fluency; (*fam*) the gift of the gab (*sl*).

labio *m* lip; edge.

labor *f* labour, task; needlework; farmwork; ploughing.

laboratorio *m* laboratory.

laboriosidad *f* laboriousness.

laborioso/sa *adj* laborious; hardworking.

labrado/da *adj* worked; carved; wrought; * *m* cultivated land.

labrador/ra *m/f* farmer; peasant.

labranza *f* farming; cultivation; farmland.

labrar *vt* to work; to carve; to farm; (*fig*) to bring about.

labriego/ga *m/f* peasant.

laca *f* lacquer; hairspray.

lacayo *m* lackey, footman.

lacerar *vt* to tear to pieces, to lacerate.

lacio/cia *adj* faded, withered; languid; lank (hair).

lacónico/ca *adj* laconic.

laconismo *m* laconic style, terseness.

lacra *f* scar; blot, blemish.

lacrar *vt* to seal (with sealing wax).

lacre *m* sealing wax.

lactancia *f* lactation; breast-feeding.

lácteo/tea *adj*: productos ~s dairy products.

ladear *vt* to move to one side; to incline; ~se *vr* to lean; to tilt.

ladera *f* slope.

ladino/na *adj* cunning, crafty.

lado *m* side; faction, party; favour,

protection; (*mil*) flank; **al ~ de** beside; **poner a un ~** to put aside; **por todos ~s** on all sides.

ladrar *vt* to bark.

ladrido *m* bark, barking.

ladrillo *m* brick.

ladrón/ona *m/f* thief, robber, burglar.

lagar *m* wine press.

lagartija *f* (small) lizard.

lagarto *m* lizard.

lago *m* lake.

lágrima *f* tear.

lagrimal *m* corner of the eye.

lagrimoso/sa *adj* weeping, shedding tears.

laguna *f* lake; lagoon; gap.

laico/ca *adj* lay.

lamedura *f* licking.

lamentable *adj* lamentable, deplorable; pitiable.

lamentación *f* lamentation.

lamentar *vt* to be sorry about; to lament, to regret; * *vi*, ~se *vr* to lament, to complain; to mourn.

lamento *m* lament.

lamer *vt* to lick, to lap.

lámina *f* plate, sheet of metal; engraving.

lámpara *f* lamp.

lamparilla *f* nightlight.

lamparón *m* grease spot.

lampiño/ña *adj* beardless.

lamprea *f* lamprey (fish).

lana *f* wool.

lance *m* cast, throw; move, play (in a game); event, incident.

lancero *m* (*mil*) lancer.

lancha *f* barge, lighter; launch.

langosta f locust; lobster.

langostino m king prawn.

languidez f langour.

lánguido/da adj languid, faint, weak.

lanudo/da adj woolly, fleecy.

lanza f lance, spear.

lanzada f stroke with a lance.

lanzadera f shuttle.

lanzamiento m throwing; (*mar*, *com*) launch, launching.

lanzar vt to throw; (*dep*) to bowl, to pitch; to launch, to fling; (*jur*) to evict.

lapicero m pencil, ballpoint pen.

lápida f flat stone, tablet.

lapidario m; ~/ria adj lapidary.

lápiz m pencil; mechanical pencil.

lapso m interval; error.

lapsus m error, mistake.

largamente adv for a long time.

largar vt to loosen, to slacken; to let go; to launch; to throw out; ~se (*fam*) to beat it (*sl*).

largo/ga adj long; lengthy, generous; copious; **a la ~a** in the end, eventually.

largueza f liberality, generosity.

largura f length.

laringe f larynx.

laringitis f laryngitis.

las art fpl the; * pn them; you.

lascivia f lasciviousness; lewdness.

lascivo/va adj lascivious, lewd.

láser m laser.

lasitud f lassitude, weariness.

lástima f compassion, pity; shame.

lastimar vt to hurt; to wound; to feel pity for; ~se vr to hurt oneself.

lastimero/ra adj pitiful, pathetic.

lastimoso/sa adj pathetic, mournful.

lastrar vt to ballast (a ship).

lastre m ballast; good sense.

lata f tin; can; (*fam*) nuisance.

lateral adj lateral.

latido m (heart)beat.

latifundio m large estate.

latigazo m lash, crack (of a whip).

látigo m whip.

latín m Latin.

latinizar vt to Latinize.

latino/na adj Latin.

Latinoamérica f Latin America.

latinoamericano/na adj, m/f Latin American.

latir vi to beat, to palpitate.

latitud f latitude.

latón m brass.

latoso/sa adj annoying; boring.

latrocinio m theft, robbery.

laúd f lute (musical instrument).

laudable adj laudable, praiseworthy.

láudano m laudanum.

laureado/da adj honoured; * m laureate.

laurel m (*bot*) laurel; reward.

lava f lava.

lavabo m washbasin; washroom.

lavadero m washing place; laundry.

lavado m washing; laundry.

lavadora f washing machine.

lavanda f lavender.

lavandera f laundress.

lavandería f laundry; ~ **automática** Launderette™.

lavaparabrisas m invar windscreen washer.

lavaplatos m invar dishwasher.

lavar vt to wash; to wipe away; ~se vr to wash oneself.

lavativa f (*med*) enema; (*fig*) nuisance.

laxante m (*med*) laxative.

laxitud f laxity, slackness, laxness.

laxo/xa adj lax, slack.

lazada f bow, knot.

lazarillo m: **perro ~** guide dog.
lazo m knot; bow; snare, trap; tie; bond.
le pn him; you; (dativo) to him; to her; to it; to you.
leal adj loyal; faithful.
lealtad f loyalty.
lebrel m greyhound.
lebrillo m glazed earthenware pan.
lección f reading; lesson; lecture; class.
leche f milk.
lechera f milkmaid, dairymaid; milk churn.
lechería f dairy.
lecho m bed; layer.
lechón m sucking pig.
lechuga f lettuce.
lechuza f owl.
lector/ra m/f reader.
lectura f reading.
leer vt, vi to read.
legado m bequest, legacy; legate.
legajo m file.
legal adj legal; trustworthy.
legalidad f legality.
legalización f legalization.
legalizar vt to legalize.
legaña f sleep (in eyes).
legar vt to leave, to bequeath.
legible adj legible.
legión f legion.
legionario/ria m&f legionary.
legislación f legislation.
legislador/ra m/f legislator, lawmaker.
legislar vt to legislate.
legislativo/va adj legislative.
legislatura f legislature.
legitimar vt to legitimize.
legitimidad f legitimacy.
legítimo/ma adj legitimate, lawful; authentic.

legua f league.
legumbres fpl pulses pl.
leído/da adj well-read.
lejano/na adj distant, remote; far.
lejía f bleach.
lejos adv at a great distance, far off.
lelo/la adj stupid, ignorant; * m/f idiot.
lema m motto; slogan.
lencería f linen, drapery.
lengua f tongue; language.
lenguado m sole.
lenguaje m language.
lente m/f lens; **~ de contacto** contact lense.
lenteja f lentil.
lentilla f contact lense.
lentitud f slowness.
lento/ta adj slow.
leña f wood, timber.
leñador m woodsman, woodcutter.
leño m block, log; trunk of a tree.
leñoso/sa adj woody.
Leo m Leo (sign of the zodiac).
león m lion.
leona f lioness.
leonado/da adj lion-coloured, tawny.
leopardo m leopard.
leotardos mpl tights.
lepra f leprosy.
leproso/sa adj leprous; * m/f leper.
lerdo/da adj slow, heavy; dull; slow-witted.
les pn them; you; (dativo) to them; to you.
lesbiana f, adj lesbian.
lesión f wound; injury; damage.
letal adj mortal, deadly.
letanía f litany.
letárgico/ca adj lethargic.
letargo m lethargy.
letra f letter; handwriting; printing type; draft of a song; bill, draft; **~s** fpl letters pl, learning.

letrado/da adj learned, lettered; * m/f lawyer; counsel.

letrero m sign; label.

letrina f latrine.

leucemia f leukaemia.

leva m (mar) weighing anchor; (mil) levy.

levadizo/za adj that can be lifted or raised; **puente** ~ drawbridge.

levadura f yeast; brewer's yeast.

levantamiento m raising; insurrection.

levantar vt to raise, to lift up; to build; to elevate; to hearten, to cheer up; **~se** vr to get up; to stand up.

levante m Levant; east; east wind.

leve adj light; trivial.

levita f greatcoat, frock coat.

léxico m vocabulary.

ley f law; standard (for metal).

leyenda f legend.

liar vt to tie, to bind; to confuse.

libelo m petition; satire, lampoon.

libélula f dragonfly.

liberación f liberation; release.

liberal adj liberal, generous; * m/f liberal.

liberalidad f liberality, generosity.

libertad f liberty, freedom.

libertador/ra m/f liberator.

libertar vt to free, to set at liberty; to exempt, to clear from an obligation or debt.

libertinaje m licentiousness.

libertino/na m/f permissive person.

libra f pound; ~ **esterlina** pound sterling.

Libra f Libra (sign of the zodiac).

librar vt to free, to deliver; (com) to draw; to make out (a cheque); (jur) to exempt; to fight (a battle); **~se** vr to escape.

libre adj free; exempt; vacant.

libremente adv freely.

librería f bookshop.

librero/ra m/f bookseller.

libreta f notebook; ~ **de ahorros** savings book.

libro m book.

licencia f licence; licentiousness.

licenciado/da adj licensed; * m/f graduate.

licenciar vt to permit, to allow; to license; to discharge; to confer a degree upon; **~se** vr to graduate.

licencioso/sa adj licentious, dissolute.

liceo m lyceum; secondary school.

lícitamente adv lawfully.

lícito/ta adj lawful, fair; permissible.

licor m liquor.

licuadora f blender.

lid m contest, fight; dispute.

líder m/f leader.

liderazgo m leadership.

liebre f hare.

lienzo m linen; canvas; face or front of a building.

liga f suspender; birdlime; league; coalition; alloy.

ligadura f (med, mus) ligature; binding; bond, tie.

ligamento m ligament; tie; bond.

ligar vt to tie, to bind, to fasten; **~se** vr to commit oneself; * vi to mix, blend; (fam) to pick up.

ligazón f union, connection.

ligereza f lightness; swiftness; agility; superficiality.

ligero/ra adj light, swift; agile; superficial.

liguero m suspender belt.

lija f dogfish; sandpaper.

lijar vt to smooth, to sandpaper.

lila f lilac.

lima f file.

limadura f filing.

limar vt to file; to polish.

limitación f limitation, restriction.

limitado/da adj limited.

limitar vt to limit; to restrict; to cut down.

límite m limit, boundary.

limítrofe adj neighbouring, bordering.

limón m lemon.

limonada f lemonade.

limonar m plantation of lemon trees.

limosna f alms pl, charity.

limpiabotas m/f invar shoeshine boy/ girl.

limpiaparabrisas m invar windscreen wiper.

limpiar vt to clean; to cleanse; to purify; to polish; (fig) to clean up.

limpieza f cleanliness; cleaning; cleansing; polishing; purity.

limpio/pia adj clean; neat; pure.

linaje m lineage, family, descent.

linaza f linseed.

lince m lynx.

linchar vt to lynch.

lindar vi to be adjacent.

linde f boundary.

lindero m edge; boundary.

lindo/da adj pretty; lovely.

línea f line; cable; outline.

lineal adj linear.

lingote m ingot.

lingüista m/f linguist.

lino m flax.

linterna f lantern, lamp; torch, flashlight.

lío m bundle, parcel; (fam) muddle, mess.

liposucción f liposuction.

liquidación f liquidation.

liquidar vt to liquidate; to settle (accounts).

líquido/da adj liquid.

lira f (mus) lyre.

lirio m (bot) iris.

lirón m dormouse; (fig) sleepy- head.

lisiado/da adj injured; * m/f cripple.

lisiar vt to injure; to hurt.

liso/sa adj plain, even, flat, smooth.

lisonja f adulation, flattery.

lisonjear vt to flatter.

lisonjero/ra m/f flatterer; * adj flat- tering; pleasing.

lista f list; school register; catalogue; menu.

lista de correos f poste restante.

listo/ta adj ready; smart, clever.

listón m ribbon; strip (of wood or metal).

litera f berth; bunk, bunk bed.

literal adj literal.

literario/ria adj literary.

literato/ta adj literary; * m/f writer, literary person; ~s mpl literati pl.

literatura f literature.

litigar vt to fight; * vi (jur) to go to law; (fig) to dispute.

litigio m lawsuit.

litografía f lithography.

litográfico/ca adj lithographic.

litoral adj coastal; * m coast.

litro m litre (measure).

liturgia f liturgy.

litúrgico/ca adj liturgical.

liviandad f fickleness; triviality; lightness.

liviano/na adj light; fickle; trivial.

lívido/da adj livid.

llaga f wound; sore.

llama f flame; llama (animal).

llamada f call.

llamador m door-knocker.

llamamiento m call.

llamar vt to call; to name; to summon; to ring up, to telephone; * vi to knock at the door; to ring up, to telephone; ~se *vr* to be named.

llamarada *f* blaze; outburst.

llamativo/va *adj* showy; loud (colour).

llano/na *adj* plain; even, level, smooth; clear, evident; * *m* plain.

llanta *f* (wheel) rim; tyre; inner (tube).

llanto *m* flood of tears, crying.

llanura *f* evenness, flatness; plain, prairie.

llave *f* tap; key; ~ **maestra** master key.

llavero *m* key ring.

llegada *f* arrival, coming.

llegar *vi* to arrive; ~ **a** to reach; ~se *vr* to come near, to approach.

llenar *vt* to fill; to cover; to fill out (a form); to satisfy, to fulfil; ~se *vr* to gorge oneself.

lleno/na *adj* full, full up; complete.

llevadero/ra *adj* tolerable.

llevar *vt* to take; to wear; to carry; to convey, to transport; to drive; to lead; to bear; ~se *vr* to carry off, to take away.

llorar *vt, vi* to weep, to cry.

lloriquear *vt* to whine.

lloro *m* weeping, crying.

llorón/ona *m/f* tearful person; cry-baby.

lloroso/sa *adj* mournful, full of tears.

llover *vi* to rain.

llovizna *f* drizzle.

lloviznar *vi* to drizzle.

lluvia *f* rain; ~ **ácida** acid rain.

lluvioso/sa *adj* rainy.

lo *pn* it; him; you; * *art* the.

loable *adj* laudable.

loar *vt* to praise.

lobato *m* young wolf.

lobo *m* wolf.

lóbrego/ga *adj* murky, dark, gloomy.

lóbulo *m* lobe.

local *adj* local; * *m* place, site.

localidad *f* locality; location.

localizar *vt* to localize.

loción *f* lotion.

loco/ca *adj* mad; * *m/f* mad person.

locomotora *f* locomotive.

locuacidad *f* loquacity.

locuaz *adj* loquacious, talkative.

locución *f* expression.

locura *f* madness, folly.

locutor/ra *m/f* (*rad*) announcer; (*TV*) newsreader.

locutorio *m* telephone booth.

lodazal *m* muddy place.

lodo *m* mud, mire.

logaritmo *m* logarithm.

lógica *f* logic.

lógico/ca *adj* logical.

lograr *vt* to achieve; to gain, to obtain.

logro *m* achievement; success.

loma *f* hillock.

lombarda *f* red cabbage.

lombriz *f* worm.

lomo *m* loin; back (of an animal); spine (of a book); **llevar, traer a ~** to carry on the back.

lona *f* canvas.

loncha *f* slice; rasher.

longaniza *f* pork sausage.

longitud *f* length; longitude.

lonja[1] *f* slice; rasher.

lonja[2] *f* market, exchange; ~ **de pescado** fish market.

loro *m* parrot.

los *art mpl* the; * *pn* them; you.

losa *f* flagstone.

lote *m* lot; portion.

lotería *f* lottery.

loza *f* crockery.

lozanía *f* luxuriance, lushness; vigour; self-assurance.

lozano/na adj luxuriant, lush; sprightly.

lubricante m lubricant.

lucero m morning star, bright star.

lucha f struggle, fight.

luchador/ra m/f fighter; * m wrestler.

luchar vi to struggle; to wrestle.

lúcido/da adj lucid.

luciérnaga f glowworm.

lucimiento m splendour, lustre; brightness.

lucir vt to light (up); to show off; * vi to shine; ~**se** vr to make a fool of oneself.

lucrativo/va adj lucrative.

lucro m gain, profit.

luego adv next; afterward(s); **desde ~ of course.

lugar m place, spot; village; reason; **en ~ de** instead of, in lieu of.

lugareño/ña adj belonging to a village; * m/f inhabitant of a village.

lugarteniente m deputy.

lúgubre adj lugubrious; sad, gloomy.

lujo m luxury; abundance.

lujoso/sa adj luxurious; showy; profuse, lavish.

lujuria f lust.

lujurioso/sa adj lustful, lewd.

lumbre f fire; light.

lumbrera f luminary; skylight.

luminaria f illumination.

luminoso/sa adj luminous, shining.

luna f moon; glass plate for mirrors; lens.

lunar m mole, spot; * adj lunar.

lunático/ca adj, m/f lunatic.

lunes m invar Monday.

lupa f magnifying glass.

lupanar m brothel.

lustre m gloss, lustre; splendour.

lustro m lustrum (space of five years).

lustroso/sa adj bright, brilliant.

luteranismo m Lutheranism.

luterano/na adj, m/f Lutheran.

luto m mourning (dress); grief.

luz f light.

M

macarrones mpl macaroni.

macedonia f: ~ **de frutas** fruit salad.

macerar vt to macerate, to soften.

maceta f flowerpot.

machacar vt to pound, to crush; * vi to insist, to go on.

machacón/ona adj wearisome, tedious.

machete m machete, cutlass.

machista adj, m sexist.

macho adj male; (fig) virile; * m male; (fig) he-man.

machucar vt to pound, to bruise.

macilento/ta adj lean; haggard, withered.

macizo/za adj massive; solid; * m mass, chunk.

madeja f skein of thread; mop of hair.

madera f timber, wood.

madero m beam of timber.

madrastra f stepmother.

madraza f loving mother.

madre f mother; womb.

madreperla f mother-of-pearl.

madreselva f honeysuckle.

madrigal m madrigal.

madriguera f burrow; den.

madrina f godmother.

madroño m strawberry plant.

madrugada f dawn; **de ~** at day break.

madrugador/ra m/f early riser.

madrugar vi to get up early; to get ahead.

madurar vt to ripen; * vi to ripen, to grow ripe; to mature.

madurez f maturity; ripeness; wisdom.

maduro/ra adj ripe; mature.

maestra f mistress; schoolmistress; teacher.

maestría f mastery, skill.

maestro m master; teacher; **~/tra** adj masterly, skilled; principal.

magia f magic.

mágico/ca adj magical.

magisterio m teaching; teaching profession; teachers pl.

magistrado/da m/f magistrate.

magistral adj magisterial; masterly.

magistratura f magistracy.

magnanimidad f magnanimity.

magnánimo/ma adj magnanimous.

magnate m magnate.

magnético/ca adj magnetic.

magnetismo m magnetism.

magnetizar vt to magnetize.

magnetofón, magnetófono m tape recorder.

magnetofónico/ca adj: **cinta magnetofónica** recording tape.

magnificencia f magnificence, splendour.

magnífico/ca adj magnificent, splendid.

magnitud f magnitude.

mago/ga m/f magician.

magro/gra adj thin, lean; meagre.

magulladura f bruise.

magullar vt to bruise; to damage; to bash (sl).

mahometano/na m/f, adj Muslim.

mahometismo m Islam.

mahonesa f mayonnaise.

maíz m maize, Indian corn.

maizal m maize field.

majada f sheepfold.

majadería f absurdity; silliness.

majadero/ra adj dull; silly, stupid; * m idiot.

majestad f majesty.

majestuoso/sa adj majestic.

majo/ja adj nice; attractive; smart.

majuelo m vine newly planted; hawthorn.

mal m evil; hurt; harm, damage; misfortune; illness; * adj (before masculine nouns) bad.

malamente adv badly.

malaria f malaria.

malcriado/da adj rude, ill-behaved; naughty; spoiled.

maldad f wickedness.

maldecir vt to curse.

maldición f curse.

maldito/ta adj wicked; damned, cursed.

malear vt to damage; to corrupt.

malecón m pier.

maledicencia f slander; scandal.

maleducado/da adj bad-mannered, rude.

maleficio m curse; spell; witchcraft.

maléfico/ca adj harmful, damaging, evil.

malestar m discomfort; (fig) uneasiness; unrest.

maleta f suitcase; (auto) boot.

maletero m (auto) boot.

malevolencia f malevolence.

malévolo/la adj malevolent.

maleza f weeds pl; thicket.

malgastar vt to waste, to ruin.

malhablado/da adj foul-mouthed.

malhechor/ra m/f malefactor; criminal.

malhumorado/da *adj* cross, bad-tempered.

malicia *f* malice, wickedness; suspicion; cunning.

malicioso/sa *adj* malicious, wicked, evil; sly, crafty; spiteful.

malignidad *f* (*med*) malignancy; evil nature; malice.

maligno/na *adj* malignant; malicious.

malla *f* mesh, network; ~s *fpl* leotard.

malo/la *adj* bad; ill; wicked; * *m/f* villain.

malograr *vt* to spoil; to upset (a plan); to waste; ~se *vr* to fail; to die early.

malparado/da *adj*: **salir ~** to come off badly.

malparida *f* woman who has had a miscarriage.

malparir *vi* to miscarry, to have a miscarriage.

malsano/na *adj* unhealthy.

malteada *f* milk shake.

maltratamiento *m* ill-treatment.

maltratar *vt* to ill-treat, to abuse, to mistreat.

malva *f* (*bot*) mallow.

malvado/da *adj* wicked, villainous.

malversación *f* embezzlement.

malversador/ra *m/f* embezzler.

malversar *vt* to embezzle.

mama *f* teat; breast.

mamá *f* (*fam*) mum, mummy.

mamar *vt*, *vi* to suck.

mamarrachada *f* ridiculous sight.

mamarracho *m* mess, botch-up.

mamífero *m* mammal.

mamón/ona *m/f* small baby; scrounger.

mampara *f* partition; screen.

mampostería *f* masonry; stone-masonry.

maná *m* manna.

manada *f* flock, herd; pack; crowd.

manantial *m* source, spring; origin.

manar *vt* to run with, to flow; * *vi* to spring from; to flow; to abound.

mancha *f* stain, spot.

manchado/da *adj* spotted.

manchar *vt* to stain, to soil.

mancilla *f* spot, blemish.

manco/ca *adj* one-armed; one-handed; maimed; faulty.

mancomunar *vt* to associate, to unite; to make jointly responsible.

mancomunidad *f* union, fellowship; community; (*jur*) joint responsibility.

mandado *m* command; errand, message.

mandamiento *m* order, command; commandment.

mandar *vt* to command, to order; to bequeath; to send.

mandarín *m* mandarin.

mandarina *f* tangerine, mandarin orange.

mandatario/ria *m/f* agent; leader.

mandato *m* mandate, order; term of office.

mandíbula *f* jaw.

mandil *m* apron.

mando *m* command, authority, power; term of office; **~ a distancia** remote control.

mandón/ona *adj* bossy, domineering.

manecilla *f* small hand (of a watch or meter); book-clasp.

manejable *adj* manageable.

manejar *vt* to manage; to operate; to handle; (*auto*) to drive; ~se *vr* to manage; to behave.

manejo *m* management; handling; driving; confidence.

manera f manner; way; fashion; kind.

manga f sleeve; hose.

mango[1] m handle.

mango[2] m mango.

mangonear vi to interfere; * vt to boss about.

manguera f hose; pipe.

manguito m muff.

maní m peanut.

manía f mania; craze; dislike; spite.

maniatar vt to tie the hands of; to handcuff.

maniático/ca adj maniac, mad, frantic; * m/f maniac.

manicomio m lunatic asylum.

manicura f manicure.

manifestación f manifestation; show; demonstration; mass meeting.

manifestar vt to manifest, to declare.

manifiesto/ta adj manifest, open, clear; * m manifesto.

manija f handle.

maniobra f manoeuvring; handling; (mil) manoeuvre.

maniobrar vt to manoeuvre; to handle.

manipulación f manipulation.

manipular vt to manipulate.

maniquí m dummy; * m/f model.

manirroto/ta adj lavish, extravagant.

manivela f crank.

manjar m (tasty) dish.

mano f hand; hand (of a clock or watch); foot, paw (of an animal); coat (of paint); lot, series; hand (at game); **a ~** by hand; **a ~s llenas** liberally, generously.

manojo m handful, bunch.

manopla f glove; face cloth.

manosear vt to handle; to mess up.

manoseo m handling.

manotazo m slap, smack.

manoteo m gesticulation.

mansalva: **a ~** adv indiscriminately.

mansedumbre f meekness, gentleness.

mansión f mansion.

manso/sa adj tame; gentle, soft.

manta f blanket.

manteca f fat; **~ de cerdo** lard.

mantecado m cake eaten at Christmas; ice cream.

mantecoso/sa adj greasy.

mantel m tablecloth.

mantelería f table linen.

mantener vt to maintain, to support; to nourish; to keep; **~se** vr to hold one's ground; to support oneself.

mantenimiento m maintenance; subsistence.

mantequilla f butter.

mantilla f mantilla (head covering for women); **~s** fpl baby clothes pl.

manto m mantle; cloak, robe.

mantón m shawl.

manual adj manual; * m manual, handbook.

manufactura f manufacture.

manufacturar vt to manufacture.

manuscrito m manuscript; * adj hand-written.

manutención f support, maintenance.

manzana f apple.

manzanilla f camomile; camomile tea; manzanilla sherry.

manzano m apple tree.

maña f handiness, dexterity, cleverness, cunning; habit, custom; trick.

mañana f morning; * adv tomorrow.

mañoso/sa adj skilful, handy; cunning.

mapa m map.

mapamundi f map of the world.

maquillaje m make-up; making up.

maquillar vt to make up; **~se** vr to put on make-up.

máquina f machine; (ferro) engine; camera; (fig) machinery; plan, project.

maquinación f machination.

maquinador/ra m/f schemer, plotter.

maquinalmente adv mechanically.

maquinar vt, vi to machinate; to conspire.

maquinaria f machinery; mechanism.

maquinilla f: ~ de afeitar razor.

maquinista m (ferro) train driver; operator; (mar) engineer.

mar m/f sea.

maraña f shrub, thicket; tangle.

maravilla f wonder.

maravillar vt to astonish, to amaze; ~se vr to be amazed, to be astonished.

maravilloso/sa adj wonderful, marvellous.

marca f mark; stamp; (com) make, brand.

marcado/da adj strong, marked.

marcador m scoreboard; scorer.

marcar vt to mark; to dial; to score; to record; to set (hair); * vi to score; to dial.

marcha f march; running; gear; speed; (fig) progress.

marchar vi to go; to work; ~se vr to go away.

marchitar vt to wither; to fade.

marchito/ta adj faded; withered.

marcial adj martial, warlike.

marciano/na adj martian.

marco m frame; framework; (dep) goalposts pl.

marea f tide; ~ negra oil slick.

marear vt (mar) to sail, to navigate; to annoy, to upset; ~se vr to feel sick; to feel faint; to feel dizzy.

marejada f swell, heavy sea, surge.

mareo m sick feeling; dizziness; nuisance.

marfil m ivory.

margarina f margarine.

margarita f daisy.

margen m margin; border; * f bank (of river).

marginal adj marginal.

marginar vt to exclude; to leave margins on (a page); to make notes in the margin of.

marica m (fam) sissy.

maricón m (fam) queer (sl).

marido m husband.

mariguana, marihuana f cannabis.

marimacho f (fam) mannish woman.

marina f navy.

marinero/ra adj sea compd; seaworthy; * m sailor.

marino/na adj marine; * m sailor, seaman.

marioneta f puppet.

mariposa f butterfly.

mariquita f ladybug.

mariscal m marshal.

marisco m shellfish.

marital adj marital.

marítimo/ma adj maritime, marine.

mármol m marble.

marmóreo/rea adj marbled, marble compd.

marmota f marmot.

maroma f rope.

marqués m marquis.

marquesa f marchioness.

marrano m pig, boar.

marrón adj brown.

marrullería f plausibility; plausible excuse; ~s fpl cajolery.

marrullero/ra adj crafty, cunning.

marta f marten, sable.

Marte m Mars (planet).

martes m invar Tuesday.

martillar vt to hammer.

martilio m hammer.

mártir m/f martyr.

martirio m martyrdom.

martirizar vt to martyr.

marxismo m Marxism.

marxista adj, m/f Marxist.

marzo m March.

mas adv but, yet.

más adv more; most; besides, moreover; **a ~ tardar** at latest; **sin ~ ni ~** without more ado.

masa f dough, paste; mortar; mass.

masacre m massacre.

masaje m massage.

mascar vt to chew.

máscara m/f masked person; * f mask.

mascarada f masquerade.

mascarilla f (med) mask.

masculino/na adj masculine, male.

mascullar vt to mumble, to chew.

masivo/va adj massive, en masse.

masoquista m/f masochist.

masticación f mastication.

masticar vt to masticate, to chew.

mástil m (mar) mast.

mastín m mastiff.

masturbación f masturbation.

masturbarse vr to masturbate.

mata f shrub; sprig, blade; grove, group of trees; mop of hair.

matadero m slaughterhouse.

matador/ra adj killing; * m/f killer; * m bullfighter.

matanza f slaughtering; massacre.

matar vt to kill; to execute; to murder; **~se** vr to kill oneself, to commit suicide.

matasanos m invar quack (doctor).

matasellos m invar postmark.

mate¹ m checkmate.

mate² adj matt.

matemáticas fpl mathematics.

matemático/ca adj mathematical; * m/f mathematician.

materia m matter, materials pl; subject.

material adj material, physical; * m equipment, materials pl.

materialidad f outward appearance.

materialismo m materialism.

materialista m/f materialist.

maternal adj maternal, motherly.

maternidad f motherhood.

materno/na adj maternal.

matinal adj morning compd.

matiz m shade of colour; shading.

matizar vt to mix colours; to tinge, to tint.

matón m bully.

matorral m shrub, thicket.

matraca f rattle.

matricida m/f matricide (person).

matricidio m matricide (murder).

matrícula f register, list; (auto) registration number; numberplate.

matricular vt to register, to enrol.

matrimonial adj matrimonial.

matrimonio m marriage, matrimony.

matriz f matrix; womb; mould, form.

matrona f matron.

matutino/na adj morning.

maullar vi to mew.

maullido m mew (of a cat).

mausoleo m mausoleum.

máxima f maxim.

máxime adv principally.

máximo/ma adj maximum; top; highest.

mayo m May.

mayonesa f mayonnaise.

mayor adj main, chief; (mus) major; biggest; eldest; greater, larger; elderly; * m chief, boss; adult; **al por ~** wholesale; **~es** mpl forefathers.

mayoral *m* foreman.

mayordomo *m* steward.

mayoría *f* majority, greater part; ~ de edad coming of age.

mayorista *m/f* wholesaler.

mayormente *adv* principally, chiefly.

mayúsculo/la *adj* (*fig*) tremendous; * *f* capital letter.

maza *f* club; mace.

mazada *f* blow with a club.

mazapán *m* marzipan.

mazmorra *f* dungeon.

mazo *m* bunch; club, mallet; bat.

mazorca *f* ear of corn.

me *pn* me; to me.

mear *vi* (*fam*) to pee, to piss (*sl*).

mecánica *f* mechanics.

mecánico/ca *adj* mechanical; * *m/f* mechanic.

mecanismo *m* mechanism.

mecanografía *f* typing.

mecanógrafo/fa *m/f* typist.

mecate *m* rope.

mecedora *f* rocking chair.

mecer *vt* to rock; to dandle (a child).

mecha *f* wick; fuse.

mechar *vt* to lard; to stuff.

mechero *m* (cigarette) lighter.

mechón *m* lock of hair; large bundle of threads or fibres.

medalla *f* medal.

medallón *m* medallion.

media *f* stocking; sock; average.

mediación *f* mediation, intervention.

mediado/da *adj* half full; half complete; a ~s de in the middle of.

mediador/ra *m/f* mediator; go-between.

mediana *f* central reserve.

medianero/ra *adj* dividing; adjacent.

mediano/na *adj* medium; middling; mediocre.

medianoche *f* midnight.

mediante *prep* by means of.

mediar *vi* to intervene; to mediate.

medias *fpl* tights *pl*.

medicación *f* medication.

medicamento *m* medicine.

medicina *f* medicine.

medicinal *adj* medicinal.

médico/ca *adj* medical; * *m/f* doctor.

medida *f* measure.

medio/día *adj* half; **a medias** partly; * *m* middle; average; way, means; medium.

mediocre *adj* middling; moderate; mediocre.

mediocridad *f* mediocrity.

mediodía *m* noon, midday.

medir *vt* to measure; ~se *vr* to be moderate.

meditación *f* meditation.

meditar *vt* to meditate.

mediterráneo/nea *adj* Mediterranean; * *m*: el M~ the Mediterranean.

medrar *vi* to grow, to thrive, to prosper; to improve.

medroso/sa *adj* fearful, timid.

médula *f* marrow; essence, substance; pith.

medusa *f* jellyfish.

megáfono *m* megaphone.

mejilla *f* cheek.

mejillón *m* mussel.

mejor *adj*, *adv* better; best.

mejora *f* improvement.

mejorar *vt* to improve, to ameliorate; to enhance; * *vi* to improve; (*med*) to recover, to get better; ~se *vr* to improve, to get better.

mejoría *f* improvement; recovery.

melancolía *f* melancholy.

melancólico/ca *adj* melancholy, sad, gloomy.

melena f long hair, loose hair, mane.

melenudo/da adj long-haired.

melindroso/sa adj prudish, finicky.

mella f notch in edged tools; gap.

mellado/da adj jagged; gap-toothed.

mellar vt to notch.

mellizo/za adj, m/f twin.

melocotón m peach.

melodía f melody.

melodioso/sa adj melodious.

melodrama f melodrama.

melón m melon.

melosidad f sweetness.

meloso/sa adj honeyed; mellow.

membrana f membrane.

membranoso/sa adj membranous.

membrete m letter head.

membrillo m quince; quince tree.

membrudo/da adj strong, robust; burly.

memorable adj memorable.

memorándum m notebook; memorandum.

memoria f memory; report; record; ~s fpl memoirs pl.

memorial m memorial; petition.

mención f mention.

mencionar vt to mention.

mendigar vt to beg.

mendigo/ga m/f beggar.

mendrugo m crust.

menear vt to move from place to place; (fig) to handle; **~se** vr to move; to shake; to sway.

meneo m movement; shake; swaying.

menester m necessity; need; want; ~es mpl duties pl.

menesteroso/sa adj needy.

menestra f vegetable soup or stew.

menguante f decreasing.

menguar vi to diminish; to discredit.

menopausia f menopause.

menor m/f young person, juvenile; * adj less; smaller; minor; **al por ~** retail.

menoría f: **a ~** retail.

menos adv less; least; **a lo ~** o **por lo ~** at least; * prep except; minus.

menoscabar vt to damage; to harm; to lessen; to discredit.

menoscabo m damage; harm; loss.

menospreciar vt to undervalue; to despise, to scorn.

menosprecio m contempt, scorn; undervaluation.

mensaje m message.

mensajero/ra m/f messenger; courier.

menstruación f menstruation.

mensual adj monthly.

menta f mint.

mental adj mental; intellectual.

mentar vt to mention.

mente f mind; understanding.

mentecato/ta adj silly, stupid; * m/f idiot.

mentir vt to feign; to pretend; * vi to lie.

mentira f lie, falsehood.

mentiroso/sa adj lying; * m/f liar.

menú m menu; set meal.

menudencia f trifle, small thing; minuteness; ~s fpl odds and ends pl.

menudillos mpl giblets pl.

menudo/da adj small; minute; petty, insignificant; **a ~** frequently, often.

meñique m little finger.

meollo m marrow; (fig) core.

mequetrefe m good-for-nothing; busybody.

meramente adv merely, solely.

mercader m dealer, trader.

mercadería f commodity; trade; ~s fpl merchandise.

mercado m market; marketplace.

mercancía f commodity; ~s fpl goods pl, merchandise.

mercantil adj commercial, mercantile.

mercenario/ria adj mercenary; * m mercenary; labourer.

mercería f haberdashery, draper's shop.

mercurio m mercury.

Mercurio m Mercury (planet).

merecedor/ra adj deserving.

merecer vt to deserve, to merit.

merecido/da adj deserved.

merendar vi to have tea; to have a picnic.

merengue m meringue.

meridiano m meridian.

meridional adj southern.

merienda f (light) tea; afternoon snack; picnic.

mérito m merit; worth, value.

meritorio/ria adj meritorious.

merluza f hake.

merma f waste, leakage.

mermar vi to waste, to diminish.

mermelada f jam.

mero m pollack (fish); ~/ra adj mere, pure.

merodeador m (mil) marauder.

merodear vi to pillage, to go marauding.

mes m month.

mesa f table; desk; plateau; ~ redonda round table.

meseta f meseta, tableland.

mesón m inn.

mestizo/za adj of mixed race; crossbred; * m/f half-caste.

mesura f gravity; politeness; moderation.

mesurado/da adj moderate; dignified; courteous.

meta f goal; finish.

metabolismo m metabolism.

metafísica f metaphysics.

metafísico/ca adj metaphysical.

metáfora f metaphor.

metafórico/ca adj metaphorical.

metal m metal; (mus) brass; timbre (of the voice).

metálico/ca adj metallic.

metalurgia f metallurgy.

metamorfosis f invar metamorphosis; transformation.

meteoro m meteor.

meteorología f meteorology.

meter vt to place, to put; to insert, to put in; to involve; to make, to cause; ~se vr to meddle, to interfere.

metódico/ca adj methodical.

método m method.

metralla f (mil) shrapnel.

metralleta f submachine-gun.

métrico/ca adj metric.

metro[1] m metre.

metro[2] m underground, tube, subway.

metrópoli f metropolis; mother country.

mezcla f mixture; medley.

mezclar vt to mix; ~se vr to mix; to mingle.

mezquindad f meanness; pettiness; wretchedness.

mezquino/na adj mean; small-minded, petty; wretched.

mezquita f mosque.

mi adj my.

mí pn me; myself.

microbio m microbe.

microbús m minibus.

micrófono m microphone.

microondas m inv microwave oven.

microordenador m microcomputer.

microscópico/ca adj microscopic.

microscopio m microscope.

miedo *m* fear, dread.

miel *f* honey.

miembro *m* member.

mientras *adv* meanwhile; * *conj* while; as long as.

miércoles *m invar* Wednesday.

mierda *f* (*fam*) shit (*sl*).

mies *f* harvest.

miga *f* crumb; **~s** *fpl* fried bread-crumbs *pl*.

migaja *f* scrap, crumb.

migración *f* migration.

mijo *m* (*bot*) millet.

mil *m* one thousand.

milagro *m* miracle, wonder.

milagroso/sa *adj* miraculous.

milano *m* kite (bird).

milésimo/ma *adj*, *m* thousandth.

mili *f*: **hacer la ~** (*fam*) to do one's military service.

milicia *f* militia; military service.

miliciano *m* militiaman.

milímetro *m* millimeter.

militante *adj* militant.

militar *vt* military; * *m* soldier; * *vi* to serve in the army; (*fig*) to be a member of a party.

milla *f* mile.

millar *m* thousand.

millón *m* million.

millonario/ria *m/f* millionaire.

mimar *vt* to spoil, pamper.

mimbre *m* wicker.

mímica *f* sign language; mimicry.

mimo *m* caress; spoiling; mime.

mimoso/sa *adj* spoilt, pampered; delicate.

mina *f* mine; underground passage.

minar *vt* to undermine; to mine.

mineral *m* mineral; * *adj* mineral.

mineralogía *f* mineralogy.

minero/ra *m/f* miner.

miniatura *f* miniature.

minicadena *f* midi system.

minifalda *f* miniskirt.

mínimo/ma *adj* minimum.

ministerio *m* ministry.

ministro/ra *m/f* minister.

minoría *f* minority.

minucioso/sa *adj* meticulous; very detailed.

minúsculo/la *adj* minute; * *f* small letter.

minusválido/da *adj* (physically) handicapped; * *m/f* (physically) handicapped person.

minuta *f* minute, first draft; menu.

minutero *m* minute hand (of a watch or clock).

minuto *m* minute.

mío/mía *adj* mine.

miope *adj* short-sighted.

mira *f* sight of a gun; (*fig*) aim.

mirada *f* glance; gaze.

mirador *m* viewpoint, vantage point.

miramiento *m* consideration; circumspection.

mirar *vt* to look at; to observe; to consider; * *vi* to look; **~se** *vr* to look at oneself; to look at one another.

mirilla *f* peephole.

mirlo *m* blackbird.

mirón/ona *m/f* spectator, onlooker, bystander; voyeur.

misa *f* mass; **~ del gallo** midnight mass.

misal *m* missal.

misantropía *f* misanthropy.

misántropo/pa *m/f* misanthropist.

miserable *adj* miserable; mean; squalid (place); (*fam*) despicable; * *m/f* rotter.

miseria *f* misery; poverty; meanness; squalor.

misericordia *f* mercy.

misil m missile.

misión f mission.

misionero/ra m/f missionary.

mismo/ma adj same; very.

misterio m mystery.

misterioso/sa adj mysterious.

mística f mysticism.

místico/ca adj mystic(al); * m/f mystic.

mitad f half; middle.

mitigación f mitigation.

mitigar vt to mitigate.

mitin m (political) rally.

mito m myth.

mitología f mythology.

mitológico/ca adj mythological.

mitones mpl mittens pl.

mixto/ta adj mixed.

mobiliario m furniture.

mochila f backpack.

mochuelo m red owl.

moción f motion.

moco m snot (sl), mucus.

moda f fashion, style.

modales mpl manners pl.

modalidad f kind, variety.

modelar vt to model, to form.

modelo m model, pattern.

módem m modem.

moderación f moderation.

moderado/da adj moderate.

moderar vt to moderate.

moderno/na adj modern.

modestia f modesty, decency.

modesto/ta adj modest.

módico/ca adj moderate.

modificación f modification.

modificar vt to modify.

modisto/ta m/f dressmaker.

modo m mode, method, manner.

modorra f drowsiness.

modulación f modulation.

modular vt to modulate.

mofa f mockery.

mofarse vr: ~ de to mock, to scoff at.

moflete m fat cheek.

moho m rust; mould, mildew.

mohoso/sa adj mouldy, musty.

mojar vt to wet, to moisten; ~se vr to get wet.

mojigato adj hypocritical.

mojón m landmark.

molde m mould; pattern; model.

moldura f moulding.

mole f bulk; pile.

molécula f molecule.

moler vt to grind, to pound; to tire out; to annoy, to bore.

molestar vt to annoy, to bother; to trouble; * vi to be a nuisance.

molestia f trouble; inconvenience; (med) discomfort.

molesto/ta adj annoying; inconvenient; uncomfortable; annoyed.

molinero m miller.

molinillo m: ~ de café coffee grinder.

molino m mill.

molusco m mollusc.

momentáneo/nea adj momentary.

momento m moment.

momia f mummy.

monacal adj monastic.

monaguillo m acolyte.

monarca m/f monarch.

monarquía f monarchy.

monárquico/ca adj monarchical; * m/f royalist, monarchist.

monasterio m monastery, convent.

monástico/ca adj monastic.

mondadientes m invar toothpick.

mondar vt to clean; to cleanse; to peel; ~se vr: ~ de risa (fam) to split one's sides laughing.

mondo/da adj clean; pure; ~ y lirondo bare, plain; pure and simple.

moneda f money; currency; coin.

monedero *m* purse.
monería *f* funny face; mimicry; prank; trifle.
monetario/ra *adj* monetary, financial.
monitor *m* monitor.
monja *f* nun.
monje *f* monk.
mono[1] *m/f* monkey; ape.
mono[2] *m* dungarees *pl*; overalls *pl*.
mono/na *adj* lovely; pretty; nice.
monólogo *m* monologue.
monopolio *m* monopoly.
monopolista *m* monopolist.
monosílabo/ba *adj* monosyllabic.
monotonía *f* monotony.
monótono/na *adj* monotonous.
monovolumen *m* people mover.
monstruo *m* monster.
monstruosidad *f* monstrosity.
monstruoso/sa *adj* monstrous.
monta *f* amount, sum total.
montaje *m* assembly; decor (of theatre); montage.
montaña *f* mountain.
montañés/esa *adj* mountain *compd*; * *m/f* highlander.
montañoso/sa *adj* mountainous.
montar *vt* to mount, to get on (a bicycle, horse, etc); to assemble, to put together; to overlap; to set up (a business); to beat, to whip (in cooking); * *vi* to mount; to ride; ~ **a** to amount to.
montaraz *adj* mountainous; wild, untamed.
monte *m* mountain; woodland; ~ **alto** forest; ~ **bajo** scrub.
montería *f* hunting, chase.
montés/esa *adj* wild, untamed.
montón *m* heap, pile; mass; **a ~ones**, abundantly, by the score.
montura *f* mount; saddle.

monumento *m* monument.
monzón *m* monsoon.
moño *m* bun.
moquillo *m* distemper (disease in dogs).
mora *f* blackberry.
morada *f* home, abode, residence.
morado/da *adj* violet, purple.
morador/ra *m/f* inhabitant.
moral[1] *m* mulberry tree.
moral[2] *f* morals *pl*, ethics *pl*; * *adj* moral.
moraleja *f* moral.
moralidad *f* morality.
moralista *m/f* moralist.
moralizar *vi* to moralize.
moralmente *adv* morally.
morar *vi* to inhabit, to dwell.
moratoria *f* moratorium.
mórbido/da *adj* morbid, diseased.
morboso/sa *adj* diseased, morbid.
morcilla *f* black pudding.
mordacidad *f* sharpness, pungency.
mordaz *adj* biting, scathing; pungent.
mordaza *f* gag; clamp.
mordedura *f* bite.
morder *vt* to bite; to nibble; to corrode, to eat away.
mordisco *m* bite.
moreno/na *adj* brown; swarthy; dark-skinned.
moribundo/da *adj* dying.
morigeración *f* temperance.
morir *vi* to die; to expire; to die down; ~**se** *vr* to die; (*fig*) to be dying.
morisco/ca *adj* Moorish.
moro/ra *adj* Moorish.
morosidad *f* slowness, sluggishness.
moroso/sa *adj* slow, sluggish; (*com*) slow to pay up.
morral *m* haversack.
morriña *f* depression; sadness.

morro *m* snout; nose (of car, plane, etc).

morsa *f* walrus.

mortaja *f* shroud; mortise; cigarette paper.

mortal *adj* mortal; fatal, deadly.

mortalidad *f* mortality.

mortandad *f* death toll.

mortero *m* mortar (cannon).

mortífero/ra *adj* deadly, fatal.

mortificación *f* mortification.

mortificar *vt* to mortify.

mortuorio *m* mortuary.

moruno/na *adj* Moorish.

mosca *f* fly.

moscardón *m* botfly, blowfly; pest (*fam*), bore.

moscatel *adj, m* muscatel.

moscón *m* pest (*fam*), bore.

mosquearse *vr* (*fam*) to get cross; (*fam*) to take offence.

mosquetero *m* musketeer.

mosquitero *m* mosquito net.

mosquito *m* gnat, mosquito.

mostaza *f* mustard.

mosto *m* must, new wine.

mostrador *m* counter.

mostrar *vt* to show, to exhibit; to explain; **~se** *vr* to appear, to show oneself.

mota *f* speck, tiny piece; dot; defect, fault.

mote *m* nickname.

motejar *vt* to nickname.

motín *m* revolt; mutiny.

motivar *vt* to motivate; to explain; to justify.

motivo *m* motive, cause, reason.

moto (*fam*), **motocicleta** *f* motorcycle.

motor *m* engine, motor.

motriz *adj* driving, motive.

movedizo/za *adj* movable; variable; changeable; fickle.

mover *vt* to move; to shake; to drive; (*fig*) to cause; **~se** *vr* to move; (*fig*) to get a move on.

móvil *adj* mobile, movable; moving; * *m* motive; mobile phone.

movilidad *f* mobility.

movimiento *m* movement, motion.

mozo/za *adj* young; * *m/f* youth, young man/girl; waiter/waitress.

muchacho/a *m/f* boy/girl; * *f* maid(servant).

muchedumbre *f* crowd.

mucho/cha *adj* a lot of, much; * *adv* much, a lot; long.

muda *f* change of clothes.

mudable *adj* changeable, variable; mutable.

mudanza *f* change; move.

mudar *vt* to change; to shed, to moult; **~se** *vr* to change one's clothes; to change house; * *vi* to change;

mudo/da *adj* dumb; silent, mute.

mueble *m* piece of furniture; **~s** *mpl* furniture.

mueca *f* grimace, funny face.

muela *f* tooth, molar.

muelle *m* spring; regulator; quay, wharf.

muérdago *m* (*bot*) mistletoe.

muerte *f* death.

muerto *m* corpse; **~/ta** *adj* dead.

muesca *f* notch, groove.

muestra *f* pattern; indication; demonstration; proof; sample; token; model.

mugido *m* lowing.

mugir *vi* to low, to bellow.

mugre *m* dirt, filth.

mugriento/ta *adj* greasy; dirty, filthy.

mujer *f* woman.

mulato/ta *adj* mulatto.

muleta *f* crutch.

mullido/da *adj* soft; springy.
mulo/la *m/f* mule.
multa *f* fine, penalty.
multar *vt* to fine.
multimedia *adj* multimedia.
múltiple *adj* multiple; **~s** many, numerous.
multiplicación *f* multiplication.
multiplicado *m (mat)* multiplicand.
multiplicar *vt* to multiply.
multiplicidad *f* multiplicity.
multitud *f* multitude.
mundano/na *adj* worldly; mundane.
mundial *adj* world-wide; world *compd.*
mundo *m* world.
munición *f* ammunition.
municipio *m* town council; municipality.
municipal *adj* municipal.
muñeca *f* wrist; child's doll.
muñeco *m* puppet; figure.
muñón *m* stump.
muralla *f* rampart, wall.
murciélago *m* bat.
murmullo *m* murmur, mutter.
murmuración *f* backbiting, gossip.

murmurador/ra *m/f* detractor, backbiter.
murmurar *vi* to murmur; to gossip, to backbite.
muro *m* wall.
muscular *adj* muscular.
músculo *m* muscle.
muselina *f* muslin.
museo *m* museum.
musgo *m* moss.
música *f* music.
musical *adj* musical.
músico/ca *m/f* musician; * *adj* musical.
muslo *m* thigh.
mustio/tia *adj* parched, withered; sad, sorrowful.
musulmán/ana *adj, m/f* Muslim.
mutabilidad *f* mutability.
mutación *f* mutation, change.
mutilación *f* mutilation.
mutilar *vt* to mutilate, to maim.
mutuo/tua *adj* mutual, reciprocal.
mutuamente *adv* mutually.
muy *adv* very; too; greatly; **~ ilustre** most illustrious.

N

nabo *m* turnip.
nácar *m* mother-of-pearl, nacre.
nacarado/da *adj* mother-of-pearl *compd*; pearl-coloured.
nacer *vi* to be born; to bud, to shoot (of plants); to rise; to grow.
nacido/da *adj* born; **recién ~** newborn.
nacimiento *m* birth; nativity.
nación *f* nation.
nacional *adj* national.
nacionalidad *f* nationality.

nacionalizar *vt* to nationalize; **~se** to become naturalized.
nada *f* nothing; * *adv* no way, not at all, by no means.
nadador/ra *m/f* swimmer.
nadar *vi* to swim.
nadie *pn* nobody, no one.
nado *adv*: **a ~** afloat.
nafta *f* petrol.
naipe *m* (playing) card.
nalgas *fpl* buttocks *pl.*
naranja *f* orange.

naranjada f orangeade.

naranjal m orange grove.

naranjo m orange tree.

narciso m (bot) daffodil; narcissus (flower); fop.

narcótico/ca adj narcotic; * m drug, narcotic.

narcotraficante m/f drug trafficker.

nardo m spikenard.

narigón/ona, narigudo/da adj bignosed.

nariz f nose; sense of smell.

narración f narration.

narrar vt to narrate, to tell.

narrativa f narrative; story.

nata f cream.

natación f swimming.

natal adj natal, native.

natalicio m birthday.

natillas fpl custard.

natividad f nativity.

nativo/va adj, m/f native.

natural m temper; natural disposition; native; * adj natural; native; common, usual; al ~ unaffectedly.

naturaleza f nature.

naturalidad f naturalness.

naturalista m naturalist.

naturalizar vi to naturalize; ~se vr to become naturalized; to become acclimatized.

naturalmente adv in a natural way; i~! of course!

naturópata m/f naturopath.

naufragar vi to be shipwrecked; to suffer ruin in one's affairs.

naufragio m shipwreck.

náufrago/ga adj shipwrecked.

nauseabundo/da adj nauseating.

náuseas fpl nauseousness, nausea.

náutica f nautics.

navaja f penknife; razor.

naval adj naval.

nave f ship; nave.

navegable adj navigable.

navegación f navigation; sea journey.

navegador m browser.

navegante m navigator.

navegar vt, vi to navigate; to sail; to fly.

navidad f Christmas.

navideño/ña adj Christmas compd.

navío m ship.

nazi adj, m/f Nazi.

neblina f mist; fine rain, drizzle.

nebuloso/sa adj misty; cloudy; nebulous; foggy; hazy; drizzling; * f nebula.

necedad f gross ignorance, stupidity; imprudence.

necesario/ria adj necessary.

neceser m toilet bag; holdall.

necesidad f necessity, need, want.

necesitado/da adj necessitous, needy.

necesitar vt to need; * vi to want, to need.

necio/cia adj ignorant; stupid, foolish; imprudent.

necrología f obituary.

nectarina f nectarine.

néctar m nectar.

nefando/da adj base, nefarious, abominable.

nefasto/ta adj unlucky.

negación f negation; denial.

negado/da adj incapable, unfit.

negar vt to deny; to refuse; ~se vr: ~ a hacer to refuse to do.

negativo/va adj, m negative; * f negative; refusal.

negligencia f negligence.

negligente adj negligent; careless, heedless.

negociación f negotiation; commerce.

negociante m/f trader, dealer.

negociar vt, vi to negotiate.

negocio m business, affair; transaction; firm; place of business.

negro/gra adj black; dark; * m black; * m/f black person.

negrura f blackness.

negruzco/ca adj blackish.

nene m, **nena** f baby.

nenúfar m water lily.

neófito m neophyte.

Neptuno m Neptune (planet).

nervio m nerve.

nervioso/sa adj nervous.

neto/ta adj neat, pure; net.

neumático/ca adj pneumatic; * m tyre.

neurona f neurone.

neutral adj neutral; neuter.

neutralidad f neutrality.

neutralizar vt to neutralize; to counteract.

neutro/tra adj neutral; neuter.

neutrón m neutrone.

nevada f heavy fall of snow.

nevar vi to snow.

nevera f icebox.

nevería f ice-cream parlour.

nexo m link.

ni conj neither, nor.

nicho m niche.

nido m nest; hiding place.

niebla f fog; mist.

nieta f granddaughter.

nieto m grandson.

nieve f snow.

nigromancia f necromancy.

nimiedad f small-mindedness; triviality.

nimio/mia adj trivial.

ninfa f nymph.

ningún, ninguno/na adj no; * pn nobody; none; not one; neither.

niña f little girl; pupil, (of eye).

niñera f nursemaid.

niñería f childishness; childish act.

niñero/ra adj fond of children.

niñez f childhood.

niño/ña adj childish; * m/f child; infant; **desde ~** from infancy, from a child; * m boy.

níspero m medlar.

nitidez f clarity; brightness; sharpness.

nitrato m (quím) nitrate.

nitrógeno m nitrogen.

nivel m level; standard; height; **a ~** perfectly level.

niveladora f bulldozer.

nivelar vt to level; to even up; to balance.

no adv no; not; * excl no!

noble adj noble, illustrious; generous.

nobleza f nobleness, nobility.

noción f notion, idea.

nocivo/va adj harmful.

nocturno/na adj nocturnal, nightly; * m nocturne.

noche f night; evening; darkness; **¡buenas ~s!** good night!

Nochebuena f Christmas Eve.

Nochevieja f New Year's Eve.

nodriza f nurse.

nogal m walnut tree.

nómada adj nomadic; * m/f nomad.

nombramiento m nomination; appointment.

nombrar vt to name; to nominate; to appoint.

nombre m name; title; reputation.

nomenclatura f nomenclature.

nómina f list; (com) payroll.

nominador m nominator.

nominal adj nominal.

nominativo m (gr) nominative.

non adj odd, uneven; * m odd number.

nonagenario/ria adj ninety-year-old; * m/f nonagenarian.

no obstante adv nevertheless, notwithstanding.

nor(d)este adj northeast, northeastern; * m northeast.

nórdico/ca adj northern; Nordic.

noria f water wheel; big wheel.

normal adj normal; usual.

normalizar vt to normalize; to standardize; ~**se** vr to return to normal.

noroeste adj northwest, northwestern; * m northwest.

norte m north, northern; * m north; (fig) rule, guide.

nos pn us; to us; for us; from us; to ourselves.

nosotros/tras pn we; us.

nostalgia f homesickness.

nota f note; notice, remark; mark.

notable adj notable, remarkable.

notar vt to note; to mark; to remark; ~**se** vr to be obvious.

notaría f profession of a notary; notary's office.

notario m notary.

noticia f notice; knowledge, information; note; ~**s** fpl news.

noticiario m newsreel; news bulletin.

noticiero m news bulletin.

notificación f notification.

notificar vt to notify, to inform.

notoriedad f notoriety.

notorio/ria adj notorious.

novato/ta adj inexperienced; * m/f beginner; fresher.

novecientos/tas adj nine hundred.

novedad f novelty; modernness; newness; piece of news; change.

novela f novel.

novelero/ra adj highly imaginative.

novelesco/ca adj fictional; romantic; fantastic.

noveno/na adj ninth.

noventa adj, m ninety.

novia f bride; girlfriend; fiancée.

noviazgo m engagement.

novicio m novice.

noviembre m November.

novilla f heifer.

novillada f drove of young bulls; fight of young bulls.

novillo m young bull or ox.

novio m bridegroom; boyfriend; fiancé.

nubarrón m large cloud.

nube f cloud.

nublado/da adj cloudy; * m storm cloud.

nublarse vr to grow dark.

nuca f nape (of the neck); scruff of the neck.

nuclear adj nuclear.

núcleo m core; nucleus.

nudillo m knuckle.

nudo m knot.

nuera f daughter-in-law.

nuestro/tra adj our; * pn ours.

nuevamente adv again; anew.

nueve m, adj nine.

nuevo/va adj new; modern; fresh; * f piece of news; ¿qué hay de ~? is there any news?, what's new?

nuez f nut; walnut; Adam's apple; ~ **moscada** nutmeg.

nulidad f incompetence; nullity.

nulo/la adj useless; drawn; null.

numeración f numeration.

numerador m numerator.

numeral m numeral.

numerar vt to number.

numérico/ca adj numerical.

número m number; cipher.

numeroso/sa adj numerous.

nunca *adv* never.
nuncio *m* nuncio.
nupcial *adj* nuptial.
nupcias *fpl* nuptials *pl*, wedding.
nutria *f* otter.

nutrición *f* nutrition.
nutrir *vt* to nourish; to feed.
nutritivo/va *adj* nutritious, nourishing.
nylon *m* nylon.

Ñ

ñato/ta *adj* snubnosed.
ñoñería *f* insipidness.

ñoño/ña *adj* insipid; spineless; silly.

O

o *conj* or; either.
oasis *m invar* oasis.
obcecación *f* obduracy.
obcecar *vt* to blind; to darken.
obedecer *vt* to obey.
obediencia *f* obedience.
obediente *adj* obedient.
obelisco *m* obelisk.
obertura *f* (*mus*) overture.
obesidad *f* obesity.
obeso/sa *adj* obese, fat.
obispado *m* bishopric, episcopate.
obispo *m* bishop.
objeción *f* objection, opposition, exception.
objetar *vi* to object.
objetor *m* **~ de conciencia** conscientious objector.
objetivo/va *adj*, *m* objective.
objeto *m* object; aim.
oblea *f* wafer.
oblicuo/cua *adj* oblique.
obligación *f* obligation; (*com*) bond.
obligar *vt* to force; **~se** *vr* to bind oneself.
obligatorio/ria *adj* obligatory.
oblongo/ga *adj* oblong.
oboe *m* oboe.

obra *f* work; building, construction; play; **por ~ de** thanks to.
obrar *vt* to work, to operate; to put into practice; * *vi* to behave, to act; to have an effect.
obrero/ra *adj* working; labour *compd*; * *m/f* workman; labourer.
obscenidad *f* obscenity.
obsceno/na *adj* obscene.
obsequiar *vt* to lavish attention on; **~ con** to present with.
obsequio *m* gift; courtesy.
obsequioso/sa *adj* obsequious, compliant; officious.
observación *f* observation; remark.
observador/ra *m/f* observer.
observancia *f* observance.
observar *vt* to observe; to notice.
observatorio *m* observatory.
obsesión *f* obsession.
obsesionar *vt* to obsess.
obstáculo *m* obstacle, impediment, hindrance.
obstar *vi*: **~ a**, **~ para** to oppose, to obstruct, to hinder.
obstetricia *f* obstetrics.
obstinación *f* obstinacy, stubbornness.

obstinado/da *adj* obstinate.

obstinarse *vr* to be obstinate; **~ en** to persist in.

obstrucción *f* obstruction.

obstruir *vt* to obstruct; **~se** *vr* to be blocked up, to be obstructed.

obtener *vt* to obtain; to gain.

obtuso/sa *adj* obtuse, blunt.

obús *m* (mil) shell.

obviar *vt* to obviate, to remove.

obvio/via *adj* obvious, evident.

ocasión *f* occasion, opportunity.

ocasional *adj* occasional.

ocasionar *vt* to cause, to occasion.

ocaso *m* (fig) decline.

occidental *adj* occidental, western.

occidente *m* occident, west.

océano *m* ocean.

ochenta *m*, *adj* eighty.

ocho *m*, *adj* eight.

ochocientos *m*, *adj* eight hundred.

ocio *m* leisure; pastime.

ociosidad *f* idleness, leisure.

ocioso/sa *adj* idle; useless.

ocre *m* ochre.

octavilla *f* pamphlet.

octavo/va *adj* eighth.

octogenario/ria *adj*, *m/f* octogenarian.

octubre *m* October.

ocular *adj* ocular; eye *compd*.

oculista *m/f* oculist.

ocultar *vt* to hide, to conceal.

oculto/ta *adj* hidden, concealed; secret.

ocupación *f* occupation; business; employment.

ocupado/da *adj* busy; occupied; engaged.

ocupar *vt* to occupy; to hold (an office); **~se vr ~ de, ~ en** to concern oneself with; to look after.

ocurrencia *f* event; bright idea.

ocurrir *vi* to occur, to happen.

oda *f* ode.

odiar *vt* to hate;**~se** *vr* to hate one another.

odio *m* hatred.

odioso/sa *adj* odious, hateful.

odontólogo/ga *m/f* dentist.

odorífero/ra *adj* odoriferous, odorous.

oeste *adj* west, western; * *m* west.

ofender *vt* to offend; to injure **~se** *vr* to be vexed; to take offence.

ofensa *f* offence; injury.

ofensivo/va *adj* offensive, injurious.

ofensor *m* offender.

oferta *f* offer; offering.

oficial *adj* official; * *m* officer; official.

oficiar *vi* to officiate, to minister (of clergymen, etc).

oficina *f* office.

oficio *m* office; employment, occupation; ministry; function; trade, business; **~s** *mpl* divine service.

oficiosidad *f* diligence; officiousness; importunity.

oficioso/sa *adj* officious; diligent; unofficial, informal.

ofimática *f* office automation.

ofrecer *vt* to offer; to present; to exhibit; **~se** *vr* to offer oneself; to occur, to present itself.

ofrecimiento *m* offer, promise.

ofrenda *f* offering, oblation.

ofrendar *vt* to offer, to contribute.

oftalmólogo/ga *m/f* ophthalmologist.

ofuscación *f* dimness of sight; obfuscation.

ofuscar *vt* to darken, to render obscure; to bewilder.

oídas *fpl*: **de ~** by hearsay.

oído *m* hearing; ear.

oír *vt, vi* to hear; to listen (to).

ojal *m* buttonhole.

¡ojalá! *conj* if only!, would that!

ojeada *f* glance.

ojear *vt* to eye; to view; to glance.

ojera *f* bag under the eyes.

ojeriza *f* spite, grudge, ill-will.

okupa *m/f (fam)* squatter.

ojo *m* eye; sight; eye of a needle; arch of a bridge.

ola *f* wave.

oleada *f* surge; violent emotion.

oleaje *m* succession of waves, sea swell.

óleo *m* oil.

oler *vt* to smell, to scent; * *vi* to smell; ~ **a** to smack of.

olfatear *vt* to smell; (fig) to sniff out.

olfato *m* sense of smell.

oligarquía *f* oligarchy.

oligárquico/ca *adj* oligarchical.

olimpíada *f*: **las O~s** the Olympics.

olímpico/ca *adj* olympic.

oliva *f* olive.

olivar *m* olive grove.

olivo *m* olive tree.

olla *f* pan; stew; ~ **podrida** dish composed of different boiled meats and vegetables; ~ **exprés**, ~ **a presión** pressure cooker.

olmo *m* elm tree.

olor *m* smell, odour; scent.

oloroso/sa *adj* fragrant; odorous.

olvidadizo/za *adj* forgetful.

olvidar *vt* to forget.

olvido *m* forgetfulness.

ombligo *m* navel.

omisión *f* omission.

omitir *vt* to omit.

omnipotencia *f* omnipotence.

omnipotente *adj* omnipotent, almighty.

once *m, adj* eleven.

onda *f* wave.

ondear *vi* to undulate; to fluctuate.

ondulado/da *adj* wavy.

oneroso/sa *adj* burdensome.

opa *f* takeover bid.

opacidad *f* opacity; gloom, darkness.

opaco/ca *adj* opaque; dark.

opción *f* option, choice.

ópera *f* opera.

operación *f* operation; ~ **de cesárea** *f* caesarean section, caesarean operation.

operador/ra *m/f* operator; projectionist; cameraman/woman.

operar *vi* to operate; to act.

opinar *vt* to think; * *vi* to give one's opinion.

opinión *f* opinion.

opio *m* opium.

oponente *m/f* opponent.

oponer *vt* to oppose; ~**se** *vr* to be opposed, ~ **a** to oppose.

oportunidad *f* opportunity.

oportunismo *m* opportunism.

oportuno/na *adj* seasonable, opportune.

oposición *f* opposition; ~**ones** *fpl* public examinations *pl*.

opositor/ra *m/f* opponent; candidate (in public examination).

opresión *f* oppression.

opresivo/va *adj* oppressive.

opresor *m* oppressor.

oprimir *vt* to oppress; to crush; to press; to squeeze.

optar *vt* to choose, to elect.

optativo/va *adj* optional.

óptica *f* optics.

óptico/ca *adj* optical; * *m/f* optician.

optimista *m/f* optimist.

óptimo/ma *adj* best.

opuesto/ta *adj* opposite; contrary; adverse.

opulencia f wealth, riches pl.

opulento/ta adj opulent, wealthy.

oración f oration, speech; prayer.

orador/ra m/f orator.

oral adj oral.

orangután m orang-utan.

orar vi to pray.

oratoria f oratory, rhetorical skill.

órbita f orbit.

orden m/f order; ~ **del día** order of the day; **órdenes sagradas** holy orders pl.

ordenación f arrangement; ordination; edict, ordinance.

ordenado/da adj methodical; orderly.

ordenador m computer.

ordenanza f order; statute, ordinance; ordination.

ordenar vt to arrange; to order; to ordain; ~**se** vr to take holy orders.

ordeñar vt to milk.

ordinal adj ordinal.

ordinario/ria adj ordinary, common; **de** ~ regularly, commonly, ordinarily.

orégano m oregano.

oreja f ear.

orejera f earflap.

orfanato m orphanage.

orfandad f orphanhood.

orgánico/ca adj organic; harmonious.

organigrama m flowchart.

organismo m organism; organization.

organista m/f organist.

organización f organization; arrangement.

organizar vt to organize.

órgano m organ.

orgasmo m orgasm.

orgía f orgy.

orgullo m pride, haughtiness.

orgulloso/sa adj proud, haughty.

orientación f position; direction.

oriental adj oriental, eastern.

orientar vt to orient; to point; to direct; to guide; ~**se** vr to get one's bearings; to decide on a course of action.

oriente m orient.

orificio m orifice; mouth; aperture.

origen m origin, source; native country; family, extraction.

original adj original, primitive; * m original, first copy.

originalidad f originality.

originar vt, vi to originate.

originario/ria adj original.

orilla f limit, border, margin; edge (of cloth); shore.

orín m rust.

orina f urine.

orinal m chamber pot.

orinar vi to pass water.

oriundo/da adj: ~ **de** native of.

ornamento m ornament, embellishment.

ornitología f ornithology.

oro m gold; ~**s** mpl diamonds pl (at cards).

orquesta f orchestra.

orquídea f orchid.

ortiga f (bot) nettle.

ortodoxia f orthodoxy.

ortodoxo/xa adj orthodox.

ortografía f orthography.

ortográfico/ca adj orthographical.

oruga f (bot) caterpillar.

orza f jar.

orzuelo m (med) stye.

os pn you; to you.

osa f she-bear; **O~ Mayor/Menor** Great/Little Bear.

osadamente adv boldly, daringly.

osadía f boldness, intrepidity; zeal, fervour.

osamenta f skeleton.

osar vi to dare, to venture.

óscar m Oscar.

oscilación f oscillation.

oscilar vi to oscillate.

oscurecer vt to obscure; to dark- en; * vi to grow dark; **~se** vr to disappear.

oscuridad f obscurity; darkness.

oscuro/ra adj obscure; dark.

osificarse vr to ossify.

oso m bear; **~ blanco** polar bear.

ostensible adj ostensible, apparent.

ostentación f ostentation, ambitious display, show.

ostentar vt to show; * vi to boast, to brag.

ostentoso/sa adj sumptuous, ostentatious.

ostra f oyster.

otitis f earache.

otoñal adj fall, autumnal.

otoño m fall, autumn.

otorgamiento m granting; execution.

otorgar vt to concede; to grant.

otorrino/na, otorrinolaringólogo/ga m/f ear, nose and throat specialist.

otro/tra adj another; other.

ovación f ovation.

ovalado/da adj oval.

óvalo m oval.

ovario m ovary.

oveja f sheep.

overol m overalls pl.

ovillo m ball of wool.

ovíparo/ra adj oviparous, egg-bearing.

ovulación f ovulation.

óvulo m ovum.

oxidación f rusting.

oxidar vt to rust; **~se** vr to go rusty.

óxido f (quím) oxide.

oxígeno m (quím) oxygen.

oyente m/f listener, hearer.

P

pabellón m pavilion; summer house; block, section.

pábilo m wick.

pacer vt to pasture, to graze.

paciencia f patience.

paciente adj, m/f patient.

pacificación f pacification.

pacificar vt to pacify, to appease.

pacífico/ca adj pacific, peaceful; * m: **el P~** the Pacific.

pacotilla f: **de ~** third-rate; cheap.

pactar vt to covenant; to contract; to stipulate.

pacto m contract, pact.

padecer vt to suffer; to sustain (an injury); to put up with.

padecimiento m suffering, sufferance.

padrastro m stepfather.

padrazo m loving, over-indulgent father.

padre m father; **~s** mpl parents pl.

padrino m godfather.

padrón m census; register; pattern; model.

paella f paella (dish of rice with shellfish, meat, etc).

paga f payment, fee.

pagadero/ra adj payable.

paganismo m paganism, heathenism.

pagano/na adj, m/f heathen, pagan.

pagar *vt* to pay; to pay for; (*fig*) to repay; * *vi* to pay.

pagaré *m* bond, note of hand, promissory note, IOU (I owe you).

página *f* page.

pago *m* payment; reward.

país *m* country; region.

paisaje *m* landscape.

paisano/na *adj* of the same country; * *m/f* fellow countryman/woman.

paja *f* straw; (*fig*) trash.

pajar *m* straw loft.

pajarita *f* bow tie.

pájaro *m* bird; sly, acute fellow.

pajarraco *m* large bird; cunning fellow.

paje *m* page.

pajita *f* (drinking) straw.

pajizo/za *adj* straw-coloured.

pala *f* spade, shovel.

palabra *f* word; **de ~** by word of mouth.

palabrota *f* swearword.

palaciego/ga *adj* pertaining or relating to the palace; * *m* courtier.

palacio *m* palace.

paladar *m* palate; taste, relish.

paladear *vt* to taste.

palanca *f* lever.

palangana *f* basin.

palco *m* box (in a theatre).

paleta *f* bat; palette; trowel.

paleto/ta *m/f* rustic.

paliar *vt* to mitigate.

paliativo/va *adj, m* palliative.

palidecer *vi* to turn pale.

palidez *f* paleness, wanness.

pálido/da *adj* pallid, pale.

palillo *m* small stick; toothpick; **~s** *mpl* chopsticks *pl*.

paliza *f* beating, thrashing.

palma *f* palm tree; palm of the hand; palm leaf.

palmada *f* slap, clap; **~s** *fpl* clapping of hands, applause.

palmatoria *f* candlestick; cane.

palmear *vi* to slap; to clap.

palmera *f* palm tree.

palmeta *f* cane.

palmo *m* palm; small amount.

palmotear *vi* to slap; to applaud.

palmoteo *m* clapping of hands.

palo *m* stick; cudgel; blow given with a stick; post; mast; bat; suit (at cards).

paloma *f* pigeon, dove; **~ torcaz** ring dove or wood pigeon; **~ mensajera** carrier pigeon, homing pigeon.

palomar *m* pigeon house.

palomilla *f* moth; wing nut; angle iron.

palomino *m* young pigeon.

palomitas *fpl* popcorn.

palpable *adj* palpable, evident.

palpar *vt* to feel, to touch.

palpitación *f* palpitation; panting.

palpitante *adj* palpitating; (*fig*) burning.

palta *f* avocado (pear).

paludismo *m* malaria.

palpitar *vi* to palpitate.

palurdo/da *adj* rustic, clownish, rude.

pampa *f* pampa(s), prairie.

pámpano *m* vine branch.

pamplina *f* trifle.

pan *m* bread; loaf.

pana *f* corduroy.

panacea *f* panacea, universal medicine.

panadería *f* baker's (shop).

panadero/ra *m/f* baker.

panal *m* honeycomb; sweet rusk.

pañal *m* nappy.

pancarta *f* placard.

panda *m* panda.

pandereta *f* tambourine.

pandilla f group; gang; clique.

panegírico/ca adj panegyrical; * m eulogy.

panel m panel.

panfleto m pamphlet.

pánico m panic.

panorama m panorama.

pantalla f screen; lampshade.

pantalón m, pantalones mpl trousers pl, pants pl.

pantano m fen; marsh; reservoir; obstacle, difficulty.

pantanoso/sa adj marshy, fenny, boggy.

panteísta f pantheist.

panteón m: ~ familiar family tomb.

pantera f panther.

pantomima f pantomime.

pantorrilla f calf (of the leg).

pantufla f slipper.

panza f belly, paunch.

panzada f bellyful of food.

panzudo/da adj big-bellied.

pañal m diaper, nappy.

paño m cloth; piece of cloth; duster, rag.

pañuelo m handkerchief.

papa f potato; * m el P~ the Pope.

papá m (fam) dad, pop.

papada f double chin.

papagayo m parrot.

papal adj papal.

papanatas m invar (fam) simpleton.

paparrucha f piece of nonsense.

papaya f papaya, papaw.

papel m paper; writing; part, role (acted in a play); ~ de estraza brown paper; ~ sellado stamped paper.

papeleo m red tape.

papelera f writing desk; wastepaper basket.

papelería f stationer's (shop).

papeleta f slip of paper; ballot paper; report.

paperas fpl mumps.

papilla f baby food.

papista m papist.

paquete m packet; parcel; package tour.

par adj equal; alike; even; * m pair; couple; peer; sin ~ matchless.

para prep for; to, in order to; toward(s).

parabién m congratulation; felicitation.

parábola f parable; parabola.

parabólico/ca adj parabolic(al).

parabrisas m invar windscreen.

paracaídas m invar parachute.

paracaidista m/f parachutist; (mil) paratrooper.

parachoques m invar bumper; shock absorber.

parada f halt; suspension; pause; stop; shutdown; stopping place; ~ a petición request stop; ~ de autobús bus stop.

paradero m halting place; term, end.

parado/da adj motionless; at a standstill; stopped; standing (up); unemployed; * m/f unemployed person.

paradoja f paradox.

parador m parador, state-owned hotel.

parafrasear vt to paraphrase.

paráfrasis f invar paraphrase.

paraguas m invar umbrella.

paraíso m paradise.

paraje m place, spot.

paralelo/la adj, m parallel.

paralítico/ca adj paralytic, palsied.

paralizar vt to paralyse; ~se vr to become paralysed; (fig) to come to a standstill.

páramo *m* desert; wilderness.

parangón *m* paragon, model; comparison.

paranoico/ca *m/f* paranoiac.

parapente *m* paragliding.

parapeto *m* parapet.

parar *vi* to stop, to halt; * *vt* to stop, to detain; **sin ~** instantly, without delay; **~se** *vr* to stop, to halt; to stand up.

pararrayos *m invar* lightning conductor.

parásito *m* parasite; (*fig*) sponger.

parasol *m* parasol.

parcela *f* piece of ground.

parche *m* patch.

parcial *adj* partial.

parcialidad *f* prejudice; bias.

parco/ca *adj* sober, moderate.

pardo/da *adj* gray.

parear *vt* to match, to pair, to couple.

parecer *m* opinion, advice, counsel; countenance; **sin**, mien; * *vi* to appear; to seem; **~se** *vr*: **~ a** to resemble.

parecido/da *adj* resembling, like.

pared *f* wall; **~ medianera** partywall.

pareja *f* pair, couple; timber beam that serves as a support, brace.

parejo/ja *adj* equal; even.

parentela *f* parentage, kindred.

parentesco *m* relationship.

paréntesis *m invar* parenthesis.

parida *f* woman who has recently given birth.

paridad *f* parity, equality.

pariente/ta *m/f* relative, relation.

parir *vt* to give birth to; * *vi* to give birth.

parking *m* car park.

parlamentar *vi* to parley.

parlamentario/ria *m/f* member of parliament; * *adj* parliamentary.

parlamento *m* parliament.

parlanchín/ina *adj*, *m/f* chatterer, jabberer.

parlotear *vi* to prattle, to chatter, to gossip.

paro *m* strike; unemployment.

parodia *f* parody.

parpadear *vi* to blink; to flicker.

párpado *m* eyelid.

parque *m* park; **~ eólico** wind farm.

parque de bomberos *m* .fire station.

parquímetro *m* parking meter.

parra *f* vine raised on stakes or nailed to a wall.

párrafo *m* paragraph.

parricida *m/f* parricide (person).

parricidio *m* parricide (murder).

parrilla *f* grill; grille.

párroco *m* parish priest.

parroquia *f* parish; customers *pl*.

parroquial *adj* parochial.

parroquiano *m* parishioner; customer; **~/na** *adj* parochial.

parsimonia *f* parsimony.

parte *f* message; report; * *f* part; side; party; **de ocho días a esta ~** within these last eight days; **de ~ a ~** from side to side, through and through.

partera *f* midwife.

partición *f* partition, division.

participación *f* participation.

participante *m* participant.

participar *vi* to participate, to partake.

partícipe *m/f* participant.

participio *m* participle.

partícula *f* particle.

particular *adj* particular, special; * *m* private individual; particular matter or subject treated upon.

particularidad f particularity.

particularizar vt, vr to particularize; to distinguish; to specify.

partida f departure; party; item in an account; parcel; game.

partidario/ria adj partisan; * m/f supporter.

partido m party; match; team.

partidor m parter, divider.

partir vt to part; to divide, to separate; to cut; to break; * vi to depart; ~se vr to break (in two, etc).

parto m birth.

parvulario m nursery school.

pasa f raisin.

pasada f passage, passing; **de** ~ on the way, in passing.

pasadizo m narrow passage; narrow, covered way.

pasado/da adj past; bad; overdone; out of date; ~ **mañana** the day after tomorrow; **la semana pasada** last week; * m past.

pasador m bolt; hair slide; grip.

pasaje m passage; fare; passengers pl.

pasajero/ra adj transient; transitory; fugitive; * m/f traveller; passenger.

pasamanos m invar (hand)rail; banister.

pasamontañas m invar balaclava helmet.

pasaporte m passport.

pasar vt to pass; to surpass; to suffer; to strain; to dissemble; * vi to pass; to happen; ~se vr to go over (to another party); to go bad or off.

pasarela f footbridge; gangway.

pasatiempo m pastime, amusement.

Pascua f Passover; Easter.

pase m pass; showing; permit.

paseante m walker.

pasear vt to walk; vi, ~se vr to walk; to walk about.

paseo m walk; shopping mall.

pasillo m passage.

pasión f passion.

pasionaria f passionflower.

pasivo/va adj passive.

pasmar vt to amaze; to numb; to chill; ~se vr to be astonished.

pasmo m astonishment, amazement.

pasmoso/sa adj marvellous, wonderful.

paso m pace, step; passage; manner of walking; flight of steps; accident; (ferro) ~ **a nivel** level crossing; **al** ~ on the way, in passing.

paso de peatones m pedestrian crossing.

pasota adj, m/f (fam) dropout; **ser un** ~ not to care about anything.

pasta f paste; dough; pastry; (fam) dough; ~**s** fpl pastries pl; pasta; ~ **de dientes** toothpaste.

pastar vt to pasture, to graze.

pastel m cake; pie; crayon (for drawing).

pastelería f cake shop.

pasteurizado/da adj pasteurized.

pastilla f bar (of soap); tablet, pill.

pasto m pasture; pasture-ground; **a** ~ abundantly.

pastor m shepherd; pastor.

pastoso/sa adj mellow; doughy.

pata f leg (of animal or furniture); foot; **a la** ~ **coja** hopscotch (children's game); **a** ~ (fam) on foot; **meter la** ~ to put one's foot in it.

patada f kick.

patalear vi to kick violently.

pataleo m act of stamping one's foot.

pataleta f fit; swoon.

patán m clown; churl, countryman.

patata f potato.

patatús m swoon, fainting fit.

paté m pâté.

patear vt to kick; to stamp on.

patente adj patent, manifest, evident; * f patent; warrant.

paternal adj paternal, fatherly.

paternidad f paternity, fatherhood.

paterno/na adj paternal, fatherly.

patético/ca adj pathetic.

patíbulo m gallows.

patillas fpl sideburns pl.

patín m skate; runner.

patinaje m skating.

patinar vi to skate; to skid; (fam) to blunder.

patio m courtyard; playground (in schools).

patizambo/ba adj knock-kneed.

pato m duck.

patochada f blunder, folly; nonsense.

patología f pathology.

patológico/ca adj pathological.

patoso/sa adj (fam) clumsy.

patraña f lie.

patria f native country.

patriarca m patriarch.

patriarcado m patriarchy.

patriarcal adj patriarchal.

patrimonial adj patrimonial.

patrimonio m patrimony.

patrio/tria adj native; paternal.

patriota m/f patriot.

patriótico/ca adj patriotic.

patriotismo m patriotism.

patrocinar vt to sponsor; to back, to support.

patrocinio m sponsorship; backing, support.

patrón/ona m/f boss, master/mistress; landlord/lady; patron saint; * m pattern.

patronal adj: **la clase ~** management.

patronato m patronage, sponsorship; trust, foundation.

patronímico m patronymic.

patrulla f patrol.

patrullar vi to patrol.

paulatino/na adj gradual, slow.

pausa f pause; repose.

pausado/da adj slow, deliberate; calm, quiet.

pausar vi to pause.

pauta f guideline.

pavesa f embers pl, hot cinders pl.

pavía f peach with hard stone.

pavimento m pavement; paving.

pavo m turkey; **~ real** peacock.

pavonearse vr to strut, to walk with affected dignity.

pavor m dread, terror.

pavoroso/sa adj awful, formidable.

payaso/sa m/f clown.

payo/ya m/f non-Gypsy (for a Gypsy).

paz f peace; tranquillity, ease.

peaje m toll.

peana f pedestal; footstool.

peatón m pedestrian.

peca f freckle; spot.

pecado m sin.

pecador/ra m/f sinner.

pecaminoso/sa adj sinful.

pecar vi to sin.

pecho m chest; breast(s) (pl); teat; bosom; (fig) courage, valour; **dar el ~ a** to breast-feed; **tomar a ~** to take to heart.

pechuga f breast (of a fowl); (fam) bosom.

pecoso/sa adj freckled.

peculiar adj peculiar; special.

pecuniario/ria adj pecuniary.

pedagogía f pedagogy.

pedagógico/ca adj pedagogic.

pedagogo/ga *m/f* pedagogue.
pedal *m* pedal.
pedalear *vi* to pedal.
pedante *adj* pedantic; * *m/f* pedant.
pedantería *f* pedantry.
pedazo *m* piece, bit.
pedernal *m* flint.
pedestal *m* pedestal, foot.
pediatra *m/f* pediatrician.
pediatría *f*. paediatrics *pl*.
pedicuro/ra *m/f* chiropodist, podiatrist.
pedido *m* (*com*) order; request.
pedir *vt* to ask for; to petition; to beg; to order; to need; to solicit; * *vi* to ask.
pedo *m* (*fam*) fart (*sl*); **tirarse un ~** to fart (*sl*).
pedrada *f* throw (of a stone).
pedregal *m* stony place.
pedregoso/sa *adj* stony.
pedrería *f* (collection of) precious stones *pl*.
pedrisco *m* hailstone.
pedrusco *m* rough piece of stone.
pegadizo/za *adj* clammy, sticky; catchy; contagious.
pegajoso/sa *adj* sticky, viscous; contagious; attractive.
pegamento *m* glue.
pegar *vt* to cement; to join, to unite; to beat; **~ fuego a** to set fire to; * *vi* to stick; to match; **~se** *vr* to intrude; to steal in.
pegatina *f* sticker.
pegote *m* sticking plaster; intruder; hanger-on, sponger (*sl*).
peinado *m* hairstyle.
peinar *vt* to comb; to style.
peine *m* comb.
peineta *f* convex comb for women.
peladilla *f* sugared almond, burnt almond; small pebble.

pelado/da *adj* peeled; shorn; bare; broke; * *m* (*fam*) haircut.
peladura *f* peeling; plucking.
pelaje *m* fur coat; (*fig*) appearance.
pelar *vt* to cut (hair); to strip off (feathers); to peel; **~se** *vr* to peel off; to have one's hair cut.
peldaño *m* step (of a flight of stairs).
pelea *f* battle, fight; quarrel.
pelear *vt* to fight, to combat; **~se** *vr* to scuffle.
pelele *m* dummy; man of straw.
peletería *f* fur store.
peletero *m* furrier.
peliagudo/da *adj* tricky; arduous, difficult.
pelícano *m* pelican.
película *f* film; pellicle.
peligrar *vi* to be in danger; **~ de** to risk.
peligro *m* danger, peril; risk.
peligroso/sa *adj* dangerous, perilous.
pelirrojo/ja *m/f* redhead; * *adj* redhaired.
pellejo *m* skin; hide, pelt; peel; wine skin, leather bag for wine; oilskin; drunkard.
pelliza *f* fur jacket.
pellizcar *vt* to pinch.
pellizco *m* pinch; nip; small bit; (*fig*) remorse.
pelma/pelmazo/za *m/f* (*fam*) pain (in the neck).
pelo *m* hair; pile; flaw (in precious stones).
pelón/ona *adj* hairless, bald.
pelota *f* ball.
pelotazo *m* blow with a ball.
pelotera *f* quarrel.
pelotón *m* large ball; (*mil*) platoon (in the neck).
peluca *f* wig.
peluche *m*: **muñeco de ~** soft toy.

peludo/da *adj* hairy.

peluquería *f* hairdresser's; barber's (shop).

peluquero/ra *m/f* hairdresser; barber.

pelusa *f* bloom (on fruit); fluff.

pena *f* punishment, pain; **a duras ~s** with great difficulty or trouble.

penacho *m* tuft on the heads of some birds; crest.

penal *adj* penal.

penalidad *f* suffering, trouble; hardship; penalty.

penalti/penalty *m* penalty (kick).

penar *vi* to suffer pain; * *vt* to chastise.

pendencia *f* quarrel, dispute.

pendenciero/ra *adj* quarrelsome.

pender *vi* to hang; to be pending; to depend.

pendiente *f* slope, declivity; * *m* earring; * *adj* pending; unsettled.

pendón *m* standard; banner.

péndulo *m* pendulum.

pene *m* penis.

penetración *f* penetration; perception.

penetrante *adj* deep; sharp; piercing; searching; biting.

penetrar *vt* to penetrate.

penicilina *f* penicillin.

península *f* peninsula.

penique *m* penny.

penitencia *f* penitence; penalty, fine.

penitenciaría *f* prison.

penitente *adj* penitent, repentant; * *m* penitent.

penoso/sa *adj* painful.

pensador/ra *m/f* thinker.

pensamiento *m* thought, thinking.

pensar *vi* to think.

pensativo/va *adj* pensive, thoughtful.

pensión *f* guest-house; pension; worry; regret.

pensionista *m/f* pensioner; lodger.

Pentecostés *m* Pentecost, Whitsuntide.

penúltimo/ma *adj* penultimate, last but one.

penumbra *f* half-light.

penuria *f* penury, poverty, neediness, extreme want.

peña *f* rock, large stone.

peñasco *m* large rock.

peñón *m* rocky mountain.

peón *m* (day)labourer; foot soldier; pawn (at chess).

peonía *f* (*bot*) peony.

peonza *f* spinning top.

peor *adj*, *adv* worse; **cada vez ~** worse and worse.

pepinillo *m* gherkin.

pepino *m* cucumber.

pepita *f* kernel; pip.

pepitoria *f* fricassee.

pequeñez *f* smallness; childhood, infancy; triviality.

pequeño/ña *adj* little, small; young.

pera *f* pear.

peral *m* pear tree.

percance *m* perquisite; bad luck, setback.

percatarse *vr:* **~ de** to notice.

percepción *f* perception; notion.

perceptible *adj* perceptible, perceivable.

percha *f* coat hook; coat hanger; perch.

percibir *vt* to receive; to perceive, to comprehend.

percusión *f* percussion.

perder *vt* to lose; to waste; to miss; **~se** *vr* to go astray; to be lost; to be spoiled.

perdición *f* loss, losing; perdition, ruin.

pérdida *f* loss, damage; lost object.

perdido/da adj lost; stray.

perdigón m young partridge; ~ones mpl buckshot, pellets.

perdiz f partridge.

perdón m pardon; mercy; ¡~! sorry!; excuse me!

perdonable adj pardonable.

perdonar vt to pardon, to forgive; to excuse.

perdurable adj perpetual, everlasting.

perdurar vi to last; to still exist.

perecedero/ra adj perishable.

perecer vi to perish, to die; to shatter (an object).

peregrinación f pilgrimage.

peregrinar vi to go on a pilgrimage.

peregrino/na adj (fig) strange; * m/f pilgrim.

perejil m parsley.

perenne adj perennial; perpetual.

perentorio/ria adj peremptory; urgent.

pereza f laziness, idleness.

perezoso/sa adj lazy, idle.

perfección f perfection.

perfeccionar vt to perfect; to complete, to finish.

perfecto/ta adj perfect; complete.

perfidia f perfidy.

pérfido/da adj perfidious.

perfil m profile.

perfilado/da adj well-formed, delicate (of features).

perfilar vt to outline; ~se vr: ~ en to show up against.

perforar vt to perforate; to drill; to punch a hole in; * vi to drill.

perfumador m perfumer.

perfumar vt to perfume.

perfume m perfume.

perfumería f perfumery.

pergamino m parchment.

pericia f skill, knowledge; expertise.

periferia f periphery; outskirts pl.

periférico m ring-road.

perifrasis f invar periphrasis, circumlocution.

perímetro m perimeter; circumference.

periódico/ca adj periodical; * m newspaper.

periodista m/f journalist.

período, periodo m period.

peripecia f vicissitude; sudden change.

peripuesto/ta adj dressed up, very spruce.

periquito m budgie.

perito/ta adj skilful, experienced; * m/f expert; skilled worker; technician.

perjudicar vt to prejudice, to damage; to injure, to hurt.

perjudicial adj prejudicial, damaging.

perjuicio m damage, harm.

perjurar vi to perjure, to swear falsely; to swear.

perjurio m perjury; false oath.

perjuro/ra adj perjured; * m/f perjurer.

perla f pearl; **de ~s** fine.

permanecer vi to stay; to continue to be.

permanencia f permanence; stay.

permanente adj permanent.

permiso m permission, leave, licence.

permitir vt to permit, to allow.

permuta f permutation, exchange.

permutar vt to exchange, to permute.

pernera f trouser leg.

pernicioso/sa adj pernicious, destructive; wicked.

pernio m hinge.

perno m bolt.

pernoctar vi to spend the night.

pero m kind of apple; * conj but, yet.

perogrullada f truism, platitude.

perol m large metal pan.

perorata f harangue, speech.

perpendicular adj perpendicular.

perpetrar vt to perpetrate, to commit (a crime).

perpetuar vt to perpetuate.

perpetuidad f perpetuity.

perpetuo/tua adj perpetual.

perplejidad f perplexity.

perplejo/ja adj perplexed.

perra f bitch; (fam) money.

perrera f kennel.

perro m dog.

persecución f persecution; toil, trouble; fatigue.

perseguidor m persecutor.

perseguir vt to pursue; to persecute; to chase after.

perseverancia f perseverance, constancy.

perseverante adj persistent.

perseverar vi to persevere, to persist.

persiana f (Venetian) blind.

persignarse vr to make the sign of the cross.

persistencia f persistence; steadiness.

persistir vi to persist.

persona f person; **de ~ a ~** from person to person.

personaje m personage; character.

personal adj personal; single; * m personnel.

personalidad f personality.

personarse vr to appear in person.

personificar vt to personify.

perspectiva f perspective; view; outlook.

perspicacia f perspicacity, clear-sightedness.

perspicaz adj perspicacious, clear-sighted.

persuadir vt to persuade; **~se** vr to be persuaded.

persuasión f persuasion.

persuasivo/va adj persuasive.

pertenecer vi: **~ a** to belong to; to appertain, to concern.

pertenencia f ownership; **~s** fpl possessions pl.

perteneciente adj: **~ a** belonging to.

pértiga f long pole or rod.

pertinacia f pertinacity; obstinacy, stubbornness.

pertinaz adj pertinacious; obstinate.

pertinente adj relevant; appropriate.

pertrechar vt to supply with ammunition and other warlike stores; to dispose; to arrange, to prepare; **~se** vr to be provided with the necessary defensive stores and arms.

pertrechos mpl tools pl, instruments pl; ammunition.

perturbación f perturbation; disturbance.

perturbado/da adj mentally unbalanced.

perturbador m disturber.

perturbar vt to perturb, to disturb.

perversidad f perversity.

perversión f perversion; depravation, corruption.

perverso/sa adj perverse; extremely wicked.

pervertido/da adj perverted; * m/f pervert.

pervertir vt to pervert; to corrupt.

pesa f weight.

pesadez f heaviness; weight; gravity; slowness; peevishness, fretfulness; trouble; fatigue.

pesadilla f nightmare.
pesado/da adj peevish; troublesome; cumbersome; tedious; heavy, weighty.
pesadumbre f weightiness; gravity; quarrel, dispute; grief; trouble.
pésame m message of condolence.
pesar m sorrow, grief; repentance; **a ~ de** in spite of, notwithstanding; * vi to weigh; to repent; * vt to weigh.
pesario m pessary.
pesaroso/sa adj sorrowful, full of repentance; restless, uneasy.
pesca f fishing.
pescadería f fish market, fishmonger, fish shop.
pescado m fish (in general).
pescador m fisher, fisherman.
pescar vt to fish for, to catch (fish); * vi to fish.
pescuezo m neck.
pesebre m crib, manger.
peseta f peseta.
pesimista m pessimist.
pésimo/ma adj very bad.
peso m weight, heaviness; balance scales pl.
pespunte m back-stitching.
pesquero/ra adj fishing compd.
pesquisa f inquiry, examination.
pestaña f eyelash.
pestañear vi to blink.
pestañeo m blink.
peste f pest, plague, pestilence.
pesticida m pesticide.
pestífero/ra adj pestilential.
pestilencia f pestilence.
pestillo m bolt.
petaca f covered hamper; tobacco pouch.
pétalo m petal.
petardo m cheat, fraud; imposition.
petate m straw bed; sleeping mat of the Indians; (mar) sailors' bedding on board ship; (mar) passengers' baggage; poor fellow.
petición f petition, demand.
peto m breastplate; bodice.
petrificar(se) vt (vr) to petrify.
petróleo m oil, petroleum.
petrolero/ra adj petroleum compd; * m (oil) tanker; (com) oil man.
petulancia f petulance; insolence.
petulante adj petulant; insolent.
peyorativo/va adj pejorative.
pez[1] m fish.
pez[2] f pitch.
pezón m nipple.
pezuña f hoof.
piadoso/sa adj pious; mild; merciful; moderate.
pianista m/f pianist.
piano m piano.
piar vi to squeak; to chirp.
piara f herd (of swine); flock (of sheep).
pibe/ba m/f boy/girl.
pica f pike.
picacho m sharp point.
picadero m riding school.
picadillo m minced meat.
picado/da adj pricked; minced, chopped; bad (tooth); cross.
picador m riding master; picador.
picadura f prick; puncture.
picante adj hot, spicy; racy.
picapedrero m stonecutter.
picaporte m door handle; latch.
picar vt to prick; to sting; to mince; to nibble; * vi to prick; to sting; to itch; **~se** vr to be piqued; to take offence; to be moth-eaten; to begin to rot.
picardía f roguery; deceit; malice; lewdness.
picaresco/ca adj roguish; picaresque.

pícaro/ra adj roguish; mischievous; malicious; sly; * m/f rogue, knave.

picazón f itching; stinging; displeasure.

pichón m young pigeon.

pico m beak; bill, nib; peak; pickaxe.

picotazo m peck (of a bird).

picotear vt to peck (of birds).

picudo/da adj with a beak; sharp-pointed.

pie m foot; leg; basis; trunk (of trees); foundation; occasion; a ~ on foot.

piedad f piety; mercy, pity.

piedra f stone.

piel f skin; hide; peel.

pienso m fodder.

pierna f leg.

pieza f piece; room.

pigmeo/mea m/f, adj pigmy.

pijama m pyjamas pl.

pila f battery; trough; font; sink; pile, heap; nombre de ~ first name.

pilar' m basin.

pilar m pillar, column; pillar box; mainstay.

píldora f pill.

pileta f basin; swimming pool.

pillaje m pillage, plunder.

pillar vt to pillage, to plunder; to foray, to seize; to catch onto; to catch.

pillo/lla m, adj rascal, scoundrel.

pilotaje m pilotage.

piloto m pilot.

piltrafa f piece of meat that is nearly all skin.

pimentón m paprika.

pimienta f pepper.

pimiento m pepper, pimiento.

pinacoteca f art gallery.

pináculo m pinnacle.

pinar m grove of pines.

pincel m paintbrush.

pincelada f dash with a paintbrush.

pinchar vt to prick; to puncture.

pinchazo m prick; puncture; (fig) prod.

pinchito m small snack.

pincho m thorn; snack.

pingajo m rag, tatter.

ping-pong m table tennis.

pingüe adj fat, greasy; fertile.

pingüino m penguin.

pino m (bot) pine.

pinta f spot, blemish; scar; mark (on playing cards); pint.

pintado/da adj painted, mottled; venir ~ to fit exactly.

pintar vt to paint; to picture; to describe; to exaggerate; * vi to paint; (fam) to count, to be important; ~se vr to put on make-up.

pintarrajear vt to daub.

pintarrajo m daub.

pintor/ra m/f painter.

pintoresco/ca adj picturesque.

pintura f painting.

pinza f claw; clothes peg; pincers pl; ~s fpl tweezers pl.

piña f pineapple; fir cone; group.

piñón m pine nut; pinion.

pío/pía adj pious, devout; merciful.

piojo m louse; troublesome hanger-on.

piojoso/sa adj lousy; miserable, stingy.

pionero/ra adj pioneering; m/f pioneer.

pipa f pipe; sunflower seed.

pipí m (fam): hacer ~ to have to go (wee-wee).

pique m pique, offence taken; rivalry; echar a ~ to sink a ship; a ~ in danger; a ~ de on the point of.

piquete m slight prick or sting; picket.

pira f funeral pyre.

piragua f canoe.

piragüismo m canoeing.

piramidal adj pyramidal.

pirámide f pyramid.

pirata m pirate.

piropo m compliment; flattery.

pirotecnia f fireworks pl.

pirueta f pirouette.

pisada f footstep; footprint.

pisar vt to tread, to trample; to stamp on (the ground); to hammer down; * vi to tread, to walk.

piscina f swimming pool; ~ **para niños** paddling pool.

Piscis m Pisces (sign of the zodiac).

piso m flat, apartment; tread, trampling; floor, pavement; floor, storey.

pisotear vt to trample, to tread under foot.

pista f trace, footprint; clue.

pisto m thick broth.

pistola f pistol.

pistolera f pistol holster.

pistolero/ra m/f gunman/woman, gangster.

pistoletazo m pistol shot.

pistón m piston; (musical) key.

pita f (bot) any plant of the family Agavaceae with tall flowers and thick, fleshy leaves.

pitar vt to blow; to whistle at; * vi to whistle; to toot one's horn; to smoke.

pitillo m cigarette.

pito m whistle; horn.

pitón m python.

pitonisa f sorceress, enchantress.

pitorreo m joke; **estar de** ~ to be joking.

pizarra f slate.

pizarral m slate quarry, slate pit.

pizca f mite; pinch.

placa f plate; badge; ~ **de matrícula** numberplate.

placentero/ra adj joyful, merry.

placer m pleasure; delight; * vt to please.

plácido/da adj placid.

plaga f plague.

plagar vt to plague, to torment.

plagio m plagiarism.

plan m plan; design; plot.

plana f trowel; page (of a book); level; ~ **mayor** (mil) staff.

plancha f plate; iron; gangway; press-up.

planchar vt to iron.

planchuela n nameplate f.

planeador m glider.

planear vt to plan; * vi to glide.

planeta m planet.

planetario/ria adj planetary.

planicie f plain.

planificación f planning; ~ **familiar** family planning.

plano/na adj plain, level, flat; * m plan; ground plot; ~ **inclinado** (ferro) dead level.

planta f plant; plantation.

plantación f plantation.

plantar vt to plant; to fix upright; to strike or hit (a blow); to found; to establish; ~**se** vr to stand upright.

plantear vt to plan; to implant.

plantilla f personnel; insole of a shoe.

plantón m long wait; (mil) sentry.

plañir vi to lament, to grieve, to bewail.

plasmar vt to mould; to represent.

plasta f paste, soft clay; mess.

plástico/ca adj plastic; * m plastic; f (art of) sculpture.

plata f silver; plate (wrought silver); cash; **en** ~ briefly.

plataforma f platform; ~ **giratoria** (ferro) turntable.

plátano m banana; plane tree.

plateado/da adj silvered; plated.

platería f silversmith's shop; trade of silversmith.

plática f discourse, conversation.

platicar vi to converse.

platillo m saucer; ~s mpl cymbals pl; ~ volador, ~ volante flying saucer.

platino m platinum; ~s mpl contact points pl.

plato m dish; plate.

platónico/ca adj platonic.

plausible adj plausible.

playa f beach.

playera f T-shirt; ~s fpl canvas shoes pl.

plaza f square; place; office, employment; room; seat.

plazo m term; instalment; expiry date.

pleamar f (mar) high water.

plebe f common people pl, populace.

plebeyo/ya adj plebeian; * m commoner.

plebiscito m plebiscite.

plegable adj pliable; folding.

plegar vt to fold; to plait.

plegaria f prayer.

pleitear vi to plead, to litigate.

pleito m contract, bargain; dispute, controversy, debate; lawsuit.

plenamente adv fully; completely.

plenario/ria adj complete; full.

plenilunio m full moon.

plenipotenciario m plenipotentiary.

plenitud f fullness; abundance.

pleno/na adj full; complete; * m plenum.

pliego m sheet of paper.

pliegue m fold; plait.

plisado/da adj pleated; * m pleating.

plomero m plumber.

plomizo/za adj leaden.

plomo m lead; a ~ perpendicularly.

pluma f feather, plume.

plumaje m plumage; plume.

plumero m bunch of feathers; feather duster.

plumón m felt-tip pen; marker; down.

plural adj (gr) plural.

pluralidad f plurality.

Plutón m Pluto (planet).

población f population; town.

poblado m town; village; inhabited place.

poblador/ra m/f populator, founder.

poblar vt to populate, to people; to fill, to occupy.

pobre adj poor.

pobreza f poverty, poorness.

pocilga f pig sty.

pocillo m coffee cup.

pócima, poción f potion.

poco/ca adj little, scanty; (pl) few; * adv little; ~ a ~ gently; little by little; * m small part; little.

poda f pruning (of trees).

podadera f pruning knife.

podar vt to prune.

podenco m hound.

poder m power, authority; command; force; * vi to be able to; to possess the power of doing or performing.

poderío m power, authority; wealth, riches pl.

poderoso/sa adj powerful; eminent, excellent.

podredumbre f putrid matter; grief.

podrido/da adj rotten, bad; (fig) rotten.

podrir vt to rot, to putrefy; ~se vr to rot, to decay.

poema m poem.

poesía f poetry.
poeta m poet.
poético/ca adj poetical.
poetisa f poetess.
poetizar vt to poetize.
polar adj polar.
polea f pulley; (mar) tackle-block.
polémica f polemic.
polémico/ca adj polemical.
polen m pollen.
policía f police; * m/f policeman/woman.
polideportivo m sports centre.
poligamia f polygamy.
polígamo m polygamist.
polígono m polygon.
polilla f moth.
polio f polio.
pólipo m polypus.
politécnico/ca adj polytechnic.
politeísmo m polytheism.
política f politics; policy.
político/ca adj political; * m/f politician.
póliza f written order; policy.
polizón m stowaway.
pollera f skirt.
pollería f poulterer's (shop).
pollo m chicken.
polo m pole; ice lolly; polo; polo neck.
polución f pollution.
polvareda f cloud of dust.
polvera f powder compact.
polvo m powder, dust.
pólvora f gunpowder.
polvoriento/ta adj dusty.
polvorín m powder reduced to the finest dust; powder flask.
pomada f cream, ointment.
pomelo m grapefruit.
pómez f: **piedra ~** pumice stone.
pompa f pomp; bubble.

pomposo/sa adj pompous.
pómulo m cheekbone.
ponche m punch.
poncho/cha adj soft, mild; * m poncho.
ponderación f pondering, considering; exaggeration.
ponderar vt to ponder, to weigh; to exaggerate.
ponedero/ra adj egg-laying; capable of being laid or placed; * m nest; nest egg.
poner vt to put, to place; to put on; to impose; to lay (eggs); **~se** vr to oppose; to set (of stars); to become.
poniente m west; west wind.
pontificado m pontificate.
pontífice m Pope, pontiff.
pontificio/cia adj pontifical.
pontón m pontoon.
ponzoña f poison.
ponzoñoso/sa adj poisonous.
popa f (mar) poop, stern.
populacho m populace, mob.
popular adj popular.
popularidad f popularity.
popularizarse vr to become popular.
populoso/sa adj populous.
poquedad f paucity, smallness; cowardice.
por prep for; by; about; by means of; through; on account of.
porcelana f porcelain, china.
porcentaje m percentage.
porción f part, portion; lot.
porcuno/na adj hoggish.
pordiosero/ra m/f beggar.
porfiar vt to dispute obstinately; to persist in a pursuit.
pormenor m detail.
pornografía f pornography.
poro m pore.

porosidad f porosity.

poroso/sa adj porous.

porque conj because; since; so that.

porqué m cause, reason.

porquería f nastiness, foulness; brutishness, rudeness; trifle; dirty action.

porqueriza f pig sty.

porra f cudgel.

porrillo: a ~ adv copiously, abundantly.

porrón m spouted wine jar.

portada f portal, porch; frontispiece.

portador/ra m/f carrier, porter.

portaequipajes m invar boot (in car); baggage rack.

portal m porch; portal.

portamonedas m invar purse.

portarse vr to behave.

portátil adj portable; * m laptop..

portaaviones m invar aircraft carrier.

portavoz m/f spokesman/woman.

portazo m bang of a door; banging a door in one's face.

porte m transportation (charges pl); deportment, demeanour, conduct.

portento m prodigy, portent.

portentoso/sa adj prodigious, marvellous, strange.

portería f porter's office; goal.

portero/ra m/f porter; caretaker; gatekeeper; goalkeeper.

portezuela f little door.

pórtico m portico, porch, lobby.

portilla f, **portillo** m aperture in a wall; gate; gap, breach.

portón m main door (of a house).

porvenir m future.

pos prep: **en ~ de** after, behind; in pursuit of.

posada f shelter; inn, hotel.

posaderas fpl buttocks pl.

posadero m innkeeper.

posar vi to sit, to pose; * vt to lay down (a burden); ~**se** vr to settle; to perch; to land.

posdata f postscript.

pose f pose.

poseedor/ra m/f owner, possessor; holder.

poseer vt to hold, to possess.

poseído/da adj possessed by the devil.

posesión f possession.

posesivo/va adj possessive.

posesor/ra m/f possessor.

posibilidad f possibility.

posibilitar vt to make possible; to make feasible.

posible adj possible.

posición f position; posture; situation.

positivo/va adj positive.

poso m sediment, dregs pl.

posponer vt to postpone.

posta f: **a ~** on purpose.

postal adj postal; * f postcard.

poste m post, pillar.

póster m poster.

postergación f missing out, passing over; putting over.

postergar vt to leave behind; to postpone.

posteridad f posterity.

posterior adj posterior.

posterioridad f: **con ~** subsequently, later.

postigo m wicket; postern; pane or sash of a window.

postizo/za adj artificial (not natural); * m wig.

postor m bidder at a public sale; better.

postración f prostration.

postrar vt to humble, to humiliate; ~**se** vr to prostrate oneself.

postre *m* dessert.

postrer(o)/ra *adj* last, hindmost.

postrimerías *fpl* dying moments *pl*; final stages *pl*.

póstumo/ma *adj* posthumous.

postura *f* posture, position; attitude; bet, wager; agreement, convention.

potable *adj* drinkable.

potaje *m* pottage; drink made up of several ingredients; medley of various useless things.

pote *m* pot, jar; flower pot.

potencia *f* power; mightiness.

potencial *m* potential.

potentado *m* potentate; prince.

potente *adj* potent, powerful, mighty.

potestad *f* power; dominion; jurisdiction.

potro/ra *m/f* colt; foal.

poyo *m* bench (near street door).

pozo *m* well.

práctica *f* practice.

practicable *adj* practicable, feasible.

practicante *adj* practising; * *m/f* practitioner.

practicar *vt* to practise.

práctico/ca *adj* practical; skilful, experienced.

pradera *f* meadow.

prado *m* lawn; meadow.

pragmático/ca *adj* pragmatic.

preámbulo *m* preamble; circumlocution.

prebenda *f* prebend.

precampaña *f* run-up to the election campaign.

precario/ria *adj* precarious.

precaución *f* precaution.

precaver *vt* to prevent; to guard against.

precedencia *f* precedence; preference; superiority.

precedente *adj* preceding, foregoing.

preceder *vt* to precede, to go before.

precepto *m* precept, order.

preceptor/ra *m/f* master, teacher, preceptor.

preciado/da *adj* esteemed, valued.

preciarse *vr* to boast; ~ **de** to take pride in.

precinto *m* seal.

precio *m* price; value.

preciosidad *f* excellence; preciousness.

precioso/sa *adj* precious; (*fam*) beautiful.

precipicio *m* precipice; violent, sudden fall; ruin, destruction.

precipitación *f* precipitation, rush.

precipitado/da *adj* precipitate, headlong, hasty.

precipitar *vt* to precipitate; ~**se** *vr* to act hastily; to rush.

precisamente *adv* precisely; exactly.

precisar *vt* to compel, to oblige; to need.

precisión *f* necessity, compulsion; preciseness.

preciso/sa *adj* necessary, requisite; precise, exact; abstracted.

precocidad *f* precocity.

preconizar *vt* to proclaim; to recommend.

precoz *adj* precocious.

precursor/ra *m/f* harbinger, forerunner.

predecesor/ra *m/f* predecessor.

predecir *vt* to foretell.

predestinación *f* predestination.

predestinar *vt* to predestine.

predicación *f* preaching; sermon.

predicado *m* predicate.

predicador *m* preacher.

predicar *vt* to preach.

predicción f prediction.
predilección f predilection.
predilecto/ta adj darling, favourite.
predisponer vt to predispose; to prejudice.
predisposición f inclination; prejudice.
predominar vi to predominate, to prevail.
predominio m predominant power, superiority.
preeminencia f pre-eminence; superiority.
preeminente adj pre-eminent; superior.
preescolar adj pre-school.
preexistencia f pre-existence.
preexistente adj pre-existent.
preexistir vt to pre-exist, to exist before.
prefabricado/da adj prefabricated.
prefacio m preface.
prefecto m prefect.
prefectura f prefecture.
preferencia f preference.
preferible adj preferable.
preferir vt to prefer.
prefijar vt (gr) to prefix; to fix beforehand.
prefijo m dialling code.
pregón m proclamation; hue and cry.
pregonar vt to proclaim.
pregonero m town crier.
pregunta f question; inquiry.
preguntar vt to ask; to question; to demand; to inquire.
preguntón/ona m/f inquisitive person.
prehistórico/ca adj prehistoric.
prejuicio m prejudgement; preconception; prejudice.
prelado m prelate.
preliminar adj, m preliminary.

preludio m prelude.
prematuro/ra adj premature.
premeditación f premeditation, forethought.
premeditar vt to premeditate, to think out.
premiar vt to reward, to remunerate.
premio m reward, recompense; premium.
premisa f premise.
premura f pressure, haste, hurry.
prenatal adj pre-natal.
prenda f pledge; garment; sweetheart; person or thing dearly loved; ~**s** fpl accomplishments pl, talents pl.
prendar vt to enchant; ~**se** vr: ~ **de** to fall in love with.
prendedor m brooch.
prender vt to seize, to catch, to lay hold of; to imprison; ~**se** vr to catch fire; * vi to take root.
prendimiento m seizure; capture.
prensa f press.
prensar vt to press.
preñado/da adj pregnant.
preñez f pregnancy.
preocupación f worry, preoccupation.
preocupado/da adj worried, anxious.
preocupar(se) vt (vr) to worry.
preparación f preparation.
preparador/ra m/f trainer.
preparar vt to prepare; ~**se** vr to be prepared.
preparativo/va adj preparatory; preliminary; qualifying; * m preparation.
preparatorio/ria adj preparatory.
preponderancia f preponderance.
preponderar vi to preponderate, to prevail.
preposición f (gr) preposition.
prepucio m foreskin.

prerrogativa f prerogative, privilege.
presa f capture, seizure; dike, dam.
presagiar vt to presage, to forebode.
presagio m omen.
presbítero m priest, clergyman.
presciencia f prescience, fore-knowledge.
prescindir vi: ~ **de** to do without; to dispense with.
prescribir vt to prescribe.
prescripción f prescription.
presencia f presence.
presenciar vt to attend; to be present at; to witness.
presentación f presentation.
presentador/ra m/f (rad, TV) presenter; compere.
presentar vt to present; to introduce; to offer; to show; ~**se** vr to present oneself; to appear; to run (as candidate); to apply.
presente m present, gift; * adj present.
presentemente adv presently, now.
presentimiento m presentiment.
presentir vt to have a premonition of.
preservación f preservation.
preservar vt to preserve; to defend.
preservativo m condom, sheath.
presidencia f presidency.
presidente/ta m/f president.
presidiario/ria m/f convict.
presidio m penitentiary, prison.
presidir vt to preside at.
presilla f clip; loop (in clothes).
presión f pressure, pressing; ~ **de los neumáticos** tyre pressure.
presionar vt to press; (fig) to put pressure on.
preso/sa m/f prisoner.
prestado/da adj on loan; **pedir** ~ to borrow.

prestamista m borrower, lender.
préstamo m loan.
prestar vt to lend.
presteza f quickness; haste, speed.
prestigio m prestige.
presto/ta adj quick; prompt; ready; * adv soon; quickly.
presumible adj presumable.
presumido/da adj presumptuous, arrogant.
presumir vt to presume, to conjecture; * vi to be conceited.
presunción f presumption, conjecture; conceit.
presunto/ta adj supposed; so-called.
presuntuoso/sa adj presumptuous.
presuponer vt to presuppose.
presupuesto m estimate; budget.
presuroso/sa adj hasty, quick; prompt; nimble.
pretencioso/sa adj pretentious.
pretender vt to pretend, to claim; to try, to attempt.
pretendiente m pretender; suitor.
pretensión f pretension.
pretérito/ta adj past.
pretextar vt to plead, use as an excuse.
pretexto m pretext, pretence; plea, excuse.
prevalecer vi to prevail; to triumph; to take root.
prevención f disposition, preparation; supply of provisions; foresight; prevention; (mil) police guard.
prevenido/da adj prepared; careful, cautious; foreseeing.
prevenir vt to prepare; to foresee; to know in advance; to prevent; to warn; ~**se** vr to be prepared; to be predisposed.
preventivo/va adj preventive.
prever vt to foresee, to forecast.
previo/via adj previous.

previsión f foresight, prevision; forecast.

previsor/ra adj far-sighted.

prima f bonus; (female) cousin.

primacía f priority; primacy.

primado m primate.

primario/ria adj primary.

primavera f spring (the season).

primeramente adv in the first place, mainly.

primer adj = **primero.**

primer(o)/ra adj first; prior; former; * adv first; rather, sooner.

primicias fpl first fruits pl.

primitivo/va adj primitive; original.

primo/ma m cousin.

primogénito/ta adj, m/f first-born.

primogenitura f primogeniture.

primor m beauty; dexterity, ability.

primordial adj basic, fundamental.

primoroso/sa adj neat, elegant; fine, excellent; handsome.

princesa f princess.

principal adj; m principal, chief.

príncipe m prince.

principiante m beginner, learner.

principiar vt, vi to commence, to begin.

principio m beginning, commencement; principle.

pringoso/sa adj greasy; sticky.

pringue m/f grease; lard; dripping.

prioridad f priority.

prisa f speed; hurry; urgency; promptness.

prisión f prison; imprisonment.

prisionero m prisoner.

prisma m prism.

prismáticos mpl binoculars pl.

privación f deprivation, want.

privado/da adj private; particular.

privar vt to deprive; to prohibit; ~se vr to deprive oneself.

privativo/va adj private, one's own; particular, peculiar.

privilegiado/da adj privileged; very good.

privilegiar vt to privilege.

privilegio m privilege.

pro m/f profit; benefit; advantage.

proa f (mar) prow.

probabilidad f probability, likelihood.

probable adj probable, likely.

probado/da adj proved, tried.

probador m fitting room.

probar vt to try; to prove; to taste; * vi to try.

probeta f test tube.

problema m problem.

problemático/ca adj problematic.

procedencia f derivation.

procedente adj reasonable; proper; ~ de coming from.

proceder m procedure; * vi to proceed, to go on; to act.

procedimiento m proceeding; legal procedure.

procesado/da m/f accused.

procesador m: ~ de textos word processor.

procesar vt to put on trial.

procesión f procession.

proceso m process; lawsuit.

proclama f proclamation, publication.

proclamación f proclamation; acclamation.

proclamar vt to proclaim.

procreación f procreation, generation.

procrear vt to procreate, to generate.

procurador/ra m/f procurer; attorney; solicitor.

procurar vt to try; to obtain; to produce.

prodigalidad f plenty, abundance.

prodigar vt to waste, to lavish.

prodigio *m* prodigy; monster.

prodigioso/sa *adj* prodigious, monstrous; exquisite; excellent.

pródigo/ga *adj* prodigal.

producción *f* production.

producir *vt* to produce; (*jur*) to produce as evidence; **~se** *vr* to come about; to arise; to be made; to break out.

productividad *f* productivity.

productivo/va *adj* productive.

producto *m* product.

productor/ra *adj* productive; * *m/f* producer.

proeza *f* prowess, valour, bravery.

profanación *f* desecration.

profanar *vt* to profane, to desecrate.

profano/na *adj* profane.

profecía *f* prophecy.

profesar *vt* to profess, to practise.

profesión *f* profession.

profesional *adj*, *m/f* professional.

profeso/sa *adj* professed.

profesor/ra *m/f* teacher; lecturer.

profesorado *m* teaching profession.

profeta *m* prophet.

profético/ca *adj* prophetic.

profetizar *vt* to prophesy.

prófugo/ga *m/f* fugitive.

profundidad *f* profundity, profoundness; depth; grandeur.

profundizar *vt* to go deeply into; to deepen; to penetrate.

profundo/da *adj* profound.

profusamente *adv* profusely.

profusión *f* profusion; prodigality.

progenie *f* progeny, offspring; race; generation.

progenitor *m* progenitor, ancestor, forefather.

programa *m* program(me).

programación *f* computer programming.

programador/ra *m/f* programmer.

programar *vt* to program(me).

progresar *vi* to progress.

progresión *f* progression.

progresista *adj*, *m/f* progressive.

progreso *m* progress.

progresivo/va *adj* progressive.

prohibición *f* prohibition, ban.

prohibir *vt* to prohibit, to forbid; to hinder.

prójimo *m* fellow creature; neighbour.

prole *f* offspring, progeny; race.

proletariado *m* proletariat.

proletario/ria *adj* proletarian.

proliferación *f* proliferation.

proliferar *vi* to proliferate.

prolífico/ca *adj* prolific.

prolijidad *f* prolixity; minute attention to detail.

prolijo/ja *adj* prolix; tedious.

prólogo *m* prologue.

prolongación *f* prolongation.

prolongar *vt* to prolong.

promedio *m* average; middle.

promesa *f* promise.

prometer *vt* to promise; to assure; **~se** *vr* to become engaged.

prometido/da *adj* promised; engaged; * *m/f* fiancé/fiancée.

prominencia *f* protuberance.

prominente *adj* prominent, jutting out.

promiscuo/cua *adj* promiscuous; confusedly mingled; ambiguous.

promoción *f* promotion.

promontorio *m* promontory, cape.

promotor *m* promoter.

promover *vt* to promote, to advance; to stir up.

promulgación *f* promulgation.

promulgar *vt* to promulgate, to publish.

pronombre m (gr) pronoun.

pronosticar vt to predict, to foretell; to conjecture.

pronóstico m prediction; forecast.

prontitud f promptness.

pronto/ta adj prompt; ready; * adv promptly.

pronunciación f pronunciation.

pronunciamiento m (jur) publication; insurrection, sedition.

pronunciar vt to pronounce; to deliver; ~**se** vr to rebel.

propagación f propagation; extension.

propagador/ra m/f propagator.

propaganda f propaganda; advertising.

propagar vt to propagate.

propasar vt to go beyond, to exceed.

propender vi to incline.

propensión f propensity, inclination.

propenso/sa adj prone, inclined.

propiamente adv properly; really.

propiciar vt to favour; to cause.

propiciatorio/ria adj propitiatory.

propicio/cia adj propitious.

propiedad f property, possessions pl; right of property; propriety.

propietario/ria adj proprietary; * m/f proprietor.

propina f tip.

propinar vt to hit; to give.

propio/pia adj proper; own; typical; very.

proponer vt to propose.

proporción f proportion; symmetry.

proporcionado/da adj proportionate; fit; **bien** ~ well-proportioned.

proporcional adj proportional.

proporcionar vt to provide; to adjust, to adapt.

proposición f proposition.

propósito m aim, purpose; **a** ~ on purpose.

propuesta f proposal, offer; representation.

propulsar vt to propel; (fig) to promote.

prórroga f prolongation; extension; extra time.

prorrogable adj extendable.

prorrogar vt to extend; to postpone.

prorrumpir vi to break forth, to burst forth.

prosa f prose.

prosaico/ca adj prosaic.

proscribir vt to proscribe, to outlaw.

proscripción f proscription.

proscrito/ta adj banned.

prosecución f continuation.

proseguir vt to continue; * vi to continue, to go on.

prospección f exploration; prospecting.

prospecto m prospectus.

prosperar vi to prosper, to thrive.

prosperidad f prosperity.

próspero/ra adj prosperous.

prostíbulo m brothel.

prostitución f prostitution.

prostituir vt to prostitute.

prostituta f prostitute.

protagonista m/f protagonist.

protagonizar vt to take the chief role in.

protección f protection.

protector m to protect.

proteger vt to protector.

proteína f protein.

protesta f protest.

protestante m/f Protestant.

protestar vt to protest; to make public declaration (of faith); * vi to protest.

protocolo m protocol.

prototipo m prototype.

provecho m profit; advantage.

provechoso/sa adj profitable; advantageous.

proveedor/ra m/f purveyor.

proveer vt to provide; to provision; to decree.

provenir vi to arise, to originate; to issue.

proverbial adj proverbial.

proverbio m proverb; **~s** mpl Book of Proverbs.

providencia f providence; foresight; divine providence.

providencial adj providential.

provincia f province.

provincial adj, m provincial.

provinciano/na adj provincial; country compd.

provisión f provision; store.

provisional adj provisional.

provisionalmente adv provisionally.

provocación f provocation.

provocador/ra adj provocative.

provocar vt to provoke; to lead to; to excite.

provocativo/va adj provocative.

próximamente adv soon.

proximidad f proximity, closeness.

próximo/ma adj next; neighbouring; close, nearby.

proyección f projection; showing; influence.

proyectar vt to throw; to cast; to screen; to plan.

proyectil m projectile, missile.

proyecto m plan; project.

proyector m projector.

prudencia f prudence, wisdom.

prudente adj prudent.

prueba f proof; reason; argument; token; experiment; essay; attempt; relish, taste.

prurito m itching.

psicoanálisis m psychoanalysis.

psicoanalista m/f psychoanalist.

psicología f psychology.

psicólogo/ga m/f psychologist.

psiquiatra m/f psychiatrist.

psiquiátrico/ca adj psychiatric.

psíquico/ca adj psychic(al).

púa f sharp point, prickle; shoot; pick.

pubertad f puberty.

publicación f publication.

publicar vt to publish; to make public.

publicidad f publicity.

público/ca adj public; * m public; audience; crowd.

puchero m pot; stew.

púdico/ca adj chaste, pure.

pudiente adj rich, opulent.

pudor m bashfulness.

pudrir vt to rot, to putrefy; **~se** vr to decay, to rot.

pueblo m people pl; town, village; population; populace.

puente m bridge.

puenting m bungee-jumping.

puerco/ca adj nasty; filthy, dirty; rude, coarse; * m pig, hog; **~ espín** porcupine.

pueril adj childish; puerile.

puerilidad f puerility.

puerro m leek.

puerta f door; doorway; gateway; **~ trasera** back door.

puerto m port, harbour; haven; pass; narrow pass.

pues adv then; therefore; well; i**~**! well, then.

puesto m place; particular spot; post, employment; barracks pl; stand.

púgil m boxer.

pugilato m boxing.

pugna f combat, battle.

pugnar vi to fight, to combat; to struggle.

pujante adj powerful, strong; robust; stout, strapping.

pujanza f power, strength.

pujar vt to outbid; to strain.

pulcritud f beauty.

pulcro/cra adj beautiful; affected.

pulga f flea; **tener malas ~s** to be easily piqued; to be ill-tempered.

pulgada f inch.

pulgar m thumb.

pulir vt to polish; to put the last touches to.

pulla f smart repartee; obscene expression.

pulmón m lung.

pulmonía f pneumonia.

pulpa f pulp; soft part (of fruit).

pulpería f small grocery store.

púlpito m pulpit.

pulpo m octopus.

pulsación f pulsation.

pulsador m push button.

pulsar vt to touch; to play; to press.

pulsera f bracelet.

pulso m pulse; wrist; firmness or steadiness of the hand.

pulular vi to swarm.

pulverización f pulverization.

pulverizador m spray gun.

pulverizar vt to pulverize.

puna f (med) mountain sickness.

pungir vt to punch, to prick.

punición f punishment, chastisement.

punitivo/va adj punitive.

punta f point; end; trace.

puntada f stitch.

puntal m prop, stay; buttress.

puntapié m kick.

puntear vt to tick; to pluck (the guitar); to stitch.

puntería f aiming.

puntero m pointer; ~ra adj leading.

puntiagudo/da adj sharp-pointed.

puntilla f narrow lace edging; **de ~s** on tiptoe.

punto m point; end; spot; stitch.

puntuación f punctuation.

puntual adj punctual; exact; reliable.

puntualidad f punctuality.

puntualizar vt to fix; to specify.

puntuar vt to punctuate; to evaluate.

punzada f prick; sting; pain; compunction.

punzante adj sharp.

punzar vt to punch; to prick; to sting.

punzón m punch.

puñado m handful.

puñal m dagger.

puñalada f stab.

puñetazo m punch.

puño m fist; handful; wrist-band; cuff; handle.

pupila f pupil (of eye).

pupitre m desk.

puré m puree; (thick) soup; ~ **de patatas** mashed potatoes pl.

pureza f purity, chastity.

purga f purge.

purgante m purgative.

purgar vt to purge; to purify; to atone, to expiate.

purgativo/va adj purgative, purging.

purgatorio m purgatory.

purificación f purification.

purificador/ra m/f purifier; * adj purifying.

purificar vt to purify.

purismo m purism.

purista m purist.

puritano/na adj puritanical; * m/f Puritan.

puro/ra adj pure; mere; clear; genuine.

púrpura f purple.
purpúreo/rea adj purple.
purulento/ta adj purulent.
pus m pus.
pusilánime adj pusillanimous, faint-hearted.

pusilanimidad f pusillanimity.
pústula f pustule, pimple.
puta f whore.
putrefacción f putrefaction.
pútrido/da adj putrid, rotten.

Q

que pn that; who; which; what; * conj that; than.
qué adj what; which; * pn what; which.
quebrada f broken, uneven ground.
quebradero m breaker; ~ **de cabeza** worry.
quebradizo/za adj brittle; flexible.
quebrado m (mat) fraction.
quebradura f fracture; rupture, hernia.
quebrantamiento m fracture; rupture; breaking; weariness, fatigue; violation (of the law).
quebrantar vt to break; to crack; to burst; to pound, to grind; to violate; to fatigue; to weaken.
quebranto m weakness; great loss, severe damage.
quebrar vt to break; to transgress; to violate (a law); * vi to go bankrupt; ~**se** vr to break into pieces; to be ruptured.
queda f resting time; (mil) tattoo.
quedar vi to stay; ~**se** vr to remain.
quedo/da adj quiet, still; * adv softly, gently.
quehacer m task.
queja f complaint.
quejarse vr to complain of.
quejido m complaint.
quejoso/sa adj complaining, querulous.

quejumbroso/sa adj complaining, plaintive.
quema f burning, combustion; fire.
quemador m burner.
quemadura f burn.
quemar vt to burn; to kindle; ~**se** vr to be parched with heat; to burn oneself; * vi to be too hot.
quemarropa f: **a** ~ adv point-blank.
quemazón f burn; itch.
querella f charge; dispute; complaint.
querellarse vr to complain; to file a complaint.
querer vt to want; to desire; to will; to love; * m will, desire.
querido/da adj dear, beloved; * m/f darling; lover; ~ **mío**, ~**da mía** my dear, my love, my darling.
queroseno n paraffin m.
querubín m cherub.
quesería f cheesemonger, cheese shop.
queso m cheese.
quicio m hook, hinge (of a door).
quiebra f break, fracture; bankruptcy; slump.
quiebro m break, fracture; bankruptcy; slump.
quien pn who; whom.
quién pn who; whom.
quienquiera adj whoever.
quieto/ta adj still, peaceable.
quietud f quietness, peace, tranquillity, calmness.
quijada f jaw; jawbone.

quijotada f quixotic action.
quijote m quixotic person.
quijotesco/ca adj quixotic.
quilate m carat.
quilla f keel.
quimera f chimera.
quimérico/ca adj chimerical, fantastic.
química f chemistry.
químico/ca m/f chemist; * adj chemical.
quimioterapia f chemotheraphy.
quina f Peruvian bark, quinine.
quincalla f hardware.
quince adj, m fifteen; fifteenth.
quincena f fortnight.
quiniela f pools coupon; ~s fpl football pools pl.
quinientos/tas adj five hundred.
quinina f quinine.
quinquenal adj quinquennial.
quinquenio m space of five years.
quinqui m delinquent.
quinta f country house; levy, drafting of soldiers.

quintaesencia f quintessence.
quintilla f (poet) metrical composition of five verses.
quinto adj fifth; * m fifth; drafted soldier.
quíntuplo/pla adj quintuple, five-fold.
quiosco m bandstand; news stand.
quirófano m operating theatre.
quiromancia f palmistry.
quirúrgico/ca adj surgical.
quisquilloso/sa adj difficult, touchy; peevish, irritable.
quiste m cyst.
quitaesmalte m nail-polish remover.
quitamanchas m invar stain remover.
quitanieves m invar snowplough.
quitar vt to take away, to remove; to take off; to relieve; to annul; ~se vr to take off (clothes, etc); to withdraw.
quitasol m parasol.
quizá, quizás adv perhaps.

R

rabadilla f coccyx; rump, croup (of a horse or other four-legged animal).
rábano m radish.
rabí m rabbi.
rabia f rage, fury.
rabiar vi to be furious, to rage.
rabieta f touchiness, petulance; fit of bad temper.
rabino m rabbi.
rabioso/sa adj rabid; furious.
rabo m tail.
racha f gust of wind; **buena/mala ~** spell of good/bad luck.
racial adj racial, race compd.

racimo m bunch of grapes.
raciocinio m reasoning; argument.
ración f ration.
racional adj rational; reasonable.
racionalidad f rationality.
racionar vt to ration (out).
racismo m racialism.
racista adj, m/f racist.
radar m radar.
radiación f radiation.
radiactivo/va, radioactivo/va adj radioactive.
radiador m radiator.
radiante adj radiant.
radiar vt to radiate.

radicación f taking root; becoming rooted (of a habit).

radical adj radical.

radicar vt to take root; **~se** vr to establish oneself.

radio f radio; radio (set); * m radius; ray.

radiografía f X-ray.

radioterapia f radiotherapy.

raer vt to scrape; to grate; to erase.

ráfaga f gust; flash; burst.

rafting m rafting.

raído/da adj scraped; worn-out; impudent.

raíz f root; base, basis; origin; **bienes raíces** mpl landed property.

raja f splinter, chip (of wood); chink, fissure.

rajar vt to split; to chop, to cleave.

rajatabla f: **a ~** adv strictly.

ralea f race; breed, species.

ralladura f small particles pl taken off by grating.

rallar vt to grate.

ralo/la adj thin, rare.

rama f branch (of a tree, of a family); printer's chase, form.

ramadán m Ramadan.

ramaje m branches pl.

rambla f avenue.

ramera f whore, prostitute.

ramificación f ramification.

ramificarse vr to ramify.

ramillete m bunch.

ramo m branch (of a tree).

rampa f ramp.

rampante adj rampant.

rana f frog.

ranchero m rancher; smallholder.

rancho m grub; ranch; small farm.

rancio/cia adj stale; musty; rancid.

rango m rank, standing.

ranúnculo m (bot) buttercup.

ranura f groove; slot.

rapacidad f rapacity.

rapadura f shaving; baldness.

rapar vt to shave; to plunder.

rapaz/za adj rapacious; * m/f young boy/girl.

rape m shaving; monkfish.

rapé m snuff.

rapidez f speed, rapidity.

rápido/da adj quick, rapid, swift.

rapiña f robbery.

rappel m abseiling.

raptar vt to kidnap.

rapto m kidnapping; (fig) ecstasy, rapture.

raqueta f racket.

raquítico/ca adj stunted; (fig) inadequate.

rareza f rarity, rareness.

raro/ra adj rare, scarce; extraordinary.

ras m: **a ~** de level with; **a ~ de tierra** at ground level.

rasar vt to level.

rascacielos m invar skyscraper.

rascar vt to scratch, to scrape.

rasgar vt to tear, to rip.

rasgo m dash, stroke; grand/magnanimous gesture; **~s** mpl features pl.

rasguear vi to form bold strokes with a pen; (mus) to strum.

rasguñar vt to scratch, to scrape.

rasguño m scratch.

raso m satin; glade; **~/sa** adj plain; flat; **al ~** in the open air.

raspa f beard (of an ear of corn); backbone (of fish); stalk (of grapes); rasp.

raspadura f filing, scraping; filings pl.

raspar vt to scrape, to rasp.

rastra f rake; **a ~s** by dragging.

rastreador m tracker.

rastrear vt to trace; to inquire into;

* *vi* to skim along close to the ground (of birds).

rastrero/ra *adj* creeping; low, humble, cringing.

rastrillar *vt* to rake.

rastrillo *m* rake.

rastro *m* track; rake; trace.

rastrojera *f* stubble ground.

rastrojo *m* stubble.

rasurador *m*, **rasuradora** *f* electric shaver.

rasurarse *vr* to shave.

rata *f* rat.

ratería *f* larceny, petty theft.

ratero/ra *adj* creeping, mean, vile; * *m/f* pickpocket; burglar.

ratificación *f* ratification.

ratificar *vt* to ratify; to approve of.

rato *m* moment; **a ~s perdidos** in leisure time.

ratón *m* mouse.

ratonera *f* mousetrap.

raudal *m* torrent.

raya *f* stroke; line; part; frontier; ray (fish); roach (fish).

rayado/da *adj* ruled; crossed; striped; rifled (of firearms).

rayar *vt* to draw lines on; to cross out; to underline; to cross; to rifle.

rayo *m* ray, beam (of light).

rayón *m* rayon.

raza *f* race, lineage; quality.

razón *f* reason; right; reasonableness; account; calculation.

razonable *adj* reasonable.

razonado/da *adj* rational; prudent.

razonamiento *m* reasoning; discourse.

razonar *vi* to reason; to discourse, to talk.

reacción *f* reaction.

reaccionar *vi* to react.

reaccionario/ria *adj* reactionary.

reacio/cia *adj* stubborn.

reactor *m* reactor.

reajuste *m* readjustment.

real *adj* real, actual; royal; * *m* (*mil*) camp.

realce *m* embossment; flash; lustre, splendour.

realidad *f* reality; sincerity.

realista *m* realist; royalist.

realizador/ra *m/f* producer (in TV etc).

realizar *vt* to realize; to achieve; to undertake.

realmente *adv* really, actually.

realzar *vt* to raise, to elevate; to emboss; to heighten.

reanimar *vt* to cheer, to encourage; to reanimate.

reanudar *vt* to renew; to resume.

reaparición *f* reappearance.

reasumir *vt* to retake, to resume.

reata *f* collar, leash; string (of horses).

rebaja *f* abatement; deduction; **~s** *fpl* sale.

rebajar *vt* to abate, to lessen, to diminish; to lower.

rebanada *f* slice.

rebaño *m* flock (of sheep), herd (of cattle).

rebasar *vt* to exceed.

rebatir *vt* to resist; to parry, to ward off; to refute; to repress.

rebeca *f* cardigan.

rebelarse *vr* to revolt; to rebel; to resist.

rebelde *m/f* rebel; * *adj* rebellious.

rebeldía *f* rebelliousness, disobedience; (*jur*) contumacy; **en ~** by default.

rebelión *f* rebellion, revolt.

rebosar *vi* to run over, to overflow; to abound.

rebotar vt to bounce; to clinch; to repel; * vi to rebound.

rebote m rebound; **de ~** on the rebound.

rebozado/da adj fried in batter or breadcrumbs.

rebozar vt to wrap up; to fry in batter or breadcrumbs.

rebullir vi to stir, to begin to move.

rebuscado/da adj affected; recherché; far-fetched.

rebuznar vi to bray.

rebuzno m braying (of an ass).

recabar vt to obtain by entreaty.

recado m message; gift.

recaer vi to fall back.

recaída f relapse.

recalcar vt to stress, to emphasize.

recalcitrante adj recalcitrant.

recalentamiento m overheating.

recalentar vt to heat again; to overheat.

recámara f bedroom.

recambio m spare; refill.

recapacitar vt to reflect.

recapitulación f recapitulation.

recapitular vt to recapitulate.

recargado/da adj overloaded.

recargar vt to overload; to recharge; to charge again.

recargo m extra load; new charge or accusation.

recatado/da adj prudent; circumspect; modest.

recato m prudence; circumspection; modesty; bashfulness.

recaudación f take; recovery of debts; collector's office.

recaudador m tax collector.

recaudar vt to gather; to obtain; to recover.

recelar vt to fear; to suspect; to doubt.

recelo m dread; suspicion, mistrust.

receloso/sa adj mistrustful; shy.

recepción f reception.

recepcionista m/f receptionist.

receptáculo m receptacle.

receptor m receiver; investigating official.

recesión f (com) recession.

receta f recipe; prescription.

recetar vt to prescribe.

recetario m register of prescriptions.

rechazar vt to refuse; to repulse; to contradict.

rechazo m rebound; denial; recoil.

rechifla f booing; (fig) derision.

rechiflar vt to boo.

rechinar vi to gnash (teeth).

rechistar vi: **sin ~** without a murmur.

rechoncho/cha adj chubby.

recibidor m entrance hall.

recibimiento m reception.

recibir vt to receive, to accept; to let in; to go to meet; **~se** vr: **~ de** to qualify as.

recibo m receipt.

reciclado/da adj recycled.

reciclar vt to recycle.

recién adv recently, lately.

reciente adj recent; new, fresh; modern.

recinto m district, precinct.

recio/cia adj stout; strong, robust; coarse, thick; rude; arduous, rigid; * adv strongly, stoutly; **hablar ~** to talk loud.

recipiente m container.

reciprocidad f reciprocity.

recíproco/ca adj reciprocal, mutual.

recitación f recitation.

recital m recital; reading.

recitar vt to recite.

recitativo/va adj recitative.

reclamación f claim; reclamation; protest.

reclamar vt to claim.

reclamo m claim; advertisement; attraction; decoy bird; catchword (in printing).

reclinar vt to recline; **~se** vr to lean back.

recluir vt to shut up.

reclusión f seclusion; prison.

recluta f recruitment; * m/f recruit.

reclutador m recruitment officer.

reclutar vt to recruit.

recobrar vt to recover; **~se** vr to recover (from sickness).

recodo m corner or angle jutting out.

recogedor m scraper (instrument).

recoger vt to collect; to retake, to take back; to get; to gather; to shelter; to compile; **~se** vr to take shelter or refuge; to retire; to withdraw from the world.

recogido/da adj retired, secluded; quiet.

recogimiento m collection; retreat; shelter; abstraction from all worldly concerns.

recolección f summary; recollection.

recomendación f recommendation.

recomendar vt to recommend.

recompensa f compensation; recompense, reward.

recompensar vt to recompense; to reward.

recomponer vt to recompose; to mend.

reconcentrar vt to concentrate on.

reconciliación f reconciliation.

reconciliar vt to reconcile; **~se** vr to make one's peace.

recóndito/ta adj recondite, secret, concealed.

reconfortar vt to comfort.

reconocer vt to recognize; to examine closely; to acknowledge; to consider; (mil) to reconnoitre.

reconocido/da adj recognized; grateful.

reconocimiento m recognition; acknowledgement; gratitude; confession; search; submission; inquiry; (mil) reconnaissance.

reconquista f reconquest.

reconquistar vt to reconquer.

reconstituyente m tonic.

reconstruir vt to reconstruct.

reconvenir vt to return the accusations of.

reconversión f: **~ industrial** industrial rationalization.

recopilación f summary, abridgement.

recopilador m compiler.

recopilar vt to compile.

récord adj invar record; * m record.

recordar vt to remember; to remind; * vi to remember.

recorrer vt to run over, to peruse; to cover.

recortar vt to cut out.

recorte m cutting; trimming.

recostar vt to lean, to recline; **~se** vr to lie down.

recoveco m cubby hole; bend.

recrear vt to amuse; to entertain; to delight.

recreativo/va adj recreational.

recreo m recreation; playtime (at school).

recriminación f recrimination.

recriminar vt to recriminate.

recrudecer vt, vi, **~se** vr to worsen.

recrudecimiento m upsurge.

recta f straight line.

rectángulo/la adj rectangular; * m rectangle.

rectificación f rectification.

rectificar vt to rectify.

rectilíneo/nea adj rectilinear.

rectitud f straightness; rectitude; justness, honesty; exactitude.

recto/ta adj straight; right; just, honest; * m rectum.

rector/ra m/f superior of a community or establishment; vice-chancellor (of a university); curate, rector; * adj governing.

rectorado m rectorship; vice-chancellorship.

rectoría f rectory; rectorship.

recua f drove of beasts of burden.

recuadro m box; inset.

recuento m inventory.

recuerdo m souvenir; memory.

recular vi to fall back, to recoil.

recuperable adj recoverable.

recuperación f recovery.

recuperar vt to recover; ~se vr to recover (from sickness).

recurrir vi: ~ a to resort to.

recurso m recourse.

recusación f refusal.

recusar vt to refuse; to refuse to admit.

red f net; network; snare.

redacción f editing; editor's office.

redactar vt to draft; to edit.

redactor/ra m/f editor.

redada f: ~ policial police raid.

redecilla f hairnet.

rededor m environs pl; al ~ round about.

redención f redemption.

redentor/ra m/f redeemer.

redescubrir vt to rediscover.

redicho/cha adj affected.

redil m sheepfold.

redimible adj redeemable.

redimir vt to redeem; to ransom.

rédito m revenue, rent.

redoblado/da adj redoubled; stout and thick; reinforced.

redoblar vt to redouble; to rivet.

redoble m doubling, repetition; (mil) roll of a drum.

redomado/da adj sly; utter.

redondear vt to round.

redondel m circle; traffic roundabout.

redondez f roundness, circular form.

redondo/da adj round; complete.

reducción f reduction.

reducible adj reducible; convertible.

reducido/da adj reduced; limited; small.

reducir adj to reduce; to limit; ~se vr to diminish.

reducto m (mil) redoubt.

redundancia f superfluity, redundancy, excess.

redundar vt to redound; to contribute.

reelegir vt to re-elect, to elect again.

reembolsar vt to refund; to reimburse.

reembolso m reimbursement; refund; contra ~ C.O.D.

reemplazar vt to replace; to restore.

reemplazo m replacement; reserve.

reenganchar vt (mil) to re-enlist; ~se vr to enlist again.

referencia f reference.

referéndum m referendum.

referir vt to refer, to relate, to report; ~se vr to refer or relate to.

refilón m: de ~ adv obliquely.

refinado/da adj refined; subtle, artful.

refinar vt to refine.

refinería f refinery.

reflejar vt to reflect.

reflejo m reflex; reflection.

reflexión f meditation, reflection.

reflexionar vt to reflect on; * vi to reflect, to meditate.

reflexivo/va adj reflexive; thoughtful.

reflujo m reflux, ebb; **flujo y ~ the** tides pl.

reforma f reform; correction; repair.

reformar vt to reform; to correct; to restore; **~se** vr to mend; to have one's manners reformed or corrected.

reformatorio m reformatory.

reforzar vt to strengthen, to fortify; to encourage.

refracción f refraction.

refractario/ria adj refractory.

refrán m proverb.

refregar vt to scrub.

refrenar vt to refrain; to check.

refrendar vt to countersign; to approve.

refrescante adj refreshing.

refrescar vt to refresh; **~se** vr to get cooler; to go out for a breath of fresh air; * vi to cool down.

refresco m refreshment.

refriega f affray, skirmish, fray.

refrigerador m, **refrigeradora** f refrigerator, fridge.

refrigerar vt to cool; to refresh; to refrigerate; to comfort.

refrigerio m refrigeration; refreshment; consolation, comfort.

refuerzo m reinforcement.

refugiado/da m/f refugee.

refugiar vt to shelter; **~se** vr to take refuge.

refugio m refuge, asylum.

refulgir vi to shine.

refunfuñar vi to snarl; to growl; to grumble.

refutación f refutation.

refutar vt to refute.

regadera f watering can.

regadío m irrigated land.

regalar vt to give (as present); to give away; to pamper; to caress.

regalía f regalia; bonus; royalty; privilege.

regaliz m liquorice.

regalo m present, gift; pleasure; comfort.

regañadientes: a ~ adv reluctantly.

regañar vt to scold; * vi to growl; to grumble; to quarrel.

regañón/ona adj snarling, growling, grumbling; troublesome.

regar vt to water, to irrigate.

regata f irrigation ditch; regatta.

regatear vt (com) to bargain over; to be mean with; * vi to haggle; to dribble (in sport).

regateo m haggling; bartering; dribbling.

regazo m lap.

regencia f regency.

regeneración f regeneration.

regenerar vt to regenerate.

regentar vt to rule; to govern.

regente m regent; manager.

régimen m regime, management; diet; (gr) rules pl of verbs.

regimiento m regime; (mil) regiment.

regio/gia adj royal, regal.

región f region.

regir vt to rule, to govern; to direct; * vi to apply.

registrador/ra m/f registrar; controller.

registrar vt to survey; to inspect, to examine; to record, to enter in a register; **~se** vr to register; to happen.

registro m examining; enrolling office; register; registration.

regla f rule, ruler; period.

reglamentar vt to regulate.

reglamentario/ria adj statutory.

reglamento m regulation; by-law.

regocijar vt to gladden; ~**se** vr to rejoice.

regocijo m joy, pleasure; merriment, rejoicing.

regodearse vr to be delighted; to trifle, to play the fool; to joke, to jest.

regodeo m joy, merriment.

regordete adj chubby, plump.

regresar vi to return, to go back.

regreso m return, regression.

reguero m small rivulet; trickle of spilt liquid; drain, gutter.

regulación f regulation.

regulador/ra m/f regulator; knob, control.

regular vt to regulate, to adjust; * adj regular; ordinary.

regularidad f regularity.

regularizar vt to regularize.

rehabilitación f rehabilitation.

rehabilitar vt to rehabilitate.

rehacer vt to repair, to make again; to redo; ~**se** vr to recover; (mil) to rally.

rehén m hostage.

rehuir vt to avoid.

rehusar vt to refuse, to decline.

reimpresión f reprint.

reimprimir vt to reprint.

reina f queen.

reinado m reign.

reinante adj (fig) prevailing.

reinar vi to reign, to govern.

reincidencia f relapse.

reincidir vi: ~ **en** to relapse into, to fall back into.

reino m kingdom, reign.

reintegración f reintegration, restoration.

reintegrar vt to reintegrate, to restore; ~**se** vr to be reinstated or restored.

reintegro m reintegration.

reir(se) vi (vr) to laugh.

reiteración f repetition, reiteration.

reiterar vt to reiterate, to repeat.

reivindicación f claim; vindication.

reivindicar vt to claim.

reja f ploughshare; lattice, grating.

rejilla f grating, grille; vent; luggage rack.

rejoneador m mounted bullfighter.

rejonear vt to spear (bulls).

rejuvenecer vt, vi to rejuvenate.

relación f relation; relationship; report; account.

relacionar vt to relate.

relajación f relaxation; remission; laxity.

relajar vt to relax, to slacken; ~**se** vr to relax.

relamerse vr to lick one's lips; to relish.

relamido/da adj affected; overdressed.

relámpago m flash of lightning.

relampaguear vi to flash.

relatar vt to relate, to tell.

relativo/va adj relative.

relato m story; recital.

relax m relaxation.

releer vt to reread.

relegación f relegation; exile.

relegar vt to relegate; to banish, to exile.

relente m evening dew.

relevante adj excellent, great; eminent.

relevar vt to emboss, to work in relief; to exonerate; to relieve; to assist.

relevo m (mil) relief.

relicario m reliquary.

relieve m relief; (*fig*) prominence.
religión f religion.
religiosidad f religiousness.
religioso/sa adj religious.
relinchar vi to neigh.
relincho m neigh, neighing.
reliquia f residue, remains pl; (saintly) relic.
rellano m landing (of stairs).
rellenar vt to fill up; to stuff.
relleno/na adj satiated, full up; stuffed; * m stuffing.
reloj m clock; watch.
relojero m watchmaker.
relucir vi to shine, to glitter; to excel, to be brilliant.
relumbrar vi to sparkle, to shine.
remachar vt to rivet; (*fig*) to drive home.
remanente m remainder; (*com*) balance; surplus.
remangar vt to roll up.
remansarse vr to form a pool.
remanso m stagnant water; quiet place.
remar vi to row.
rematadamente adv entirely, totally.
rematado/da adj utter, complete.
rematar vt to terminate, to finish; to sell off cheaply; * vi to end.
remate m end, conclusion; shot; tip; last or best bid.
remedar vt to copy, to imitate; to mimic.
remediable adj remediable.
remediar vt to remedy; to assist, to help; to free from danger; to avoid.
remedio m amendment, correction; recourse; refuge.
remedo m imitation, copy.
remendar vt to patch, to mend; to correct.

remero m rower, oarsman.
remesa f shipment; remittance.
remiendo m patch; mend.
remilgado/da adj prim; affected.
remilgo m affected nicety or gravity.
reminiscencia f reminiscence, recollection.
remiso/sa adj remiss, careless; indolent.
remitente m sender.
remitir vt to remit, to send; to pardon (a fault); to suspend, to put off; * vi, ~se vr to slacken.
remo m oar; rowing.
remojar vt to steep; to dunk.
remojo m steeping, soaking.
remolacha f beet.
remolcar vt to tow.
remolino m whirlwind; whirlpool; crowd.
remolón/ona adj stubborn; lazy.
remolque m tow, towing; tow rope.
remontar vt to mend; ~se vr to tower, to soar.
remorder vt to disturb.
remordimiento m remorse.
remoto/ta adj remote, distant; far.
remover vt to stir; to move around.
remozar vt to rejuvenate; to renovate.
remuneración f remuneration, recompense.
remunerador/ra m/f remunerator.
remunerar vt to reward, to remunerate.
renacer vi to be born again; to revive.
renacimiento m regeneration; rebirth.
renacuajo m tadpole.
renal adj renal, kidney compd.
rencilla f quarrel.
rencor m rancour, grudge.

rencoroso/sa adj rancorous.
rendición f surrender; profit.
rendido/da adj submissive; exhausted.
rendija f crevice, crack, cleft.
rendimiento m output; efficiency.
rendir vt to subject; to subdue; ~**se** vr to yield; to surrender; to be tired out.
renegado m apostate; wicked person.
renegar vt to deny; to disown; to detest, to abhor; * vi to apostatize; to blaspheme; to curse.
renglón m line; item.
renombrado/da adj renowned.
renombre m renown.
renovación f renovation; renewal.
renovar vt to renew; to renovate; to reform.
renquear vi to limp.
renta f income; rent; profit.
renuncia f renunciation; resignation.
renunciar vt to renounce; * vi to resign.
reñido/da adj at variance, at odds; hard-fought.
reñir vt, vi to wrangle, to quarrel; to scold, to chide.
reo m offender, criminal.
reojo m: mirar de ~ to look at furtively.
reparación f repair; reparation.
reparar vt to repair; to consider, to observe; to parry * vi: ~ **en** to notice; to pass (at cards).
reparo m repair, reparation; consideration; difficulty.
repartición f distribution.
repartidor m/f distributor; assessor of taxes.
repartir vt to distribute; to deliver.

reparto m distribution; delivery; cost; property development.
repasar vt to repass; to revise; to check; to mend.
repaso m revision; check-up.
repatriar vt to repatriate.
repecho m slope.
repelente adj repellent, repulsive.
repeler vt to repel; to refute, to reject.
repente: de ~ adv suddenly.
repentino/na adj sudden, unforeseen.
repercusión f reverberation.
repercutir vi to reverberate; to rebound.
repertorio m repertory; index; list.
repetición f repetition; (mus) encore.
repetidor/ra m/f repeater.
repetir vt, vi to repeat.
repicar vt to ring.
repique m chime.
repiquetear vt to ring merrily.
repisa f pedestal, stand; shelf; windowsill.
replegar vt to redouble; to fold over; ~**se** vr (mil) to fall back.
repleto/ta adj replete, very full.
réplica f reply, answer; repartee.
replicar vi to reply.
repoblación f repopulation; restocking; ~ **forestal** reafforestation.
repoblar vt to repopulate; to reafforest.
repollo m cabbage.
reponer vt to replace; to restore; ~**se** vr to recover lost health or property.
reportaje m report, article.
reportero/ra m/f reporter.
reposado/da adj quiet, peaceful; settled (wine).

reposar vi to rest, to repose.

reposición f replacement; remake.

reposo m rest, repose.

repostería f confectioner's (shop).

repostero m confectioner.

reprender vt to reprimand.

represa f dam; lake.

represalia f reprisal.

representación f representation; authority.

representante m/f representative; understudy (stage).

representar vt to represent; to play on the stage; to look (age).

representativo/va adj representative.

represión f repression.

reprimenda f reprimand.

reprimir vt to repress; to check; to contain.

reprobable adj reprehensible.

reprobación f reprobation, reproof.

reprobar vt to reject; to condemn, to upbraid.

réprobo m reprobate.

reprochar vt to reproach.

reproche m reproach.

reproducción f reproduction.

reproducir vt to reproduce.

reptil m reptile.

república f republic.

republicano/na adj, m/f republican.

repudiar vt to repudiate.

repudio m repudiation.

repuesto m supply; spare part.

repugnancia f reluctance; repugnance.

repugnante adj repugnant.

repugnar vt to disgust.

repulsa f refusal.

repulsar vt to reject; to decline, to refuse.

repulsión f repulsion.

repulsivo/va adj repulsive.

reputación f reputation, renown.

reputar to consider.

requebrar vt to woo, to court.

requerimiento m request; requisition; intimation; summons.

requerir vt to intimate, to notify; to request; to require, to need; to summon.

requesón m cottage cheese.

requiebro m endearing expression.

réquiem m requiem.

requisa f inspection; (mil) requisition.

requisito m requisite.

res f head of cattle.

resabio m (unpleasant) aftertaste; vicious habit, bad custom.

resaca f surge, surf; (fig) backlash; (fam) hangover.

resaltar vi to rebound; to jut out; to be evident; to stand out.

resarcimiento m compensation, reparation.

resarcir vt to compensate, to make amends for.

resbaladizo/za adj slippery.

resbalar(se) vi (vr) to slip, to slide.

resbalón m slip, slide.

rescatar vt to ransom, to redeem.

rescate m ransom.

rescindir vt to rescind, to annul.

rescisión f rescindment, revocation.

rescoldo m embers pl, cinders pl.

resecarse vr to dry up.

reseco/ca adj very dry.

resentido/da adj resentful.

resentimiento m resentment.

resentirse vr: ~ **de** to suffer; ~ **con** to resent.

reseña f review; account.

reseñar vt to describe; to review.

reserva f reserve; reservation.

reservado/da adj reserved, cautious, circumspect.

reservar vt to keep; to reserve; ~**se** vr to preserve oneself; to keep to oneself.

resfriado m cold.

resfriarse vr to catch cold.

resguardar vt to preserve, to defend; ~**se** vr to be on one's guard.

resguardo m guard; security, safety; voucher; receipt.

residencia f residence.

residente adj residing, resident; * m/f resident.

residir vi to reside, to dwell.

residuo m residue, remainder.

resignación f resignation.

resignadamente adv resignedly.

resignarse vr to resign oneself.

resina f resin.

resinoso/sa adj resinous.

resistencia f resistance, opposition.

resistente adj strong; resistant.

resistir vt to resist, to oppose; to put up with; * vi to resist; to hold out.

resma f ream (of paper).

resol m glare (of the sun).

resollar vi to wheeze; to take breath.

resolución f resolution, boldness; decision.

resolver vt to resolve, to decide; to analyse; ~**se** vr to resolve, to determine.

resonar vi to resound.

resoplar vi to snore; to snort.

resoplido m heavy breathing.

resorte m spring.

respaldar vt to endorse; ~**se** vr to lean back.

respaldo m backing; endorsement; back of a seat.

respectivo/va adj respective.

respecto m respect; relation; **al** ~ on this matter.

respetable adj respectable.

respetar vt to respect; to revere.

respeto m respect, regard, consideration; homage.

respetuoso/sa adj respectful.

respingar vi to shy.

respingo m start; jump.

respiración f respiration, breathing.

respiradero m vent, breathing hole; rest, repose.

respirar vi to breathe.

respiratorio/ria adj respiratory.

respiro m breathing; (fig) respite.

resplandecer vi to shine; to glisten.

resplandeciente adj resplendent.

resplandor m splendour, brilliance.

responder vt to answer; * vi to answer; to correspond; ~ **de** to be responsible for.

respondón/ona adj ever ready to reply; cheeky.

responsable adj responsible; accountable, answerable.

responsabilidad f responsibility.

responsabilizarse vr to take charge.

responso m prayer for the dead.

respuesta f answer, reply.

resquemor m resentment.

resquicio m crack, cleft; (fig) chance.

restablecer vt to re-establish; ~**se** vr to recover.

restablecimiento m re-establishment.

restallar vi to crack; to click.

restante adj remaining.

restar vt to subtract, to take away; * vi to be left.

restauración f restoration.

restaurante m restaurant.

restaurar vt to restore.

restitución f restitution.

restituir vt to restore; to return.

resto m remainder, rest.

restregar vt to scrub, to rub.

restricción f restriction, limitation.

restringir vt to restrict, to limit; to restrain.

resucitar vt to resuscitate, to revive; to renew.

resuello m breath, breathing.

resuelto/ta adj resolute, determined; prompt.

resultado m result, consequence.

resultar vi to be; to turn out; to amount to.

resumen m summary.

resumidamente adv summarily.

resumir vt to abridge; to sum up; to summarize.

resurrección f resurrection, revival.

retablo m picture drawn on a board; splendid altarpiece.

retaguardia f rearguard.

retahíla f range, series.

retal m remnant.

retar vt to challenge.

retardar vt to retard; to delay.

retardo m delay.

retazo m remnant; cutting.

retención f retention.

retener vt to retain, to keep back.

retentiva f memory.

reticencia f reticence.

retina f retina.

retintín m tinkling sound; affected tone of voice.

retirada f (mil) retreat, withdrawal; recall.

retirar vt to withdraw, to retire; to remove; **~se** vr to retire, to retreat; to go to bed.

retiro m retreat, retirement; pension.

reto m challenge; threat, menace.

retocar vt to retouch; to mend; to finish off (work).

retoñar vi to sprout.

retoño m sprout; offspring.

retoque m finishing stroke; retouching.

retorcer vt to twist; to wring.

retorcimiento m twisting, contortion.

retórica f rhetoric.

retórico/ca adj rhetorical; * f rhetoric; affectedness.

retornar vt, vi to return.

retorno m return; barter, exchange.

retortero: andar al ~ to bustle about.

retortijón m twisting; **~ de tripas** stomach cramp.

retozar vi to frisk, to skip.

retozo m romp.

retozón/ona adj wanton; romping.

retracción f retraction.

retractar vr to retract.

retraer vt to draw back; to dissuade; **~se** vr to take refuge; to flee.

retraído/da adj shy.

retransmisión f broadcast.

retransmitir vt to broadcast; to relay; to retransmit.

retrasado/da adj late; (med) mentally retarded; backward.

retraso m delay; slowness; backwardness; lateness; (ferro): **el tren ha tenido ~** the train is overdue or late.

retratar vt to portray; to photograph; to describe.

retrato m portrait, effigy.

retreta f (mil) retreat.

retrete m toilet, lavatory.

retribución f retribution.

retribuir vt to repay.

retroacción f retroaction.

retroactivo/va adj retroactive.

retroceder vi to go backward(s); to fly back; to back down.

retrógrado/da adj retrograde; reactionary.

retrospectivo/va *adj* retrospective.

retrovisor *m* rear-view mirror.

retumbar *vi* to resound, to jingle.

reuma *f* rheumatism.

reumático/ca *adj* rheumatic.

reumatismo *m* rheumatism.

reunión *f* reunion, meeting.

reunir *vt* to reunite; to unite; **~se** *vr* to gather, to meet.

revalidación *f* confirmation, ratification.

revalidar *vt* to ratify, to confirm.

revancha *f* revenge.

revelación *f* revelation.

revelado *m* developing.

revelar *vt* to reveal; to develop (photographs).

reventar *vi* to burst, to crack; to explode; to toil, to drudge.

reventón *m* (*auto*) blow-out.

reverberación *f* reverberation.

reverberar *vi* to reverberate.

reverdecer *vi* to grow green again; to revive.

reverencia *f* reverence, veneration, respect.

reverenciar *vt* to venerate, to revere.

reverendo/da *adj* reverend.

reverente *adj* respectful, reverent.

reverso *m* reverse.

revés *m* back; wrong side; disappointment, setback.

revestir *vt* to put on; to coat, to cover.

revisar *vt* to revise, to review.

revisión *f* revision.

revisor/ra *m/f* inspector; ticket collector.

revista *f* magazine; review, revision.

revivir *vi* to revive.

revocación *f* revocation.

revocar *vt* to revoke.

revolcarse *vr* to wallow.

revolotear *vi* to flutter.

revoloteo *m* fluttering.

revoltijo *m* confusion, disorder.

revoltoso/sa *adj* rebellious, unruly.

revolución *f* revolution.

revolucionario/ria *adj*, *m/f* revolutionary.

revolver *vt* to move about; to turn around; to mess up; to revolve; **~se** *vr* to turn round; to change (of the weather).

revólver *m* revolver.

revuelo *m* fluttering; (*fig*) commotion.

revuelta *f* turn; disturbance, revolt.

rey *m* king; king (in cards or chess).

reyerta *f* quarrel, brawl.

rezagar *vt* to leave behind; to defer; **~se** *vr* to remain behind.

rezar *vi* to pray, to say one's prayers.

rezo *m* prayer.

rezongar *vi* to grumble.

rezumar *vi* to ooze, to leak.

ría *f* estuary.

riada *f* flood.

ribera *f* shore, bank.

ribereño/ña *adj* coastal; riverside.

ribete *m* trimming; seam, border.

ribetear *vt* to hem, to border.

ricino *m*: **aceite de ~** castor oil.

rico/ca *adj* rich; delicious; lovely; cute.

ridiculez *f* absurdity.

ridiculizar *vt* to ridicule.

ridículo/la *adj* ridiculous.

riego *m* irrigation.

riel *m* (*ferro*) rail.

rienda *f* rein of a bridle; **dar ~ suelta** to give free rein to.

riesgo *m* risk, danger.

rifa *f* raffle, lottery.

rifar *vt* to raffle.

rifle *m* rifle.

rigidez *f* rigidity.

rígido/da adj rigid, inflexible; severe.
rigor m rigour.
riguroso/sa adj rigorous.
rima f rhyme.
rimar vi to rhyme.
rimbombante adj pompous.
rímel, rimmel m mascara.
rincón m (inside) corner.
rinoceronte m rhinoceros.
riña f quarrel, dispute.
riñón m kidney.
río m river, stream.
rioja m rioja (wine).
riqueza f riches pl, wealth.
risa f laugh, laughter.
risco m steep rock.
risible adj risible, laughable.
risotada f loud laugh.
ristra f string.
risueño/ña adj smiling.
rítmico/ca adj rhythmic.
ritmo m rhythm.
rito m rite, ceremony.
ritual adj, m ritual.
rival adj, m/f rival.
rivalidad f rivalry.
rivalizar vi: ~ **con** to rival, to vie with.
rizado/da adj curly.
rizar vt to curl (hair).
rizo m curl; ripple (on water).
robar vt to rob; to steal; to break into.
roble m oak tree.
robledal m oakwood.
robo m robbery; theft.
robot m robot.
robustez f robustness.
robusto/ta adj robust, strong.
roca f rock.
rocalla f pebbles pl.
roce m rub; brush; friction.
rociada f sprinkling; spray, shower.
rociar vt to sprinkle; to spray.
rocín m nag; hack; stupid person.

rocío m dew.
rocoso/sa adj rocky.
rodada f rut, track of a wheel.
rodadura f act of rolling.
rodaja f slice.
rodaje m filming; **en** ~ (auto) running in.
rodar vi to roll.
rodear vi to make a detour; * vt to surround, to enclose.
rodeo m detour; subterfuge; evasion; rodeo.
rodilla f knee; **de** ~**s** on one's knees.
rodillo m roller.
roedor/ra adj gnawing; * m rodent.
roedura f gnawing.
roer vt to gnaw; to corrode.
rogar vt, vi to ask for; to beg, to entreat; to pray.
rogativa f supplication, prayer.
rojez f redness.
rojizo/za adj reddish.
rojo/ja adj red; ruddy.
rol m list, roll, catalogue; role.
rollizo/za adj round; plump, chubby.
rollo m roll; coil.
romance m Romance language; romance.
romancero m collection of romances or ballads.
romanticismo m romanticism.
romántico/ca adj romantic.
rombo m rhombus.
romboide m rhomboid.
romería f pilgrimage.
romero m (bot) rosemary.
romo/ma adj blunt; snub-nosed.
rompecabezas m invar riddle; jigsaw.
romper vt to break; to tear up; to wear out; to break up (land); * vi to break (of waves); to break through.

rompimiento m tearing, breaking; crack.

ron m rum.

roncar vi to snore; to roar.

roncha f weal, bruise.

ronco/ca adj hoarse; husky; raucous.

ronda f night patrol; round (of drinks, cards etc).

rondar vt, vi to patrol; to prowl around.

ronquera f hoarseness.

ronquido m snore; roar.

ronzal m halter.

ronronear vi to purr.

ropa f clothes pl; clothing; dress.

ropaje m gown, robes pl; drapery.

ropero m linen cupboard; closet.

rosa f rose; birthmark.

rosado/da adj pink; rosy.

rosal m rosebush.

rosario m rosary.

rosca f thread (of a screw); coil, spiral.

rosetón m rosette; rose window.

rosquilla f doughnut.

rostro m face.

rotación f rotation.

roto/ta adj broken, destroyed; debauched.

rótula f kneecap; ball-and-socket joint.

rotulador m felt-tip pen.

rotular vt to inscribe; to label.

rótulo m inscription; label, ticket; placard, poster.

rotundo/da adj round; emphatic.

rotura f breaking; crack; tear.

roturar vt to plough.

rozadura f graze, scratch.

rozar vt to rub; to chafe; to nibble (the grass); to scrape; to touch lightly.

rubí m ruby.

rubicundo/da adj reddish.

rubio/bia adj fair-haired, blond/blonde; * m/f blond/blonde.

rubor m blush; bashfulness.

rúbrica f red mark; flourish at the end of a signature; title, heading, rubric.

rubricar vt to sign with a flourish; to sign and seal.

rudeza f roughness, rudeness; stupidity.

rudimento m principle; beginning; ~s mpl rudiments pl.

rudo/da adj rough, coarse; plain, simple; stupid.

rueca f distaff.

rueda f wheel; circle; slice, round.

ruedo m rotation; border, selvage; arena, bullring.

ruego m request, entreaty.

rufián m pimp, pander; lout.

rugby m rugby.

rugido m roar.

rugir vi to roar, to bellow.

rugoso/sa adj wrinkled.

ruibarbo m rhubarb.

ruido m noise, sound; din, row; fuss.

ruidoso/sa adj noisy, loud.

ruin adj mean, despicable; mean, stingy.

ruina f ruin, collapse; downfall, destruction; ~s fpl ruins pl.

ruindad f meanness, lowness; mean act.

ruinoso/sa adj ruinous, disastrous.

ruiseñor m nightingale.

ruleta f roulette.

rulo m curler.

rumba f rumba.

rumbo m (mar) course, bearing; road, route, way; course of events, pomp, ostentation.

rumboso/sa adj generous, lavish.
rumiante m ruminant.
rumiar vt to chew; * vi to ruminate.
rumor m rumour; murmur.
runrún m rumour; sound of voices, whirr.

ruptura f rupture.
rural adj rural.
rusticidad f rusticity; coarseness.
rústico/ca adj rustic; * m/f peasant.
ruta f route, itineráry.
rutina f routine; habit.

S

sábado m Saturday; (Jewish) Sabbath.
sábana f sheet; altar cloth.
sabandija f bug, insect.
sabañón m chilblain.
sabelotodo m/f invar know-all.
saber vt to know; to be able to; to find out, to learn; to experience; * vi: ~ a to taste of; * m learning, knowledge.
sabiduría f learning, knowledge; wisdom.
sabiendas adv: a ~ knowingly.
sabihondo/da adj know-all; pedantic.
sabio/bia adj sage, wise; * m/f sage, wise person.
sablazo m sword wound; (fam) sponging, scrounging.
sable m sabre, cutlass.
sabor m taste, savour, flavour.
saborear vt to savour, to taste; to enjoy.
sabotaje m sabotage.
saboteador/ora m/f saboteur.
sabotear vt to sabotage.
sabroso/sa adj tasty, delicious; pleasant; salted.
sabueso m bloodhound.
sacacorchos m invar corkscrew.
sacapuntas m invar pencil sharpener.
sacar vt to take out, to extract; to get

out; to bring out (a book etc); to take off (clothes); to receive, to get; (dep) to serve.
sacarina f saccharin(e).
sacerdotal adj priestly.
sacerdote m priest.
sacerdotisa f priestess.
saciar vt to satiate.
saciedad f satiety.
saco m bag, sack; jacket; ~ de dormir sleeping bag.
sacramental adj sacramental.
sacramento m sacrament.
sacrificar vt to sacrifice.
sacrificio m sacrifice.
sacrilegio m sacrilege.
sacrilego/ga adj sacrilegious.
sacristán m sacristan, sexton.
sacristía f sacristy, vestry.
sacro/cra adj holy, sacred.
sacrosanto/ta adj sacrosanct.
sacudida f shake, jerk.
sacudir vt to shake, to jerk; to beat, to hit.
sádico/ca adj sadistic; * m/f sadist.
sadismo m sadism.
saeta f arrow, dart.
sagacidad f shrewdness, cleverness, sagacity.
sagaz adj shrewd, clever, sagacious.
Sagitario m Sagittarius (sign of the zodiac).
sagrado/da adj sacred, holy.

sagrario m shrine; tabernacle.

sainete m (teat) farce; flavour, relish; seasoning.

sal f salt.

sala f large room; (teat) house, auditorium; public hall; (jur) court; (med) ward.

salado/da adj salted; witty, amusing.

salamandra f salamander.

salar vt to salt.

salarial adj wage compd, salary compd.

salario m salary.

salazón f salting.

salchicha f sausage.

salchichón m (salami-type) sausage.

saldar vt to pay; to sell off; (fig) to settle.

saldo m settlement; balance; remainder; ~s mpl sale.

saledizo/za adj projecting, salient.

salero m salt cellar.

saleroso/sa adj witty, amusing.

salida f exit, way out; leaving, departure; production, output; (com) sale; sales outlet.

saliente adj projecting; rising; (fig) outstanding.

salina f saltworks, salt mine.

salino/na adj saline.

salir vi to go out, to leave; to depart, to set out; to appear; to turn out, to prove; ~se vr to escape, to leak.

salitre m saltpetre.

saliva f saliva.

salmo m psalm.

salmón m salmon.

salmonete m red mullet.

salmuera f brine.

salobre adj brackish, salty.

salón m living room, lounge; public hall.

salpicadero m dashboard.

salpicar vt to sprinkle, to splash, to spatter.

salpicón m salmagundi.

salpimentar vt to season with pepper and salt.

salsa f sauce.

salsera f sauce boat; gravy boat.

saltamontes m invar grasshopper.

saltar vt to jump; to leap; to skip, to miss out; * vi to leap, to jump; to bounce; (fig) to explode, to blow up.

salteador m highwayman.

saltear vt to rob in a hold-up; to assault; to sauté (in cooking).

saltimbanqui m/f acrobat.

salto m leap, jump.

saltón/ona adj bulging; protruding.

salubre adj healthy.

salubridad f healthiness.

salud f health.

saludable adj healthy.

saludar vt to greet; (mil) to salute.

saludo m greeting.

salutación f salutation, greeting.

salva f (mil) salute, salvo.

salvación f salvation; rescue.

salvado m bran.

salvaguardar vt to safeguard.

salvaguardia m safeguard.

salvaje adj savage.

salvajismo m savagery.

salvar vt to save; to rescue; to overcome; to cross, to jump across; to cover, to travel; to exclude; ~se vr to escape from danger.

salvavidas adj invar: **bote ~** lifeboat; **chaleco ~** life jacket.

salvia f (bot) sage.

salvo/va adj safe; * adv save, except (for).

salvoconducto m safe-conduct.

san adj saint (as title).

sanamente adv healthily.

sanar vt, vi to heal.

sanatorio m sanatorium; nursing home.

sanción f sanction.

sancionar vt to sanction.

sandalia f sandal.

sándalo m sandal, sandalwood.

sandez f folly, stupidity.

sandía f watermelon.

sandwich m sandwich.

saneamiento m sanitation.

sanear vt to drain.

sangrar vt, vi to bleed.

sangre f blood; **a ~ fría** in cold blood; **a ~ y fuego** without mercy.

sangría f sangria (drink); bleeding.

sangriento/ta adj bloody, blood-stained, gory; cruel.

sanguijuela f leech.

sanguinario/ria adj bloodthirsty, cruel.

sanguíneo/nea adj blood compd.

sanidad f sanitation; health.

sanitario/ria adj sanitary; health; ~s mpl toilets pl.

sano/na adj healthy, fit; intact, sound.

santiamén m: **en un ~** in no time at all.

santidad f sanctity.

santificar vt to sanctify; to make holy.

santiguarse vr to make the sign of the cross.

santo/ta adj holy; sacred; * m/f saint; **~ y seña** watchword.

santuario m sanctuary.

saña f anger, passion.

sañudo/da adj furious, enraged.

sapo m toad.

saque m (dep) serve, service (in tennis); throw-in (in soccer).

saqueador/ra m/f ransacker, looter.

saquear vt to ransack, to plunder.

saqueo m looting, sacking.

sarampión m measles.

sarao m evening party, soiree.

sarcasmo m sarcasm.

sarcástico/ca adj sarcastic.

sarcófago m sarcophagus.

sardina f sardine.

sardónico/ca adj sardonic; ironic(al).

sargento m sergeant.

sarmiento m vine shoot.

sarna f itch; mange; (med) scabies.

sarnoso/sa adj itchy, scabby, mangy.

sarpullido m (med) rash.

sarro m (med) tartar.

sarta f string of beads, etc; string, row.

sartén f frying pan.

sastre m tailor.

sastrería f tailor's shop.

Satanás m Satan.

satélite m satellite.

sátira f satire.

satírico/ca adj satirical.

satirizar vt to satirize.

sátiro m satyr.

satisfacción f satisfaction; apology.

satisfacer vt to satisfy; to pay (a debt); **~se** vr to satisfy oneself; to take revenge.

satisfactorio/ria adj satisfactory.

satisfecho/cha adj satisfied.

saturación f (quím) saturation.

Saturno m Saturn (planet).

sauce m (bot) willow.

saúco m (bot) elder.

sauna f sauna.

savia f sap.

saxofón m saxophone.

sazonado/da adj flavoured, seasoned.

sazonar vt to ripen; to season.

se pn reflexivo: himself; herself; itself; yourself; themselves; yourselves; each other; one another; oneself.

sebo m fat, grease.

seboso/sa adj fat, greasy.

secador m: ~ de pelo hairdryer.

secadora f tumble drier.

secamente adv dryly, curtly.

secano m dry, arable land which is not irrigated.

secar vt to dry; ~**se** vr to dry up; to dry oneself.

sección f section.

seco/ca adj dry; dried up; skinny; cold (of character); brusque, sharp; bare.

secretaría f secretariat.

secretario/ria m/f secretary.

secreto/ta adj secret; hidden; * m secret; secrecy.

secta f sect.

sectario/ria adj, m/f sectarian.

sector m sector.

secuela f sequel; consequence.

secuencia f sequence.

secuestrador/ra m/f kidnapper.

secuestrar vt to kidnap; to confiscate.

secuestro m kidnapping; confiscation.

secular adj secular.

secularización f secularization.

secularizar vt to secularize.

secundar vt to second.

secundario/ria adj secondary.

sed f thirst; **tener** ~ to be thirsty.

seda f silk.

sedal m fishing line.

sedante m sedative.

sede f see; seat; headquarters.

sedentario/ria adj sedentary.

sedición f sedition.

sedicioso/sa adj seditious, mutinous.

sediento/ta adj thirsty; eager.

sedoso/sa adj silky.

seducción f seduction.

seducir vt to seduce; to bribe; to charm, to attract.

seductor/ra adj seductive; charming; attractive; * m/f seducer.

segador/ra m/f reaper, harvester.

segadora-trilladora f combine harvester.

segar vt to reap, to harvest; to mow.

seglar adj secular, lay.

segmento m segment.

segregación f segregation, separation.

segregar vt to segregate, to separate.

seguido/da adj continuous; successive; long-lasting; * adv straight (on); after; often.

seguidor/ra m/f follower; supporter.

seguimiento m pursuit; continuation.

seguir vt to follow; to pursue; to continue; * vi to follow; to carry on; ~**se** vr to follow, to ensue.

según prep according to.

segundo/da adj second; * m second (of time).

seguramente adv surely; for sure.

seguridad f security; certainty; safety; confidence; stability.

seguro/ra adj safe, secure; sure, certain; firm, constant; * adv for sure; * m safety device; insurance; safety, certainty.

seis adj, m six; sixth.

seiscientos/tas adj six hundred.

seísmo m earthquake.

selección f selection, choice.

seleccionar vt to select, to choose.

selecto/ta adj select, choice.

sellar vt to seal; to stamp (a document).

sello m seal; stamp.

selva f forest.

semáforo m traffic lights pl; signal.

semana f week.

semanal adj weekly.

semanario/ria m weekly (magazine).

semblante m face; (fig) look; appearance.

sembrado m sown field.

sembrar vt to sow; to sprinkle, to scatter.

semejante adj similar, like; * m fellow man.

semejanza f resemblance, likeness.

semejar vi to resemble; ~se vr to look alike.

semen m semen.

semental m stud.

sementera f sowing; land sown with seed.

semestral adj half-yearly.

semicircular adj semicircular.

semicírculo m semicircle.

semifinal f semi-final.

semilla f seed.

semillero m seed plot.

seminario m seedbed; seminary.

seminarista m seminarist.

sémola f semolina.

sempiterno/na adj everlasting.

senado m senate.

senador/ra m/f senator.

sencillez f plainness; simplicity; naturalness.

sencillo/lla adj simple; natural; unaffected; single.

senda f m path, footpath.

senderismo m hillwalking.

senderista m/f hillwalker.

sendero m path, footpath.

senil adj senile.

seno m bosom; lap; womb; hole, cavity; sinus; ~s mpl breasts pl.

sensación f sensation, feeling; sense.

sensacional adj sensational.

sensato/ta adj sensible.

sensibilidad f sensibility, sensitivity.

sensible adj sensitive; perceptible, appreciable; regrettable.

sensitivo/va adj sense compd., sensitive.

sensorial adj sensorial, sensory.

sensual adj sensuous, sensual.

sensualidad f sensuousness; sensuality; sexiness.

sentado/da adj sitting, seated; sedate; settled.

sentar vt to seat; (fig) to establish; * vi to suit; ~se vr to sit down.

sentencia f (jur) sentence; opinion; saying.

sentenciar vt (jur) to sentence, to pass judgement on; * vi to give one's opinion.

sentencioso/sa adj sententious.

sentido m sense; feeling; meaning; ~/da adj regrettable; sensitive.

sentimental adj sentimental.

sentimiento m feeling, emotion, sentiment; sympathy; regret, grief.

sentir vt to feel; to hear; to perceive; to sense; to suffer from; to regret, to be sorry for; ~se vr to feel; to feel pain; to crack (of walls, etc); * m opinion, judgement.

seña f sign, mark, token; signal; (mil) password; ~s fpl address.

señal f sign, token; symptom; signal; landmark; (com) deposit.

señalado/da adj distinct; special; distinguished, notable.

señalar vt to stamp, to mark; to signpost; to point out; to fix, to settle;

~se vr to distinguish oneself, to excel.

señor m man; gentleman; master; Mr; sir.

señora f lady; Mrs; madam; wife.

señorita f Miss; young lady.

señorito m young gentleman; rich kid.

señuelo m decoy; bait, lure.

separable adj separable.

separación f separation.

separar vt to separate; **~se** vr to separate; to come away, to come apart; to withdraw.

septentrional adj north, northern.

septiembre m September.

séptimo/ma adj seventh.

sepulcral adj sepulchral.

sepulcro m sepulchre, grave, tomb.

sepultar vt to bury, to inter.

sepultura f burial, interment; grave, tomb.

sepulturero m gravedigger, sexton.

sequedad f dryness; brusqueness.

sequía f dryness; thirst; drought.

séquito m retinue, suite; group of supporters; aftermath.

ser vi to be; to exist; **~ de** to come from; to be made of; to belong to; * m being.

serenarse vr to calm down.

serenata f (mus) serenade.

serenidad f serenity.

sereno m night watchman; **~/na** adj serene, calm, quiet.

serial m serial.

serie f series; sequence.

seriedad f seriousness, gravity; reliability; sincerity.

serio/ria adj serious; grave; reliable.

sermón m sermon.

sermonear vt to lecture; * vi to sermonize.

seronegativo/va adj HIV-negative.

seropositivo/va adj HIV-positive.

serpentear vi to wriggle; to wind, to snake.

serpentina f streamer.

serpiente f snake.

serranía f range of mountains; mountainous country.

serrano/na m/f highlander.

serrar vt to saw.

serrín m sawdust.

serrucho m handsaw.

servible adj serviceable.

servicial adj helpful, obliging.

servicio m service; service charge; service, set of dishes; **~s** mpl toilets pl.

servidor/ra m/f servant.

servidumbre f servitude; servants pl, staff.

servil adj servile.

servilleta f napkin, serviette.

servir vt to serve; to wait on; * vi to serve; to be of use; to be in service; **~se** vr to serve oneself; to help oneself; to deign, to please; to make use of.

sesenta m, adj sixty; sixtieth.

sesentón/ona m/f person of about sixty years of age.

sesgar vt to slope, to slant.

sesgo m slope.

sesión f session; sitting; performance; showing.

seso m brain.

sestear vi to take a nap.

sesudo/da adj sensible, prudent.

seta f mushroom.

setecientos/tas adj seven hundred.

setenta adj, m seventy.

setiembre m September.

seto m fence; enclosure; hedge.

seudo ... pref pseudo. ...

seudónimo *m* pseudonym.

severidad *f* severity.

severo/ra *adj* severe, strict; grave, serious.

sexagenario/ria *adj* sixty years old.

sexagésimo/ma *adj* sixtieth.

sexenio *m* space of six years.

sexo *m* sex.

sexto/ta *adj*, *m* sixth.

sexual *adj* sexual.

si *conj* whether; if.

sí *adv* yes; certainly; indeed; * *pn* oneself; himself; herself; itself; yourself; themselves; yourselves; each other; one another.

siderúrgico/ca *adj* iron and steel *compd*.

sidra *f* cider.

siega *f* harvest, mowing.

siembra *f* sowing time.

siempre *adv* always; all the time; ever; still; ~ **jamás** for ever and ever.

sien *f* temple (of the head).

sierra *f* saw; range of mountains.

siervo/va *m/f* slave.

siesta *f* siesta, afternoon nap.

siete *adj*, *m* seven.

sietemesino/na *adj* born seven months after conception; premature; (*fig*) half-witted.

sífilis *f* syphilis.

sifón *m* syphon; soda.

sigilo *m* secrecy.

sigiloso/sa *adj* reserved; silent.

sigla *f* acronym; abbreviation.

siglo *m* century.

significación *f* significance, meaning.

significado *m* significance, meaning.

significar *vt* to signify, to mean; to make known, to express.

significativo/va *adj* significant.

signo *m* sign, mark.

siguiente *adj* following, successive, next.

sílaba *f* syllable.

silbar *vt*, *vi* to hiss; to whistle.

silbato *m* whistle.

silbido, silbo *m* hiss; whistling.

silencio *m* silence; i~! silence! quiet!

silencioso/sa *adj* silent.

silla *f* chair; saddle; seat; ~ **de ruedas** wheelchair.

sillón *m* armchair, easy chair; rocking chair.

silo *m* silo; underground store for wheat.

silogismo *m* syllogism.

silueta *f* silhouette; outline; figure.

silvestre *adj* wild, uncultivated; rustic.

sima *f* abyss; pothole, cavern.

simbólico/ca *adj* symbolic.

simbolizar *vt* to symbolize.

símbolo *m* symbol.

simetría *f* symmetry.

simétrico/ca *adj* symmetrical.

simiente *f* seed.

similar *adj* similar.

similitud *f* similarity, similitude.

simio *m* ape.

simpatía *f* liking; kindness; solidarity; affection.

simpático/ca *adj* pleasant; kind.

simpatizante *m/f* sympathizer.

simpatizar *vi*: ~ **con** to get on well with.

simple *adj* single; simple, easy; mere; sheer; silly; * *m/f* simpleton.

simpleza *f* simpleness, gullibility; silliness.

simplicidad *f* simplicity.

simplificar *vt* to simplify.

simulación *f* simulation.

simulacro *m* simulacrum, idol.

simuladamente *adv* deceptively, hypocritically.

simular *vt* to simulate.

simultaneidad *f* simultaneity.

simultáneo/nea *adj* simultaneous.

sin *prep* without.

sinagoga *f* synagogue.

sinceridad *f* sincerity.

sincero/ra *adj* sincere.

síncope *f* (*med*) syncope, fainting fit.

sincronizar *vt* to synchronize.

sindical *adj* union *compd*.

sindicato *m* trade(s) union; syndicate.

sinfín *m*: **un ~ de** a great many.

sinfonía *f* symphony.

singular *adj* singular; exceptional; peculiar, odd.

singularidad *f* singularity.

singularizar *vt* to distinguish; to singularize; **~se** *vr* to distinguish oneself; to stand out.

siniestro/tra *adj* left; (*fig*) sinister; * *m* accident.

sinnúmero *m* = **sinfín**.

sino *conj* but; except; save; only; * *m* fate.

sinónimo/ma *adj* synonymous; * *m* synonym.

sinsabor *m* unpleasantness; disgust.

sintaxis *m* syntax.

síntesis *f* synthesis.

sintético/ca *adj* synthetic.

sintetizar *vt* synthesize.

síntoma *m* symptom.

sinuosidad *f* sinuosity; curve, wave.

sinuoso/sa *adj* sinuous; wavy.

sinvergüenza *m/f* rogue.

siquiera *conj* even if, even though; * *adv* at least.

sirena *f* siren; mermaid; car hooter/horn.

sirviente/ta *m/f* servant.

sisa *f* petty theft; cut, percentage.

sisear *vt*, *vi* to hiss.

sistema *m* system.

sistemático/ca *adj* systematic.

sitiar *vt* to besiege.

sitio *m* place; spot; site, location; room, space; job, post; (*mil*) siege, blockade.

situación *f* situation, position; standing.

situar *vt* to place, to situate; to invest; **~se** *vr* to be established in place or business.

slip *m* pants pl, briefs pl.

smoking *m* dinner-jacket.

sobaco *m* armpit, armhole.

sobar *vt* to handle, to soften; to knead; to massage, to rub hard; to rumple (clothes); to fondle.

soberanía *f* sovereignty.

soberano/na *adj*, *m/f* sovereign.

soberbia *f* pride, haughtiness; magnificence.

soberbio/bia *adj* proud, haughty; magnificent.

sobornar *vt* to suborn, to bribe.

soborno *m* subornation, bribe.

sobra *f* surplus, excess; **de ~** spare, surplus, extra.

sobradamente *adv* too; amply.

sobrante *adj* remaining; * *m* surplus, remainder.

sobrar *vt* to exceed, to surpass; * *vi* to be more than enough; to remain, to be left.

sobrasada *f* pork sausage spread.

sobre *prep* on; on top of; above, over; more than; besides; * *m* envelope.

sobreabundancia *f* superabundance.

sobreabundar *vi* to superabound.

sobrecarga *f* extra load; (*com*) surcharge.

sobrecargar vt to overload; (com) to surcharge.

sobrecoger vt to surprise.

sobredosis f invar overdose.

sobreentender vt to deduce; ~se vr: se sobreentiende que . . . it is implied that.

sobrehumano/na adj superhuman.

sobrellevar vt to carry; to tolerate.

sobremanera adv excessively.

sobremesa f: de ~ immediately after dinner.

sobrenatural adj supernatural.

sobrenaturalmente adv supernaturally.

sobrenombre m nickname.

sobrepasar vt to surpass.

sobreponer vt to put (something) over or on top of; ~se vr to pull through.

sobresaliente adj projecting; (fig) outstanding.

sobresalir vi to project; (fig) to stand out.

sobresaltar vt to frighten.

sobresalto m start, scare; sudden shock.

sobreseer vt: ~ una causa (jur) to stay a case; * vi: ~ de to desist from.

sobreseimiento m dismissal, suspension.

sobrevenir vi to happen, to come unexpectedly; to supervene.

sobreviviente adj surviving; * m/f survivor.

sobrevivir vi to survive.

sobrevolar vt to fly over.

sobriedad f sobriety.

sobrino/na m/f nephew/niece.

sobrio/ria adj sober, frugal.

socarrón/ona adj sarcastic; ironic(al).

socarronería f sarcasm; irony.

socavar vt to undermine.

socavón m hole.

sociabilidad f sociability.

sociable adj sociable.

social adj social.

socialdemócrata adj, m/f social democrat.

socialista adj, m/f socialist.

sociedad f society.

socio/cia m/f associate, member.

sociología f sociology.

sociólogo/ga m/f sociologist.

socorrer vt to help.

socorrido/da adj well stocked or supplied.

socorrista m/f first aider; lifeguard.

socorro m help, aid, assistance, relief.

soda f soda; soda water.

sodomía f sodomy.

sodomita m sodomite.

soez adj dirty, obscene.

sofá m sofa.

sofisma m sophism.

sofista m/f sophist.

sofisticación f sophistication.

sofocar vt to suffocate.

software m software.

soga f rope.

soja f soya.

sojuzgar vt to conquer, to subdue.

sol m sun; sunshine, sunlight.

solamente adv only, solely.

solapa f lapel.

solapado/da adj cunning, crafty, artful.

solar m building site; piece of land; ancestral home of a family; * adj solar.

solariego/ga adj belonging to the ancestral home of a family.

solaz m recreation, relaxation; solace, consolation.

solazar vt to provide relaxation for; to comfort.

soldada f wages pl.

soldadesca f military profession.

soldado m/f soldier; ~ **raso** private.

soldador m welder; soldering iron.

soldadura f soldering; solder.

soldar vt to solder; to weld; to unite.

soleado/da adj sunny.

soledad f solitude; loneliness.

solemne adj solemn; impressive, grand.

solemnidad f solemnity.

solemnizar vt to solemnize; to praise.

soler vi to be accustomed to, to be in the habit of.

solfeo m (mus) solfa.

solicitar vt to ask for, to seek; to apply for (a job); to canvass for; to chase after, to pursue.

solícito/ta adj diligent; solicitous.

solicitud f care, solicitude; request, petition.

solidaridad f solidarity.

solidario/ria adj joint; mutually binding.

solidez f solidity.

sólido/da adj solid.

soliloquio m soliloquy, monologue.

solista m/f soloist.

solitario/ria adj lonely, solitary; * m solitaire; * m/f hermit.

sollozar vi to sob.

sollozo m sob.

solo m (mus) solo; ~**la** adj alone, single; **a solas** alone, unaided.

sólo adv only.

solomillo m sirloin.

solsticio m solstice.

soltar vt to untie, to loosen; to set free, to let out; ~**se** vr to get loose; to come undone.

soltero/ra m/f bachelor/single woman; * adj single, unmarried.

soltura f looseness, slackness; agility, activity; fluency.

soluble adj soluble; solvable.

solución f solution; denouement.

solucionar vt to solve; to resolve.

solvente adj, m solvent.

sombra f shade; shadow.

sombrear vt to shade.

sombrero m hat.

sombrilla f parasol.

sombrío/bría adj shady, gloomy; sad.

somero/ra adj superficial.

someter vt to conquer (a country); to subject to one's will; to submit; to subdue; ~**se** vr to give in, to submit.

sometimiento m submission.

somnífero m sleeping pill.

somnolencia f sleepiness, drowsiness.

son m sound; rumour.

sonado/da adj celebrated; famous; generally reported.

sonaja f (mus) timbrel.

sonajero m (mus) small timbrel.

sonámbulo/la m/f sleep-walker; somnambulist.

sonar vt to ring; * vi to sound; to make a noise; to be pronounced; to be talked of; to sound familiar; ~**se** vr to blow one's nose.

sonata f (mus) sonata.

sonda f sounding; (med) probe.

sondear vt (mar) to sound; to probe; to bore.

sondeo m sounding; boring; (fig) poll.

soneto m sonnet.

sónico/ca adj sonic.

sonido m sound.

sonoro/ra adj sonorous.

sonreír(se) vi (vr) to smile.

sonrisa f smile.

sonrojarse vr to blush.

sonrojo m blush.

sonsacar vt to wheedle, cajole; to obtain by cunning.

sonsonete m tapping noise; monotonous voice.

soñador/ra m/f dreamer.

soñar vt, vi to dream.

soñoliento/ta adj sleepy, drowsy.

sopa f soup; sop.

sopapo m punch, thump.

sopera f soup dish.

sopero m soup plate.

sopetón m: de ~ suddenly.

soplar vt to blow away, to blow off; to blow up, to inflate; * vi to blow, to puff.

soplete m blowlamp.

soplo m blowing; puff of wind; (fam) tip-off.

soplón/ona m/f telltale.

sopor m drowsiness, sleepiness.

soporífero/ra adj soporific; * m sleeping pill.

soportable adj tolerable, bearable.

soportal m portico.

soportar vt to suffer, to tolerate; to support.

sorber vt to sip; to inhale; to swallow; to absorb.

sorbete m sherbet; iced fruit drink.

sorbo m sip; gulp, swallow.

sordera f deafness.

sordidez f sordidness; dirtiness; meanness.

sórdido/da adj sordid; dirty; mean.

sorda/da adj deaf; silent, quiet; * m/ f deaf person.

sordomudo/da adj deaf and dumb.

sorna f slyness; sarcasm; slowness.

soroche m mountain sickness.

sorprender vt to surprise.

sorpresa f surprise.

sortear vt to draw or cast (lots); to raffle; to avoid.

sorteo m draw; raffle.

sortija f ring; ringlet, curl.

sortilegio m sorcery.

sosegado/da adj quiet, peaceful.

sosegar vt to appease, to calm; * vi to rest.

sosería f insipidness; dullness.

sosiego m tranquility, calmness.

soslayar vt to do or place (something) obliquely.

soslayo adv: al o de ~ obliquely, sideways.

soso/sa adj insipid, tasteless; dull.

sospecha f suspicion.

sospechar vt to suspect.

sospechoso/sa adj suspicious; suspect; * m/f suspect.

sostén m support; bra; sustenance.

sostener vt to sustain, to maintain; ~se vr to support or maintain oneself; to contrive, to remain.

sostenimiento m support; maintenance; sustenance.

sota f knave (at cards).

sotana f cassock.

sótano m basement, cellar.

sotavento m (mar) leeward, lee.

soto m grove, thicket.

squash m squash.

status m invar status.

su pn his, her, its, one's; their; your.

suave adj smooth, soft; delicate; gentle; mild, meek.

suavidad f softness, sweetness; suavity.

suavizar vt to soften.

subalterno/na adj secondary; auxiliary.

subasta f auction.

subastar vt to sell by auction.

subcampeón/ona m/f runner-up.

subconsciente adj, m subconscious.

subdesarrollado/da adj underdeveloped.

subdesarrollo m underdevelopment.

subdirector/ora m/f assistant director.

súbdito/ta adj, m/f subject.

subdividir vt to subdivide.

subdivisión f subdivision.

subestimar vt to underestimate.

subida f climb, ascent, rise in value or price.

subido/da adj deep-coloured; high (price).

subir vt, vi to raise, to lift up; to go up; to climb, to ascend; to increase, to swell; to get in, to get on, to board; to rise (in price).

súbito/ta adj sudden, hasty; unforeseen.

subjetivo/va adj subjective.

subjuntivo m (gr) subjunctive.

sublevación f sedition, revolt.

sublevar vt to excite (a rebellion); to incite (a revolt); **~se** vr to revolt.

sublime adj sublime.

sublimidad f sublimity.

submarino/na adj underwater; * m submarine.

subnormal adj subnormal; * m/f subnormal person.

subordinación f subordination.

subrayar vt to underline.

subrepticio/cia adj surreptitious.

subsanar vt to excuse; to mend, to repair; to overcome.

subsidio m subsidy, aid; benefit, allowance.

subsistencia f subsistence.

subsistir vi to subsist.

su(b)stancia f substance.

su(b)stancial adj substantial.

su(b)stancioso/sa adj substantial; nutritious.

su(b)stracción f removal; (mat) subtraction.

su(b)straer vt to remove; (mat) to subtract; **~se** vr to avoid; to withdraw.

subterfugio m subterfuge.

subterráneo/nea adj subterranean; underground; * m underground passage; (ferro) underground (railway).

suburbio m slum quarter; suburbs pl.

subvencionar vt to subsidize.

subversión f subversion, overthrow.

subversivo/va adj subversive.

subvertir vt to subvert, to overthrow.

subyugar vt to subdue, to subjugate.

sucedáneo/nea adj substitute; * m substitute (food).

suceder vt to succeed, to inherit; * vi to happen.

sucesión f succession; issue, offspring; inheritance.

sucesivamente adv: **y así ~** and so on.

sucesivo/va adj successive.

suceso m event; incident.

sucesor/ra m/f successor; heir.

suciedad f dirtiness, filthiness; dirt.

sucinto/ta adj succinct, concise.

sucio/cia adj dirty, filthy; obscene; dishonest.

suculento/ta adj succulent, juicy.

sucumbir vi to succumb.

sucursal f branch (office).

sudar vt, vi to sweat.

sudeste adj southeast, southeastern; * m southeast.

sudoeste adj southwest, southwestern; * m southwest.

sudor m sweat.

sudorífico/ca adj sweaty.

suegra f mother-in-law.

suegro m father-in-law.

suela f sole (shoe).

sueldo m wages pl, salary.

suelo m ground; floor; soil, surface.

suelto/ta adj loose; free; detached; swift; * m loose change.

sueño m sleep; dream.

suero m (med) serum; whey.

suerte f fate, destiny, chance, lot, fortune, good luck; kind, sort.

suéter m sweater.

suficiencia f sufficiency, competence, fitness.

suficiente adj enough, sufficient; fit, capable.

sufragar vt to aid, to assist.

sufragio m vote, suffrage; aid, assistance.

sufrible adj bearable.

sufrido/da adj long-suffering, patient; hard-wearing.

sufrimiento m suffering; patience.

sufrir vt to suffer; to bear, to put up with; to support.

sugerencia f suggestion.

sugerir vt to suggest.

sugestión f suggestion.

suicida adj suicidal; * m/f suicide; suicidal person.

suicidio m suicide.

sujeción f subjection.

sujetador m fastener; bra.

sujetar vt to fasten, to hold down; to subdue; to subject; ~se vr to subject oneself.

sujeto/ta adj fastened, secure; subject, liable; * m subject; individual.

sulfúrico adj sulphuric.

sultán m sultan.

sultana f sultana.

suma f total, sum; adding up; summary.

sumamente adv extremely.

sumar vt to add, to add up; to collect, to gather; * vi to add up.

sumario/ria adj brief, concise; * m summary.

sumergir vt to submerge, to sink; to immerse.

sumidero m sewer, drain.

suministrador/ra m/f provider, supplier.

suministrar vt to supply, to furnish.

sumir vt to sink, to submerge; (fig) to plunge.

sumisión f submission.

sumiso/sa adj submissive, docile.

sumo/ma adj great, extreme; highest, greatest; **a lo ~** at most.

suntuosidad f sumptuousness.

suntuoso/sa adj sumptuous.

súper f four-star (petrol).

superable adj surmountable.

superabundancia f superabundance.

superabundar vi to superabound.

superar vt to surpass; to overcome; to exceed, to go beyond.

superficial adj superficial; shallow.

superficie f surface; area.

superfluo/lua adj superfluous.

superintendencia f supervision.

superintendente m/f superintendent, supervisor; floorwalker.

superior adj superior; upper; higher; better; * m/f superior.

superioridad f superiority.

superlativo/va adj, m (gr) superlative.

supermercado m supermarket.

superstición f superstition.

supersticioso/sa adj superstitious.

supervisor/ra *m/f* supervisor.

supervivencia *f* survival.

superviviente *m/f* survivor; * *adj* surviving.

suplantación *f* supplanting.

suplantar *vt* to supplant.

suplemento *m* supplement.

suplente *m/f* substitute.

supletorio/ria *adj* supplementary.

súplica *f* petition, request; supplication.

suplicante *adj, m/f* applicant; suppliant.

suplicar *vt* to beg (for), to plead (for); to beg; to plead with.

suplicio *m* torture.

suplir *vt* to supply; to make good, to make up for; to replace.

suponer *vt* to suppose; * *vi* to have authority.

suposición *f* supposition; authority.

supremo/ma *adj* supreme.

supresión *f* suppression; abolition; removal; deletion.

suprimir *vt* to suppress; to abolish; to remove; to delete.

supuesto *m* assumption; ~/ta *adj* supposed; ~ que *conj* since, granted that.

supuración *f* suppuration.

supurar *vt* to suppurate.

sur *adj* south, southern; * *m* south; south wind.

surcar *vt* to furrow; to cut, to score.

surco *m* furrow; groove.

surgir *vi* to emerge; to crop up.

surtido *m* assortment, supply.

surtir *vt* to supply, to furnish, to provide; * *vi* to spout, to spurt.

susceptible *adj* susceptible; impressionable.

suscitar *vt* to excite, to stir up.

suscribir *vt* to sign; to subscribe to.

suscripción *f* subscription.

suscriptor/ra *m/f* subscriber.

susodicho/cha *adj* above-mentioned.

suspender *vt* to suspend, to hang up; to stop; to fail (an exam etc).

suspensión *f* suspension; stoppage.

suspenso/sa *adj* hanging; suspended, failed.

suspicacia *f* suspicion, mistrust.

suspicaz *adj* suspicious, mistrustful.

suspirar *vi* to sigh.

suspiro *m* sigh.

sustancia *f* = **substancia**.

sustancial *adj* = **substancial**.

sustancioso *adj* = **substancioso**.

sustantivo/va *adj, m* (*gr*) substantive, noun.

sustentar *vt* to sustain; to support, to nourish.

sustento *m* food, sustenance; support.

sustitución *f* substitution.

sustituir *vt* to substitute.

sustituto/ta *adj, m/f* substitute.

susto *m* fright, scare.

sustracción *f* subtraction.

sustraer *vt* to take away; to subtract.

susurrar *vi* to whisper; to murmur; to rustle; **~se** *vr* to be whispered about.

susurro *m* whisper; murmur.

sutil *adj* subtle; thin; delicate; very soft; keen, observant.

sutileza *f* subtlety; thinness; keenness.

suyo/ya *adj* his; hers; theirs; one's; his; her; its own; one's own; their own; **de ~** per se; **los ~s** *mpl* his own, near friends, relations, family, supporters.

T

tabaco *m* tobacco; (*fam*) cigarettes *pl*.

tábano *m* horsefly.

taberna *f* bar, tavern.

tabernero/ra *m/f* barman/barmaid, bartender.

tabicar *vt* to wall up.

tabique *m* thin wall; partition wall.

tabla *f* board; shelf; plank; slab; index of a book; bed of earth in a garden.

tablado *m* scaffold; platform; stage.

tablero *m* plank, board; chessboard; draughtsboard; (*auto*) dashboard; bulletin board; gambling den.

tableta *f* tablet; (chocolate) bar.

tablilla *f* small board; (*med*) splint.

tablón *m* plank; beam; ~ **de anuncios** bulletin board.

tabú *m* taboo.

taburete *m* stool.

tacañería *f* meanness; craftiness.

tacaño/ña *adj* mean, stingy; crafty.

tacha *f* fault, defect; small nail.

tachar *vt* to find fault with; to cross out, to erase.

tachuela *f* tack, nail.

tácito/ta *adj* tacit, silent; implied.

taciturno/na *adj* tacit, silent; sulky.

taco *m* stopper, plug; heel (of a shoe); wad; book of coupons; billiard cue.

tacón *m* heel.

taconear *vi* to stamp with one's heels; to walk on one's heels.

taconeo *m* stamping of the heels in dancing.

táctica *f* tactics *pl*.

tacto *m* touch, feeling; tact.

tafetán *m* taffeta.

tafilete *m* morocco leather.

tahona *f* bakery.

tahúr *m* gambler; cheat.

taimado/da *adj* sly, cunning, crafty.

tajada *f* slice; (*med*) hoarseness.

tajante *adj* sharp.

tajar *vt* to cut; to chop; to slice.

tajo *m* cut, incision; cleft, sheer drop; working area; chopping block.

tal *adj* such; **con ~ que** provided that; **no hay ~** no such thing.

tala *f* felling of trees.

taladrar *vt* to bore; to pierce.

taladro *m* drill; borer, gimlet.

talante *m* mood; appearance; aspect; will.

talar *vt* to fell (trees); to desolate.

talco *m* talc.

talega *f*, **talego** *m* bag; bagful.

talento *m* talent.

talismán *m* talisman.

talla *f* raised work; sculpture; stature, size; measure (of anything); hand, draw, turn (at cards).

tallado/da *adj* cut; carved; engraved.

tallador *m* engraver.

tallar *vt* to cut, to chop; to carve in wood; to engrave; to measure.

tallarines *mpl* noodles.

talle *m* shape; size; proportion; waist.

taller *m* workshop, laboratory.

tallo *m* shoot, sprout.

talón *m* heel; receipt; cheque.

talonario *m* cheque book; receipt book.

tamaño *m* size, shape, bulk.

tamarindo *m* tamarind tree.

tambalearse *vr* to stagger, to waver.

tambaleo m staggering, reeling.

también adv also, as well; likewise; besides.

tambor m drum; drummer; eardrum.

tamborilear vi to drum.

tamborilero m drummer.

tamiz m fine sieve.

tampoco adv neither, nor.

tampón m tampon.

tan adv so.

tanda f turn; rotation; task; gang; number of persons employed in a workforce.

tangente f tangent.

tangible adj tangible.

tanque m tank; tanker.

tantear vt to reckon (up); to measure, to proportion; to consider; to examine.

tanteo m computation, calculation; valuation; test; scoring.

tanto m certain sum or quantity; point; goal; ~/ta adj so much, as much; very great; * adv so much, as much; so long, as long.

tañido m tune; sound; clink.

tapa f lid, cover; snack; (fam) ~ de los sesos skull.

tapadera f lid (of a pot), cover.

tapar vt to stop up, to cover; to conceal, to hide.

taparrabo m loincloth.

tapete m table cover.

tapia f wall.

tapiar vt to brick up; to stop up (a passage).

tapicería f tapestry; upholstery; upholsterer's shop.

tapicero m tapestry-maker; upholsterer.

tapiz m tapestry; carpet.

tapizar vt to upholster.

tapón m cork, plug, bung.

taquigrafía f shorthand.

taquilla f booking office; takings pl.

taquillero/ra m/f ticket clerk.

tara f tare.

tarántula f tarantula.

tardanza f slowness, delay.

tardar vi to delay; to take a long time; to be late.

tarde f afternoon; evening; * adv late.

tardío/día adj late; slow, tardy.

tardo/da adj sluggish, tardy.

tarea f task.

tarifa f tariff; price list.

tarima f platform; step.

tarjeta f card; visiting card; ~ postal postcard; ~ de crédito credit card.

tarro m pot.

tarta f tart; cake.

tartamudear vi to stutter, to stammer.

tartamudo/da adj stammering.

tarugo m wooden peg or pin.

tasa f rate; measure, rule; valuation; ~s de aeropuerto airport tax.

tasación f valuation, appraisal.

tasador m appraiser.

tasar vt to appraise, to value.

tasca f pub, bar.

tatarabuelo/la m/f great-great-grandfather/mother.

tataranieto/ta m/f great-great-grandson/daughter.

tatuaje m tattoo; tattooing.

tatuar vt to tattoo.

taurino/na adj bullfighting compd.

Tauro m Taurus (sign of the zodiac).

taxi m taxi.

taxista m/f taxi driver.

taza f cup; basin of a fountain.

té m (bot) tea.

te pn you.

tea f torch.

teatral adj theatrical.

teatro m theatre, playhouse.

tebeo m comic.

techo m roof; ceiling.

techumbre f upper roof, ceiling.

tecla f key (of an organ, piano, etc.).

teclado m keyboard.

técnico/ca adj technical.

tecnología f technology.

tedio m boredom; dislike, abhorrence.

teja f tile.

tejado m roof covered with tiles.

tejanos mpl jeans pl.

tejar vt to tile.

tejedor m weaver.

tejemaneje m artfulness, cleverness; restlessness.

tejer vt to weave.

tejido m texture; web.

tejo m quoit (a ring of iron, plastic etc used in the game of quoits); hopscotch; (bot) yew tree.

tejón m badger.

tela f cloth; material.

telar m loom.

telaraña f cobweb.

tele f (fam) telly.

telebanca f telephone banking.

telecomedia f sitcom.

telediario m television news.

telefax m invar fax; fax (machine).

telefonear vt to telephone.

telefónico/ca adj telephone compd.

teléfono m (tele)phone.

teléfono público m payphone.

telegráfico/ca adj telegraphic.

telégrafo m telegraph.

telegrama m telegram.

telescopio m telescope.

teletienda f home shopping programme.

teletrabajador/ra m/f teleworker.

teletrabajo m teleworking.

televidente m/f viewer.

televisar vt to televise.

televisión f television; ~ por cable cable television.

televisor m television set.

télex m telex.

telón m curtain, drape.

tema m theme.

temblar vi to tremble.

temblón/ona adj trembling.

temblor m trembling; earthquake.

temer vt to fear, to doubt; * vi to be afraid.

temerario/ria adj rash.

temeridad f temerity, imprudence.

temeroso/sa adj timid; frightful.

temible adj dreadful, terrible.

temor m dread, fear.

témpano m ice-floe.

temperamento m temperament.

temperatura f temperature.

tempestad f tempest, storm; violent commotion.

tempestuoso/sa adj tempestuous, stormy.

templado/da adj temperate, tempered.

templanza f temperance, moderation.

templar vt to temper, to moderate, to cool; to tune; ~se vr to be moderate.

temple m temperature; tempera; temperament; tuning; al ~ painted in distemper.

templo m temple.

temporada f time, season; epoch, period.

temporal adj temporary, temporal; * m tempest, storm.

temprano/na adj early, anticipated; * adv early; very early, prematurely.

tenacidad f tenacity; obstinacy.

tenacillas fpl small tongs pl.

tenaz adj tenacious; stubborn.

tenaza(s) f (pl) tongs pl, pincers pl.

tenazmente adv tenaciously; obstinately.

tendedero m clothes line.

tendencia f tendency.

tender vt to stretch out; to expand; to extend; to hang out; to lay; ~**se** vr to stretch oneself out.

tenderete m stall; display of goods.

tendero/ra m/f shopkeeper.

tendido/da adj lying down; hanging; * m row of seats for the spectators at a bullfight.

tendón m tendon, sinew.

tenebroso/sa adj dark, obscure.

tenedor m holder, keeper, tenant; fork.

tenencia f possession; tenancy; tenure.

tener vt to have; to take; to hold; to possess; ~**se** vr to stand upright; to stop, to halt; to resist; to adhere.

tenia f tapeworm.

teniente m lieutenant.

tenis m tennis.

tenista m/f tennis player.

tenor m meaning; (mus) tenor.

tensar vt to tauten; to draw.

tensión f tension.

tenso/sa adj tense.

tentación f temptation.

tentador/ra m/f tempter.

tentar vt to touch; to try; to tempt; to attempt.

tentativa f attempt.

tentempié m (fam) snack.

tenue adj thin; tenuous, slender.

tenuidad f slenderness; weakness; trifle.

teñir vt to tinge, to dye.

teología f theology, divinity.

teológico/ca adj theological.

teólogo m theologian, divine.

teorema f theorem.

teoría, teórica f theory.

teórico/ca adj theoretical.

terapéutico/ca adj therapeutic.

terapia f therapy.

tercermundista adj Third World compd.

tercer(o)/ra adj third; * m (jur) third party.

terceto m (mus) trio.

terciar vt to put on sideways; to divide into three parts; to plough the third time; * vi to mediate; to take part.

tercio/cia adj third; * m third part.

terciopelo m velvet.

terco/ca adj obstinate.

tergiversación f distortion; evasion.

tergiversar vt to distort.

termal adj thermal.

termas fpl thermal waters pl.

terminación f termination; conclusion; last syllable of a word.

terminal adj, m/f terminal.

terminante adj decisive; categorical.

terminar vt to finish; to end; to terminate; * vi to end; to stop.

término m term; end; boundary; limit; terminus.

terminología f terminology.

termodinámico/ca adj thermodynamic.

termómetro m thermometer.

termo m flask.

termostato m thermostat.

ternero/ra m/f calf; veal; heifer.

ternilla f gristle.

ternilloso/sa adj gristly.

terno m three-piece suit.

ternura f tenderness.

terquedad f stubbornness, obstinacy.
terrado m terrace.
terraplén m terrace; platform.
terrateniente m/f landowner.
terraza f balcony; (flat) roof; terrace (in fields).
terremoto m earthquake.
terrenal adj terrestrial, earthly.
terreno/na adj earthly, terrestrial; * m land, ground, field.
terrestre adj terrestrial.
terrible adj terrible, dreadful; ferocious.
territorial adj territorial.
territorio m territory.
terrón m clod of earth; lump; ~ones mpl landed property.
terror m terror, dread.
terrorismo m terrorism.
terrorista m/f terrorist.
terso/sa adj smooth, glossy.
tersura f smoothness; shine.
tertulia f club, assembly, circle.
tesis f invar thesis.
tesón m tenacity, firmness.
tesorero m treasurer.
tesoro m treasure; exchequer.
testamentaría f testamentary execution.
testamentario m executor of a will; ~/ria adj testamentary.
testamento m will, testament.
testar vt, vi to make one's will.
testarudo/da adj obstinate.
testículo m testicle.
testificación f attestation.
testificar vt to attest, to witness.
testigo m witness, deponent.
testimoniar vt to attest, to bear witness to.
testimonio m testimony.
teta f teat.
tétanos m tetanus.

tetera f teapot.
tetilla f nipple; teat (of a bottle).
tétrico/ca adj gloomy, sullen, surly.
textil adj textile compd.
texto m text.
textual adj textual.
textura f texture.
tez f complexion, hue.
ti pn you; yourself.
tía f aunt; (fam) bird.
tiara f tiara.
tibieza f lukewarmness.
tibio/bia adj lukewarm.
tiburón m shark.
tiempo m time; term; weather; (gr) tense; occasion, opportunity; season.
tienda f tent; awning; tilt; shop.
tiento m touch; circumspection; a ~ or a tientas gropingly.
tierno/na adj tender.
tierra f earth; land, ground; native country.
tieso/sa adj stiff, hard, firm; robust; valiant; stubborn.
tiesto m large earthen pot.
tifón m typhoon.
tifus m typhus.
tigre m tiger.
tijeras fpl scissors pl.
tijeretada f cut (with scissors), clip.
tijereta f earwig.
tijeretear vt to cut (with scissors).
tildar vt to brand, to stigmatize.
tilde f tilde (ñ).
tilo m lime tree.
timar vt to steal; to swindle.
timbrar vt to stamp.
timbre m stamp; bell; timbre; stamp duty.
timidez f timidity.
tímido/da adj timid; cowardly.
timo m swindle.

timón *m* helm, rudder.

tímpano *m* ear-drum; small drum.

tina *f* tub; bath (tub).

tinaja *f* large earthenware jar.

tinglado *m* shed; trick; intrigue.

tinieblas *fpl* darkness; shadows *pl.*

tino *m* skill; judgement, prudence.

tinta *f* ink; tint, dye; colour.

tinte *m* tint, dye; dry cleaner's.

tintero *m* inkwell.

tinto/ta *adj* dyed; * *m* red wine.

tintorería *f* dry cleaner's.

tintura *f* tincture; dyeing.

tiña *f* scab.

tiñoso/sa *adj* scabby, scurvy; niggardly.

tío *m* uncle; (*fam*) guy.

tiovivo *m* merry-go-round.

típico/ca *adj* typical.

tiple *m* (*mus*) treble; * *f* soprano.

tipo *m* type; norm; pattern; guy.

tipografía *f* typography.

tipográfico/ca *adj* typographical.

tipógrafo *m* printer.

tiquet *m* ticket; cash slip.

tiquismiquis *m invar* fussy person.

tira *f* abundance; strip.

tirabuzón *m* curl.

tirachinas *m invar* catapult.

tirado/da *adj* dirt-cheap; (*fam*) very easy; * *f* cast; distance; series; edition.

tirador *m* handle.

tiranía *f* tyranny.

tiránico/ca *adj* tyrannical.

tiranizar *vt* to tyrannize.

tirano/na *m/f* tyrant.

tirante *m* joist; stay; strap; brace; * *adj* taut, extended, drawn.

tirantez *f* tension; tautness.

tirar *vt* to throw; to pull; to draw; to drop; to tend, to aim at; * *vi* to shoot; to pull; to go; to tend to.

Tirita® *f* (sticking) plaster.

tiritar *vi* to shiver.

tiritona *f* shiver; shaking with cold.

tiro *m* throw, shot; prank; set of coach-horses; **errar el ~** to miss (at shooting).

tirón *m* pull, haul, tug.

tirotear *vt* to shoot at.

tiroteo *m* shooting; sharpshooting.

tirria *f* antipathy.

tísico/ca *adj* consumptive.

tisis *f* tuberculosis.

títere *m* puppet; ridiculous little fellow.

titiritero/ra *m/f* puppeteer.

titubear *vi* to stammer; to stagger; to hesitate.

titubeo *m* staggering; hesitation.

titular *adj* titular; * *m/f* occupant; * *m* headline; * *vt* to title; **~se** *vr* to obtain a title.

título *m* title; name; **a ~** on pretence, under pretext.

tiza *f* chalk.

tiznar *vt* to stain; to tarnish.

tizne *m* soot; smut.

tiznón *m* spot, stain.

tizón *m* half-burnt wood.

toalla *f* towel.

tobillo *m* ankle.

tobogán *m* toboggan; roller-coaster; slide.

toca *f* head-dress.

tocadiscos *m invar* record player.

tocado *m* head-dress, headgear.

tocador *m* dressing table; ladies' room.

tocante *prep:* ~ **a** concerning, relating to.

tocar *vt* to touch; to strike; (*mus*) to play; to ring (a bell); * *vi* to belong; to concern; to knock; to call; to be a duty or obligation.

tocayo/ya m/f namesake.
tocino m bacon.
todavía adv even; yet, still.
todo/da adj all, entire; every; * pn everything, all; * m whole.
todopoderoso/sa adj almighty.
todoterreno m all-terrain vehicle.
toga f toga; gown.
toldo m awning; parasol.
tolerable adj tolerable.
tolerancia f tolerance, indulgence.
tolerante adj tolerant.
tolerar vt to tolerate, to suffer.
toma f taking; dose; ~ (de corriente) socket.
tomar vt to take; to seize, to grasp; to understand; to interpret, to perceive; to drink; to acquire; * vi to drink; to take.
tomate m tomato.
tomavistas m invar cine-camera.
tomillo m thyme.
tomo m bulk; tome; volume.
ton m: sin ~ ni son without rhyme or reason.
tonada f tune, melody.
tonadilla f interlude of music; short tune.
tonalidad f tone.
tonel m cask, barrel.
tonelada f ton; (mar) tonnage duty.
tónico/ca adj tonic, strengthening; * m tonic; * f tonic (water); (mus) tonic; (fig) keynote.
tonificar vt to tone up.
tono m tone.
tono de marcar m dialling tone.
tontada f nonsense.
tontear vi to talk nonsense; to act foolishly.
tontería f foolery, nonsense.
tonto/ta adj stupid, foolish.
topacio m topaz.

topar vt to run into; to find.
tope m butt; scuffle; ~s mpl (ferro) buffers pl.
topera f molehill.
tópico/ca adj topical.
topo m mole; stumbler.
topografía f topography.
topográfico/ca adj topographical.
toque m touch; bell-ringing; crisis.
toquilla f head-scarf; shawl.
tórax m thorax.
torbellino m whirlwind.
torcedura f twisting.
torcer vt to twist, to curve; to turn; to sprain; ~se vr to bend; to go wrong; * vi to turn off.
torcido/da adj oblique; crooked.
torcimiento m bending; deflection; circumlocution.
tordo m thrush; ~/da adj speckled black and white.
torear vt to avoid; to tease; * vi to fight bulls.
toreo m bullfighting.
torero m bullfighter.
toril m bull pen (at bullfight).
tormenta f storm, tempest.
tormento m torment, pain, anguish; torture.
tornar vt to return; to restore; ~se vr to become; * vi to return; ~ a hacer to do again.
tornasolado adj iridescent; shimmering.
torneo m tournament.
tornillo m screw.
torniquete m turnstile; (med) tourniquet.
torno m winch; revolution.
toro m bull.
toronja f grapefruit.
torpe adj dull, heavy; stupid.
torpedo m torpedo.

torpeza *f* heaviness, dullness; torpor; stupidity.

torre *f* tower; turret; steeple of a church.

torrefacto/ta *adj* roasted.

torrente *m* torrent.

tórrido/da *adj* torrid, parched, hot.

torrija *f* French toast.

torso *m* torso.

torta *f* cake; (*fam*) slap.

tortícolis *f invar* stiff neck.

tortilla *f* omelette; pancake.

tórtola *f* turtledove.

tortuga *f* tortoise.

tortuoso/sa *adj* tortuous, circuitous.

tortura *f* torture.

torvo/va *adj* stern, grim.

tos *f* cough.

toscamente *adv* coarsely, grossly.

tosco/ca *adj* coarse, ill-bred, clumsy.

toser *vi* to cough.

tostada *f* slice of toast.

tostado/da *adj* parched; sunburnt; light-yellow; light-brown.

tostador *m* toaster.

tostar *vt* to toast, to roast.

total *m* whole, totality; * *adj* total, entire; * *adv* in short.

totalidad *f* totality.

totalitario/ria *adj* totalitarian.

tóxico/ca *adj* toxic; * *m* poison.

toxicómano/na *m/f* drug addict.

tozudo/da *adj* obstinate.

traba *f* obstacle, impediment; trammel, fetter.

trabajador/ra *adj* working; * *m/f* worker.

trabajar *vt* to work, to labour; to persuade; to push; * *vi* to strive.

trabajo *m* work, labour, toil; difficulty; ~s *mpl* troubles *pl*.

trabajoso/sa *adj* laborious; painful.

trabalenguas *m invar* tongue twister.

trabar *vt* to join, to unite; to take hold of; to fetter, to shackle.

trabucarse *vr* to mistake.

tracción *f* traction; ~ delantera/ trasera front-wheel/rear-wheel drive.

tractor *m* tractor.

tradición *f* tradition.

traducción *f* translation.

traducir *vt* to translate.

traductor/ra *m/f* translator.

traer *vt* to bring, to carry; to attract; to persuade; to wear; to cause.

traficante *m* merchant, dealer.

traficar *vi* to trade, to do business, to deal.

tráfico *m* traffic, trade.

tragaldabas *m/f invar* glutton.

tragaluz *m* skylight.

tragaperras *m/f invar* slot machine.

tragar *vt* to swallow; to swallow up.

tragedia *f* tragedy.

trágico/ca *adj* tragic.

trago *m* drink; gulp; adversity, misfortune.

tragón/ona *adj* gluttonous.

traición *f* treason.

traicionar *vt* to betray.

traicionero/ra *adj* treacherous.

traidor/ra *m/f* traitor; * *adj* treacherous.

traje *m* suit; dress; costume.

trajín *m* haulage; (*fam*) bustle.

trajinar *vt* to carry; * *vi* to bustle about; to travel around.

trama *f* plot; woof.

tramar *vt* to weave; to plot.

tramitar *vt* to transact; to negotiate; to handle.

trámite *m* path; (*jur*) procedure.

tramo *m* section; piece of ground; flight of stairs.

tramoya *f* scene, theatrical decoration; trick.

tramoyista *m* scene-painter; swindler.

trampa *f* trap, snare; trapdoor; fraud.

trampear *vt* to swindle, to deceive; * *vi* to cheat.

trampolín *m* trampoline; diving board.

tramposo/sa *adj* deceitful, swindling.

tranca *f* bar, crossbeam.

trance *m* danger; last stage of life; trance.

tranco *m* long step or stride.

tranquilidad *f* tranquillity; repose, heart's ease.

tranquilizar *vt* to calm; to reassure.

tranquilo/la *adj* tranquil, calm, quiet.

transacción *f* transaction.

transbordador *m* ferry.

transbordar *vt* to transfer.

transbordo *m* transfer; **hacer ~ to** change (trains).

transcribir *vt* to transcribe; to copy.

transcurrir *vi* to pass; to turn out.

transcurso *m*: **~ del tiempo** course of time.

transeúnte *adj* transitory; * *m* passer-by.

transferencia *f* transference; (*com*) transfer.

transferir *vt* to transfer; to defer.

transfiguración *f* transformation, transfiguration.

transformación *f* transformation.

transformador *m* transformer.

transformar *vt* to transform; **~se** *vr* to change one's sentiments or manners.

tránsfuga, tránsfugo *m* deserter; fugitive; defector.

transfusión *f* transfusion.

transgresión *f* transgression.

transgresor *m* transgressor.

transición *f* transition.

transido/da *adj* worn out with anguish; overcome.

transigir *vi* to compromise.

transistor *m* transistor.

transitar *vi* to travel, to pass through a place.

transitivo/va *adj* transitive.

tránsito *m* passage; transition; road, way; change; removal; death of holy or virtuous persons.

transitorio/ria *adj* transitory.

transmisión *f* transmission; transfer; broadcast.

transmitir *vt* to transmit; to broadcast.

transmutación *f* transmutation.

transmutar *vt* to transmute.

transparencia *f* transparency; clearness; slide.

transparentarse *vr* to be transparent; to shine through.

transparente *adj* transparent.

transpiración *f* perspiration; transpiration.

transpirar *vt* to perspire; to transpire.

transportar *vt* to transport, to convey.

transporte *m* transportation.

transposición *f* transposition, transposal.

transversal *adj* transverse; collateral.

tranvía *m* tram.

trapacería *f* fraud, deceit.

trapacero/ra *adj* deceitful.

trapecio *m* trapeze.

trapecista *m/f* trapeze artist.

trapero/ra *m/f* dealer in rags.

trapicheo *m* (*fam*) fiddle.

trapo *m* rag, tatter.

tráquea *f* windpipe.

traqueteo *m* rattling.

tras *prep* after, behind.

trascendencia *f* transcendency; penetration.

trascendental *adj* transcendental.

trascender *vi* to smell; to come out; ~ **de** to go beyond.

trasegar *vt* to move about; to decant.

trasero/ra *adj* back; * *m* bottom.

trasfondo *m* background.

trasgredir *vt* to contravene.

trashumante *adj* migrating.

trasiego *m* removal; decanting (of drinks).

trasladar *vt* to transport; to transfer; to postpone; to transcribe, to copy; ~**se** *vr* to move.

traslado *m* move; removal.

traslucirse *vr* to be transparent; to conjecture.

trasluz *m* reflected light.

trasnochar *vi* to watch, to sit up the whole night.

traspapelarse *vr* to get mislaid among other papers.

traspasar *vt* to remove, to transport; to transfix, to pierce; to return; to exceed (the proper bounds); to transfer.

traspaso *m* transfer, sale.

traspié *m* trip; slip, stumble.

trasplantar *vt* to transplant.

trasplante *m* transplant.

trasquilar *vt* to shear (sheep); to clip.

trasquilón *m* cut (of the shears); badly cut hair.

traste *m* fret (of a guitar); **dar al** ~ **con algo** to ruin something.

trastear *vt* to move (furniture).

trastienda *f* back room behind a shop.

trasto *m* piece of junk; useless person.

trastornado/da *adj* crazy.

trastornar *vt* to overthrow, to overturn; to confuse; ~**se** *vr* to go crazy.

trastorno *m* overturning; confusion.

trastrocar *vt* to invert (the order of things).

tratable *adj* friendly.

tratado *m* treaty, convention; treatise.

tratamiento *m* treatment; style of address.

tratante *m* dealer.

tratar *vt* to traffic, to trade; to use; to treat; to handle; to address; ~**se** *vr* to treat each other.

trato *m* treatment; manner, address; trade, traffic; conversation; (*com*) agreement.

trauma *m* trauma.

través *m* (*fig*) reverse; **de** *o* **al** ~ across, crossways; **a** ~ **de** *prep* across; over; through.

travesaño *m* cross timber; transom.

travesía *f* crossing; cross-street; trajectory; (*mar*) side wind.

travesura *f* wit; wickedness.

travieso/sa *adj* restless, uneasy, fidgety; turbulent; lively; naughty.

trayecto *m* road; journey, stretch; course.

trayectoria *f* trajectory; path.

traza *f* first sketch; trace, outline; project; manner; means; appearance.

trazar *vt* to plan out; to project; to trace.

trazo *m* sketch, plan, design.

trébedes *fpl* trivet, tripod.

trébol *m* trefoil, clover.

trece *adj*, *m* thirteen; thirteenth.

trecho *m* space, distance of time or place; **a** ~**s** at intervals.

tregua *f* truce, cessation of hostilities.

treinta adj, m thirty.

tremendo/da adj terrible, formidable; awful, grand.

tremolar vt to hoist (the colours); to wave.

trémulo/la adj tremulous, trembling.

tren m train, retinue; show, ostentation; (ferro) train; ~ **de alta velocidad** high-speed train; ~ **de mercancías** freight train, luggage-train.

trenza f plait (in hair), plaited silk.

trenzar vt to braid.

trepar vi to climb; to crawl.

tres adj, m three.

tresillo m three-piece suite; (mus) triplet.

treta f thrust (fencing); trick.

triangular adj triangular.

triángulo m triangle.

tribu f tribe.

tribulación f tribulation, affliction.

tribuna f tribune.

tribunal m tribunal, court of justice.

tributar vt to pay; to contribute to; to pay (homage, respect).

tributario/ria adj tributary.

tributo m tribute.

tricolor adj tricoloured.

tricotar vi to knit.

tridente m trident.

trienal adj triennial.

trienio m period of three years.

trigal m wheat field.

trigésimo/ma adj, m thirtieth.

trigo m wheat.

trigueño/ña adj corn-coloured; olive-skinned.

trillado/da adj beaten; trite, stale, hackneyed; **camino** ~ common routine.

trilladora f threshing machine.

trillar vt to thresh.

trimestral adj quarterly, three-monthly.

trimestre m period of three months.

trinar vi to trill, to quaver; to be angry.

trincar vt to tie up; to pinion.

trinchante m carver; carving knife.

trinchar vt to carve, to divide (meat).

trinchera f trench, entrenchment.

trineo m sledge.

Trinidad f Trinity.

trino m trill.

trío m (mus) trio.

tripa f gut, intestine; ~**s** fpl guts; tripe.

triple adj triple, treble.

triplicar vt to treble.

trípode m tripod, trivet.

tripulación f crew.

tripulante m/f crewman/woman.

tripular vt to man; to drive.

triquiñuela f trick.

triquitraque m clack, clatter; clashing.

tris m invar: **estar en un** ~ **de** to be on the point of.

triste adj sad, mournful, melancholy.

tristeza f sadness, mourning.

trituración f pulverization.

triturar vt to reduce to powder; to grind, to pound.

triunfal adj triumphal.

triunfar vi to triumph; to trump (at cards).

triunfo m triumph; trump (at cards).

trivial adj trivial.

trivialidad f triviality.

triza f: **hacer** ~**s** to smash to bits; to tear to shreds.

trocar vt to exchange.

trocha f short cut.

troche: a ~ **y moche** adv helter-skelter.

trofeo m trophy.

tromba f whirlwind.

trombón m trombone.

trombosis f invar thrombosis.

trompa f trumpet; proboscis; spinning top.

trompazo m heavy blow; accident.

trompeta f trumpet; * m trumpeter.

trompetilla f small trumpet; speaking-trumpet.

trompicón m stumble.

trompo m spinning top.

tronar vi to thunder; to rage.

troncar vt to truncate, to mutilate.

tronchar vt to cut off; to shatter; to tire out.

troncho m sprig, stem or stalk.

tronco m trunk; log of wood; stock.

tronera m loophole; small window; pocket (of a billiard table).

trono m throne.

tropa f troop.

tropel m confused noise; hurry; bustle, confusion; heap of things; crowd; **en ~** in a tumultuous and confused manner.

tropelía f outrage.

tropezar vi to stumble; * vt to meet accidentally.

tropezón/ona adj stumbling; * m trip; **a ~ones** by fits and starts.

tropical adj tropical.

trópico m tropic.

tropiezo m stumble, trip; obstacle; slip, fault; quarrel; dispute.

trotamundos m invar globetrotter.

trotar vi to trot.

trote m trot; travelling.

trovador/ra m/f troubadour.

trozo m piece.

trucha f trout.

truco m knack; trick.

trueno m thunderclap.

trueque m exchange.

trufa f truffle.

truhán adj rogue.

truncado/da adj truncated.

truncamiento m truncation.

truncar vt to truncate, to maim.

tu adj your.

tú pn you.

tubérculo m tuber.

tuberculosis f tuberculosis.

tubería f pipe; pipeline.

tubo m tube.

tuerca f screw.

tuerto/ta adj one-eyed; squint-eyed; * m/f one-eyed person.

tuétano f marrow.

tufarada f strong scent or smell.

tufo m warm vapour arising from the earth; offensive smell.

tugurio m slum.

tul m tulle.

tulipán m tulip.

tullido/da adj crippled, maimed.

tumba f tomb.

tumbar vt to knock down; * vi to tumble (to fall down); **~se** vr to lie down to sleep.

tumbo m fall; jolt.

tumbona f easy chair; beach chair.

tumor m tumour, growth.

túmulo m tomb; sepulchral monument.

tumulto m tumult, uproar.

tumultuoso/sa adj tumultuous.

tuna f student music group.

tunda f beating.

túnel m tunnel.

túnica f tunic.

tuno m rogue.

tupé m toupee, wig or hairpiece.

tupido/da adj dense.

tupir vt to press close; **~se** vr to stuff oneself.

turbación f perturbation, confusion; trouble, disorder.

turbado/da adj disturbed.

turbante m turban.

turbar vt to disturb, to trouble; **~se** vr to be disturbed.

turbina f turbine.

turbio/bia adj muddy; troubled.

turbulencia f turbulence; disturbance.

turbulento/ta adj muddy; turbulent.

turismo m tourism; **~ rural** rural tourism.

turista m/f tourist, holiday-maker.

turístico/ca adj tourist compd.

turnar vi to alternate.

turno m turn; shift; opportunity.

turquesa f turquoise.

turrón m nougat (almond cake).

tutear vt to address as 'tu'.

tutela f guardianship, tutelage.

tutelar vt tutelar, tutelary.

tutor m guardian, tutor.

tutora f tutoress.

tutoría f tutelage.

tuyo/ya adj yours; **~s** pl friends and relations of the party addressed.

U

u conj or (instead of o before an o or ho).

ubicar vt to place; **~se** to be located.

ubre f udder.

ufanarse vr to boast.

ufano/na adj haughty, arrogant.

ujier m usher.

úlcera f ulcer.

ulcerar vi to ulcerate.

ulterior adj ulterior; farther, further.

últimamente adv lately.

ultimar vt to finalize; to finish.

ultimátum m ultimatum.

último/ma adj last; latest; bottom; top.

ultrajar vt to outrage; to despise; to abuse.

ultraje m outrage.

ultramar adj, m overseas.

ultramarinos mpl groceries.

ultrasónico/ca adj ultrasonic.

umbilical adj umbilical.

umbral m threshold.

un/una art a, an; * adj, m one (for uno).

unánime adj unanimous.

unanimidad f unanimity.

unción f unction; extreme or last unction.

ungir vt to anoint.

ungüento m ointment.

únicamente adv only, simply.

único/ca adj only; singular, unique.

unicornio m unicorn.

unidad f unity; unit; conformity; union.

unificar vt to unite.

uniformar vt to make uniform.

uniforme adj uniform; * m (mil) uniform, regimentals pl.

uniformidad f uniformity.

unilateral adj unilateral.

unión f union; **~ Europea** European Union.

unir vt to join, to unite; to mingle; to bind, to tie; **~se** vr to associate.

unísono/na adj unison.

universal adj universal.

universalidad f universality.

universidad f university.

universitario/ria adj university compd; * m/f student.

universo m universe.

uno m one; **~/una** adj one; sole, only; **~ a otro** one another; **~ a ~** one by one; **a una** jointly together.

untar vt to anoint; to grease; (fam) to bribe.

uña f nail; hoof; claw, talon.

¡upa! up! up!

urbanidad f urbanity, politeness.

uranio m uranium.

Urano m Uranus (planet).

urbanismo m town planning.

urbanización f housing estate.

urbano/na adj urban; urbane, polite.

urdimbre f warp; intrigue.

urdir vt to warp; to contrive.

urgencia f urgency; emergency; need, necessity.

urgente adj urgent.

urgentemente adv urgently.

urgir vi to be urgent.

urinario/ria adj urinary; * m urinal.

urna f urn; ballot box.

urraca f magpie.

usado/da adj used; experienced; worn.

usanza f usage, use, custom.

usar vt to use, to make use of; to wear; **~se** vr to be used.

uso m use, service; custom; mode.

usted pn you.

usuario m user.

usufructo m (jur) usufruct, use.

usura f usury.

usurario/ria adj usurious.

usurero m usurer.

usurpación f usurpation.

usurpar vt to usurp.

utensilio m utensil.

uterino/na adj uterine.

útero m uterus, womb.

útil adj useful, profitable; * m utility.

utilidad f utility.

utilizar vt to use; to make useful.

utopía f Utopia.

utópico/ca adj Utopian.

uva f grape.

V

vaca f cow; beef.

vacaciones fpl vacation; holidays pl.

vacante adj vacant; * f vacancy.

vaciar vt to empty, to clear; to mould; * vi to fall, to decrease (of waters); * se vr to empty.

vacilación f hesitation; irresolution.

vacilar vi to hesitate; to falter; to fail.

vacío/cía adj void, empty; unoccupied; concave; vain; presumptuous; * m vacuum; emptiness.

vacuna f vaccine.

vacunar vt to vaccinate.

vacuno/na adj bovine, cow compd.

vadear vt to wade, to ford.

vagabundo/da adj wandering; * m vagrant, bum, tramp.

vagancia f vagrancy.

vagar vi to rove or loiter about; to wander.

vagido m cry of a child; convulsive sob.

vagina f vagina.

vago/ga adj vagrant; restless; vague.

vagón m (ferro) wagon; carriage; **~ de mercancías** goods wagon.

vaguear vi to rove, to loiter; to wander.

vahído m vertigo, giddiness.

vaho m steam, vapour.

vaina f scabbard (of a sword); pod, husk.

vainilla f (bot) vanilla.

vaivén m fluctuation, instability; giddiness.

vajilla f crockery.

vale m farewell; promissory note, IOU

valedero/ra adj valid; efficacious; binding.

valentía f valour, courage.

valentón m braggart.

valentonada f brag, boast.

valer vi to be valuable; to be deserving; to cost; to be valid; to be worth; to produce; to be current; * vt to protect, to favour; to be worth; to be equivalent to; ~se vr to employ, to make use of; to have recourse to.

valeroso/sa adj valiant, brave; strong, powerful.

valía f valuation; worth.

validar vt to validate.

validez f validity; stability.

válido/da adj valid.

valiente adj robust, vigorous; valiant, brave; boasting.

valija f suitcase.

valioso/sa adj valuable.

valla f fence; hurdle; barricade.

vallar vt to fence in.

valle m valley.

valor m value; price; validity; force; power; courage, valour.

valoración f valuation.

valorar vt to value; to evaluate.

valuación f valuation.

vals m invar waltz.

válvula f valve.

vampiro m vampire.

vanagloriarse vr to boast.

vandalismo m vandalism.

vándalo/la m, adj vandal.

vanguardia f vanguard.

vanidad f vanity; ostentation.

vanidoso/sa adj vain, showy; haughty; conceited.

vano/na adj vain; useless, frivolous; arrogant; futile; **en ~** in vain.

vapor m vapour, steam; breath.

vaporizador m atomizer.

vaporizar vt to vaporize.

vaporoso/sa adj vaporous.

vapular vt to whip, to flog.

vaquerizo/za adj cattle compd; * m cowherd.

vaquero m cowherd, cowman; ~/ra adj belonging to a cowherd; ~s mpl jeans pl.

vara f rod; pole, staff; stick.

variable adj variable, changeable.

variación f variation.

variado/da adj varied; variegated.

variar vt to vary; to modify; to change; * vi to vary.

varices fpl varicose veins pl.

variedad f variety; inconstancy.

varilla f small rod; curtain rod; spindle, pivot.

vario/ria adj varied, different; vague; variegated; ~s pl some; several.

varón m man, male.

varonil adj male, masculine; manful.

vasco/ca adj, m/f Basque.

vascuence m Basque.

Vaselina® f Vaseline® .

vasija f vessel.

vaso m glass; vessel; vase.

vástago m bud, shoot; offspring.

vasto/ta adj vast, huge.

vaticinar vt to divine, to foretell.

vaticinio m prophecy.

vatio m watt.

vecindad f inhabitants of a place; neighbourhood.

vecindario *m* number of inhabitants of a place; neighbourhood.

vecino/na *adj* neighbouring; near; * *m* neighbour, inhabitant.

veda *f* prohibition.

vedar *vt* to prohibit, to forbid; to impede.

vegetación *f* vegetation.

vegetal *adj* vegetable.

vegetar *vi* to vegetate.

vegetariano/na *adj, m/f* vegetarian.

vehemencia *f* vehemence, force.

vehemente *adj* vehement, violent.

vehículo *m* vehicle.

veinte *adj, m* twenty.

veintena *f* twentieth part; score.

vejación *f* vexation; embarrassment.

vejar *vt* to vex, to humiliate.

vejestorio *m* old man.

vejez *f* old age.

vejiga *f* bladder.

vela *f* wakefulness; vigil; night work; candle; sail; **hacerse a la ~** to set sail.

velado/da *adj* veiled; blurred; * *f* soiree.

velador *m* night watchman; observer; candlestick; pedestal table.

velar *vi* to stay awake; to be attentive; * *vt* to guard, to watch.

veleidad *f* feeble will; inconstancy.

velero/ra *adj* swift-sailing.

veleta *f* weather cock.

vello *m* down; gossamer; short downy hair.

vellón *m* fleece.

velludo/da *adj* shaggy, woolly.

velo *m* veil; pretext.

velocidad *f* speed; velocity.

velocímetro *m* speedometer.

veloz(mente) *adj* (*adv*) swift(ly), fast.

vena *f* vein.

venado *m* deer; venison.

vencedor/ra *m/f* conqueror, victor, winner.

vencer *vt* to defeat; to conquer, to vanquish; * *vi* to win; to expire.

vencido/da *adj* defeated; due.

vencimiento *m* victory; maturity.

vendaje *m* bandage, dressing for wounds.

vendal *f* bandage.

vendar *vt* to bandage; to hoodwink.

vendaval *m* gale.

vendedor/ra *m/f* seller; **~ de periódicos** newsagent; **~ ambulante** pedlar.

vender *vt* to sell.

vendimia *f* grape harvest; vintage.

vendimiador/ra *m/f* vintage.

vendimiar *vt* to harvest; to gather (the vintage).

veneno *m* poison, venom.

venenoso/sa *adj* venomous, poisonous.

venerable *adj* venerable.

veneración *f* veneration, worship.

venerar *vt* to venerate, to worship.

venéreo/rea *adj* venereal.

venganza *f* revenge, vengeance.

vengar *vt* to revenge, to avenge; **~se** *vr* to take revenge.

vengativo/va *adj* revengeful.

venia *f* pardon; leave, permission; bow.

venial *adj* venial.

venida *f* arrival; return; overflow of a river.

venidero/ra *adj* future; **~s** *mpl* posterity.

venir *vi* to come, to arrive; to follow, to succeed; to happen; to spring from; **~se** *vr* to ferment.

venta *f* sale.

ventaja *f* advantage.

ventajoso/sa *adj* advantageous.

ventana *f* window; window shutter; nostril.

ventanilla *f* window.

venta por correo *f* mail order.

ventarrón *m* violent wind.

ventilación *f* ventilation; draught.

ventilar *vt* to ventilate; to fan; to discuss.

ventisca *f*, **ventisco** *m* snowstorm.

ventiscar *vi* to drift, to lie in drifts (snow).

ventisquero *m* snowdrift; **~s** *mpl* glaciers *pl*.

ventolera *f* gust; pride, loftiness.

ventosidad *f* flatulence.

ventoso/sa *adj* windy; flatulent.

ventrículo *m* ventricle.

ventrílocuo *m* ventriloquist.

ventura *f* happiness; luck, chance, fortune; **por ~** by chance.

venturoso/sa *adj* lucky, fortunate, happy.

Venus *f* Venus (planet).

ver *vt* to see, to look at; to observe; to visit; * *vi* to understand; to see; **~se** *vr* to be seen; to be conspicuous; to find oneself; **~se con uno** to have a bone to pick with someone; * *m* sense of sight; appearance.

vera *f* edge; bank.

veracidad *f* truth; veracity.

veranear *vi* to spend the summer holiday, to vacation.

veraneo *m* summer holiday.

veraniego/ga *adj* summer.

verano *m* summer.

veras *fpl* truth, sincerity; **de ~ en** truth, really.

veraz *adj* truthful.

verbal *adj* verbal.

verbena *f* fair; dance.

verbo *m* word, term; (*gr*) verb.

verbosidad *f* verbosity.

verdad *f* truth, veracity; reality; reliability.

verdaderamente *adv* truly, in fact.

verdadero/ra *adj* true; real; sincere.

verde *m, adj* green.

verdear, verdecer *vi* to turn green.

verdín *m* bright green; verdure.

verdor *m* greenness; verdure; youth.

verdoso/sa *adj* greenish, greeny.

verdugo *m* hangman; very cruel person.

verdulero/ra *m/f* greengrocer.

verdura *f* verdure; vegetables *pl*, greens *pl*.

vereda *f* path; pavement, sidewalk.

veredicto *m* verdict.

vergel *m* orchard.

vergonzoso/sa *adj* bashful; shamefaced.

vergüenza *f* shame; bashfulness; confusion.

vericueto *m* rough road.

verídico/ca *adj* truthful.

verificación *f* verification.

verificar *vt* to check, to verify; **~se** *vr* to happen.

verisímil *adj* probable.

verja *f* grate, lattice.

vermut *m* vermouth.

verosímil *adj* likely; credible.

verosimilitud *f* likeliness; credibility.

verraco *m* boar.

verruga *f* wart, pimple.

versado/da *adj* versed.

versátil *adj* versatile.

versículo *m* versicle; verse of a chapter.

versificar *vt* to versify.

versión *f* translation, version.

verso *m* verse.

vértebra *f* vertebra.

vertedero *m* sewer, drain; tip.

verter *vt* to pour; to spill; to empty; * *vi* to flow.

vertical *adj* vertical.

vértice *m* vertex, zenith; crown of the head.

vertiente *f* slope; waterfall, cascade.

vertiginoso/sa *adj* giddy.

vértigo *m* giddiness, vertigo.

vesícula *f* blister.

vespertino/na *adj* evening *compd*.

vestíbulo *m* vestibule, lobby; foyer.

vestido *m* dress; clothes *pl*.

vestidura *f* dress; clothing.

vestigio *m* vestige; footstep; trace.

vestimenta *f* clothing.

vestir *vt* to put on; to wear; to dress; to adorn; to cloak, to disguise; * *vi* to dress; ~**se** to get dressed.

vestuario *m* clothes *pl*; uniform; vestry; changing room.

veta *f* vein (in mines, wood, etc); streak; grain.

vetado/da *adj* striped, veined.

vetar *vt* to veto.

veterano/na *adj* experienced, practised; * *m* veteran, old soldier.

veterinario/ria *m/f* vet; * *f* veterinary science.

veto *m* veto.

vez *f* time; turn; return; **cada** ~ each time; **una** ~ once; **a veces** sometimes, by turns.

vía *f* way; road, route; mode, manner, method; (*ferro*) railway line.

viajante *m* sales representative.

viajar *vi* to travel.

viaje *m* journey; voyage; travel.

viajero/ra *m/f* traveller.

vial *adj* road *compd*.

viático *m* viaticum; travel allowance.

víbora *f* viper.

vibración *f* vibration.

vibrador *m* vibrator.

vibrante *adj* vibrant.

vibrar *vt*, *vi* to vibrate.

vicaría *f* vicarship; vicarage.

vice- *pref* vice- (deputy, etc).

vicealmirante *m* vice-admiral.

viceconsulado *m* vice-consulate.

vicepresidente/ta *m/f* vice-president.

viciar *vt* to vitiate; to corrupt; to annul; to deprave.

vicio *m* vice.

vicioso/sa *adj* vicious; depraved.

vicisitud *f* vicissitude.

víctima *f* victim; sacrifice.

victoria *f* victory.

victorioso/sa *adj* victorious.

vicuña *m* vicuna.

vid *f* (*bot*) vine.

vida *f* life.

vidriado *m* glazed earthenware, crockery.

vídeo *m* video.

videocámara *f* video camera, camcorder.

videocasete *m* video cassette.

videoclip *m* pop video.

videojuego *m* video game.

vidriar *vt* to glaze.

vidriera *f* stained-glass window; shop window.

vidriero *m* glazier.

vidrio *m* glass.

vidrioso/sa *adj* glassy; brittle; slippery; very delicate.

vieira *f* scallop.

viejo/ja *adj* old; ancient, antiquated.

viento *m* wind; air.

vientre *m* belly.

viernes *m invar* Friday; **V~ Santo** Good Friday.

viga *f* beam; girder.

vigencia *f* validity.

vigente *adj* in force.

vigésimo/ma adj, m twentieth.
vigía f (mar) lookout; * m watchman.
vigilancia f vigilance, watchfulness.
vigilante adj watchful, vigilant.
vigilar vt to watch over; * vi to keep watch.
vigilia f vigil; watch.
vigor m vigour, strength.
vigoroso/sa adj vigorous.
vil adj mean, sordid, low; worthless; infamous; ungrateful.
vileza f meanness, lowness; abjectness.
vilipendiar vt to despise, to revile.
villa f villa; small town.
villancico m Christmas carol.
villano/na adj rustic, clownish; villainous; * m villain; rustic.
villorio m one horse town; (fam) dump; shanty town.
vilo: en ~ adv in the air; in suspense.
vinagre m vinegar.
vinagrera f vinegar cruet.
vinagreta f vinaigrette.
vinculación f link; linking.
vincular vt to link.
vínculo m tie, link, chain; entail.
vindicación f revenge.
vindicar vt to avenge.
vindicativo/va adj vindictive.
vinicultura f wine growing.
vino m wine; ~ **tinto** red wine.
viña f vineyard.
viñedo m vineyard.
viñeta f vignette.
viola f viola.
violación f violation; rape.
violado/da adj violet-coloured; violated.
violador/ra m/f rapist; violator; profaner.
violar vt to rape; to violate; to profane.

violencia f violence.
violentar vt to force.
violento/ta adj violent; forced; absurd; embarrassing.
violeta f violet.
violín m violin, fiddle.
violinista m violinist.
violón m double bass.
violoncelo, violonchelo m violoncello, cello.
vip m/f VIP.
viperino/na adj viperish.
viraje m turn; bend.
virar vi to swerve.
virgen m/f virgin.
virginidad f virginity.
Virgo f Virgo (sign of the zodiac).
viril adj virile, manly.
virilidad f virility, manhood.
virrey m viceroy.
virtual adj virtual.
virtud f virtue.
virtuoso/sa adj virtuous.
viruela f smallpox.
virulencia f virulence.
virulento/ta adj virulent.
virus m invar virus.
visa f, **visado** m visa.
viscosidad f viscosity.
viscoso/sa adj viscous, glutinous.
visera f visor.
visibilidad f visibility.
visible adj visible; apparent.
visillos mpl lace curtains pl.
visión f sight, vision; fantasy.
visionario/ria adj visionary.
visita f visit; visitor.
visitar vt to visit.
vislumbrar vt to catch a glimpse of; to perceive indistinctly.
visón m mink.
víspera f eve; evening before; ~**s** pl vespers.

vista f sight, view; vision; eyesight; appearance; looks pl; prospect; intention; (jur) trial; * m customs officer.

vistazo m glance.

visto: ~ **que** conj considering that.

vistoso/sa adj colourful, attractive, lively.

visual adj visual.

vital adj life compd; vital.

vitalicio/cia adj for life.

vitalidad f vitality.

vitamina f vitamin.

viticultor/ra m/f wine grower.

viticultura f wine growing.

vitorear vt to shout, to applaud.

vítreo/trea adj vitreous.

vitriolo m vitriol.

vitrina f showcase.

vituperación f condemnation, censure.

vituperar vt to condemn, to censure.

vituperio m condemnation, censure; insult.

viuda f widow.

viudedad f widowhood; widow's pension.

viudez f widowhood.

viudo m widower.

vivacidad f vivacity, liveliness.

vivamente adv in lively fashion.

vivaracho/cha adj lively, sprightly; bright.

vivaz adj lively.

víveres mpl provisions.

vivero m nursery (for plants); fish farm.

viveza f liveliness; sharpness.

vividor/ra adj (pej) sharp, clever; unscrupulous.

vivienda f housing; flat, apartment.

viviente adj living.

vivificar vt to vivify, to enliven.

vivíparo/ra adj viviparous.

vivir vt to live through; to go through; * vi to live; to last.

vivo/va adj living; lively; **al** ~ to the life; very realistically.

vizconde m viscount.

vocablo m word, term.

vocabulario m vocabulary.

vocación f vocation.

vocacional adj vocational.

vocal f vowel; * m/f member (of a committee); * adj vocal, oral.

vocativo m (gr) vocative.

vocear vt to cry; to shout; to cheer; to shriek; * vi to yell.

vocería f, **vocerío** m shouting.

vociferar vt to shout; to proclaim in a loud voice; * vi to yell.

vodka m/f vodka.

volador/ra adj flying; fast.

volandas: en ~ adv in the air; (fig) swiftly.

volante adj flying; * m (auto) steering wheel; note; pamphlet; shuttlecock.

volar vi to fly; to pass swiftly (of time); to rush, to hurry; * vt to blow up, to explode.

volatería f fowling; fowls pl.

volátil adj volatile; changeable.

volatilizar vt to volatilize, to vaporize.

volcán m volcano.

volcánico adj volcanic.

volcar vt to upset, to overturn; to make giddy; to empty out; to exasperate; ~**se** vr to tip over.

voleibol m volleyball.

voleo m volley.

volquete m tipper truck; dump truck.

voltaje m voltage.

voltear vt to turn over; to overturn; * vi to roll over, to tumble.

voltereta *f* tumble; somersault.
voltio *m* volt.
voluble *adj* unpredictable; fickle.
volumen *m* volume; size.
voluminoso/sa *adj* voluminous.
voluntad *f* will, willpower; wish, desire.
voluntario/ria *adj* voluntary; * *m/f* volunteer.
voluptuoso/sa *adj* voluptuous.
volver *vt* to turn (over); to turn upside down; to turn inside out; * *vi* to return, to go back; ~**se** *vr* to turn around.
vomitar *vt, vi* to vomit.
vómito *m* vomiting; vomit.
vomitona *f* violent vomiting.
voracidad *f* voracity.
voraz(mente) *adj (adv)* voracious(ly).
vórtice *m* whirlpool.
vos *pn* you.
vosotros/tras *pn pl* you.

votación *f* voting; vote.
votar *vi* to vote; to vote.
voto *m* vow; vote; opinion; advice; swearword; curse; ~**s** *mpl* good wishes *pl*.
voz *f* voice; shout; rumour; word, term.
vuelco *m* overturning.
vuelo *m* flight; wing; projection of a building; ruffle, frill; **cazar al ~** to catch in flight; ~ **chárter** charter flight.
vuelta *f* turn; circuit; return; row of stitches; cuff; change; bend, curve; reverse, other side; return journey.
vuestro/tra *adj* your; * *pn* yours.
vulgar *adj* vulgar, common.
vulgaridad *f* vulgar, common.
vulgaridad *f* vulgarity, commonness.
vulgo *m* common people *pl*.
vulnerable *adj* vulnerable.

W

wáter *m* toilet.
whisky *m* whisky.

windsurf *m* windsurfing.
windsurfista *m/f* windsurfer.

X

xenofobia *f* xenophobia.
xilófono *m* xylophone.
xilógrafo *m* xylographer (person

who prints from wooden blocks); wood engraver.

Y

y *conj* and.
ya *adv* already; now; immediately; at once; soon; * *conj:* ~ **que** since, seeing that; ¡~! of course!, sure!

yacer *vi* to lie, to lie down.
yacimiento *m* deposit.
yanqui *m/f* Yankee.
yate *m* yacht, sailing boat.

yedra f ivy.
yegua f mare.
yema f bud; leaf; yolk; **~ del dedo** tip of the finger.
yermo m wasteland, wilderness; **~/ma** adj waste; (fig) barren.
yerno m son-in-law.
yerro m error, mistake, fault.
yerto/ta adj stiff, inflexible; rigid.
yesca f tinder.
yeso m gypsum; plaster; **~ mate** plaster of Paris.
yo pn I; **~ mismo** I myself.
yodo m iodine.
yogur m yoghurt.
yugo m yoke.
yugular adj jugular.
yunque m anvil.
yunta f yoke; **~s** fpl couple, pair.
yute m jute.
yuxtaponer vt to juxtapose.
yuxtaposición f juxtaposition.

Z

zafar vt to loosen, to untie; to lighten (a ship); **~se** vr to escape; **~se de** to avoid; to free oneself from (trouble).
zafio/fia adj uncouth, coarse.
zafiro m sapphire.
zaga f rear; **a la ~** behind.
zagal/la m/f boy/girl.
zaguán m porch, hall.
zaherir vt to criticize; to upbraid.
zahorí m clairvoyant.
zalamería f flattery.
zalamero/ra adj flattering; * m/f wheedler.
zamarra f sheepskin; sheepskin jacket.
zambo/ba adj knock-kneed.
zamba f rural drum.
zambullida f plunge, dive; dipping, submersion.
zambullirse vr to plunge into water, to dive.
zampar vt to gobble down; to put away hurriedly; **~se** vr to thrust oneself suddenly into any place; to crash, to hurtle.
zanahoria f carrot.
zancada f stride.

zancadilla f trip; trick.
zanco m stilt.
zancudo/da adj long-legged; * m mosquito.
zángano m drone; idler, slacker.
zanja f ditch, trench.
zanjar vt to dig (ditches); (fig) to surmount; to resolve.
zapador m (mil) sapper.
zapata f boot; **~ de freno** (auto) brake shoe.
zapatazo m (dancing) stamp.
zapatear vt to tap with the shoe; to beat time with the sole of the shoe.
zapatería f shoemaking; shoe shop; shoe factory.
zapatero/ra m/f shoemaker; **~ de viejo** cobbler.
zapatilla f slipper; pump (shoe); (dep) **~s de lona** fpl trainers pl.
zapato m shoe.
zapping m channel-hopping.
zar m czar.
zarandear vt to shake vigorously.
zarcillo m earring; tendril.
zarpa f dirt on clothes; claw.
zarpar vi to weigh anchor.
zarpazo m thud.

zarrapastroso/sa *adj* shabby, rough-looking.

zarza *f* bramble.

zarzal *m* bramble patch.

zarzamora *f* blackberry.

zarzuela *f* Spanish light opera.

zigzag *adj* zigzag.

zigzaguear *vi* to zigzag.

zinc *m* zinc.

zócalo *m* plinth, base; skirting board.

zodiaco *m* zodiac.

zona *f* zone; area, belt.

zoo *m* zoo.

zoología *f* zoology.

zoológico/ca *adj* zoological; * *m* zoo.

zoólogo/ga *m/f* zoologist.

zopenco/ca *adj* dull, very stupid.

zoquete *m* block; crust of bread; (*fam*) blockhead.

zorra *f* fox; vixen; (*fam*) whore, tart (*sl*).

zorro *m* male fox; cunning person.

zozobra *f* (*mar*) capsizing; uneasiness, anxiety.

zozobrar *vi* (*mar*) to founder; to capsize; (*fig*) to fail; to be anxious.

zueco *m* wooden shoe; clog.

zumba *f* banter, teasing; beating.

zumbar *vt* to hit; **~se** *vr* to hit each other; * *vi* to buzz.

zumbido *m* humming, buzzing sound.

zumbón/ona *adj* waggish, funny, teasing.

zumo *m* juice.

zurcir *vt* to darn; (*fig*) to join, to unite; to hatch (lies).

zurdo/da *adj* left; left-handed.

zurra *f* flogging; drudgery.

zurrar *vt* (*fam*) to flog, to lay into; (*fig*) to criticize harshly.

zurrón *m* pouch.

zutano/na *m/f* so-and-so; ~ **y fulano** such and such a one, so and so.

English–Spanish
Dictionary

A

a *art* un, uno, una; * *prep* a, al, en.

aback *adv* detrás, atrás; **to be taken ~** quedar consternado/da.

abacus *n* ábaco *m*.

abandon *vt* abandonar, dejar.

abandonment *n* abandono *m*; desamparo *m*.

abase *vt* abatir, humillar.

abasement *n* abatimiento *m*; humillación *f*.

abash *vt* avergonzar, causar confusión.

abate *vt* disminuir, rebajar; * *vi* disminuirse.

abatement *n* rebaja, disminución *f*.

abbess *n* abadesa *f*.

abbey *n* abadía *f*.

abbot *n* abad *m*.

abbreviate *vt* abreviar, acortar.

abbreviation *n* abreviatura *f*.

abdicate *vt* abdicar; renunciar.

abdication *n* abdicación *f*; renuncia *f*.

abdomen *n* abdomen *m*.

abdominal *adj* abdominal.

abduct *vt* secuestrar.

abductor *n* músculo abductor *m*.

abed *adv* en (la) cama.

aberrant *adj* anormal.

aberration *n* error *m*; aberración *f*.

abet *vt*: **to aid and ~** ser cómplice de.

abeyance *n* desuso *m*.

abhor *vt* aborrecer, detestar.

abhorrence *n* aborrecimiento, odio *m*.

abhorrent *adj* repugnante.

abide *vt* soportar, sufrir.

ability *n* habilidad, capacidad, aptitud *f*; **abilities** *pl* talento *m*.

abject *adj* vil, despreciable, bajo/ja; **~ly** *adv* vilmente, bajamente.

abjure *vt* abjurar; renunciar.

ablative *n* (*gr*) ablativo *m*.

ablaze *adj* en llamas.

able *adj* capaz, hábil; **to be ~** poder.

able-bodied *adj* robusto/ta, vigoroso/sa.

ablution *n* ablución *f*.

ably *adv* con habilidad.

abnegation *n* abnegación, resignación *f*.

abnormal *adj* anormal.

abnormality *n* anormalidad *f*.

aboard *adv* a bordo.

abode *n* domicilio *m*.

abolish *vt* abolir, anular, revocar.

abolition *n* abolición, anulación *f*.

abominable *adj* abominable, detestable; **~bly** *adv* abominablemente.

abomination *n* abominación *f*.

aboriginal *adj* aborigen.

aborigines *n* aborígenes *mpl*.

abort *vi* abortar.

abortion *n* aborto *m*.

abortive *adj* fracasado/da.

abound *vi* abundar; **to ~ with** abundar en.

about *prep* acerca de, acerca; **I carry no money ~ me** no traigo dinero; * *adv* aquí y allá; **to be ~ to** estar a punto de; **to go ~** andar acá y acullá; **to go ~ a thing** emprender alguna cosa; **all ~** en todo lugar.

above *prep* encima; * *adv* arriba; **~ all** sobre todo, principalmente; **~ mentioned** ya mencionado.

aboveboard *adj* legítimo/ma.

abrasion *n* abrasión *f*.

abrasive *adj* abrasivo/va.

abreast *adv* de costado.

abridge vt abreviar, compendiar; acortar.

abridgement n compendio m, recopilación f.

abroad adv en el extranjero; **to go ~** salir del país.

abrogate vt abrogar, anular.

abrogation n abrogación, anulación f.

abrupt adj brusco/ca; **~ly** adv precipitadamente; bruscamente.

abscess n absceso m.

abscond vi esconderse; huir.

abseiling n rappel m.

absence n ausencia f.

absent adj ausente; * vi ausentarse.

absentee n ausente m.

absenteeism n absentismo m.

absent-minded adj distraído/da.

absolute adj absoluto/ta; categórico/ca; **~ly** adv totalmente.

absolution n absolución f.

absolutism n absolutismo m.

absolve vt absolver.

absorb vt absorber.

absorbent adj absorbente.

absorbent cotton n algodón hidrófilo m.

absorption n absorción f.

abstain vi abstenerse, privarse.

abstemious adj abstemio/mia, sobrio/ria; **~ly** adv moderadamente.

abstemiousness n sobriedad, abstinencia f.

abstinence n abstinencia f; templanza f.

abstinent adj abstinente, sobrio/ria.

abstract adj abstracto/ta; * n extracto m; sumario m; **in the ~** de modo abstracto.

abstraction n abstracción f.

abstractly adv en abstracto.

abstruse adj oscuro/ra; **~ly** adv oscuramente.

absurd adj absurdo/da; **~ly** adv absurdamente.

absurdity n absurdidad f.

abundance n abundancia f.

abundant adj abundante; **~ly** adv abundantemente.

abuse vt abusar; maltratar; * n abuso m; injurias fpl.

abusive adj abusivo/va, ofensivo/va; **~ly** adv abusivamente.

abut vi confinar.

abysmal adj abismal; insondable.

abyss n abismo m.

acacia n acacia f.

academic adj académico/ca.

academician n académico m.

academy n academia f.

accede vi acceder.

accelerate vt acelerar.

accelerator n acelerador m.

acceleration n aceleración f.

accent n acento m; tono m; * vt acentuar.

accentuate vt acentuar.

accentuation n acentuación f.

accept vt aceptar; admitir.

acceptable adj aceptable.

acceptability n aceptabilidad f.

acceptance n aceptación f.

access n acceso m; entrada f.

accessible adj accesible.

accession n acceso m.

accessory n accesorio m; (law) cómplice m.

accident n accidente m; casualidad f.

accidental adj casual; **~ly** adv por casualidad.

acclaim vt aclamar, aplaudir.

acclamation n aclamación f; aplauso m.

acclimatize vt aclimatar.

accommodate vt alojar; complacer.

accommodating adj servicial.

accommodations npl alojamiento m.
accompaniment n (mus) acompañamiento m.
accompanist n (mus) acompañante m.
accompany vt acompañar.
accomplice n cómplice m.
accomplish vt efectuar, completar.
accomplished adj elegante, consumado/da.
accomplishment n cumplimiento m; ~s pl talentos, conocimientos mpl.
accord n acuerdo, convenio m; **with one** ~ unánimemente; **of one's own** ~ espontáneamente.
accordance n: **in** ~ **with** de acuerdo con.
according prep según, conforme; ~ **as** según que, como; ~**ly** adv por consiguiente.
accordion n (mus) acordeón m.
accost vt trabar conversación con.
account n cuenta f; **on no** ~ de ninguna manera; **bajo ningún concepto**; **on** ~ **of** por motivo de; **to call to** ~ pedir cuenta; **to turn to** ~ hacer provechoso; * vt **to** ~ **for** explicar.
accountability n responsabilidad f.
accountable adj responsable.
accountancy n contabilidad f.
accountant n contable, contador m.
account book n libro de cuentas m.
account number n número m de cuenta.
accrue vi resultar, provenir.
accumulate vt acumular; amontonar; * vi crecer.
accumulation n acumulación f; amontonamiento m.
accuracy n exactitud f.
accurate adj exacto/ta; ~**ly** adv exactamente.

accursed adj maldito/ta.
accusation n acusación f.
accusative n (gr) acusativo m.
accusatory adj acusatorio/ria.
accuse vt acusar; culpar.
accused n acusado m.
accuser n acusador/a m/f.
accustom vt acostumbrar.
accustomed adj acostumbrado/da, habitual.
ace n as m; **within an** ~ **of** . . . casi; **por poco no** . . .
acerbic adj mordaz.
acetate n (chem) acetato m.
ache n dolor m; * vi doler.
achieve vt realizar; obtener.
achievement n realización f; hazaña f.
acid adj ácido/da; agrio/ria; * n ácido m.
acid rain n lluvia ácida f.
acidity n acidez f.
acknowledge vt reconocer, confesar.
acknowledgment n reconocimiento m; gratitud f.
acme n apogeo m.
acne n acne m.
acorn n bellota f.
acoustics n acústica f.
acquaint vt informar, avisar.
acquaintance n conocimiento m; conocido m.
acquiesce vi someterse, consentir, asentir.
acquiescence n consentimiento m.
acquiescent adj deferente.
acquire vt adquirir.
acquisition n adquisición, obtención f.
acquit vt absolver.
acquittal n absolución f.
acre n acre m.
acrid adj acre.
acrimonious adj mordaz.

acrimony *n* acrimonia, acritud *f*.
across *adv* de una parte a otra; * *prep* a través de; **to come ~** toparse con.
act *vt* representar; * *vi* hacer; * *n* acto, hecho *m*; acción *f*; **~s of the apostles** Hechos *mpl* de los Apóstoles.
acting *adj* interino/na.
action *n* acción *f*; batalla *f*.
action replay *n* repetición *f*.
activate *vt* activar.
active *adj* activo/va; **~ly** *adv* activamente.
activity *n* actividad *f*.
actor *n* actor *m*.
actress *n* actriz *f*.
actual *adj* real; efectivo/va; **~ly** *adv* en efecto, realmente.
actuary *n* actuario de seguros *m*.
acumen *n* agudeza, perspicacia *f*.
acupuncture *n* acupuntura *f*.
acute *adj* agudo/da; ingenioso/sa; **~ accent** *n* acento agudo *m*; **~ angle** *n* ángulo agudo *m*; **~ly** *adv* con agudeza.
acuteness *n* perspicacia, sagacidad *f*.
adage *n* proverbio *m*.
adamant *adj* inflexible.
adapt *vt* adaptar, acomodar; ajustar.
adaptability *n* facilidad de adaptarse *f*.
adaptable *adj* adaptable.
adaptation *n* adaptación *f*.
adaptor *n* adaptador *m*.
add *vt* añadir, agregar; **to ~ up** sumar.
addendum *n* suplemento *m*.
adder *n* culebra *f*; víbora *f*.
addict *n* drogadicto *m*.
addiction *n* dependencia *f*.
addictive *adj* que crea dependencia.
addition *n* adición *f*.
additional *adj* adicional; **~ly** *adv* en o por adición.

additive *n* aditivo *m*.
address *vt* dirigir; * *n* dirección *f*; discurso *m*.
adduce *vt* alegar, aducir.
adenoids *npl* vegetaciones adenoideas *fpl*.
adept *adj* hábil.
adequacy *n* suficiencia *f*.
adequate *adj* adecuado/da; suficiente; **~ly** *adv* adecuadamente.
adhere *vi* adherir.
adherence *n* adherencia *f*.
adherent *n* adherente, partidario *m*.
adhesion *n* adhesión *f*.
adhesive *adj* pegajoso/sa.
adhesiveness *n* adhesividad *f*.
adieu *adv* adiós; * *n* despedida *f*.
adipose *adj* adiposo/sa.
adjacent *adj* adyacente, contiguo/gua.
adjectival *adj* adjetivado/da; **~ly** *adv* como adjetivo.
adjective *n* adjetivo *m*.
adjoin *vi* estar contiguo/gua.
adjoining *adj* contiguo/gua.
adjourn *vt* aplazar.
adjournment *n* prórroga *f*.
adjudicate *vt* adjudicar.
adjunct *n* adjunto *m*.
adjust *vt* ajustar, acomodar.
adjustable *adj* ajustable.
adjustment *n* ajustamiento, arreglo *m*.
adjutant *n* (*mil*) ayudante *m*.
ad lib *vt* improvisar.
administer *vt* administrar; gobernar; **to ~ an oath** prestar juramento.
administration *n* administración *f*; gobierno *m*.
administrative *adj* administrativo/va.
administrator *n* administrador/a *m/f*.
admirable *adj* admirable; **~bly** *adv* admirablemente.

admiral n almirante m.
admiralship n almirante f.
admiralty n almirantazgo m.
admiration n admiración f.
admire vt admirar.
admirer n admira/a m/f.
admiringly adv con admiración.
admissible adj admisible.
admission adj entrada f.
admit vt admitir; to ~ to confesarse culpable de.
admittance n entrada f.
admittedly adj de acuerdo que.
admixture n mixtura, mezcla f.
admonish vt amonestar, reprender.
admonition n amonestación f; consejo, aviso m.
admonitory adj exhortatorio/ria.
ad nauseam adv hasta el cansancio.
adolescence n adolescencia f.
adopt vt adoptar.
adopted adj adoptivo/va.
adoption n adopción f.
adoptive adj adoptivo/va.
adorable adj adorable.
adorably adv de adorable adorable.
adoration n adoración f.
adore vt adorar.
adorn vt adornar.
adornment n adorno m.
adrift adv a la deriva.
adroit adj diestro/tra, hábil.
adroitness n destreza f.
adulation n adulación, zalamería f.
adulatory adj lisonjero/ra.
adult adj adulto/ta; * n adulto m; adulta f.
adulterate vt adulterar, corromper; * adj adulterado/da, falsificado/da.
adulteration n adulteración, corrupción f.
adulterer n adúltero m.
adulteress n adúltera f.

adulterous adj adúltero/ra.
adultery n adulterio m.
advance vt avanzar; promover; pagar por adelantado; * vi hacer progresos; to make ~s insinuarse; * n avance m; paga adelantada f.
advanced adj avanzado/da.
advancement n adelantamiento m; progreso m; promoción f.
advantage n ventaja f; to take ~ of sacar provecho de.
advantageous adj ventajoso/sa; ~ly adv ventajosamente.
advantageousness n ventaja, utilidad f.
advent n venida f; Advent n Adviento m.
adventitious adj adventicio/cia.
adventure n aventura f.
adventurer n aventurero m.
adventurous adj intrépido/da; valeroso/sas; ~ly adv arriesgadamente.
adverb n adverbio m.
adverbial adj adverbial; ~ly adv como adverbio.
adversary n adversario, enemigo m.
adverse adj adverso/sa, contrario/ria.
adversity n calamidad f; infortunio m.
advertise vt anunciar.
advertisement n anuncio m.
advertising n publicidad f.
advice n consejo m; aviso m.
advisability n prudencia, conveniencia f.
advisable adj prudente, conveniente.
advise vt aconsejar; avisar.
advisedly adv prudentemente, avisadamente.
advisory adj consultivo/va.
advocacy n defensa f.

advocate n abogado m; protector m;
* vt abogar por.
advocateship n abogacía f.
aerial n antena f.
aerobics npl aerobic m.
aerometer n areómetro m.
aeroplane n avión m.
aerosol n aerosol m.
aerostat n globo aerostático m.
aesthetic adj estético/ca; ~s npl estética f.
afar adv lejos, distante; **from** ~ desde lejos.
affability n afabilidad, urbanidad f.
affable adj afable, complaciente;
~**bly** adv afablemente.
affair n asunto m; negocio m.
affect vt conmover; afectar.
affectation n afectación f.
affected adj afectado/da, lleno/na de afectación; ~**ly** adv con afectación.
affectingly adv con afecto.
affection n cariño m.
affectionate adj afectuoso/sa; ~**ly** adv cariñosamente.
affidavit n declaración jurada f.
affiliate vt afiliar.
affiliation n afiliación f.
affinity n afinidad f.
affirm vt afirmar, declarar.
affirmation n afirmación f.
affirmative adj afirmativo/va; ~**ly** adv afirmativamente.
affix vt pegar; * n (gr) afijo m.
afflict vt afligir.
affliction n aflicción f; dolor m.
affluence n abundancia f.
affluent adj opulento/ta.
afflux n confluencia, afluencia f.
afford vt dar; proveer.
affray n asalto m; tumulto m.
affront n afrenta, injuria f; * vt afrentar, insultar, ultrajar.

aflame adv en llamas.
afloat adv flotante, a flote.
afraid adj espantado/da, tímido/da; I
am ~ temo.
afresh adv de nuevo, otra vez.
aft adv (mar) a popa.
after prep después; detrás; según;
* adv después; ~ **all** después de todo.
afterbirth n secundinas fpl.
after-effects npl consecuencias fpl.
afterlife n vida venidera f.
aftermath n consecuencias fpl.
afternoon n tarde f.
aftershave n aftershave m.
aftertaste n resabio m.
afterwards adv después.
again adv otra vez; ~ **and** ~ muchas veces; **as much** ~ otra vez tanto.
against prep contra; ~ **the grain** a contrapelo; de mala gana.
agate n ágata f.
age n edad f; **under** ~ menor; * vt envejecer.
aged adj viejo/ja, anciano/na.
agency n agencia f.
agenda n orden del día m.
agent n agente m.
agglomerate vt aglomerar.
agglomeration n aglomeración f.
aggrandizement n engrandecimiento m.
aggravate vt agravar, exagerar.
aggravation n agravación f.
aggregate n agregado m.
aggregation n agregación f.
aggression n agresión f.
aggressive adj ofensivo/va.
aggressor n agresor m.
aggrieved adj ofendido/da.
aghast adj horrorizado/da.
agile adj ágil; diestro/tra.
agility n agilidad f; destreza f.

agitate *vt* agitar.

agitation *n* agitación *f*; perturbación *f*.

agitator *n* agitador, incitador *m*.

ago *adv* pasado, largo tiempo; después; how long ~? ¿cuánto hace?

agog *adj* emocionado/da.

agonizing *adj* atroz.

agony *n* agonía *f*.

agree *vt* convenir; * *vi* estar de acuerdo/da.

agreeable *adj* agradable; amable; ~bly *adv* agradablemente; ~ with según, conforme a.

agreeableness *n* amabilidad, gracia *f*.

agreed *adj* establecido/da, convenido/da; ~! ide acuerdo!

agreement *n* acuerdo *m*.

agricultural *adj* agrario/ria.

agriculture *n* agricultura *f*.

agriculturist *n* agricultor *m*.

agronomy *n* agronomía *f*.

aground *adv* (mar) encallado/da.

ah! *excl* iah!, iay!

ahead *adv* más allá, delante de otro; (mar) por la proa.

ahoy! *excl* (mar) iohe!

aid *vt* ayudar, socorrer; to ~ and abet ser cómplice de; * *n* ayuda *f*; auxilio, socorro *m*.

aide-de-camp *n* (mil) ayudante de campo *m*.

AIDS *n* SIDA *m*.

ail *vt* afligir, molestar.

ailing *adj* doliente.

ailment *n* dolencia, indisposición *f*.

aim *vt* apuntar aspirar a; intentar; * *n* designio *m*; puntería *f*.

aimless *adj* sin designio, sin objeto; ~ly a la deriva.

air *n* aire *m*; * *vt* airear; ventilar.

airbag *n* airbag *m*.

air balloon *n* globo aerostático *m*.

airborne *adj* aerotransportado/da.

air-conditioned *adj* climatizado/da.

air conditioning *n* aire acondicionado *m*.

aircraft *n* avión *m*.

air cushion *n* cojinete rellenado de aire *m*.

air force *n* fuerzas aéreas *fpl*.

air freshener *n* ambientador *m*.

air gun *n* escopeta de aire comprimido *f*.

air hole *n* respiradero *m*.

airless *adj* falto de ventilación, sofocado/da.

airlift *n* puente aéreo *m*.

airline *n* línea aérea *f*.

airmail *n*: by ~ por avión.

airport *n* aeropuerto *m*.

airport tax *n* tasas de aeropuerto *f*.

air pump *n* bomba de aire *f*.

airsick *adj* mareado/da.

airstrip *n* pista de aterrizaje *f*.

air terminal *n* terminal *f*.

airtight *adj* herméticamente cerrado/da.

airy *adj* bien ventilado/da.

aisle *n* nave de una iglesia *f*.

ajar *adj* entreabierto/ta.

akimbo *adj* corvo/va.

akin *adj* parecido/da.

alabaster *n* alabastro *m*; * *adj* alabastrino/na.

alacrity *n* presteza *f*.

alarm *n* alarma *f*; * *vt* alarmar; inquietar.

alarm bell *n* timbre de alarma *m*.

alarmist *n* alarmista *m*.

alas *adv* desgraciadamente.

albeit *conj* aunque.

album *n* álbum *m*.

alchemist *n* alquimista *m*.

alchemy *n* alquimia *f*.

alcohol n alcohol m.

alcoholic adj alcohólico/ca; * n alcoholizado m.

alcove n nicho m.

alder n aliso m.

ale n cerveza f.

alert adj vigilante; alerto/ta; * n alerta f.

alertness n cuidado m; vigilancia f.

algae npl alga f.

algebra n álgebra f.

algebraic adj algebraico/ca.

alias adj alias.

alibi n (law) coartada f.

alien adj ajeno/na; * n forastero m.

alienate vt enajenar.

alienation n enajenación f.

alight vi apearse; * adj encendido/da.

align vt alinear.

alike adj semejante, igual; * adv igualmente.

alimentation n alimentación f.

alimony n alimentos mpl.

alive adj vivo/va, viviente; activo/va.

alkali n álcali m.

alkaline adj alcalino/na.

all adj todo/da; * adv totalmente; ~ **at once**, ~ **of a sudden** de repente; ~ **the same** sin embargo; **the better** tanto mejor; **not at** ~l ino hay de qué!; **once for** ~ una vez por todas; * n todo m.

allay vt aliviar.

all clear n luz verde f.

allegation n alegación f.

allege vt alegar; declarar.

allegiance n lealtad, fidelidad f.

allegorical adj alegórico/ca; **~ly** adv alegóricamente.

allegory n alegoría f.

allegro n (mus) alegro m.

allergy n alergia f.

alleviate vt aliviar, aligerar.

alleviation n alivio m; mitigación f.

alley n callejuela f.

alliance n alianza f.

allied adj aliado/da.

alligator n caimán m.

alliteration n aliteración f.

all-night adj abierto/ta toda la noche.

allocate vt repartir.

allocation n cuota f.

allot vt asignar.

allow vt conceder; permitir; dar, pagar; **to** ~ **for** tener en cuenta.

allowable adj admisible, permitido/da.

allowance n concesión f.

alloy n liga, mezcla, aleación f.

all right adv bien.

all-round adj completo/ta.

allspice n pimienta de Jamaica f.

allude vt aludir.

allure n fascinación f.

alluring adj seductor/a; **~ly** adv seductoramente.

allurement n aliciente, atractivo m.

allusion n alusión f.

allusive adj alusivo/va; **~ly** adv de modo alusivo.

alluvial adj aluvial.

ally n aliado m; * vt aliar.

almanac n almanaque m.

almighty adj omnipotente, todopoderoso/sa.

almond n almendra f.

almond tree n almendro m.

almost adv casi; cerca de.

alms n limosna f.

aloft prep arriba.

alone adj solo; * adv solamente, sólo; **to leave** ~ dejar en paz.

along adv a lo largo; ~ **side** al lado.

aloof adv lejos.

aloud adj en voz alta.
alphabet n alfabeto m.
alphabetical adj alfabético/ca; **~ly** adv por orden alfabético.
alpine adj alpino/na.
already adv ya.
also adv también, además.
altar n altar m.
altarpiece n retablo m.
alter vt modificar.
alteration n alteración f.
altercation n altercado m.
alternate adj alterno/na; * vt alternar, variar; **~ly** adv alternativamente.
alternating adj alterno/na.
alternation n alternación f.
alternator n alternador m.
alternative n alternativa f; * adj alternative; **~ly** adv si no.
although conj aunque, no obstante.
altitude n altitud, altura f.
altogether adv del todo.
alum n alumbre m.
aluminium n aluminio m.
aluminous adj aluminoso/sa.
always adv siempre, constantemente.
a.m. adv de la mañana.
amalgam n amalgama f.
amalgamate vt, vi amalgamar(se).
amalgamation n amalgamación f.
amanuensis n amanuense, secretario m.
amaryllis n (bot) amarillas f.
amass vt acumular, amontonar.
amateur n aficionado m, amateur m/f.
amateurish adj torpe.
amatory adj amatorio/ria; erótico/ca.
amaze vt asombrar.
amazement n asombro m.
amazing adj pasmoso/sa; **~ly** adv extraordinariamente.

amazon n amazona f.
ambassador n embajador m.
ambassadress n embajadora f.
amber n ámbar m; * adj ambarino/na.
ambidextrous adj ambidextro/tra, ambidiestro/tra.
ambient adj ambiente.
ambiguity n ambigüedad, duda f.
ambiguous adj ambiguo; **~ly** adv ambiguamente.
ambition n ambición f.
ambitious adj ambicioso/sa; **~ly** adv ambiciosamente.
amble vi andar sin prisa.
ambulance n ambulancia f.
ambush n emboscada f; **to lie in ~** estar emboscado/da; * vt tender una emboscada a.
ameliorate vt mejorar.
amelioration n mejoramiento m.
amenable adj sensible.
amend vt enmendar.
amendable adj reparable, corregible.
amendment n enmienda f.
amends npl compensación f.
amenities npl comodidades fpl.
America n América f.
American adj americano/na.
amethyst n amatista f.
amiability n amabilidad f.
amiable adj amable.
amiableness n amabilidad f.
amiably adv amablemente.
amicable adj amigable, amistoso/sa; **~bly** adv amistosamente.
amid(st) prep entre, en medio de.
amiss adv: **something's ~** algo pasa.
ammonia n amoniaco m.
ammunition n municiones fpl.
amnesia n amnesia f.

amnesty n amnistía f.

among(st) prep entre, en medio de.

amoral adv amoral.

amorous adj amoroso/sa; **~ly** adv amorosamente.

amorphous adj informe.

amount n importe m; cantidad f; * vi sumar.

amp(ere) n amperio m.

amphibian n anfibio m.

amphibious adj anfibio/bia.

amphitheatre n anfiteatro m.

ample adj amplio/lia.

ampleness n amplitud, abundancia f.

amplification n amplificación f; extensión f.

amplifier n amplificador m.

amplify vt ampliar, extender.

amplitude n amplitud, extensión f.

amply adv ampliamente.

amputate vt amputar.

amputation n amputación f.

amulet n amuleto m.

amuse vt entretener, divertir.

amusement n diversión f, pasatiempo, entretenimiento m.

amusing adj divertido/da; **~ly** adv entretenidamente.

an art un, uno, una.

anachronism n anacronismo m.

anaemia n anemia f.

anaemic adj (med) anémico/ca.

anaesthetic n anestesia f.

analog adj (comput) analógico/ca.

analogous adj análogo.

analogy n analogía f.

analyse vt analizar.

analysis n análisis m invar.

analyst n analizador/a m/f.

analytical adj analítico/ca; **~ly** adv analíticamente.

anarchic adj anárquico/ca.

anarchist adj anarquista.

anarchy n anarquía f.

anatomical adj anatómico/ca; **~ly** adv anatómicamente.

anatomize vt anatomizar.

anatomy n anatomía f.

ancestor n: **~s** pl antepasados mpl.

ancestral adj hereditario/ria.

ancestry n raza, alcurnia f.

anchor n ancla f; * vi anclar; **to weigh ~** zarpar.

anchorage n fondeadero m.

anchovy n anchoa f.

ancient adj antiguo.

ancillary adj auxiliar.

and conj y, e.

anecdotal adj anecdótico/ca.

anecdote n anécdota f.

anemone n (bot) anémona f.

anew adv de nuevo, nuevamente.

angel n ángel m.

angelic adj angélico/ca.

anger n cólera f; * vt enojar, irritar.

angle n ángulo m; * vt pescar con caña.

angled adj anguloso/sa.

angler n pescador/a de caña m/f.

anglicism n anglicismo m.

angling n pesca con caña f.

angrily adv enojado.

angry adj enojado/da.

anguish n ansia, angustia f.

angular adj angular.

angularity n forma angular f.

animal n adj animal m.

animate vt animar; * adj viviente.

animated adj vivo/va.

animation n animación f.

animosity n rencor m.

animus n odio m.

anise n anís m.

aniseed n anís m.

ankle n tobillo m; **~ bone** hueso del tobillo m.

annals n anales mpl.

annex vt anejar; * n anejo m.

annexation n anexión f.

annihilate vt aniquilar.

annihilation n aniquilación f.

anniversary n aniversario m.

annotate vi anotar.

annotation n anotación f.

announce vt anunciar, publicar.

announcement n anuncio m.

announcer n locutor/a m/f.

annoy vt molestar.

annoyance n molestia f.

annoying adj molesto/ta; fastidioso/sa.

annual adj anual; ~ly adv anualmente, cada año.

annuity n renta vitalicia f.

annul vt anular.

annulment n anulación f.

annunciation n anunciación f.

anodyne adj anodino/na.

anoint vt untar, ungir.

anomalous adj anómalo.

anomaly n anomalía, irregularidad f.

anon adv más tarde.

anonymity n anonimato m.

anonymous adj anónimo/ma; ~ly adj anónimamente.

anorexia n anorexia f.

another adj otro/tra, diferente; **one ~** uno a otro.

answer vt responder, replicar; corresponder; **to ~ for** responder de o por; **to ~ to** corresponder a; * n respuesta, réplica f.

answerable adj responsable.

answering machine n contestador automático m.

ant n hormiga f.

antagonism n antagonismo m; rivalidad f.

antagonist n antagonista m.

antagonize vt provocar.

antarctic adj antártico/ca.

anteater n oso hormiguero m.

antecedent n: ~s pl antecedentes mpl.

antechamber n antecámara f.

antedate vt antedatar.

antelope n antílope m.

antenna npl antena f.

anterior adj anterior, precedente.

anthem n himno m.

ant hill n hormiguero m.

anthology n antología f.

anthracite n antracita f.

anthropologist n antropólogo/ga m/f.

anthropology n antropología f.

anti-aircraft adj antiaéreo/rea.

antibiotic n antibiótico m.

antibody n anticuerpo m.

Antichrist n Anticristo m.

anticipate vt anticipar, prevenir.

anticipation n anticipación f.

anticlockwise adv en sentido contrario al de las agujas del reloj.

antidote n antídoto m.

antifreeze n anticongelante m.

antimony n antimonio m.

antipathy n antipatía f.

antipodes npl antípodas fpl.

antiquarian n anticuario m.

antiquated adj antiguo/gua; * n antigüedad f.

antiquity n antigüedad f.

antiseptic adj antiséptico/ca.

antisocial adj antisocial.

antithesis n antítesis f.

antler n cuerna f.

anvil n yunque m.

anxiety n ansiedad f, ansia f; afán m, zozobra f.

anxious adj ansioso/sa; ~ly adv ansiosamente; **to be ~** vi zozobrar.

any *adj pn* cualquier, cualquiera; alguno, alguna; todo; ~**body** alguien, nadie, cualquiera; ~**how** de cualquier manera; ~**more** más; ~**place** en ninguna parte; ~**thing** algo, nada, cualquier cosa.
apace *adv* rápidamente.
apart *adv* aparte, separadamente.
apartment *n* apartamento, departamento *m*.
apartment house *n* casa de apartamentos *f*.
apathetic *adj* apático/ca.
apathy *n* apatía *f*.
ape *n* mono *m*; * *vt* remedar.
aperture *n* abertura *f*.
apex *n* ápice *m*.
aphorism *n* aforismo *m*; máxima *f*.
apiary *n* colmenar *m*.
apiece *adv* por cabeza, por persona.
aplomb *n* aplomo *m*.
Apocalypse *n* Apocalipsis *m*.
apocrypha *npl* libros apócrifos *mpl*.
apocryphal *adj* apócrifo/fa, no canónico/ca.
apologetic *adj* de disculpa.
apologist *n* apologista *m*.
apologize *vt* disculpar.
apology *n* apología, defensa *f*.
apoplexy *n* apoplejía *f*.
apostle *n* apóstol *m*.
apostolic *adj* apostólico/ca.
apostrophe *n* apóstrofe *m*.
apotheosis *n* apoteosis *f*.
appal *vt* espantar, aterrar.
appalling *adj* espantoso/sa.
apparatus *n* aparato *m*.
apparel *n* traje, vestido *m*.
apparent *adj* evidente, aparente; ~**ly** *adv* por lo visto.
apparition *n* aparición, visión *f*.
appeal *vi* apelar, recurrir a un tribunal superior; * *n* (*law*) apelación *f*.

appealing *adj* atractivo/va.
appear *vi* aparecer.
appearance *n* apariencia *f*.
appease *vt* aplacar.
appellant *n* (*law*) apelante *m*.
append *vt* anejar.
appendage *n* cosa accesoria *f*.
appendicitis *n* apendicitis *f*.
appendix *n* apéndice *m*.
appertain *vi* tocar a.
appetite *n* apetito *m*.
appetizing *adj* apetitivo/va.
applaud *vi* aplaudir.
applause *n* aplausos *mpl*.
apple *n* manzana *f*.
apple pie *n* pastelillo de manzanas *m*; **in ~ order** en sumo orden.
apple tree *n* manzano *m*.
appliance *n* aparato *m*.
applicability *n* aplicabilidad *f*.
applicable *adj* aplicable.
applicant *n* aspirante, candidato *m*.
application *n* aplicación *f*; solicitud *f*.
applied *adj* aplicado/da.
apply *vt* aplicar; * *vi* dirigirse a, recurrir a.
appoint *vt* nombrar.
appointee *n* persona nombrada *f*.
appointment *n* cita *f*; nombramiento *m*.
apportion *vt* repartir.
apportionment *n* repartición *f*.
apposite *adj* adaptado/da.
apposition *n* aposición *f*.
appraisal *n* estimación *f*.
appraise *vt* tasar; estimar.
appreciable *adj* sensible.
appreciably *adv* sensiblemente.
appreciate *vt* apreciar; agradecer.
appreciation *n* aprecio *m*.
appreciative *adj* agradecido/da.
apprehend *vt* arrestar.
apprehension *n* aprensión *f*.

apprehensive *adj* aprensivo/va, tímido/da.

apprentice *n* aprendiz *m*; * *vt* poner de aprendiz.

apprenticeship *n* aprendizaje *m*.

apprise *vt* informar.

approach *vt* (*vi*) aproximar(se); * *n* acceso *m*.

approachable *adj* accesible.

approbation *n* aprobación *f*.

appropriate *vt* apropiarse de; * *adj* apropiado/da.

approval *n* aprobación *f*.

approve (of) *vt* aprobar.

approximate *vi* acercarse; * *adj* aproximativo/va; **~ly** *adv* aproximadamente.

approximation *n* aproximación *f*.

apricot *n* damasco, albaricoque *m*.

April *n* abril *m*.

apron *n* delantal *m*.

apse *n* ábside *m*.

apt *adj* apto/ta, idóneo/nea; **~ly** *adv* oportunamente.

aptitude *n* aptitud *f*.

aqualung *n* escafandra autónoma *f*.

aquarium *n* acuario *m*.

Aquarius *n* Acuario *m*.

aquatic *adj* acuático/ca.

aqueduct *n* acueducto *m*.

aquiline *adj* aguileño/ña.

arabesque *n* arabesco *m*.

arable *adj* labrantío/tía.

arbiter *n* árbitro *m*.

arbitrariness *n* arbitrariedad *f*.

arbitrary *adj* arbitrario/ria.

arbitrate *vt* arbitrar, juzgar como árbitro.

arbitration *n* arbitrio *m*.

arbitrator *n* árbitro *m*.

arbour *n* emparrado *m*; enramada *f*.

arcade *n* galería *f*.

arch *n* arco *m*; * *adj* malicioso/sa.

archaeological *adj* arqueológico/ca.

archaeologist *n* arqueólogo/ga *m/f*.

archaeology *n* arqueología *f*.

archaic *adj* arcaico/ca.

archangel *n* arcángel *m*.

archbishop *n* arzobispo *m*.

archbishopric *n* arzobispado *m*.

archer *n* arquero *m*.

archery *n* tiro con arco *m*.

architect *n* arquitecto/ta *m/f*.

architectural *adj* arquitectónico/ca.

architecture *n* arquitectura *f*.

archives *npl* archivos *mpl*.

archivist *n* archivero/ra *m/f*.

archly *adv* maliciosamente.

archway *n* arcada, bóveda *f*.

arctic *adj* ártico/ca.

ardent *adj* apasionado/da; **~ly** *adv* con pasión.

ardour *n* ardor *m*; vehemencia *f*; pasión *f*.

arduous *adj* arduo, difícil.

area *n* área *f*; espacio *m*, zona *f*.

arena *n* arena *f*.

arguably *adv* posiblemente.

argue *vi* discutir; * *vt* sostener.

argument *n* argumento *m*, controversia *f*.

argumentation *n* argumentación *f*.

argumentative *adj* discutidor/a.

aria *n* (*mus*) aria *f*.

arid *adj* árido/da, estéril.

aridity *n* sequedad *f*.

Aries *n* Aries *m*.

aright *adv* bien; **to set ~** rectificar.

arise *vi* levantarse; nacer.

aristocracy *n* aristocracia *f*.

aristocrat *n* aristócrata *m/f*.

aristocratic *adj* aristocrático/ca; **~ally** *adv* aristocráticamente.

arithmetic *n* aritmética *f*.

arithmetical *adj* aritmético/ca; **~ly** *adv* aritméticamente.

ark n arca f.

arm n brazo m; arma f; * vt, vi armar(se).

armament n armamento m.

armchair n sillón m.

armed adj armado/da.

armful n brazada f.

armhole n sobaco m.

armistice n armisticio m.

armour n armadura f.

armoured car n carro blindado m.

armoury n arsenal m.

armpit n sobaco m.

armrest n apoyabrazos m invar.

army n ejército m; tropas fpl.

aroma n aroma m.

aromatherapy n aromaterapia f.

aromatic adj aromático/ca.

around prep alrededor de; * adv alrededor.

arouse vt despertar; excitar.

arraign vt acusar.

arraignment n acusación f; proceso criminal m.

arrange vt organizar.

arrangement n colocación f; arreglo.

arrant adj consumado/da.

array n serie f.

arrears npl resto de una deuda m; atraso m.

arrest n arresto m; * vt detener, arrestar.

arrival n llegada f.

arrive vi llegar.

arrogance n arrogancia, presunción f.

arrogant adj arrogante, presuntuoso/sa; ~ly adv arrogantemente.

arrogate vt arrogarse.

arrogation n arrogación f.

arrow n flecha f.

arsenal n (mil) arsenal m; (mar) atarazana, armería f.

arsenic n arsénico m.

arson n fuego incendiario m.

art n arte m.

arterial adj arterial.

artesian well n pozo artesiano m.

artery n arteria f.

artful adj ingenioso/sa.

artfulness n astucia, habilidad f.

art gallery n pinacoteca f.

arthritis n artritis f.

artichoke n alcachofa f.

article n artículo m.

articulate vt articular, pronunciar distintamente.

articulated adj articulado/da.

articulation n articulación f.

artifice n artificio, fraude m.

artificial adj artificial; artificioso/sa; ~ly adv artificialmente; artificiosamente.

artificial insemination n inseminación artificial f.

artificiality n artificialidad f.

artillery n artillería f.

artisan n artesano/na m/f.

artist n artista m.

artistic adj artístico/ca.

artistry n habilidad f.

artless adj sencillo, simple; ~ly adv sencillamente, naturalmente.

artlessness n sencillez f.

as conj como; mientras; también; visto que, puesto que; ~ for, ~ to en cuanto a.

asbestos n asbesto, amianto m.

ascend vi ascender, subir.

ascendancy n dominio m.

ascension n ascensión f.

ascent n subida f.

ascertain vt establecer.

ascetic adj ascético/ca; * n asceta m.

ascribe vt atribuir.

ash n (bot) fresno m; ceniza f.

ashamed *adj* avergonzado/da.

ashore *adv* en tierra, a tierra; **to go ~** desembarcar.

ashtray *n* cenicero *m*.

Ash Wednesday *n* miércoles de ceniza *m*.

aside *adv* a un lado.

ask *vt* pedir, rogar; **to ~ after** preguntar por; **to ~ for** pedir; **to ~ out** invitar.

askance *adv* desconfiado/da.

askew *adv* de lado.

asleep *adj* dormido/da; **to fall ~** dormirse.

asparagus *n* espárrago *m*.

aspect *n* aspecto *m*.

aspen *n* álamo temblón *m*.

aspersion *n* calumnia *f*.

asphalt *n* asfalto *m*.

asphyxia *n* (*med*) asfixia *f*.

asphyxiate *vt* asfixiar.

asphyxiation *n* asfixia *f*.

aspirant *n* aspirante *m*.

aspirate *vt* aspirar, pronunciar con aspiración; * *n* sonido aspirado *m*.

aspiration *n* aspiración *f*.

aspire *vi* aspirar, desear.

aspirin *n* aspirina *f*.

ass *n* asno *m*; **she ~** burra *f*.

assail *vt* asaltar, atacar.

assailant *n* asaltante *m/f*, agresor/a *m/f*.

assassin *n* asesino/na *m/f*.

assassinate *vt* asesinar.

assassination *n* asesinato *m*.

assault *n* asalto *m*; * *vt* acometer, asaltar.

assemblage *n* multitud *f*.

assemble *vt* reunir, convocar; * *vi* juntarse.

assembly *n* asamblea, junta *f*; congreso *m*.

assembly line *n* cadena de montaje *f*.

assent *n* asentimiento *m*; * *vi* asentir.

assert *vt* sostener, mantener; afirmar.

assertion *n* aserción *f*.

assertive *adj* perentorio/ria.

assess *vt* valorar.

assessment *n* valoración *f*.

assessor *n* asesor/a *m/f*.

assets *npl* bienes *mpl*.

assiduous *adj* diligente, aplicado/da; **~ly** *adv* diligentemente.

assign *vt* asignar.

assignation *n* cita *f*.

assignment *n* asignación *f*; tarea *f*.

assimilate *vt* asimilar.

assimilation *n* asimilación *f*.

assist *vt* asistir, ayudar, socorrer.

assistance *n* asistencia *f*; socorro *m*.

assistant *n* asistente, ayudante *m*.

associate *vt* asociar; * *adj* asociado/da; * *n* socio *m*.

association *n* asociación, sociedad *f*.

assonance *n* asonancia *f*.

assorted *adj* surtido/da.

assortment *n* surtido *m*.

assuage *vt* mitigar, suavizar.

assume *vt* asumir; suponer.

assumption *n* supuesto *m*.

Assumption *n* Asunción *f*.

assurance *n* seguro *m*.

assure *vt* asegurar.

assuredly *adv* sin duda.

asterisk *n* asterisco *m*.

astern *adv* (*mar*) a popa.

asthma *n* asma *f*.

asthmatic *adj* asmático/ca.

astonish *vt* pasmar, sorprender.

astonishing *adj* asombroso/sa; **~ly** *adv* asombrosamente.

astonishment *n* asombro *m*.

astound *vt* pasmar.

astray *adv*: **to go ~** extraviarse; **to lead ~** llevar por mal camino.

astride *adv* a horcajadas.

astringent *adj* astringente.
astrologer *n* astrólogo/ga *m/f*.
astrological *adj* astrológico/ca.
astrology *n* astrología *f*.
astronaut *n* astronauta *m/f*.
astronomer *n* astrónomo *m*.
astronomical *adj* astronómico/ca.
astronomy *n* astronomía *f*.
astute *adj* astuto/ta.
asylum *n* asilo, refugio *m*.
at *prep* a; en; ~ **once** en seguida; ya; ~ **all** en absoluto; ~ **all events** en todo caso; ~ **first** al principio; ~ **last** por fin.
atheism *n* ateísmo *m*.
atheist *n* ateo *m*, atea *f*.
athlete *n* atleta *m/f*.
athletic *adj* atlético/ca.
atlas *n* atlas *m invar*.
atmosphere *n* atmósfera *f*.
atmospheric *adj* atmosférico/ca.
atom *n* átomo *m*.
atom bomb *n* bomba atómica *f*.
atomic *adj* atómico/ca.
atone *vt* expiar.
atonement *n* expiación *f*.
atop *adv* encima.
atrocious *adj* atroz; ~ly *adv* atrozmente.
atrocity *n* atrocidad, enormidad *f*.
atrophy *n* (*med*) atrofia *f*.
attach *vt* adjuntar.
attaché *n* agregado *m*.
attachment *n* afecto *m*.
attack *vt* atacar; acometer; * *n* ataque *m*.
attacker *n* asaltante *m*.
attain *vt* conseguir, obtener.
attainable *adj* asequible.
attempt *vt* intentar; probar, experimentar; * *n* intento *m*, tentativa *f*.
attend *vt* servir; asistir; **to ~ to** ocuparse de; * *vi* prestar atención.

attendance *n* presencia *f*.
attendant *n* sirviente *m*.
attention *n* atención *f*; cuidado *m*.
attentive *adj* atento/ta; cuidadoso/sa; ~ly *adv* con atención.
attenuate *vt* atenuar, disminuir.
attest *vt* atestiguar.
attic *n* desván *m*; guardilla *f*.
attire *n* atavío *m*.
attitude *n* actitud, postura *f*.
attorney *n* abogado/da *m/f*.
attract *vt* atraer.
attraction *n* atracción *f*; atractivo *m*.
attractive *adj* atractivo/va.
attribute *vt* atribuir; * *n* atributo *m*.
attrition *n* agotamiento *m*.
auburn *adj* moreno/na, castaño/ña.
auction *n* subasta *f*.
auctioneer *n* subastador/a, rematador/a *m/f*.
audacious *adj* audaz, temerario/ria; ~ly *adv* atrevidamente.
audacity *n* audacia, osadía *f*.
audible *adj* perceptible al oído; ~ly *adv* de manera audible.
audience *n* audiencia *f*; auditorio *m*.
audit *n* auditoría *f*; * *vt* auditar.
auditor *n* censor/a de cuentas *m/f*.
auditory *adj* auditivo/va.
augment *vt* aumentar, acrecentar; * *vi* crecer.
augmentation *n* aumentación *f*; aumento *m*.
August *n* agosto *m*.
august *adj* majestuoso/sa.
aunt *n* tía *f*.
au pair *n* au pair *f*.
aura *n* aura *f*.
auspices *npl* auspicios *mpl*.
auspicious *adj* propicio/cia; ~ly *adv* favorablemente.
austere *adj* austero/ra, severo/ra; ~ly *adv* austeramente.

austerity n austeridad f.

authentic adj auténtico/ca; **~ly** adv auténticamente.

authenticate vt autenticar.

authenticity n autenticidad f.

author n autor/a m/f; escritor/a m/f.

authoress n autora; escritora f.

authoritarian adj autoritario/ria.

authoritative adj autoritativo/va; **~ly** adv autoritativamente, con autoridad.

authority n autoridad f.

authorization n autorización f.

authorize vt autorizar.

authorship n autoría f.

automobile n coche, auto m.

autocrat n autócrata m.

autocratic adj autocrático/ca.

autograph n autógrafo m.

automated adj automatizado/da.

automatic adj automático/ca.

automaton n autómata m.

autonomy n autonomía f.

autopsy n autopsia f.

autumn n otoño m.

autumnal adj otoñal.

auxiliary adj auxiliar, asistente.

avail vt: to ~ **oneself of** aprovecharse de; * n: to no ~ en vano.

available adj disponible.

avalanche n alud m.

avarice n avaricia f.

avaricious adj avaro/ra.

avenge vt vengarse, castigar.

avenue n avenida f.

aver vt afirmar, declarar.

average vt tomar un término medio; * n término medio m.

aversion n aversión f, disgusto m.

avert vt desviar, apartar.

aviary n pajarera f.

avoid vt evitar, escapar, huir; * vr zafarse de.

avoidable adj evitable.

await vt aguardar.

awake vt despertar; * vi despertarse; * adj despierto/ta.

awakening n despertar.

award vt otorgar; * n premio m; sentencia, decisión f.

aware adj consciente; vigilante.

awareness n conciencia f.

away adv ausente, fuera; ~! ¡fuera! , ¡quita de ahí!, ¡marcha! **far and ~** de mucho, con mucho.

away game n partido fuera de casa m.

awe n miedo, temor m.

awe-inspiring, awesome adj imponente.

awful adj tremendo/da; horroroso/sa; **~ly** adv terriblemente.

awhile adv un rato, algún tiempo.

awkward adj torpe, rudo/da, poco diestro/tra; **~ly** adv groseramente, toscamente.

awkwardness n tosquedad, grosería, poca habilidad f.

awl n lezna f.

awning n (mar) toldo m.

awry adv oblicuamente, torcidamente, al través.

axe n hacha f; * vt despedir; cortar.

axiom n axioma m.

axis n eje m.

axle n eje m.

ay(e) excl sí.

B

baa n balido m; * vi balar.

babble vi charlar, parlotear; ~, **babbling** n charla, cháchara f.

babbler n charlador/a, charlatán/ana m/f.

babe, baby n niño/a, pequeño/a, nene/a m/f; **small** ~ mamón/ona m/f.

baboon n babuino m.

babyhood n niñez f.

babyish adj niñero/ra; pueril.

baby carriage n cochecito m.

baby linen n ropita de niño f.

bachelor n soltero m; bachiller m.

bachelorship n soltería f; bachillerato m.

back n dorso m; revés de la mano m; * adv atrás, detrás; **a few years** ~ hace algunos años; * vt sostener, apoyar, favorecer.

backbite vt hablar mal del que está ausente; difamar.

backbiter n detractor/a m/f.

backbone n hueso dorsal, espinazo m.

backdate vt antedatar.

backdoor n puerta trasera f.

backer n partidario/ria m/f.

backgammon n backgammon m.

background n fondo m.

backlash n reacción f.

backlog n trabajo acumulado m.

back number n número atrasado m.

backpack n mochila f.

back payment n paga atrasada f.

backside n trasero m.

back-up lights npl (auto) luces de marcha atrás fpl.

backward adj tardo/da, lento/ta; * adv hacia atrás.

bacon n tocino m.

bad adj mal/malo; perverso/sa; infeliz; dañoso/sa; indispuesto/ta; ~**ly** adv malamente.

badge n señal f; símbolo m; divisa f.

badger n tejón m; * vt fatigar; cansar, atormentar.

badminton n bádminton m.

badness n maldad, mala calidad f.

baffle vt confundir, hundir; acosar.

bag n saco m; bolsa f.

baggage n bagaje, equipaje m.

bagpipe n gaita f.

bail n fianza, caución (juratoria) f; fiador m; * vt caucionar, fiar.

bailiff n alguacil m; mayordomo m.

bait vt cebar; atraer; * n cebo m; anzuelo m.

baize n bayeta f.

bake vt cocer en horno.

bakery n panadería f.

baker n hornero/ra, panadero/ra m/f; ~**'s dozen** trece piezas.

baking n cocción f.

baking powder n levadura f.

balance n balanza f; equilibrio m; saldo de una cuenta m; **to lose one's** ~ caerse, dar en tierra; * vt pesar en balanza; contrapesar; saldar; considerar, examinar.

balance sheet n balance m.

balcony n balcón m.

bald adj calvo/va.

baldness n calvicie f.

bale n bala f; * vt embalar; tirar el agua del bote.

baleful adj triste, funesto/ta; ~**ly** adv tristemente; míseramente.

ball n bola f; pelota f; baile m; balón m.

ballad n balada f.

ballast n lastre, m; * vt lastrar.

ballerina n bailarina f.

ballet n ballet m.

ballistic adj balístico/ca.

balloon n globo m.

ballot n voto m; escrutinio m; * vi votar.

ballpoint (pen) n bolígrafo m.

ballroom n salón de baile m.

balm, balsam n bálsamo m; * vt untar con bálsamo.

balmy adj balsámico/ca; fragante.

balustrade n balaustrada f.

bamboo n bambú m.

bamboozle vt (fam) engañar.

ban n prohibición f; * vt prohibir.

banal adj vulgar.

banana n plátano m.

band n faja f; cuadrilla f; banda (de soldados) f; orquesta f.

bandage n venda f, vendaje m; * vt vendar.

bandit n bandido/da m/f.

bandstand n quiosco m.

bandy vt pelotear; discutir.

bandy-legged adj patizambo/ba.

bang n golpe m; * vt golpear; cerrar con violencia.

bangle n brazalete m.

bangs npl flequillo m.

banish vt desterrar, echar fuera, proscribir, expatriar.

banishment n destierro m.

banister(s) n(pl) pasamanos m.

banjo n banjo m.

bank n orilla (de río) f; montón de tierra m; banco m; dique m; escollo m; * vt poner dinero en un banco; **to ~ on** contar con.

bank account n cuenta de banco f.

bank card n tarjeta bancaria f.

banker n banquero/ra m/f.

banking n banca f; **electronic ~** banca electrónica.

banknote n billete de banco m.

bankrupt adj insolvente; * n fallido/da, quebrado/da m.

bankruptcy n bancarrota, quiebra f.

bank statement n detalle de cuenta m.

banner n bandera f; estandarte m.

banquet n banquete m.

banter n zumba f.

baptism n bautismo m.

baptismal adj bautismal.

baptistery n bautisterio m.

baptize vt bautizar.

barbarian n bárbaro/ra m/f; * adj bárbaro/ra.

barbaric adj bárbaro/ra.

barbarism n (gr) barbarismo m; crueldad f.

barbarity n barbaridad, inhumanidad f.

barbarous adj bárbaro/ra, cruel.

barbecue n barbacoa f.

barber n peluquero m.

bar code n código de barras m.

bard n bardo m; poeta m.

bare adj desnudo/da, descubierto/ta; simple; puro/ra; * vt desnudar, descubrir.

barefaced adj desvergonzado/da, impudente.

barefoot(ed) adj descalzo, sin zapatos.

bareheaded adj descubierto/ta.

barelegged adj con las piernas desnudas.

barely adv apenas, solamente.

bareness n desnudez f.

bargain n ganga f; contrato, pacto m; * vi pactar; negociar; **to ~ for** esperar.

bar n bar m; barra f; tranca f; obstáculo m; (law) abogacía f; * vt impedir; prohibir; excluir.

barge n barcaza f.

baritone n (mus) barítono m.

bark n corteza f; ladrido m (del perro); * vi ladrar.

barley n cebada f.

barmaid n camarera f.

barman n barman m.

barn n granero, pajar m.

barnacles npl percebe m.

barometer n barómetro m.

baron n barón m.

baroness n baronesa f.

baronial adj de barón.

barracks npl cuartel m.

barrage n descarga f; (fig) lluvia f.

barrel n barril m; cañón de escopeta m.

barrel organ n organillo de cilindro m.

barren adj estéril, infructuoso/sa; (fig) yermo/ma.

barricade n barricada f; estacada f; barrera f; * vt cerrar con barreras, empalizar.

barrier n barrera f; obstáculo m.

barring adv excepto, fuera de.

barrow n carretilla f.

bartender n barman m.

barter vi baratar; * vt cambiar, trocar.

base n fondo m; base f; basa f; pedestal m; zócalo m; * vt apoyar; * adj bajo/ja, vil.

baseball n béisbol m.

baseless adj sin fondo o base.

basement n sótano m.

baseness n bajeza, vileza f.

bash vt golpear.

bashful adj vergonzoso/sa, modesto/ta, tímido/da; ~ly adv vergonzosamente.

basic adj básico/ca, ~ally adv básicamente.

basilisk n basilisco m.

basin n jofaina, bacía f.

basis n base f; fundamento m.

bask vi ponerse a tomar el sol.

basket n cesta, canasta f.

basketball n baloncesto m.

bass n (mus) contrabajo m.

bassoon n bajón m.

bass viol n viola f.

bass voice n bajo cantante m.

bastard n, adj bastardo/da m/f.

bastardy n bastardía f.

baste vt pringar; hilvanar.

basting n hilván m; apaleamiento m; paliza f.

bastion n (mil) bastión m.

bat n murciélago m.

batch n serie f.

bath n baño m.

bathe vt (vi) bañar(se).

bathing suit n traje de baño m.

bathos n estilo bajo en la poesía m.

bathroom n (cuarto de) baño m.

baths npl piscina f.

bathtub n baño m, bañera f.

baton n batuta f.

battalion n (mil) batallón m.

batter vt apalear; batir, cañonear; * n batido m.

battering ram n (mil) ariete m.

battery n batería f.

battle n combate m; batalla f; * vi batallar, combatir.

battle array n orden de batalla f.

battlefield n campo de batalla m.

battlement n muralla almenada f.

battleship n acorazado m.

bawdy adj indecente.

bawl vi gritar, vocear.

bay n bahía f; laurel, lauro m; * vi balar; * adj bayo.

bayonet n bayoneta f.

bay window n ventana saldiza f.

bazaar n bazar m.

be vi ser; estar.

beach n playa, orilla f.

beacon n almenara f.

bead n cuenta f; ~s npl rosario m.

beagle n sabueso m.

beak n pico m.

beaker n taza con pico f.

beam n rayo de luz m; travesaño m; pareja f; * vi brillar.

bean n alubia f, frijol m, judía f; **green ~, French ~** judía verde f.

beansprouts npl brotes de soja mpl.

bear vt llevar; sostener; soportar; producir; parir; * vi sufrir (algún dolor).

bear n oso m; **she ~** osa f.

bearable adj soportable.

beard n barba f.

bearded adj barbado/da.

bearer n portador/a m/f; árbol fructífero m.

bearing n relación f.

beast n bestia f; hombre brutal m; ~ **of burden** acémila f.

beastliness n bestialidad, brutalidad f.

beastly adj bestial, brutal; * adv brutalmente.

beat vt golpear; tocar (un tambor); **to ~ time** (with the sole of the shoe) zapatear; * vi pulsar, palpitar; * n golpe m; pulsación f.

beatific adj beatífico/ca.

beatify vt beatificar, santificar.

beating n paliza, zurra f, pulsación f, zumba f.

beatitude n beatitud, felicidad f.

beautiful adj hermoso/sa, bello; **~ly** adv con belleza o perfección.

beautify vt hermosear; embellecer; adornar.

beauty n hermosura, belleza f; ~

salon n salón de belleza m; ~ **spot** n lunar m.

beaver n castor m.

because conj porque, a causa de.

beckon vi hacer seña con la cabeza o la mano.

become vt convenir; estar bien; * vi hacerse, convertirse, venir a parar.

becoming adj decente, conveniente.

bed n cama f.

bedclothes npl cobertores npl, mantas o colchas fpl.

bedding n ropa de cama f.

bedecked adj adornado/da.

bedlam n manicomio m.

bedpost n pilar de cama m.

bedridden adj postrado/da en cama, encamado/da.

bedroom n dormitorio m.

bedspread n colcha f.

bedtime n hora de irse a la cama f.

bee n abeja f.

beech n haya f.

beef n carne de vaca f.

beefburger n hamburguesa f.

beefsteak n bistec m.

beehive n colmena f.

beeline n línea recta f.

beer n cerveza f.

beeswax n cera f.

beet n remolacha f.

beetle n escarabajo m.

befall vi suceder, acontecer, sobrevenir.

befit vt convenir, acomodarse a.

before adv, prep antes de; delante, enfrente; ante.

beforehand adv de antemano, anticipadamente.

befriend vt proteger, amparar.

beg vt mendigar, rogar; suplicar; suponer; * vi vivir de limosna.

beget vt engendrar.

beggar n mendigo/ga m/f.

begin vt, vi comenzar, empezar.

beginner n principiante m; novicio/cia m/f.

beginning n principio, origen m.

begrudge vt envidiar.

behalf n on ~ of de parte de.

behave vi comportarse, portarse, conducirse.

behaviour n conducta f; modo de portarse m.

behead vt decapitar, cortar la cabeza.

behind prep detrás; atrás; a la, en zaga; * adv atrasadamente.

behold vt ver, contemplar, observar.

behove vi importar, ser útil; incumbir.

beige adj color beige.

being n existencia f; estado m; ser m.

belated adj atrasado/da.

belch vi eructar, vomitar; * n eructo m.

belfry n campanario m.

belie vt desmentir, calumniar.

belief n fe, creencia f; opinión f; credo m.

believable adj creíble.

believe vt creer; * vi pensar, imaginar.

believer n creyente, fiel, cristiano/na m/f.

belittle vt minimizar.

bell n campana f.

bellicose adj belicoso/sa.

belligerent adj beligerante.

bellow vi bramar; rugir; vociferar; * n bramido m.

bellows npl fuelle m.

belly n vientre m; panza f.

bellyful n panzada f; hartura f.

belong vi pertenecer.

belongings npl pertenencias fpl.

beloved adj querido/da, amado/da.

below adv, prep debajo, inferior; abajo.

belt n cinturón, cinto m; zona f.

bemoan vt deplorar, lamentar.

bemused adj confundido/da.

bench n banco m, banquillo m.

bend vt encorvar, inclinar, plegar; hacer una reverencia; * vi encorvarse, inclinarse; * n curva f.

beneath adv, prep debajo, abajo.

benediction n bendición f.

benefactor n bienhechor m.

benefice n beneficio m; beneficio eclesiástico m.

beneficent adj benéfico/ca.

beneficial adj beneficioso/sa, provechoso/sa, útil.

beneficiary n beneficiario/ria m.

benefit n beneficio m; utilidad f; provecho m; * vt beneficiar; * vi utilizarse; prevalerse.

benefit night n representación dramática a beneficio de un actor o de una actriz f.

benevolence n benevolencia f; donativo gratuito m.

benevolent adj benévolo/la.

benign adj benigno/na; afable; liberal.

bent n inclinación f.

benzine n (chem) bencina f.

bequeath vt legar en testamento.

bequest n legado m.

bereave vt privar.

bereavement n pérdida f.

beret n boina f.

berm n arcén m.

berry n baya f.

berserk adj loco/ca.

berth n (mar) amarradero m, camarote m.

beseech vt suplicar, implorar, conjurar, rogar.

beset vt acosar.

beside(s) prep al lado de; excepto; sobre; fuera de; * adv por otra parte.

besiege vt sitiar, bloquear.

best adj mejor; * adv (lo) mejor; * n lo mejor m.

bestial adj bestial, brutal; ~**ly** adv bestialmente.

bestiality n bestialidad, brutalidad f.

bestow vt dar, conferir; otorgar.

bestseller n bestseller m.

bet n apuesta f; * vt apostar.

betray vt traicionar; divulgar algún secreto.

betrayal n traición f.

betroth vt contraer esponsales.

betrothal n esponsales mpl.

better adj, adv mejor; **so much the ~** tanto mejor; * vt mejorar, reformar.

betting n juego m.

between prep entre, en medio de.

bevel n cartabón m.

beverage n bebida f; trago m.

bevy n bandada (de aves) f.

beware vi guardarse.

bewilder vt pasmar.

bewilderment n perplejidad f.

bewitch vt encantar, hechizar.

beyond prep más allá, más adelante, fuera de.

bias n propensión, inclinación f; sesgo m; prejuicio m.

bib n babador m.

Bible n Biblia f.

biblical adj bíblico/ca.

bibliography n bibliografía f.

bicarbonate of soda n bicarbonato de soda m.

bicker vi escaramucear, reñir, disputar.

bicycle n bicicleta f.

bid vt mandar, ordenar; ofrecer; * n oferta f; tentativa f.

bidding n orden f; mandato m; ofrecimiento m.

bide vt sufrir, aguantar.

biennial adj bienal.

bifocals npl gafas bifocales fpl.

bifurcated adj bifurcado/da.

big adj grande, lleno/na; inflado/da.

bigamist n bígamo/ma m/f.

bigamy n bigamia f.

big dipper n montaña rusa f.

bigheaded adj engreído/da.

bigness n grandeza f.

bigot n fanático/ca m/f.

bigoted adj fanático/ca.

bike n bici f; bicicleta f; **mountain ~** bicicleta de montaña.

bikini n bikini m.

bilberry n arándano m.

bile n bilis f.

bilingual adj bilingüe.

bilious adj bilioso/sa.

bill n pico de ave m; billete m; cuenta f.

billboard n cartelera f.

billet n alojamiento m.

billiards npl billar m.

billiard-table n mesa de billar f.

billion n mil millones mpl, millardo m.

billy n porra f.

bin n cubo de la basura m.

bind vt atar; unir; encuadernar.

binder n encuadernador/a m/f.

binding n venda, faja f.

binge n juerga f.

bingo n bingo m.

biochemistry n bioquímica f.

biodegradable adj biodegradable.

biodiversity n biodiversity f.

binoculars npl prismáticos m.

biographer n biógrafo/fa m/f.

biographical adj biográfico/ca.

biography n biografía f.

biological adj biológico/ca.

biology n biología f.

biped n bípedo m.

birch n abedul m.

bird n ave f; pájaro m.

bird's-eye view n vista de pájaro f.

bird-watcher n ornitólogo/ga m/f.

birth n nacimiento m; origen m; partom.

birth certificate n partida de nacimiento f.

birth control n control de natalidad m.

birthday n cumpleaños m invar.

birthplace n lugar de nacimiento m.

birthright n derechos de nacimiento mpl; primogenitura f.

biscuit n bizcocho m; galleta f.

bisect vt bisecar.

bishop n obispo m.

bison n bisonte m.

bit n bocado m; pedacito m.

bitch n perra f; (fig) zorra f.

bite vt morder; picar; ~ **the dust** (fam) morder la tierra, morir; * n mordedura f.

bitter adj amargo/ga, áspero/ra; mordaz, satírico/ca; penoso/sa; ~**ly** adv amargamente; con pena; severamente.

bitterness n amargor m; rencor m; pena f; dolor m.

bitumen n betún m.

bizarre adj raro/ra, extravagante.

blab vi chismear.

black adj negro/gra, oscuro/ra; funesto/ta; * n color negro m.

blackberry n zarzamora f.

blackbird n mirlo m.

blackboard n pizarra f.

black box n caja negra f.

blacken vt teñir de negro; ennegrecer.

black ice n hielo invisible m.

blackjack n veintiuna f.

blackleg n esquirol m.

blacklist n lista negra f.

blackmail n chantaje m; * vt chantajear.

black market n mercado negro m.

blackness n negrura f.

black pudding n morcilla f.

black sheep n oveja negra f.

blacksmith n herrero m.

blackthorn n endrino m.

bladder n vejiga f.

blade n hoja f; filo m; escobilla f.

blame vt culpar; * n culpa f.

blameless adj inocente, irreprensible, puro/ra; ~**ly** adv inocentemente.

blanch vt blanquear.

bland adj blando/da, suave, dulce, apacible.

blank adj blanco/ca; pálido/da; * n blanco m.

blank cheque n cheque en blanco m.

blanket n manta f.

blare vi resonar.

blasé adj indiferente.

blaspheme vt blasfemar, jurar, decir blasfemias.

blasphemous adj blasfemo/ma.

blasphemy n blasfemia f.

blast n soplo de aire m; carga explosiva f; * vt volar.

blast-off n lanzamiento m.

blatant adj obvio.

blaze n llama f; * vi encenderse en llamas; brillar; resplandecer.

bleach vt blanquear al sol; * vi blanquear; * n lejía f.

bleached adj teñido/da de rubio; descolorado/da.

bleachers npl gradas al sol fpl.

bleak adj pálido/da, descolorido/da; frío, helado/da.

bleakness n frialdad f; palidez f.

bleary(-eyed) adj legañoso/sa.

bleat n balido m; * vi balar.

bleed vi, vt sangrar.

bleeding n sangría f.

bleeper n busca m.

blemish vt manchar, ensuciar; infamar; * n tacha f; deshonra, infamia f.

blend vt mezclar.

bless vt bendecir.

blessing n bendición f; beneficio m; ventaja f.

blight vt arruinar.

blind adj ciego/ga; ~ **alley** n callejón sin salida m; * vt cegar; deslumbrar; * n velo m; **(Venetian)** ~ persiana f.

blinders npl anteojeras fpl.

blindfold vt vendar los ojos; ~**ed** adj con los ojos vendados.

blindly adv ciegamente, a ciegas.

blindness n ceguera f.

blind side n punto ciego m.

blind spot n punto ciego m.

blink vi parpadear.

blinkers npl anteojeras fpl.

bliss n felicidad (eterna) f.

blissful adj feliz en sumo grado; beato/ta, bienaventurado/da; ~**ly** adv felizmente.

blissfulness n suprema felicidad f.

blister n ampolla f; * vi ampollarse.

blitz n bombardeo aéreo m.

blizzard n ventisca f.

bloated adj hinchado/da.

blob n gota f.

bloc n bloque m.

block n bloque m; obstáculo m; zoquete m; manzana f; ~ **(up)** vt bloquear.

blockade n bloqueo f; * vt bloquear.

blockage n obstrucción f.

blockbuster n éxito de público m.

blockhead n bruto, necio, zopenco m; (fam) zoquete m.

blond adj rubio/bia; * n rubio/bia m/f.

blood n sangre f.

blood donor n donante de sangre m/f.

blood group n grupo sanguíneo m.

bloodhound n sabueso m.

bloodily adv sangrientamente, inhumanamente.

bloodiness n (fig) crueldad f.

bloodless adj exangüe; sin efusión de sangre.

blood poisoning n septicemia f.

blood pressure n presión sanguínea f.

bloodshed n efusión de sangre f; matanza f, derramamiento de sangre m.

bloodshot adj ensangrentado/da.

bloodstream n corriente sanguínea f.

bloodsucker n sanguijuela f; (fig) desollador/a m/f.

blood test n análisis de sangre m invar.

bloodthirsty adj sanguinario/ria.

blood transfusion n transfusión sanguínea f.

blood vessel n vena f; vaso sanguíneo m.

bloody adj sangriento/ta, ensangrentado/da; cruel; ~ **minded** adj sanguinario/ria.

bloom n flor f; (also fig); * vi florecer.

blossom n flor f.

blot vt manchar (lo escrito); cancelar; denigrar; * n mancha f.

blotchy adj muy manchado/da.

blotting paper n papel secante m.

blouse n blusa f.

blow vi soplar; sonar; * vt soplar; inflar; **to ~ up** volar; * n golpe m.

blowout n pinchazo m.

blowpipe n soplete m.

blubber n grasa de ballena f; * vi lloriquear.

bludgeon n cachiporra f; palocorto m.

blue adj azul.

bluebell, harebell n (bot) campanilla f.

blue berets npl cascos azules mpl.

bluebottle n moscarda f.

blueness n color azul m.

blueprint n (fig) anteproyecto m.

bluff n farol m; * vt farolear.

bluish adj azulado/da.

blunder n metedura de pata f; error craso m; * vi meter la pata.

blunt adj obtuso/sa; grosero/ra; * vt embotar.

bluntly adv sin artificio; claramente; obtusamente.

bluntness n embotadura, franqueza f.

blur n contorno borroso m; * vt hacer borroso.

blurt out vt descolgarse con.

blush n rubor m; sonrojo m; * vi ponerse colorado/da, sonrojarse.

blustery adj tempestuoso/sa.

boa n boa f (serpiente).

boar n verraco m; **wild ~** jabalí m.

board n tabla f; mesa f; consejo m; * vt embarcarse en; subir a.

boarder n pensionista m/f.

boarding card n tarjeta de embarque f.

boarding house n pensión f, casa de huéspedes f.

boarding school n internado m.

boast vi jactarse; * n jactancia f; ostentación f.

boastful adj jactancioso/sa.

boat n barco m; bote m; barca f.

boating n canotaje m; paseo en barquilla m; regata f.

bobsleigh n bob m.

bode vt presagiar, pronosticar.

bodice n corsé m.

bodily adj, adv corpóreo/rea; corporalmente.

body n cuerpo m; individuo m; gremio m; **any ~** cualquier; **every ~** cada uno.

body-building n culturismo m.

bodyguard n guardaespaldas m/f invar.

bodywork n (auto) carrocería f.

bog n pantano m.

boggy adj pantanoso/sa, palustre.

bogus adj postizo.

boil vi hervir; bullir; hervirle a uno la sangre; * vt cocer; * n furúnculo m.

boiled egg n huevo duro m, huevo pasado por agua m.

boiled potatoes npl patatas hervidas fpl.

boiler n marmita f; caldero m.

boiling point n punto de ebullición m.

boisterous adj borrascoso/sa, tempestuoso/sa; violento/ta; **~ly** adv tumultuosamente, furiosamente.

bold adj ardiente, valiente; audaz; temerario/ria; impudente; **~ly** adv descaradamente.

boldness n intrepidez f; valentía f; osadía f.

bolster n travesero m; cabezal m; * vt reforzar.

bolt n cerrojo m; * vt cerrar con cerrojo.

bomb n bomba f; **~ disposal** desactivación de explosivos f.

bombard vt bombardear.

bombardier n bombardero m.

bombardment n bombardeo m.

bombshell n (fig) bomba f.

bond n ligadura f, vínculo m; vale m; obligación f.

bondage n esclavitud, servidumbre f.
bond holder n titular de bonos m/f.
bone n hueso m; * vt desosar.
boneless adj sin huesos; desosado/da.
bonfire n hoguera f.
bonnet n gorra f; bonete m.
bonny adj bonito/ta.
bonsai n bonsái m.
bonus n cuota, prima f.
bony adj osudo/da.
boo vt abuchear.
booby trap n trampa explosiva f.
book n libro m; **to bring to ~** vt pedir cuentas a alguien.
bookbinder n encuadernador/a m/f.
bookcase n estantería f.
bookkeeper n tenedor/a de libros m/f.
bookkeeping n teneduría de libros f.
bookmaker n corredor de apuestas m.
bookmarker n registro de un libro m.
bookseller n librero/ra m/f.
bookstore n librería f.
bookworm n polilla f; ratón de biblioteca m.
boom n trueno m; boom m; * vi retumbar.
boon n presente, regalo m; favor m.
boor n patán, villano/na m/f.
boorish adj rústico/ca, agreste.
boost n estímulo m; vt estimular.
booster n reinyección f.
boot n(aut) maletero m; bota f; zapata f; **to ~** adv además.
booth n barraca, cabaña f.
booty n botín m; presa f; saqueo m.
booze vi emborracharse; * n bebida f.
border n orilla f; borde m; margen f; frontera f; * vt lindar con.
borderline n frontera f.
bore vt taladrar; barrenar; fastidiar; * n taladro m; calibre m; pelmazo/za m/f.

boredom n aburrimiento m.
borehole n barreno m.
boring adj aburrido/da.
born adj nacido/da; destinado/da.
borrow vt pedir prestado/da.
borrower n prestamista m.
bosom n seno, pecho m.
bosom friend n amigo/ga íntimo/ma m/f.
boss n jefe m; patrón/ona m/f.
botanic(al) adj botánico/ca.
botanist n botánico m.
botany n botánica f.
botch vt chapuzar.
botch-up n mamarracho m.
both adj ambos, entrambos; ambas, entrambas; * conj tanto como.
bother vt preocupar; fastidiar; * n molestia f.
bottle n botella f; * vt embotellar.
bottleneck n embotellamiento m.
bottle-opener n abrebotellas m invar.
bottom n fondo m; fundamento m; * adj más bajo/ja; último/ma.
bottomless adj insondable; excesivo/va; impenetrable.
bough n brazo del árbol m; ramo m.
boulder n canto rodado m.
bounce vi rebotar; ser rechazado/da; * n rebote m.
bound n límite m; salto m; repercusión f; * vi resaltar; * adj destinado/da.
boundary n límite m; frontera f.
boundless adj ilimitado/da, infinito/ta.
bounteous, bountiful adj liberal, generoso/sa, bienhechor.
bounty n liberalidad, bondad f.
bouquet n ramillete de flores m.
bourgeois adj burgués/esa.
bout n ataque m; encuentro m.

bovine adj bovino/na.

bow[1] vt encorvar, doblar; * vi encorvarse; hacer una reverencia; * n reverencia, inclinación f.

bow[2] n arco m; arco de violín; corbata f; nudo m.

bowels npl intestinos mpl; entrañas fpl.

bowl n taza; bola f; * vi jugar a las bochas.

bowler hat n hongo m.

bowling n bolos mpl.

bowling alley n bolera f.

bowling-green n campo m para jugar a las bochas.

bowstring n cuerda del arco f.

bow tie n pajarita f.

box n caja, cajita f; palco de teatro m; ~ **on the ear** bofetada f; * vt encajonar; * vi boxear.

boxer n boxeador m.

boxing n boxeo m.

boxing gloves npl guantes de boxeo mpl.

boxing ring n cuadrilátero m.

box office n taquilla f.

box-seat n asiento de palco m.

boy n muchacho m; niño m; zagal m.

boycott vt boicotear; * n boicot m.

boyfriend n novio m.

boyish adj pueril; frívolo.

bra n sujetador m.

brace n abrazadera f; corrector m.

bracelet n brazalete m.

bracing adj vigorizante.

bracken n (bot) helecho m.

bracket n puntal m; paréntesis m; corchete m; * **to ~ with** vt unir, ligar.

bracing adj vigorizante.

brag n jactancia f; * vi jactarse, fanfarronear.

braid n trenza f; * vt trenzar.

brain n cerebro m; seso; juicio m; * vt descerebrar, matar a uno.

brainchild n parto del ingenio m.

brainwash vt lavar el cerebro.

brainwave n idea luminosa f.

brainy adj inteligente.

brainless adj tonto/ta, insensato/ta.

brake n freno m; * vt, vi frenar.

brake fluid n líquido de frenos m.

brake light n luz de frenado f.

brake shoe n (auto) zapata de freno f.

bramble n zarza, espina f.

bramble patch n zarzal m.

bran n salvado m.

branch n ramo m; rama f; * vt, vi ramificar(se).

branch line n (rail) empalme, ramal m.

brand n marca f; hierro m; * vt marcar (con un hierro incandescente).

brandish vt blandir, ondear.

brand-new adj flamante.

brandy n coñac m.

brash adj tosco/ca; descarado/da.

brass n bronce m.

brassiere n sujetador m.

brat n crío m.

bravado n baladronada f.

brave adj bravo/va, valiente, atrevido/da; * vt desafiar; * n bravo m; **~ly** adv bravamente.

bravery n valor m; magnificencia f.

brawl n pelea, camorra f; * vi pelearse.

brawn n fuerza muscular f; carne de verraco f.

bray n rebuznar; * n rebuzno (del asno) m.

braze vt soldar con latón; broncear.

brazen adj de latón; desvergonzado/da; impudente; * vi hacerse descarado/da.

brazier n brasero m.

breach n rotura f; brecha f; violación f.

bread n pan m; (fig) sustento m;
brown ~ pan moreno m.
breadbox n panera f.
breadcrumbs npl migajas fpl.
breadth n anchura f.
breadwinner n sostén de la familia m.
break vt romper; quebrantar; violar;
arruinar; interrumpir; * vi romperse; **to ~ into** forzar; **to ~ out** abrirse salida; * n rotura, abertura f;
interrupción f; **~ of day** despuntar
del día m, aurora f.
breakage n rotura f.
breakdown n avería f; descalabro m.
breakfast n desayuno m; * vi desayunar.
breaking n rompimiento m; principio de las vacaciones en las escue-
las m; fractura f.
breakthrough n avance m.
breakwater n rompeolas m invar.
breast n pecho, seno m; pechuga f;
corazón m.
breastbone n esternón m.
breastplate n peto m; pectoral m;
coraza f.
breaststroke n braza f.
breath n aliento m, respiración f; soplo de aire m.
breathe vt, vi respirar; exhalar.
breathing n respiración f; aliento m.
breathing space n descanso, reposo m.
breathless adj falto/ta de aliento;
desalentado/da.
breathtaking adj pasmoso/sa.
breed n casta, raza f; * vt procrear,
engendrar; producir; educar; * vi
multiplicarse.
breeder n criador/a m/f.
breeding n crianza f; buena educación f.
breeze n brisa f.

breezy adj refrescado/da con brisas.
brethren n pl de **brother** hermanos
mpl (en estilo grave).
breviary n breviario m.
brevity n brevedad, concisión f.
brew vt hacer; tramar, mezclar; * vi
hacerse; tramarse; * n brebaje m.
brewer n cervecero m.
brewery n cervecería f.
briar, brier n zarza f, espino m.
bribe n cohecho, soborno m; * vt cohechar, corromper, sobornar.
bribery n cohecho, soborno m.
bric-a-brac n baratijas fpl.
brick n ladrillo m; * vt enladrillar.
bricklayer n albañil m.
bricklaying n albañilería f.
bridal adj nupcial.
bride n novia f.
bridegroom n novio m.
bridesmaid n madrina de boda f.
bridge n puente m/f; caballete de la
nariz m; puente de violín m; **to
build a ~ (over)** vt construir un
puente (sobre).
bridle n brida f freno m; * vt embri-
dar; reprimir, refrenar.
brief adj breve, conciso/sa, sucinto/
ta; * n compendio m; breve m.
briefcase n cartera f.
briefly adv brevemente, en pocas palabras.
brier n = **briar.**
brigade n (mil) brigada f.
brigadier n (mil) general de brigada m.
brigand n bandido m.
bright adj claro/ra, luciente, brillante; **~ly** adv espléndidamente.
brighten vt pulir, dar lustre; ilustrar;
* vi aclararse.
brightness n esplendor m, brillantez
f; agudeza f; claridad f.

brilliance n brillo m.

brilliant adj brillante; ~ly adv espléndidamente.

brim n borde extremo m; orilla f.

brimful(l) adj lleno/na hasta el borde.

bring vt llevar, traer; conducir; inducir, persuadir; to ~ about efectuar; to ~ forth producir; parir; to ~ up educar.

brink n orilla f; margen m/f, borde m.

brisk adj vivo/va, alegre, jovial; fresco/ca.

brisket n pecho (de un animal) m.

briskly adv vigorosamente; alegremente; vivamente.

bristle n cerda, seta f; * vi erizarse.

bristly adj cerdoso/sa, lleno/na de cerdas.

brittle adj quebradizo, frágil.

broach vt comenzar a hablar de.

broad adj ancho.

broad bean n (bot) haba f; ~s haba gruesa fpl.

broadcast n emisión f; * vt, vi emitir; transmitir.

broadcasting n radiodifusión f.

broaden vt (vi) ensanchar(se).

broadly adv anchamente.

broad-minded adj tolerante.

broadness n ancho m; anchura f.

broadside n costado de navío m; andanada f.

broadways adv a lo ancho, por lo ancho.

brocade n brocado m.

broccoli n brécol m.

brochure n folleto m.

brogue n abarca f; acento irlandés m.

broil vt asar a la parrilla.

broken adj roto/ta, interrumpido/da; ~ English inglés mal articulado m.

broker n corredor/a m/f.

brokerage n corretaje m.

bronchial adj bronquial.

bronchitis n bronquitis f.

bronze n bronce m; * vt broncear.

brooch n broche m.

brood vi empollar; meditar; * n raza f; nidada f.

brood-hen n pan moreno m; ~ sugar n empolladora f.

brook n arroyo m.

broom n retama f; escoba f.

broomstick n palo de escoba m.

broth n caldo m.

brothel n burdel m.

brother n hermano m.

brotherhood n hermandad f; fraternidad f.

brother-in-law n cuñado m.

brotherly adj, adv fraternal; fraternalmente.

brow n caja f; frente f; cima f.

browbeat vt intimidar.

brown adj moreno/na; castaño/ña; ~ paper n papel de estraza m; ~ bread n pan moreno m; ~ sugar n azúcar terciado m; * n color moreno m; * vt volver moreno/na.

browse vt ramonear; * vi pacer la hierba.

browser n navegador m.

bruise vt magullar; * n magulladura, contusión f; roncha f.

brunch n desayuno-almuerzo m.

brunette n morena f.

brunt n choque m.

brush n cepillo m; escobilla f; combate m; * vt cepillar.

brushwood n breñal, zarzal m.

brusque adj brusco/ca.

Brussels sprout n col de Bruselas f.

brutal adj brutal; ~ly adv brutalmente.

brutality n brutalidad f.

brutalize vt, vi embrutecer(se).

brute n bruto m; * adj feroz, bestial; irracional.

brutish adj brutal, bestial; feroz; ~ly adv brutalmente.

bubble n burbuja f; * vi burbujear, bullir.

bubblegum n chicle m.

bucket n cubo, pozal m.

buckle n hebilla f; * vt hebillar; abrochar; * vi encorvarse.

buckshot n perdigones mpl.

bucolic adj bucólico/ca.

bud n pimpollo, botón, capullo m; yema f; * vi brotar.

Buddhism n Budismo m.

budding adj en ciernes.

buddy n compañero m.

budge vi moverse, menearse.

budgerigar n periquito m.

budget n presupuesto m.

buff n entusiasta m.

buffalo n búfalo m.

buffers npl (rail) parochoques m invar, topes mpl.

buffet n buffet m; * vt abofetear.

buffoon n bufón, chocarrero m.

bug n chinche m.

bugbear n espantajo, coco m.

bugle(horn) n trompa de caza f.

build vt edificar; construir.

builder n constructor/a m/f; maestro/tra de obras m/f.

building n edificio m; construcción f.

bulb n bulbo m; cebolla f.

bulbous adj bulboso/sa.

bulge vi combarse; * n bombeo m.

bulk n masa f; volumen m; grosura f; mayor parte f; capacidad de un buque f; in ~ a granel.

bulky adj grueso/sa, grande.

bull n toro m.

bulldog n dogo m.

bulldozer n aplanadora f.

bullet n bala f.

bulletin board n tablón de anuncios m.

bulletproof adj a prueba de balas.

bullfight n corrida de toros f.

bullfighter n torero m.

bullfighting n toreo m.

bullion n oro o plata en barras m o f.

bullock n novillo capado m.

bullring n plaza de toros f.

bull's-eye n centro del blanco m.

bully n valentón m; * vt tiranizar.

bulwark n baluarte m.

bum n vagabundo m/f.

bumblebee n abejorro, zángano m.

bump n hinchazón f; jiba f; bollo m; barriga f; * vt chocar contra.

bumper n parachoques m invar.

bumpkin n patán m; villano/na m/f.

bumpy adj bacheado/da.

bun n bollo m; mono m.

bunch n ramo m; grupo m.

bundle n fardo m, haz m (de leña etc); paquete m; rollo m; * vt atar, hacer un lío.

bung n tapón m; * vt atarugar.

bungalow n bungalow m.

bungee-jumping n puenting m.

bungle n chapucear; * vi hacer algo chabacanamente.

bunion n juanete m.

bunk n litera f.

bunker n refugio m; búnker m.

buoy n (mar) boya f.

buoyancy n capacidad para flotar f.

buoyant adj boyante.

burden n carga f; * vt cargar.

bureau n armario m; escritorio m.

bureaucracy n burocracia f.

bureaucrat n burócrata m/f.

burglar n ladrón/ona m/f.

burglar alarm n alarma antirrobo f.

burglary n robo en una casa m.

burial n enterramiento m; exequias fpl; sepultura f.

burial place n cementerio m.

burlesque n, adj lengua burlesca f; burlesco/ca m/f.

burly adj fornido/da.

burn vt quemar, abrasar, incendiar; * vi arder; * n quema dura f.

burner n quemador m; mechero m.

burning adj ardiente.

burrow n madriguera f; * vi esconderse en la madriguera.

bursar n tesorero/ra f.

burse n bolsa, lonja f.

burst vi reventar; abrirse; **to ~ into tears** prorrumpir en lágrimas; **to ~ out laughing** estallarse de risa; * vt **to ~ into** irrumpir en; * n reventón m; rebosadura f.

bury vt enterrar, sepultar; esconder.

bus n autobús m.

bush n arbusto, espinal m; cola de zorro f.

bushy adj espeso/sa, lleno/na de arbustos.

busily adv diligentemente, apresuradamente.

business n asunto m; negocios mpl; empleo m; ocupación f.

businesslike adj serio/ria.

businessman n hombre de negocios m.

business trip n viaje de negocios m.

businesswoman n mujer de negocios f.

bus lane n carril bus m.

bust n busto m.

bus stop n parada de autobuses f.

bustle vi hacer ruido; menearse; andar al retortero; * n baraúnda f; ruido m.

bustling adj animado/da.

busy adj ocupado/da; entrometido/da.

busybody n entrometido m.

but conj pero; mas; excepto, menos; solamente.

butcher n carnicero/ra m/f; * vt matar atrozmente.

butcher's (shop) n carnicería f.

butchery n matadero m.

butler n mayordomo m.

butt n colilla f; cabo, extremo m; * vt topar.

butter n mantequilla f; * vt untar con mantequilla.

buttercup n (bot) ranúnculo m.

butterfly n mariposa f.

buttermilk n suero de manteca m.

buttocks npl posaderas fpl.

button n botón m; * vt abotonar.

buttonhole n ojal m.

buttress n estribo m; apoyo m; * vt estribar.

buxom adj frescachona, rolliza.

buy vt comprar.

buyer n comprador/a m/f.

buzz, buzzing n susurro, zumbido m; * vi zumbar.

buzzer n timbre m.

buzzard n ratonero común m.

by prep por; a, en; de; cerca, al lado de; **~ and ~** de aquí a poco, ahora; **~ the ~** de paso; **~ much** con mucho; **~ all means** por supuesto.

bygone adj pasado/da.

by-law n ordenanza municipal f.

bypass n carretera de circunvalación f.

by-product n derivado m.

by-road n camino secundario m.

bystander n mirador m.

byte n (comput) byte m.

byword n proverbio, refrán m.

C

cab n taxi m.

cabbage n berza, col f.

cabin n cabaña, cámara de navío f.

cabinet n consejo de ministros m; gabinete m; escritorio m.

cabinet-maker n ebanista m.

cable n cable m.

cable car n teleférico m.

cable television n televisión por cable f.

caboose n (mar) cocina f.

cache n alijo m.

cackle vi cacarear, graznar; * n cacareo m; charla f.

cactus n cacto m, cactus m invar.

cadence n (mus) cadencia f.

cadet n cadete m.

cadge vt mangar.

caesarean section, ~ operation n (med) (operación de) cesárea f.

café n café m.

cafeteria n café m.

caffeine n cafeína f.

cage n jaula f; prisión f; * vt enjaular.

cagey adj cauteloso/sa.

cajole vt lisonjear, adular; sonsacar.

cake n bollo m; tortita f.

calamitous adj calamitoso/sa.

calamity n calamidad, miseria f.

calculable adj calculable.

calculate vt calcular, contar.

calculation n cálculo m.

calculator n calculadora f.

calculus n cálculo m.

calendar n calendario m.

calf n ternero m; ternera f; carne de ternero f.

calibre n calibre m.

call vt llamar, nombrar; llamar por teléfono; convocar, citar; apelar; **to ~ for** preguntar por, ir a buscar; **to ~ on** visitar; **to ~ attention** llamar la atención; **to ~ names** insultar; * n llamada f; instancia f; invitación f; urgencia f; vocación f; profesión f.

caller n visitador/a m/f.

calligraphy n caligrafía f.

calling n profesión, vocación f.

callisthenics n calistenia f.

callous adj calloso/sa, endurecido/da; insensible.

calm n calma, tranquilidad f; * adj quieto/ta, tranquilo/la; * vt calmar; aplacar, aquietar; **~ly** adv tranquilamente.

calmness n tranquilidad, calma f.

calorie n caloría f.

calumny n calumnia f.

Calvary n calvario m.

calve vi parir.

Calvinist n calvinista m/f.

camcorder n videocámara f.

camel n camello m.

cameo n camafeo m.

camera n máquina fotográfica f; cámara f.

cameraman n cámara m.

camomile n manzanilla f.

camouflage n camuflaje m.

camp n campo m; * vi acampar; **refugee** ~ campo de refugiados.

campaign n campana f; **run-up-to-the-election** ~ precampaña f; * vi hacer campana.

campaigner n defensor/a m/f.

camper n campista m/f.

camping n camping m.

camphor n alcanfor m.

campsite n camping m.

campus n ciudad universitaria f, campus m invar.

can ví poder; * n lata f.

canal n estanque m; canal m.

cancel vt cancelar; anular, invalidar.

cancellation n cancelación f.

cancer n cáncer m.

Cancer n Cáncer m (signo del zodiaco).

cancerous adj canceroso/sa.

candid adj cándido/da, sencillo/lla, sincero/ra; ~**ly** adv cándidamente, francamente.

candidate n candidato/a m/f.

candied adj azucarado/da.

candle n candela f; vela f.

candlelight n luz de candela f.

candlestick n candelero m.

candour n candor m; sinceridad f.

candyfloss n algodón azucarado m.

cane n cana f; bastón m.

canine adj canino/na, perruno/na.

canister n bote m.

cannabis n cannabis m.

cannibal n caníbal m/f; antropófago/ga m/f.

cannibalism n canibalismo m.

cannon n cañón m.

cannonball n bala de artillería f.

canny adj cuerdo/da, discreto/ta.

canoe n canoa f.

canon n canon m; regla f; ~**law** derecho canónico m.

canonization n canonización f.

canonize vt canonizar.

can opener n abrelatas m invar.

canopy n dosel, pabellón m.

cantankerous adj áspero/ra, fastidioso/sa.

canteen n cantina f.

canter n medio galope m.

canvas n cañamazo m.

canvass vt escudriñar, examinar; controvertir; * ví solicitar votos; pretender.

canvasser n solicitador/a m/f.

canyon n cañón m.

canyoning n barranquismo m.

cap n gorra f.

capability n capacidad f, aptitud, inteligencia f.

capable adj capaz.

capacitate vt hacer capaz.

capacity n capacidad f; inteligencia, habilidad f.

cape n cabo, promontorio m.

caper n cabriola f; alcaparra f; * ví hacer cabriolas.

capillary adj capilar.

capital adj capital; principal; * n capital f (la ciudad principal); capital, fondo m; mayúscula f.

capitalism n capitalismo m.

capitalist n capitalista m.

capitalize vt capitalizar; **to ~ on** aprovechar.

capital punishment n pena de muerte f.

Capitol n Capitolio m.

capitulate ví capitular.

capitulation n capitulación f.

caprice n capricho m; extravagancia f.

capricious adj caprichoso/sa; ~**ly** adv caprichosamente.

Capricorn n Capricornio m (signo del zodiaco).

capsize vt (mar) volcar, zozobrar.

capsizing n (mar) zozobra f.

capsule n cápsula f.

captain n capitán/ana m/f.

captaincy, captainship n capitanía f.

captivate vt cautivar.

captivation n atractivo m.

captive n cautivo/va, esclavo/va m/f.

captivity n cautividad, esclavitud f, cautiverio m.

capture n captura f; presa f; * vt apresar, capturar.

car n coche, carro m; vagón m.

carafe n garrafa f.

caramel n caramelo m.

carat n quilate m.

caravan n caravana f.

caraway n (bot) alcaravea f.

carbohydrates npl hidratos de carbono mpl.

car bomb n coche bomba m.

carbon n carbono m, carbón m.

carbon copy n copia al carbón f.

carbonize vt carbonizar.

carbon paper n papel carbón m.

carbuncle n carbúnculo, rubí m; carbunco, tumor maligno m.

carburettor n carburador m.

carcass n cadáver m.

carcinogenic adj cancerígeno/na.

card n naipe m; carta f; pack of ~s baraja f.

cardboard n cartón m.

card game n juego de naipes m.

cardiac adj cardíaco/ca, cardiaco/ca.

cardinal n cardinal, principal; * n cardenal m.

card table n mesa para jugar f.

care n cuidado m; solicitud f; * vi cuidar, tener cuidado o pena, inquietarse; what do I ~? ¿a mí que me importa?; to ~ for vt cuidar a; querer.

career n carrera f; curso m; * vi correr a carrera tendida.

carefree n despreocupado/da.

careful adj cuidadoso/sa, diligente, prudente; ~ly adv cuidadosamente.

careless adj descuidado/da, negli-

gente; indolente; ~ly adv descuidadamente.

carelessness n negligencia, indiferencia f.

caress n caricia f; * vt acariciar, halagar.

caretaker n portero m, conserje m/f.

car-ferry n transbordador para coches m.

cargo n cargamento m.

car hire n alquiler de coches m.

caricature n caricatura f; * vt hacer caricaturas, ridiculizar.

caries n caries f.

caring n humanitario/ria.

Carmelite n carmelita m.

carnage n carnicería, matanza f.

carnal adj carnal; sensual; ~ly adv carnalmente.

carnation n clavel m.

carnival n carnaval m.

carnivorous adj carnívoro/ra.

carol n villancico m, canción de alegría o piedad f.

car park n aparcamiento, estacionamiento m.

carpenter n carpintero m; ~'s bench banco de carpintero m.

carpentry n carpintería f.

carpet n alfombra f; * vt cubrir con alfombras.

carpeting n alfombrado m.

car radio n autorradio m.

carriage n porte m; coche m; vehículo m.

carriage-free adj franco de porte.

carrier n portador, carretero m.

carrier pigeon n paloma correo o mensajera f.

carrion n carroña f.

carrot n zanahoria f.

carry vt llevar, conducir; to ~ out ejecutar; * vi oírse; to ~ the day quedar victorioso/sa; **to ~ on** seguir.

cart n carro m; carreta f; * vt llevar (en carro).

cartel n cartel m.

carthorse n caballo de tiro m.

Carthusian n cartujo (monje) m.

cartilage n cartílago m.

cartload n carretada f.

carton n caja f.

cartoon n dibujo animado m; tira cómica f.

cartridge n cartucho m.

carve vt cincelar; trinchar; grabar.

carving n escultura f.

carving knife n cuchillo de trinchar m.

car wash n lavado de coches m.

case n caja f; maleta f; caso m; estuche m; vaina f; **in ~** por si acaso.

cash n dinero contante m; * vt cobrar.

cash card n tarjeta de cajero automático f.

cash dispenser, cash machine n cajero automático m.

cashier n cajero m.

cashmere n cachemira f.

casing n forro m; cubierta f.

casino n casino m.

cask n barril, tonel m.

casket n ataúd m.

casserole n cazuela f.

cassette n casete, cassette m.

cassette player, recorder n casete, cassette m.

cassock n sotana f.

cast vt tirar, lanzar; modelar; * n reparto m; forma f.

castanets npl castañuelas fpl.

castaway n réprobo m.

caste n casta f.

castigate vt castigar.

casting vote n voto de calidad m.

cast iron n hierro colado m.

castle n castillo m; fortaleza f.

castor oil n aceite de ricino m.

castrate vt castrar.

castration n capadura f.

cast steel n acero fundido m.

casual adj casual, fortuito/ta; **~ly** adv casualmente, fortuitamente.

casualty n víctima f; baja f.

cat n gato m; gata f.

catalogue n catálogo m.

catalyst n catalizador m.

catalytic converter n catalizador m.

catamaran n catamarán m.

catapult n catapulta, honda f.

cataract n cascada f; catarata f.

catarrh n catarro m; reuma f.

catastrophe n catástrofe f.

catcall n silbido m; reclamo m.

catch vt coger, agarrar, asir; atrapar; pillar; sorprender; **to ~ cold** resfriarse; **to ~ fire** encenderse; * n presa f; captura f; (mus) canon m; trampa f.

catching adj contagioso/sa.

catch phrase n lema m.

catchword n reclamo m.

catchy adj pegadizo/za.

catechism n catecismo m.

catechize vt catequizar, examinar.

categorical adj categórico/ca; **~ly** adv categóricamente.

categorize vt clasificar.

category n categoría f.

cater vi abastecer, proveer.

caterer n proveedor/a, abastecedor/a m/f.

catering n alimentación f.

caterpillar n oruga f.

catgut n cuerda de violín f.

cathedral n catedral f.

catholic adj, n católico/ca m/f.

Catholicism n catolicismo m.

cattle n ganado m.

cattle show *n* feria de ganado *f*.

caucus *n* junta electoral *f*.

cauliflower *n* coliflor *f*.

cause *n* causa *f*; razón *f*; motivo *m*; proceso *m*; * *vt* causar.

causeway *n* arrecife *m*.

caustic *adj*, *n* cáustico *m*.

cauterize *vt* cauterizar.

caution *n* prudencia, precaución *f*; aviso *m*; * *vt* avisar; amonestar; advertir.

cautionary *adj* de escarmiento.

cautious *adj* prudente, circunspecto/ta, cauto/ta.

cavalier *adj* arrogante.

cavalry *n* caballería *f*.

cave *n* caverna *f*; bodega *f*.

caveat *n* aviso *m*; advertencia *f*; (*law*) notificación *f*.

cavern *n* caverna *f*; bodega *f*.

cavernous *adj* cavernoso/sa.

caviar *n* caviar *m*.

cavity *n* hueco *m*; caries *f invar*.

CD-ROM *n* cederrón *m*.

cease *vt* parar, suspender; * *vi* desistir.

cease-fire *n* alto el fuego *m*.

ceaseless *adj* incesante, continuo/nua; ~ly *adv* perpetuamente.

cedar *n* cedro *m*.

cede *vt* ceder, transferir.

ceiling *n* techo *m*.

celebrate *vt* celebrar.

celebration *n* celebración *f*.

celebrity *n* celebridad, fama *f*.

celery *n* apio *m*.

celestial *adj* celeste, divino/na.

celibacy *n* celibato *m*, soltería *f*.

celibate *adj* soltero; soltera.

cell *n* celdilla *f*; célula *f*; cueva *f*.

cellar *n* sótano *m*; bodega *f*.

cello *n* violoncelo *m*.

Cellophane® *n* celofán *m*.

cellular *adj* celular.

cellulitis *n* celulitis *f*.

cellulose *n* (*chem*) celulosa *f*.

cement *n* cemento *m*; (*fig*) vínculo *m*; * *vt* pegar con cemento.

cemetery *n* cementerio *m*.

cenotaph *n* cenotafio *m*.

censor *n* censor/a *m/f*; crítico/ca *m/f*.

censorious *adj* severo/ra, crítico/ca.

censorship *n* censura *f*.

censure *n* censura, reprensión *f*; * *vt* censurar, reprender; criticar.

census *n* censo *m*.

cent *n* centavo *m*.

centenarian *n* centenario *m*; centenaria *f*.

centenary *n* centena *f*; * *adj* centenario/ria.

centennial *adj* centenario/ria.

centigrade *adj* centígrado *m*.

centilitre *n* centilitro *m*.

centimetre *n* centímetro *m*.

centipede *n* escolopendra *f*.

central *adj* central; ~ly *adv* centralmente, en el centro.

central reserve *n* mediana *f*.

centralize *vt* centralizar.

centre *n* centro *m*; * *vt* centrar; concentrar; * *vi* concentrarse.

centrifugal *adj* centrífugo/ga.

century *n* siglo *m*.

ceramic *adj* cerámico/ca.

cereals *npl* cereales *fpl*.

cerebral *adj* cerebral.

ceremonial *adj*, *n* ceremonial *m*; rito externo *m*.

ceremonious *adj* ceremonioso/sa; ~ly *adv* ceremoniosamente.

ceremony *n* ceremonia *f*.

certain *adj* cierto/ta, evidente; seguro/ra; ~ly *adv* ciertamente, sin duda.

certainty, certitude *n* certeza *f*; seguridad *f*.

certificate n certificado, testimonio m.

certification n certificado m.

certified mail n correo certificado m.

certify vt certificar, afirmar.

cervical adj cervical.

cessation n cesación f.

cesspool n cloaca f; sumidero m.

chafe vt frotar; enojar, irritar.

chaff n paja menuda f.

chaffinch n pinzón m.

chagrin n disgusto m.

chain n cadena f; serie, sucesión f; * vt encadenar, atar con cadena.

chain reaction n reacción en cadena f.

chain store n gran almacén m.

chair n silla f; * vt presidir.

chairman n presidente m.

chalice n cáliz m.

chalk n creta f; tiza f.

challenge n desafío m; * vt desafiar, impugnar.

challenger n desafiador/a m/f.

challenging adj desafiante.

chamber n cámara f; aposento m.

chambermaid n moza de cámara f.

chameleon n camaleón m.

chamois leather n gamuza f.

champagne n champaña f.

champion n campeón m; * vt defender.

championship n campeonato m.

chance n ventura, suerte f; oportunidad f; **by ~** por acaso; * vt arriesgar.

chancellor n canciller m.

chancery n chancillería f.

chandelier n araña de luces f; candelero m.

change vt cambiar; * vi variar, alterarse; * n mudanza, variedad f; vicisitud f; cambio m.

changeable adj variable, inconstante; mudable.

changeless adj constante, inmutable.

changing adj cambiante.

channel n canal m; estrecho m; * vt encauzar.

channel-hopping n zapping m.

chant n canto (llano) m; * vt cantar.

chaos n caos m; confusión f.

chaotic adj confuso/sa.

chapel n capilla f.

chaplain n capellán m.

chapter n capítulo m.

char vt chamuscar.

character n carácter m; personaje m.

characteristic adj característico/ca; **~ally** adv característicamente.

characterize vt caracterizar.

characterless adj sin carácter.

charade n charada f.

charcoal n carbón de leña m.

chard n (bot) acelga f.

charge vt cargar; acusar, imputar; * n cargo m; acusación f; (mil) ataque m; depósito m; carga f.

chargeable adj imputable.

charge card n tarjeta de compra f.

charitable adj caritativo/va; benigno/na, clemente; **~bly** adv caritativamente.

charity n caridad, benevolencia f; limosna f.

charlatan n charlatán/tana m/f.

charm n encanto m; atractivo m; * vt encantar, embelesar, atraer.

charming adj encantado/da.

chart n carta de navegar f.

charter n carta f; privilegio m; * vt fletar un buque; alquilar.

charter flight n vuelo chárter m, charter m.

chase vt cazar; perseguir; * n caza f.

chasm n vacío m.

chaste adj casto/ta; puro/ra; honesto/ta.

chasten vt corregir, castigar.
chastise vt castigar, reformar, corregir.
chastisement n castigo m.
chastity n castidad, pureza f.
chat vi charlar; * n charla, cháchara f.
chatter vi cotorrear; rechinar; charlar; * n chirrido m; charla f.
chatterbox n parlero/ra, hablador/a, gárrulo/la m/f.
chatty adj locuaz, parlanchín/china.
chauffeur n chófer m.
chauvinist n machista m.
cheap adj barato/ta; **~ly** adv a bajo precio.
cheapen vt regatear; abaratar.
cheaper adj más barato/ta.
cheat vt engañar, defraudar; * n trampa f; fraude, engaño m; tramposo/sa m/f.
check vt comprobar; contar; reprimir, refrenar; regañar; registrar; * n restricción f; freno m.
checkmate n mate m.
checkout n caja f.
checkpoint n control m.
check-up n reconocimiento médico m.
cheek n mejilla f; (fam) desvergüenza f; atrevimiento m.
cheekbone n hueso del carrillo m.
cheeky adj descarado/da.
cheer n alegría f; aplauso m; buen humor m; * vt animar, alentar.
cheerful adj alegre, vivo/va, jovial; **~ly** adv alegremente.
cheerfulness, cheeriness n alegría f; buen humor m.
cheese n queso m.
cheesemonger, cheese shop n quesería f.
chef n jefe de cocina m.
chemical adj químico/ca.
chemist n químico m.

chemistry n química f.
chemotherapy n quimioterapia f.
cheque n cheque m.
cheque account n cuenta corriente f.
chequerboard, draughtboard n tablero de damas m.
chequered adj accidentado/da.
cherish vt fomentar, proteger.
cheroot n puro m.
cherry n cereza f; * adj bermejo/ja.
cherry tree n cerezo m.
cherub n querubín m.
chess n ajedrez m.
chessboard n tablero de ajedrez m.
chessman n pieza de ajedrez f.
chest n pecho m; arca f; **~ of drawers** cómoda f.
chestnut n castaña f; color de castaña m.
chestnut tree n castaño m.
chew vt mascar, masticar.
chewing gum n chicle m.
chic adj elegante.
chicanery n quisquilla f.
chick n polluelo m; (col) chica f.
chicken n pollo m.
chickenpox n varicela f.
chickpea n garbanzo m.
chicory n achicoria f.
chide vt reprobar, regañar.
chief adj principal, capital; **~ly** adv principalmente; * n jefe, principal m.
chief executive n director/a general m/f.
chieftain n jefe, comandante m.
chiffon n gasa f.
chilblain n sabañón m.
child n niño m; niña f; hijo m; hija f; **from a ~** desde niño/ña; **with ~** preñada, embarazada.
childbirth n parto m.
childhood n infancia, niñez f; pequeñez f.

childish *adj* frívolo/la, pueril; **~ly**
adv puerilmente.

childishness *n* puerilidad *f*.

childless *adj* sin hijos.

childlike *adj* pueril.

children *npl de* **child** niños *mpl*.

chill *adj* frío/ría, friolero/ra; * *n* frío
m; * *vt* enfriar; helar.

chilly *adj* friolero/ra, friolento/ta.

chime *n* armonía *f*; clave *m*; * *vi* sonar con armonía; concordar.

chimney *n* chimenea *f*.

chimpanzee *n* chimpancé *m*.

chin *n* barbilla *f*.

china(ware) *n* porcelana *f*.

chink *n* grieta, hendedura *f*; * *vi* resonar.

chip *vt* astillar; * *vi* picarse; * *n* astilla *f*; chip *m*; patata o papa frita *f*.

chiropodist, podiatrist *n* pedi-
curo/ra *m/f*.

chirp *vi* chirriar, gorjear; * *n* gorjeo,
chirrido *m*.

chirping *n* canto de las aves *m*.

chisel *n* cincel *m*; * *vt* cincelar, grabar.

chitchat *n* charla *f*.

chivalrous *adj* caballeresco/ca.

chivalry *n* caballería *f*.

chives *npl* cebollinos *f*.

chlorine *n* cloro *m*.

chloroform *n* cloroformo *m*.

chock-full *adj* de bote en bote, completamente lleno/na.

chocolate *n* chocolate *m*.

choice *n* elección, preferencia *f*; se-
lecto *m*; * *adj* selecto/ta, exquisito/
ta, excelente.

choir *n* coro *m*.

choke *vt* sofocar; oprimir; tapar.

cholera *n* cólera *m*.

choose *vt* escoger, elegir.

chop *vt* tajar, cortar; * *n* chuleta *f*;
~s *pl* (*sl*) quijadas *fpl*.

chopper *n* helicóptero *m*.

chopping block *n* tajo de cocina *m*.

chopsticks *npl* palillos *mpl*.

chore *n* faena *f*.

choral *adj* coral.

chord *n* cuerda *f*.

chorist, chorister *n* corista *m*.

chorus *n* coro *m*.

Christ *n* Cristo *m*.

christen *vt* bautizar.

Christendom *n* cristianismo *m*; cristiandad *f*.

christening *n* bautismo *m*.

Christian *adj*, *n* cristiano/na *m/f*; **~**
name nombre de pila *m*.

Christianity *n* cristianismo *m*; cristiandad *f*.

Christmas *n* Navidad *f*.

Christmas card *n* tarjeta de Navidad *f*.

Christmas Eve *n* Nochebuena *f*.

chrome *n* cromo *m*.

chronic *adj* crónico/ca.

chronicle *n* crónica *f*.

chronicler *n* cronista *m*.

chronological *adj* cronológico/ca;
~ly *adv* cronológicamente.

chronology *n* cronología *f*.

chronometer *n* cronómetro *m*.

chubby *adj* gordo/da.

chuck *vt* lanzar.

chuckle *vi* reírse a carcajadas.

chug *vi* resoplar.

chum *n* compañero/ra, compinche
m/f.

chunk *n* trozo *m*.

church *n* iglesia *f*.

churchyard *n* cementerio *m*.

churlish *adj* hosco/ca, grosero/ra;
tacaño/ña.

churn *n* mantequera *f*; * *vt* batir la
leche para hacer manteca.

cider *n* sidra *f*.

cigar *n* cigarro *m*.

cigarette n cigarrillo m.
cigarette case n pitillera f.
cigarette end n colilla f.
cigarette holder n boquilla f.
cinder n carbonilla f.
cinema n cine m.
cinnamon n canela f.
cipher n cifra f.
circle n círculo m; corrillo m; asamblea f; * vt circundar; cercar; * vi circular.
circuit n circuito m; recinto m.
circuitous adj circular, tortuoso/sa.
circular adj circular, redondo/da; * n carta circular f.
circulate vi circular; moverse alrededor.
circulation n circulación f.
circumcise vt circuncidar.
circumcision n circuncisión f.
circumference n circunferencia f; circuito m.
circumflex n acento circunflejo m.
circumlocution n circunlocución f.
circumnavigate vt circunnavegar.
circumnavigation n circunnavegación f.
circumscribe vt circunscribir.
circumspect adj circunspecto/ta, prudente, reservado/da.
circumspection n circunspección, prudencia f.
circumstance n circunstancia, condición f; incidente m.
circumstantial adj accidental; accesorio/ria.
circumstantiate vt circunstanciar, detallar.
circumvent vt burlar.
circumvention n evasión f.
circus n circo m.
cistern n cisterna f.
citadel n ciudadela, fortaleza f.

citation n citación, cita f.
cite vt citar (a juicio); alegar; referirse a.
citizen n ciudadano/na m/f.
citizenship n ciudadanía f.
city n ciudad f.
civic adj cívico/ca.
civil adj civil, cortés; ~ly adv civilmente.
civil defence n protección civil f.
civil engineer n ingeniero/ra civil m/f.
civilian n paisano m.
civility n civilidad, urbanidad, cortesía f.
civilization n civilización f.
civilize vt civilizar.
civil law n derecho civil m.
civil war n guerra civil f.
clad adj vestido/da, cubierto/ta.
claim vt pedir en juicio, reclamar; * n demanda f; derecho m.
claimant n reclamante m; demandador/a m/f.
clairvoyant n clarividente m/f; zahorí m.
clam n almeja f.
clamber vi gatear, trepar.
clammy adj viscoso/sa.
clamour n clamor, grito m; * vi vociferar, gritar.
clamp n abrazadera f; * vt afianzar; to ~ down on reforzar la lucha contra.
clan n familia, tribu, raza f.
clandestine adj clandestino/na, oculto/ta.
clang n rechino, sonido desapacible m; * vt rechinar.
clap vt aplaudir.
clapping n palmada f; aplauso, palmoteo m.
claret n clarete m.

clarification n clarificación f.

clarify vt clarificar, aclarar.

clarinet n clarinete m.

clarity n claridad f.

clash vi chocar; * n estruendo m; choque m.

clasp n broche m; hebilla f; abrazo m; * vt abrochar; abrazar.

class n clase f; orden f; * vt clasificar, coordinar.

classic(al) adj clásico/ca; * n autor clásico m.

classification n clasificación f.

classified advertisement n anuncio por palabras m.

classify vt clasificar.

classmate n compañero/ra de clase m/f.

classroom n aula f.

clatter vi resonar; hacer ruido; * n ruido m.

clause n cláusula f; artículo m; estipulación f.

claw n garra f; zarpa f; * vt desgarrar, arañar.

clay n arcilla f.

clean adj limpio/pia; casto/ta; * vt limpiar.

cleaning n limpieza f.

cleanliness n limpieza f.

cleanly adj limpio/pia; * adv limpiamente, aseadamente.

cleanness n limpieza f; pureza f.

cleanse vt limpiar, purificar; purgar.

clear adj claro/ra; neto/ta; diáfano/na; evidente; * adv claramente; * vt clarificar, aclarar; justificar, absolver; * vi aclararse.

clearance n despeje m; acreditación f.

clear-cut adj bien definido/da.

clearly adv claramente, evidentemente.

cleaver n cuchillo de carnicero m.

clef n clave f.

cleft n hendedura, abertura f.

clemency n clemencia f.

clement adj clemente, benigno/na.

clenched adj cerrado/da.

clergy n clero m.

clergyman n eclesiástico m.

clerical adj clerical, eclesiástico/ca.

clerk n dependiente m; oficinista m.

clever adj listo/ta; hábil, mañoso/sa; ~**ly** adv diestramente, hábilmente.

click vt chasquear; * vi taconear.

client n cliente m/f.

cliff n acantilado m.

climate n clima m; temperatura f.

climatic adj climático/ca.

climax n clímax m.

climb vt escalar, trepar; * vi subir.

climber n alpinista m/f.

climbing n alpinismo m.

clinch vt cerrar; remachar.

cling vi colgar, adherirse, pegarse.

clinic n clínica f.

clink vt hacer resonar; * vi resonar; * n retintín m.

clip vt cortar; * n clip m; horquilla f.

clipping n recorte m.

clique n camarilla f.

cloak n capa f; pretexto m; * vt encapotar.

cloakroom n guardarropa m.

clock n reloj m.

clockwork n mecanismo de un reloj m; * adj sumamente exacto y puntual.

clod n terrón m.

clog n zueco m; * vi atascarse.

cloister n claustro, monasterio m.

clone n clon m; * vt clonar.

cloned adj clónico/ca.

cloning n clonación f.

close vt cerrar; concluir, terminar; * vi cerrarse; * n fin m; conclusión f; * adj cercano/na; estrecho/cha; ajustado/da; denso/sa; reservado/da; * adv de cerca; ~ by muy cerca; junto.

closed adj cerrado/da.

closely adv estrechamente; de cerca.

closeness n proximidad f; estrechez; reclusión f.

closet n armario m.

close-up n primer plano m.

closure n cierre m; conclusión f.

clot n grumo m; embolia f.

cloth n paño m; mantel m; vestido m; lienzo m.

clothe vt vestir, cubrir.

clothes npl ropa f; ropaje m; ropa de cama f; bed ~ cobertores mpl.

clothes basket n cesta grande f.

clotheshorse n tendedero m.

clothesline n cuerda (de tendedero) f.

clothespin n pinza f.

clothing n vestidos mpl.

cloud n nube f; nublado m; (fig) adversidad f; * vt anublar; oscurecer; * vi anublarse; oscurecerse.

cloudiness n nubosidad f; oscuridad f.

cloudy adj nublado/da; oscuro/ra; sombrío/ría, melancólico/ca.

clout n tortazo m.

clove n clavo m.

clover n trébol m.

clown n payaso m.

club n cachiporra f.

club car n coche restaurante m.

clue n pista f, indicios m; idea f.

clump n grupo m.

clumsily adv torpemente.

clumsiness n torpeza f.

clumsy adj torpe, pesado/da; sin arte.

cluster n racimo m; manada f; pelotón m; * vt agrupar; * vi arracimarse.

clutch n embrague m; apretón m; * vt empuñar.

clutter vt atestar.

coach n autocar, autobús m; vagón m; entrenador/a m/f; * vt entrenar; enseñar.

coach trip n excursión en autocar f.

coagulate vt coagular, cuajar; * vi coagularse, cuajarse, espesarse.

coal n carbón m.

coalesce vi juntarse, incorporarse.

coalfield n yacimiento de carbón m.

coalition n coalición, confederación f.

coalman n carbonero m.

coalmine n mina de carbón, carbonería f.

coarse adj basto/ta; grosero/ra; zafio/fia; ~ly adv groseramente.

coast n costa f.

coastal adj costero/ra; ribereño/ña.

coastguard n guardacostas m invar.

coastline n litoral m.

coat n chaqueta f; abrigo m; capa f; * vt cubrir.

coat hanger n percha f.

coat hook n percha f.

coating n revestimiento m.

coax vt lisonjear.

cob n mazorca de maíz f.

cobbler n zapatero/ra m/f.

cobbles, cobblestones npl adoquines mpl.

cobweb n telaraña f.

cocaine n cocaína f.

coccyx n rabadilla f.

cock n gallo m; macho m; * vt armar el sombrero; amartillar, montar una escopeta.

cock-a-doodle-doo n quiquiriquí m.

cockcrow n canto del gallo m.

cockerel n gallito m.

cockfight(ing) n pelea de gallos f.

cockle n berberecho m.

cockpit n cabina f.

cockroach n cucaracha f.

cocktail n cóctel m.

cocoa n cacao m; cacao m.

coconut n coco m.

cocoon n capullo (del gusano de seda) m.

cod n bacalao m.

code n código m; prefijo m.

cod-liver oil n aceite de hígado de bacalao m.

coefficient n coeficiente m.

coercion n coerción f.

coexistence n coexistencia f.

coffee n café m.

coffee break n descanso m.

coffee house n café m.

coffee-pot n cafetera f.

coffee table n mesita f.

coffer n cofre m; caja f.

coffin n ataúd m.

cog n diente (de rueda) m.

cogency n fuerza, urgencia f.

cogent adj convincente, urgente; ~ly adv de modo convincente.

cognac n coñac m.

cognate adj cognado/da.

cognition n conocimiento m; convicción f.

cognizance n conocimiento m; competencia f.

cognizant adj informado/da; (law) competente.

cogwheel n rueda dentada f.

cohabit vi cohabitar.

cohabitation n cohabitación f.

cohere vi pegarse; unirse.

coherence n coherencia, conexión f.

coherent adj coherente; consiguiente.

cohesion n coherencia f.

cohesive adj cohesivo/va.

coil n rollo m; bobina f; * vt enrollar.

coin n moneda f; * vt acuñar.

coincide vi coincidir, concurrir, convenir.

coincidence n coincidencia f.

coincidental adj fortuito; coincidente.

coke n coque m.

Coke® n Coca-Cola® f.

colander n colador, pasador m.

cold adj frío/ría; indiferente, insensible; reservado/da; ~ly adv fríamente; indiferentemente; * n frío m; frialdad f; resfriado m.

cold-blooded adj impasible.

coldness n frialdad f; indiferencia, insensibilidad, apatía f.

cold sore n herpes labial m.

coleslaw n ensalada de col f.

colic n cólico m.

collaborate vt cooperar.

collaboration n cooperación f.

collapse vi hundirse; * n hundimiento; (med) colapso m.

collapsible adj plegable.

collar n cuello m.

collarbone n clavícula f.

collate vt comparar, confrontar.

collateral adj colateral; * n garantía subsidiaria f.

collation n colación f.

colleague n colega, compañero/ra m/f.

collect vt recoger; coleccionar.

collection n colección f; compilación f.

collective adj colectivo/va, congregado/da; ~ly colectivamente.

collector n coleccionista m/f.

college n colegio m.

collide vi chocar.

collision n choque m, colisión f.

colloquial adj familiar; coloquial; ~ly adv familiarmente.

colloquialism n lengua usual f.

collusion n colusión f.

colon n dos puntos mpl; (med) colon m.

colonel n (mil) coronel m.

colonial adj colonial.

colonist n colono m.

colonize vt colonizar.

colony n colonia f.

colossal adj colosal.

colossus n coloso m.

colour n color m; **~s** pl bandera f; * vt colorar; pintar; * vi ponerse colorado/da.

colour-blind adj daltónico/ca.

colourful adj lleno de color.

colouring n colorido m.

colourless adj descolorido/da, sin color.

colour television n televisión en color f.

colt n potro m.

column n columna f.

columnist n columnista m.

coma n coma f.

comatose adj comatoso/sa.

comb n peine m; * vt peinar.

combat n combate m; batalla f; **single ~** duelo m; * vt combatir.

combatant n combatiente m.

combative adj combativo/va.

combination n combinación, coordinación f.

combine vt combinar; * vi unirse.

combustion n combustión f.

come vi venir; **to ~ across/upon** vt topar con; dar con; **to ~ by** vi conseguir; **to ~ down** vi bajar; ser derribado/da; **to ~ from** vt ser de; **to ~ in for** vt merecer; **to ~ into** vt heredar; **to ~ round/to** vi volver en sí; **to ~ up with** vt sugerir.

comedian n comediante, cómico m.

comedienne n cómica f.

comedy n comedia f.

comet n cometa m.

comfort n confort m; ayuda f; consuelo m; comodidad f; * vt confortar; alentar, consolar.

comfortable adj cómodo/da.

comfortably adv agradablemente; cómodamente.

comforter n chupete m.

comic(al) adj cómico/ca, burlesco/ca; **~ly** adv cómicamente.

coming n venida, llegada f; * adj venidero/ra.

comma n (gr) coma f.

command vt comandar, ordenar; * n orden f.

commander n comandante m.

commandment n mandamiento, precepto m.

commando n comando m.

commemorate vt conmemorar; celebrar.

commemoration n conmemoración f.

commence vt, vi comenzar.

commencement n principio m.

commend vt encomendar; alabar; enviar.

commendable adj recomendable.

commendably adv loablemente.

commendation n recomendación f.

commensurate adj proporcionado/da.

comment n comentario m; * vt comentar; glosar.

commentary n comentario m; interpretación f.

commentator n comentarista m/f.

commerce n comercio, tráfico, trato, negocio m.

commercial adj comercial.

commiserate vt compadecer, tener compasión.

commiseration n conmiseración, piedad f.

commissariat n comisaría f.

commission n comisión f; * vt comisionar; encargar.

commissioner n comisionado/da, delegado/da m/f.

commit vt cometer; depositar; encargar.

commitment n compromiso m.

committee n comité m.

commodity n comodidad f.

common adj común; bajo/ja; in ~ comúnmente; * n pastos comunales mpl.

commoner n plebeyo m.

common law n derecho consuetudinario m.

commonly adv comúnmente, frecuentemente.

commonplace n lugar común m; * adj trivial.

common sense n sentido común m.

commonwealth n república f.

commotion n tumulto m; perturbación del ánimo f.

commune vt conversar, conferir.

communicable adj comunicable, impartible.

communicate vt comunicar, participar; * vi comunicarse.

communication n comunicación f.

communicative adj comunicativo/va.

communion n comunión f.

communiqué n comunicado m.

communism n comunismo m.

communist n comunista m/f.

community n comunidad f; colectividad f.

community centre n centro social m.

community chest n arca comunitaria f.

commutable adj conmutable, cambiable.

commutation ticket n billete de abono m.

commute vt conmutar.

compact adj compacto/ta, sólido/da, denso/sa; * n pacto, convenio m; ~ly adv estrechamente; en pocas palabras.

compact disc, CD n compact disc m, disco compacto m.

companion n compañero/ra, socio/cia, compinche m/f.

companionship n sociedad, compañía f.

company n compañía, sociedad f; compañía de comercio f.

comparable adj comparable.

comparative adj comparativo/va; ~ly adv comparativamente.

compare vt comparar.

comparison n comparación f.

compartment n compartimento m.

compass n brújula f.

compassion n compasión, piedad f.

compassionate adj compasivo/va.

compatibility n compatibilidad f.

compatible adj compatible.

compatriot n compatriota m/f.

compel vt compeler, obligar, constreñir.

compelling adj convicente.

compensate vt compensar.

compensation n compensación f; resarcimiento m.

compere n (rad, TV) presentador/a m/f.

compete vi concurrir, competir.

competence n competencia f; suficiencia f.

competent adj competente, adecuado/da; ~ly adv competentemente.

competition n competencia f; concurrencia f.

competitive *adj* competitivo/va.

competitive scheduling *n* contraprogramación *f*.

competitor *n* competidor/a *m/f*, rival *m*.

compilation *n* compilación *f*.

compile *vt* compilar.

complacency *n* autocomplacencia *f*.

complacent *adj* complaciente.

complain *vi* quejarse, lamentarse, lastimarse, dolerse.

complaint *n* queja *f*; reclamación *f*.

complement *n* complemento *m*.

complementary *adj* complementario/ria.

complete *adj* completo/ta, perfecto/ta; ~ly *adv* completamente; * *vt* completar, acabar.

completion *n* terminación *f*.

complex *adj* complejo/ja.

complexion *n* tez *f*; aspecto *m*.

complexity *n* complejidad *f*.

compliance *n* complacencia, sumisión *f*.

compliant *adj* complaciente, oficioso/sa.

complicate *vt* complicar.

complication *n* complicación *f*.

complicity *n* complicidad *f*.

compliment *n* cumplido *m*; * *vt* cumplimentar; hacer cumplidos.

complimentary *adj* elogioso/sa, ceremonioso/sa.

comply *vi* cumplir; condescender, conformarse.

component *n* componente.

compose *vt* componer; sosegar.

composed *adj* compuesto/ta, moderado/da.

composer *n* compositor/a *m/f*.

composite *adj* compuesto/ta.

composition *n* composición *f*.

compositor *n* cajista *m*.

compost *n* abono, estiércol *m*.

composure *n* composición *f*; tranquilidad, sangre fría *f*.

compound *vt* componer, combinar; * *adj*, *n* compuesto/ta.

comprehend *vt* comprender, contener; entender.

comprehensible *adj* comprensible; ~ly *adv* comprensiblemente.

comprehension *n* comprensión *f*; inteligencia *f*.

comprehensive *adj* comprensivo/va; ~ly *adv* comprensivamente.

compress *vt* comprimir, estrechar; * *n* cabezal *m*.

comprise *vt* comprender, incluir.

compromise *n* compromiso *m*; * *vt* comprometer.

compulsion *n* compulsión *f*; apremio *m*.

compulsive *adj* compulsivo/va; ~ly *adv* compulsivamente.

compulsory *adj* obligatorio/ria.

compunction *n* compunción, contrición *f*.

computable *adj* computable, calculable.

computation *n* computación *f*, cómputo *m*.

compute *vt* computar, calcular.

computer *n* ordenador *m*.

computer graphics *n* infografía *f*.

computerize *vt* computerizar, informatizar.

computer programming *n* programación *f*.

computer science *n* informática *f*.

comrade *n* camarada, compañero/ra *m/f*.

comradeship *n* compañerismo *m*.

con *vt* estafar; * *n* estafa *f*.

concave *adj* cóncavo/va.

concavity *n* concavidad *f*.

conceal *vt* ocultar, esconder.

concealment *n* ocultación *f*; encubrimiento *m*.

concede *vt* conceder, asentir.

conceit *n* concepto *m*; capricho *m*; pensamiento *m*; presunción *f*.

conceited *adj* afectado/da, vano/na, presumido/da.

conceivable *adj* concebible, inteligible.

conceive *vt* concebir, comprender; * *vi* concebir.

concentrate *vt* concentrar.

concentration *n* concentración *f*.

concentration camp *n* campo de concentración *m*.

concentric *adj* concéntrico/ca.

concept *n* concepto *m*.

conception *n* concepción *f*; sentimiento *m*.

concern *vt* concernir, importar; * *n* negocio *m*; asunto *m*; preocupación *f*.

concerning *prep* tocante a.

concert *n* concierto *m*.

concerto *n* concierto *m*.

concession *n* concesión *f*; privilegio *m*.

conciliate *vt* conciliar.

conciliation *n* conciliación *f*.

conciliatory *adj* conciliador/a.

concise *adj* conciso/sa, sucinto/ta; ~ly *adv* concisamente.

conclude *vt* concluir; decidir; determinar.

conclusion *n* conclusión, determinación *f*; fin *m*.

conclusive *adj* decisivo/va, conclusivo/va; ~ly *adv* concluyentemente.

concoct *vt* cocer, digerir; (*fig*) zurcir.

concoction *n* confección *f*; cocción *f*.

concomitant *adj* concomitante.

concord *n* concordia, armonía *f*.

concordance *n* concordancia *f*.

concordant *adj* concordante, conforme.

concourse *n* concurso *m*; multitud *f*; gentío *m*.

concrete *n* concreto *m*; * *vt* concretar.

concubine *n* concubina *f*.

concur *vi* concurrir; juntarse.

concurrence *n* concurrencia *f*; unión *f*; asistencia *f*.

concurrently *adv* al mismo tiempo.

concussion *n* conmoción cerebral *f*.

condemn *vt* condenar; desaprobar; vituperar.

condemnation *n* condena *f*.

condensation *n* condensación *f*.

condense *vt* condensar.

condescend *vi* condescender; consentir.

condescending *adj* condescendiente.

condescension *n* condescendencia *f*.

condiment *n* condimento *m*; salsa *f*.

condition *n* condicionar; * *n* situación, condición, calidad *f*; estado *m*.

conditional *adj* condicional, hipotético/ca; ~ly *adv* condicionalmente.

conditioned *adj* condicionado/da.

conditioner *n* acondicionador *m*.

condolences *npl* pésame *m*.

condom *n* condón *m*.

condominium *n* condominio *m*.

condone *vt* perdonar.

conducive *adj* conducente, oportuno/na.

conduct *n* conducta *f*; manejo, proceder *m*; * *vt* conducir, guiar.

conductor *n* conductor *m*; guía, director *m*; conductor de electricidad *m*.

conduit *n* conducto *m*; cano *m*.

cone *n* cono *m*.

confection n confitura f; confección f.

confectioner n confitero/ra m/f.

confectioner's (shop) n pastelería f; confitería f.

confectionery n caramelo m.

confederacy n confederación f.

confederate vi confederarse; * adj, n confederado/da m/f.

confer vi conferenciar; * vt conferir, comparar.

conference n conferencia f.

confess vt (vi) confesar(se).

confession n confesión f.

confessional n confesionario m.

confessor n confesor m.

confetti n confeti m.

confidant n confidente, amigo/ga íntimo/ma m/f.

confide vt, vi confiar; fiarse.

confidence n confianza, seguridad f.

confidence trick n timo m.

confident adj cierto/ta, seguro/ra; confiado/da.

confidential adj confidencial.

configuration n configuración f.

confine vt limitar; aprisionar.

confinement n prisión f; confinación f.

confirm vt confirmar; ratificar.

confirmation n confirmación f; ratificación f; prueba f.

confirmed adj empedernido/da.

confiscate vt confiscar.

confiscation n confiscación f.

conflagration n conflagración f; incendio m.

conflict n conflicto m; combate m; pelea f.

conflicting adj contradictorio/ria.

confluence n confluencia f; concurso m.

conform vt (vi) conformar(se).

conformity n conformidad, conveniencia f.

confound vt turbar, confundir.

confront vt afrontar; confrontar; comparar.

confrontation n enfrentamiento m.

confuse vt confundir; desordenar.

confusing adj confuso/sa.

confusion n confusión f; perturbación f; desorden m.

congeal vt (vi) helar, congelar(se).

congenial adj congenial.

congenital adj congénito/ta.

congested adj atestado/da.

congestion n congestión f; acumulación f.

conglomerate vt conglomerar, aglomerar; * adj aglomerado/da; * n (com) conglomerado m.

conglomeration n aglomeración f.

congratulate vt congratular, felicitar.

congratulations npl felicidades fpl; * interj enhorabuena.

congratulatory adj congratulatorio/ria.

congregate vt congregar, reunir.

congregation n congregación, reunión f.

congress n congreso m; conferencia f.

congressman n miembro del Congreso m.

congruity n congruencia f.

congruous adj idóneo/nea, congruo/rua, apto/ta.

conic(al) adj cónico/ca.

conifer n conífera f.

coniferous adj (bot) conífero/ra.

conjecture n conjetura, apariencia f; * vt conjeturar; pronosticar.

conjugal adj conyugal, matrimonial.

conjugate vt (gr) conjugar.

conjugation n conjugación f.

conjunction n conjunción f; unión f.

conjuncture n coyuntura f; ocasión f; tiempo crítico m.

conjure vi conjurar, suplicar.

conjurer n conjurador/a, encantador/a m/f.

con man n timador m.

connect vt juntar, unir, enlazar.

connection n conexión f.

connivance n connivencia f.

connive vi tolerar.

connoisseur n conocedor/a m/f.

conquer vt conquistar; vencer.

conqueror n vencedor/a, conquistador/a m/f.

conquest n conquista f.

conscience n conciencia f; escrúpulo m.

conscientious adj concienzudo/da, escrupuloso/sa; **~ly** adv concienzudamente.

conscientious objector n objetor de conciencia m.

conscious adj sabedor, consciente; **~ly** adv a sabiendas.

consciousness n conciencia f.

conscript n conscripto m.

conscription n reclutamiento m.

consecrate vt consagrar; dedicar.

consecration n consagración f.

consecutive adj consecutivo/va; **~** adv consecutivamente.

consensus n consenso m.

consent n consentimiento m; aprobación f; * vi consentir; aprobar.

consequence n consecuencia f; importancia f.

consequent adj consecutivo/va, concluyente; **~ly** adv consiguientemente.

conservation n conservación f.

conservative adj conservador/a m/f.

conservatory n conservatorio m.

conserve vt conservar; * n conserva f.

consider vt considerar, examinar; * vi pensar, deliberar.

considerable adj considerable; importante; **~bly** adv considerablemente.

considerate adj considerado/da, prudente, discreto/ta; **~ly** adv juiciosamente; prudentemente.

consideration n consideración f; deliberación f; importancia f; valor, mérito m.

considering conj en vista de; **~ that** a causa de; visto que, en razón a.

consign vt consignar.

consignment n consignación f.

consist vi consistir.

consistency n consistencia f.

consistent adj consistente; conveniente, conforme; solido/da, estable; **~ly** adv conformemente.

console n consola f.

consolable adj consolable.

consolation n consolación f; consuelo m.

consolatory adj consolatorio/ria.

console vt consolar.

consolidate vt, vi consolidar(se).

consolidation n consolidación f.

consonant adj consonante, conforme; * n (gr) consonante f.

consort n consorte, socio m.

conspicuous adj conspicuo/cua, aparente; notable; **~ly** adv claramente.

conspiracy n conspiración f.

conspirator n conspirador/a m/f.

conspire vi conspirar, maquinar.

constancy n constancia f, perseverancia, persistencia f.

constant adj constante; perseverante; **~ly** adv constantemente.

constellation n constelación f.

consternation n consternación f; terror m.

constipated adj estreñido/da.

constituency n circunscripción electoral f.

constituent n constitutivo m; * adj constituyente.

constitute vt constituir; establecer.

constitution n constitución f; estado m; temperamento m.

constitutional adj constitucional.

constrain vt constreñir, forzar; restringir.

constraint n constreñimiento m; fuerza, violencia f.

constrict vt constreñir, estrechar.

construct vt construir, edificar.

construction n construcción f.

construe vt construir; interpretar.

consul n cónsul m.

consular adj consular.

consulate, consulship n consulado m.

consult vt (vi) consultar(se); aconsejar(se).

consultant n asesor m.

consultation n consulta, deliberación f.

consume vt consumir; disipar; * vi consumirse.

consumer n consumidor/a m/f.

consumer goods npl bienes de consumo mpl.

consumerism n consumismo m.

consumer society n sociedad de consumo f.

consummate vt consumar, acabar, perfeccionar; * adj cumplido/da, consumado/da.

consummation n consumación, perfección f.

consumption n consumo m.

contact n contacto m.

contact lenses npl lentes de contacto fpl.

contagious adj contagioso/sa.

contain vt contener, comprender; caber, reprimir, refrenar.

container n recipiente m.

contaminate vt contaminar; corromper; ~d adj contaminado/da, corrompido/da.

contamination n contaminación f.

contemplate vt contemplar.

contemplation n contemplación f.

contemplative adj contemplativo/va.

contemporaneous, contemporary adj contemporáneo/nea.

contempt n desprecio, desdén m.

contemptible adj despreciable, vil; ~bly adv vilmente.

contemptuous adj desdeñoso/sa, insolente; ~ly adv con desdén.

contend vi contender, disputar, afirmar.

content adj contento/ta, satisfecho/cha; * vt contentar, satisfacer; * n contenido m; ~s pl contenido m; tabla de materias f.

contentedly adv de un modo satisfecho/cha; con paciencia.

contention n contención, altercación f.

contentious adj contencioso/sa, litigioso/sa; ~ly adv contenciosamente.

contentment n contentamiento, placer m.

contest vt contestar, disputar, litigar; * n concurso m; contestación, altercación f.

contestant n concursante/ta m/f.

context n contexto m; contextura f.

contiguous adj contiguo/gua, vecino/na.

continent *adj* continente; * *n* continente *m*.

continental *adj* continental.

contingency *n* contingencia *f*; acontecimiento *m*; eventualidad *f*.

contingent *n* contingente *m*; cuota *f*; * *adj* contingente, casual; ~ly *adv* casualmente.

continual *adj* continuo/nua; ~ly *adv* continuamente.

continuation *n* continuación, serie *f*.

continue *vt* continuar; * *vi* durar, perseverar, persistir.

continuity *n* continuidad *f*.

continuous *adj* continuo/nua, unido/da; ~ly *adv* continuadamente.

contort *vt* torcer.

contortion *n* contorsión *f*.

contour *n* contorno *m*.

contraband *n* contrabando *m*; * *adj* prohibido/da, ilegal.

contraception *n* contracepción *f*.

contraceptive *n* anticonceptivo *m*; * *adj* anticonceptivo/va.

contract *vt* contraer; abreviar; contratar; *vi* contraerse; * *n* contrato, pacto *m*.

contraction *n* contracción *f*; abreviatura *f*.

contractor *n* contratante *m/f*.

contradict *vt* contradecir.

contradiction *n* contradicción, oposición *f*.

contradictory *adj* contradictorio/ria.

contraption *n* artilugio *m*.

contrariness *n* contrariedad, oposición *f*.

contrary *adj* contrario/ria, opuesto/ta; * *n* contrario *m*; on the ~ al contrario.

contrast *n* contraste *m*; oposición *f*; * *vt* contrastar, oponer.

contrasting *adj* opuesto/ta.

contravention *n* contravención *f*.

contribute *vt* contribuir, ayudar.

contributory *adj* contributario/ria.

contribution *n* contribución *f*; tributo *m*.

contributor *n* contribuidor/a *m/f*.

contributory *adj* contribuyente.

contrite *adj* contrito/ta, arrepentido/da.

contrition *n* penitencia, contrición *f*.

contrivance *n* designio *m*; invención *f*; concepto *m*.

contrive *vt* inventar, trazar, maquinar; manejar; combinar.

control *n* control *m*; inspección *f*; * *vt* controlar; manejar; restringir; gobernar.

control room *n* sala de mando *f*.

control tower *n* torre de control *f*.

controversial *adj* polémico/ca.

controversy *n* controversia *f*.

contusion *n* contusión *f*, magullamiento *m*.

conundrum *n* problema *m*.

conurbation *n* conurbación *f*.

convalesce *vi* convalecer.

convalescence *n* convalecencia *f*.

convalescent *adj* convaleciente.

convene *vt* convocar; juntar, unir; * *vi* convenir, juntarse.

convenience *n* conveniencia, comodidad, conformidad *f*.

convenient *adj* conveniente, apto/ta, cómodo/da, propio/pia; ~ly *adv* cómodamente, oportunamente.

convent *n* convento, claustro, monasterio *m*.

convention *n* convención *f*; contrato, tratado *m*.

conventional *adj* convencional, estipulado/da.

converge *vi* converger.

convergence *n* convergencia *f*.

convergent *adj* convergente.

conversant *adj* versado en; íntimo; ma.

conversation *n* conversación *f*.

converse *vi* conversar; platicar.

conversely *adv* mutuamente, recíprocamente.

conversion *n* conversión, transmutación *f*.

convert *vt* (*vi*) convertir(se); * *n* converso, convertido *m*.

convertible *adj* convertible, transmutable; * *n* descapotable *m*.

convex *adj* convexo/xa.

convexity *n* convexidad *f*.

convey *vt* transportar; transmitir, transferir.

conveyance *n* transporte *m*; conducción *f*; escritura de traspaso *f*.

conveyancer *n* notario *m*.

convict *vt* probar un delito; * *n* convicto/ta *m/f*.

conviction *n* convicción *f*.

convince *vt* convencer, poner en evidencia.

convincing *adj* convincente.

convincingly *adv* de modo convincente.

convivial *adj* sociable; hospitalario/ ria.

conviviality *n* sociabilidad *f*.

convoke *vt* convocar, reunir.

convoy *n* convoy *m*.

convulse *vt* conmover, convulsionar.

convulsion *n* convulsión *f*; conmoción *f*; tumulto *m*.

convulsive *adj* convulsivo/va; ~ly *adv* convulsivamente.

coo *vi* arrullar.

cook *n* cocinero/ra *m/f*; * *vt* cocinar; * *vi* cocinar; guisar.

cookbook *n* libro de cocina *m*.

cooker *n* cocina *f*.

cookery *n* arte culinario *m*, cocina *f*; * *n* frescura *f*; * *vt* enfriar, refrescar.

cool *adj* fresco/ca; indiferente; * *n* frescura *f*; * *vt* enfriar, refrescar.

coolly *adv* frescamente; indiferentemente.

coolness *n* fresco *m*; frialdad, frescura *f*.

cooperate *vi* cooperar.

cooperation *n* cooperación *f*.

cooperative *adj* cooperativo/va; cooperante.

coordinate *vt* coordinar.

coordination *n* coordinación, elección *f*.

cop *n* (*fam*) poli *m*.

copartner *n* compañero/ra, socio/cia *m/f*.

cope *vi* arreglárselas.

copier *n* copiadora *f*.

copious *adj* copioso/sa, abundante; ~ly *adv* en abundancia.

copper *n* cobre *m*.

coppice, copse *n* bosquecillo *m*.

copulate *vi* copular.

copy *n* copia *f*; original *m*; ejemplar *m*; * *vt* copiar; imitar.

copybook *n* copiador de cartas (libro) *m*.

copying machine *n* copiadora *f*.

copyist *n* copista *m/f*.

copyright *n* propiedad de una obra literaria *f*; derechos de autor *mpl*.

coral *n* coral *m*.

coral reef *n* arrecife de coral *m*.

cord *n* cuerda *f*; cable *m*.

cordial *adj* cordial, de corazón, amistoso/sa; ~ly *adv* cordialmente.

corduroy *n* pana *f*.

core *n* cuesco *m*; interior, centro, corazón *m*; materia *f*.

cork n alcornoque m; corcho m; * vt encorchar.

corkscrew n sacacorchos m invar.

corn n maíz m; grano m; callo m.

corncob n mazorca f.

cornea n córnea f.

corned beef n carne acecinada f.

corner n rincón m; esquina f.

cornerstone n piedra angular f.

cornet n corneta f.

cornfield n maizal m.

cornflakes npl copos de maíz mpl.

cornflour n harina de maíz f.

cornice n cornisa f.

corollary n corolario m.

coronary n infarto m.

coronation n coronación f.

coroner n oficial que hace la inspección jurídica de los cadáveres m.

coronet n corona pequeña f.

corporal n cabo m.

corporate adj corporativo/va.

corporation n corporación f; gremio m.

corporeal adj corpóreo/rea.

corps n cuerpo (de ejército) m; regimiento m.

corpse n cadáver m.

corpulent adj corpulento/ta, gordo/da.

corpuscle n corpúsculo, átomo m.

corral n corral m.

correct vt corregir; enmendar; * adj correcto/ta, justo/ta; ~ly adv correctamente.

correction n corrección f; enmienda f; censura f.

corrective adj correctivo/va; * n correctivo m; restricción f.

correctness n exactitud f.

correlation n correlación f.

correlative adj correlativo/va.

correspond vi corresponder; corresponderse.

correspondence n correspondencia f.

correspondent adj correspondiente, conforme; * n corresponsal m.

corridor n pasillo m.

corroborate vt corroborar.

corroboration n corroboración f.

corroborative adj corroborativo/va.

corrode vt corroer.

corrosion n corrosión f.

corrosive adj, n corrosivo m.

corrugated iron n chapa ondulada f.

corrupt vt corromper; sobornar; * vi corromperse, pudrirse; * adj corrompido/da; depravado/da.

corruptible adj corruptible.

corruption n corrupción f; depravación f.

corruptive adj corruptivo/va.

corset n corsé, corpiño m.

cortege n cortejo m.

cosily adv cómodamente, con facilidad.

cosmetic adj cosmético/ca; * n cosmético m.

cosmic adj cósmico/ca.

cosmonaut n cosmonauta m/f.

cosmopolitan adj cosmopolita.

cosset vt mimar.

cost n coste, precio m; * vi costar.

costly adj costoso/sa, caro/ra.

costume n traje m.

cosy adj cómodo/da.

cottage n casita, casucha f.

cotton n algodón m.

cotton mill n hilandería de algodón.

cotton wool n algodón hidrófilo m.

couch n sofá m.

couchette n litera f.

cough n tos f; * vi toser.

council n concilio, consejo m.

councillor n concejal/a m/f.

counsel n consejo, aviso m; abogado/da m/f.

counsellor n consejero/ra m/f; abogado/da m/f.

count vt contar, numerar; calcular; **to ~ on** contar con; * n cuenta f; cálculo m; conde m.

countdown n cuenta atrás f.

countenance n rostro m; aspecto m; (buena o mala) cara f.

counter n mostrador m; (games) ficha f.

counteract vt contrariar, impedir, estorbar; frustrar.

counterbalance vt contrapesar; igualar, compensar; * n contrapeso m.

counterfeit vt contrahacer, imitar, falsear; * adj falsificado/da; fingido/da.

countermand vt contramandar; revocar.

counterpart n parte correspondiente f.

counterproductive adj contraproducente.

countersign vt refrendar; firmar un decreto.

countess n condesa f.

countless adj innumerable.

countrified adj rústico/ca; tosco/ca, rudo/da.

country n país m; campo m; región f; patria f; * adj rústico/ca; campestre, rural.

country house n casa de campo, granja f.

countryman n paisano m; compatriota m.

county n condado m.

coup n golpe m.

coupé n (auto) cupé m.

couple n par m; lazo m; yuntas fpl; * vt unir, parear; casar.

couplet n copla f; par m.

coupon n cupón m.

courage n coraje, valor f.

courageous adj corajudo/da, valeroso/sa; ~ly adv valerosamente.

courier n correo, mensajero/ra m/f, expreso m.

course n curso m; carrera f; camino m; ruta f; método m; **of ~** por supuesto, sin duda.

court n corte f; palacio m; tribunal de justicia m; * vt cortejar; solicitar, adular.

courteous adj cortés; benévolo/la; ~ly adv cortésmente.

courtesan n cortesana f.

courtesy n cortesía f; benignidad f.

courthouse n palacio de justicia m.

courtly adj cortesano/na, elegante.

court martial n consejo de guerra m.

courtroom n sala de justicia f.

courtyard n patio m.

cousin n primo m; prima f; **first ~** primo hermano m.

cove n (mar) ensenada, caleta f.

covenant n contrato m; convención f; * vi pactar, estipular.

cover n cubierta f; abrigo m; pretexto m; * vt cubrir; tapar; ocultar; proteger.

coverage n alcance m.

coveralls npl mono m.

covering n ropa f; vestido m.

cover letter n carta de explicación f.

covert adj cubierto/ta; oculto/ta, secreto/ta; ~ly adv secretamente.

cover-up n encubrimiento m.

covet vt codiciar, desear con ansia.

covetous adj avariento/ta, sórdido/da.

cow n vaca f.

coward n cobarde m/f.

cowardice n cobardía, timidez f.

cowardly adj, adv cobarde; pusilánime.

cowboy n vaquero m.

cower vi agacharse.

cowherd n vaquero m; vaquerizo m.

coy adj recatado/da, modesto/ta; esquivo/va; ~ly adv con esquivez.

coyness n esquivez, modestia f.

crab n cangrejo m; manzana silvestre f.

crab apple n manzana silvestre f; ~ **tree** n manzano silvestre m.

crack n crujido m; hendedura, quebraja f; * vt hender, rajar; romper; **to ~ down** vi reprimandar fuertemente; * vi reventar.

cracker n buscapiés m invar; galleta f.

crackle vi crujir, chillar.

crackling n estallido, crujido m.

cradle n cuna f; * vt acunar.

craft n arte m; artificio m; barco m.

craftily adv astutamente.

craftiness n astucia, estratagema f.

craftsman n artífice, artesano m.

craftsmanship n artesanía f.

crafty adj astuto/ta, artificioso/sa.

crag n despeñadero m.

cram vt embutir; engordar; empujar; * vi empollar.

crammed adj atestado/da.

cramp n calambre m; * vt constreñir.

cramped adj apretado/da.

crampon n crampón m.

cranberry n arándano agrio m.

crane n grulla f; grúa f.

crash vi estallar; * vr zamparse; * n estallido m; choque m.

crash helmet n casco m.

crash landing n aterrizaje forzoso m.

crass adj craso/sa, grueso/sa, basto/ta, tosco/ca, grosero/ra.

crate n cesta grande f.

crater n cráter m; boca de volcán f.

cravat n pañuelo m.

crave vt rogar, suplicar.

craving adj insaciable, pedigüeño/ña; * n deseo ardiente m.

crawl vi arrastrar; **to ~ with** hormiguear.

crayfish n cangrejo de río m.

crayon n lápiz m.

craze n manía f.

craziness n locura f.

crazy adj loco/ca.

creak vi crujir, chirriar.

cream n crema f; * adj color crema.

creamy adj cremoso/sa.

crease n pliegue m; * vt plegar.

create vt crear; causar.

creation n creación f; elección f.

creative adj creativo/va.

creator n creador/a m/f.

creature n criatura f.

credence n creencia, fe f; renombre m.

credentials npl (cartas) credenciales fpl.

credibility n credibilidad f.

credible adj creíble.

credit n crédito m; reputación f; autoridad f; * vt creer, fiar, acreditar.

creditable adj estimable, honorífico/ca; ~bly adv honorablemente.

credit card n tarjeta de crédito f.

creditor n acreedor m.

credulity n credulidad f.

credulous adj crédulo/la; ~ly adv con credulidad.

creed n credo m.

creek n arroyo m.

creep vi arrastrar, serpear; complacer bajamente.

creeper n (bot) enredadera f.

creepy adj horripilante.

cremate vt incinerar cadáveres.

cremation n cremación f.

crematorium n crematorio m.

crescent adj creciente; * n cuarto creciente m.

cress n berro m.

crest n cresta f.

crested adj crestado/da.

crestfallen adj acobardado/da, abatido/da de espíritu.

crevasse n grieta (de glaciar) f.

crevice n raja, hendedura f.

crew n banda, tropa f; tripulación f.

crib n cuna f; pesebre m.

cricket n grillo m; críquet m.

crime n crimen m; culpa f.

criminal adj criminal, reo/rea; ~ly adv criminalmente; * n criminal m/f.

criminality n criminalidad f.

crimson adj, n carmesí m.

cripple n, adj cojo/ja m/f; * vt lisiar; (fig) estropear.

crisis n crisis f invar.

crisp adj crujiente.

crispness n sequedad f.

criss-cross adj entrelazado/da.

criterion n criterio m.

critic n crítico m; crítica f.

critic(al) adj crítico/ca; exacto/ta; delicado/da; ~ally adv exactamente, rigurosamente.

criticism n criticismo m.

criticize vt criticar, censurar; zaherir; (fig) zurrar.

croak vi graznar.

crochet n ganchillo m; * vt, vi hacer ganchillo.

crockery n loza f; vasijas de barro fpl.

crocodile n cocodrilo m.

crony n amigote m; compinche m.

crook n (fam) ladrón m; cayado m.

crooked adj torcido/da; perverso/sa.

crop n cultivo m; cosecha f; * vt recortar.

cross n cruz f; carga f; * adj mal humorado/da; * vt atravesar, cruzar; to ~ over traspasar.

crossbar n travesaño m.

crossbreed n raza cruzada f.

cross-country n carrera a campo traviesa f.

cross-examine vt preguntar a un testigo.

crossfire n fuego cruzado m.

crossing n cruce m; paso a nivel m.

cross-purpose n disposición contraria f; contradicción f; to be at ~s entenderse mal.

cross-reference n remisión f.

crossroad n encrucijada f.

crotch n entrepierna f.

crouch vi agacharse, bajarse.

crow n cuervo m; canto del gallo m; * vi cantar el gallo.

crowd n público m; muchedumbre f; * vt amontonar; * vi reunirse.

crown n corona f; cumbre f; * vt coronar.

crown prince n príncipe real m.

crucial adj crucial.

crucible n crisol m.

crucifix n crucifijo m.

crucifixion n crucifixión f.

crucify vt crucificar; atormentar.

crude adj crudo/da, imperfecto/ta; ~ly adv crudamente.

cruel adj cruel, inhumano/na; ~ly adv cruelmente.

cruelty n crueldad f.

cruet n vinagrera f.

cruise n crucero m; * vi hacer un crucero.

cruiser n crucero m.

crumb n miga f.

crumble vt desmigajar, desmenuzar; * vi desmigajarse.

crumple vt arrugar.

crunch vt ronzar; * n (fig) crisis f invar.

crunchy adj crujiente.

crusade n cruzada f.

crush vt apretar, oprimir; * n choque m.

crust n costra f; corteza f; zoquete m.

crusty adj costroso/sa; bronco/ca, áspero/ra.

crutch n muleta f.

crux n lo esencial.

cry vt, vi gritar; exclamar; llorar; * n grito m; lloro m; clamor m.

crypt n cripta f.

cryptic adj enigmático/ca.

crystal n cristal m.

crystal-clear adj claro/ra como el agua.

crystalline adj cristalino/na; transparente.

crystallize vt (vi) cristalizar(se).

cub n cachorro m.

cube n cubo m.

cubic adj cúbico/ca.

cuckoo n cuco m.

cucumber n pepino m.

cud n: **to chew the ~** rumiar; (fig) reflexionar.

cuddle vt abrazar; * vi abrazarse; * n abrazo m.

cudgel n garrote, palo m.

cue n taco (de billar) m.

cuff n puñada f; vuelta f.

culinary adj culinario/ria, de la cocina.

cull vt escoger, elegir.

culminate vi culminar.

culmination n colmo m.

culpability n culpabilidad f.

culpable adj culpable, criminal; ~bly adv culpablemente, criminalmente.

culprit n culpable m/f.

cult n culto f.

cultivate vi cultivar, mejorar; perfeccionar.

cultivation n cultivo m.

cultural adj cultural.

culture n cultura f.

cumbersome adj engorroso/sa, pesado/da, confuso/sa.

cumulative adj cumulativo/va.

cunning adj astuto/ta; intrigante; ~ly adv astutamente; expertamente; * n astucia, sutileza f; ~ **person** zorro m.

cup n taza, jícara f; (bot) cáliz m.

cupboard n armario m.

curable adj curable.

curate n teniente de cura m; párroco m.

curator n curador/a m/f; guardián/ana m/f.

curb n freno m; bordillo m; * vt refrenar, contener, moderar.

curd n cuajada f.

curdle vt (vi) cuajar(se), coagular(se).

cure n cura f; remedio m; * vt curar, sanar.

curfew n toque de queda m.

curing n curación f.

curiosity n curiosidad f; rareza f.

curious adj curioso/sa; ~ly adv curiosamente.

curl n rizo de pelo m; * vt rizar; ondear; * vi rizarse.

curling iron n, **curling tongs** npl tenacillas de rizar fpl.

curly adj rizado/da.

currant n pasa f.

currency n moneda f; circulación f; duración f.

current adj corriente, común; * n curso, progreso m; marcha f; corriente f.

current affairs npl actualidades fpl.

currently adv actualmente.

curriculum vitae n currículum m.

curry n curry m.

curse vt maldecir; * vi imprecar; blasfemar; * n maldición f.

cursor n cursor m.
cursory adj precipitado/da, inconsiderado/da.
curt adj sucinto/ta.
curtail vt acortar.
curtain n cortina f; telón (en teatro) m.
curtain rod n varilla de cortinaje f.
curtsy n reverencia f; * vi hacer una reverencia.
curvature n curvatura f.
curve vt encorvar; * n curva f.
cushion n cojín m; almohada f.
custard n natillas fpl.
custodian n custodio m.
custody n custodia f; prisión f.
custom n costumbre f, uso m.
customary adj usual, acostumbrado/da, ordinario/ria.
customer n cliente m/f.
customs npl aduana f.
customs duty n derechos de aduana mpl.
customs officer n aduanero/ra m/f.
cut vt cortar; separar; herir; dividir; cortar los naipes; **to ~ short** interrumpir, cortar la palabra; **to ~ teeth** nacerle los dientes (a un niño); * vi traspasar; cruzarse; * n

corte m; cortadura f; herida f; ~ **and dried** adj rutinario/ria.
cutback n reducción f.
cute adj lindo/da.
cutlery n cuchillería f.
cutlet n chuleta f.
cut-rate adj a precio reducido.
cut-throat n asesino m; * adj encarnizado/da.
cutting n cortadura f; * adj cortante; mordaz.
cyanide n cianuro m.
cyberspace n ciberespacio m.
cycle n ciclo m; bicicleta f; * vi ir en bicicleta.
cycling n ciclismo m.
cyclist n ciclista m/f.
cyclone n ciclón m.
cygnet n pollo del cisne m.
cylinder n cilindro m; rollo m.
cylindric(al) adj cilíndrico/ca.
cymbals n címbalo m.
cynic(al) adj cínico/ca; obsceno/na; * n cínico m (filósofo).
cynicism n cinismo m.
cypress n ciprés m.
cyst n quiste m.
czar n zar m.

D

dab n pedazo pequeño m; toque m.
dabble vi chapotear.
dad(dy) n papa m.
daddy-long-legs n típula f.
daffodil n narciso m.
dagger n puñal m.
daily adj diario/ria, cotidiano/na; * adv diariamente, cada día; * n diario m.
daintily adv delicadamente.

daintiness n elegancia f; delicadeza f.
dainty adj delicado/da, elegante.
dairy n lechería f.
dairy farm n vaquería f.
dairy produce n productos lácteos mpl.
daisy n margarita, maya f.
dale n valle m.
dally vi tardar.
dam n presa f; * vt represar.

damage n daño m; perjuicio m;
  * dañar; perjudicar.
damask n damasco m; * adj de damasco.
dame n dama f.
damn vt condenar; * adj maldito/ta.
damnable adj maldito/ta; ~**bly** adv
  terriblemente.
damnation n perdición f.
damning adj irrecusable.
damp adj húmedo/da; * n humedad
  f; * vt mojar.
dampen vt mojar.
dampness n humedad f.
damson n damascena f (ciruela).
dance n danza f; baile m; * vi bailar.
dance hall n salón de baile m.
dancer n bailarín m, bailarina f.
dandelion n diente de león m.
dandruff n caspa f.
dandy n mono/na.
danger n peligro, riesgo m.
dangerous adj peligroso/sa; ~**ly** adv
  peligrosamente.
dangle vi estar colgado/da.
dank adj húmedo/da.
dapper adj apuesto/ta.
dappled adj rodado/da.
dare vi atreverse; * vt desafiar.
daredevil n atrevido m.
daring n osadía f; * adj atrevido/da;
  ~**ly** adv atrevidamente,
  osadamente.
dark adj oscuro/ra; negro/gra; * n oscuridad f; ignorancia f.
darken vt (vi) oscurecer(se).
dark glasses npl gafas de sol fpl.
darkness n oscuridad f.
darkroom n cuarto oscuro m.
darling n, adj querido/m, n.
darn vt zurcir.
dart n dardo m.
dartboard n diana f.

dash vi irse de prisa; * n pizca f; **at
  one** ~ de un golpe.
dashboard n tablero de instrumen-
  tos m.
dashing adj gallardo/da.
dastardly adj cobarde.
data n datos mpl.
database n base de datos f.
data processing n proceso de datos m.
date n fecha f; cita f; (bot) dátil m;
  * vt fechar; salir con.
dated adj anticuado/da.
dative n dativo m.
daub vt manchar.
daughter n hija f; ~ **in-law** nuera f.
daunting adj desalentador/a.
dawdle vi gastar tiempo.
dawn n alba f; * vi amanecer.
day n día m; luz f; **by** ~ de día; **by**
  ~ de día en día.
daybreak n alba f.
day labourer n jornalero m.
daylight n luz del día, luz natural f;
  ~ **saving time** n hora de verano f.
daytime n día m.
daze vt aturdir.
dazed adj aturdido/da.
dazzle vt deslumbrar.
dazzling adj deslumbrante.
deacon n diácono m.
dead adj muerto/ta, marchito/ta;
  ~**wood** n lastre m; ~ **silence** n
  silencio profundo m; **the** ~ npl los
  muertos.
dead-drunk adj borracho como una
  cuba.
deaden vt amortiguar.
dead heat n empate m.
deadline n fecha tope f.
deadlock n punto muerto m.
deadly adj mortal; * adv terriblemente.

dead march *n* marcha fúnebre *f*.

deadness *n* inercia *f*.

deaf *adj* sordo/da.

deafen *vt* ensordecer.

deaf-mute *n* sordomudo/da *m./f*.

deafness *n* sordera *f*.

deal *n* convenio *m*; transacción *f*; **a great** ~ mucho; **a good** ~ bastante; * *vt* distribuir; dar; * *vi* comerciar; **to** ~ **in/with** tratar en/con.

dealer *n* comerciante *m/f*; traficante *m/f*; mano *f*.

dealings *npl* trato *m*.

dean *n* deán *m*.

dear *adj* querido/da; caro/ra, costoso/sa; ~**ly** *adv* caro.

dearness *n* carestía *f*.

dearth *n* escasez *f*.

death *n* muerte *f*.

deathbed *n* lecho de muerte *m*.

deathblow *n* golpe mortal *m*.

death certificate *n* partida de defunción *f*.

death penalty *n* pena de muerte *f*.

death throes *npl* agonía *f*.

death warrant *n* sentencia de muerte *f*.

debacle *n* desastre *m*.

debar *vt* excluir, no admitir.

debase *vt* degradar.

debasement *n* degradación *f*.

debatable *adj* discutible.

debate *n* debate *m*; polémica *f*; * *vt* discutir; examinar.

debauched *adj* vicioso/sa.

debauchery *n* libertinaje *m*.

debilitate *vt* debilitar.

debit *n* debe *m*; * *vt* (*com*) cargar en una cuenta.

debt *n* deuda *f*; obligación *f*; **to get into** ~ contraer deudas.

debtor *n* deudor/a *m/f*.

debunk *vt* desacreditar.

decade *n* década *f*.

decadence *n* decadencia *f*.

decaffeinated *adj* descafeinado/da.

decanter *n* garrafa *f*.

decapitate *vt* decapitar, degollar.

decapitation *n* decapitación *f*.

decay *vi* decaer; pudrirse; * *n* decadencia *f*; caries *f*.

deceased *adj* muerto/ta.

deceit *n* engaño *m*.

deceitful *adj* engañoso/sa; ~**ly** *adv* falsamente.

deceive *vt* engañar.

December *n* diciembre *m*.

decency *n* decencia *f*; modestia *f*.

decent *adj* decente, razonable; ~**ly** *adv* decentemente.

deception *n* engaño *m*.

deceptive *adj* engañoso/sa.

decibel *n* decibelio *m*.

decide *vt*, *vi* decidir; resolver.

decided *adj* decidido/da.

decidedly *adv* decididamente.

deciduous *adj* (*bot*) de hoja caduca.

decimal *adj* decimal.

decimate *vt* diezmar.

decipher *vt* descifrar.

decision *n* decisión, determinación *f*.

decisive *adj* decisivo/va; ~**ly** *adv* de modo decisivo.

deck *n* cubierta *f*; * *vt* adornar.

deckchair *n* tumbona *f*.

declaim *vi* declamar.

declamation *n* declamación *f*.

declaration *n* declaración *f*.

declare *vt* declarar, manifestar.

declension *n* declinación *f*.

decline *vt* (*gr*) declinar; evitar; * *vi* decaer; * *n* decadencia *f*.

declutch *vi* desembragar.

decode *vt* descifrar.

decoder (TV) *n* descodificador *m*.

decompose *vt* descomponer.

decomposition n descomposición f.

decor n decoración f.

decorate vt decorar, adornar.

decoration n decoración f.

decorative adj decorativo/va.

decorator n pintor (decorador) m.

decorous adj decoroso/sa; ~ly adv decorosamente.

decorum n decoro, garbo m.

decoy n señuelo m.

decrease vt disminuir; * n disminución f.

decree n decreto m; * vt decretar; ordenar.

decrepit adj decrépito/ta.

decry vt desacreditar, censurar.

dedicate vt dedicar; consagrar.

dedication n dedicación f; dedicatoria f.

deduce vt deducir; concluir.

deduct vt restar.

deduction n deducción f; descuento m.

deed n acción f; hecho m; hazaña f.

deem vi juzgar.

deep adj profundo/da.

deepen vt profundizar.

deep-freeze n congeladora f.

deeply adv profundamente.

deepness n profundidad f.

deer n ciervo m.

deface vt desfigurar, afear.

defacement n desfiguración f.

defamation n difamación f.

default n defecto m; falta f; * vi faltar.

defaulter n (law) moroso/sa m/f.

defeat n derrota f; * vt derrotar; frustrar.

defect n defecto m; falta f.

defection n deserción f.

defective adj defectuoso/sa.

defend vt defender; proteger.

defendant n acusado/da m/f.

defence n defensa f; protección f.

defenceless adj indefenso/sa.

defensive adj defensivo/va; ~ly adv de modo defensivo.

defer vt aplazar.

deference n deferencia f; respeto m.

deferential adj respetuoso/sa.

defiance n desafío m.

defiant adj insolente.

deficiency n defecto m; falta f.

deficient adj insuficiente.

deficit n déficit m.

defile vt ensuciar.

definable adj definible.

define vt definir.

definite adj definido/da, preciso/sa; ~ly adv no cabe duda.

definition n definición f.

definitive adj definitivo/va; ~ly adv definitivamente.

deflate vt desinflar.

deflect vt desviar.

deflower vt desvirgar.

deform vt desfigurar.

deformity n deformidad f.

defraud vt estafar.

defray vt costear.

defrost vt deshelar; descongelar.

defroster n luneta térmica f.

deft adj diestro/tra; ~ly adv hábilmente.

defunct adj difunto/ta.

defuse vt desactivar.

degenerate vi degenerar; * adj degenerado/da.

degeneration n degeneración f.

degradation n degradación f.

degrade vt degradar.

degree n grado m; título m.

dehydrated adj deshidratado/da.

de-ice vt deshelar.

deign vi dignarse.

deity n deidad, divinidad f.
dejected adj desanimado/da.
dejection n desaliento m.
delay vt demorar; * n retraso m.
delectable adj deleitoso/sa.
delegate vt delegar; * n delegado m.
delegation n delegación f.
delete vt tachar; borrar.
deliberate vt deliberar; * adj intencionado/da; ~ly adv a propósito.
deliberation n deliberación f.
deliberative adj deliberativo/va.
delicacy n delicadeza f.
delicate adj delicado/da, exquisito/ta; ~ly adv delicadamente.
delicious adj delicioso/sa, exquisito/ta; ~ly adv deliciosamente.
delight n delicia f; gozo, encanto m; * vt (vi) deleitar(se).
delighted adj encantado/da.
delightful adj encantador/a; ~ly adv en forma encantadora.
delineate vt delinear.
delineation n delineación f.
delinquency n delincuencia f.
delinquent n delincuente m/f.
delirious adj delirante.
delirium n delirio m.
deliver vt entregar; pronunciar.
deliverance n liberación f.
delivery n entrega f; parto m.
delude vt engañar.
deluge n diluvio m.
delusion n engaño m; ilusión f.
delve vi hurgar.
demagogue n demagogo/a m/f.
demand n demanda f; reclamación f; * vt exigir; reclamar.
demanding adj exigente.
demarcation n demarcación f.
demean vi rebajarse.
demeanour n conducta f.
demented adj demente.

demise n desaparición f.
democracy n democracia f.
democrat n demócrata m/f.
democratic adj democrático/ca.
demolish vt demoler.
demolition n demolición f.
demon n demonio, diablo m.
demonstrable adj demostrable; ~bly adv manifiestamente.
demonstrate vt demostrar, probar; * vi manifestarse.
demonstration n demostración f; manifestación f.
demonstrative adj demostrativo/va.
demonstrator n manifestante m/f.
demoralization n desmoralización f.
demoralize vt desmoralizar.
demote vt degradar.
demur vi objetar.
demure adj modesto/ta; ~ly adv modestamente.
den n guarida f.
denatured alcohol n alcohol desnaturalizado m.
denial n negación f.
denims npl vaqueros mpl.
denomination n valor m.
denominator n (math) denominador m.
denote vt denotar, indicar.
denounce vt denunciar.
dense adj denso/sa, espeso/sa.
density n densidad f.
dent n abolladura f; * vt abollar.
dental adj dental.
dentifrice n dentífrico m.
dentist n dentista m/f.
dentistry n odontología f.
denture npl dentadura postiza f.
denude vt desnudar, despojar.
denunciation n denuncia f.
deny vt negar.
deodorant n desodorante m.

deodorize vt desodorizar.

depart vi partir.

department n departamento m.

department store n gran almacén m.

departure n partida f.

departure lounge n sala de embarque f.

depend vi depender; ~ **on/upon** contar con.

dependable adj seguro/ra, serio/ria.

dependant n dependiente m.

dependency n dependencia f.

dependent adj dependiente.

depict vt pintar, retratar; describir.

depleted adj reducido/da.

deplorable adj deplorable, lamentable; ~**bly** adv deplorablemente.

deplore vt deplorar, lamentar.

deploy vt (mil) desplegar.

depopulated adj despoblado/da.

depopulation n despoblación f.

deport vt deportar.

deportation n deportación f; destierro m.

deportment n conducta f.

deposit vt depositar; * n depósito m; yacimiento m.

deposition n deposición f.

depositor n depositante m.

depot n depósito m.

deprave vt depravar, corromper.

depraved adj depravado/da.

depravity n depravación f.

deprecate vt lamentar.

depreciate vi depreciarse.

depreciation n depreciación f.

depredation n pillaje m.

depress vt deprimir.

depressed adj deprimido/da.

depression n depresión f.

deprivation n privación f.

deprive vt privar.

deprived adj necesitado/da.

depth n profundidad f.

deputation n diputación f.

depute vt diputar, delegar.

deputize vi suplir a.

deputy n diputado/da m/f.

derail vt descarrilar.

deranged adj trastornado/da.

derelict adj abandonado/da.

deride vt burlar.

derision n mofa f.

derisive adj irrisorio/ria.

derivable adj deducible.

derivation n derivación f.

derivative n derivado m.

derive vt (vi) derivar(se).

dermatologist n dermatólogo/ga m/f.

dermatology n dermatología f.

derogatory adj despectivo/va.

derrick n torre de perforación f.

desalinate vt desalinizar.

desalination plant n desalinizadora f.

descant n (mus) discante m.

descend vi descender.

descendant n descendiente m.

descent n descenso m.

describe vt describir.

description n descripción f.

descriptive adj descriptivo/va.

descry vt divisar.

desecrate vt profanar.

desecration n profanación f.

desert¹ n desierto m; * adj desierto/ta.

desert² vt abandonar; desertar; * n mérito m.

deserter n desertor/a m/f.

desertion n deserción f.

deserve vt merecer; ser digno/na.

deservedly adv merecidamente.

deserving adj meritorio/ria.

deshabille, dishabille n deshabillé m.

desideratum n desiderátum m.

design vt diseñar; * n diseño m; dibujo m.
designate vt nombrar; designar.
designation n designación f.
designedly adv a propósito.
designer n diseñador m; modisto m.
desirability n conveniencia f.
desirable adj deseable.
desire n deseo m; * vt desear.
desirous adj deseoso/sa, ansioso/sa.
desist vi desistir.
desk n escritorio m.
desktop publishing n autoedición f.
desolate adj desierto/ta.
desolation n desolación f.
despair n desesperación f; * vi desesperarse.
despairingly adj desesperadamente.
despatch = dispatch.
desperado n bandido/da m/f.
desperate adj desesperado/da; **~ly** adv desesperadamente; sumamente.
desperation n desesperación f.
despicable adj despreciable.
despise vt despreciar.
despite prep a pesar de.
despoil vt despojar.
despondency n abatimiento m.
despondent adj abatido/da.
despot n déspota m/f.
despotic adj despótico/ca, absoluto/ta; **~ally** adv despóticamente.
despotism n despotismo m.
dessert n postre m.
destination n destino m.
destine vt destinar.
destiny n destino m; suerte f.
destitute adj indigente.
destitution n miseria f.
destroy vt destruir, arruinar.
destruction n destrucción f, ruina f.
destructive adj destructivo/va.

desultory adj irregular; sin método.
detach vt separar.
detachable adj desmontable; de quitapón.
detachment n (mil) destacamento m.
detail n detalle m; **in ~** detalladamente; * vt detallar.
detain vt retener; detener.
detect vt detectar.
detection n descubrimiento m.
detective n detective m/f.
detector n detector m.
detention n detención f.
deter vt disuadir.
detergent n detergente m.
deteriorate vt deteriorar.
deterioration n deterioro m.
determination n resolución f.
determine vt determinar, decidir.
determined adj resuelto/ta.
deterrent n fuerza de disuasión f.
detest vt detestar, aborrecer.
detestable adj detestable, abominable.
dethrone vt destronar.
dethronement n destronamiento m.
detonate vi detonar.
detonation n detonación f.
detour n desviación f.
detract vt desvirtuar.
detriment n perjuicio m.
detrimental adj perjudicial.
deuce n deuce m.
devaluation n devaluación f.
devastate vt devastar.
devastating adj devastador.
devastation n devastación, ruina f.
develop vt desarrollar.
development n desarrollo m.
deviate vi desviarse.
deviation n desviación f.
device n mecanismo m.
devil n diablo, demonio m.

devilish adj diabólico/ca; **~ly** adv diabólicamente.

devious adj taimado/da.

devise vt inventar; idear.

devoid adj desprovisto/ta.

devolve vt delegar.

devote vt dedicar; consagrar.

devoted adj fiel.

devotee n partidario/a m/f.

devotion n devoción f.

devotional adj devoto/ta.

devour vt devorar.

devout adj devoto/ta, piadoso/sa; **~ly** adv piadosamente.

dew n rocío m.

dewy adj rociado/da.

dexterity n destreza f.

dexterous adj diestro/tra, hábil.

diabetes n diabetes f.

diabetic n diabético/ca m/f.

diabolic adj diabólico/ca; **~ally** adv diabólicamente.

diadem n diadema f.

diagnosis n (med) diagnóstico m.

diagnostic adj, n diagnóstico m; **~s** pl diagnóstica f.

diagonal adj, n diagonal f; **~ly** adv diagonalmente.

diagram n diagrama m.

dial n cuadrante m; disco m.

dialect n dialecto m.

dialling code n prefijo m.

dialling tone n tono de marcar m.

dialogue n diálogo m.

diameter n diámetro m.

diametrical adj diametral; **~ly** adv diametralmente.

diamond n diamante m.

diamond-cutter n diamantista m/f.

diamonds npl (cards) diamantes mpl.

diaphragm n diafragma m.

diarrhoea n diarrea f.

diary n diario m.

dice npl dados mpl.

dictate vt dictar; * n dictado m.

dictation n dictado m.

dictatorial adj autoritativo/va, magistral.

dictatorship n dictadura f.

diction n dicción f

dictionary n diccionario m.

didactic adj didáctico/ca.

die[1] vi morir; **to ~ away** perderse; **to ~ down** apagarse.

die[2] n dado m.

diehard n reaccionario/ria m/f.

diesel n diesel m.

diet n dieta f; régimen m; * vi estar a dieta.

dietary adj dietético/ca.

differ vi diferenciarse.

difference n diferencia, disparidad f.

different adj diferente; **~ly** adv diferentemente.

differentiate vt diferenciar.

difficult adj difícil.

difficulty n dificultad f.

diffidence n timidez f.

diffident adj desconfiado/da; **~ly** adv desconfiadamente.

diffraction n difracción f.

diffuse vt difundir, esparcir; * adj difuso/sa.

diffusion n difusión f.

dig vt cavar; **to ~ ditches** zanjar; * n empujón m.

digest vt digerir.

digestible adj digerible.

digestion n digestión f.

digestive adj digestivo/va.

digger n excavadora f.

digit n dígito m.

digital adj digital.

digitize vt digitalizar.

dignified adj grave.

dignitary n dignatario m.
dignity n dignidad f.
digress vi divagar.
digression n digresión f.
dike n dique m.
dilapidated adj desmoronado/da.
dilapidation n ruina f.
dilate vt, vi dilatar(se).
dilemma n dilema m.
diligence n diligencia f.
diligent adj diligente, asiduo/dua; ~ly adv diligentemente.
dilute vt diluir.
dim adj turbio/bia; lerdo/da; oscuro/ra; * vt bajar.
dime n moneda de diez centavos f.
dimension n dimensión, extensión f.
diminish vt (vi) disminuir(se).
diminution n disminución f.
diminutive n diminutivo m.
dimly adv indistintamente.
dimmer n interruptor m.
dimple n hoyuelo m.
din n alboroto m.
dine vi cenar.
dinghy n lancha neumática f.
dingy adj sombrío/ría.
dinner n cena f.
dinner-jacket n smoking m.
dinner time n hora de comer f.
dinosaur n dinosaurio m.
dint n: by ~ of a fuerza de.
diocese n diócesis f invar.
dip vt mojar; * n zambullida f.
diphtheria n difteria f.
diphthong n diptongo m.
diploma n diploma m.
diplomacy n diplomacia f.
diplomat n diplomático/ca m/f.
diplomatic adj diplomático/ca.
dipsomania n dipsomanía f.
dipstick n (auto) varilla de nivel f.
dire adj calamitoso/sa.

direct adj directo/ta; * vt dirigir.
direction n dirección f; instrucción f.
directly adj directamente; inmediatamente.
director n director/a m/f.
directory n guía f.
dirt n suciedad f; ~ on clothes zarpa f.
dirtiness n suciedad f.
dirty adj sucio/cia; vil, bajo/ja.
disability n discapacidad f.
disabled adj discapacitado/da.
disabuse vt desengañar.
disadvantage n desventaja f; * vt perjudicar.
disadvantageous adj desventajoso/sa.
disaffected adj descontento/ta.
disagree vi no estar de acuerdo.
disagreeable adj desagradable; ~bly adv desagradablemente.
disagreement n desacuerdo m.
disallow vt rechazar.
disappear vi desaparecer; ausentarse.
disappearance n desaparición f.
disappoint vt decepcionar.
disappointed adj decepcionado/da.
disappointing adj decepcionante.
disappointment n decepción f.
disapproval n desaprobación, censura f.
disapprove vt desaprobar.
disarm vt desarmar.
disarmament n desarme m.
disarray n desarreglo m.
disaster n desastre m.
disastrous adj desastroso/sa, calamitoso/sa.
disband vt disolver.
disbelief n incredulidad f.
disbelieve vt desconfiar.
disburse vt desembolsar, pagar.
disc, disk n disco m.

discard *vt* descartar.

discern *vt* discernir, percibir.

discernible *adj* perceptible.

discerning *adj* perspicaz.

discernment *n* perspicacia *f*.

discharge *vt* descargar; pagar (una deuda); cumplir; * *n* descarga *f*; descargo *m*.

disciple *n* discípulo/la *m/f*.

discipline *n* disciplina *f*; * *vt* disciplinar.

disclaim *vt* negar.

disclaimer *n* negación *f*.

disclose *vi* revelar.

disclosure *n* revelación *f*.

discolour *vt* descolorar.

discolouration *n* descolorimiento *m*.

discomfort *n* incomodidad *f*.

disconcert *vt* desconcertar.

disconnect *vt* desconectar.

disconsolate *adj* inconsolable; **~ly** *adv* desconsoladamente.

discontent *n* descontento/ta *m/f*; * *adj* descontento/ta.

discontented *adj* descontento/ta.

discontinue *vi* interrumpir.

discord *n* discordia *f*.

discordant *adj* discordante.

discotheque, disco *n* discoteca *f*.

discount *n* descuento *m*; rebaja *f*; * *vt* descontar.

discourage *vt* desalentar, desanimar.

discouraged *adj* desalentado/da.

discouragement *n* desaliento *m*.

discouraging *adj* desalentador/a.

discourse *n* discurso *m*.

discourteous *adj* descortés, grosero; ra; **~ly** *adv* descortésmente.

discourtesy *n* descortesía *f*.

discover *vt* descubrir.

discovery *n* descubrimiento *m*; revelación *f*.

discredit *vt* desacreditar.

discreditable *adj* ignominioso/sa.

discreet *adj* discreto/ta; **~ly** *adv* discretamente.

discrepancy *n* discrepancia, diferencia *f*.

discretion *n* discreción *f*.

discretionary *adj* discrecional.

discriminate *vt* distinguir.

discrimination *n* discriminación *f*.

discursive *adj* discursivo/va.

discuss *vt* discutir.

discussion *n* discusión *f*.

disdain *vt* desdeñar; * *n* desdén, desprecio *m*.

disdainful *adj* desdeñoso/sa; **~ly** *adv* desdeñosamente.

disease *n* enfermedad *f*.

diseased *adj* enfermo/ma.

disembark *vt*, *vi* desembarcar.

disembarkation *n* desembarco *m*.

disenchant *vt* desencantar.

disenchanted *adj* desilusionado/da.

disenchantment *n* desilusión *f*.

disengage *vt* soltar.

disentangle *vt* desenredar.

disfigure *vt* desfigurar, afear.

disgrace *n* ignominia *f*; escándalo *m*; * *vt* deshonrar.

disgraceful *adj* ignominioso/sa; **~ly** *adv* vergonzosamente.

disgruntled *adj* descontento/ta.

disguise *vt* disfrazar; * *n* disfraz *m*.

disgust *n* aversión *f*; * *vt* repugnar.

disgusting *adj* repugnante.

dish *n* fuente *f*; plato *m*; taza *f*; * *vt* servir en fuente; **to ~ up** servir.

dishcloth *n* paño de cocina *m*.

dishearten *vt* desalentar.

dishevelled *adj* desarreglado/da.

dishonest *adj* deshonesto/ta; **~ly** *adv* deshonestamente.

dishonesty *n* falta de honradez *f*.

dishonour n deshonra, ignominia f;
* vt deshonrar.
dishonourable adj deshonroso/sa;
~**bly** adv deshonrosamente.
dishtowel n trapo de fregar m.
dishwarmer n escalfador m.
dishwasher n lavaplatos m/f; lavava-
jillas m invar.
disillusion vt desilusionar.
disillusioned adj desilusionado/da.
disincentive n freno m.
disinclination n aversión f.
disinclined adj reacio/cia.
disinfect vt desinfectar.
disinfectant n desinfectante m.
disinherit vt desheredar.
disintegrate vi disgregarse.
disinterested adj desinteresado/da;
~**ly** adv desinteresadamente.
disjointed adj inconexo/xa.
diskette n disco, disquete m.
dislike n aversión f; * vt tener antipatía.
dislocate vt dislocar.
dislocation n dislocación f.
dislodge vt, vi desalojar.
disloyal adj desleal; ~**ly** adv desleal-
mente.
disloyalty n deslealtad f.
dismal adj triste.
dismantle vt desmontar.
dismay n consternación f.
dismember vt despedazar.
dismiss vt despedir.
dismissal n despedida f.
dismount vt desmontar; * vi apearse.
disobedience n desobediencia f.
disobedient adj desobediente.
disobey vt desobedecer.
disorder n desorden m; confusión f.
disorderly adj desarreglado/da,
confuso/sa.
disorganization n desorganización f.

disorganized adj desorganizado/da.
disorientated adj desorientado/da.
disown vt desconocer.
disparage vt despreciar.
disparaging adj despreciativo/va.
disparity n disparidad f.
dispassionate adj desapasio-
nado/da.
dispatch vt enviar; * n envío m; informe m.
dispel vt disipar.
dispensary n dispensario m.
dispense vt dispensar; distribuir.
disperse vt dispersar.
dispirited adj desalentado/da.
displace vt desplazar.
display vt exponer; * n ostentación f;
despliegue m.
displeased adj disgustado/da.
displeasure n disgusto m.
disposable adj desechable.
disposal n disposición f.
dispose vt disponer; arreglar.
disposed adj dispuesto/ta.
disposition n disposición f.
dispossess vt desposeer.
disproportionate adj desproporcio-
nado/da.
disprove vt refutar.
dispute n disputa, controversia f;
* vt disputar.
disqualify vt incapacitar.
disquiet n inquietud f.
disquieting adj inquietante.
disquisition n disquisición f.
disregard vt desatender; * n desdén m.
disreputable adj de mala fama.
disrespect n irreverencia f.
disrespectful adj irreverente; ~**ly**
adv irreverentemente.
disrobe vt desnudar.
disrupt vt interrumpir.

disruption n interrupción f.

dissatisfaction n descontento/ta, disgusto m.

dissatisfied adj insatisfecho/cha.

dissect vt disecar.

dissection n disección f.

disseminate vt diseminar.

dissension n disensión f.

dissent vi disentir; * n disensión f.

dissenter n disidente m.

dissertation n disertación f.

dissident n disidente m.

dissimilar adj distinto/ta.

dissimilarity n disimilitud f.

dissimulation n disimulo m.

dissipate vt disipar.

dissipation n disipación f.

dissociate vt disociar.

dissolute adj libertino/na.

dissolution n disolución f.

dissolve vt disolver; * vi disolverse, derretirse.

dissonance n disonancia f.

dissuade vt disuadir.

distance n distancia f; **at a ~** de lejos; * vt apartar.

distant adj distante.

distaste n disgusto m.

distasteful adj desagradable.

distend vt hinchar.

distil vt destilar.

distillation n destilación f.

distillery n destilería f.

distinct adj distinto/ta, diferente; claro/ra; **~ly** adv distintamente.

distinction n distinción f.

distinctive adj distintivo/va.

distinctness n claridad f.

distinguish vt distinguir; discernir.

distort vt retorcer.

distorted adj distorsionado/da.

distortion n distorción f.

distract vt distraer.

distracted adj distraído/da; **~ly** adj distraídamente.

distraction n distracción f; confusión f.

distraught adj enloquecido/da.

distress n angustia f; * vt angustiar.

distressing adj penoso/sa.

distribute vt distribuir, repartir.

distribution n distribución f.

distributor n distribuidor m.

district n distrito m.

distrustful adj desconfiado/da; sospechoso/sa.

disturb vt molestar.

disturbance n disturbio m.

disturbed adj preocupado/da.

disturbing adj inquietante.

disuse n desuso m.

disused adj abandonado/da.

ditch n zanja f.

dither vi vacilar.

ditto adv ídem.

ditty n cancioneta f.

diuretic adj (med) diurético/ca.

dive vi sumergirse; bucear; * vr zambullirse; * n zambullida f.

diver n buzo m.

diverge vi divergir.

divergence n divergencia f.

divergent adj divergente.

diverse adj diverso/sa, diferente; **~ly** adv diversamente.

diversion n diversión f.

diversity n diversidad f.

divert vt desviar; divertir.

divest vt desnudar; despojar.

divide vt dividir; * vi dividirse.

dividend n dividendo m.

dividers npl (math) compás de puntas m.

divine adj divino/na.

divinity n divinidad f.

diving n salto m; buceo m.

diving board n trampolín m.
divisible adj divisible.
division n (math) división f; desunión f.
divisor n (math) divisor m.
divorce n divorcio m; * vi divorciarse.
divorced adj divorciado/da.
divulge vt divulgar, publicar.
dizziness n vértigo m.
dizzy adj mareado/da.
DJ n pinchadiscos m.
do vt hacer, obrar.
docile adj dócil, apacible.
dock n muelle m; * vi atracar.
docker n estibador m.
dockyard n (mar) astillero m.
doctor n médico/ca m/f.
doctrinal adj doctrinal.
doctrine n doctrina f.
document n documento m.
documentary adj documental.
dodge vt esquivar.
doe n gama f; ~ **rabbit** coneja f.
dog n perro m.
dogged adj tenaz; ~**ly** adv tenazmente.
dog kennel n perrera f.
dogmatic adj dogmático/ca; ~**ly** adv dogmáticamente.
doings npl hechos mpl; eventos mpl.
do-it-yourself n bricolaje m.
doleful adj lúgubre, triste.
doll n muñeca f.
dollar n dólar m.
dolphin n delfín m.
domain n campo m.
dome n cúpula f.
domestic adj doméstico/ca.
domesticate vt domesticar.
domestication n domesticación f.
domesticity n domesticidad f.
domicile n domicilio m.
dominant adj dominante.

dominate vi dominar.
domination n dominación f.
domineer vi dominar.
domineering adj dominante.
dominion n dominio m.
dominoes npl dominó m.
donate vt donar.
donation n donación f.
done adj hecho/cha; cocido/da.
donkey n asno, borrico m.
donor n donante m/f.
doodle vi garabatear.
doom n suerte f.
door n puerta f.
doorbell n timbre m.
door handle n tirador m.
doorman n portero m.
doormat n felpudo m.
doorstep n peldaño m.
doorway n entrada f.
dormant adj latente.
dormer window n buhardilla f.
dormitory n dormitorio m.
dormouse n lirón m.
dosage n dosis f invar.
dose n dosis f invar; * vt disponer la dosis de.
dossier n expediente m.
dot n punto m.
dote vi adorar.
dotingly adv con cariño excesivo.
double adj doble; * vt doblar; duplicar; * n doble m.
double bed n cama matrimonial f.
double-breasted adj cruzado/da.
double chin n papada f.
double-dealing n duplicidad f.
double-edged adj de doble filo.
double entry n (com) partida doble f.
double-lock vt echar la segunda vuelta a la llave a.
double room n habitación doble f.

doubly adj doblemente.
doubt n duda, sospecha f; * vt dudar; sospechar.
doubtful adj dudoso/sa.
doubtless adv sin duda.
dough n masa f.
douse vt apagar.
dove n paloma f.
dovecot(e) n palomar m.
dowdy adj mal vestido/da.
down n plumón m; flojel m; * prep abajo; **to sit ~** sentarse; **upside ~** al revés.
downcast adj cabizbajo/ja.
downfall n ruina f.
downhearted adj desanimado/da.
downhill adv cuesta abajo/ja.
down payment n entrada f.
downpour n aguacero m.
downright adj manifiesto/ta.
downstairs adv abajo/ja.
down-to-earth adj práctico/ca.
downtown adv al centro (de la ciudad).
downward(s) adv hacia abajo.
dowry n dote f.
doze vi dormitar.
dozen n docena f.
dozy adj somnoliento/ta.
drab adj gris.
draft n borrador m; quinta f; corriente de aire f.
drafty adj expuesto/ta al aire.
drag vt arrastrar; tirar con fuerza; * n lata f.
dragnet n red barredera f.
dragon n dragón m.
dragonfly n libélula f.
drain vt desaguar; secar; * n desaguadero m.
drainage n desagüe m.
draining board n escurridor m.
drainpipe n desagüe m.

drake n ánade macho m.
dram n traguito m.
drama n drama m.
dramatic adj dramático/ca; **~ally** adv dramáticamente.
dramatist n dramaturgo/ga m/f.
dramatize vt dramatizar.
drape vt cubrir.
drastic adj drástico/ca.
draughtboard n tablero de damas m.
draughts npl juego de damas m.
draw vt tirar; dibujar; **to ~ nigh** acercarse.
drawback n desventaja f.
drawer n cajón m.
drawing n dibujo m.
drawing board n tablero de dibujo m.
drawing pin n chincheta f.
drawing room n salón m.
drawl vi hablar con pesadez.
dread n terror, espanto m; * vt temer.
dreadful adj espantoso/sa; **~ly** adv terriblemente.
dream n sueño m; * vi soñar.
dreary adj triste.
dredge vt dragar.
dregs npl heces fpl.
drench vt empapar.
dress vt vestir; vendar; * vi vestirse; * n vestido m.
dresser n aparador m.
dressing n vendaje m; aliño m.
dressing gown n bata f.
dressing room n tocador m.
dressing table n tocador m.
dressmaker n modista f.
dressy adj elegante.
dribble vi caer gota a gota, babear.
dribbling n regateo m.
dried adj seco/ca.
drift n montón m; ventisquero m; significado m; * vi ir a la deriva.

driftwood n madera de deriva f.
drill n taladro m; (mil) instrucción f; * vt taladrar.
drink vt, vi beber; * n bebida f.
drinkable adj potable.
drinker n bebedor/a m/f.
drinking bout n borrachera f.
drinking water n agua potable f.
drip vi gotear; * n gota f; goteo m.
dripping n pringue m/f.
drive vt conducir, manejar; empujar; * vi conducir, manejar; * n paseo en coche m; entrada f.
drivel n baba f; * vi babear.
driver n conductor/a m/f; chofer m.
driver's licence n carnet m de conducir, carnet m de manejar.
driveway n entrada f.
driving n conducción f, manejo m.
driving instructor n profesor/a de autoescuela m/f.
driving school n autoescuela f.
driving test n examen de conducir, examen de manejo m.
drizzle vi lloviznar.
droll adj gracioso/sa.
drone n zumbido m; zángano m.
drool vi babear.
droop vi decaer.
drop n gota f; * vt dejar caer; * vi bajar; **to ~ out** retirarse.
drop-out n marginado m.
dropper n cuentagotas m invar.
dross n escoria f.
drought n sequía f.
drove n: **in ~s** en tropel.
drown vt anegar; * vi anegarse.
drowsiness n somnolencia f.
drowsy adj somnoliento/ta.
drudgery n trabajo monótono m; zurra f.
drug n droga f; * vt drogar.
drug addict n drogadicto/ta m/f.

drug addiction n drogadicción f.
drug trafficker n narcotraficante m/f.
drum n tambor m; **rural ~** zambomba f; * vi tocar el tambor.
drum majorette n batonista f.
drummer n batería m.
drumstick n palillo de tambor m.
drunk adj borracho/cha.
drunkard n borracho m.
drunken adj borracho/cha.
drunkenness n borrachera f.
dry adj seco/ca; * vt secar; * vi secarse.
dry-cleaning n lavado en seco m.
dryness n sequedad f.
dry rot n podredumbre f.
dual adj doble.
dual-purpose adj de doble uso.
dubbed adj doblado/da.
dubious adj dudoso/sa.
duck n pato m; * vt (vi) zambullir(se).
duckling n patito m.
dud adj estropeado/da.
due adj debido/da, apto/ta; * adv exactamente; * n derecho m.
duel n duelo m.
duet n (mus) dúo m.
dull adj lerdo/da; insípido/da; zopenco/ca; gris; * vt aliviar.
duly adv debidamente; puntualmente.
dumb adj mudo/da; **~ly** adv sin chistar.
dumbbell n pesa f.
dumbfounded adj pasmado/da.
dummy n chupete m.
dump n montón m; * vt dejar.
dumping n (com) dumping m.
dumpling n bola de masa f.
dumpy adj gordito/ta.
dunce n zopenco m.
dune n duna f.
dung n estiércol m.
dungarees npl mono m.

dungeon n calabozo m.

dupe n bobo m; * vt engañar, embaucar.

duplex n dúplex m.

duplicate n duplicado m; copia f; * vt multicopiar.

duplicity n duplicidad f.

durability n durabilidad f.

durable adj duradero/ra.

duration n duración f.

during prep mientras, durante el tiempo que.

dusk n crepúsculo m.

dust n polvo m; * vt desempolvar.

dustbin n cubo de la basura m.

dustbin man, dustman n basurero m.

duster n plumero m.

dusty adj polvoriento/ta.

Dutch courage n valor fingido m.

duteous adj fiel, leal.

dutiful adj obediente, sumiso/sa; ~ly adv obedientemente.

duty n deber m; obligación f.

duty-free adj libre de derechos de aduana.

dwarf n enano m; enana f; * vt empequeñecer.

dwell vi habitar, morar.

dwelling n habitación f; domicilio m.

dwindle vi mermar, disminuirse.

dye vt teñir; * n tinte m.

dyer n tintorero/ra m/f.

dyeing n tintorería f; tintura f.

dye-works npl taller del tintorero m.

dying adj agonizante, moribundo/da; * n muerte f; ~ **moments** postrimerías fpl.

dynamic adj dinámico/ca.

dynamics n dinámica f.

dynamite n dinamita f.

dynamiter n dinamitero/ra m/f.

dynamo n dinamo f.

dynasty n dinastía f.

dysentery n disentería f.

dyspepsia n (med) dispepsia f.

dyspeptic adj dispéptico/ca.

E

each pn cada uno, cada una; ~ **other** unos a otros, unas a otras, mutuamente.

eager adj entusiasmado/da; ~ly adv con entusiasmo.

eagerness n ansia f; anhelo m.

eagle n águila f.

eagle-eyed adj con vista de lince.

eaglet n aguilucho m.

ear n oreja f; oído m; espiga f; **by** ~ de oreja.

earache n dolor de oídos m.

eardrum n tímpano (del oído) m.

early adj temprano/na; adv temprano.

earmark vt destinar a.

earn vt ganar; conseguir.

earnest adj serio/ria; en serio; ~ly adv seriamente.

earnestness n seriedad f.

earnings npl ingresos mpl.

earphones npl auriculares mpl.

earring n zarcillo, pendiente m.

earth n tierra f; * vt conectar a tierra.

earthen adj de tierra.

earthenware n loza de barro f.

earthquake n terremoto m.

earthworm n lombriz f.

earthy adj sensual.

earwig n tijereta f.

ease n comodidad f; facilidad f; **at** ~ con desahogo; * vt aliviar; mitigar.

easel n caballete m.

easily adv fácilmente.

easiness n facilidad f.

east n este m; oriente m.

Easter n Pascua de Resurrección; Semana Santa f.

Easter egg n huevo de Pascua m.

easterly adj del este.

eastern adj del este, oriental.

eastward(s) adv hacia el este.

easy adj fácil; cómodo/da, ~ going acomodadizo/za.

easy chair n sillón m.

eat vt comer; * vi alimentarse.

eatable adj comestible; * ~s npl víveres mpl.

eaves npl alero m.

eau de Cologne n agua de Colonia f.

eavesdrop vt escuchar a escondidas.

ebb n reflujo m; * vi menguar; decaer, disminuir.

ebony n ébano m.

eccentric adj excéntrico/ca.

eccentricity n excentricidad f.

ecclesiastic adj eclesiástico/ca.

echo n eco m; * vi resonar, repercutir.

eclectic adj ecléctico/ca.

eclipse n eclipse m; * vt eclipsar.

ecologist, environmentalist n ecologista m/f.

ecology n ecología f.

e-commerce n comercio electrónico m.

economic(al) adj económico/ca, frugal, moderado/da.

economics npl economía f.

economist n economista m/f.

economize vt economizar.

economy n economía f; frugalidad f.

ecosystem n ecosistema m.

ecotax n ecotasa f.

ecotourism n ecoturismo m.

ecstasy n éxtasis m; rapto m.

ecstatic adj extático/ca; ~ally adv en éxtasis.

eczema n eczema m.

eddy n reflujo de agua m; remolino m; * vi arremolinarse.

edge n filo m; punta f; margen m/f; acrimonia f; * vt ribetear; introducir.

edgeways, edgewise adv de lado.

edging n orla, orilla f.

edgy adj nervioso/sa.

edible adj comestible.

edict n edicto, mandato m.

edification n edificación f.

edifice n edificio m; fábrica f.

edify vt edificar.

edit vt dirigir; redactar; cortar.

edition n edición f; publicación f; impresión f.

editor n director/a m/f; redactor/a m/f.

editorial adj, n editorial m.

educate vt educar; enseñar.

education n educación f.

eel n anguila f.

eerie adj espeluznante.

efface vt borrar, destruir.

effect n efecto m; realidad f; ~s npl efectos, bienes mpl; * vt efectuar, ejecutar.

effective adj eficaz; efectivo/va; ~ly adv efectivamente, en efecto.

effectiveness n eficacia f.

effectual adj eficiente, eficaz; ~ly adv eficazmente.

effeminacy n afeminación f.

effeminate adj afeminado/da.

effervescence n efervescencia f; hervor m.

effete adj estéril.

efficacy n eficacia f.

efficiency n eficiencia, virtud f.

efficient adj eficaz.

effigy n efigie, imagen f; retrato m.
effort n esfuerzo, empeño m.
effortless adj sin esfuerzo.
effrontery n descaro m; impudencia, desvergüenza f.
effusive adj efusivo/va.
egg n huevo m; * **to ~ on** vt animar.
eggcup n huevera f.
eggplant n berenjena f.
eggshell n cáscara de huevo f.
ego(t)ism n egoísmo m.
ego(t)ist n egoísta m/f.
ego(t)istical adj egotista.
eiderdown n edredón m.
eight adj, n ocho.
eighteen adj, n dieciocho.
eighteenth adj, n decimoctavo.
eighth adj, n octavo.
eightieth adj, n octogésimo/ma.
eighty adj, n ochenta.
either pn cualquiera; * conj o, sea, ya.
ejaculate vt exclamar; eyacular.
ejaculation n exclamación f; eyaculación f.
eject vt expeler, desechar.
ejection n expulsión f.
ejector seat n asiento eyectable m.
eke vt alargar; prolongar; hacer crecer.
elaborate vt elaborar; * adj elaborado/da; **~ly** adv cuidadosamente.
elapse vi pasar, correr (el tiempo).
elastic adj elástico/ca.
elasticity n elasticidad f.
elated adj regocijado/da.
elation n regocijo m.
elbow n codo m; * vt codear.
elbow-room n anchura f; espacio suficiente m; (fig) libertad, latitud f.
elder n saúco m (árbol); * adj mayor.
elderly adj anciano/na.

elders npl ancianos, antepasados mpl.
eldest adj el mayor, la mayor.
elect vt elegir; * adj elegido/da, escogido/da.
election n elección f.
electioneering n electoralismo m.
elective adj facultativo/va.
elector n elector/a m/f.
electoral adj electoral.
electorate n electorado m.
electric(al) adj eléctrico/ca; ~ **domestic appliance** electrodoméstico m.
electric blanket n manta eléctrica f.
electric cooker n cocina eléctrica f.
electric fire n estufa eléctrica f.
electrician n electricista m/f.
electricity n electricidad f.
electrify vt electrizar.
electrocardiogram n electrocardiograma m.
electron n electrón m.
electronic adj electrónico/ca; **~s** npl electrónica f.
elegance n elegancia f.
elegant adj elegante, delicado/da; **~ly** adv elegantemente.
elegy n elegía f.
element n elemento m; fundamento m.
elemental, elementary adj elemental.
elephant n elefante m.
elephantine adj inmenso/sa.
elevate vt elevar, alzar, exaltar.
elevation n elevación f; altura f; alteza (de pensamientos) f.
elevator n ascensor m.
eleven adj, n once.
eleventh adj, n undécimo.
elf n duende m.
elicit vt sacar de.

eligibility n elegibilidad f.
eligible adj elegible.
eliminate vt eliminar, descartar.
elk n alce m.
elliptic(al) adj elíptico/ca.
elm n olmo m.
elocution n elocución f.
elocutionist n profesor de elocución m.
elongate vt alargar.
elope vi escapar, huir, evadirse.
elopement n fuga, huida, evasión f.
eloquence n elocuencia f.
eloquent adj elocuente; ~**ly** adv elocuentemente.
else pn otro/ra.
elsewhere adv en otra parte.
elucidate vt explicar.
elucidation n elucidación, explicación f.
elude vt eludir, evitar.
elusive adj esquivo/va.
emaciated adj demacrado/da.
e-mail n correo electrónico m.
emanate (from) vi emanar.
emancipate vt emancipar; dar libertad.
emancipation n emancipación f.
embalm vt embalsamar.
embankment n terraplén m.
embargo n embargo m.
embark vt embarcar.
embarkation n embarque m.
embarrass vt avergonzar.
embarrassed adj avergonzado/da.
embarrassing adj violento/ta; embarazoso/sa.
embarrassment n desconcierto m.
embassy n embajada f.
embed vt empotrar; clavar.
embellish vt hermosear, adornar.
embellishment n adorno m.
embers npl rescoldo m.

embezzle vt desfalcar.
embezzlement n desfalco m.
embitter vt amargar.
emblem n emblema m.
emblematic(al) adj emblemático/ca, simbólico/ca.
embodiment n incorporación f.
embody vt incorporar.
embrace vt abrazar; contener; * n abrazo m.
embroider vt bordar.
embroidery n bordado m; bordadura f.
embroil vt embrollar; confundir.
embryo n embrión m.
emendation n enmienda, corrección f.
emerald n esmeralda f.
emerge vi salir, proceder.
emergency n emergencia f; necesidad urgente f.
emergency cord n timbre de alarma m.
emergency exit n salida de emergencia f.
emergency landing n aterrizaje forzoso m.
emergency meeting n reunión extraordinaria f.
emery n esmeril m.
emigrant n emigrante m/f.
emigrate vi emigrar.
emigration n emigración f.
eminence n altura f; eminencia, excelencia f.
eminent adj eminente, elevado/da; distinguido/da; ~**ly** adv eminentemente.
emission n emisión f.
emit vt emitir; arrojar, despedir.
emolument n emolumento, provecho m.
emotion n emoción f.

emotional *adj* emocional.

emotive *adj* emotivo/va.

emperor *n* emperador *m*.

emphasis *n* énfasis *m*.

emphasize *vt* hablar con énfasis.

emphatic *adj* enfático/ca; ~ally *adv* enfáticamente.

empire *n* imperio *m*.

employ *vt* emplear, ocupar.

employee *n* empleado/da *m/f*.

employer *n* patrón *m*; empresario/ ria *m/f*.

employment *n* empleo *m*; trabajo *m*.

emporium *n* emporio *m*.

empress *n* emperatriz *f*.

emptiness *n* vaciedad *f*; futilidad *f*.

empty *adj* vacío/cía; vano/na; ignorante; * *vt* vaciar, evacuar.

empty-handed *adj* con las manos vacías.

emulate *vt* emular, competir; imitar.

emulsion *n* emulsión *f*.

enable *vt* capacitar.

enact *vt* promulgar; representar; hacer.

enamel *n* esmalte *m*; * *vt* esmaltar.

enamour *vt* enamorar.

encamp *vi* acamparse.

encampment *n* campamento *m*.

encase *vt* encajar, encajonar.

enchant *vt* encantar.

enchanting *adj* encantador/a.

enchantment *n* encanto *m*.

encircle *vt* cercar, circundar.

enclose *vt* cercar, circunvalar, circundar; incluir.

enclosure *n* cercamiento *m*; cercado *m*.

encompass *vt* abarcar.

encore *adv* otra vez, de nuevo.

encounter *n* encuentro *m*; duelo *m*; pelea *f*; * *vt* encontrar.

encourage *vt* animar, alentar.

encouragement *n* estímulo, patrocinio *m*.

encroach *vt* usurpar, avanzar gradualmente.

encroachment *n* usurpación, intrusión *f*.

encrusted *adj* incrustado/da.

encumber *vt* embarazar, cargar.

encumbrance *n* embarazo, impedimento *m*.

encyclical *adj* encíclico/ca, circular.

encyclopaedia *n* enciclopedia *f*.

end *n* fin *m*; extremidad *f*; término *m*; resolución *f*; to the ~ that para que; to no ~ en vano; on ~ en pie, de pie; * *vt* terminar, concluir, fenecer; * *vi* acabar, terminar.

endanger *vt* peligrar, arriesgar.

endear *vt* encarecer.

endearing *adj* simpático/ca.

endearment *n* ternura *f*.

endeavour *vi* esforzarse; intentar; * *n* esfuerzo *m*.

endemic *adj* endémico/ca.

ending *n* conclusión *f*; desenlace *m*; terminación *f*.

endive *n* (*bot*) endibia *f*.

endless *adj* infinito/ta, perpetuo/ tua; ~ly *adv* sin fin, perpetuamente.

endorse *vt* endosar; aprobar.

endorsement *n* endoso *m*; aprobación *f*.

endow *vt* dotar.

endowment *n* dote, dotación *f*.

endurable *adj* sufrible, tolerable.

endurance *n* duración *f*; paciencia *f*; sufrimiento *m*.

endure *vt* sufrir, soportar; * *vi* durar.

endways, endwise *adv* de punta, derecho.

enemy *n* enemigo/ga, antagonista *m/f*.

energetic *adj* enérgico/ca, vigoroso/sa.

energy *n* energía, fuerza *f*; **renewable forms of ~** energía renovables.

enervate *vt* enervar, debilitar.

enfeeble *vt* debilitar.

enfold *vt* envolver.

enforce *vt* hacer cumplir.

enforced *adj* forzoso/sa.

enfranchise *vt* emancipar.

engage *vt* llamar; abordar; contratar.

engaged *adj* prometido/da.

engagement *n* empeño *m*; combate *m*; pelea *f*; obligación *f*.

engagement ring *n* anillo de prometida *m*.

engaging *adj* atractivo/va.

engender *vt* engendrar; producir.

engine *n* motor *m*; locomotora *f*.

engine driver *n* maquinista *m/f*.

engineer *n* ingeniero/ra *m/f*; maquinista *m/f*.

engineering *n* ingeniería *f*.

engrave *vt* grabar; esculpir; tallar.

engraving *n* grabado *m*; estampa *f*.

engrossed *adj* absorto/ta.

engulf *vt* sumergir.

enhance *vt* aumentar, realzar.

enigma *n* enigma *m*.

enjoy *vt* gozar; poseer.

enjoyable *adj* agradable; divertido/da.

enjoyment *n* disfrute *m*; placer *m*; fruición *f*.

enlarge *vt* engrandecer, dilatar, extender.

enlargement *n* aumento *m*; ampliación *f*, soltura *f*.

enlighten *vt* iluminar; instruir.

enlightened *adj* iluminado/da.

Enlightenment *n*: **the ~** el Siglo de las Luces *m*, la Ilustración *f*.

enlist *vt* alistar.

enlistment *n* alistamiento *m*.

enliven *vt* animar; avivar; alegrar.

enmity *n* enemistad *f*; odio *m*.

enormity *n* enormidad *f*; atrocidad *f*.

enormous *adj* enorme; **~ly** *adv* enormemente.

enough *adv* bastante; basta; * *n* bastante *m*.

enounce *vt* declarar.

enquire, inquire *vt*, *vi* preguntar; **to ~ about** informarse de; **to ~ after** *vt* preguntar por; **to ~ into** *vt* investigar, indagar, inquirir.

enquiry *n* pesquisa *f*.

enrage *vt* enfurecer, irritar.

enrapture *vt* arrebatar, entusiasmar; encantar.

enrich *vt* enriquecer; adornar.

enrichment *n* enriquecimiento *m*.

enrol *vt* registrar; arrollar.

enrolment *n* inscripción *f*.

en route *adv* durante el viaje.

ensign *n* (*mil*) bandera *f*; abanderado *m*; (*mar*) alférez *m*.

enslave *vt* esclavizar, cautivar.

ensue *vi* seguirse; suceder.

ensure *vt* asegurar.

entail *vt* suponer.

entangle *vt* enmarañar, embrollar.

entanglement *n* enredo *m*.

enter *vt* entrar; admitir; registrar; **to ~ for** presentarse para; **to ~ into** establecer; formar parte de/en; firmar.

enterprise *n* empresa *f*.

enterprising *adj* emprendedor/a.

entertain *vt* divertir; hospedar; mantener.

entertainer *n* artista *m/f*.

entertaining *adj* divertido/da.

entertainment *n* entretenimiento, pasatiempo *m*.

enthralled *adj* encantado/da.

enthralling *adj* cautivador/a.
enthrone *vt* entronizar.
enthusiasm *n* entusiasmo *m*.
enthusiast *n* entusiasta *m/f*.
enthusiastic *adj* entusiasta.
entice *vt* tentar; seducir.
entire *adj* entero/ra, completo/ta, perfecto/ta; ~**ly** *adv* enteramente.
entitle *vt* intitular; conferir algún derecho.
entitled *adj* titulado/da.
entity *n* entidad, existencia *f*.
entourage *n* séquito *m*.
entrails *npl* entrañas *fpl*; asadura *f*.
entrance *n* entrada *f*; admisión *f*; principio *m*.
entrance examination *n* examen de ingreso *m*.
entrance fee *n* cuota *f*.
entrance hall *n* pórtico, vestíbulo *m*.
entrant *n* participante *m*; candidato *m*.
entrap *vt* enredar; engañar.
entreat *vt* rogar, suplicar.
entreaty *n* petición, suplica, instancia *f*.
entrepreneur *n* empresario/ria *m/f*.
entrust *vt* confiar.
entry *n* entrada *f*.
entry phone *n* portero automático *m*.
entwine *vt* entrelazar, enroscar, torcer.
enumerate *vt* enumerar, numerar.
enunciate *vt* enunciar, declarar.
enunciation *n* enunciación *f*.
envelop *vt* envolver.
envelope *n* sobre *m*.
enviable *adj* envidiable.
envious *adj* envidioso/sa; ~**ly** *adv* envidiosamente.
environment *n* medio ambiente *m*.
environmental *adj* ambiental, medioambiental.

environs *npl* vecindad *f*; contornos *mpl*.
envisage *vt* prever; concebir.
envoy *n* enviado/da *m/f*; mensajero/ra *m/f*.
envy *n* envidia, malicia *f*; * *vt* envidiar.
ephemeral *adj* efímero/ra.
epic *adj* épico/ca; * *n* épica *f*.
epidemic *adj* epidémico/ca; * *n* epidemia *f*.
epilepsy *n* epilepsia *f*.
epileptic *adj* epiléptico/ca.
epilogue *n* epílogo *m*.
Epiphany *n* Epifanía *f*.
episcopacy *n* episcopado *m*.
Episcopal *adj* episcopal.
Episcopalian *n* anglicano/na *m/f*.
episode *n* episodio *m*.
epistle *n* epístola *f*.
epistolary *adj* epistolar.
epithet *n* epíteto *m*.
epitome *n* epítome, compendio *m*.
epitomize *vt* epitomar, abreviar.
epoch *n* época *f*.
equable *adj* uniforme; ~**bly** *adv* uniformemente.
equal *adj* igual; justo/ta; semejante; * *n* igual *m*; compañero *m*; * *vt* igualar; compensar.
equalize *vt* igualar.
equalizer *n* igualada *f*.
equality *n* igualdad, uniformidad *f*.
equally *adv* igualmente.
equanimity *n* ecuanimidad *f*.
equate *vt* equiparar (con).
equation *n* ecuación *f*.
equator *n* ecuador *f*.
equatorial *adj* ecuatorial, ecuatorio/ria.
equestrian *adj* ecuestre.
equilateral *adj* equilátero/ra.
equilibrium *n* equilibrio *m*.

equinox n equinoccio m.

equip vt equipar, pertrechar.

equipment n equipaje m.

equitable adj equitativo/va, imparcial; ~bly adv equitativamente.

equity n equidad, justicia, imparcialidad f.

equivalent adj, n equivalente m.

equivocal adj equívoco/ca, ambiguo/gua; ~ly adv equivocadamente, ambiguamente.

equivocate vt equivocar, usar equívocos.

equivocation n equívoco m.

era n era f.

eradicate vt desarraigar, extirpar.

eradication n extirpación f.

erase vt borrar.

eraser n goma de borrar f.

erect vt erigir; establecer; * adj derecho/ha, erguido/da, vertical.

erection n establecimiento m; estructura f; erección f.

ermine n armiño m.

erode vt erosionar; corroer.

erotic adj erótico/ca.

err vi vagar, errar; desviarse.

errand n recado, mensaje m.

errand boy n recadero m.

errata npl fe de erratas f.

erratic adj errático/ca, errante; irregular.

erroneous adj erróneo/nea; falso/sa; ~ly adv erróneamente.

error n error m; yerro m.

erudite adj erudito/ta.

erudition n erudición f; doctrina f.

erupt vi entrar en erupción; hacer erupción.

eruption n erupción f.

escalate vi extenderse.

escalation n intensificación f.

escalator n escalera mecánica f.

escapade n travesura f.

escape vt evitar; escapar; * vi evadirse, salvarse; * vr zafarse; * n escapada, huida, fuga f; inadvertencia f; to make one's ~ poner los pies en polvorosa.

escapism n escapismo m.

eschew vt huir, evitar, evadir.

escort n escolta f; * vt escoltar.

esoteric adj esotérico/ca.

especial adj especial; ~ly adv especialmente.

espionage n espionaje m.

esplanade n (mil) esplanada f.

espouse vt desposar.

essay n ensayo m.

essence n esencia f.

essential n esencia f; * adj esencial, substancial, principal; ~ly adv esencialmente.

establish vt establecer, fundar, fijar; confirmar.

establishment n establecimiento m; fundación f; institución f.

estate n estado m; hacienda f; bienes mpl.

esteem vt estimar, apreciar; pensar; * n estima f; consideración f.

estimate vt estimar, apreciar, tasar; * n presupuesto m.

estimation n estimación, valuación f; opinión f.

estrange vt extrañar, apartar, enajenar.

estranged adj separado/da.

estrangement n enajenación f; extrañeza, distancia f.

estuary n estuario m, ría f.

etch vt grabar al aguafuerte.

etching n grabado al aguafuerte m.

eternal adj eterno/na, perpetuo/tua, inmortal; ~ly adv eternamente.

eternity n eternidad f.

ether *n* éter *m*.

ethical *adj* ético/ca; **~ly** *adv* moralmente.

ethics *npl* ética *f*.

ethnic *adj* étnico/ca.

ethos *n* genio *m*.

etiquette *n* etiqueta *f*.

etymological *adj* etimológico/ca.

etymologist *n* etimólogo/ga *m/f*, etimologista *m/f*.

etymology *n* etimología *f*.

Eucharist *n* Eucaristía *f*.

eulogy *n* elogio, encomio *m*; alabanza *f*.

eunuch *n* eunuco *m*.

euphemism *n* eufemismo *m*.

euro *n* euro *m*.

Euro MP *n* eurodiputado/da *m/f*.

Europe *n* Europa *f*.

European Community *n* Comunidad Europea *f*.

European Parliament *n* eurocámara *f*.

European Union *n* unión Europea *f*.

Eurosceptic *n* euroescéptico/ca *m/f*.

Eurotunnel, Channel Tunnel *n* eurotúnel *m*.

evacuate *vt* evacuar.

evacuation *n* evacuación *f*.

evade *vt* evadir, escapar, evitar.

evaluate *vt* evaluar; interpretar.

evangelic(al) *adj* evangélico/ca.

evangelist *n* evangelista *m*.

evaporate *vt* evaporar; * *vi* evaporarse; disiparse.

evaporated milk *n* leche evaporada *f*.

evaporation *n* evaporación *f*.

evasion *n* evasión *f*; escape *m*.

evasive *adj* evasivo/va; **~ly** *adv* con evasivas.

eve *n* víspera *f*.

even *adj* llano/na, igual; par, semejante; * *adv* aun; aun cuando, supuesto que; no obstante; * *vt* igualar, allanar; * *vi*: **to ~ out** nivelarse.

even-handed *adj* imparcial, equitativo/va.

evening *n* tarde *f*.

evening class *n* clase nocturna *f*.

evening dress *n* traje de etiqueta *m*; traje de noche *m*.

evenly *adv* igualmente, llanamente.

evenness *n* igualdad *f*; uniformidad *f*; llanura *f*; imparcialidad *f*.

event *n* acontecimiento, evento *m*; suceso *m*.

eventful *adj* lleno de acontecimientos.

eventual *adj* final; **~ly** *adv* por fin.

eventuality *n* eventualidad *f*.

ever *adv* siempre; **for ~ and ~** siempre jamás, eternamente; **~ since** después.

evergreen *adj* de hoja perenne; * *n* árbol de hoja perenne *m*.

everlasting *adj* eterno/na.

evermore *adv* eternamente, para siempre jamás.

every *adj* cada uno, cada una; **~ where** en *o* por todas partes; **~ thing** todo; **~ one**, **~ body** todos, todo el mundo.

evict *vt* desahuciar.

eviction *n* desahucio *m*.

evidence *n* evidencia *f*; testimonio *m*; prueba *f*; * *vt* evidenciar.

evident *adj* evidente; patente, manifiesto/ta; **~ly** *adv* evidentemente.

evil *adj* malo/la, depravado/da, pernicioso/sa; dañoso/sa; * *n* mal *m*; maldad *f*.

evil-minded *adj* malicioso/sa, mal intencionado/da.

evocative *adj* sugestivo/va.

evoke *vt* evocar.

evolution n evolución f.

evolve vt, vi evolucionar; desenvolver; desplegarse.

ewe n oveja f.

exacerbate vt exacerbar.

exact adj exacto/ta; * vt exigir.

exacting adj exigente.

exaction n exacción, extorsión f.

exactly adj exactamente.

exactness, exactitude n exactitud f.

exaggerate vt exagerar.

exaggeration n exageración f.

exalt vt exaltar, elevar; alabar; realzar.

exaltation n exaltación, elevación f.

exalted adj exaltado/da; muy animado/da.

examination n examen m.

examine vt examinar; escudriñar.

examiner n inspector/a m/f.

example n ejemplar m; ejemplo m.

exasperate vt exasperar, irritar, enojar, provocar; agravar; amargar.

exasperation n exasperación, irritación f.

excavate vt excavar, ahondar.

excavation n excavación f.

exceed vt exceder; sobrepujar.

exceedingly adv extremamente, en sumo grado.

excel vt sobresalir, exceder; * vi descollar.

excellence n excelencia f; preeminencia f.

Excellency n Excelencia (título) f.

excellent adj excelente; ~ly adv excelentemente.

except vt exceptuar, excluir; ~(ing) prep excepto, a excepción de.

exception n excepción, exclusión f.

exceptional adj excepcional.

excerpt n extracto m.

excess n exceso m.

excessive adj excesivo/va; ~ly adv excesivamente.

exchange vt cambiar; trocar, permutar; * n cambio m; bolsa f.

exchange rate n tipo de cambio m.

excise n impuestos sobre el consumo mpl.

excitability n excitabilidad f.

excitable adj excitable.

excite vt excitar; estimular.

excited adj emocionado/da.

excitement n estímulo, excitación f.

exciting adj emocionante.

exclaim vi exclamar.

exclamation n exclamación f; clamor m.

exclamation mark n punto de admiración m.

exclamatory adj exclamatorio/ria.

exclude vt excluir; exceptuar.

exclusion n exclusión, exclusiva, excepción f.

exclusive adj exclusivo/va; ~ly adv exclusivamente.

excommunicate vt excomulgar.

excommunication n excomunión f.

excrement n excremento m.

excruciating adj atroz, enorme, grave.

exculpate vt disculpar; justificar.

excursion n excursión f; digresión f.

excusable adj excusable.

excuse vt disculpar; perdonar; * n disculpa, excusa f; pretexto m; ~ me! interj ¡perdón!.

execute vt ejecutar.

execution n ejecución f.

executioner n ejecutor/a m/f; verdugo m.

executive adj ejecutivo/va.

executor n testamentario/ria, albacea m/f.

exemplary adj ejemplar.

exemplify vt ejemplificar.

exempt adj exento/ta.

exemption n exención f.

exercise n ejercicio m; ensayo m; tarea f; practica f; * vi hacer ejercicio; * vt ejercer; valerse de.

exercise book n cuaderno m.

exert vt emplear; **to ~ oneself** esforzarse.

exertion n esfuerzo m.

exhale vt exhalar.

exhaust n escape m; * vt agotar.

exhausted adj agotado/da.

exhaustion n agotamiento m; extenuación f.

exhaustive adj comprensivo/va.

exhibit vt exhibir; mostrar; * n (law) objeto expuesto m.

exhibition n exposición, presentación f.

exhilarating adj estimulante.

exhilaration n alegría f; buen humor, regocijo m.

exhort vt exhortar, excitar.

exhortation n exhortación f.

exhume vt exhumar, desenterrar.

exile n destierro m; * vt desterrar, deportar.

exist vi existir.

existence n existencia f.

existent adj existente.

existing adj actual, presente.

exit n salida f; * vi hacer mutis.

exodus n éxodo m.

exonerate vt exonerar, descargar.

exoneration n exoneración f.

exorbitant adj exorbitante, excesivo/va.

exorcise vt exorcizar, conjurar.

exorcism n exorcismo m.

exotic adj exótico/ca, extranjero/ra.

expand vt extender, dilatar.

expanse n extensión f.

expansion n expansión f.

expansive adj expansivo/va.

expatriate vt expatriar.

expect vt esperar, aguardar.

expectance, expectancy n expectación, esperanza f.

expectant adj expectante.

expectant mother n mujer encinta f.

expectation n expectación, expectativa f.

expediency n conveniencia, oportunidad f.

expedient adj oportuno/na, conveniente; * n expediente m; **~ly** adv convenientemente.

expedite vt acelerar; expedir.

expedition n expedición f.

expeditious adj pronto/ta, expedito/ta; **~ly** adv prontamente.

expel vt expeler, desterrar.

expend vt expender; desembolsar.

expendable adj prescindible.

expenditure n gasto, desembolso m.

expense n gasto m; coste m.

expense account n cuenta de gastos f.

expensive adj caro/ra; costoso/sa; **~ly** adv costosamente.

experience n experiencia f; práctica f; * vt experimentar.

experienced adj experimentado/da.

experiment n experimento m; * vt experimentar.

experimental adj experimental; **~ly** adv experimentalmente.

expert adj experto/ta, diestro/tra.

expertise n pericia f.

expiration n expiración f; muerte f.

expire vi expirar.

explain vt explanar, explicar.

explanation n explicación f.

explanatory adj explicativo/va.

expletive adj expletivo/va.

explicable adj explicable.

explicit adj explícito/ta; **~ly** adv explícitamente.

explode vt, vi estallar, explotar.

exploit vt explotar; * n hazaña f; hecho heroico m.

exploitation n explotación f.

exploration n exploración f; examen m.

exploratory adj exploratorio/ria.

explore vt explorar, examinar; sondear.

explorer n explorador/a m/f.

explosion n explosión f.

explosive adj, n explosivo m.

exponent n (math) exponente m.

export vt exportar.

export, exportation n exportación f.

exporter n exportador/a m/f.

expose vt exponer; mostrar; descubrir; poner en peligro.

exposed adj expuesto/ta.

exposition n exposición f; interpretación f.

expostulate vi debatir, contender.

exposure n exposición f; velocidad de obturación f; fotografía f.

exposure meter n fotómetro m.

expound vt exponer; interpretar.

express vt exprimir; representar; * adj expreso/sa, claro/ra; a propósito; * n expreso, correo m; (rail) tren expreso m.

expression n expresión f; locución f.

expressionless adj sin expresión (cara).

expressive adj expresivo/va; **~ly** adv expresivamente.

expressly adv expresamente.

expressway n autopista f.

expropriate vt expropiar (por causa de utilidad pública).

expropriation n (law) expropiación f.

expulsion n explosión f.

expurgate vt expurgar.

exquisite adj exquisito/ta, perfecto/ta, excelente; **~ly** adv exquisitamente.

extant adj existente.

extempore adv de improviso.

extemporize vi improvisar.

extend vt extender; amplificar; * vi extenderse.

extension n extensión f.

extensive adj extenso/sa, dilatado/da; **~ly** adv extensivamente.

extent n extensión f.

extenuate vt extenuar, disminuir, atenuar.

extenuating adj atenuante.

exterior adj, n exterior m.

exterminate vt exterminar; extirpar.

extermination n exterminación, extirpación f.

external adj externo/na; **~ly** adv exteriormente; **~s** npl exterior m.

extinct adj extinto/ta; abolido/da.

extinction n extinción f; abolición f.

extinguish vt extinguir; suprimir.

extinguisher n extintor m.

extirpate vt extirpar.

extol vt alabar, magnificar, alzar, exaltar.

extort vt sacar por la fuerza.

extortion n extorsión f.

extortionate adj excesivo/va.

extra adv extra; * n extra m.

extract vt extraer; extractar; * n extracto m; compendio m.

extraction n extracción f; descendencia f.

extracurricular adj extraescolar.

extradite vt extraditar.

extradition n (law) extradición f.

extramarital adj extramatrimonial.

extramural adj extraescolar.

extraneous adj extraño/ña, ajeno/na.

extraordinarily adv extraordinaria- mente.

extraordinary adj extraordinario/ ria.

extravagance n extravagancia f; gas- tos, excesivos mpl.

extravagant adj extravagante, exor- bitante; pródigo/ga; ~ly adv extra- vagantemente.

extreme adj extremo/ma, supremo/ ma; último/ma; * n extremo m; ~ly adv extremamente.

extremist adj, n extremista m/f.

extremity n extremidad f.

extricate vt desembarazar, desenre- dar.

extrinsic(al) adj extrínseco/ca, exte- rior.

extrovert adj, n extrovertido m.

exuberance n exuberancia, suma abundancia f.

exuberant adj exuberante, abundan- tísimo/ma; ~ly adv exuberante- mente.

exude vi transpirar.

exult vt exultar, regocijarse, triunfar.

exultation n exultación f; regocijo m.

eye n ojo m; * vt ojear, contemplar, observar.

eyeball n globo del ojo m.

eyebrow n ceja f.

eyelash n pestaña f.

eyelid n párpado m.

eyesight n vista f.

eyesore n monstruosidad f.

eyetooth n colmillo m.

eyewitness n testigo ocular m.

eyrie n nido de águila m.

F

fable n fábula f; ficción f.

fabric n tejido m.

fabricate vt fabricar, edificar.

fabrication n fabricación f.

fabulous adj fabuloso/sa; ~ly adv fa- bulosamente.

facade n fachada f.

face n cara, faz f; superficie f; facha- da f; aspecto m; apariencia f; * vt encararse; hacer frente; **to ~ up to** hacer frente a.

face cream n crema facial f.

face-lift n lifting m.

face powder n polvos mpl.

facet n faceta f.

facetious adj chistoso/sa, alegre, gracioso/sa; ~ly adv chistosamente.

face value n valor nominal m.

facial adj facial.

facile adj fácil, afable.

facilitate vt facilitar.

facility n facilidad, ligereza f; afabili- dad f.

facing n paramento m; * prep en- frente.

facsimile n facsímil m; fax m.

fact n hecho m; realidad f; **in ~** en efecto.

faction n facción f; disensión f.

factor n factor m.

factory n fábrica f.

factual adj basado/da en hechos rea- les.

faculty n facultad f; personal docen- te m.

fad n moda f.

fade vi decaer, marchitarse, fallecer.

fail vt suspender, reprobar; fallar a; * vi suspender; fracasar; fallar; (fig) zozobrar.

failing n falta f; defecto m.

failure n falta f; culpa f; descuido m; quiebra, bancarrota f.

faint vi desmayarse, debilitarse; * n desmayo m; * adj débil; **~ly** adv débilmente.

fainthearted adj cobarde, medroso/sa, pusilánime.

faintness n flaqueza f; desmayo m.

fair adj hermoso/sa, bello/lla; blanco/ca; rubio/bia; claro/ra, sereno/na; favorable; recto/ta, justo/ta; franco/ca; * adv limpio; * n feria f.

fairly adv justamente; completamente.

fairness n hermosura f; justicia f.

fair play n juego limpio m.

fair trade n comercio justo m.

fairy n hada f.

fairy tale n cuento de hadas m.

faith n fe f; dogma de fe m; fidelidad f.

faithful adj fiel, leal; **~ly** adv fielmente.

faithfulness n fidelidad, lealtad f.

fake n falsificación f; impostor/a m/f; * adj falso/sa; * vt fingir; falsificar.

falcon n halcón m.

falconry n cetrería f.

fall vi caer(se); perder el poder; disminuir, decrecer en precio; **to ~ asleep** dormirse; **to ~ back** retroceder; **to ~ back on** recurrir a; **to ~ behind** quedarse atrás; **to ~ down** caerse; **to ~ for** dejarse engañar; enamorarse de; **to ~ in** hundirse; **to ~ short** faltar; **to ~ sick** enfermar; **to ~ in love** enamorarse; **to ~ off** caerse; disminuir; **to ~ out** reñir, disputar; * n caída f; otoño m.

fallacious adj falaz, fraudulento/ta; **~ly** adv falzamente.

fallacy n falacia, sofistería f; engaño m.

fallibility n falibilidad f.

fallible adj falible.

fallow adj en barbecho; **~ deer** n gamo m.

false adj falso/sa; **~ly** adv falsamente.

false alarm n falsa alarma f.

falsehood, falseness n falsedad f.

falsify vt falsificar.

falsity n falsedad, mentira f.

falter vi tartamudear; faltar.

faltering adj vacilante.

fame n fama f; renombre m.

famed adj celebrado/da, famoso/sa.

familiar adj familiar; casero/ra; **~ly** adv familiarmente.

familiarity n familiaridad f.

familiarize vt familiarizar.

family n familia f; linaje m; clase, especie f.

family business n negocio familiar m.

family doctor n médico de familia m.

famine n hambre f; carestía f.

famished adj hambriento/ta.

famous adj famoso/sa, afamado/da; **~ly** adv famosamente.

fan n abanico m; aficionado m; fan m/f; * vt abanicar; atizar.

fanatic adj, n fanático/ca m/ca.

fanaticism n fanatismo m.

fan belt n correa del ventilador f.

fanciful adj imaginativo/va, caprichoso/sa; **~ly** adv caprichosamente.

fancy n fantasía, imaginación f; capricho m; * vt tener ganas de; imaginarse.

fancy-goods npl novedades, modas fpl.

fancy-dress ball n baile de disfraces m.

fanfare n (mus) fanfarria f.

fang n colmillo m.

fantastic adj fantástico/ca; caprichoso/sa; ~ally adv fantásticamente.

fantasy n fantasía f.

far adv lejos, a una gran distancia; * adj lejano/na, distante, remoto/ta; ~ and away con mucho, de mucho; ~ off lejano/na.

faraway adj remoto/ta.

farce n farsa f.

farcical adj burlesco/ca.

fare n precio m; tarifa f; comida f; viajero m; pasaje m.

farewell n despedida f; ~! excl ¡adiós!

farm n finca f, granja f; * vt cultivar.

farmer n agricultor/a m/f; granjero/ra m/f.

farmhand n peón m.

farmhouse n casa de hacienda f, granja f.

farming n agricultura f.

farmland n tierra de cultivo f.

farmyard n corral m.

far-reaching adj de gran alcance.

fart n (sl) pedo; * vi tirarse un pedo.

farther adv más lejos; más adelante; * adj más lejos, ulterior.

farthest adv lo más lejos; lo más tarde; a lo más.

fascinate vt fascinar, encantar.

fascinating adj fascinante.

fascination n fascinación f; encanto m.

fascism n fascismo.

fascist n fascista m/f.

fashion n moda f; forma, figura f; uso m; manera f; estilo m; people of ~ gente de tono f; * vt formar, amoldar.

fashionable adj a la moda; elegante; the ~ world el gran mundo; ~bly adv a o según la moda.

fashion show n desfile de modelos m.

fast vi ayunar; * n ayuno m; * adj rápido/da; firme, estable; * adv rápidamente; firmemente; estrechamente.

fasten vt abrochar; afirmar, asegurar, atar; fijar; * vi fijarse, establecerse.

fastener, fastening n cierre m; cerrojo m.

fast food n comida rápida f.

fastidious adj fastidioso/sa, desdeñoso/sa; ~ly adv fastidiosamente.

fat adj gordo/da; * n grasa f; pringue m/f.

fatal adj fatal; funesto/ta; ~ly adv fatalmente.

fatalism n fatalismo m.

fatalist n fatalista m/f.

fatality n fatalidad, predestinación f.

fate n hado, destino m.

fateful adj fatídico/ca.

father n padre m; loving (over-indulgent) ~ padrazo m.

fatherhood n paternidad f.

father-in-law n suegro m.

fatherland n patria f.

fatherly adj paternal.

fathom n braza (medida) f; * vt sondar; penetrar.

fatigue n fatiga f; * vt fatigar, cansar.

fatten vt, vi engordar.

fatty adj graso/sa.

fatuous adj fatuo/tua, tonto/ta, imbécil.

fault n falta, culpa f; delito m; defecto m; yerro m.

faultfinder n censurador/a m/f.

faultless adj perfecto/ta, cumplido/da.

faulty adj defectuoso/sa.

fauna n fauna f.

faux pas n metedura de pata f.

favour n favor, beneficio m; patrocinio m; blandura f; * vt favorecer, proteger.

favourable adj favorable, propicio/cia; ~bly adv favorablemente.

favoured adj favorecido/da.

favourite n favorito/ta m/f; * adj favorecido/da.

favouritism n favoritismo m.

fawn n cervatillo m; * vi adular servilmente.

fawningly adv lisonjeramente, con adulación servil.

fax n facsímil(e) m; fax m; * vt mandar por fax.

fear vi temer; * n miedo m.

fearful adj medroso/sa, temeroso/sa; tímido/da; ~ly adv medrosamente, temerosamente.

fearless adj intrépido/da, atrevido/da; ~ly adv sin miedo.

fearlessness n intrepidez f.

feasibility n posibilidad f.

feasible adj factible, viable.

feast n banquete, festín m; fiesta f; * vi banquetear.

feat n hecho m; acción, hazaña f.

feather n pluma f;.

feather bed n plumón m.

feature n característica f; rasgo m; forma f; * vi figurar.

feature film n largometraje m.

February n febrero m.

federal adj federal.

federalist n federalista m/f.

federate vt, vi federar(se).

federation n federación f.

fed-up adj harto/ta.

fee n honorarios mpl; cuota f.

feeble adj flaco/ca, débil.

feebleness n debilidad f.

feebly adv débilmente.

feed vt nutrir; alimentar; **to ~ on**

alimentarse de; * vi nutrirse; engordar; * n comida f; pasto m.

feedback n reacción f.

feel vt sentir; tocar; creer; **to ~ around** tantear; * n sensación f; tacto, sentido m.

feeler n antena f; (fig) tentativa f.

feeling n tacto m; sensibilidad f; corazonada f.

feelingly adv sensiblemente.

feign vt inventar, fingir; disimular.

feline adj felino/na.

fellow n tipo, tío m; socio/cia m/f.

fellow citizen n conciudadano/na m/f.

fellow countryman n compatriota m/f.

fellow feeling n simpatía f.

fellow men npl semejantes mpl.

fellowship n compañerismo m; beca f (en un colegio) f.

fellow student n compañero/ra de curso m/f.

fellow traveller n compañero/ra de viaje m/f.

felon n criminal m/f.

felony n crimen m.

felt n fieltro m.

felt-tip pen n rotulador m.

female n hembra f; * adj femenino/na.

feminine adj femenino/na.

feminism n feminismo m.

feminist n feminista m/f.

fen n pantano m.

fence n cerca f; defensa f; * vt cercar; * vi esgrimir.

fencing n esgrima f.

fennel n (bot) hinojo m.

ferment n agitación f; * vi fermentar.

fern n (bot) helecho m.

ferocious adj feroz; fiero/ra; ~ly adv ferozmente.

ferocity n ferocidad, fiereza f.
ferret n hurón m; * vt huronear; **to ~ out** descubrir, echar fuera.
ferry n transbordador, ferry m; * vt transportar.
fertile adj fértil, fecundo/da.
fertility n fertilidad, fecundidad f.
fertilization n fertilización f.
fertilize vt fertilizar.
fertilizer n abono m.
fervent adj ferviente; fervoroso/sa; **~ly** adv con fervor.
fervid adj ardiente, vehemente.
fervour n fervor, ardor m.
fester vi encenarse, inflamarse.
festival n fiesta f; festival m.
festive adj festivo/va.
festivity n festividad f.
fetch vt ir a buscar.
fetching adj atractivo/va.
fete n fiesta f.
fetid, foetid adj fétido/da, hediondo/da.
feud n riña, contienda f.
feudal adj feudal.
feudalism n feudalismo m.
fever n fiebre f.
feverish adj febril.
few adj poco/ca; **a ~** algunos; **~ and far between** pocos.
fewer adj menor; * adv menos.
fewest adj los menos.
fiancé n novio m.
fiancée n novia f.
fib n mentira f; * vi mentir.
fibre n fibra, hebra f.
fibreglass n fibra de vidrio f.
fickle adj voluble, inconstante, mudable, ligero/ra.
fiction n ficción f; invención f.
fictional adj novelesco/ca.
fictitious adj ficticio/cia; fingido/da; **~ly** adv fingidamente.

fiddle n violín m; trampa f; * vi tocar el violín.
fiddler n violinista m/f.
fidelity n fidelidad, lealtad f.
fidget vi inquietarse.
fidgety adj inquieto/ta, impaciente.
field n campo m; campaña f; espacio m.
field day n (mil) día de maniobras m.
fieldmouse n ratón de campo m.
fieldwork n trabajo de campo m.
fiend n enemigo m; demonio m.
fiendish adj demoniaco/ca.
fierce adj fiero/ra, feroz; cruel, furioso/sa; **~ly** adv furiosamente.
fierceness n fiereza, ferocidad f.
fiery adj ardiente; apasionado/da.
fifteen adj, n quince.
fifteenth adj, n decimoquinto/ta.
fifth adj, n quinto/ta; **~ly** adv en quinto lugar.
fiftieth adj, n quincuagésimo/ma.
fifty adj, n cincuenta.
fig n higo m.
fight vt, vi reñir; batallar; combatir; * n batalla f; combate m; pelea f.
fighter n combatiente m; luchador/a m/f; caza m.
fighting n combate m.
fig-leaf n hoja de higuera f.
fig tree n higuera f.
figurative adj figurativo/va; **~ly** adv figuradamente.
figure n figura, forma f; imagen f; cifra f; * vi figurar; ser lógico/ca; **to ~ out** comprender.
figurehead n testaferro m.
filament n filamento m; fibra f.
filch vi ratear.
filcher n ratero/ra, ladroncillo/lla m/f.
file n hilo m; lista f; (mil) fila, hilera f; lima f; carpeta f; fichero m; * vt

enhilar; limar; clasificar; presentar;
* vi to ~ in/out entrar/salir en fila;
to ~ past desfilar ante.

filing cabinet n archivador m.

fill vt llenar; hartar; to ~ in rellenar;
to ~ up llenar (hasta el borde).

fillet n filete m.

fillet steak n filete de ternera m.

filling station n estación de servicio
f; gasolinera f.

fillip n (fig) estímulo m.

filly n potra f.

film n película f; film m; capa f; * vt
filmar; * vi rodar.

film star n estrella de cine f.

film strip n tira de película f.

filter n filtro m; * vt filtrar.

filter-tipped adj con filtro.

filth(iness) n inmundicia, porquería
f; fango, lodo m.

filthy adj sucio/cia, puerco/ca.

fin n aleta f.

final adj final, último/ma; ~ly finalmente; ~ stages postrimerías
fpl.

finale n final m.

finalist n finalista m/f.

finalize vt concluir.

finance n fondos mpl.

financial adj financiero/ra.

financier n financiero/ra m/f.

find vt hallar, descubrir; to ~ out
averiguar; descubrir; to ~ one's
self hallarse; * n hallazgo m.

findings npl fallo m;
recomendaciones fpl.

fine adj fino/na; agudo/da, cortante;
claro/ra, trasparente; delicado/da;
astuto/ta; elegante; bello/la; * n
multa f; * vt multar.

fine arts npl bellas artes fpl.

finely adv con elegancia.

finery n adorno, atavío m.

finesse n sutileza f.

finger n dedo m; * vt tocar, manosear; manejar.

fingernail n uña f.

fingerprint n huella dactilar f.

fingertip n yema del dedo f.

finicky adj delicado/da.

finish vt acabar, terminar, concluir;
to ~ off acabar (con); to ~ up terminar; * vi: to ~ up ir a parar.

finishing line n línea de llegada, línea de meta f.

finishing school n academia para
señoritas f.

finite adj finito/ta; conjugado/da.

fir n (bot) abeto m.

fire n fuego m; incendio m; * vt disparar; incendiar; despertar; * vi
encenderse.

fire alarm n alarma de incendios f.

firearm n arma de fuego f.

fireball n bola f de fuego.

firebreak, fire line n cortafuegos m.

fire engine n coche de bomberos m.

fire escape n escalera de incendios f.

fire extinguisher n extintor m.

firefly n luciérnaga f.

fireman n bombero m.

fireplace n hogar, fogón m.

fireproof adj a prueba de fuego.

fireside n chimenea f.

fire station n parque de bomberos m.

firewater n aguardiente m.

firewood n leña f.

fireworks npl fuegos artificiales mpl.

firing n disparos mpl.

firing squad n pelotón de ejecución m.

firm adj firme, estable, constante; * n
(com) firma f; ~ly adv firmemente.

firmament n firmamento m.

firmness n firmeza f; constancia f.

first *adj* primero/ra; * *adv* primeramente; at ~ al principio; ~ly *adv* en primer lugar.

first aid *n* primeros auxilios *mpl*.

first-aid kit *n* botiquín *m*.

first-class *adj* de primera (clase).

first-hand *adj* de primera mano.

first name *n* nombre de pila *m*.

first-rate *adj* de primera (clase).

fiscal *adj* fiscal.

fish *n* pez *m*; * *vi* pescar.

fishbone *n* espina *f*.

fisherman *n* pescador *m*.

fish farm *n* piscifactoría *f*.

fishing *n* pesca *f*.

fishing line *n* sedal *m*.

fishing rod *n* caña de pescar *f*.

fishing tackle *n* aparejo *m*.

fish market *n* lonja de pescado *f*.

fishseller *n* pescadero/ra *m/f*.

fishmonger, fish shop *n* pescadería *f*.

fishy *adj* (*fig*) sospechoso/sa.

fissure *n* grieta, hendedura *f*.

fist *n* puño *m*.

fit *n* paroxismo *m*; convulsión *f*; * *adj* en forma; apto/ta, idóneo/nea, justo/ta; * *vt* ajustar, acomodar, adaptar; to ~ out proveer; * *vi* convenir; to ~ in encajarse; llevarse bien (con todos).

fitness *n* salud *f*; aptitud, conveniencia *f*.

fitted carpet *n* moqueta *f*.

fitted kitchen *n* cocina amueblada *f*.

fitter *n* ajustador *m*.

fitting *adj* conveniente, idóneo/nea, justo/ta; * *n* conveniencia *f*; ~s *pl* guarnición *f*.

five *adj*, *n* cinco.

fix *vt* fijar, establecer; to ~ up arreglar.

fixation *n* obsesión *f*.

fixed *adj* fijo/ja.

fixture *n* encuentro *m*.

fizz(le) *vi* silbar.

fizzy *adj* gaseoso/sa.

flabbergasted *adj* pasmado/da.

flabby *adj* blando/da, flojo/ja, lacio/cia.

flaccid *adj* flojo/ja, flaco/ca; fláccido/da.

flag *n* bandera *f*; losa *f*; * *vi* debilitarse.

flagpole *n* asta de bandera *f*.

flagrant *adj* flagrante; notorio/ria.

flagship *n* buque insignia *m*.

flair *n* aptitud especial *f*.

flak *n* fuego antiaéreo *m*; lluvia de críticas.

flake *n* copo *m*; lámina *f*; * *vi* romperse en láminas.

flaky *adj* escamoso/sa, desmenuzable.

flamboyant *adj* vistoso/sa.

flame *n* llama *f*; fuego (del amor) *m*.

flamingo *n* flamenco *m*.

flammable *adj* inflamable.

flank *n* ijada *f*; (*mil*) flanco *m*; * *vt* flanquear.

flannel *n* franela, flanela *f*.

flap *n* solapa *f*; hoja *f*; aletazo *m*; * *vi* aletear; * *vi* ondear.

flare *n* lucir, brillar; to ~ up encenderse; encolerizarse; estallar; * *n* llama *f*.

flash *n* flash *m*; relámpago *m*; * *vt* to ~ on and off encender y apagar.

flashbulb *n* bombilla de flash *f*.

flash cube *n* cubo de flash *m*.

flashlight *n* linterna *f*.

flashy *adj* superficial.

flask *n* frasco *m*; botella *f*.

flat¹ *adj* llano/na, plano/na; insípido/da; * *n* llanura *f*; plano *m*; (*mus*) bemol *m*; ~ly *adv* horizontalmente; llanamente; enteramente; de plano, de nivel; francamente.

flat² n apartamento, departamento m.

flatness n llanura f; insipidez f.

flatten vt allanar; abatir.

flatter vt adular; lisonjear.

flattering adj halagüeño/ña, zalamero/ra.

flattery n adulación, lisonja f; zalamería f.

flatulence n (med) flatulencia f.

flaunt vt ostentar.

flavour n sabor m; * vt sazonar.

flavoured adj con sabor (a).

flavourless adj soso/sa.

flaw n falta, tacha f; defecto m.

flawless adj sin defecto.

flax n lino m.

flea n pulga f.

flea bite n picadura de pulga f.

fleck n mota f; punto m.

flee vt huir de; * vi escapar; huir.

fleece n vellón m; * vt (sl) pelar.

fleet n flota f; escuadra f.

fleeting adj pasajero/ra, fugitivo/va.

flesh n carne f.

flesh wound n herida superficial f.

fleshy adj carnoso/sa, pulposo/sa.

flex n cordón m; * vt tensar.

flexibility n flexibilidad f.

flexible adj flexible.

flick n golpecito m; * vt dar un golpecito a.

flicker vi aletear; fluctuar.

flier n aviador/a m/f.

flight n vuelo m; huida, fuga f; bandada (de pájaros) f; (fig) elevación f.

flight attendant n auxiliar de vuelo m/f.

flight deck n cabina de mandos f.

flimsy adj débil; fútil.

flinch vi encogerse.

fling vt lanzar, echar.

flint n pedernal m.

flip vt arrojar, lanzar.

flippant adj petulante, locuaz.

flipper n aleta f.

flirt vi coquetear; * n coqueta f.

flirtation n coquetería f.

flit vi volar, huir; aletear.

float vt hacer flotar; lanzar; * vi flotar; * n flotador m; carroza f; reserva f.

flock n manada f; rebaño m; gentío m; * vi congregarse.

flog vt azotar; (fam) zurrar.

flogging n tunda, zurra f.

flood n diluvio m; inundación f; flujo m; * vt inundar.

flooding n inundación f.

floodlight n foco m.

floor n suelo, piso m; piso (de una casa); * vt dejar sin respuesta.

floorboard n tabla f.

floor lamp n lámpara de pie f.

floor show n cabaret m.

flop n fracaso m.

floppy adj flojo/ja.

floppy disk n floppy m, disquete m.

flora n flora f.

floral adj floral.

florescence n florescencia f.

florid adj florido/da.

florist n florista m/f.

florist's (shop) n floristería f.

flotilla n (mar) flotilla f.

flounder n platija (pez de mar) f; * vi tropezar.

flour n harina f.

flourish vi florecer; gozar de prosperidad; * n belleza f; lazo m; (mus) floreo, preludio m.

flourishing adj floreciente.

flout vt burlarse de.

flow vi fluir, manar; crecer la marea; ondear; * n flujo de la marea m ; abundancia f; flujo m.

flow chart n organigrama m.

flower n flor f; * vi florear; florecer.

flowerbed n parterre m.

flowerpot n tiesto m, maceta f.

flowery adj florido/da.

flower show n exposición de flores f.

fluctuate vi fluctuar.

fluctuation n fluctuación f.

fluency n fluidez f.

fluent adj fluido/da; fácil; ~ly adv con fluidez.

fluff n pelusa f; ~y adj velloso/sa.

fluid adj, n fluido/da m.

fluidity n fluidez f.

fluke n (sl) chiripa f.

fluoride n fluoruro f.

flurry n ráfaga f; agitación f.

flush vt: **to ~ out** levantar; desalojar; * vi ponerse colorado/da; * n rubor m; resplandor m.

flushed adj ruborizado/da.

fluster vt confundir.

flustered adj aturdido/da.

flute n flauta f.

flutter vi revolotear; estar en agitación; * n confusión f; agitación f.

flux n flujo m.

fly vt pilotar; transportar; * vi volar; huir, escapar; **to ~ away/off** emprender el vuelo; * n mosca f; bragueta f.

flying n aviación f.

flying saucer n platillo volante m.

flypast n desfile aéreo m.

flysheet n doble techo m.

foal n potro m.

foam n espuma f; * vi espumar.

foam rubber n espuma de caucho f.

foamy adj espumoso/sa.

focus n foco m.

fodder n forraje m.

foe n adversario/ria m/f, enemigo/ga m/f.

foetus n feto m.

fog n niebla f.

foggy adj nebuloso/sa, brumoso/sa.

fog light n faro antiniebla m.

foible n debilidad, parte flaca f.

foil vt frustrar; * n hoja f; florete m.

fold n redil m; pliegue m; * vt plegar; * vi: **to ~ up** plegarse, doblarse; quebrar.

folder n carpeta f; folleto m.

folding adj plegable.

folding chair n silla de tijera f.

foliage n follaje m.

folio n folio m.

folk n gente f.

folklore n folklore m.

folk music n folk m.

folk song n canción folklórica f.

follow vt seguir; acompañar; imitar; **to ~ up** responder a; investigar; * vi seguir, resultar, provenir.

follower n seguidor/a m/f; imitador/a m/f; secuaz, partidario/ria m/f; adherente m; compañero/ra m/f.

following adj siguiente; * n afición f.

folly n extravagancia, bobería f.

foment vt fomentar; proteger.

fond adj cariñoso/sa; ~ly adv cariñosamente.

fondle vt acariciar.

fondness n gusto m; cariño m.

font n pila bautismal f.

food n comida f.

food mixer n batidora f.

food poisoning n intoxicación alimentaria f.

food processor n robot de cocina m.

foodstuffs npl comestibles mpl.

fool n loco/ca, tonto/ta m/f; * vt engañar.

foolhardy adj temerario/ria.

foolish adj, bobo/ba, tonto/ta; ~ly adv tontamente.

foolproof *adj* infalible.

foolscap *n* papel tamaño folio *m*.

foot *n* pie *m*; pata *f*; paso *m*; **on, by ~** a pie.

footage *n* imágenes *fpl*.

football *n* balón *m*; fútbol *m*.

footballer *n* futbolista *m/f*; jugador/a de fútbol *m/f*.

football pools *npl* quinielas *fpl*.

football pools coupon *n* quiniela *f*.

footbrake *n* freno de pie *m*.

footbridge *n* puente peatonal *m*.

foothills *npl* estribaciones *fpl*.

foothold *n* pie firme *m*.

footing *n* base *f*; estado *m*; condición *f*; fundamento *m*.

footlights *npl* candilejas *fpl*.

footman *n* lacayo *m*; soldado de infantería *m*.

footnote *n* nota de pie *f*.

footpath *n* senda *f*.

footprint *n* huella, pisada *f*.

footsore *adj* con los pies doloridos.

footstep *n* paso *m*; huella *f*.

footwear *n* calzado *m*.

for *prep* por, a causa de; para; * *conj* porque, para que; por cuanto; **as ~ me** tocante a mí; **what ~?** ¿para qué?

forage *n* forraje *m*; * *vt* forrajear; saquear.

foray *n* incursión *f*.

forbid *vt* prohibir, vedar; impedir; **God ~!** ¡Dios no quiera!

forbidding *adj* inhóspito/ta; severo/ra.

force *n* fuerza *f*; poder, vigor *m*; violencia *f*; necesidad *f*; **~s** *pl* tropas *fpl*; * *vt* forzar, violentar; esforzar; constreñir.

forced *adj* forzado/da.

forced march *n* (*mil*) marcha forzada *f*.

forceful *adj* enérgico/ca.

forceps *n* fórceps *m*.

forcible *adj* fuerte, eficaz, poderoso/sa; **~bly** *adv* fuertemente, forzadamente.

ford *n* vado *m*; * *vt* vadear.

fore *n*: **to the ~** en evidencia.

forearm *n* antebrazo *m*.

foreboding *n* presentimiento *m*.

forecast *vt* pronosticar; * *n* pronóstico *m*.

forecourt *n* patio *m*.

forefather *n* abuelo, antecesor *m*.

forefinger *n* índice *m*.

forefront *n*: **in the ~ of** en la vanguardia de.

forego *vt* ceder, abandonar; preceder.

foregone *adj* pasado/da; anticipado/da.

foreground *n* delantera *f*.

forehead *n* frente *f*; insolencia *f*.

foreign *adj* extranjero/ra; extraño/ña.

foreigner *n* extranjero/ra, forastero/ra *m/f*.

foreign exchange *n* divisas *fpl*.

foreleg *n* pata delantera *f*.

foreman *n* capataz *m*; (*law*) presidente del jurado *m*.

foremost *adj* principal.

forenoon *n* mañana *f*.

forensic *adj* forense; **~ scientist** *n* forense *m/f*.

forerunner *n* precursor/a *m/f*; predecesor/a *m/f*.

foresee *vt* prever.

foreshadow *vt* pronosticar; simbolizar.

foresight *n* previsión *f*; presciencia *f*.

forest *n* bosque *m*; selva *f*.

forestall *vt* anticipar; prevenir.

forester *n* guardabosque *m/f*.

forestry *n* silvicultura *f*.

foretaste n muestra f.

foretell vt predecir, profetizar.

forethought n providencia f; premeditación f.

forever adv para siempre.

forewarn vt prevenir de antemano.

foreword n prefacio m.

forfeit n confiscación f; * vt perder derecho a.

forge n fragua f; fábrica de metales f; * vt forjar; falsificar; inventar; * vi: **to ~ ahead** avanzar constantemente.

forger n falsificador/a m/f.

forgery n falsificación f.

forget vt olvidar; * vi olvidarse.

forgetful adj olvidadizo/za; descuidado/da.

forgetfulness n olvido m; negligencia f.

forget-me-not n (bot) nomeolvides m.

forgive vt perdonar.

forgiveness n perdón m; remisión f.

fork n tenedor m; horca f; * vi bifurcarse; **to ~ out** (sl) desembolsar.

forked adj horcado/da.

fork-lift truck n carretilla elevadora f.

forlorn adj abandonado/da, perdido/da.

form n forma f; modelo m; modo m; formalidad f; método m; molde m; * vt formar.

formal adj formal, metódico/ca; ceremonioso/sa; **~ly** adv formalmente.

formality n formalidad f; ceremonia f.

format n formato m; * vt formatear.

formation n formación f.

formative adj formativo/va.

former adj precedente; anterior; pasado/da; **~ly** adv antiguamente, en tiempos pasados.

formidable adj formidable, terrible.

formula n fórmula f.

formulate vt formular, articular.

forsake vt dejar, abandonar.

fort n castillo m; fortaleza f.

forte adj fuerte.

forthcoming adj venidero/ra.

forthright adj franco/ca.

forthwith adj inmediatamente, sin tardanza.

fortieth adj, n cuadragésimo m.

fortification n fortificación f.

fortify vt fortificar; corroborar.

fortitude n fortaleza f; valor m.

fortnight n quince días mpl; dos semanas fpl; **~ly** adj, adv cada quince días.

fortress n (mil) fortaleza f.

fortuitous adj impensado/da; casual; **~ly** adv fortuitamente.

fortunate adj afortunado/da; **~ly** adv felizmente.

fortune n fortuna, suerte f.

fortune-teller n sortílego/ga, adivino/na m/f.

forty adj, n cuarenta.

forum n foro m.

forward adj avanzado/da; delantero/ra; presumido/da; **~(s)** adv adelante, más allá; * vt remitir; promover, patrocinar.

forwardness n precocidad f; audacia f.

fossil adj, n fósil m.

foster vt criar, nutrir.

foster child n hijo/ja adoptivo/va m/f.

foster father n padre adoptivo m.

foster mother n madre adoptiva f.

foul adj sucio/cia, puerco/ca; impuro/ra, detestable; * **copy** n borrador m; **~ly** adv suciamente; ilegítimamente; * vt ensuciar.

foul play n mala jugada f; muerte violenta f.

found *vt* fundar, establecer; edificar; fundir.

foundation *n* fundación *f*; fundamento *m*.

founder *n* fundador/a *m/f*; fundidor *m*; * *vi* (*mar*) irse a pique; zozobrar.

foundling *n* niño/ña expósito/ta *m/f*.

foundry *n* fundición *f*.

fount, fountain *n* fuente *f*.

fountainhead *n* origen de fuente *m*.

four *adj*, *n* cuatro.

fourfold *adj* cuádruple.

four-poster (bed) *n* cama de dosel *f*.

foursome *n* grupo de cuatro personas *m*.

fourteen *adj*, *n* catorce.

fourteenth *adj*, *n* decimocuarto/ta.

fourth *adj*, *n* cuarto/ta; * *n* cuarto *m*; **~ly** *adv* en cuarto lugar.

fowl *n* ave *f* de corral.

fox *n* zorra *f*; (*fig*) zorro *m*.

foyer *n* vestíbulo *m*.

fracas *n* riña *f*.

fraction *n* fracción *f*.

fracture *n* fractura *f*; * *vt* fracturar, romper.

fragile *adj* frágil; débil.

fragility *n* fragilidad *f*; debilidad, flaqueza *f*.

fragment *n* fragmento *m*.

fragmentary *adj* fragmentario/ria.

fragrance *n* fragancia *f*.

fragrant *adj* fragante, oloroso/sa; **~ly** *adv* con fragancia.

frail *adj* frágil, débil.

frailty *n* fragilidad *f*; debilidad *f*.

frame *n* armazón *m*; marco, cerco *m*; cuadro de vidriera *m*; estructura *f*; montura *f*; * *vt* encuadrar; componer, construir, formar.

frame of mind *n* estado de ánimo m.

framework *n* estructura *f*; esqueleto *m*, armazón *f*.

franchise *n* sufragio *m*; concesión *f*.

frank *adj* franco/ca, liberal.

frankly *adv* francamente.

frankness *n* franqueza *f*.

frantic *adj* frenético/ca, furioso/sa.

fraternal *adj*, **~ly** *adv* fraternal(mente).

fraternity *n* fraternidad *f*.

fraternize *vi* hermanarse.

fratricide *n* fratricidio *m*; fratricida *m/f*.

fraud *n* fraude, engaño *m*.

fraudulence *n* fraudulencia *f*.

fraudulent *adj* fraudulento/ta; **~ly** *adv* fraudulentamente.

fraught *adj* cargado/da, lleno/na.

fray *n* riña, disputa, querella *f*.

freak *n* fantasía *f*; fenómeno *m*.

freckle *n* peca *f*.

freckled *adj* pecoso/sa.

free *adj* libre; liberal; suelto/ta; exento/ta; desocupado/da; gratis; * *vt* soltar; librar; eximir; * *vr*: **to ~ oneself from trouble** zafarse de.

freedom *n* libertad *f*.

freehold *n* propiedad absoluta *f*.

free-for-all *n* trifulca *f*.

free gift *n* prima *f*.

free kick *n* tiro libre *m*.

freelance *adj*, *adv* por cuenta propia.

freely *adv* libremente; espontáneamente; liberalmente, gratis.

freemason *n* francmasón *m*, masón *m*.

freemasonry *n* francmasonería *f*, masonería *f*.

freepost *n* franqueo pagado *m*.

free-range *adj* de granja.

freethinker *n* librepensador/a *m/f*.

freethinking *n* librepensamiento *m*.

free trade *n* libre comercio *m*.

freeway *n* autopista *f*.

freewheel *vi* ir en punto muerto.

free will *n* libre albedrío *m*.
freeze *vi* helar(se); * *vt* congelar; helar.
freeze-dried *adj* liofilizado/da.
freezer *n* congelador *m*.
freezing *adj* helado/da.
freezing point *n* punto de congelación *m*.
freight *n* carga *f*; flete *m*.
freighter *n* fletador *m*.
freight train *n* tren de mercancías *m*.
French bean *n* judía verde *f*.
French fries *npl* patatas *o* papas fritas *fpl*.
French window *n* puertaventana *f*.
frenzied *adj* loco/ca, delirante.
frenzy *n* frenesí *m*; locura *f*.
frequency *n* frecuencia *f*.
frequent *adj*, ~**ly** *adv* frecuente(mente); * *vt* frecuentar.
fresco *n* fresco *m*.
fresh *adj* fresco/ca; nuevo/va, reciente; ~ **water** *n* agua dulce *f*.
freshen *vt* (*vi*) refrescar(se).
fresher *n* novato *m*.
freshly *adv* nuevamente; recientemente.
freshness *n* frescura *f*; fresco *m*.
freshwater *adj* de agua dulce.
fret *vi* agitarse, enojarse.
friar *n* fraile *m*.
friction *n* fricción *f*.
Friday *n* viernes *m*; **Good** ~ Viernes Santo *m*.
friend *n* amigo/ga *m/f*.
friendless *adj* sin amigos.
friendliness *n* amistad, benevolencia, bondad *f*.
friendly *adj* amistoso/sa.
friendship *n* amistad *f*.
frieze *n* friso *m*.
frigate *n* (*mar*) fragata *f*.
fright *n* espanto, terror *m*.
frighten *vt* espantar.

frightened *adj* asustado/da.
frightening *adj* espantoso/sa.
frightful *adj* espantoso/sa, horrible; ~**ly** *adv* espantosamente, terriblemente.
frigid *adj* frío/ría, frígido/da; ~**ly** *adv* fríamente.
fringe *n* franja *f*.
fringe benefits *npl* ventajas adicionales *fpl*.
frisk *vt* cachear.
frisky *adj* juguetón/ona.
fritter *vt*: **to ~ away** desperdiciar.
frivolity *n* frivolidad *f*.
frivolous *adj* frívolo/la, vano/na.
frizz(le) *vt* frisar; rizar.
frizzy *adj* rizado/da.
fro *adv*: **to go to** and ~ ir y venir.
frog *n* rana *f*.
frolic *vi* juguetear.
frolicsome *adj* juguetón/ona, travieso/sa.
from *prep* de; después; desde.
front *n* parte delantera *f*; fachada *f*; paseo marítimo *m*; frente *m*; apariencias *fpl*; * *adj* delantero/ra; primero/ra.
frontal *adj* de frente.
front door *n* puerta principal *f*.
frontier *n* frontera *f*.
front page *n* primera plana *f*.
front-wheel drive *n* (*auto*) tracción delantera *f*.
frost *n* helada *f*; hielo *m*; * *vt* escarchar.
frostbite *n* congelación *f*.
frostbitten *adj* helado/da, con síntomas de congelación.
frosted *adj* deslustrado/da.
frosty *adj* helado/da, frío/ría como el hielo.
froth *n* espuma (de algún líquido) *f*; * *vi* espumar.

frothy adj espumoso/sa.

frown vt mirar con ceño; * n ceño m.

frozen adj helado/da.

frugal adj frugal; económico/ca; sobrio/ria; **~ly** adv frugalmente.

fruit n fruta f; fruto m; producto m.

fruiterer n frutero/ra m/f.

fruitful adj fructífero/ra, fértil; provechoso/sa, útil; **~ly** adv con fertilidad.

fruitfulness n fertilidad f.

fruition n realización f.

fruit juice n zumo de fruta m.

fruitless adj estéril; inútil; **~ly** adv vanamente, inútilmente.

fruit salad n ensalada de frutas f, macedonia f.

fruit seller, greengrocer n frutero/ra m.

fruit shop, greengrocer's shop n frutería f.

fruit tree n frutal m.

frustrate vt frustrar; anular.

frustrated adj frustrado/da.

frustration n frustración f.

fry vt freír.

frying pan n sartén f.

fuchsia n (bot) fucsia f.

fudge n caramelo blando m.

fuel n combustible m.

fuel tank n depósito m de combustible.

fugitive adj, n fugitivo/va m/f.

fugue n (mus) fuga f.

fulcrum n fulcro m.

fulfil vt cumplir; realizar.

fulfilment n cumplimiento m.

full adj lleno/na, repleto/ta, completo/ta; perfecto/ta; * adv enteramente, del todo.

full-blown adj hecho/cha y derecho/cha.

full-fledged adj hecho/cha y derecho/cha.

full-length adj de cuerpo entero/ra; completo/ta.

full moon n plenilunio m; luna llena f.

fullness n plenitud, abundancia f.

full-scale adj en gran escala; de tamaño natural.

full-time adj de tiempo completo.

fully adv llenamente, enteramente, ampliamente.

fulsome adj exagerado/da.

fumble vi manejar torpemente.

fumes npl humo m.

fumigate vt fumigar.

fun n diversión f; alegría f.

function n función f.

functional adj funcional.

fund n fondo m; fondos públicos mpl; * vt costear.

fundamental adj fundamental; **~ly** adv fundamentalmente.

fundamentalism n fundamentalismo m.

fundamentalist n fundamentalista m/f.

funeral service n misa de difuntos f, funeral m.

funeral n funeral m.

funereal adj funeral, fúnebre.

fungus n hongo m; seta f.

funnel n embudo m; cañón (de chimenea) m.

funny adj divertido/da; curioso/sa; zumbón/ona.

fur n piel f.

fur coat n abrigo de pieles m.

furious adj furioso/sa, frenético/ca; **~ly** adv con furia.

furlong n estadio m; (octava parte de una milla).

furlough n (mil) licencia f; permiso m.

furnace n horno m; hornaza f.

furnish vt amueblar; facilitar; suministrar.

furnishings npl muebles mpl.

furniture n muebles mpl.

furrow n surco m; * vt surcar; estriar.

furry adj peludo/da.

further adj nuevo/va; más lejano/na; * adv más lejos, más allá; aún; además; * vt adelantar, promover, ayudar.

further education n educación para adultos f.

furthermore adv además.

furthest adv lo más lejos, lo más remoto.

furtive adj furtivo/va; secreto/ta; ~ly adv furtivamente.

fury n furor m; furia f; ira f.

fuse vt, vi fundir; derretirse; * n fusible m; n mecha f.

fuse box n caja de fusibles f.

fusion n fusión f.

fuss n lío m; alboroto m.

fussy adj jactancioso/sa.

futile adj fútil, frívolo/la.

futility n futilidad, vanidad f.

future adj futuro/ra; * n futuro m; porvenir m.

fuzzy adj borroso/sa; muy rizado/da.

G

gab n (fam) charla f.

gabble vi charlar, parlotear; * n algarabía f.

gable n gablete m.

gadget n dispositivo m.

gaffe n plancha f.

gag n mordaza f; chiste m; * vt amordazar.

gaiety n alegría f.

gaily adv alegremente.

gain n ganancia f; interés, provecho m; * vt ganar; conseguir.

gait n marcha f; porte m.

gala n fiesta f.

galaxy n galaxia f.

gale n vendaval m.

gall n hiel f.

gallant adj galante.

gall bladder n vesícula biliar f.

gallery n galería f.

galley n cocina f; galera f.

gallon n galón m (medida).

gallop n galope m; * vi galopar.

gallows n horca f.

gallstone n cálculo biliar m.

galore adv en abundancia.

galvanize vt galvanizar.

gambit n estrategia f.

gamble vi jugar; especular; * n riesgo m; apuesta f.

gambler n jugador/a m/f.

gambling n juego m.

game n juego m; pasatiempo m; partido m; partida f; caza f; * vi jugar.

gamekeeper n guardabosques m invar.

gaming n juego m.

gammon n jamón m.

gamut n (mus) gama f.

gander n ganso m.

gang n pandilla, banda f.

gangrene n gangrena f.

gangster n gángster m.

gangway n pasarela f.

gap n hueco m; claro m; intervalo m.

gape vi boquear; estar con la boca abierta.

gaping adj muy abierto/ta.

garage n garaje m.
garbled adj falsificado/da.
garden n jardín m.
garden-hose n regadera f.
gardener n jardinero/ra m/f.
gardening n jardinería f.
gargle vi hacer gárgaras.
gargoyle n gárgola f.
garish adj ostentoso/sa.
garland n guirnalda f.
garlic n ajo m.
garment n prenda f.
garnish vt guarnecer, adornar; * n guarnición f; adorno m.
garret n guardilla f; desván m.
garrison n (mil) guarnición f; * vt (mil) guarnecer.
garrotte, garrote vt estrangular.
garrulous adj gárrulo/la, locuaz, charlador/a.
garter n liga f.
gas n gas m; gasolina f.
gas burner n mechero de gas m.
gas cylinder n bombona de gas f.
gaseous adj gaseoso/sa.
gas fire n estufa de gas f.
gash n cuchillada f; raja f; * vt acuchillar.
gasket n junta de culata f.
gas mask n careta antigás f.
gas meter n contador de gas m.
gasp vi jadear; * n boqueada f.
gas ring n hornillo de gas m.
gassy adj gaseoso/sa.
gas tap n llave del gas f.
gastric adj gástrico/ca.
gastronomic adj gastronómico/ca.
gasworks npl fábrica de gas f.
gate n puerta f.
gateway n puerta f.
gather vt recoger, amontonar; entender; plegar; * vi juntarse.
gathering n reunión f; colecta f.

gauche adj torpe.
gaudy adj chillón/ona.
gauge n calibre m; entrevía f; indicador m; * vt medir.
gaunt adj flaco/ca, delgado/da.
gauze n gasa f.
gay adj alegre; vivo/va; gay.
gaze vi contemplar, considerar; * n mirada f.
gazelle n gacela f.
gazette n gaceta f.
gazetteer n gacetero m; diccionario geográfico m.
gear n atavío m; vestido m; aparejo m; tirantes mpl; velocidad f.
gearbox n caja de cambios f.
gear lever n palanca de cambios f.
gear wheel n rueda dentada f.
gel n gel m.
gelatin(e) n gelatina, jalea f.
gelignite n gelignita f.
gem n gema f.
Gemini n Géminis m (signo del zodiaco).
gender n género m.
gene n gen m.
genealogical adj genealógico/ca.
genealogy n genealogía f.
general adj general, común, usual; in ~ por lo general; ~ly adv generalmente; * n general m; generala f.
general election n elecciones generales fpl.
generality n generalidad, mayor parte f.
generalization n generalización f.
generalize vt generalizar.
generate vt engendrar; producir; causar.
generation n generación f.
generator n generador m.
generic adj genérico/ca.

generosity n generosidad, liberalidad f.

generous adj generoso/sa.

genetic engineering n ingeniería genética f.

genetics npl genética f.

genial adj genial, natural; alegre.

genitals npl genitales mpl.

genitive n genitivo m.

genius n genio m.

genteel adj refinado/da, elegante.

gentile adj gentil, pagano/na m/f.

gentle adj suave, dócil, manso/sa, moderado/da; benigno/na.

gentleman n caballero m.

gentleness n dulzura, suavidad f.

gently adv suavemente.

gentry n alta burguesía f.

gents n aseos mpl.

genuflection n genuflexión f.

genuine adj genuino/na, puro/ra; **~ly** adv puramente, naturalmente.

genus n género m.

geographer n geógrafo/fa m/f.

geographical adj geográfico/ca.

geography n geografía f.

geological adj geológico/ca.

geologist n geólogo/ga m/f.

geology n geología f.

geometric(al) adj geométrico/ca.

geometry n geometría f.

geranium n (bot) geranio m.

geriatric n, adj geriátrico/ca m/f.

germ n germen m, microbio m.

germinate vi brotar.

gesticulate vi gesticular.

gesture n gesto, movimiento expresivo m.

get vt ganar; conseguir, obtener, alcanzar; coger; agarrar; * vi hacerse, ponerse; prevalecer; introducirse; **to ~ the better** salir vencedor/a, sobrepujar.

geyser n géiser m; calentador de agua m.

ghastly adj espantoso/sa.

gherkin n pepinillo, cohombrillo m.

ghetto n gueto m.

ghost n fantasma m; espectro m.

ghostly adj fantasmal.

giant n gigante m.

gibberish n jerigonza f.

gibe vi escarnecer, burlarse, mofar; * n mofa, burla f.

giblets npl menudillos mpl.

giddiness n vértigo m.

giddy adj vertiginoso/sa.

gift n regalo m; don m; dádiva f; talento m.

gifted adj dotado/da.

gift voucher n vale de regalo m.

gigantic adj gigantesco/ca.

giggle vi reírse tontamente.

gild vt dorar.

gilding, gilt n doradura f.

gill n cuarta parte de pinta f; **~s** pl agallas fpl.

gilt-edged adj de máxima garantía.

gimmick n truco m.

gin n ginebra f.

ginger n jengibre m.

gingerbread n pan de jengibre m.

ginger-haired adj pelirrojo/ja.

giraffe n jirafa f.

girder n viga f.

girdle n faja f; cinturón m.

girl n muchacha, chica f, zagala f.

girlfriend n amiga; novia f.

girlish adj de niña.

giro n giro postal m.

girth n cincha f; circunferencia f.

gist n punto principal m.

give vt, vi dar, donar; conceder; abandonar; pronunciar; aplicarse; dedicarse; **to ~ away** regalar; traicionar; revelar; **to ~ back**

devolver; **to ~ in** vi ceder; vt entregar; **to ~ off** despedir; **to ~ out** distribuir; **to ~ up** vi rendir; vt renunciar a.

gizzard n molleja f.

glacial adj glacial.

glacier n glaciar m.

glad adj alegre, contento/ta, agradable; **I am ~ to see** me alegro de ver; **~ly** adv alegremente.

gladden vt alegrar.

gladiator n gladiador m.

glamorous adj atractivo/va.

glamour n encanto, atractivo m.

glance n ojeada f; * vi mirar; echar una ojeada.

glancing adj oblicuo/cua.

gland n glándula f.

glare n deslumbramiento m; mirada feroz y penetrante f; * vi deslumbrar, brillar; echar miradas de indignación.

glaring adj deslumbrante; manifiesto/ta; notorio/ria.

glass n vidrio m, cristal m; telescopio m; vaso m; espejo m; **~es** pl gafas fpl; * adj vítreo/rea.

glassware n cristalería f.

glassy adj vítreo/rea, cristalino/na, vidrioso/sa.

glaze vt, vi driar; embarnizar.

glazier n vidriero m, cristalero m.

gleam n relámpago, rayo m; * vi relampaguear, brillar.

gleaming adj reluciente.

glean vt espigar; recoger.

glee n alegría f; gozo m; jovialidad f.

glen n valle m; llanura f.

glib adj con lab; **~ly** adv con labia.

glide vi resbalar; planear.

gliding n vuelo sin motor m.

glimmer n vislumbre f; * vi vislumbrarse.

glimpse n vislumbre f; relámpago m;

ojeada f; * vt entrever, percibir.

glint vi centellear.

glisten, glitter vi relucir, brillar.

gloat vi relamerse; saborear.

global adj mundial.

globalization n globalización f.

global warming n calentamiento global m.

globe n globo m; esfera f.

gloom, gloominess n oscuridad f; melancolía, tristeza f; **~ily** adv oscuramente; tristemente.

gloomy adj sombrío/ría, oscuro/ra; cubierto de nubes; triste, melancólico/ca.

glorification n glorificación, alabanza f.

glorify vt glorificar, celebrar.

glorious adj glorioso/sa, ilustre; **~ly** adv gloriosamente.

glory n gloria, fama, celebridad f.

gloss n glosa f; lustre m; * vt glosar, interpretar; **to ~ over** encubrir.

glossary n glosario m.

glossy adj lustroso/sa, brillante.

glove n guante m.

glove compartment n guantera f.

glow vi arder; inflamarse; relucir; * n color vivo m; viveza de color f; vehemencia de una pasión f.

glower vi mirar con ceño.

glue n cola f; cemento m; * vt pegar.

gluey adj viscoso/sa, pegajoso/sa.

glum adj abatido/da, triste.

glut n hartura, abundancia f.

glutinous adj glutinoso/sa, viscoso/sa.

glutton n glotón/ona, tragón/ona m/f.

gluttony n glotonería f.

glycerine n glicerina f.

gnarled adj nudoso/sa.

gnash vt, vi rechinar.

gnat n mosquito m.

gnaw *vt* roer.

gnome *n* gnomo *m*.

go *vi* ir, irse, marchar; huir; pasar; partir(se); marcharse; to ~ **ahead** seguir adelante; to ~ **away** marcharse; to ~ **back** volver; to ~ **by** pasar; to ~ **for** ir por; gustar; to ~ **in** entrar; to ~ **off** irse; pasarse; to ~ **on** seguir; pasar; to ~ **out** salir; apagarse; to ~ **up** subir.

goad *n* aguijada, aijada *f*; * *vt* aguijar; estimular, incitar.

go-ahead *adj* emprendedor/a; * *n* luz verde *f*.

goal *n* meta *f*; fin *m*.

goalkeeper *n* portero/ra *m/f*.

goalpost *n* poste (de la portería) *m*.

goatherd *n* cabrero/ra *m/f*.

gobble *vt* engullir, tragar; to ~ **down** zampar.

go-between *n* mediador/a *m/f*.

goblet *n* copa *f*.

goblin *n* espíritu ambulante, duende *m*.

God *n* Dios *m*.

godchild *n* ahijado, hijo de pila *m*.

goddaughter *n* ahijada, hija de pila *f*.

goddess *n* diosa *f*.

godfather *n* padrino *m*.

godforsaken *adj* dejado/da de la mano de Dios.

godhead *n* deidad, divinidad *f*.

godless *adj* infiel, impío/pía, sin Dios, ateo/tea.

godlike *adj* divino/na.

godliness *n* piedad, devoción, santidad *f*.

godly *adj* piadoso/sa, devoto/ta, religioso/sa; recto/ta, justificado/da.

godmother *n* madrina *f*.

godsend *n* don del cielo *m*.

godson *n* ahijado *m*.

goggle-eyed *adj* con ojos desorbitados.

goggles *npl* gafas *fpl*; gafas de bucear *fpl*.

going *n* ida *f*; salida *f*; partida *f*; progreso *m*.

gold *n* oro *m*.

golden *adj* áureo/rea, de oro; excelente; ~ **rule** *n* regla de oro *f*.

goldfish *n* pez de colores *m*.

gold-plated *adj* chapado/da en oro.

goldsmith *n* orfebre *m*.

golf *n* golf *m*.

golf ball *n* pelota de golf *f*.

golf club *n* club de golf *m*.

golf course *n* campo de golf *m*.

golfer *n* golfista *m/f*.

gondolier *n* gondolero/ra *m/f*.

gone *adj* ido/da; perdido/da; pasado/da; gastado/da; muerto/ta.

gong *n* atabal chino, gong *m*.

good *adj* bueno/na, benévolo/la, cariñoso/sa; conveniente, apto/ta; * *adv* bien; * *n* bien *m*; prosperidad, ventaja *f*; ~**s** *pl* bienes muebles *mpl*; mercaderías *fpl*.

goodbye! *excl* ¡adiós!

Good Friday *n* Viernes Santo *m*.

goodies *npl* golosinas *fpl*.

good-looking *adj* guapo/pa.

good nature *n* bondad *f*.

good-natured *adj* bondadoso/sa.

goodness *n* bondad *f*.

goodwill *n* benevolencia, bondad *f*.

goose *n* ganso *m*; oca *f*.

gooseberry *n* grosella espinosa *f*.

goose bumps, goose flesh *npl* carne de gallina *f*.

goose-step *n* paso de la oca *m*.

gore *n* sangre cuajada *f*; * *vt* cornear.

gorge *n* barranco *m*; * *vt* engullir, tragar.

gorgeous adj maravilloso/sa.

gorilla n gorila m.

gorse n aulaga f.

gory adj sangriento/ta.

goshawk n azor m.

gospel n evangelio m.

gossamer n vello m; pelusa (de frutas) f.

gossip n cotilleo m; * vi cotillear.

gothic adj gótico/ca.

gout n gota f (enfermedad).

govern vt gobernar, dirigir, regir.

governess n gobernadora f.

government n gobierno m; administración pública f.

governor n gobernador/a m/f.

gown n toga f; vestido de mujer m; bata f.

grab vt agarrar.

grace n gracia f; favor m; merced f; perdón m; gracias fpl; to say ~ bendecir la mesa; * vt adornar; agraciar.

graceful adj gracioso/sa, primoroso/sa; ~ly adv elegantemente, con gracia.

gracious adj gracioso/sa; favorable; ~ly adv graciosamente.

gradation n gradación f.

grade n grado m; curso m.

gradient n (rail) pendiente.

gradual adj gradual; ~ly adv gradualmente.

graduate vi graduarse.

graduation n graduación f.

graffiti n pintadas fpl.

graft n injerto m; * vt injertar, ingerir.

grain n grano m; semilla f; cereales mpl.

gram n gramo m (peso).

grammar n gramática f.

grammatical adj gramatical; ~ly adv gramaticalmente.

granary n granero m.

grand adj grande, ilustre.

grandchild n nieto/ta m/f.

grandad n abuelo m.

granddaughter n nieta f; great ~ bisnieta f.

grandeur n grandeza f; pompa f.

grandfather n abuelo m; great ~ bisabuelo m.

grandiose adj grandioso/sa.

grandma n abuelita f.

grandmother n abuela f; great ~ bisabuela f.

grandparents npl abuelos mpl.

grand piano n piano de cola m.

grandson n nieto m; great ~ bisnieto m.

grandstand n tribuna f.

granite n granito m.

granny n abuelita f.

grant vt conceder; to take for ~ed presuponer; * n beca f; concesión f.

granulate vt granular.

granule n gránulo m.

grape n uva f; bunch of ~s racimo de uvas m.

grapefruit n toronja f, pomelo m.

graph n gráfica f.

graphic(al) adj gráfico/ca; pintoresco/ca; ~ally adv gráficamente.

graphics n artes gráficas fpl; gráficos mpl.

grapnel n (mar) arpeo m.

grasp vt empuñar, asir, agarrar; * n puño m; comprensión f; poder m.

grasping adj avaro/ra.

grass n hierba f.

grasshopper n saltamontes m invar.

grassland n pampa, pradera f.

grass-roots adj popular.

grass snake n culebra de agua f.

grassy adj herboso/sa.

grate n reja, verja, rejilla f; * vt rallar; rechinar (los dientes); enrejar.

grateful adj grato/ta, agradecido/da; ~ly adv agradecidamente.

gratefulness n gratitud f.

gratification n gratificación f.

gratify vt contentar; gratificar.

gratifying adj grato/ta.

grating n rejado m; * adj áspero/ra; ofensivo/va.

gratis adv gratis.

gratitude n gratitud f.

gratuitous adj gratuito/ta, voluntario/ria; ~ly adv gratuitamente.

gratuity n gratificación, recompensa f.

grave vt sepultura f; * adj grave, serio/ria; ~ly adv con gravedad, seriamente.

grave digger n sepulturero m.

gravel n cascajo m.

gravestone n lápida f.

graveyard n cementerio m.

gravitate vi gravitar.

gravitation n gravitación f.

gravity n gravedad f.

gravy n jugo de la carne f; salsa f.

graze vt pastorear; tocar ligeramente; * vi pacer.

grease n grasa f; pringue m/f; * vt untar.

greaseproof adj a prueba de grasa.

greasy adj grasiento/ta.

great adj gran, grande; principal; ilustre; noble, magnánimo/ma; ~ly adv muy, mucho.

greatcoat n sobretodo m.

greatness n grandeza f; dignidad f; poder m; magnanimidad f.

greedily adv vorazmente, ansiosamente.

greediness, greed n gula f; codicia f.

greedy adj avaro/ra, codicioso/sa; goloso/sa, glotón/ona.

Greek n griego (idioma) m.

green adj verde, fresco/ca, reciente; no maduro/ra; * n verde m; llanura verde f; ~s pl verduras fpl.

green belt n zona verde f.

greenery n verdura f.

greengrocer n verdulero/ra m/f.

greenhouse n invernadero m.

greenhouse effect n efecto invernadero m.

greenish adj verdoso/sa.

green movement n ecologismo m.

greenness n verdor, vigor m; frescura, falta de experiencia f; novedad f.

greet vt saludar, congratular.

greeting n saludo m.

greeting(s) card n tarjeta de felicitación f.

grenade n (mil) granada f.

grenadier n granadero m.

grey adj gris; cano/na; * n gris m.

grey-haired adj canoso/sa.

greyhound n galgo m.

greyish adj grisáceo/a; entrecano/na.

greyness n color gris m.

grid n reja f; red f.

gridiron n parrilla f; campo de fútbol americano m.

grief n dolor m; aflicción, pena f.

grievance n pesar m; molestia f; agravio m; injusticia f; perjuicio m.

grieve vt agraviar, afligir; * vi afligirse; llorar.

grievous adj doloroso/sa; enorme, atroz; ~ly adv penosamente; cruelmente.

griffin n grifo m.

grill n parrilla f; * vt interrogar.

grille n reja f.

grim adj feo, fea; horrendo/da; ceñludo/da.

grimace n mueca f.

grime n porquería f.

grimy adj ensuciado/da.

grin n mueca f; * vi sonreír.

grind vt moler; pulverizar; afilar; picar; rechinar los dientes.

grinder n molinero m; molinillo m; amolador m.

grip n asimiento m; asidero m; maletín m; * vt agarrar.

gripping adj absorbente.

grisly adj horroroso/sa.

gristle n tendón, cartílago m.

gristly adj tendinoso/sa, cartilaginoso/sa.

grit n gravilla f; valor m.

groan vi gemir, suspirar; * n gemido, suspiro m.

grocer n tendero/ra, abarrotero/ra m/f.

groceries npl comestibles mpl.

grocer's shop n tienda de comestibles f.

groggy adj atontado/da.

groin n ingle f.

groom n establero m; criado m; novio m; * vt cuidar, almohazar.

groove n ranura f.

grope vt, vi tentar, buscar a oscuras; andar a tientas.

gross adj grueso/sa, corpulento/ta, espeso/sa; grosero/ra; estúpido/da; **~ly** adv enormemente.

grotesque adj grotesco/ca.

grotto n gruta f.

ground n tierra f; terreno, suelo, pavimento m; fundamento m; razón fundamental f; campo (de batalla) m; fondo m; * vt mantener en tierra; conectar con tierra.

ground floor n planta baja f.

grounding n conocimientos básicos mpl.

groundless adj infundado/da; **~ly** adv sin motivo.

ground staff n personal de tierra m.

groundwork n preparación f.

group n grupo m; * vt agrupar.

grouse n lagópodo escocés m; * vi quejarse.

grove n arboleda f.

grovel vi arrastrarse.

grow vt cultivar; * vi crecer, aumentarse; **~ up** crecer.

grower n cultivador/a m/f; productor/a m/f.

growing adj creciente.

growl vi regañar, gruñir; * n gruñido m.

grown-up n adulto/ta m/f.

growth n crecimiento m.

grub n gusano m.

grubby adj sucio/cia.

grudge n rencor, odio m; envidia f; * vt, vi envidiar.

grudgingly adv de mala gana.

gruelling adj penoso/sa, duro/ra.

gruesome adj horrible.

gruff adj brusco/ca; **~ly** adv bruscamente.

gruffness n aspereza, severidad f.

grumble vi gruñir; murmurar.

grumpy adj regañón/ona.

grunt vi gruñir; * n gruñido m.

G-string n taparrabo m.

guarantee n garantía f; * vt garantizar.

guard n guardia f; * vt guardar; defender.

guarded adj cauteloso/sa, mesurado/da.

guardroom n (mil) cuarto de guardia m.

guardian n tutor/ra m/f; curador/a m/f; guardián/dana m/f.

guardianship n tutela f.
guerrilla n guerrillero/ra m/f.
guerrilla group n guerrilla f.
guerrilla warfare n guerra de guerrillas f.
guess vt, vi conjeturar; adivinar; suponer; * n conjetura f.
guesswork n conjeturas fpl.
guest n huésped/a, convidado/da m/f.
guest room n cuarto de huéspedes m.
guffaw n carcajada f.
guidance n gobierno m; dirección f.
guide vt guiar, dirigir; * n guía m.
guide dog n perro lazarillo m.
guidelines npl directiva f.
guidebook n guía f.
guild n gremio m; corporación f.
guile n astucia f.
guillotine n guillotina f; * vt guillotinar.
guilt n culpabilidad f.
guiltless adj inocente, libre de culpa.
guilty adj reo, rea, culpable.
guinea pig n cobaya f, conejillo de Indias m.
guise n manera f.
guitar n guitarra f.
gulf n golfo m; abismo m.
gull n gaviota f.
gullet n esófago m.
gullibility n credulidad f; simpleza f.
gullible adj crédulo/la.
gully n barranco m.
gulp n trago m; * vi tragar saliva; * vt tragarse.
gum n goma f; cemento m; encía f; chicle m; * vt pegar con goma.

gum tree n árbol gomero m.
gun n pistola f; escopeta f.
gunboat n cañonera f.
gun carriage n cureña f.
gunfire n disparos mpl.
gunman n pistolero m.
gunmetal n bronce de cañones m.
gunner n artillero m.
gunnery n artillería f.
gunpoint n: at ~ a punta de pistola; a mano armada.
gunpowder n pólvora f.
gunshot n escopetazo m.
gunsmith n armero/ra m/f.
gurgle vi gorgotear.
guru n gurú m.
gush vi brotar; chorrear; * n chorro m.
gushing adj superabundante.
gusset n escudete m.
gust n ráfaga f; soplo de aire m, racha f.
gusto n entusiasmo m.
gusty adj tempestuoso/sa.
gut n intestino m; ~s npl valor m; * vt destripar.
gutter n canalón m; arroyo m.
guttural adj gutural.
guy n tío m; tipo m.
guzzle vt engullir.
gym(nasium) n gimnasio m.
gymnast n gimnasta m/f.
gymnastic adj gimnástico/ca; ~s npl gimnástica f.
gynaecologist n ginecólogo/ga m/f.
gypsy n gitano/na m/f.
gypsum n yeso m.
gyrate vi girar.

H

haberdasher n camisero/ra m/f.

haberdashery n camisería f; mercería f; prendas de caballero fpl.

habit n costumbre f.

habitable adj habitable.

habitat n hábitat m.

habitual adj habitual; ~ly adv por costumbre.

hack n corte m; gacetillero/ra m/f; * vt tajar, cortar.

hackneyed adj trillado/da.

haddock n especie de bacalao f.

haemorrhage n hemorragia f.

haemorrhoids npl hemorroides mpl.

hag n bruja f.

haggard adj ojeroso/sa.

haggle vi regatear.

hail n granizo m; * vt saludar; * vi granizar.

hailstone n piedra de granizo f.

hair n pelo; cabello m.

hairbrush n cepillo m.

haircut n corte de pelo m.

hairdresser n peluquero/ra m/f.

hairdryer n secador de pelo m.

hairless adj calvo/va.

hairnet n redecilla f.

hairpiece n tupé m.

hairpin n horquilla f.

hairpin curve n curva muy cerrada f.

hair remover n depilatorio m.

hairspray n laca f.

hairstyle n peinado m.

hairy adj peludo/da, cabelludo/da.

hale adj sano/na, vigoroso/sa.

half n mitad f; * adj medio/dia.

half-caste adj mestizo/za.

half-hour n media hora f.

half-moon n media luna f.

half-price adj a mitad de precio.

half-time n descanso m.

halfway adv a medio camino.

hall n vestíbulo m; hall m.

hallmark n contraste m.

hallow vt consagrar, santificar.

hallucination n alucinación f.

halo n halo m.

halt vi parar; * n parada f; alto m.

halve vt partir por la mitad.

ham n jamón m.

hamburger n hamburguesa f.

hamlet n aldea f.

hammer n martillo m; * vt martillar.

hammock n hamaca f.

hamper n cesto f; * vt estorbar.

hamstring vt desjarretar.

hand n mano f; brazo m; aguja f; at ~ a mano; * vt alargar.

handbag n cartera f.

handbell n campanilla f.

handbook n manual m.

handbrake n freno de mano m.

handcuff n esposa f.

handful n puñado m.

handicap n desventaja f.

handicapped adj minusválido/da.

handicraft n artesanía f.

handiwork n obra f.

handkerchief n pañuelo m.

handle n mango, puño m; asa; manija f; * vt manejar; tratar.

handlebars npl manillar m.

handling n manejo m.

handrail n pasamanos m.

handshake n apretón de manos m.

handsome adj guapo/pa; ~ly adv primorosamente.

handwriting n letra f.
handy adj práctico/ca; diestro/tra.
hang vt colgar; ahorcar; * vi colgar; ser ahorcado/da.
hanger n percha f.
hanger-on n parásito m.
hangings npl tapicería f.
hangman n verdugo m.
hangover n resaca f.
hang-up n complejo m.
hanker vi ansiar, apetecer.
haphazard adj fortuito/ta.
hapless adj desgraciado/da.
happen vi pasar; acontecer, acaecer.
happening n suceso m.
happily adv felizmente.
happiness n felicidad f.
happy adj feliz.
harangue n arenga f; * vi arengar.
harass vt cansar, fatigar.
harbinger n precursor m.
harbour n puerto m; * vt albergar.
hard adj duro/ra, firme; difícil; penoso/sa; severo/ra, rígido/da; ~ of hearing medio sordo/da; ~ by muy cerca.
harden vt (vi) endurecer(se).
hard-headed adj realista.
hard-hearted adj duro de corazón, insensible.
hardiness n robustez f.
hardly adv apenas.
hardness n dureza f; dificultad f; severidad f.
hardship n penas fpl.
hard-up adj sin plata.
hardware n hardware m; quincallería f.
hardwearing adj resistente.
hardy adj fuerte, robusto/ta.
hare n liebre f.
hare-brained adj atolondrado/da.
hare-lipped adj labihendido/da.
haricot n alubia f.

harlequin n arlequín m.
harm n mal, daño m; perjuicio m; * vt dañar.
harmful adj perjudicial.
harmless adj inocuo/cua.
harmonic adj armónico/ca.
harmonious adj armonioso/sa; ~ly adv armoniosamente.
harmonize vt armonizar.
harmony n armonía f.
harness n arreos de un caballo mpl; * vt enjaezar.
harp n arpa f.
harpist n arpista m/f.
harpoon n arpón m.
harpsichord n clavicordio m.
harrow n grada f; rastro m.
harry vt hostigar.
harsh adj duro/ra; austero/ra; ~ly adv severamente.
harshness n aspereza, dureza f; austeridad f.
harvest n cosecha f; * vt cosechar.
harvester n cosechadora f.
hash n hachís m; picadillo m.
hassock n cojín de paja m.
haste n apuro m; to be in ~ estar apurado/da.
hasten vt acelerar, apresurar; * vi tener prisa.
hastily adv precipitadamente.
hastiness n precipitación f.
hasty adj apresurado/da.
hat n sombrero m.
hatbox n sombrerera f.
hatch vt incubar; tramar; to ~ a plot or scheme zurcir; * n escotilla f.
hatchback n tres puertas, cinco puertas m invar.
hatchet n hacha f.
hatchway n (mar) escotilla f.
hate n odio, aborrecimiento m; * vt odiar, detestar.

hateful *adj* odioso/sa.
hatred *n* odio, aborrecimiento *m*.
hatter *n* sombrerero *m*.
haughtily *adv* orgullosamente.
haughtiness *n* orgullo *m*; altivez *f*.
haughty *adj* altanero/ra, orgulloso/sa.
haul *vt* tirar; * *n* botín *m*.
hauler *n* transportista *m/f*.
haunch *n* anca *f*.
haunt *vt* frecuentar, rondar; * *n* guarida *f*; costumbre *f*.
have *vt* haber; tener; poseer.
haven *n* asilo *m*; puerto *m*.
haversack *n* mochila *f*.
havoc *n* estrago *m*.
hawk *n* halcón *m*; * *vi* cazar con halcón.
hawthorn *n* espino blanco *m*.
hay *n* heno *m*.
hay fever *n* fiebre del heno *f*.
hayloft *n* henil *m*.
hayrick, haystack *n* almiar *m*.
hazard *n* riesgo *m*; * *vt* arriesgar.
hazardous *adj* arriesgado/da, peligroso/sa.
haze *n* niebla *f*.
hazel *n* avellano *m*; * *adj* castaño/ña.
hazelnut *n* avellana *f*.
hazy *adj* oscuro/ra.
he *pn* él.
head *n* cabeza *f*; jefe *m*; juicio *m*; * *vt* encabezar; **to ~ for** dirigirse a.
headache *n* dolor de cabeza *m*.
headdress *n* cofia *f*; tocado *m*.
headland *n* promontorio *m*.
headlight *n* faro *m*.
headline *n* titular *m*.
headlong *adv* precipitadamente.
headmaster *n* director *m*.
head office *n* oficina central *f*.
headphones *npl* auriculares *mpl*.
headquarters *npl* (*mil*) cuartel general *m*; sede central *f*.

headroom *n* altura *f*.
headstrong *adj* testarudo/da, cabezudo/da.
headwaiter *n* maître *m*.
headway *n* progresos *mpl*.
heady *adj* cabezón/ona.
heal *vt, vi* curar.
health *n* salud *f*; brindis *m invar*.
healthiness *n* sanidad *f*.
healthy *adj* sano/na.
heap *n* montón *m*; * *vt* amontonar.
hear *vt* oír; escuchar; * *vi* oír; escuchar.
hearing *n* oído *m*.
hearing aid *n* audífono *m*.
hearsay *n* rumor *m*; fama *f*.
hearse *n* coche fúnebre *m*.
heart *n* corazón *m*; **by ~ de** memoria; **with all my ~** con toda mi alma.
heart attack *n* infarto, infarto de miocardio *m*.
heartbreaking *adj* desgarrador.
heartburn *n* ardor de estómago *m*.
heart failure *n* fallo cardíaco *m*.
heartfelt *adj* sincero/ra.
hearth *n* hogar *m*.
heartily *adv* sinceramente, cordialmente.
heartless *n* cordialidad, sinceridad *f*.
heartless *adj* cruel; **~ly** *adv* cruelmente.
hearty *adj* cordial.
heat *n* calor *m*; * *vt* calentar.
heater *n* calentador *m*.
heather *n* (*bot*) brezo *m*.
heathen *n* pagano/na *m/f*; **~ish** *adj* salvaje.
heating *n* calefacción *f*.
heat wave *n* ola de calor *f*.
heave *vt* alzar; tirar; * *n* tirón *m*.
heaven *n* cielo *m*.
heavenly *adj* divino/na.

heavily adv pesadamente.
heaviness n pesadez f.
heavy adj pesado/da; opresivo/va.
Hebrew n hebreo m.
heckle vt interrumpir.
hectic adj agitado/da.
hedge n seto m; * vt cercar con seto.
hedgehog n erizo m.
heed vt hacer caso de; * n cuidado m; atención f.
heedless adj descuidado/da, negligente; ~ly adv negligentemente.
heel n talón m; **to take to one's ~s** apretar los talones, huir.
hefty adj grande.
heifer n ternera f.
height n altura f; altitud f.
heighten vt realzar; adelantar, mejorar; exaltar.
heinous adj atroz.
heir n heredero/ra m/f; **~ apparent** heredero/ra forzoso/sa m/f.
heiress n heredera f.
heirloom n reliquia de familia f.
helicopter n helicóptero m.
hell n infierno m.
hellish adj infernal.
helm n (mar) timón m.
helmet n casco m.
help vt, vi ayudar, socorrer; **I cannot ~ it** no puedo remediarlo; no lo puedo evitar; * n ayuda f; socorro, remedio m.
helper n ayudante m/f.
helpful adj útil.
helping n ración f.
helpless adj indefenso/sa; ~ly adv irremediablemente.
helter-skelter adv a trochemoche, en desorden.
hem n ribete m; * vt ribetear.
he-man n macho m.
hemisphere n hemisferio m.

hemp n cáñamo m.
hen n gallina f.
henchman n secuaz m.
henceforth, **henceforward** adv de aquí en adelante.
henhouse n gallinero m.
hepatitis n hepatitis f.
her pn su; ella; de ella; a ella.
herald n heraldo m.
heraldry n heráldica f.
herb n hierba f; **~s** pl hierbas fpl.
herbaceous adj herbáceo/cea.
herbalist n herbolario m.
herbivorous adj herbívoro/ra.
herd n rebaño m.
here adv aquí, acá.
hereabout(s) adv aquí alrededor.
hereafter adv en el futuro.
hereby adv por esto.
hereditary adj hereditario/ria.
heredity n herencia f.
heresy n herejía f.
heretic n hereje m/f; * adj herético/ca.
herewith adv con esto.
heritage n patrimonio m.
hermetic adj hermético/ca; ~ly adv herméticamente.
hermit n ermitaño/ña m/f.
hermitage n ermita f.
hernia n hernia f.
hero n héroe m.
heroic adj heroico/ca; ~ally adv heroicamente.
heroine n heroína f.
heroism n heroísmo m.
heron n garza f.
herring n arenque m.
hers pn suyo, de ella.
herself pn ella misma.
hesitant adj vacilante.
hesitate vt dudar; tardar.
hesitation n duda, irresolución f.

heterogeneous *adj* heterogéneo/nea.

heterosexual *adj, n* heterosexual *m*.

hew *vt* tajar; cortar; picar.

heyday *n* apogeo *m*.

hi *excl* ¡hola!

hiatus *n* (*gr*) hiato *m*.

hibernate *vi* invernar.

hiccup *n* hipo *m*; * *vi* tener hipo.

hickory *n* nogal americana *m*.

hide *vt* esconder; * *n* cuero *m*; piel *f*.

hideaway *n* escondite *m*.

hideous *adj* horrible; ~**ly** *adv* horriblemente.

hiding place *n* escondite, escondrijo *m*.

hierarchy *n* jerarquía *f*.

hieroglyphic *adj* jeroglífico/ca; * *n* jeroglífico *m*.

hi-fi *n* estéreo, hi-fi *m*.

higgledy-piggledy *adv* confusamente.

high *adj* alto/ta; elevado/da.

high altar *n* altar mayor *m*.

highchair *n* silla alta *f*.

high-handed *adj* despótico/ca.

highlands *npl* tierras montañosas, tierras altas *fpl*.

highlight *n* punto culminante *m*.

highly *adv* en sumo grado.

highness *n* altura *f*; alteza *f*.

highly strung *adj* hipertenso/sa.

high water *n* marea alta *f*.

highway *n* carretera *f*.

hike *vi* ir de excursión.

hijack *vt* secuestrar.

hijacker *n* secuestrador/a *m/f*.

hilarious *adj* alegre.

hill *n* colina *f*.

hillock *n* colina *f*.

hillside *n* ladera *f*.

hilly *adj* montañoso/sa.

hilt *n* puño de espada *m*.

him *pn* le, lo, el.

himself *pn* él mismo, se, si mismo.

hind *adj* trasero/ra, posterior; * *n* cierva *f*.

hinder *vt* impedir.

hindrance *n* impedimento, obstáculo *m*.

hindquarter *n* cuarto trasero *m*.

hindsight *n*: **with** ~ en retrospectiva.

hinge *n* bisagra *f*.

hint *n* indirecta *f*; * *vt* insinuar; sugerir.

hip *n* cadera *f*.

hippopotamus *n* hipopótamo *m*.

hire *vt* alquilar; * *n* alquiler *m*.

hire purchase *n* compra a plazos *f*.

his *pn* su, suyo, de él.

Hispanic *adj* hispano/na; hispánico/ca; * *n* hispanoamericano/na *m/f*.

hiss *vt, vi* silbar.

historian *n* historiador/a *m/f*.

historic(al) *adj* histórico/ca; ~**ally** *adv* históricamente.

history *n* historia *f*.

histrionic *adj* teatral.

hit *vt* golpear; alcanzar; zumbar; **to ~ each other** *vr* zumbarse; * *n* golpe *m*; éxito *m*.

hitch *vt* atar; * *n* problema *m*.

hitchhike *vi* hacer autoestop.

hitchhiker *n* autoestopista *m/f*.

hitchhiking *n* autoestop *f*.

hitherto *adv* hasta ahora, hasta aquí.

hive *n* colmena *f*.

HIV-negative *adj* seronegativo/va.

HIV-positive *adj* seropositivo/va.

hoard *n* montón *m*; tesoro escondido *m*; * *vt* acumular.

hoarfrost *n* escarcha *f*.

hoarse *adj* ronco/ca; ~**ly** *adv* roncamente.

hoarseness *n* ronquera, carraspera *f*.

hoax n trampa f; * vt engañar, burlar.

hobble vi cojear.

hobby n pasatiempo m, afición f.

hobbyhorse n caballo de batalla m.

hockey n hockey m.

hodgepodge n mezcolanza f.

hoe n azadón m; * vt azadonar.

hoist vt alzar; * n grúa f.

hold v tener; detener; contener; celebrar; **to ~ on to** agarrarse a; * vi valer; * n presa f; poder m.

holder n poseedor/a m/f; titular m/f.

holding n tenencia, posesión f.

hold-up n atraco m; retraso m.

hole n agujero m.

holiday n día de fiesta m; **~s** pl vacaciones fpl.

holiday-maker n turista m/f.

holiness n santidad f.

hollow adj hueco/ca; * n hoyo m; * vt excavar, ahuecar.

holly n (bot) acebo m.

hollyhock n malva hortense f.

holocaust n holocausto m.

holster n pistolera f.

holy adj santo/ta, pío, pía; consagrado/da.

holy water n agua bendita f.

holy week n semana santa f.

homage n homenaje m.

home n casa f; patria f; domicilio m; **~ly** adj casero/ra.

home address n domicilio m.

homeless adj sin casa.

homeliness n simpleza f.

homely adj casero/ra.

home-made adj casero/ra.

homeopathist n homeópata m/f.

homeopathy n homeopatía f.

home shopping programme (TV) n teletienda f.

homesick adj nostálgico/ca.

homesickness n nostalgia f.

hometown n ciudad natal f.

homeward adj hacia casa; hacia su país.

homework n deberes mpl.

homicidal adj homicida.

homicide n homicidio m; homicida m/f.

homogeneous adj homogéneo/nea.

homosexual adj, n homosexual m.

honest adj honrado/da; **~ly** adv honradamente.

honesty n honradez f.

honey n miel f.

honeycomb n panal m.

honeymoon n luna de miel f.

honeysuckle n (bot) madreselva f.

honorary adj honorario/ria.

honour n honra f; honor m; * vt honrar.

honourable adj honorable; ilustre.

honourably adv honorablemente.

hood n capo m; capucha f.

hoodlum n matón m.

hoof n pezuña f.

hook n gancho m; anzuelo m; **by ~ or by crook** de un modo u otro; * vt enganchar.

hooked adj encorvado/da.

hooligan n gamberro/rra m/f.

hoop n aro m.

hooter n sirena f.

hop n (bot) lúpulo m; salto m; * vi saltar, brincar.

hope n esperanza f; * vi esperar.

hopeful adj esperanzador/a; **~ly** adv con esperanza.

hopefulness n buena esperanza f.

hopeless adj desesperado/da; **~ly** adv sin esperanza.

hopscotch n tejo m.

horde n horda f.

horizon n horizonte m.

horizontal adj horizontal; **~ly** adv horizontalmente.
hormone n hormona f.
horn n cuerno m; (auto) sirena f.
horned adj cornudo/da.
hornet n avispón m.
horny adj calloso/sa.
horoscope n horóscopo m.
horrendous adj horrendo/da.
horrible adj horrible, terrible.
horribly adv horriblemente; enormemente.
horrid adj horrible.
horrific adj horroroso/sa.
horrify vt horrorizar.
horror n horror, terror m.
horror film n película de horror f.
hors d'oeuvre n entremeses mpl.
horse n caballo m; caballete m.
horseback adv: on ~ a caballo.
horse-breaker n domador/a de caballos m/f.
horse chestnut n castaño de Indias m.
horsefly n moscarda f; moscardón m.
horseman n jinete m.
horsemanship n equitación f.
horsepower n caballo de fuerza m.
horse race n carrera de caballos f.
horseracing n hípica f.
horseradish n rábano silvestre m.
horseshoe n herradura de caballo f.
horsewoman n jineta f.
horticulture n horticultura, jardinería f.
horticulturist n jardinero/ra m/f.
hosepipe n manguera f.
hosiery n calcetería f.
hospitable adj hospitalario/ria.
hospitably adv con hospitalidad.
hospital n hospital m.
hospitality n hospitalidad f.

host n anfitrión m; hostia f.
hostage n rehén m.
hostess n anfitriona f.
hostile adj hostil.
hostility n hostilidad f.
hot adj caliente; cálido/da.
hotbed n semillero m.
hotdog n perro caliente m.
hotel n hotel m.
hotelier n hotelero/ra m/f.
hot-headed adj exaltado/da.
hothouse n invernadero m.
hotline n línea directa f.
hotplate n hornillo m.
hotly adv con calor; violentamente.
hound n perro de caza m.
hour n hora f.
hour-glass n reloj de arena m.
hourly adv cada hora.
house n casa f; familia f; * vt alojar.
houseboat n casa flotante f.
housebreaker n ladrón/ona de casa m/f.
housebreaking n allanamiento de morada m.
household n familia f.
householder n amo de casa, padre de familia m; dueño/ña de la casa m/f.
housekeeper n ama de llaves f.
housekeeping n trabajos domésticos mpl.
house-warming party n fiesta de estreno de una casa f.
housewife n ama de casa f.
housework n faenas de la casa fpl.
housing n vivienda f.
housing development n urbanización f.
hovel n choza, cabaña f.
hover vi flotar.
how adv cómo, como; ~ **do you do!** ¡encantado!

however adv comoquiera, comoquiera que sea; aunque; no obstante.
howl vi aullar; * n aullido m.
hub n centro m.
hubbub n barullo m.
hubcap n tapacubos m invar.
hue n color m; matiz m.
huff n: in a ~ picado/da.
hug vt abrazar; * n abrazo m.
huge adj vasto/ta, enorme; **~ly** adv inmensamente.
hulk n (mar) casco m; armatoste m.
hull n (mar) casco m.
hum vi canturrear.
human adv humano/na.
humane adv humano/na; benigno/na; **~ly** adv humanamente.
humanist n humanista m/f.
humanitarian adj humanitario/ria.
humanity n humanidad f.
humanize vt humanizar.
humanly adv humanamente.
humble adj humilde, modesto/ta; * vt humillar, postrar.
humbleness n humildad f.
humbly adv con humildad.
humbug n tonterías fpl.
humdrum adj monótono/na.
humid adj húmedo/da.
humidity n humedad f.
humiliate vt humillar.
humiliation n humillación f.
humility n humildad f.
humming n zumbido m.
humming-bird n colibrí m.
humorist n humorista m/f
humorous adj gracioso/sa; **~ly** adv con gracia.
humour n sentido del humor m, humor m; jocosidad f; * vt complacer.
hump n giba, joroba f.
hunch n corazonada f; **~backed** adj jorobado/da, jiboso/sa.

hundred adj ciento; * n centenar m; un ciento.
hundredth adj centésimo.
hundredweight n quintal m.
hunger n hambre f; * vi hambrear.
hunger strike n huelga de hambre f.
hungrily adv con apetito.
hungry adj hambriento/ta.
hunt vt cazar; perseguir; buscar; * vi andar a caza; * n caza f.
hunter n cazador/a m/f.
hunting n caza f.
huntsman n cazador m.
hurdle n valla f.
hurl vt tirar con violencia; arrojar.
hurricane n huracán m.
hurried adj hecho/cha de prisa; **~ly** adv con prisa.
hurry vt acelerar, apresurar; * vi apresurarse; * n prisa f.
hurt vt hacer daño; ofender; * n mal, daño m.
hurtful adj dañoso/sa; **~ly** adv dañosamente.
hurtle vi zamparse.
husband n marido m.
husbandry n agricultura f.
hush! ¡chitón!, ¡silencio!; * vt hacer callar; * vi estar quieto/ta.
husk n cáscara f.
huskiness n ronquedad f.
husky adj ronco/ca.
hustings n tribuna para las elecciones f.
hustle vt empujar con fuerza.
hut n cabaña, barraca f.
hutch n conejera f.
hyacinth n jacinto m.
hydrant n boca de incendios f.
hydraulic adj hidráulico/ca; **~s** npl hidráulica f.
hydroelectric adj hidroeléctrico/ca.
hydrofoil n hidroala f.

hydrogen *n* hidrógeno *m*.
hydrophobia *n* hidrofobia *f*.
hyena *n* hiena *f*.
hygiene *n* higiene *f*.
hygienic *adj* higiénico/ca.
hymn *n* himno *m*.
hyperbole *n* hipérbole *f*; exageración *f*.
hypermarket *n* hipermercado *m*.
hyphen *n* (*gr*) guión *m*.
hypochondria *n* hipocondria *f*.

hypochondriac *adj*, *n* hipocondríaco/ca *m/f*.
hypocrisy *n* hipocresía *f*.
hypocrite *n* hipócrita *m/f*.
hypocritical *adj* hipócrita.
hypothesis *n* hipótesis *f*.
hypothetical *adj* hipotético/ca; ~ly *adv* hipotéticamente.
hysterical *adj* histérico/ca.
hysterics *npl* histeria *f*.

I

I *pn* yo; ~ **myself** yo mismo.
ice *n* hielo *m*; * *vt* helar.
ice-axe *n* piqueta *f*.
iceberg *n* iceberg *m*.
ice-bound *adj* rodeado/da de hielos.
icebox *n* nevera *f*.
ice cream *n* helado *m*.
ice rink *n* pista de hielo *f*.
ice skating *n* patinaje sobre hielo *m*.
icicle *n* carámbano *m*.
iconoclast *n* iconoclasta *m/f*.
icy *adj* helado/da; frío/ría.
idea *n* idea *f*.
ideal *adj* ideal; ~ly *adv* idealmente.
idealist *n* idealista *m/f*.
identical *adj* idéntico/ca.
identification *n* identificación *f*.
identify *vt* identificar.
identity *n* identidad *f*.
ideology *n* ideología *f*.
idiom *n* idioma *m*.
idiomatic *adj* idiomático/ca.
idiosyncrasy *n* idiosincrasia *f*.
idiot *n* idiota, necio/cia *m/f*.
idiotic *adj* tonto/ta, bobo/ba.
idle *adj* desocupado/da; holgazán/zana; inútil.
idleness *n* pereza *f*.

idler *n* holgazán/zana *m/f*; zángano *m*.
idly *adv* ociosamente; vanamente.
idol *n* ídolo *m*.
idolatry *n* idolatría *f*.
idolize *vt* idolatrar.
idyllic *adj* idílico/ca.
i.e. *adv* esto es.
if *conj* si, aunque; ~ **not** si no.
igloo *n* iglú *m*.
ignite *vt* encender.
ignition *n* (*chem*) ignición *f*; encendido *m*.
ignition key *n* llave de contacto *f*.
ignoble *adj* innoble; bajo/ja.
ignominious *adj* ignominioso/sa; ~ly *adv* ignominiosamente.
ignominy *n* ignominia, infamia *f*.
ignoramus *n* ignorante, tonto/ta *m/f*.
ignorance *n* ignorancia *f*.
ignorant *adj* ignorante; ~ly *adv* ignorantemente.
ignore *vt* no hacer caso de.
ill *adj* malo/la, enfermo/ma; * *n* mal, infortunio *m*; * *adv* mal.
ill-advised *adj* imprudente.
illegal *adj*, ~ly *adv* ilegal(mente).
illegality *n* ilegalidad *f*.
illegible *adj* ilegible.

illegibly adv de modo ilegible.
illegitimacy n ilegitimidad f.
illegitimate adj ilegítimo/ma; ~ly adv ilegítimamente.
ill feeling n rencor m.
illicit adj ilícito/ta.
illiterate adj analfabeto/ta.
illness n enfermedad f.
illogical adj ilógico/ca.
ill-timed adj inoportuno/na.
ill-treat vt maltratar.
illuminate vt iluminar.
illumination n iluminación f.
illusion n ilusión f.
illusory adj ilusorio/ria.
illustrate vt ilustrar; explicar.
illustration n ilustración f; elucidación f.
illustrative adj explicativo/va.
illustrious adj ilustre, insigne.
ill-will n rencor m.
image n imagen f.
imagery n imágenes fpl.
imaginable adj concebible.
imaginary adj imaginario/ria.
imagination n imaginación f.
imaginative adj imaginativo/va.
imagine vt imaginarse; idear, inventar.
imbalance n desequilibrio m.
imbecile adj imbécil, necio/cia.
imbibe vt beber.
imbue vt infundir.
imitate vt imitar, copiar.
imitation n imitación, copia f.
imitative adj imitativo/va.
immaculate adj inmaculado/da, puro/ra.
immaterial adj poco importante.
immature adj inmaduro/ra.
immeasurable adj inconmensurable.
immeasurably adv inmensamente.

immediate adj inmediato/ta; ~ly adv inmediatamente; ya.
immense adj inmenso/sa; vasto/ta; ~ly adv inmensamente.
immensity n inmensidad f.
immerse vt sumergir.
immersion n inmersión f.
immigrant n inmigrante m/f.
immigrate vi inmigrar.
immigration n inmigración f.
imminent adj inminente.
immobile adj inmóvil.
immobility n inmovilidad f.
immoderate adj inmoderado/da, excesivo/va; ~ly adv inmoderadamente.
immodest adj inmodesto/ta.
immoral adj inmoral.
immorality n inmoralidad f.
immortal adj inmortal.
immortality n inmortalidad f.
immortalize vt inmortalizar, eternizar.
immune adj inmune.
immunity n inmunidad f.
immunize vt inmunizar.
immutable adj inmutable.
imp n diablillo, duende m.
impact n impacto m.
impair vt disminuir.
impale vt empalar.
impalpable adj impalpable.
impart vt comunicar.
impartial adj, ~ly adv imparcial(mente).
impartiality n imparcialidad f.
impassable adj intransitable.
impasse n punto muerto m.
impassive adj impasible.
impatience n impaciencia f.
impatient adj, ~ly adv impaciente(mente).
impeach vt acusar, denunciar.

impeccable *adj* impecable.

impecunious *adj* indigente.

impede *vt* estorbar.

impediment *n* obstáculo *m*.

impel *vt* impeler, impulsar.

impending *adj* inminente.

impenetrable *adj* impenetrable.

impenitent *adj* impenitente.

imperative *adj* imperativo/va.

imperceptible *adj* imperceptible.

imperceptibly *adv* imperceptiblemente.

imperfect *adj* imperfecto/ta, defectuoso/sa; ~**ly** *adv* imperfectamente; * *n* (*gr*) pretérito imperfecto *m*.

imperfection *n* imperfección *f*, defecto *m*.

imperial *adj* imperial.

imperialism *n* imperialismo *m*.

imperious *adj* imperioso/sa; arrogante; ~**ly** *adv* imperiosamente, arrogantemente.

impermeable *adj* impermeable.

impersonal *adj*, ~**ly** *adv* impersonal(mente).

impersonate *vt* hacerse pasar por; imitar.

impertinence *n* impertinencia *f*; descaro *m*.

impertinent *adj* impertinente; ~**ly** *adv* impertinentemente.

imperturbable *adj* imperturbable.

impervious *adj* impermeable.

impetuosity *n* impetuosidad *f*.

impetuous *adj* impetuoso/sa; ~**ly** *adv* impetuosamente.

impetus *n* ímpetu *m*.

impiety *n* impiedad *f*.

impinge (on) *vt* tener influjo en.

impious *adj* impío/pía, irreligioso/sa.

implacable *adj* implacable.

implacably *adv* implacablemente.

implant *vt* implantar; plantear.

implement *n* herramienta *f*; utensilio *m*.

implicate *vt* implicar.

implication *n* implicación *f*.

implicit *adj* implícito/ta; ~**ly** *adv* implícitamente.

implore *vt* suplicar.

imply *vt* suponer.

impolite *adj* maleducado/da.

impoliteness *n* falta de educación *f*.

impolitic *adj* imprudente; impolítico/ca.

import *vt* importar; * *n* importación *f*.

importance *n* importancia *f*.

important *adj* importante.

importation *n* importación *f*.

importer *n* importador/a *m*/*f*.

importunate *adj* importuno/na.

importune *vt* importunar.

importunity *n* importunidad *f*.

impose *vt* imponer.

imposing *adj* imponente.

imposition *n* imposición, carga *f*.

impossibility *n* imposibilidad *f*.

impossible *adj* imposible.

impostor *n* impostor *m*.

impotence *n* impotencia *f*.

impotent *adj* impotente; ~**ly** *adv* sin poder.

impound *vt* embargar.

impoverish *vt* empobrecer.

impoverished *adj* necesitado/da.

impoverishment *n* empobrecimiento *m*.

impracticability *n* inviabilidad *f*.

impracticable *adj* impracticable, inviable.

impractical *adj* poco práctico/ca.

imprecation *n* imprecación, maldición *f*.

imprecise *adj* impreciso/sa.

impregnable *adj* inexpugnable.

impregnate *vt* impregnar.

impregnation n fecundación f; impregnación f.
impress vt impresionar.
impression n impresión f; edición f.
impressionable adj impresionable.
impressive adj impresionante.
imprint n sello m; * vt imprimir; estampar.
imprison vt encarcelar.
imprisonment n encarcelamiento m.
improbability n improbabilidad f.
improbable adj improbable.
impromptu adj de improviso.
improper adj impropio/pia, indecente; ~ly adv impropiamente.
impropriety n impropiedad f.
improve vt, vi mejorar.
improvement n progreso m, mejora f.
improvident adj impróvido/da, imprudente.
improvise vt improvisar.
imprudence n imprudencia f.
imprudent adj imprudente.
impudence n impudencia f.
impudent adj impudente; ~ly adv desvergonzadamente.
impugn vt impugnar.
impulse n impulso m.
impulsive adj impulsivo/va.
impunity n impunidad f.
impure adj impuro/ra; ~ly adv impuramente.
impurity n impureza f.
in prep en.
inability n incapacidad f.
inaccessible adj inaccesible.
inaccuracy n inexactitud f.
inaccurate adj inexacto/ta.
inaction n inacción f.
inactive adj inactivo/va, perezoso/sa.
inactivity n inactividad f.
inadequate adj inadecuado/da, defectuoso/sa.

inadmissible adj inadmisible.
inadvertently adv sin querer.
inalienable adj inalienable.
inane adj necio/cia.
inanimate adj inanimado/da.
inapplicable adj inaplicable.
inappropriate adj impropio/pia.
inasmuch adv visto que; en tanto en cuanto.
inattentive adj desatento/ta.
inaudible adj inaudible.
inaugural adj inaugural.
inaugurate vt inaugurar.
inauguration n inauguración f.
inauspicious adj poco propicio/cia.
in-between adj intermedio/dia.
inborn, inbred adj innato/ta.
incalculable adj incalculable.
incandescent adj incandescente.
incantation n conjuro m.
incapable adj incapaz.
incapacitate vt inhabilitar.
incapacity n incapacidad f.
incarcerate vt encarcelar.
incarnate adj encarnado/da.
incarnation n encarnación f.
incautious adj incauto/ta; ~ly adv incautamente.
incendiary n bomba incendiaria f.
incense n incienso m; * vt exasperar.
incentive n incentivo m.
inception n principio m.
incessant adj incesante, constante; ~ly adv continuamente.
incest n incesto m.
incestuous adj incestuoso/sa.
inch n pulgada f; ~ **by** ~ palmo a palmo.
incidence n frecuencia f.
incident n incidente m.
incidental adj casual; ~ly adv a propósito.
incinerator n incinerador m.

incipient *adj* incipiente.

incise *vt* tajar, cortar.

incision *n* incisión *f*.

incisive *adj* incisivo/va.

incisor *n* incisivo *m*.

incite *vt* incitar, estimular.

inclement *adj* feo, fea.

inclination *n* inclinación, propensión *f*.

incline *vt* (*vi*) inclinar(se); * *n* cuesta *f*.

include *vt* incluir, comprender.

including *prep* incluso.

inclusion *n* inclusión *f*.

inclusive *adj* inclusivo/va.

incognito *adv* de incógnito.

incoherence *n* incoherencia *f*.

incoherent *adj* incoherente, inconsecuente; ~**ly** *adv* de modo incoherente.

income *n* renta *f*; ingresos *mpl*.

income tax *n* impuesto sobre la renta *m*.

incoming *adj* entrante.

incomparable *adj* incomparable.

incomparably *adv* incomparablemente.

incompatibility *n* incompatibilidad *f*.

incompatible *adj* incompatible.

incompetence *n* incompetencia *f*.

incompetent *adj*, ~**ly** *adv* incompetente(mente).

incomplete *adj* incompleto/ta.

incomprehensibility *n* incomprensibilidad *f*.

incomprehensible *adj* incomprensible.

inconceivable *adj* inconcebible.

inconclusive *adj* no concluyente; * *adv* sin conclusión.

incongruity *n* incongruencia *f*.

incongruous *adj* incongruo/rua; ~**ly** *adv* incongruamente.

inconsequential *adj* inconsecuente.

inconsiderate *adj* desconsiderado/da; ~**ly** *adv* desconsideradamente.

inconsistency *n* inconsecuencia *f*.

inconsistent *adj* inconsecuente.

inconsolable *adj* inconsolable.

inconspicuous *adj* discreto/ta.

incontinence *n* incontinencia *f*.

incontinent *adj* incontinente.

incontrovertible *adj* incontrovertible.

inconvenience *n* incomodidad *f*; * *vt* incomodar.

inconvenient *adj* incómodo/da; ~**ly** *adv* incómodamente.

incorporate *vt* (*vi*) incorporar(se).

incorporated company (inc) *n* sociedad anónima *f*.

incorporation *n* incorporación *f*.

incorrect *adj* incorrecto/ta; ~**ly** *adv* incorrectamente.

incorrigible *adj* incorregible.

incorruptibility *n* incorruptibilidad *f*.

incorruptible *adj* incorruptible.

increase *vt* acrecentar, aumentar; * *vi* crecer; * *n* aumento *m*.

increasing *adj* creciente; ~**ly** *adv* cada vez más.

incredible *adj* increíble.

incredulity *n* incredulidad *f*.

incredulous *adj* incrédulo/la.

increment *n* incremento *m*.

incriminate *vt* incriminar.

incrust *vt* incrustar.

incubate *vi* incubar.

incubator *n* incubadora *f*.

inculcate *vt* inculcar.

incumbent *adj* obligatorio/ria; * *n* beneficiado/da *m/f*.

incur *vt* incurrir.

incurability *n* lo incurable.

incurable *adj* incurable.

incursion *n* incursión, invasión *f*.

indebted *adj* agradecido/da.

indecency n indecencia f.
indecent adj indecente; ~**ly** adv indecentemente.
indecision n irresolución f.
indecisive adj indeciso/sa.
indecorous adj indecente.
indeed adv verdaderamente, de veras.
indefatigable adj incansable.
indefinite adj indefinido/da; ~**ly** adv indefinidamente.
indelible adj indeleble.
indelicacy n falta de delicadeza, grosería f.
indelicate adj poco delicado/da.
indemnify vt indemnizar.
indemnity n indemnidad f.
indent vt mellar.
independence n independencia f.
independent adj independiente; ~**ly** adv independientemente.
indescribable adj indescriptible.
indestructible adj indestructible.
indeterminate adj indeterminado/da.
index n índice m.
index card n ficha f.
indexed adj indexado/da.
index finger n dedo índice m.
indicate vt indicar.
indication n indicación f; indicio m.
indicative adj, n (gr) indicativo m.
indicator n indicador m.
indict vt acusar.
indictment n acusación f.
indifference n indiferencia f.
indifferent adj indiferente; ~**ly** adv indiferentemente.
indigenous adj indígena.
indigent adj indigente.
indigestible adj indigerible.
indigestion n indigestión f.
indignant adj indignado/da.
indignation n indignación f.

indignity n indignidad f.
indigo n añil m.
indirect adj indirecto/ta; ~**ly** adv indirectamente.
indiscreet adj indiscreto/ta; ~**ly** adv indiscretamente.
indiscretion n indiscreción f.
indiscriminate adj indistinto/ta; ~**ly** adv sin distinción.
indispensable adj indispensable.
indisposed adj indispuesto/ta.
indisposition n indisposición f.
indisputable adj indiscutible.
indisputably adv indisputablemente.
indistinct adj indistinto/ta, confuso/sa; ~**ly** adv indistintamente.
indistinguishable adj indistinguible.
individual adj individual; ~**ly** adv individualmente; * n individuo m.
individuality n individualidad f.
indivisible adj indivisible; ~**bly** adv indivisiblemente.
indoctrinate vt adoctrinar.
indoctrination n adoctrinamiento m.
indolence n indolencia, pereza f.
indolent adj indolente; ~**ly** adv con negligencia.
indomitable adj indomable.
indoors adv dentro.
indubitably adv indudablemente.
induce vt inducir, persuadir; causar.
inducement n aliciente m.
induction n inducción f.
indulge vt, vi conceder; ser indulgente.
indulgence n indulgencia f.
indulgent adj indulgente; ~**ly** adv de modo indulgente.
industrial adj industrial.
industrialist n industrial m/f.
industrialization n industrialización f.
industrialize vt industrializar.

industrial park n polígono industrial m.

industrious adj trabajador/a.

industry n industria f.

inebriated adj embriagado/da.

inebriation n embriaguez f.

inedible adj incomestible.

ineffable adj inefable.

ineffective, ineffectual adj ineficaz; ~**ly** adv sin efecto.

inefficiency n ineficacia f.

inefficient adj ineficaz.

ineligible adj inelegible.

inept adj incompetente.

ineptitude n incompetencia f.

inequality n desigualdad f.

inert adj inerte, perezoso/sa.

inertia n inercia f.

inescapable adj ineludible.

inestimable adj inestimable, inapreciable.

inevitable adj inevitable.

inevitably adv inevitablemente.

inexcusable adj inexcusable.

inexhaustible adj inagotable.

inexorable adj inexorable.

inexpedient adj imprudente.

inexpensive adj económico/ca.

inexperience n inexperiencia f.

inexperienced adj inexperto/ta.

inexpert adj inexperto/ta.

inexplicable adj inexplicable.

inexpressible adj indecible.

inextricably adv indisolublemente.

infallibility n infalibilidad f.

infallible adj infalible; indefectible.

infamous adj vil, infame; ~**ly** adv infamemente.

infamy n infamia f.

infancy n infancia f; pequeñez f.

infant n niño/ña m/f.

infanticide n infanticidio m; infanticida m/f.

infantile adj infantil.

infantry n infantería f.

infatuated adj chiflado/da.

infatuation n infatuación f.

infect vt infectar.

infection n infección f.

infectious adj contagioso/sa; infeccioso/sa.

infer vt inferir.

inference n inferencia f.

inferior adj inferior; * n subordinado/da m/f.

inferiority n inferioridad f.

infernal adj infernal.

inferno n infierno m.

infest vt infestar.

infidel n infiel, pagano m.

infidelity n infidelidad f.

infiltrate vi infiltrarse.

infinite adj infinito/ta; ~**ly** adv infinitamente.

infinitive n infinitivo m.

infinity n infinito m; infinidad f.

infirm adj enfermo/ma, débil.

infirmary n enfermería f.

infirmity n fragilidad, enfermedad f.

inflame vt (vi) inflamar(se).

inflammation n inflamación f.

inflammatory adj inflamatorio/ria.

inflatable adj inflable.

inflate vt inflar, hinchar.

inflation n inflación f.

inflection n inflexión f; modulación de la voz f.

inflexibility n inflexibilidad f.

inflexible adj inflexible; yerto/ta.

inflexibly adv inflexiblemente.

inflict vt imponer.

influence n influencia f; * vt influir.

influential adj influyente.

influenza n gripe f.

influx n afluencia f.

inform vt informar.

informal adj informal.
informality n informalidad f.
informant n informante m/f.
information n información f; ~ **super highway** autopista de la información f.
infraction n infracción f.
infra-red adj infrarrojo/ja.
infrastructure n infraestructura f.
infrequent adj raro/ra; **~ly** adv raramente.
infringe vt infringir; violar.
infringement n infracción f.
infuriate vt enfurecer.
infuse vt infundir.
infusion n infusión f.
ingenious adj ingenioso/sa; **~ly** adv ingeniosamente.
ingenuity n ingeniosidad f.
ingenuous adj ingenuo/nua, sincero/ra; **~ly** adv ingenuamente.
inglorious adj ignominioso/sa, vergonzoso/sa; **~ly** adv ignominiosamente.
ingot n lingote m.
ingrained adj inveterado/da.
ingratiate vi congraciarse.
ingratitude n ingratitud f.
ingredient n ingrediente m.
inhabit vt, vi habitar.
inhabitable adj habitable.
inhabitant n habitante m/f.
inhale vt inhalar.
inherent adj inherente.
inherit vt heredar.
inheritance n herencia f.
inheritor n heredero/ra m/f.
inhibit vt inhibir.
inhibited adj cohibido/da.
inhibition n inhibición f.
inhospitable adj inhospitalario/ria.
inhospitality n inhospitalidad f.
inhuman adj inhumano/na, cruel; **~ly** adv inhumanamente.

inhumanity n inhumanidad, crueldad f.
inimical adj enemigo/ga.
inimitable adj inimitable.
iniquitous adj inicuo/cua, injusto/ta.
iniquity n iniquidad, injusticia f.
initial adj inicial; * n inicial f.
initially adv al principio.
initiate vt iniciar.
initiation n principio m; iniciación f.
initiative n iniciativa f.
inject vt inyectar.
injection n inyección f.
injudicious adj poco juicioso/sa.
injunction n entredicho m.
injure vt herir.
injury n daño m.
injury time n descuento m.
injustice n injusticia f.
ink n tinta f.
inkling n sospecha f.
inkstand n tintero m.
inlaid adj taraceado/da.
inland adj interior; * adv tierra adentro.
in-laws npl suegros mpl.
inlay vt taracear.
inlet n ensenada f.
inmate n preso m.
inmost adj más íntimo/ma.
inn n posada f; mesón m.
innate adj innato/ta.
inner adj interior.
innermost adj más íntimo/ma.
inner tube n cámara f.
innkeeper n posadero/ra, mesonero/ra m/f.
innocence n inocencia f.
innocent adj inocente; **~ly** adv inocentemente.
innocuous adj inocuo/cua; **~ly** adv inocentemente.

innovate *vt* innovar.

innovation *n* innovación *f*.

innuendo *n* indirecta, insinuación *f*.

innumerable *adj* innumerable.

inoculate *vt* inocular.

inoculation *n* inoculación *f*.

inoffensive *adj* inofensivo/va.

inopportune *adj* inconveniente, inoportuno/na.

inordinately *adv* desmesuradamente.

inorganic *adj* inorgánico/ca.

inpatient *n* paciente interno/na *m/f*.

input *n* entrada *f*.

inquest *n* encuesta judicial *f*.

inquire *vt, vi* preguntar; to ~ about informarse de; to ~ after *vt* preguntar por; to ~ into *vt* investigar, indagar, inquirir.

inquiry *n* pesquisa *f*.

inquisition *n* inquisición *f*.

inquisitive *adj* curioso/sa.

inroad *n* incursión, invasión *f*.

insane *adj* loco/ca, demente.

insanity *n* locura *f*.

insatiable *adj* insaciable.

inscribe *vt* inscribir; dedicar.

inscription *n* inscripción *f*; dedicatoria *f*.

inscrutable *adj* inescrutable.

insect *n* insecto *m*.

insecticide *n* insecticida *m*.

insecure *adj* inseguro/ra.

insecurity *n* inseguridad *f*.

insemination *n* inseminación *f*.

insensible *adj* inconsciente.

insensitive *adj* insensible.

inseparable *adj* inseparable.

insert *vt* introducir.

insertion *n* inserción *f*.

inshore *adj* costero/ra.

inside *n* interior *m*; * *adv* dentro.

inside out *adv* al revés; a fondo.

insidious *adj* insidioso/sa; ~ly *adv* insidiosamente.

insight *n* perspicacia *f*.

insignia *npl* insignias *fpl*.

insignificant *adj* insignificante, frívolo/la.

insincere *adj* poco sincero/ra.

insincerity *n* falta de sinceridad *f*.

insinuate *vt* insinuar.

insinuation *n* insinuación *f*.

insipid *adj* insípido/da; insulso/sa; ñoño/ña.

insipidness *n* ñoñería *f*.

insist *vi* insistir.

insistence *n* insistencia *f*.

insistent *adj* insistente.

insole *n* plantilla *f*.

insolence *n* insolencia *f*.

insolent *adj* insolente; ~ly *adv* insolentemente.

insoluble *adj* insoluble.

insolvency *n* insolvencia *f*.

insolvent *adj* insolvente.

insomnia *n* insomnio *m*.

insomuch *conj* puesto que.

inspect *vt* examinar, inspeccionar.

inspection *n* inspección *f*.

inspector *n* inspector, superintendente *m*.

inspiration *n* inspiración *f*.

inspire *vt* inspirar.

instability *n* inestabilidad *f*.

install, instal *vt* instalar.

installation *n* instalación *f*.

instalment *n* instalación *f*; plazo *m*.

instance *n* ejemplo *m*; for ~ por ejemplo.

instant *adj* inmediato/ta; ~ly *adv* en seguida; * *n* instante, momento *m*.

instantaneous *adj* instantáneo/nea; ~ly *adv* instantáneamente.

instead (of) *prep* por, en lugar de, en vez de.

instep n empeine m.

instigate vt instigar.

instigation n instigación f.

instil vt inculcar.

instinct n instinto m.

instinctive adj instintivo/va; ~ly adv por instinto.

institute vt establecer; * n instituto m.

institution n institución f.

instruct vt instruir, enseñar; illustrar.

instruction n instrucción f.

instructive adj instructivo/va.

instructor n instructor/a m/f.

instrument n instrumento m.

instrumental adj instrumental.

insubordinate adj insubordinado/da.

insubordination n insubordinación f.

insufferable adj insoportable.

insufferably adv de modo insoportable.

insufficiency n insuficiencia f.

insufficient adj insuficiente; ~ly adv insuficientemente.

insular adj insular.

insulate vt aislar.

insulating tape n cinta aislante f.

insulation n aislamiento m.

insulin n insulina f.

insult vt insultar; * n insulto m.

insulting adj insultante.

insuperable adj insuperable.

insurance n (com) seguro m.

insurance policy n póliza de seguros f.

insure vt asegurar.

insurgent n insurgente, rebelde m.

insurmountable adj insuperable.

insurrection n insurrección f.

intact adj intacto/ta.

intake n admisión f; entrada f.

integral adj íntegro/gra; (chem) integrante; * n todo m.

integrate vt integrar.

integration n integración f.

integrity n integridad f.

intellect n intelecto m.

intellectual adj intelectual.

intelligence n inteligencia f.

intelligent adj inteligente.

intelligentsia n intelectualidad f.

intelligible adj inteligible.

intelligibly adv inteligiblemente.

intemperate adj inmoderado/da; ~ly adv inmoderadamente.

intend vi tener intención de.

intendant n intendente m.

intended adj deseado/da.

intense adj intenso/sa, hondo/da; ~ly adv intensamente.

intensify vt intensificar.

intensity n intensidad f.

intensive adj intensivo/va.

intensive care unit n unidad de vigilancia intensiva, unidad de cuidados intensivos f.

intent adj atento/ta, cuidadoso/sa; ~ly adv con aplicación; * n designio m.

intention n intención f; designio m.

intentional adj intencional; ~ly adv a propósito.

inter vt enterrar.

interaction n interacción f.

intercede vi interceder.

intercept vt interceptar.

intercession n intercesión, mediación f.

interchange n intercambio m.

intercom n interfono m.

intercourse n coito m.

interest vt interesar; * n interés m.

interesting adj interesante.

interest rate n tipo de interés m.

interface n interfaz, interface f.

interfere vi entrometerse.

interference *n* interferencia *f.*
interim *adj* provisional.
interior *adj* interior.
interior design *n* interiorismo *m.*
interior designer *n* interiorista *m/f.*
interjection *n* (*gr*) interjección *f.*
interlock *vi* endentarse.
interlocutor *n* interlocutor/a *m/f.*
interloper *n* intruso/sa *m/f.*
interlude *n* intermedio *m.*
intermarriage *n* matrimonio mixto *m.*
intermediary *n* intermediario/ria *m/f.*
intermediate *adj* intermedio/dia.
interment *n* entierro *m;* sepultura *f.*
interminable *adj* inacabable.
intermingle *vt, vi* entremezclar; mezclarse.
intermission *n* descanso *m.*
intermittent *adj* intermitente.
intern *n* interno *m.*
internal *adj* interno/na; ~ly *adv* internamente.
international *adj* internacional.
Internet café *n* cibercafé *m.*
interplay *n* interacción *f.*
interpose *vt* interponer.
interpret *vt* interpretar.
interpretation *n* interpretación *f.*
interpreter *n* intérprete *m/f.*
interracial *adj* interracial.
interregnum *n* interregno *m.*
interrelated *adj* interrelacionado/da.
interrogate *vt* interrogar.
interrogation *n* interrogatorio *m.*
interrogative *adj* interrogativo/va.
interrupt *vt* interrumpir.
interruption *n* interrupción *f.*
intersect *vi* cruzarse.
intersection *n* cruce *m.*
intersperse *vt* esparcir.
intertwine *vt* entretejer.
interval *n* intervalo *m.*
intervene *vi* intervenir; ocurrir.

intervention *n* intervención *f.*
interview *n* entrevista *f;* * *vt* entrevistar.
interviewer *n* entrevistador/a *m/f.*
interweave *vt* entretejer.
intestate *adj* intestado/da.
intestinal *adj* intestinal.
intestine *n* intestino *m.*
intimacy *n* intimidad *f.*
intimate *n* amigo/ga íntimo/ma *m/f;* * *adj* íntimo/ma; ~ly *adv* íntimamente; * *vt* insinuar, dar a entender.
intimidate *vt* intimidar.
into *prep* en, dentro, adentro.
intolerable *adj* intolerable.
intolerably *adv* intolerablemente.
intolerance *n* intolerancia *f.*
intolerant *adj* intolerante.
intonation *n* entonación *f.*
intoxicate *vt* embriagar.
intoxication *n* embriaguez *f.*
intractable *adj* intratable.
intransitive *adj* (*gr*) intransitivo/va.
intravenous *adj* intravenoso/sa.
in-tray *n* bandeja de entrada *f.*
intrepid *adj* intrépido/da; ~ly *adv* intrépidamente.
intrepidity *n* intrepidez *f.*
intricacy *n* complejidad *f.*
intricate *adj* intrincado/da, complicado/da; ~ly *adv* intrincadamente.
intrigue *n* intriga *f;* * *vi* intrigar.
intriguing *adj* fascinante.
intrinsic *adj* intrínseco/ca; ~ally *adv* intrínsecamente.
introduce *vt* introducir.
introduction *n* introducción *f.*
introductory *adj* introductorio/ria.
introspection *n* introspección *f.*
introvert *n* introvertido/da *m/f.*
intrude *vi* entrometerse.
intruder *n* intruso/sa *m/f.*
intrusion *n* invasión *f.*

intuition n intuición f.
intuitive adj intuitivo/va.
inundate vt inundar.
inundation n inundación f.
inure vt acostumbrar, habituar.
invade vt invadir.
invader n invasor/a m/f.
invalid adj inválido/da, nulo/la; * n minusválido m.
invalidate vt invalidar, anular.
invaluable adj inapreciable.
invariable adj invariable.
invariably adv invariablemente.
invasion n invasión f.
invective n invectiva f.
inveigle vt seducir, persuadir.
invent vt inventar.
invention n invento m.
inventive adj inventivo/va.
inventor n inventor m.
inventory n inventario m.
inverse adj inverso/sa.
inversion n inversión f.
invert vt invertir.
invest vt invertir.
investigate vt investigar.
investigation n investigación, pesquisa f.
investigator n investigador/a m/f.
investment n inversión f.
inveterate adj inveterado/da.
invidious adj odioso/sa.
invigilate vt vigilar.
invigorating adj vigorizante.
invincible adj invencible.
invincibly adv invenciblemente.
inviolable adj inviolable.
invisible adj invisible.
invisibly adv invisiblemente.
invitation n invitación f.
invite vt invitar.
inviting adj atractivo/va.
invoice n (com) factura f.

invoke vt invocar.
involuntarily adv involuntariamente.
involuntary adj involuntario/ria.
involve vt implicar.
involved adj complicado/da.
involvement n compromiso m.
invulnerable adj invulnerable.
inward adj interior; interno/na; ~, ~s adv hacia dentro.
iodine n (chem) yodo m.
IOU (I owe you) n pagaré m.
irascible adj irascible.
irate, ireful adj enojado/da.
iris n iris m.
irksome adj fastidioso/sa.
iron n hierro m, plancha f; * adj férreo/rea; * vt planchar.
ironic adj irónico/ca; ~ly adv con ironía.
ironing n planchado m.
ironing board n tabla de planchar f.
iron ore n mineral de hierro m.
ironwork n herraje m; ~s pl herrería f.
irony n ironía f.
irradiate vt irradiar.
irrational adj irracional.
irreconcilable adj irreconciliable.
irregular adj, ~ly adv irregular(mente).
irregularity n irregularidad f.
irrelevant adj impertinente.
irreligious adj irreligioso/sa.
irreparable adj irreparable.
irreplaceable adj irreemplazable.
irrepressible adj incontenible.
irreproachable adj irreprensible.
irresistible adj irresistible.
irresolute adj irresoluto/ta; ~ly adv irresolutamente.
irresponsible adj irresponsable.
irretrievably adv irreparablemente.
irreverence n irreverencia f.

irreverent adj irreverente; **~ly** adv irreverentemente.
irrigate vt regar.
irrigation n riego m.
irritability n irritabilidad f.
irritable adj irritable.
irritant n (med) irritante m.
irritate vt irritar.
irritating adj fastidioso/sa.
irritation n fastidio m; picazón f.
Islam n islam m.
Islamic adj islámico/ca.
island n isla f.
islander n isleño/ña m/f.
isle n isla f.
isolate vt aislar.

isolation n aislamiento m.
issue n asunto m; * vt expedir; publicar; repartir.
isthmus n istmo m.
it pn él, ella, ello, lo, la, le.
italic n cursiva f.
itch n picazón f; * vi picar.
item n artículo m.
itemize vt detallar.
itinerant n ambulante, errante m.
itinerary n itinerario m.
its pn su, suyo.
itself pn se, por sí mismo.
ivory n marfil m.
ivy n hiedra f; yedra f.

J

jab vt clavar.
jabber vi farfullar.
jack n gato m; sota f.
jackal n chacal m.
jackboots npl botas militares fpl.
jackdaw n grajo m.
jacket n chaqueta; funda f.
jack-knife vi colear.
jackpot n premio gordo m.
jacuzzi n jacuzzi m.
jade n jade m.
jagged adj dentado/da.
jaguar n jaguar m.
jail, gaol n cárcel f.
jailbird n preso/sa m/f.
jailer n carcelero/ra m/f.
jam n conserva f; mermelada de frutas f; (auto) embotellamiento m.
jangle vi sonar.
January n enero m.
jar vi chocar; (mus) discordar; reñir; * n jarra f.
jargon n jerigonza f.

jasmine n jazmín m.
jaundice n ictericia f.
jaunt n excursión f.
jaunty adj alegre.
javelin n jabalina f.
jaw n mandíbula f.
jay n arrendajo m.
jazz n jazz m.
jealous adj celoso/sa; envidioso/sa.
jealousy n celos mpl; envidia f.
jeans npl vaqueros mpl.
Jeep® n jeep m.
jeer vi befar, mofar; * n burla f.
jelly n jalea, gelatina f.
jellyfish n medusa f, aguamar m.
jeopardize vt arriesgar, poner en riesgo.
jerk n sacudida f; * vt tirar.
jerky adj espasmódico/ca.
jersey n jersey m.
jest n broma f.
jester n bufón/ona m/f.
jestingly adv de burlas.

Jesuit n jesuita m.
Jesus n Jesús m.
jet n avión a reacción m; azabache m.
jet engine n motor a reacción m, reactor m.
jettison vt desechar.
jetty n muelle m.
Jew n judío/día m/f.
jewel n joya f.
jeweller n joyero/ra m/f.
jeweller's shop n joyería f.
jewellery n joyería f.
Jewish adj judío/día.
jib n (mar) foque m.
jibe n mofa f.
jig n giga f.
jigsaw n rompecabezas m invar.
jilt vt dejar.
jinx n gafe m.
job n trabajo m.
jockey n jinete m/f.
jocular adj jocoso/sa, alegre.
jocularity n jocosidad f.
jog vi hacer footing.
jogging n footing m.
join vt juntar, unir; (fig) zurcir; **to ~ in** participar en; * vi unirse, juntarse.
joiner n carpintero/ra m/f.
joinery n carpintería f.
joint n articulación f; * adj común.
jointly adv conjuntamente.
joint-stock company n (com) sociedad por acciones f.
joke n broma f; * vi bromear.
joker n comodín m.
jollity n alegría f.
jolly adj alegre.
jolt vt sacudir; * n sacudida f.
jostle vt codear.
journal n revista f.
journalism n periodismo m.
journalist n periodista m/f.
journey n viaje m; * vt viajar.

jovial adj jovial, alegre; **~ly** adv con jovialidad.
joy n alegría f; júbilo m.
joyful, joyous adj alegre, gozoso/sa; **~ly** adv alegremente.
joystick n palanca de control f, joystick m.
jubilant adj jubiloso/sa.
jubilation n júbilo/la, regocijo m.
jubilee n jubileo m.
Judaism n judaísmo m.
judge n juez/a m/f; * vt juzgar.
judgement n juicio m.
judicial adj, **~ly** adv judicial(mente).
judiciary n poder judicial m, judicatura f.
judicious adj prudente.
judo n judo m.
jug n jarro m.
juggle vi hacer juegos malabares.
juggler n malabarista m/f.
jugular adj yugular.
juice n zumo, jugo m.
juicy adj jugoso/sa.
jukebox n gramola f.
July n julio m.
jumble vt mezclar; * n revoltijo m.
jump vi saltar, brincar; * n salto m.
jumper n suéter, jersey m.
jumpy adj nervioso/sa.
juncture n coyuntura f.
June n junio m.
jungle n selva f.
junior adj más joven.
juniper n (bot) enebro m.
junk n basura f; baratijas fpl.
junk food n comida basura f.
junta n junta f.
jurisdiction n jurisdicción f.
jurisprudence n jurisprudencia f.
jurist n jurista m/f.
juror, juryman n jurado/da m/f.
jury n jurado m.

just *adj* justo/ta; * *adv* justamente, exactamente; ~ **as** como; ~ **now** ahora mismo.
justice *n* justicia *f*.
justifiably *adv* con justificación.
justification *n* justificación *f*.
justify *vt* justificar.

justly *adv* justamente.
justness *n* justicia *f*.
jut *vi*; **to ~ out** sobresalir.
jute *n* yute *m*.
juvenile *adj* juvenil.
juxtapose *vt* yuxtaponer.
juxtaposition *n* yuxtaposición *f*.

K

kaleidoscope *n* caleidoscopio *m*.
kangaroo *n* canguro *m*.
karaoke *n* karaoke *m*.
karate *n* kárate *m*.
kebab *n* pincho *m* moruno.
keel *n* (*mar*) quilla *f*.
keen *adj* agudo/da; vivo/va.
keenness *n* entusiasmo *m*.
keep *vt* mantener; guardar; conservar.
keeper *n* guardián/ana *m/f*.
keepsake *n* recuerdo *m*.
keg *n* barril *m*.
kennel *n* perrera *f*.
kernel *n* fruta *f*; meollo *m*.
ketchup *n* catsup, ketchup *m*.
kettle *n* hervidor *m*.
kettle-drum *n* timbal *m*.
key *n* llave *f*; (*mus*) clave *f*; tecla *f*.
keyboard *n* teclado *m*.
keyhole *n* ojo de la cerradura *m*.
keynote *n* (*mus*) tónica *f*.
key ring *n* llavero *m*.
keystone *n* piedra clave *f*.
khaki *n* caqui *m*.
kick *vt, vi* patear; * *n* puntapié *m*; patada *f*.
kid *n* chico/ca *m/f*.
kidnap *vt* secuestrar.
kidnapper *n* secuestrador/a *m/f*.
kidnapping *n* secuestro *m*; rapto *m*.
kidney *n* riñón *m*.
killer *n* asesino/na *m/f*.

killing *n* asesinato *m*.
kiln *n* horno *m*.
kilo *n* kilo *m*.
kilobyte *n* kilobyte *m*.
kilogram *n* kilo *m*.
kilometre *n* kilómetro *m*.
kilt *n* falda escocesa *f*.
kin *n* parientes *mpl*; **next of** ~ pariente próximo *m*, pariente próxima *f*.
kind *adj* cariñoso/sa; * *n* género *m*.
kindergarten *n* jardín de infancia *m*.
kind-hearted *adj* bondadoso/sa.
kindle *vt, vi* encender.
kindliness *n* benevolencia *f*.
kindly *adj* bondadoso/sa.
kindness *n* bondad *f*.
kindred *adj* emparentado/da.
kinetic *adj* cinético/ca.
king *n* rey *m*.
kingdom *n* reino *m*.
kingfisher *n* martín pescador *m*.
king prawn *n* langostino *m*.
kiosk *n* quiosco *m*.
kiss *n* beso *m*; * *vt* besar.
kissing *n* besos *mpl*.
kit *n* equipo *m*.
kitchen *n* cocina *f*.
kitchen garden *n* huerta *f*.
kitchen maid *n* fregona *f*.
kite *n* cometa *f*.
kitten *n* gatito *m*.
knack *n* don *m*.

knapsack n mochila f.
knave n bribón, pícaro m; (cards) sota f.
knead vt amasar.
knee n rodilla f.
knee-deep adj metido hasta las rodillas.
kneel vi arrodillarse.
knell n toque de difuntos m.
knife n cuchillo m.
knight n caballero m.
knit vt, vi tejer, tricotar; **to ~ the brows** fruncir el ceño.
knitter n calcetero/ra, mediero/ra m/f.
knitting needle n aguja de tejer f.
knitwear n prendas de punto fpl.
knob n bulto m; nudo en la madera m; botón de las flores m.

knock vt, vi golpear, tocar; **to ~ down** derribar; * n golpe m.
knocker n aldaba f.
knock-kneed adj patizambo/ba; zambo/ba.
knock-out n K.O. m.
knoll n cima de una colina f.
knot n nudo m; lazo m; * vt anudar.
knotty adj escabroso/sa.
know vt, vi conocer; saber.
know-all n sabelotodo m/f.
know-how n conocimientos mpl.
knowing adj entendido/da; **~ly** adv a sabiendas.
knowledge n conocimiento m.
knowledgeable adj bien informado/da.
knuckle n nudillo m.

L

laboratory n laboratorio m.
laborious adj laborioso/sa; difícil; **~ly** adv laboriosamente.
labour n trabajo m; **to be in ~** estar de parto; * vt trabajar.
labourer n peón m.
labyrinth n laberinto m.
lace n cordón; encaje m; * vt abrochar.
lacerate vt lacerar.
lack vt, vi faltar; * n falta f.
lackadaisical adj descuidado/da.
lackey n lacayo m.
laconic adj lacónico/ca.
lacquer n laca f.
lad n muchacho m.
ladder n escalera f.
ladle n cucharón m.
ladleful n cucharada f.
lady n señora f.

ladybird n mariquita f.
lady-killer n casanova m.
ladylike adj fino/na.
ladyship n señoría f.
lag vi quedarse atrás.
lager n cerveza (rubia) f.
lagoon n laguna f.
laid-back adj relajado/da.
lair n guarida f.
laity n laicado m.
lake n lago m; laguna f.
lamb n cordero m; * vi parir.
lame adj cojo/ja.
lament vt (vi) lamentar(se); * n lamento m.
lamentable adj lamentable, deplorable.
lamentation n lamentación f.
laminated adj laminado/da; plastificado/da.

lamp n lámpara f.

lampoon n sátira f.

lampshade n pantalla f.

lance n lanza f; * vt abrir con lanceta.

lancet n lanceta f.

land n país m; tierra f; * vt, vi desembarcar.

land forces npl tropas de tierra fpl.

land-holder n hacendado m.

landing n desembarco m.

landing strip n pista de aterrizaje f.

landlady n propietaria f.

landlord n propietario m.

landlubber n marinero de agua dulce m.

landmark n lugar conocido; hito m.

landowner n terrateniente m/f.

landscape n paisaje m.

landslide n corrimiento de tierras m.

lane n callejuela f.

langoustine n langostino m.

language n lengua f; lenguaje m.

languid adj lánguido/da, débil; ~ly adv lánguidamente, débilmente.

languish vi languidecer.

lank adj lacio/cia.

lanky adj larguirucho/cha.

lantern n linterna f; farol m.

lap n regazo m; * vt lamer.

lapdog n perro faldero m.

lapel n solapa f.

lapse n lapso m; * vi transcurrir.

laptop n portátil m.

larceny n latrocinio m.

larch n alerce m.

lard n manteca de cerdo f.

larder n despensa f.

large adj grande; at ~ en libertad; ~ly adv en gran parte.

large-scale adj en gran escala.

largesse n liberalidad f.

lark n alondra f.

larva n larva, oruga f.

laryngitis n laringitis f.

larynx n laringe f.

lascivious adj lascivo/va; ~ly adv lascivamente.

laser n láser m.

laser printer n impresora láser f.

lash n latigazo m; * vt dar latigazos; atar.

lasso n lazo m.

last adj último/ma; pasado/da; at ~ por fin; ~ly adv finalmente; * n horma de zapatero f; * vi durar.

last-ditch adj último/ma.

lasting adj duradero/ra, permanente; ~ly adv perpetuamente.

last-minute adj de última hora.

latch n picaporte m.

latch-key n llave maestra f.

late adj tarde; difunto/ta; (rail) **the train is ten minutes ~** el tren tiene un retraso de diez minutos; * adv tarde; ~ly adv recientemente.

latecomer n recién llegado/da m/f.

latent adj latente.

lateral adj, ~ly adv lateral(mente).

lathe n torno m.

lather n espuma f.

latitude n latitud f.

latrine n letrina f.

latter adj último/ma; ~ly adv últimamente, recientemente.

lattice n celosía f.

laudable adj loable.

laudably adv loablemente.

laugh vi reír; to ~ at vt reírse de; * n risa f.

laughable adj absurdo/da.

laughing stock n hazmerreír m.

laughter n risa f.

launch vt (vi) lanzar(se); * n (mar) lancha f.

launching n lanzamiento m.

launching pad n plataforma de lanzamiento f.

launder vt lavar.

Launderette™ n lavandería automática f.

laundry n lavandería f.

laurel n laurel m.

lava n lava f.

lavatory n cuarto de baño m.

lavender n (bot) espliego m, lavanda f.

lavish adj pródigo/ga; ~ly adv pródigamente; * vt disipar.

law n ley f; derecho m.

law-abiding adj respetuoso/sa con la ley.

law and order n orden público m.

law court n tribunal m.

lawful adj legal; legítimo/ma; ~ly adv legalmente.

lawless adj anárquico/ca.

lawlessness n anarquía f.

lawmaker, lawgiver n legislador/a m/f.

lawn n pasto m.

lawnmower n cortacésped m.

law school n facultad de derecho f.

lawsuit n proceso m.

lawyer n abogado/da m/f.

lax adj laxo/xa; flojo/ja.

laxative n laxante m.

laxity n laxitud f; flojedad f.

lay vt poner; **to ~ claim** reclamar; pretender; **to ~ into** (fam) zurrar; * vi poner.

layabout n vago/ga m/f.

layer n capa f.

layette n ajuar de niño m.

layman n lego, seglar m.

layout n composición f.

laze vi holgazanear.

lazily adv perezosamente; lentamente.

laziness n pereza f.

lazy adj perezoso/sa.

lead1 n plomo m.

lead2 vt conducir, guiar; * vi mandar.

leader n jefe/fa m/f.

leadership n dirección f; liderazgo m.

leading adj principal; capital; **~ article** n artículo principal m.

leaf n hoja f, yema f.

leaflet n folleto m.

leafy adj frondoso/sa.

league n liga, alianza f; legua f.

leak n escape m; * vi (mar) hacer agua.

leaky adj agujereado/da.

lean vt (vi) apoyar(se); * adj magro/ra.

leap vi saltar; * n salto m.

leapfrog n pídola f.

leap year n año bisiesto m.

learn vt, vi aprender.

learned adj docto/ta.

learner n aprendiz m.

learning n erudición f.

lease n arriendo m; * vt arrendar.

leasehold n arriendo m.

leash n correa f.

least adj mínimo/ma; **at ~** por lo menos; **not in the ~** en absoluto.

leather n cuero m.

leathery adj correoso/sa.

leave n licencia f; permiso m; **to take ~** despedirse; * vt dejar, abandonar.

leaven n levadura f; * vt fermentar.

leavings npl sobras fpl.

lecherous adj lascivo/va.

lecture n conferencia f; * vt dar una conferencia.

lecturer n conferenciante m/f; profesor/ra m/f.

ledge n reborde m.

ledger n (com) libro mayor m.

lee n (mar) sotavento m.

leech n sanguijuela f.
leek n (bot) puerro m.
leer vt mirar de manera lasciva.
lees npl sedimento, poso m.
leeward adj (mar) sotavento.
leeway n libertad de acción f.
left adj izquierdo/da; zurdo/da; on the ~ a la izquierda.
left-handed adj zurdo/da.
left luggage office n consigna f.
leftovers npl sobras fpl.
leg n pierna f; pie m.
legacy n herencia f.
legal adj legal, legítimo/ma; ~ly adv legalmente.
legal holiday n fiesta oficial f.
legality n legalidad, legitimidad f.
legalize vt legalizar.
legal tender n moneda de curso legal f.
legate n legado m.
legatee n legado m.
legation n legación f.
legend n leyenda f.
legendary adj legendario/ria.
legible adj legible.
legibly adv legiblemente.
legion n legión f.
legislate vt legislar.
legislation n legislación f.
legislative adj legislativo/va.
legislator n legislador/a m/f.
legislature n cuerpo legislativo m.
legitimacy n legitimidad f.
legitimate adj legítimo/ma; ~ly adv legítimamente; * vt legitimar.
leisure n ocio m; ~ly adj sin prisa; at ~ desocupado/da.
lemon n limón m.
lemonade n limonada f.
lemon tea n te con limón m.
lemon tree n limonero m.
lend vt prestar.

length n largo m; duración f; at ~ finalmente.
lengthen vt alargar; * vi alargarse.
lengthways, lengthwise adv a lo largo.
lenient adj largo/ga.
lenient adj indulgente.
lens n lente f.
Lent n Cuaresma f.
lentil n lenteja f.
leopard n leopardo m; mallas fpl.
leotard n leotardo m.
leper n leproso/sa m/f.
leprosy n lepra f.
lesbian n lesbiana f.
less adj menor; * adv menos.
lessen vt disminuir; * vi disminuirse.
lesser adj más pequeño/ña.
lesson n lección f.
lest conj para que no.
let vt dejar, permitir; alquilar.
lethal adj mortal.
lethargic adj letárgico/ca.
lethargy n letargo m.
letter n letra f; carta f.
letter bomb n carta bomba f.
letter box, postbox n buzón m.
lettering n letras fpl.
letter of credit n carta de crédito f.
lettuce n lechuga f.
leukaemia n leucemia f.
level adj llano/na, igual; nivelado/da; * n nivel m; * vt allanar; nivelar.
level crossing n paso a nivel m.
level-headed adj sensato/ta.
lever n palanca f.
leverage n influencia f.
levity n ligereza f.
levy n leva (de tropas) f; * vt recaudar.
lewd adj obsceno/na.
lexicon n lexicón m.

liability n responsabilidad f.
liable adj sujeto/ta; responsable.
liaise vi enlazar.
liaison n enlace m.
liar n embustero m.
libel n difamación f; * vt difamar.
libellous adj difamatorio/ria.
liberal adj liberal, generoso/sa; ~ly adv liberalmente.
liberality n liberalidad, generosidad f.
liberate vt libertar.
liberation n liberación f.
libertine n libertino m.
liberty n libertad f.
Libra n Libra f.
librarian n bibliotecario/ria m/f.
library n biblioteca f.
libretto n libreto m.
licence n licencia f; permiso m.
license vt autorizar, licenciar.
licentious adj licencioso/sa.
lichen n (bot) liquen m.
lick vt lamer.
lid n tapa f.
lie n mentira f; * vi mentir; echarse.
lie down vi yacer.
lieu n: in ~ of en vez de.
lieutenant n lugarteniente m/f; teniente m/f.
life n vida f; for ~ para toda la vida.
lifeboat n lancha de socorro f; bote salvavidas m.
lifeguard n socorrista m/f.
life jacket n chaleco salvavidas m.
lifeless adj muerto/ta; sin vida.
lifelike adj natural.
lifeline n cordón umbilical m.
life sentence n cadena perpetua f.
life-sized adj de tamaño natural.
life span n vida f.
lifestyle n estilo de vida f.
life-support system n sistema de respiración asistida m.

lifetime n vida f.
lift vt levantar.
ligament n ligamento m.
light n luz f; * adj ligero/ra; claro/ra; * vt encender; alumbrar.
light bulb n foco m; bombilla f.
lighten vi relampaguear; * vt iluminar; aligerar; (ship) zafar.
lighter n encendedor m.
light-headed adj mareado/da.
light-hearted adj alegre.
lighthouse n (mar) faro m.
lighting n iluminación f.
lightly adv ligeramente.
lightning n relámpago m.
lightning-rod n pararrayos m invar.
light pen n lápiz óptico m.
lightweight adj ligero/ra.
light year n año luz m.
ligneous adj leñoso/sa.
like adj semejante; igual; * adv como, del mismo modo que; * vt, vi gustar.
likeable adj simpático/ca.
likelihood n probabilidad f.
likely adj probable, verosímil.
liken vt comparar.
likeness n semejanza f.
likewise adv igualmente.
liking n agrado m.
lilac n lila f.
lily n lirio m; ~ of the valley lirio de los valles.
limb n miembro m.
limber adj flexible.
lime n cal f; lima f; ~ tree tilo m.
limestone n piedra caliza f.
limit n límite, término m; * vt restringir.
limitation n limitación f; restricción f.
limitless adj inmenso/sa.
limousine n limusina f.

limp *vi* cojear; * *n* cojera *f*; * *adj* flojo/ja.
limpet *n* lapa *f*.
limpid *adj* claro/ra, transparente.
line *n* línea *f*; raya *f*; * *vt* forrar; revestir.
lineage *n* linaje *m*; filiación *f*.
linear *adj* lineal.
lined *adj* rayado/da; arrugado/da.
linen *n* lino *m*.
liner *n* transatlántico *m*.
linesman *n* juez de línea *m*.
linger *vi* persistir.
lingerie *n* ropa interior *f*.
lingering *adj* lento/ta.
linguist *n* lingüista *m/f*.
linguistic *adj* lingüístico/ca.
linguistics *n* lingüística *f*.
liniment *n* linimento *m*.
lining *n* forro *m*.
link *n* eslabón *m*; * *vt* enlazar.
linnet *n* pardillo *m*.
linoleum *n* linóleo *m*.
linseed *n* linaza *f*.
lint *n* hilas *fpl*.
lintel *n* dintel, tranquero *m*.
lion *n* león *m*.
lioness *n* leona *f*.
lip *n* labio *m*; borde *m*.
liposuction *n* liposucción *f*.
lip read *vi* leer los labios.
lipstick *n* lápiz de labios *m*.
liqueur *n* licor *m*.
liquid *adj* líquido/da; * *n* líquido *m*.
liquidate *vt* liquidar.
liquidation *n* liquidación *f*.
liquidize *vt* licuar.
liquor *n* licor *m*.
liquorice *n* regaliz *m*.
lisp *vi* cecear; * *n* ceceo *m*.
list *n* lista *f*; * *vt* hacer una lista de.
listen *vi* escuchar.
listless *adj* indiferente.

litany *n* letanía *f*.
literal *adj*, ~ly *adv* literal(mente).
literary *adj* literario/ria.
literate *adj* culto/ta.
literature *n* literatura *f*.
lithe *adj* ágil.
lithograph *n* litografía *f*.
lithography *n* litografía *f*.
litigation *n* litigio *m*.
litigious *adj* litigioso/sa.
litre *n* litro *m*.
litter *n* litera *f*; camada *f*; * *vt* parir.
little *adj* pequeño/ña, poco/ca; ~ by ~ poco a poco; * *n* poco *m*.
liturgy *n* liturgia *f*.
live *vi* vivir; habitar; to ~ on alimentarse de; to ~ up to *vt* cumplir con; * *adj* vivo/va.
livelihood *n* vida *f*.
liveliness *n* vivacidad *f*; belleza *f*.
lively *adj* vivo/va.
liven up *vt* animar.
liver *n* hígado *m*.
livery *n* librea *f*.
livestock *n* ganado *m*.
livid *adj* lívido/da, cárdeno/na.
living *n* vida *f*; * *adj* vivo/va.
living room *n* sala de estar *f*.
lizard *n* lagarto *m*.
load *vt* cargar; * *n* carga *f*.
loaded *adj* cargado/da.
loaf *n* pan *m*.
loafer *n* holgazán, gandul *m*.
loam *n* marga *f*.
loan *n* préstamo *m*.
loathe *vt* aborrecer; tener hastío; * *vi* fastidiar.
loathing *n* aversión *f*.
loathsome *adj* asqueroso/sa.
lobby *n* vestíbulo *m*.
lobe *n* lóbulo *m*.
lobster *n* langosta *f*.
local *adj* local.

local anaesthetic n anestesia local f.
local government n gobierno municipal m.
locality n localidad f.
localize vt localizar.
locally adv en la vecindad.
locate vt localizar.
location n situación f.
loch n lago m.
lock n cerradura f; * vt cerrar con llave.
locker n vestuario m.
locket n medallón m.
lockout n cierre patronal m.
locksmith n cerrajero m.
lockup n garaje m, cochera f.
locomotive n locomotora f.
locust n langosta f.
lodge n casa del guarda f; * vi alojarse.
lodger n inquilino/na m/f.
loft n desván m.
lofty adj alto/ta.
log n leño m.
logbook n (mar) diario de a bordo m.
logic n lógica f.
logical adj lógico/ca.
logo n logotipo m.
loin n lomo m.
loiter vi merodear.
loll vi repantigarse.
lollipop n pirulí m, piruleta f.
lonely adj solitario/ria; solo/la.
loneliness n soledad f.
long adj largo/ga; * vi anhelar.
long-distance n: ~ **call** llamada interurbana f.
longevity n longevidad f.
long-haired adj de pelo largo.
longing n anhelo m.
longitude n longitud f.
longitudinal adj longitudinal.
long jump n salto de longitud m.
long-legged adj zancudo/da.

long-playing record n elepé m.
long-range adj de gran alcance.
long-term adj a largo plazo.
long wave n onda larga f.
long-winded adj prolijo/ja.
look vi mirar; parecer; **to** ~ **after** vt cuidar; **to** ~ **for** vt buscar; **to** ~ **forward to** vt esperar con impaciencia; **to** ~ **out for** vt aguardar; * n aspecto m; mirada f.
looking glass n espejo m.
lookout n (mil) centinela f; vigía f.
loom n telar m; * vi amenazar.
loop n lazo m.
loophole n escapatoria f.
loose adj suelto/ta; flojo/ja; ~**ly** adv aproximadamente.
loosen vt aflojar, zafar.
loot vt saquear; * n botín m.
lop vt desmochar.
lop-sided adj desequilibrado/da.
loquacious adj locuaz.
loquacity n locuacidad f.
lord n señor m.
lore n saber popular m.
lose vt perder; * vi perder; **to** ~ **weight** vi adelgazar.
loss n pérdida f; **to be at a** ~ no saber qué hacer.
lost and found n objetos perdidos mpl.
lot n suerte f; lote m; **a** ~ **much**.
lotion n loción f.
lottery n lotería, rifa f.
loud adj fuerte; ~**ly** adv fuerte.
loudspeaker n altavoz m.
lounge n salón m.
louse n (pl **lice**) piojo m.
lousy adj vil.
lout n gamberro m.
lovable adj amable.
love n amor, cariño m; **to fall in** ~ enamorarse; * vt amar; gustar.

ove letter n carta de amor f.

ove life n vida sentimental f.

ovely adj hermoso/sa.

over n amante m.

ovesick adj enamorado/da.

loving adj amoroso/sa.

low adj bajo/ja; * vi mugir.

low-cut adj escotado/da.

lower adj más bajo/ja; * vt bajar.

lowest adj más bajo/ja, ínfimo/ma.

lowland n tierra baja f.

lowliness n humildad f.

lowly adj humilde.

low water, low tide n bajamar f.

loyal adj leal; fiel; ~**ly** adv lealmente.

loyalty n lealtad f; fidelidad f.

lozenge n pastilla f.

lubricant n lubricante m.

lubricate vt lubricar.

lucid adj lúcido/da.

luck n suerte; fortuna f.

luckily adv afortunadamente.

luckless adj desdichado/da.

lucky adj afortunado/da.

lucrative adj lucrativo/va.

ludicrous adj absurdo/da.

lug vt arrastrar.

luggage n equipaje m.

lugubrious adj lúgubre, triste.

lukewarm adj tibio/bia.

lull vt acunar; * n tregua f.

lullaby n nana f.

lumbago n lumbago m.

lumberjack n maderero/ra m/f.

luminous adj luminoso/sa.

lump n terrón m; bulto m; chichón m; * vt juntar.

lump sum n suma global f.

lunacy n locura f.

lunar adj lunar.

lunatic adj loco/ca.

lunch, luncheon n almuerzo m, comida f; * vt, vi almorzar.

lungs npl pulmones mpl.

lurch n sacudida f.

lure n señuelo m; cebo m; * vt inducir.

lurid adj sensacional.

lurk vi esconderse.

luscious adj delicioso/sa.

lush adj exuberante.

lust n lujuria, sensualidad f; concupiscencia f; * vi lujuriar; **to ~ after** vt codiciar.

lustful adj lujurioso/sa, voluptuoso/sa; ~**ly** adv lujuriosamente.

lustily adv vigorosamente.

lustre n lustre m.

lusty adj fuerte, vigoroso/sa.

lute n laúd m.

Lutheran n luterano/na m/f.

luxuriance n exuberancia, superabundancia f.

luxuriant adj exuberante, superabundante.

luxuriate vi crecer con exuberancia.

luxurious adj lujoso/sa; exuberante; ~**ly** adv lujosamente.

luxury n lujo m, voluptuosidad f; exuberancia f.

lying n mentiras fpl.

lymph n linfa f.

lynch vt linchar.

lynx n lince m.

lyrical adj lírico/ca.

lyrics npl letra f.

M

macaroni n macarrones mpl.

macaroon n almendrado m.

mace n maza f; macis f invar.

macerate vt macerar; mortificar.

machination n maquinación, trama f.

machine n máquina f.

machine gun n ametralladora f.

machinery n maquinaria, mecánica f.

mackerel n caballa f.

mad adj loco/ca, furioso/sa, rabioso/sa, insensato/ta.

madam n madama, señora f.

madden vt enloquecer.

madder n (bot) rubia f.

madhouse n casa de locos f.

madly adv locamente.

madman n loco m.

madness n locura f.

magazine n revista f; almacén m.

maggot n gusano m.

magic n magia f; * adj mágico/ca; ~ally adv mágicamente.

magician n mago/ga m/f; prestidigitador/a m/f.

magisterial adj magistral; ~ly adv magistralmente.

magistracy n magistratura f.

magistrate n magistrado/a m/f.

magnanimity n magnanimidad f.

magnanimous adj magnánimo; ~ly adv magnánimamente.

magnet n iman m.

magnetic adj magnetico/ca.

magnetism n magnetismo m.

magnificence n magnificencia f.

magnificent adj magnifico; ~ly adv magníficamente.

magnify vt aumentar; exagerar.

magnifying glass n lupa f.

magnitude n magnitud f.

magpie n urraca f.

mahogany n caoba f.

maid n criada f.

maiden n doncella f.

maiden name n nombre de soltera m.

mail n correo m.

mailing list n lista de direcciones f.

mail order n venta por correo f.

mail train n (rail) tren correo m.

maim vt mutilar.

main adj principal; esencial; in the ~ en general.

mainland n continente m.

main line n (rail) línea principal f.

mainly adv principalmente.

main street n calle mayor f.

maintain vt mantener; sostener.

maintenance n mantenimiento m.

maize n maíz m.

majestic adj majestuoso/sa; ~ally adv majestuosamente.

majesty n majestad f.

major adj principal; * n (mil) comandante/a m/f.

majority n mayoría f.

make vt hacer, crear; to ~ for dirigirse hacia; to ~ up inventar; to ~ up for compensar; to ~ off with something alzar; * n marca f.

make-believe n invención f.

makeshift adj improvisado.

make-up n maquillaje m.

make-up remover n desmaquillador m.

malady n enfermedad f.

malaise n malestar m.

malaria n malaria f.

malcontent adj, n malcontento/ta m/f.

male *adj* masculino/na; * *n* macho *m*.

malevolence *n* malevolencia *f*.

malevolent *adj* malévolo/la; ~ly *adv* malignamente.

malfunction *n* mal funcionamiento, fallo *m*.

malice *n* malicia *f*.

malicious *adj* malicioso/sa; ~ly *adv* maliciosamente.

malign *adj* maligno; * *vt* calumniar.

malignant *adj* maligno/na; ~ly *adv* malignamente.

mall (shopping) *n* centro comercial; paseo *m*.

malleable *adj* maleable.

mallet *n* mazo *m*.

mallow *n* (*bot*) malva *f*.

malnutrition *n* desnutrición *f*.

malpractice *n* negligencia *f*.

malt *n* malta *f*.

maltreat *vt* maltratar.

mammal *n* mamífero *m*.

mammoth *adj* gigantesco/ca.

man *n* hombre *m*; * *vt* (*mar*) tripular.

manacle *n* manilla *f*; ~s *npl* esposas *fpl*.

manage *vt*, *vi* manejar, dirigir.

manageable *adj* manejable.

management *n* dirección *f*.

manager *n* director/a *m/f*.

manageress *n* directora *f*.

managerial *adj* directivo/va.

managing director *n* director/a general *m/f*.

mandarin *n* (*bot*) mandarina *f*; mandarín *m*.

mandate *n* mandato *m*.

mandatory *adj* obligatorio/ria.

mane *n* crines *fpl*, melena *f*.

manfully *adv* valerosamente.

manger *n* pesebre *m*.

mangle *n* rodillo *m*; * *vt* mutilar.

mangy *adj* sarnoso/sa.

manhandle *vt* maltratar.

manhood *n* madurez *f*; hombría *f*.

man-hour *n* hora hombre *f*.

mania *n* manía *f*.

maniac *n* maníaco/ca *m/f*.

manic *adj* frenético/ca.

manicure *n* manicura *f*.

manifest *adj* manifiesto/ta, patente; * *vt* manifestar.

manifestation *n* manifestación *f*.

manifesto *n* manifiesto *m*.

manipulate *vt* manejar; manipular.

manipulation *n* manejo; manipulación *f*.

mankind *n* género humano *m*.

manlike *adj* varonil.

manliness *n* valentía, hombría *f*.

manly *adj* varonil.

man-made *adj* artificial.

manner *n* manera *f*; modo *m*; forma *f*; ~s *pl* modales *mpl*.

manoeuvre *n* maniobra *f*.

manpower *n* mano de obra *f*.

mansion *n* palacio *m*, mansión *f*.

manslaughter *n* homicidio (sin premeditación) *m*.

mantelpiece *n* repisa (de chimenea) *f*.

manual *adj*, *n* manual *m*.

manufacture *n* fabricación *f*; * *vt* fabricar.

manufacturer *n* fabricante *m/f*.

manure *n* abono *m*; estiércol *m*; fiemo *m*; * *vt* abonar.

manuscript *n* manuscrito *m*.

many *adj* muchos, muchas; ~ a time muchas veces; how ~? ¿cuantos?; as ~ as tantos como.

map *n* mapa *m*; * *vt* planear, trazar el mapa de; to ~ out proyectar.

maple *n* arce *m*.

mar *vt* estropear.

marathon *n* maratón *m*.

marauder *n* merodeador/a *m/f*.

marble n mármol m; * adj marmóreo/rea.

March n marzo m.

march n marcha f; * vi marchar.

march past n desfile m.

mare n yegua f.

margarine n margarina f.

margin n margen m; borde m.

marginal adj marginal.

marigold n (bot) caléndula f.

marijuana n marihuana f.

marinate vt adobar.

marine adj marino/na; * n infante de marina m.

mariner n marinero/ra m/f.

marital adj marital.

maritime adj marítimo/ma.

marjoram n mejorana f.

mark n marca f; señal f; * vt marcar.

marker n registro m.

market n mercado m.

marketable adj vendible.

market garden n huerto de hortalizas m.

marketing n márketing m.

marketplace n mercado m.

market research n análisis de mercados m invar.

market value n valor de mercado m.

marksman n tirador m.

marmalade n mermelada de naranja f.

maroon adj marrón.

marquee n entoldado/da m/f.

marriage n matrimonio m; casamiento m.

marriageable adj casadero/ra.

marriage certificate n partida de casamiento f.

married adj casado/da; conyugal.

marrow n médula f.

marry vi casarse.

marsh n pantano m.

marshal n mariscal/a m/f.

marshy adj pantanoso/sa.

marten n marta f.

martial adj marcial; ~ **law** n ley marcial f.

martyr n mártir m.

martyrdom n martirio m.

marvel n maravilla f; * vi maravillar(se).

marvellous adj maravilloso/sa; ~**ly** adv maravillosamente.

marzipan n mazapán m.

mascara n rímel m.

masculine adj masculino/na, varonil.

mash n mezcla f.

mask n máscara f; * vt enmascarar.

masochist n masoquista m/f.

mason n albañil m.

masonry n mampostería f.

masquerade n mascarada f.

mass n masa f; misa f; montón m.

massacre n carnicería, matanza f; * vt hacer una carnicería.

massage n masaje m.

masseur n masajista m.

masseuse n masajista f.

massive adj enorme.

mass-media npl medios de comunicación de masas mpl.

mast n mástil m.

master n amo/ma, dueño/ña m/f; maestro/tra m/f; * vt dominar.

masterly adj magistral.

mastermind vt dirigir.

masterpiece n obra maestra f.

mastery n maestría f.

masticate vt masticar.

mastiff n mastín m.

mat n estera f; felpudo m.

match n fósforo m, cerilla f; partido m; * vt igualar; * vi hacer juego.

matchbox n caja de fósforos f.

matchless *adj* incomparable, sin par.
matchmaker *n* casamentero/ra *m/f*.
mate *n* compañero/ra *m/f*; * *vt* acoplar.
material *adj*, **~ly** *adv* material(mente).
materialism *n* materialismo *m*.
maternal *adj* maternal.
maternity clothes *npl* vestido premamá *m*.
maternity hospital *n* hospital de maternidad *m*.
mathematical *adj* matemático/ca; **~ly** *adv* matemáticamente.
mathematician *n* matemático/ca *m/f*.
mathematics *npl* matemáticas *fpl*.
maths *npl* mates, matemáticas *fpl*.
matinee *n* función de la tarde *f*.
mating *n* aparejamiento *m*.
matins *npl* maitines *mpl*.
matriculate *vt* matricular.
matriculation *n* matriculación *f*.
matrimonial *adj* matrimonial.
mat, matt(e) *adj* mate.
matted *adj* enmarañado/da.
matter *n* materia, substancia *f*; asunto *m*; cuestión *f*; **what is the ~?** ¿qué pasa?; **as a ~ of fact** en realidad; * *vi* importar.
mattress *n* colchón *m*.
mature *adj* maduro/ra; * *vt* madurar.
maturity *n* madurez *f*.
maul *vt* magullar.
mausoleum *n* mausoleo *m*.
mauve *adj* malva.
maxim *n* máxima *f*.
maximum *n* máximo *m*.
may *vi* poder; **~be** acaso, quizá.
May *n* mayo *m*.
Mayday *n* primero de mayo *m*.
mayonnaise *n* mayonesa *f*.
mayor *n* alcalde *m*.
mayoress *n* alcaldesa *f*.

maze *n* laberinto *m*.
me *pn* me; mí.
meadow *n* pradera *f*; prado *m*.
meagre *adj* pobre.
meagreness *n* escasez *f*.
meal *n* comida *f*; harina *f*.
mealtime *n* hora de comer *f*.
mean *adj* tacaño/ña; **~s** *npl* medios *mpl*; * *vt*, *vi* significar.
meander *vi* serpentear.
meaning *n* sentido, significado *m*.
meaningful *adj* significativo/va.
meaningless *adj* sin sentido.
meanness *n* tacañería *f*.
meantime (in the), meanwhile *adv* mientras tanto.
measles *npl* sarampión *m*.
measure *n* medida *f*; (*mus*) compás *m*; * *vt* medir.
measurement *n* medida *f*.
meat *n* carne *f*.
meatball *n* albóndiga *f*.
meaty *adj* sustancioso/sa.
mechanic *n* mecánico/ca *m/f*.
mechanical *adj* mecánico; **~ly** *adv* mecánicamente.
mechanics *npl* mecánica *f*.
mechanism *n* mecanismo *m*.
medal *n* medalla *f*.
medallion *n* medallón *m*.
medallist *n* medallero/ra *m/f*.
meddle *vi* entrometerse.
meddler *n* entrometido *m*.
media *npl* medios de comunicación *mpl*.
mediate *vi* mediar.
mediation *n* mediación, interposición *f*.
mediator *n* intermediario/ria *m/f*.
medical *adj* médico/ca.
medicate *vt* medicar.
medicated *adj* medicinal.
medicinal *adj* medicinal.

medicine n medicina f; medicamento m.

medieval adj medieval.

mediocre adj mediocre.

mediocrity n mediocridad f.

meditate vi meditar.

meditation n meditación f.

meditative adj contemplativo/va.

Mediterranean adj mediterráneo/nea; **the ~** el Mediterráneo/nea m.

medium n medio m; * adj mediano/na.

medium wave n onda media f.

medley n mezcla f.

meek adj manso/sa; **~ly** adv mansamente.

meekness n mansedumbre f.

meet vt encontrar; **to ~ with** reunirse con; * vi encontrarse; juntarse.

meeting n reunión f; congreso m.

megaphone n megáfono m.

melancholy n melancolía f; * adj melancólico/ca.

mellow adj maduro/ra; suave; * vi madurar.

mellowness n madurez f.

melodious adj melodioso/sa; **~ly** adv melodiosamente.

melody n melodía f.

melon n melón m.

melt vt derretir; * vi derretirse.

melting point n punto de fusión m.

member n miembro m/f.

membership n número de miembros m.

membrane n membrana f.

memento n recuerdo m.

memo n memorándum m.

memoir n memoria f.

memorable adj memorable.

memorandum n memorándum m.

memorial n monumento conmemorativo m.

memorize vt memorizar, aprender de memoria.

memory n memoria f; recuerdo m.

menace n amenaza f; * vt amenazar.

menacing adj amenazador/ra.

menagerie n casa de fieras f.

mend vt reparar.

mending n reparación f.

menial adj doméstico/ca.

meningitis n meningitis f.

menopause n menopausia f.

menstruation n menstruación f.

mental adj mental, intelectual.

mentality n mentalidad f.

mentally adv mentalmente, intelectualmente.

mention n mención f; * vt mencionar.

mentor n mentor m.

menu n menú m; carta f.

mercantile adj mercantil.

mercenary adj, n mercenario/ria m/f.

merchandise n mercancía f.

merchant n comerciante m/f.

merchantman n navío mercante m.

merchant marine n marina mercante f.

merciful adj compasivo/va.

merciless adj despiadado/da; **~ly** adv despiadadamente.

mercury n mercurio m.

mercy n compasión f.

mere adj mero/ra; **~ly** adv simplemente.

merge vt fundir.

merger n fusión f.

meridian n meridiano m.

meringue n merengue m.

merit n mérito m; * vt merecer.

meritorious adj meritorio/ria.

mermaid n sirena f.

merrily adv alegremente.

merriment n diversión f; regocijo m.

merry *adj* alegre.
merry-go-round *n* tiovivo *m*.
mesh *n* malla *f*.
mesmerize *vt* hipnotizar.
mess *n* lío *m*; mamarracho *m*; (*mil*) comedor *m*; to ~ up *vt* desordenar.
message *n* mensaje *m*.
messenger *n* mensajero/ra *m/f*.
metabolism *n* metabolismo *m*.
metal *n* metal *m*.
metallic *adj* metálico/ca.
metallurgy *n* metalurgía *f*.
metamorphosis *n* metamorfosis *f invar*.
metaphor *n* metáfora *f*.
metaphoric(al) *adj* metafórico/ca.
metaphysical *adj* metafísico/ca.
metaphysics *npl* metafísica *f*.
mete (out) *vt* imponer.
meteor *n* meteoro *m*.
meteorological *adj* meteorológico/ca.
meteorology *n* meteorología *f*.
meter *n* contador *m*.
method *n* método *m*.
methodical *adj* metódico/ca; ~ly *adv* metódicamente.
Methodist *n* metodista *m/f*.
metre *n* metro *m*.
metric *adj* métrico/ca.
metropolis *n* metrópoli *f*.
metropolitan *adj* metropolitano/na.
mettle *n* valor *m*.
mettlesome *adj* brioso/sa.
mew *vi* maullar.
mezzanine *n* entresuelo *m*.
microbe *n* microbio *m*.
microchip *n* microchip *m*.
microphone *n* micrófono *m*.
microscope *n* microscopio *m*.
microscopic *adj* microscópico/ca.
microwave *n* microondas *m invar*; ~ oven microondas *m*.
mid *adj* medio/dia.

midday *n* mediodía *m*.
middle *adj* medio/dia; * *n* medio, centro *m*.
middle name *n* segundo nombre *m*.
middleweight *n* peso medio *m*.
middling *adj* mediano/na.
midge *n* mosquito *m*.
midget *n* enano/na *m/f*.
midi system *n* minicadena *f*.
midnight *n* medianoche *f*.
midriff *n* diafragma *m*.
midst *n* medio, centro *m*.
midsummer *n* pleno verano *m*.
midway *adv* a medio camino.
midwife *n* partera *f*.
midwifery *n* obstetricia *f*.
might *n* poder *m*; fuerza *f*.
mighty *adj* fuerte.
migraine *n* jaqueca *f*.
migrate *vi* emigrar, migrar.
migration *n* emigración, migración *f*.
migratory *adj* migratorio/ria.
mike *n* micrófono *m*.
mild *adj* apacible; suave; ~ly *adv* suavemente.
mildew *n* moho *m*.
mildness *n* dulzura *f*.
mile *n* milla *f*.
mileage *n* kilometraje *m*.
mileometer, milometer *n* cuentakilómetros *m invar*.
milieu *n* ambiente *m*.
militant *adj* militante.
military *adj* militar.
militate *vi* militar.
militia *n* milicia *f*.
milk *n* leche *f*; * *vt* ordenar.
milkshake *n* batido de leche *m*, malteada *f*.
milky *adj* lechoso/sa; M~ Way *n* Via Lactea *f*.
mill *n* molino *m*; * *vt* moler.
millennium *n* milenio *m*.

miller n molinero/ra m/f.
millet n (bot) mijo m.
milligram n miligramo m.
millilitre n mililitro m.
millimetre n milímetro m.
milliner n sombrerero/ra m/f.
millinery n sombrerería f.
million n millón m.
millionaire n millonario/ria m/f.
millionth adj, n milinésimo/ma m/f.
millstone n piedra de molino f.
mime n mimo m.
mimic vt imitar.
mimicry n mímica f.
mince vt picar.
mind n mente f; * vt cuidar; * vi
molestar.
minded adj dispuesto/ta.
mindful adj consciente.
mindless adj sin motivo.
mine pn mío, mía, mi; * n mina; * vi
minar.
minefield n campo de minas m.
miner n minero/ra m/f.
mineral adj, n mineral m.
mineralogy n mineralogía f.
mineral water n agua mineral f.
minesweeper n dragaminas m invar.
mingle vt mezclar.
miniature n miniatura f.
minimal adj mínimo/ma.
minimize vt minimizar.
minimum n mínimo m.
mining n minería f.
minion n favorito/ta m/f.
minister n ministro/tro m/f; * vt servir.
ministerial adj ministerial.
ministry n ministerio m.
mink n visón m.
minnow n vario m (pez).
minor adj menor; * n menor (de
edad) m/f.

minority n minoría f.
minstrel n juglar m.
mint n (bot) menta f; casa de la moneda f; * vt acuñar.
minus adv menos.
minute¹ adj diminuto/ta; ~ly adv mi-
nuciosamente.
minute² n minuto m.
miracle n milagro m.
miraculous adj milagroso/sa.
mirage n espejismo m.
mire n fango m.
mirky adj turbio/bia.
mirror n espejo m.
mirth n alegría f.
mirthful adj alegre.
misadventure n desgracia f.
misanthrope, misanthropist n mi-
sántropo m.
misapply vt aplicar mal.
misapprehension n error m.
misbehave vi portarse mal.
misbehaviour n mala conducta f.
miscalculate vt calcular mal.
miscarriage n aborto (espontá-
neo) m.
miscarry vi abortar (espontáneamente); malograrse.
miscellaneous adj varios, varias.
miscellany n miscelánea f.
mischief n mal, daño m.
mischievous adj dañoso/sa; tra-
vieso/sa.
misconception n equivocación f.
misconduct n mala conducta f.
misconstrue vt interpretar mal.
miscount vt contar mal.
miscreant n malvado/da m/f.
misdeed n delito m.
misdemeanour n delito m.
misdirect vt dirigir mal.
miser n avaro/ra m/f.
miserable adj miserable, infeliz.

miserly *adj* mezquino/na, tacaño/ña.

misery *n* miseria *f*.

misfit *n* inadaptado/da *m/f*.

misfortune *n* desgracia *f*.

misgiving *n* recelo *m*; presentimiento *m*.

misgovern *vt* gobernar mal.

misguided *adj* equivocado/da.

mishandle *vt* manejar mal.

mishap *n* desgracia *f*.

misinform *vt* informar mal.

misinterpret *vt* interpretar mal.

misjudge *vi* juzgar mal.

mislay *vt* extraviar.

mislead *vt* engañar.

mismanage *vt* manejar mal.

mismanagement *n* mala administración *f*.

misnomer *n* nombre inapropiado *m*.

misogynist *n* misógino/na *m/f*.

misplace *vt* extraviar.

misprint *vt* imprimir mal; * *n* errata *f*.

misrepresent *vt* representar mal.

Miss *n* señorita *f*.

miss *vt* perder; echar de menos.

missal *n* misal *m*.

misshapen *adj* deforme.

missile *n* misil *m*.

missing *adj* perdido/da; ausente.

mission *n* misión *f*.

missionary *n* misionero/ra *m/f*.

misspent *adj* disipado/da.

mist *n* niebla *f*.

mistake *vt* entender mal; * *vi* equivocarse, engañarse; **to be mistaken** equivocarse; * *n* equivocación *f*; error *m*, yerro *m*.

Mister *n* Señor *m*.

mistletoe *n* (*bot*) muérdago *m*.

mistress *n* amante *f*.

mistrust *vt* desconfiar; * *n* desconfianza *f*.

mistrustful *adj* desconfiado/da.

misty *adj* nebuloso/sa.

misunderstand *vt* entender mal.

misunderstanding *n* malentendido *m*.

misuse *vt* maltratar; abusar de.

mitre *n* mitra *f*.

mitigate *vt* mitigar.

mitigation *n* mitigación *f*.

mittens *npl* manoplas *fpl*.

mix *vt* mezclar.

mixed *adj* surtido/da; mixto/ta.

mixed-up *adj* confuso/sa.

mixer *n* licuadora *f*.

mixture *n* mezcla *f*.

mix-up *n* confusión *f*.

moan *n* gemido *m*; * *vi* gemir; quejarse.

moat *n* foso *m*.

mob *n* multitud *f*.

mobile *adj* móvil; ~ **phone** móvil *m*.

mobile home *n* caravana *f*.

mobility *n* movilidad *f*.

mobilize *vt* (*mil*) movilizar.

moccasin *n* mocasín *m*.

mock *vt* burlarse.

mockery *n* mofa *f*.

mode *n* modo *m*.

model *n* modelo *m*; * *vt* modelar.

modem *n* módem *m*.

moderate *adj* moderado/da; **~ly** *adv* medianamente; * *vt* moderar.

moderation *n* moderación *f*.

modern *adj* moderno/na.

modernize *vt* modernizar.

modest *adj* modesto/ta; **~ly** *adv* modestamente.

modesty *n* modestia *f*.

modicum *n* mínimo *m*.

modification *n* modificación *f*.

modify *vt* modificar.

modulate *vt* modular.

modulation *n* (*mus*) modulación *f*.

module *n* módulo *m*.

mogul *n* magnate *m/f*.

mohair n mohair m.
moist adj húmedo/da.
moisten vt humedecer.
moisture n humedad f.
molars npl muelas fpl.
molasses n melaza f.
mole n topo m.
molecule n molécula f.
molehill n topera f.
molest vt importunar.
mollify vt apaciguar.
mollusc n molusco m.
mollycoddle vt mimar.
molten adj derretido/da.
moment n momento m.
momentarily adv momentáneamente.
momentary adj momentáneo/nea.
momentous adj importante.
momentum n ímpetu m.
monarch n monarca m.
monarchy n monarquía f.
monastery n monasterio m.
monastic adj monástico/ca.
Monday n lunes m.
monetary adj monetario/ria.
money n dinero m.
money laundering n blanqueo m.
money order n giro m.
Mongol n mongólico/ca m/f.
mongrel adj, n mestizo/za m/f.
monitor n monitor m.
monk n monje m.
monkey n mono m.
monochrome adj monocromo/ma.
monocle n monóculo m.
monologue n monólogo m.
monopolize vt monopolizar.
monopoly n monopolio m.
monosyllable n monosílabo m.
monotonous adj monótono/na.
monotony n monotonía f.
monsoon n (mar) monzón m.

monster n monstruo m.
monstrosity n monstruosidad f.
monstrous adj monstruoso/sa; ~ly
   adv monstruosamente.
montage n montaje m.
month n mes m.
monthly adj, adv mensual(mente).
monument n monumento m.
monumental adj monumental.
moo vi mugir.
mood n humor m.
moodiness n mal humor m.
moody adj malhumorado/da.
moon n luna f.
moonbeams npl rayos lunares mpl.
moonlight n luz de la luna f.
moor vt (mar) atracar.
mooring rope n amarra f.
moorland, moor n páramo m.
moose n alce m.
mop n fregona f; * vt fregar.
mope vi estar triste.
moped n ciclomotor m.
moral adj, ~ly adv moral(mente);
   ~s npl moralidad f.
morale n moral f.
moralist n moralista m/f.
morality n ética, moralidad f.
moralize vt, vi moralizar.
morass n pantano m.
morbid adj morboso/sa.
more adj, adv más; **never** ~ nunca
   más; **once** ~ otra vez; ~ **and** ~
   más y más, cada vez más; **so much**
   the ~ cuanto más.
moreover adv además.
morgue n depósito de cadáveres m.
morning n mañana f; **good** ~ buenos
   días mpl.
moron n imbécil m/f.
morose adj hosco/ca.
morphine n morfina f.
morsel n bocado m.

mortal adj mortal; **~ly** adv mortalmente; * n mortal m/f.
mortality n mortalidad f.
mortar n mortero m.
mortgage n hipoteca f; * vt hipotecar.
mortgage company n banco hipotecario m.
mortgager n deudor hipotecario m, deudora hipotecaria f.
mortification n mortificación f.
mortify vt mortificar.
mortuary n depósito de cadáveres m.
mosaic n mosaico m.
mosque n mezquita f.
mosquito n mosquito m; zancudo/da m.
moss n (bot) musgo m.
mossy adj cubierto/ta de musgo.
most adj la mayoría de; * adv sumamente; **at ~** a lo sumo; **~ly** adv principalmente.
motel n motel m.
moth n polilla f.
mothball n bola de naftalina f.
mother n madre f; **loving ~** madraza f.
motherhood n maternidad f.
mother-in-law n suegra f.
motherless adj sin madre.
motherly adj maternal.
mother-of-pearl n nácar m.
mother-to-be n futura madre f.
mother tongue n lengua materna f.
motif n tema m.
motion n movimiento m.
motionless adj inmóvil.
motion picture n película f.
motivated adj motivado/da.
motive n motivo m.
motley adj abigarrado/da.
motor n motor m.
motorbike n moto f.
motorboat n lancha motora f.

motorcycle n motocicleta f.
motor vehicle n automóvil m.
mottled adj multicolor.
motto n lema m.
mould n molde m; moho m; * vt moldear.
moulder vi decaer.
mouldy adj enmohecido/da.
moult vt mudar.
mound n montón m.
mount n monte m; * vt subir.
mountain n montaña f.
mountaineer n montañero/ra m/f.
mountaineering n montañismo m.
mountainous adj montañoso/sa.
mourn vt lamentar.
mourner n doliente m/f.
mournful adj triste; **~ly** adv tristemente.
mourning n luto m.
mouse n (pl **mice**) ratón m.
mouse mat n alfombrilla f.
mousse n mousse f.
moustache n bigote m.
mouth n boca f; desembocadura f.
mouthful n bocado m.
mouth organ n harmónica f.
mouthpiece n boquilla f.
mouthwash n enjuague m.
mouthwatering adj apetitoso/sa.
movable adj movible.
move vt mover; proponer; * vi moverse; * n movimiento m.
movement n movimiento m.
movie n película f.
movie camera n cámara cinematográfica f.
moving adj conmovedor/a.
mow vt segar.
mower n cortacésped m.
Mrs n señora f.
much adj, adv mucho/cha; con mucho.

muck n suciedad f.
mucous adj mocoso/sa.
mucus n moco m.
mud n barro m.
muddle vt confundir; * n confusión f.
muddy adj fangoso/sa.
mudguard n guardabarros m invar.
muffle vt embozar.
mug n jarra f.
muggy adj bochornoso/sa.
mulberry n mora f; ~ tree morera f.
mule n mulo m, mula f.
mull vt meditar.
multifarious adj múltiple.
multimedia adj multimedia.
multiple adj múltiplo/a; * n múltiplo m.
multiplication n multiplicación f; ~ table tabla de multiplicar f.
multiply vt multiplicar.
multitude n multitud f.
mumble vt, vi refunfuñar.
mummy¹ n mamá f.
mummy² n momia f.
mumps npl paperas fpl.
munch vt mascar.
mundane adj trivial.
municipal adj municipal.
municipality n municipalidad f.
munificence n munificencia f.
munitions npl municiones fpl.
mural n mural m.
murder n asesinato m; homicidio m; * vt asesinar.
murderer n asesino/na m/f.
murderess n asesina f.
murderous adj homicida.
murky adj sombrío/ría.
murmur n murmullo m;* vi murmurar.
muscle n músculo m.
muscular adj muscular.

muse vi meditar.
museum n museo m.
mushroom n (bot) seta f; champiñón m.
music n musica f.
musical adj musical; melodioso/sa.
musician n músico/ca m/f.
musk n almizcle m.
muslin n muselina f.
mussel n mejillón m.
must v aux tener que, deber; deber de.
mustard n mostaza f.
muster vt agregar.
musty adj mohoso/sa, añejo/ja.
mute adj mudo/da, silencioso/sa.
muted adj callado/da.
mutilate vt mutilar.
mutilation n mutilación f.
mutiny n motin, tumulto m; * vi amotinarse, rebelarse.
mutter vt, vi murmurar, musitar; * n murmuración f.
mutton n carnero m.
mutual adj mutuo/tua, mutual, recíproco/ca; ~ly adv mutuamente, recíprocamente.
muzzle n bozal m; hocico m; * vt embozar.
my pn mi, mis; mio, mia; mios, mias.
myriad n miríada f; gran número m.
myrrh n mirra f.
myrtle n mirto, arrayán m.
myself pn yo mismo/ma.
mysterious adj misterioso/sa; ~ly adv misteriosamente.
mystery n misterio m.
mystic(al) adj místico/ca.
mystify vt dejar perplejo/ja.
mystique n misterio m.
myth n mito m.
mythology n mitología f.

N

nab vt agarrar.

nag n jaca f; * vt regañar.

nagging adj persistente; * npl quejas fpl.

nail n uña f; garra f; clavo m; * vt clavar.

nailbrush n cepillo de uñas m.

nailfile n lima de uñas f.

nail polish n esmalte de uñas m.

nail scissors npl tijeras de manicura fpl.

naïve adj ingenuo/nua.

naked adj desnudo/da evidente; puro/ra, simple.

name n nombre m; fama, reputación f; * vt nombrar; mencionar.

nameless adj anónimo/ma.

nameplate n planchuela f.

namely adv a saber.

namesake n tocayo/ya m/f.

nanny n niñera f.

nap n sueño ligero m.

napalm n napalm m.

nape n nuca f.

napkin n servilleta f.

nappy n pañal m.

narcissus n (bot) narciso m.

narcotic adj narcótico/ca; * n narcótico m.

narrate vt narrar, relatar.

narrative adj narrativo/va; * n narrativa f.

narrow adj angosto/ta, estrecho/cha; ~ly adv estrechamente; * vt estrechar; limitar.

narrow-minded adj estrecho/cha de miras.

narrow pass n puerto m.

nasal adj nasal.

nasty adj sucio/cia, puerco/ca; obsceno/na; sórdido/da.

natal adj nativo/va; natal.

nation n nación f.

national adj, ~ly adv nacional(mente).

nationalism n nacionalismo m.

nationalist adj, n nacionalista m/f.

nationality n nacionalidad f.

nationalize vt nacionalizar.

nationwide adj a nivel nacional.

native adj nativo/va; * n natural m/f.

native language n lengua materna f.

Nativity n Navidad f.

natural adj natural; sencillo/lla; ~ly adv naturalmente.

natural gas n gas natural m.

naturalist n naturalista m/f.

naturalize vt naturalizar.

nature n naturaleza f; índole f.

naturopath n naturópata m/f.

naught n cero m.

naughty adj malo/la, malvado/da.

nausea n náuseas fpl, gana de vomitar f.

nauseate vt dar náuseas a.

nauseous adj fastidioso/sa.

nautical, naval adj náutico/ca, naval.

nave n nave (de la iglesia) f.

navel n ombligo m.

navigate vi navegar.

navigation n navegación f.

navy n marina f; armada f.

near prep cerca de, junto a; * adv casi; cerca, cerca de; * adj cercano/na, próximo/ma.

nearby adj cercano/na.

nearly adv casi.

near-sighted adj miope.

neat adj hermoso/sa, pulido/da; puro/ra; neto/ta; ~ly adv elegantemente.

nebulous adj nebuloso/sa.

necessarily adv necesariamente.

necessary adj necesario/ria.

necessitate vt necesitar.

necessity n necesidad f.

neck n cuello m; * vi besuquearse.

necklace n collar m.

nectar n néctar m.

née, nee adj: ~ Brown de soltera Brown.

need n necesidad f; pobreza f; * vt necesitar.

needle n aguja f.

needless adj superfluo/lua, inútil.

needlework n costura f; bordado de aguja m; obra de punto m.

needy adj necesitado/da, pobre.

negation n negación f.

negative adj negativo/va; ~ly adv negativamente; * n negativa f.

neglect vt descuidar, desatender; * n negligencia f.

negligee n salto de cama m.

negligence n negligencia f; descuido m.

negligent adj negligente, descuidado/da; ~ly adv negligentemente.

negligible adj insignificante.

negotiate vt, vi negociar (con).

negotiation n negociación f; negocio m.

Negress n negra f.

Negro adj negro/gra; * n negro m.

neigh vi relinchar; * n relincho m.

neighbour n vecino/na m/f; * vt confinar.

neighbourhood n vecindad f; vecindario m.

neighbouring adj vecino/na.

neighbourly adj sociable.

neither conj ni; * pn ninguno/na, ni uno ni otro, ni una ni otra.

neon n neón m.

neon light n luz de neón f.

nephew n sobrino m.

nepotism n nepotismo m.

nerve n nervio m; valor m.

nerve-racking adj espantoso/sa.

nervous adj nervioso/sa; nervudo/da.

nervous breakdown n crisis nerviosa f.

nest n nido m; nidada f.

nest egg n (fig) ahorros mpl.

nestle vt anidarse.

net n red f.

netball n nétbol m.

net curtain n visillo m.

netting n mallado m.

nettle n ortiga f.

network n red f, malla f.

neurone n neurona f.

neurosis n neurosis f invar.

neurotic adj, n neurótico/ca m/f.

neuter adj (gr) neutro/tra.

neutral adj neutral.

neutrality n neutralidad f.

neutralize vt neutralizar.

neutron n neutrón m.

neutron bomb n bomba de neutrones f.

never adv nunca, jamás; ~ mind no importa.

never-ending adj sin fin.

nevertheless adv no obstante.

new adj nuevo/va, fresco/sca, reciénte; ~ly adv nuevamente.

newborn adj recién nacido/da.

newcomer n recién llegado/da m.

new-fangled adj inventado/da por novedad.

news npl novedad, noticias fpl.

news agency n agencia de noticias f.
newsagent n vendedor/a de periódicos m/f.
newscaster n presentador/a m/f.
news flash n noticia de última hora f.
newsletter n boletín m.
newspaper n periódico m.
newsreel n noticiario m.
New Year n Año Nuevo m; ~'s Day Día de Año Nuevo m; ~'s Eve Nochevieja f.
next adj próximo/ma; **the ~ day** el día siguiente; * adv luego, inmediatamente después.
nib n pico m; punta f.
nibble vt picar, mordiscar.
nice adj simpático/ca; agradable; lindo/da; ~**ly** adv bien.
nice-looking adj guapo/pa.
niche n nicho m.
nick n mella f; * vt (sl) robar.
nickel n níquel m; moneda de cinco centavos f.
nickname n mote, apodo m; * vt poner apodos.
nicotine n nicotina f.
niece n sobrina f.
niggling adj insignificante.
night n noche f; velador m; **by ~** de noche; **good ~** buenas noches.
nightclub n cabaret m.
nightfall n anochecer m.
nightingale n ruiseñor m.
nightly adv por las noches, todas las noches; * adj nocturno/na.
nightmare n pesadilla f.
night school n clases nocturnas fpl.
night shift n turno de noche m.
night-time n noche f.
night work n vela f.
nihilist n nihilista m/f.
nimble adj ligero/ra, activo/va, listo/ta, ágil.

nine adj, n nueve.
nineteen adj, n diecinueve.
nineteenth adj, n decimonoveno/na.
ninetieth adj, n nonagésimo/ma.
ninety adj, n noventa.
ninth adj, n nono/na, noveno/na.
nip vt pellizcar; morder.
nipple n pezón m; tetilla f.
nit n liendre f.
nitrogen n nitrógeno m.
no adv no; * adj ningún, ninguno/na.
nobility n nobleza f.
noble adj noble; insigne; * n noble m/f.
nobleman n noble m.
nobody n nadie, ninguna persona f.
nocturnal adj nocturnal, nocturno/na.
nod n cabeceo m; señal f; * vi cabecear; amodorrarse.
noise n ruido, estruendo m; rumor m.
noisily adv con ruido.
noisiness n ruido, tumulto, alboroto m.
noisy adj ruidoso/sa, turbulento/ta.
nominal adj, ~**ly** adv nominal(mente).
nominate vt nombrar.
nomination n nominación f.
nominative n (gr) nominativo m.
nominee n candidato/ta m/f.
nonalcoholic adj no alcohólico/ca.
nonaligned adj no alineado/da.
nonchalant adj indiferente.
noncommittal adj reservado/da.
nonconformist n inconformista m/f.
nondescript adj no descrito/ta.
none adj nadie, ninguno/na.
nonentity n nulidad f.
nonetheless adv sin embargo.
nonexistent adj inexistente.
nonfiction n no ficción f.
nonplussed adj confuso/sa.

nonsense n disparate, absurdo m.

nonsensical adj absurdo/da.

nonsmoker n no fumador/a m/f.

nonstick adj antiadherente.

nonstop adj directo/ta; * adv sin parar.

noodles npl fideos (chinos) mpl.

noon n mediodía m.

noose n nudo corredizo m.

nor conj ni.

normal adj normal.

north n norte m; * adj del norte.

North America n América del Norte, Norteamérica f.

northeast n nor(d)este m.

northerly, northern adj norteño/ña.

North Pole n polo norte m.

northward(s) adv hacia el norte.

northwest n nor(d)oeste m.

nose n nariz f; olfato m.

nosebleed n hemorragia nasal f.

nosedive n picado vertical m.

nostalgia n nostalgia f.

nostril n ventana de la nariz f.

not adv no.

notable adj notable; memorable.

notably adv especialmente.

notary n notario/ria m/f.

notch n muesca f; * vt hacer muescas.

note n nota, marca f; señal f; aprecio m; billete m; consecuen cia f; noticia f; indirecta f; * vt notar, marcar; observar.

notebook n cuaderno m, libreta f.

noted adj afamado/da, celebre.

notepad n bloc m.

notepaper n papel de cartas m.

nothing n nada f; good for ~ lo que sirve para nada.

notice n noticia f; aviso m; * vt observar.

noticeable adj notable, reparable.

notification n notificación f.

notify vt notificar.

notion n noción f; opinión f; idea f.

notoriety n mala fama f.

notorious adj tristemente célebre; ~ly adv notoriamente.

notwithstanding conj no obstante, aunque.

nougat n turrón m.

nought n cero m.

noun n (gr) sustantivo m.

nourish vt nutrir, alimentar.

nourishing adj nutritivo/va.

nourishment n nutrimiento, alimento m.

novel n novela f.

novelist n novelista m/f.

novelty n novedad f.

November n noviembre m.

novice n novicio/cia m/f.

now adv ya, ahora, hoy (en) día; ~ and then de vez en cuando.

nowadays adv hoy (en) día.

nowhere adv en ninguna parte.

noxious adj nocivo/va, dañoso/sa.

nozzle n boquilla f.

nuance n matiz m.

nuclear adj nuclear; ~ power energía nuclear f; ~ power station n central nuclear f.

nucleus n núcleo m.

nude adj desnudo/da, en carnes, en cueros, sin vestido.

nudge vt dar un codazo a.

nudist n nudista m/f.

nudity n desnudez f.

nuisance n daño, perjuicio m; incomodidad f.

nuke n (col) bomba atómica f; * vt atacar con arma nuclear.

null adj nulo/la, inválido/da.

nullify vt anular, invalidar.

numb adj entorpecido/da; * vt entorpecer.

number n número m; cantidad f; * vt numerar.
numberplate n placa de matrícula f.
numbness n entumecimiento m.
numeral n número m.
numerical adj numérico/ca.
numerous adj numeroso/sa.
nun n monja, religiosa f.
nunnery n convento de monjas m.
nuptial adj nupcial; ~s npl nupcias fpl.
nurse n enfermera f; * vt cuidar; amamantar.

nursery n guardería infantil f; criadero m.
nursery rhyme n canción infantil f.
nursery school n parvulario m.
nursing home n clínica de reposo f.
nurture vt criar, educar.
nut n nuez f.
nutcrackers npl cascanueces m invar.
nutmeg n nuez moscada f.
nutritious adj nutritivo/va.
nutshell n cascara de nuez f.
nylon n nylon, nailon m; * adj de nylon, de nailon.

O

oak n roble m.
oar n remo m.
oasis n oasis f invar.
oath n juramento m.
oatmeal n harina de avena f.
oats npl avena f.
obedience n obediencia f.
obedient adj, ~ly adv obediente(mente).
obese adj obeso/sa, gordo/da.
obesity n obesidad f.
obey vt obedecer.
obituary n necrología f.
object n objeto m; * vt objetar.
objection n oposición, objeción, réplica f.
objectionable adj desagradable.
objective adj objetivo/va; * n objetivo m.
obligation n obligación f.
obligatory adj obligatorio/ria.
oblige vt obligar; complacer, favorecer.
obliging adj servicial.
oblique adj oblicuo/cua; indirecto/ta; ~ly adv oblicuamente.

obliterate vt borrar.
oblivion n olvido m.
oblivious adj olvidadizo/za.
oblong adj oblongo/ga.
obnoxious adj odioso/sa.
oboe n oboe m.
obscene adj obsceno/na, impúdico/ca.
obscenity n obscenidad f.
obscure adj oscuro/ra; ~ly adv oscuramente; * vt oscurecer.
obscurity n oscuridad f.
observance n observancia f; reverencia f.
observant adj observante, respetuoso/sa.
observantly adv cuidadosamente, atentamente.
observation n observación f.
observatory n observatorio m.
observe vt observar, mirar.
observer n observador/a m/f.
obsess vt obsesionar.
obsessive adj obsesivo/va.
obsolete adj obsoleto/ta.
obstacle n obstáculo m.

obstinacy *n* tenacidad *f*.
obstinate *adj* obstinado/da; ~ly *adv* obstinadamente.
obstruct *vt* obstruir; impedir.
obstruction *n* obstrucción *f*; impedimento *m*.
obtain *vt* obtener, adquirir; ~ by cunning sonsacar.
obtainable *adj* asequible.
obtrusive *adj* intruso/sa, importuno/na.
obtuse *adj* obtuso/sa, sin punta; lerdo/da, torpe.
obvious *adj* obvio/via, evidente; ~ly *adv* naturalmente.
occasion *n* ocasión *f*; momento oportuno *m*; * *vt* ocasionar, causar.
occasional *adj* ocasional, casual; ~ly *adv* ocasionalmente.
occupant, occupier *n* ocupante *m/f*; poseedor/a *m/f*; inquilino/na *m/f*.
occupation *n* ocupación *f*; empleo *m*.
occupy *vt* ocupar, emplear.
occur *vi* pasar, ocurrir.
occurrence *n* incidente *m*.
ocean *n* océano *m*; alta mar *f*.
ocean-going *adj* de alta mar.
oceanic *adj* oceánico/ca.
ochre *n* ocre *m*.
octave *n* octava *f*.
October *n* octubre *m*.
octopus *n* pulpo *m*.
odd *adj* impar; particular; extravagante; extraño/ña; ~ly *adv* extrañamente.
oddity *n* singularidad, particularidad, rareza *f*.
oddness *n* desigualdad *f*; singularidad *f*.
odds *npl* probabilidades *fpl*; apuestas *fpl*.
odious *adj* odioso/sa.

odorous *adj* odorífero/ra.
odour *n* olor *m*; fragancia *f*.
of *prep* de; tocante; según.
of course *interj* ¡naturalmente!
off *adj* desconectado/da; apagado/da; cerrado/da; cancelado/da; ~! *excl* ¡fuera!
offence *n* ofensa *f*; injuria *f*.
offend *vt* ofender, irritar; injuriar; * *vi* pecar.
offender *n* delincuente *m*.
offensive *adj* ofensivo/va; injurioso/sa; ~ly *adv* ofensivamente.
offer *vt* ofrecer; * *n* oferta *f*.
offering *n* sacrificio *m*; oferta *f*.
offhand *adj* descortés; * *adv* de repente.
office *n* oficina *f*; oficio, empleo *m*; servicio *m*.
office building *n* bloque de oficinas *m*.
office hours *npl* horas de oficina *fpl*.
officer *n* oficial/a, empleado/da *m/f*.
office worker *n* oficinista *m/f*.
official *adj* oficial; ~ly *adv* de oficio; * *n* empleado *m*.
officiate *vi* oficiar.
officious *adj* oficioso/sa; ~ly *adv* oficiosamente.
off-line *adj*, *adv* fuera de línea.
off-peak *adj* de temporada baja.
off-season *adj*, *adv* fuera de temporada, en tarifa reducida.
offset *vt* contrarrestar.
offshoot *n* ramificación *f*.
offshore *adj* costero/ra.
offside *adj* fuera de juego.
offspring *n* prole *f*; linaje *m*; descendencia *f*.
offstage *adv* entre bastidores.
off-the-peg *adj* confeccionado/da.
ogle *vt* comerse con los ojos.
oil *n* aceite *m*; óleo *m*; * *vt* engrasar.

oilcan n lata de aceite f.

oilfield n campo petrolífero m.

oil filter n filtro de aceite m.

oil painting n pintura al óleo f.

oil rig n torre de perforación f.

oil slick n marea negra f.

oil tanker n petrolero m.

oil well n pozo petrolífero m.

oily adj aceitoso/sa; grasiento/ta.

ointment n ungüento m.

OK, okay excl vale; * adj bien; * vt dar el visto bueno a.

old adj viejo/ja; antiguo/gua.

old age n vejez f.

old-fashioned adj pasado/da de moda.

olive n olivo m; oliva f.

olive oil n aceite de oliva m.

Olympic Games n las Olímpicos f.

omelette n tortilla (francesa) f.

omen n agüero, presagio m.

ominous adj ominoso/sa.

omission n omisión f; descuido m.

omit vt omitir.

omnipotence n omnipotencia f.

omnipotent adj omnipotente, todo-poderoso/sa.

on prep sobre, encima, en; de; a; * adj encendido/da; prendido/da; abierto/ta; puesto/ta.

once adv una vez; **at ~** en seguida; **all at ~** de una vez, en seguida; **~ more** otra vez.

oncoming adj que viene de frente.

one adj un, uno, una; **~ by ~** uno a uno, una a una, uno por uno, una por una.

one-day excursion n billete de ida y vuelta en un día m.

one-man n individual.

onerous adj oneroso/sa, molesto/ta.

oneself pn sí mismo; sí misma.

one-sided adj parcial.

one-to-one adj de uno a uno; cara a cara.

ongoing adj continuo/nua.

onion n cebolla f.

on-line adj, adv en línea.

onlooker n espectador/a m/f.

only adj único/ca, solo/la; * adv solamente.

onset, onslaught n acometida f; ataque m.

onus n responsabilidad f.

onward(s) adv adelante.

ooze n manar suavemente, rezumar.

opaque adj opaco/ca.

open adj abierto/ta; patente, evidente; sincero/ra, franco/ca; **~ly** adv con franqueza; * vt (vi) abrir(se); descubrir(se); **to ~ on to** dar a; **to ~ up** vt abrir; vi abrirse.

opening n abertura f; (com) salida f; principio m.

open-minded adj de mentalidad abierta.

openness n claridad f; franqueza, sinceridad f.

opera n ópera f.

opera house n teatro de la ópera m.

operate vi obrar, operar.

operating theatre n quirófano m.

operation n operación f; efecto m.

operational adj operacional.

operative adj operativo/va.

operator n operario/ria m/f; operador/a m/f.

ophthalmic adj oftálmico/ca.

opine vi opinar, juzgar.

opinion n opinión f; juicio m.

opinionated adj testarudo/da.

opinion poll n sondeo m.

opponent n antagonista m/f; adversario/ria m/f.

opportune adj oportuno/na.

opportunist *n* oportunista *m/f*.
opportunity *n* oportunidad *f*.
oppose *vt* oponerse.
opposing *adj* opuesto/ta.
opposite *adj* opuesto/ta; contrario/
ria; * *adv* enfrente; *prep* frente a;
* *n* lo contrario.
opposition *n* oposición *f*; resistencia
f; impedimento *m*.
oppress *vt* oprimir.
oppression *n* opresión *f*.
oppressive *adj* opresivo/va, cruel.
oppressor *n* opresor/a *m/f*.
optic(al) *adj* óptico/ca; ~s *npl* óptica *f*.
optician *n* óptico/ca *m/f*.
optimist *n* optimista *m/f*.
optimistic *adj* optimista.
optimum *adj* óptimo/ma.
option *n* opción *f*; deseo *m*.
optional *adj* facultativo/va.
opulent *adj* opulento/ta.
or *conj* o; u.
oracle *n* oráculo *m*.
oral *adj* oral, vocal; ~ly *adv* verbalmente, de palabra.
orange *n* naranja *f*.
orator *n* orador/a *m/f*.
orbit *n* órbita *f*.
orchard *n* huerto *m*.
orchestra *n* orquesta *f*.
orchestral *adj* orquestal.
orchid *n* orquídea *f*.
ordain *vt* ordenar; establecer.
ordeal *n* prueba rigurosa *f*.
order *n* orden *m/f*; regla *f*; mandato
m; serie, clase *f*; * *vt* ordenar, arreglar; mandar.
order form *n* hoja de pedido *f*.
orderly *adj* ordenado/da, regular.
ordinarily *adv* ordinariamente.
ordinary *adj* ordinario/ria.
ordination *n* ordenación *f*.

ordnance *n* armamento *m*; pertrechos *mpl*.
ore *n* mineral *m*.
organ *n* órgano *m*.
organic *adj* orgánico/ca.
organic farming *n* agricultura biológica *f*.
organism *n* organismo *m*.
organist *n* organista *m/f*.
organization *n* organización *f*.
organize *vt* organizar.
orgasm *n* orgasmo *m*.
orgy *n* orgía *f*.
oriental *adj* oriental.
orifice *n* orificio *m*.
origin *n* origen, principio *m*.
original *adj* original, primitivo/va;
~ly *adv* originalmente.
originality *n* originalidad *f*.
originate *vi* originar.
ornament *n* ornamento *m*; * *vt* orna-
mentar, adornar.
ornamental *adj* ornamental, deco-
rativo/va.
ornate *adj* adornado/da, ataviado/da.
ornithology *n* ornitología *f*.
orphan *n*, *adj* huérfano/na *m/f*.
orphanage *n* orfanato *m*.
orthodox *adj* ortodoxo/xa.
orthodoxy *n* ortodoxia *f*.
orthography *n* ortografía *f*.
orthopaedic *adj* ortopédico/ca.
Oscar *n* óscar *m*.
oscillate *vi* oscilar, vibrar.
osprey *n* águila pescadora *f*.
ostensibly *adv* aparentemente.
ostentatious *adj* ostentoso/sa.
osteopath *n* osteópata *m/f*.
ostracize *vt* condenar al ostracismo.
ostrich *n* avestruz *m*.
other *pn* otro, otra.
otherwise *adv* de otra manera, por
otra parte.

otter n nutria f.

ouch excl ¡ay!

ought v aux deber, ser menester.

ounce n onza f.

our, ours pn nuestro, nuestra, nuestros, nuestras.

ourselves pn pl nosotros mismos, nosotras mismas.

oust vt quitar; desposeer.

out adv fuera, afuera; apagado/da.

outboard adj: ~ **motor** fueraborda m.

outbreak n erupción f.

outburst n explosión f.

outcast n paria m/f.

outcome n resultado m.

outcry n clamor m; gríterío m.

outdated adj fuera de moda.

outdo vt exceder a otro, sobrepujar.

outdoor adj, ~s adv al aire libre.

outer adj exterior.

outermost adj extremo/ma; lo más exterior.

outer space n espacio exterior m.

outfit n vestidos mpl; ropa f.

outfitter n sastre m.

outgoing adj extrovertido/da.

outgrow vt sobrecrecer.

outhouse n dependencia (de una casa) f.

outing n excursión f.

outlandish adj estrafalario/ria.

outlaw n bandido m; * vt proscribir.

outlay n despensa f, gastos mpl.

outlet n salida f.

outline n contorno m; bosquejo m.

outlive vt sobrevivir.

outlook n perspectiva f.

outlying adj distante, lejos.

outmoded adj anticuado/da.

outnumber vt superar en número.

out-of-date adj caducado/da; pasado/da de moda.

outpatient n paciente externo/na m/f.

outpost n puesto avanzado m.

output n rendimiento m; salida f.

outrage n ultraje m; * vt ultrajar.

outrageous adj escandaloso/sa; atroz; ~ly adv escandalosamente; injuriosamente; enormemente.

outright adv absolutamente; * adj completo/ta.

outrun vt correr más que.

outset n principio m.

outshine vt exceder en brillantez, eclipsar.

outside n superficie f; exterior m; apariencia f; * adv fuera; * prep fuera de.

outsider n forástero m/f.

outsize adj de talla grande.

outskirts npl alrededores mpl.

outspoken adj muy franco/ca.

outstanding adj excepcional; pendiente.

outstretch vt extenderse, alargar.

outstrip vt dejar atrás; superar.

out-tray n bandeja de salida f.

outward adj exterior, externo/na; de ida; ~ly adv por fuera; exteriormente.

outweigh vt pesar más que.

outwit vt burlar.

oval n óvalo m; * adj oval.

ovary n ovario m.

oven n horno m.

ovenproof adj resistente al horno.

over prep sobre, encima; más de; durante; **all** ~ por todos lados; * adj terminado/da; de sobra; ~ **again** otra vez; ~ **and** ~ repetidas veces.

overall adj total; * adv en conjunto; ~s npl overol m; mono m.

overawe vt imponer respeto.

overbalance vi perder el equilibrio.

overbearing adj déspótico/ca.

overboard adv (mar) por la borda, al mar.

overbook vt sobrereservar.

overcast adj encapotado/da.

overcharge vt sobrecargar; cobrar de más.

overcoat n abrigo m.

overcome vt vencer; superar.

overconfident adj demasiado confiado/da.

overcrowded adj atestado/da; superpoblado/da.

overdo vt hacer más de lo necesario; exagerar.

overdose n sobredosis f invar.

overdraft n saldo deudor, descubierto m.

overdrawn adj en descubierto.

overdress vt engalanar con exceso.

overdue adj retrasado/da.

overeat vi comer demasiado.

overestimate vt sobreestimar.

overflow vt, vi inundar; rebosar; * n inundación f; superabundancia f.

overgrown adj invadido/da.

overgrowth n vegetación exuberante f.

overhang vt colgar sobre.

overhaul vt revisar; * n revisión f.

overhead adv sobre la cabeza, en lo alto.

overhear vt oír por casualidad.

overjoyed adj muy gozoso/sa.

overkill n exceso de medios m.

overland adj, adv por tierra.

overlap vi traslaparse.

overleaf adv al dorso.

overload vt sobrecargar.

overlook vt mirar desde lo alto; examinar; repasar; pasar por alto, tolerar; descuidar.

overnight adv durante la noche; * adj de noche.

overpass n paso superior m.

overpower vt predominar, oprimir.

overpowering adj agobiante.

overrate vt sobrevalorar.

override vt no hacer caso de; anular.

overriding adj predominante.

overrule vt denegar.

overrun vt inundar; infestar; rebasar.

overseas adv fuera del país; * adj extranjero/ra.

oversee vt inspeccionar.

overseer n superintendente m.

overshadow vt eclipsar.

overshoot vt excederse.

oversight n yerro m; equivocación f.

oversleep vi dormir demasiado.

overspill n exceso de población m.

overstate vt exagerar.

overstep vt traspasar, exceder.

overt adj abierto/ta; publico/ca; ~ly adv abiertamente.

overtake vt adelantar, sobrepasar.

overthrow vt trastornar; demoler; destruir; * n trastorno m; ruina, derrota f.

overtime n horas extra fpl.

overtone n trasfondo m.

overture n abertura f; (mus) obertura f.

overturn vt subvertir, trastornar.

overweight adj demasiado pesado/da.

overwhelm vt abrumar; oprimir; sumergir.

overwhelming adj arrollador/a; irresistible.

overwork vi trabajar demasiado.

owe vt deber, tener deudas; estar obligado/da.

owing adj que es debido/da; ~ to por causa de.

owl n búho m.

own adj propio/pia; **my** ~ mío, mía; * vt tener; poseer; **to ~ up** vi confesar.

owner n dueño/ña, propietario/ria m/f.

ownership n posesión f.

ox n buey m; ~**en** pl ganado vacuno m.

oxidize vt oxidar.

oxygen n oxígeno m.

oxygen mask n máscara de oxígeno f.

oxygen tent n tienda de oxígeno f.

oyster n ostra f.

ozone n ozono m.

P

pa n papá m.

pace n paso m; * vt regular el ritmo de; * vi pasear.

pacemaker n marcapasos m invar.

pacific adj pacífico/ca; **P~ Ocean** el Pacífico m.

pacification n pacificación f.

pacify vt pacificar.

pack n lío, fardo m; baraja (de naipes) f; cuadrilla f; * vt empaquetar; hacer la maleta; llenar.

package n paquete m; acuerdo m.

package tour n viaje organizado m.

packet n paquete m.

packing n embalaje m.

pact n pacto m.

pad n bloc m; plataforma f; (sl) casa f; * vt rellenar.

padding n relleno m; paja f.

paddle vi vadear; remar; chapotear; * n canalete m.

paddle steamer n vapor de ruedas m.

paddling pool n piscina para niños f.

paddock n corral m.

paddy field n arrozal m.

paediatrics n pediatría f.

pagan adj, n pagano/na m/f.

page n página f; paje m.

pageant n espectáculo público m.

pageantry n pompa f.

pail n cubo, pozal m.

pain n pena f; castigo m; dolor m; * vt afligir.

pained adj afligido/da.

painful adj dolorido/da; penoso/sa; ~**ly** adv dolorosamente, con pena.

painkiller n analgésico m.

painless adj sin pena; indoloro/ra.

painstaking adj laborioso/sa, meticuloso/sa.

paint vt pintar.

paintbrush n pincel m; brocha f.

painter n pintor m/f.

painting n pintura f.

paintwork n pintura f.

pair n par m; yuntas fpl.

pal n compañero/ra m/f.

palatable adj sabroso/sa.

palate n paladar m; gusto m.

palatial adj palatino/na.

palaver n lío m.

pale adj palido/da; claro/ra.

palette n paleta f.

paling n estacada, palizada f.

pall n cortina de humo f; * vi perder el sabor.

palliative adj paliativo/va; * n paliativo m.

pallid adj pálido/da.

pallor n palidez f.

palm n (bot) palma f.

palmistry n quiromancia f.

Palm Sunday n Domingo de Ramos m.

palpable adj palpable; evidente.

palpitation n palpitación f.

paltry adj irrisorio/ria; mezquino/na.
pamper vt mimar.
pamphlet n folleto m.
pan n cazuela f; sartén f; olla f.
panacea n panacea f.
panache n estilo m.
pancake n crepe f.
pandemonium n jaleo m.
pane n cristal m.
panel n panel m; paño m.
panelling n paneles mpl.
pang n angustia, congoja f.
panic adj, n pánico/ca m.
panicky adj asustadizo/za.
panic-stricken adj preso/sa del pánico.
pansy n (bot) pensamiento m.
pant vi jadear.
panther n pantera f.
panties npl bragas fpl.
pantry n despensa f.
papacy n papado m.
papal adj papal.
papaw, pawpaw, papaya n papaya f.
paper n papel m; periódico m; examen m; estudio m; ~s pl escrituras fpl; (com) fondos mpl; * adj de papel; * vt empape lar; tapizar.
paperback n libro en rústica m.
paper bag n bolsa de papel f.
paperclip n clip m.
paperweight n sujetapapeles m invar.
paperwork n papeleo m.
paprika n pimentón m, paprika f.
par n equivalencia f; igualdad f; par m; at ~ (com) a la par.
parable n parábola f.
parachute n paracaídas m invar; * vi lanzarse en paracaídas.
parade n ostentación, pompa f; (mil) parada f; * vt, vi desfilar; pasear; hacer gala.

paradise n paraíso m.
paradox n paradoja f.
paradoxical adj paradójico/ca.
paraffin n queroseno m.
paragliding n parapente m.
paragon n dechado m.
paragraph n párrafo m.
parallel adj paralelo/la; * n línea paralela f; * vt paralelizar; parangonar.
paralyse vt paralizar.
paralysis n parálisis f.
paralytic adj paralítico/ca.
paramedic n auxiliar sanitario/ria m/f.
paramount adj supremo/ma, superior.
paranoid adj paranoico/ca.
paraphernalia n parafernalia f.
parasite n parásito m.
parasol n parasol, quitasol m.
paratrooper n paracaidista m.
parcel n paquete m; porción, cantidad f; equipajes, bultos mpl; * vt empaquetar, embalar.
parch vt resecar.
parched adj reseco/ca; muerto/ta de sed.
parchment n pergamino m.
pardon n perdón m; * vt perdonar.
parent n padre m; madre f.
parentage n parentela f; extracción f.
parental adj de los padres.
parenthesis n paréntesis m invar.
parish n parroquia f; * adj parroquial.
parishioner n parroquiano/na m/f.
parity n paridad f.
park n parque m; * vt, vi aparcar, estacionar.
parking n aparcamiento, estacionamiento m.
parking meter n parquímetro m.

parking ticket *n* multa de estacionamiento *f*.

parlance *n* lenguaje *m*.

parliament *n* parlamento *m*.

parliamentary *adj* parlamentario/ria.

parlour *n* salón *m*.

parody *n* parodia *f*; * *vt* parodiar.

parole *n*: on ~ en libertad bajo palabra.

parricide *n* parricidio *m*; parricida *m/f*.

parrot *n* papagayo *m*.

parry *vt* parar.

parsley *n* (*bot*) perejil *m*.

parsnip *n* (*bot*) chirivía *f*.

part *n* parte *f*; partido *m*; oficio *m*; papel (de un actor) *m*; obligación *f*; raya *f*; ~s *pl* partes *fpl*; paraje, distrito *m*; * *vt* partir, separar, desunir; * *vi* partirse, separarse; **to ~ with** entregar; pagar; deshacerse de; ~**ly** *adv* en parte.

partial *adj*, ~**ly** *adv* parcial(mente).

participant *n* concursante *m*.

participate *vi* participar (en).

participation *n* participación *f*.

participle *n* (*gr*) participio *m*.

particle *n* partícula *f*.

particular *adj* particular, singular; ~**ly** *adv* particularmente; * *n* particular *m*; particularidad *f*.

parting *n* separación, partida *f*; raya (en los cabellos) *f*.

partisan *n* partidario/ria *m/f*.

partition *n* partición, separación *f*; * *vt* partir, dividir en varias partes.

partner *n* socio/cia, compañero/ra *m/f*.

partnership *n* compañía, sociedad de comercio *f*.

partridge *n* perdiz *f*.

party *n* partido *m*; fiesta *f*.

pass *vt* pasar; traspasar; transferir;

adelantarse a; * *vi* pasar, aprobar; * *n* permiso *m*; puerto *m*; **to ~ away** *vi* fallecer; **to ~ by** *vi* pasar; *vt* pasar por alto; **to ~ on** *vt* transmitir.

passable *adj* pasadero/ra, transitable.

passage *n* pasaje *m*; travesía *f*; pasadizo *m*.

passbook *n* libreta de depósitos *f*.

passenger *n* pasajero/ra *f*.

passer-by *n* transeúnte *m/f*.

passing *adj* pasajero/ra.

passion *n* pasión *f*; amor *m*; celo, ardor *m*.

passionate *adj* apasionado/da; ~**ly** *adv* apasionadamente; ardientemente.

passive *adj* pasivo/va; ~**ly** *adv* pasivamente.

passkey *n* llave maestra *f*.

Passover *n* Pascua *f*.

passport *n* pasaporte *m*.

passport control *n* control de pasaportes *m*.

password *n* contraseña *f*.

past *adj* pasado/da; gastado/da; * *n* (*gr*) pretérito *m*; el pasado; * *prep* más allá de; después de.

pasta *n* pasta *f*.

paste *n* pasta *f*; engrudo *m*; * *vt* engrudar.

pasteurized *adj* pasteurizado/da.

pastime *n* pasatiempo *m*; diversión *f*.

pastor *n* pastor *m*.

pastoral *adj* pastoril; pastoral.

pastry *n* pastelería *f*.

pasture *n* pasto *m*.

pasty *adj* pastoso/sa; pálido/da.

pat *vt* dar golpecillos.

patch *n* remiendo *m*; parche *m*; terreno *m*; * *vt* remendar; **to ~ up** reparar; hacer las paces en.

patchwork n obra de retacitos f; chapucería f.
pâté n paté m.
patent adj patente; privilegiado/da; * n patente f; * vt privilegiar.
patentee n poseedor/a de una patente m/f.
patent leather n charol m.
paternal adj paternal.
paternity n paternidad f.
path n senda f.
pathetic adj patético/ca; ~ally adv patéticamente.
pathological adj patológico/ca.
pathology n patología f.
pathos n patetismo m.
pathway n sendero m.
patience n paciencia f.
patient adj paciente, sufrido/da; ~ly adv con paciencia; * n enfermo/ma m/f.
patio n patio m.
patriarch n patriarca m.
patriot n patriota m.
patriotic adj patriótico/ca.
patriotism n patriotismo m.
patrol n patrulla f; * vi patrullar.
patrol car n coche patrulla m.
patrolman n policía m.
patron n patrón/ona, protector m/f.
patronage n patrocinio m; patronato, patronazgo m.
patronize vt patrocinar, proteger.
patter n golpeteo m; labia f; * vi tamborilear.
pattern n patrón m; dibujo m.
paunch n panza f; vientre m.
pauper n pobre m/f.
pause n pausa f; * vt pausar; deliberar.
pave vt empedrar; enlosar, embaldosar.
pavement n acera f.

pavilion n pabellón m.
paving stone n ladrillo m; losa f.
paw n pata f; garra f; * vt manosear.
pawn n peón m; * vt empeñar.
pawnbroker n prestamista m/f.
pawnshop n casa de empeños f.
pay vt pagar; sufrir por; to ~ back vt reembolsar; to ~ for pagar; to ~ off vt liquidar; vi dar resultados; * n paga f; salario m.
payable adj pagadero/ra.
payday n día de paga m.
payee n portador/a m/f.
pay envelope n sobre (de paga) m.
paymaster n pagador/a m/f.
payment n paga f; pagamento, pago m.
payphone n teléfono público m.
payroll n nómina f.
pea n guisante m.
peace n paz f.
peaceful adj tranquilo/la, pacífico/ca.
peach n melocotón, durazno m.
peacock n pavón, pavo real m.
peak n cima f.
peak hours, peak period n horas punta fpl.
peal n campaneo m; estruendo m.
peanut n cacahuete m; maní m.
pear n pera f.
pearl n perla f.
peasant n campesino/na m/f.
peat n turba f.
pebble n guija f; guijarro m.
peck n picotazo m; * vt picotear; picar.
pecking order n orden de jerarquía m.
peculiar adj peculiar, particular, singular; ~ly adv peculiarmente.
peculiarity n particularidad, singularidad f.
pedal n pedal m; * vi pedalear.

edant n pedante m/f.

edantic adj pedante.

edestal n pedestal m.

edestrian n peatón/ona m/f; * adj pedestre.

pedestrian crossing n paso de peatones m.

edigree n genealogía f; * adj de raza.

pedlar n vendedor/a ambulante m/f.

peek vi mirar de soslayo.

peel vt pelar; * vi desconcharse; * n piel f; cáscara f.

peer n compañero/ra m/f; par m.

peerless adj incomparable.

peeved adj enojado/da.

peevish adj regañón/ona, bronco/ca; enojadizo/za.

peg n clavija f; gancho m; * vt clavar.

pelican n pelícano m.

pellet n bolita f; ~s perdigones mpl.

pelt n pellejo, cuero m; * vt arrojar; * vi llover a cántaros.

pen n bolígrafo m; pluma f; redil m.

penal adj penal.

penalty n pena f; castigo m; multa f.

penance n penitencia f.

pence n pl de penny.

pencil n lápiz m; lapicero m.

pencil case n estuche m.

pendant n pendiente m.

pending adj pendiente.

pendulum n péndulo m.

penetrate vt penetrar.

penguin n pingüino m.

penicillin n penicilina f.

peninsula n península f.

penis n pene m.

penitence n penitencia f.

penitent adj, n penitente m.

penknife n navaja f.

pennant n banderola f.

penniless adj sin dinero.

penny n penique m.

penpal n amigo/ga por carta m/f.

pension n pensión f; * vt dar pensión a.

pensive adj pensativo/va; ~ly adv pensativamente.

pentagon n: the P~ el Pentágono.

Pentecost n Pentecostés m.

penthouse n ático m.

pent-up adj reprimido/da.

penultimate adj penúltimo/ma.

penury n penuria, carestía f.

people n pueblo m; nación f; gente f; * vt poblar.

people mover n monovolumen m.

pep n energía f; to ~ up vt animar.

pepper n pimienta f; * vt sazonar con pimienta.

peppermint n menta f.

per prep por.

per annum adv al año.

per capita adj, adv per cápita.

perceive vt percibir, comprender.

percentage n porcentaje m.

perception n percepción, idea, noción f.

perch n percha f.

perchance adv acaso, quizá.

percolate vt colar; filtrar.

percolator n cafetera de filtro f.

percussion n percusión f; golpe m.

perdition n pérdida, ruina f.

peremptory adj perentorio/ria; decisivo/va.

perennial adj perenne; perpetuo/tua.

perfect adj perfecto/ta, acabado/da; puro/ra; ~ly adv perfectamente; * vt perfeccionar, acabar.

perfection n perfección f.

perforate vt horadar.

perforated adj (of stamps) dentado/da.

perforation n perforación f.

perform vt ejecutar; efectuar; * vi representar, hacer papel.

performance n ejecución f; cumplimiento m; obra f; representación teatral, función f.

performer n ejecutor/a m/f; actor m, actriz f.

perfume n perfume m; fragancia f; * vt perfumar.

perhaps adv quizá, quizás.

peril n peligro, riesgo m.

perilous adj peligroso/sa; ~ly adv peligrosamente.

perimeter n perímetro m.

period n período m; época f; regla f.

periodic adj periódico/ca; ~ally adv periódicamente.

periodical n periódico m.

peripheral adj periférico/ca; * n periférico m.

perish vi perecer.

perishable adj perecedero/ra.

perjure vt perjurar.

perjury n perjurio m.

perk n extra m.

perky adj animado/da.

perm n permanente f.

permanent adj, ~ly adv permanente(mente).

permeate vt penetrar, atravesar.

permissible adj lícito/ta, permiso.

permission n permiso m.

permissive adj permisivo/va.

permit vt permitir; * n permiso m.

permutation n permutación f.

perpendicular adj, ~ly adv perpendicular(mente); * n línea perpendicular f.

perpetrate vt perpetrar, cometer.

perpetual adj perpetuo/tua; ~ly adv perpetuamente.

perpetuate vt perpetuar, eternizar.

perplex vt confundir.

persecute vt perseguir, importunar

persecution n persecución f.

perseverance n perseverancia f.

persevere vi perseverar.

persist vi persistir.

persistence adj persistencia f.

persistent adj persistente.

person n persona f.

personable adj atractivo/va.

personage n personaje m.

personal adj, ~ly adv personal(mente).

personal assistant n secretario/ria personal m/f.

personal column n anuncios personales mpl.

personal computer n ordenador personal m, computadora personal f.

personality n personalidad f.

personification n personificación f.

personify vt personificar.

personnel n personal m.

perspective n perspectiva f.

perspiration n transpiración f.

perspire vi transpirar.

persuade vt persuadir.

persuasion n persuasión f.

persuasive adj persuasivo/va; ~ly adv de modo persuasivo.

pert adj listo/ta, vivo/va; petulante.

pertaining: ~ to prep relacionado/da con.

pertinent adj pertinente; ~ly adv oportunamente.

pertness n impertinencia f; vivacidad f.

perturb vt perturbar.

perusal n lectura, lección f.

peruse vt leer; examinar atentamente.

pervade vt atravesar, penetrar.

erverse *adj* perverso/sa, depravado/da; **~ly** *adv* perversamente.

ervert *vt* pervertir, corromper.

essimist *n* pesimista *m/f*.

est *n* plaga *f*; molestia *f*.

ester *vt* molestar, cansar.

estilence *n* pestilencia *f*.

et *n* animal doméstico *m*; favorito/ta *m/f*; * *vt* mimar; * *vi* besuquearse.

etal *n* (*bot*) pétalo *m*.

petite *adj* chiquito/ta.

petition *n* presentación, petición *f*; * *vt* suplicar; requerir en justicia.

petrified *adj* horrorizado/da.

petrol *n* gasolina *f*; **four-star ~** súper *f*.

petroleum *n* petróleo *m*.

petticoat *n* enaguas *fpl*.

pettiness *n* mezquindad *f*; pequeñez *f*.

petty *adj* mezquino/na; insignificante.

petty cash *n* dinero para gastos menores *m*.

petty officer *n* contramaestre *m*.

petulant *adj* petulante.

pew *n* banco *m*.

pewter *n* peltre *m*.

phantom *n* fantasma *m*.

Pharisee *n* fariseo/sea *m/f*.

pharmaceutical *adj* farmacéutico/ca.

pharmacist *n* farmacéutico/ca *m/f*.

pharmacy *n* farmacia *f*.

phase *n* fase *f*.

pheasant *n* faisán *m*.

phenomenal *adj* fenomenal.

phenomenon *n* fenómeno *m*.

phial *n* vial *m*.

philanthropic *adj* filantrópico/ca.

philanthropist *n* filántropo/pa *m/f*.

philanthropy *n* filantropía *f*.

philologist *n* filólogo/ga *m/f*.

philology *n* filología *f*.

philosopher *n* filósofo/fa *m/f*.

philosophic(al) *adj* filosófico/ca; **~ally** *adv* filosóficamente.

philosophize *vi* filosofar.

philosophy *n* filosofía *f*; **natural ~** filosofía natural *f*.

phlegm *n* flema *f*.

phlegmatic(al) *adj* flemático/ca.

phobia *n* fobia *f*.

phone *n* teléfono *m*; * *vt* telefonear; **to ~ back** volver a llamar; **to ~ up** llamar por teléfono.

phone book *n* guía telefónica *f*.

phone box*n* cabina telefónica *f*.

phone call *n* llamada (telefonica) *f*.

phosphorus *n* fosforo *m*.

photocopier *n* fotocopiadora *f*.

photocopy *n* fotocopia *f*.

photograph *n* fotografía *f*; * *vt* fotografiar.

photographer *n* fotógrafo/fa *m/f*.

photographic *adj* fotográfico/ca.

photography *n* fotografía *f*.

phrase *n* frase *f*; estilo *m*; * *vt* expresar.

phrase book *n* libro de frases *m*.

physical *adj* físico/ca; **~ly** *adv* físicamente.

physical education *n* educación física *f*.

physician *n* médico/ca *m/f*.

physicist *n* físico/ca *m/f*.

physiological *adj* fisiológico/ca.

physiologist *n* fisiólogo/ga *m/f*.

physiology *n* fisiología *f*.

physiotherapy *n* fisioterapia *f*.

physique *n* físico *m*.

pianist *n* pianista *m/f*.

piano *n* piano *m*.

piccolo *n* flautín *m*.

pick *vt* escoger, elegir; recoger;

mondar, limpiar; **to ~ on** vt meterse con; **to ~ out** vt escoger; **to ~ up** vi ir mejor; recobrarse; * vt recoger; comprar; aprender; * n pico m; **the ~ of** lo más escogido de.

pickaxe n pico m.

picket n piquete m.

pickle n escabeche m; *vt escabechar.

pickpocket n carterista m/f.

pick-up (auto) furgoneta f.

picnic n picnic m.

pictorial adj pictórico/ca.

picture n pintura f; retrato m; * vt pintar; figurar.

picture book n libro de dibujos m.

picturesque adj pintoresco/ca.

pie n pastel m; tarta f; empanada f.

piece n pedazo m; pieza, obra f; * vt remendar.

piecemeal adv en pedazos; * adj dividido/da.

piecework n destajo m; * vi **to do ~** trabajar a destajo.

pier n pilar m; muelle m.

pierce vt penetrar, agujerear, taladrar.

piercing adj penetrante.

piety n piedad, devoción f.

pig n cerdo m; (sl) cochino m.

pigeon n paloma f; **carrier,homing ~** paloma mensajera f.

pigeonhole n casillero m.

piggy bank n hucha f.

pig-headed adj terco/ca.

pigsty n pocilga f.

pigtail n trenza f.

pike n lucio m; pica f.

pile n estaca f; pila f; montón m; pelo m; pelillo m; **~s** pl almorranas fpl; * vt amontonar, apilar.

pile-up n colisión múltiple f.

pilfer vt hurtar.

pilgrim n peregrino/na m/f.

pilgrimage n peregrinación f.

pill n píldora f.

pillage vt saquear.

pillar n pilar m.

pillion n asiento trasero m.

pillow n almohada f.

pillow case n funda de almohada f.

pilot n piloto m/f; * vt pilotar; (fig) guiar.

pilot light n piloto m.

pimple n grano m.

pimp n chulo, cafiche m.

pin n alfiler m; **~s and needles** npl hormigueo m; * vt prender con alfileres; fijar con clavija.

pinafore n delantal m.

pinball n flíper m.

pincers n pinzas, tenazuelas fpl.

pinch vt pellizcar; (sl) birlar; * vi apretar; * n pellizco m.

pincushion n acerico m.

pine n (bot) pino m; * vi ansiar por.

pineapple n piña f, ananás m invar.

ping n sonido agudo m.

pink n rosa f; * adj color de rosa.

pinnacle n cumbre f.

pinpoint vt precisar.

pint n pinta f.

pioneer n pionero/ra m/f.

pious adj pío, pía, devoto/ta; **~ly** adv piadosamente.

pip n pepita f.

pipe n tubo, caño m; pipa f; **~s** cañería f.

pipe cleaner n limpiapipas m invar.

pipe dream n sueño imposible m.

pipeline n tubería f; oleoducto m; gasoducto m.

piper n gaitero/ra m/f.

piping adj hirviente.

pique n pique m; desazón f; ojeriza f.

piracy n piratería f.

irate n pirata m/f.

irouette n pirueta f; vi piruetear.

Pisces n Piscis m (signo del zodiaco).

iss n (sl) meada f; * vi mear.

istol n pistola f.

iston n émbolo m.

it n hoyo m; mina f.

itch n lanzamiento m; tono m; * vt tirar, arrojar; * vi caerse; caer de cabeza.

itch-black adj negro/gra como boca de lobo.

pitcher n cántaro m.

pitchfork n horca f.

pitfall n trampa f.

pithy adj meduloso/sa.

pitiable adj lastimoso/sa.

pitiful adj lastimoso/sa, compasivo/va; ~ly adv lastimosamente.

pittance n pitanza f, ración f; porcioncilla f.

pity n piedad f, compasión f; * vt compadecer.

pivot n eje m.

pizza n pizza f.

placard n pancarta f.

placate vt apaciguar.

place n lugar, sitio m; rango, empleo m; * vt colocar; poner.

placid adj plácido/da, quieto/ta; ~ly adv plácidamente.

plagiarism n plagio m.

plague n peste, plaga f; * vt atormentar; infestar, apestar.

plaice n platija f (pez).

plaid n tartán m.

plain adj liso/sa, llano/na, abierto/ta; sincero/ra; puro/ra, simple, común; claro/ra, evidente, distinto/ta; ~ly adv llanamente; claramente; * n llano m.

plaintiff n (law) demandante m/f.

plait n pliegue m; trenza f; * vt plegar; trenzar.

plan n plano m; plan m; * vt proyectar.

plane n avión m; plano m; cepillo m; * vi allanar; acepillar.

planet n planeta m.

planetary adj planetario/ria.

plank n tabla f.

planner n planificador/a m/f.

planning n planificación f.

plant n planta f; fábrica f; maquinaria f; * vt plantar.

plantation n plantación f; colonia f.

plaque n placa f.

plaster n yeso m; emplasto m; * vt enyesar; emplastar.

plastered adj (sl) borracho/cha.

plasterer n yesero/ra m/f.

plaster of Paris n yeso mate m.

plastic adj plástico/ca.

plastic surgery n cirugía plástica f.

plate n plato m; lámina f; placa f.

plateau n meseta f.

plate glass n vidrio cilindrado m.

platform n plataforma f.

platinum n platino m.

platitude n tópico m.

platoon n (mil) pelotón m.

platter n fuente f; plato grande m.

plaudit n aplauso m.

plausible adj plausible.

play n juego m; comedia f; * vt, vi jugar; juguetear; representar; (mus) tocar; **to – down** vt quitar importancia a.

playboy n playboy m.

player n jugador/a m/f; comediante/ta m/f, actor m, actriz f.

playful adj juguetón/ona, travieso/sa; ~ly adv juguetonamente, retozando.

playmate n camarada m/f.

playground n patio m.

playgroup n parvulario m.

play-off n desempate m.

playpen n corral (de niños) m.

plaything n juguete m.

playwright n dramaturgo/ga m/f.

plea n defensa f; excusa f; pretexto m; * vt pretextar.

plead vt defender en juicio; alegar.

pleasant adj agradable; placentero/ra, alegre; **~ly** adv alegremente, placenteramente.

please vt agradar, complacer.

pleased adj contento/ta.

pleasing adj agradable, placentero/ra.

pleasure n gusto, placer m; recreo m.

pleat n pliegue m.

pledge n prenda f; fianza f; * vt empeñar, prometer.

plentiful adj copioso/sa, abundante.

plenty n copia, abundancia f.

plethora n plétora f.

pleurisy n pleuresía f.

pliable, pliant adj flexible, dócil.

pliers npl alicates mpl.

plight n situación difícil f.

plinth n plinto m; zócalo m.

plod vi afanarse mucho, ajetrearse.

plot n terreno m; plano m; conspiración, trama f; estratagema f; * vi trazar; conspirar; tramar.

plough n arado m; * vt arar, labrar la tierra; to **~ back** vt reinvertir; to **~ through** abrirse paso; roer.

ploy n truco m.

pluck vt tirar con fuerza; arrancar; desplumar; * n ánimo m.

plucky adj gallardo/da.

plug n tapón m; enchufe m; bujía f; * vt tapar.

plum n ciruela f.

plumage n plumaje m.

plumb n plomada f; * adv a plomo; * vt aplomar.

plumber n fontanero/ra, plomero/r m/f.

plume n pluma f.

plump adj gordo/da, rollizo/za.

plum tree n ciruelo m.

plunder vt saquear, pillar, robar; * n pillaje, botín m.

plunge vi sumergir(se), precipitarse; * n zambullida f.

plunger n desatascador m.

pluperfect n (gr) pluscuamperfecto m.

plural adj, n plural m.

plurality n pluralidad f.

plus n signo de más m; * prep más, y, además de.

plush adj de felpa.

ply vt trabajar con ahínco; * vi aplicarse; (mar) ir y venir.

plywood n madera contrachapada f.

pneumatic adj neumático/ca.

pneumatic drill n martillo neumático m.

pneumonia n pulmonía f.

poach vt escalfar; cazar en vedado; * vi cazar en vedado.

poached adj escalfado/da.

poacher n cazador furtivo m.

poaching n caza furtiva f.

pocket n bolsillo m; bolsa f; * vt embolsar.

pocketbook n cartera f.

pocket money n dinero para gastos m.

pod n vaina f.

podgy adj gordinflón/ona.

poem n poema m.

poet n poeta m, poetisa f.

poetic adj poético/ca.

poetry n poesía f.

poignant adj punzante.

int *n* punta *f*; punto *m*; promonto-
rio *m*; puntillo *m*; estado *m*; **~ of**
view *n* punto de vista *m*; * *vt* apuntar; aguzar; puntuar; **to ~ a gun**
encañonar.

int-blank *adv* directamente.

inted *adj* puntiagudo/da; epigra-
mático/ca; **~ly** *adv* sutilmente.

inter *n* apuntador/a *m/f*; perro de
muestra *m*.

ointless *adj* sin sentido.

oise *n* peso *m*; equilibrio *m*.

oison *n* veneno *m*; * *vt* envenenar.

oisoning *n* envenenamiento *m*.

oisonous *adj* venenoso/sa.

oke *vt* hurgar; empujar.

oker *n* atizador *m*; póker *m*.

oker-faced *adj* con cara de póker.

oky *adj* estrecho/cha.

olar *adj* polar.

ole *n* polo *m*; palo *m*; pértiga *f*.

ole bean *n* judía trepadora *f*.

pole vault *n* salto con pértiga *m*.

police *n* policía *f*.

police car *n* coche patrulla *m*.

policeman *n* policía *m*.

police state *n* estado policial *m*.

police station *n* comisaría *f*.

policewoman *n* mujer policía *f*.

policy *n* política *f*.

polio *n* polio *f*.

polish *vt* pulir, alisar; limar; **to ~ off**
vt terminar; despachar; * *n* puli-
mento *m*.

polished *adj* elegante, pulido/da.

polite *adj* pulido/da, cortés; **~ly** *adv*
cortésmente.

politeness *n* cortesía *f*.

politic *adj* político/ca; astuto/ta.

political *adj* político/ca.

political asylum *n* asilo político *m*.

politician *n* político/ca *m/f*.

politics *npl* política *f*.

polka *n* polca *f*; **~ dot** *n* lunar *m*.

poll *n* voto *m*; encuesta *f*, sondeo *m*.

pollen *n* (*bot*) polen *m*.

pollute *vt* contaminar.

pollution *n* polución, contaminación *f*.

polo *n* polo *m*.

polyester *n* poliéster *m*.

polyethylene, polythene *n* polietile-
no *m*.

polygamy *n* poligamia *f*.

polystyrene *n* poliestireno *m*.

polytechnic *n* politécnico *m*.

pomegranate *n* granada *f*.

pomp *n* pompa *f*; esplendor *m*.

pompom *n* borla *f*.

pompous *adj* pomposo/sa.

pond *n* estanque *m*.

ponder *vt* ponderar, considerar.

ponderous *adj* ponderoso/sa, pesa-
do/da.

pontiff *n* pontífice, papa *m*.

pontoon *n* pontón *m*.

pony *n* jaca *f*; potro *m*.

ponytail *n* cola de caballo *f*.

pool *n* charca *f*; piscina, alberca *f*;
* *vt* juntar; **to form a ~** remansarse.

poor *adj* pobre; humilde; de poco
valor; **~ly** *adv* pobremente; **the ~**
n los pobres *mpl*.

pop *n* pop *m*; papá *m*; gaseosa *f*;
chasquido *m*; * **to ~ in/out** *vi* entrar *o* salir un momento.

pop concert *n* concierto pop *m*.

popcorn *n* palomitas *fpl*.

Pope *n* Papa *m*.

poplar *n* álamo *m*.

poppy *n* (*bot*) amapola *f*.

populace *n* populacho *m*.

popular *adj*, **~ly** *adv* popu-
lar(mente).

popularity *n* popularidad *f*.

popularize vt popularizar.

populate vi poblar.

population n población f.

populous adj populoso/sa.

pop video n videoclip m.

porcelain n porcelana, china, loza fina f.

porch n pórtico, vestíbulo m, zaguán m.

porcupine n puerco espín m.

pore n poro m.

pork n carne de cerdo, carne de puerco f.

pornography n pornografía f.

porous adj poroso/sa.

porpoise n marsopa f.

porridge n gachas de avena fpl.

port n puerto m; (mar) babor m; vino de Oporto m.

portable adj portátil.

portal n portal m; portada f.

porter n portero m; mozo m; conserje m/f.

portfolio n cartera f.

porthole n portilla f.

portico n pórtico, portal m.

portion n porción, parte f.

portly adj rollizo/za.

portrait n retrato m.

portray vt retratar.

pose n postura f; pose f; * vi posar; * vt plantear.

posh adj elegante.

position n posición, situación f; * vt colocar.

positive adj positivo/va, real, verdadero/ra; ~ly adv positivamente; ciertamente.

posse n pelotón a m.

possess vt poseer; gozar.

possession n posesión f.

possessive adj posesivo/va.

possibility n posibilidad f.

possible adj posible; ~ly adv quizá quizás.

post n correo m; puesto m; emple m; poste m; * vt apostar; fijar.

postage n franqueo m.

postage stamp n sello de correos r estampilla f.

postal box, P O Box n apartado c correos m.

postcard n tarjeta f postal.

post code n código m postal.

postdate vt posfechar.

poster n cartel m.

poste restante n lista de correos f.

posterior n trasero m.

posterity n posteridad f.

postgraduate n posgraduado/da m/f

posthumous adj póstumo/ma.

postman n cartero m.

postmark n matasellos m.

postmaster n administrador/a de correos m/f.

post office n correos m.

postpone vt diferir, suspender; posponer.

postscript n posdata f.

posture n postura f.

post-war adj de posguerra.

postwoman n cartera f.

posy n ramillete de flores m.

pot n marmita f; olla f; (sl) marihuana f; * vt preservar en marmitas.

potato n patata f; papa f.

potato peeler n pelapatatas m invar.

potbellied adj panzudo/da.

potent adj potente, poderoso/sa, eficaz.

potential adj potencial, poderoso/sa.

pothole n bache m.

potion n poción, bebida medicinal f.

potted adj en conserva; en tiesto.

potter n alfarero/ra m/f.

pottery n cerámica f.

potty adj chiflado/da.

pouch n bolsa f; petaca f; zurrón m.

poultice n cataplasma f.

poultry n aves de corral fpl.

pound n libra f; libra esterlina f; corral m; * vt machacar; * vi dar golpes.

pour vt echar; servir; * vi fluir con rapidez; llover a cántaros.

pout vi fruncir el ceño.

poverty n pobreza f.

powder n polvo m; pólvora f; * vt polvorear.

powder compact n polvera f.

powdered milk n leche en polvo f.

powder puff n borla f.

powder room n aseos mpl.

powdery adj polvoriento/ta.

power n poder m; potestad f; imperio m; potencia f; autoridad f; fuerza f; * vt impulsar.

powerful adj poderoso/sa; ~ly adv poderosamente, con mucha fuerza.

powerless adj impotente.

power station n central eléctrica f.

practicable adj factible; viable.

practical adj práctico/ca; ~ly adv prácticamente.

practicality n viabilidad f.

practical joke n broma pesada f.

practice n práctica f; uso m; costumbre f; ~s pl intrigas fpl.

practise vi practicar, ejercer.

practitioner n médico/ca m/f.

pragmatic adj pragmático/ca.

prairie n pampa f.

praise n renombre m; alabanza f; * vt celebrar, alabar.

praiseworthy adj digno/na de alabanza.

prance vi cabriolar.

prank n travesura, extravagancia f.

prattle vi charlar; * n charla f.

prawn n gamba f.

pray vi rezar; rogar; orar.

prayer n oración, súplica f.

prayer book n devocionario m.

preach vi predicar.

preacher n pastor/a; predicador/a m/f.

preamble n preámbulo m.

precarious adj precario, incierto/ta; ~ly adv precariamente.

precaution n precaución f.

precautionary adj preventivo/va.

precede vt anteceder, preceder.

precedence n precedencia f.

precedent adj, n precedente m.

precinct n límite, lindero m; barrio m; distrito electoral m.

precious adj precioso/sa.

precipice n precipicio m.

precipitate vt precipitar; * adj precipitado/da.

precise adj preciso/sa, exacto/ta; ~ly adv precisamente, exactamente.

precision n precisión, limitación exacta f.

preclude vt prevenir, impedir.

precocious adj precoz, temprano/na, prematuro/ra.

preconceive vt preconcebir.

preconception n preconcepción f.

precondition n condición previa f.

precursor n precursor/a m/f.

predator n depredador/a m/f.

predecessor n predecesor/a, antecesor/a m/f.

predestination n predestinación f.

predicament n aprieto m; dilema m.

predict vt predecir.

predictable adj previsible.

prediction n predicción f.

predilection n predilección f.

predominant adj predominante.

predominate vt predominar.
preen vt limpiarse (las plumas).
prefab n casa prefabricada f.
preface n prefacio m.
prefer vt preferir.
preferable adj preferible.
preferably adv de preferencia.
preference n preferencia f.
preferential adj preferente.
preferment n promoción f; preferencia f.
prefix vt prefijar; * n (gr) prefijo m.
pregnancy n embarazo m.
pregnant adj embarazada.
prehistoric adj prehistórico/ca.
prejudice n perjuicio, daño m; * vt perjudicar, hacer daño.
prejudiced adj predispuesto/ta; parcial.
prejudicial adj perjudicial, dañoso/sa.
preliminary adj preliminar.
prelude n preludio m.
premarital adj premarital.
premature adj prematuro/ra; ~ly adv anticipadamente.
premeditation n premeditación f.
premier n primer ministro m, primera ministra f.
première n estreno m.
premise n premisa f.
premises npl establecimiento m.
premium n premio m; remuneración f; prima f.
premonition n presentimiento m.
preoccupied adj preocupado/da; ensimismado/da.
prepaid adj con el porte pagado.
preparation n preparación f; cosa preparada f.
preparatory adj preparatorio/ria.
prepare vt (vi) preparar(se).
prepared adj abonado/da.

preponderance n preponderancia f
preposition n preposición f.
preposterous adj absurdo/da.
prerequisite n requisito m.
prerogative n prerrogativa f.
prescribe vi prescribir; recetar.
prescription n prescripción f; receta medicinal f.
presence n presencia f; asistencia f.
present n regalo m; * adj presente; ~ly adv al presente; * vt ofrecer, presentar; regalar; acusar.
presentable adj decente, decoroso/sa.
presentation n presentación f.
present-day adj actual.
presenter n presentador/a m/f.
presentiment n presentimiento m.
preservation n preservación f.
preservative n preservativo m.
preserve vt preservar, conservar; poner en conserva; * n conserva, confitura f.
preside vi presidir; dirigir.
presidency n presidencia f.
president n presidente m/f.
presidential adj presidencial.
press vt empujar; apretar; compeler; * vi apretar; * n prensa f; armario m; apretón m; imprenta f.
press agency n agencia de prensa f.
press conference n rueda de prensa f.
pressing adj, ~ly adv urgente(mente).
press-up n plancha f.
pressure n presión f; opresión f.
pressure cooker n olla exprés, olla a presión f.
pressure group n grupo de presión m.
pressurized adj a presión.
prestige n prestigio m.
presumable adj presumible.
presumably adv es de suponer que.

resume *vt* presumir, suponer.

resumption *n* presunción *f*.

resumptuous *adj* presuntuoso/sa.

resuppose *vt* presuponer.

retence *n* pretexto *m*; pretensión *f*.

retend *vi* pretender; presumir.

retender *n* pretendiente *m/f*.

retension *n* pretensión *f*.

retentious *adj* presumido/da; ostentoso/sa.

reterite *n* preterito *m*.

retext *n* pretexto *m*; **to find a ~ for** pretextar.

pretty *adj* lindo/da, bien parecido/da; hermoso/sa; * *adv* algo, un poco.

prevail *vi* prevalecer, predominar.

prevailing *adj* dominante (uso, costumbre).

prevalent *adj* predominante, eficaz.

prevent *vt* prevenir; impedir.

prevention *n* prevención *f*.

preventive *adj* preventivo/va.

preview *n* preestreno *m*.

previous *adj* previo/via; antecedente; ~ly *adv* antes.

prewar *adj* de antes de la guerra.

prey *n* presa *f*.

price *n* precio *m*.

priceless *adj* inapreciable.

price list *n* tarifa, lista de precios *f*.

pricey *adj* carero/ra.

prick *vt* punzar, picar; apuntar; excitar; * *n* puntura *f*; pica dura *f*; punzada *f*.

prickle *n* pincho *m*; espina *f*.

prickly *adj* espinoso/sa.

pride *n* orgullo *m*; vanidad *f*; jactancia *f*.

priest *n* sacerdote *m*.

priestess *n* sacerdotisa *f*.

priesthood *n* sacerdocio *m*.

priestly *adj* sacerdotal.

priggish *adj* afectado/da.

prim *adj* peripuesto/ta, afectado/ta.

primacy *n* primacía *f*.

primarily *adv* primariamente, sobre todo.

primary *adj* primario/ria, principal, primero/ra.

primary school *n* escuela primaria *f*.

primate *n* primadoprimate *m*.

prime *n* (*fig*) flor, nata *f*; primavera *f*; principio *m*; * *adj* primero/ra; primoroso/sa, excelente; * *vt* cebar.

prime minister *n* primer ministro *m*, primera ministra *f*.

primeval *adj* primitivo/va.

priming *n* cebo *m*; imprimación *f*.

primitive *adj* primitivo/va; ~ly *adv* primitivamente.

primrose *n* (*bot*) primavera *f*.

prince *n* príncipe *m*.

princess *n* princesa *f*.

principal *adj*, ~ly *adv* principal(mente); * *n* principal, jefe *m*.

principality *n* principado/da *m*.

principle *n* principio *m*; causa primitiva *f*; fundamento, motivo *m*.

print *vt* imprimir; * *n* impresión, estampa, edición *f*; impreso *m*; **out of ~** vendido/da, agotado/da.

printed matter *n* impresos *mpl*.

printer *n* impresor/a *m/f*.

printing *n* imprenta *f*.

prior *adj* anterior, precedente; * *n* prior (prelado) *m*.

priority *n* prioridad *f*.

priory *n* priorato *m*.

prism *n* prisma *m*.

prison *n* prisión, carcel *f*.

prisoner *n* prisionero/ra *m/f*.

pristine *adj* prístino/na, antiguo/gua.

privacy *n* soledad *f*.

private *adj* secreto/ta, privado/da;

particular; ~ **soldier** *n* soldado raso *m*; **~ly** *adv* en secreto.

private eye *n* detective privado/da *m/f*.

privet *n* alheña *f*.

privilege *n* privilegio *m*.

prize *n* premio *m*; presa *f*; * *vt* apreciar, valuar; **to ~ open** abrir por fuerza.

prize-giving *n* entrega de premios *f*.

prizewinner *n* premiado/da *m/f*.

pro *prep* para.

probability *n* probabilidad, verosimilitud *f*.

probable *adj* probable, verosímil; **~bly** *adv* probablemente.

probation *n* prueba *f*.

probationary *adj* de prueba.

probe *n* sonda *f*; encuesta *f*; * *vt* sondar; investigar.

problem *n* problema *m*.

problematical *adj* problemático/ca; **~ly** *adv* problemáticamente.

procedure *n* procedimiento *m*; progreso, proceso *m*.

proceed *vi* proceder; provenir; originarse; **~s** *npl* producto *m*; rédito *m*; **gross ~s** producto íntegro; **net ~s** producto neto.

proceedings *n* procedimiento *m*; proceso *m*; conducta *f*.

process *n* proceso *m*.

procession *n* procesión *f*.

proclaim *vt* proclamar, promulgar, publicar.

proclamation *n* proclamación *f*; decreto *m*.

procrastinate *vt* diferir, retardar.

proctor *n* censor/a *m/f*.

procure *vt* procurar.

procurement *n* procuración *f*.

prod *vt* empujar.

prodigal *adj* pródigo/ga.

prodigious *adj* prodigioso/sa; **~l** *adv* prodigiosamente.

prodigy *n* prodigio *m*.

produce *vt* producir, criar; causar; * *n* producto *m*.

produce dealer *n* verdulero/ra *m/f*.

producer *n* productor/a *m/f*.

product *n* producto *m*; obra *f*; efecto *m*.

production *n* producción *f*; producto *m*.

production line *n* línea de producción *f*.

productive *adj* productivo/va.

productivity *n* productividad *f*.

profane *adj* profano/na.

profess *vt* profesar; ejercer; declarar.

profession *n* profesión *f*.

professional *adj* profesional.

professor *n* profesor/a, catedratico/ca *m/f*.

proficiency *n* capacidad *f*.

proficient *adj* proficiente, adelantado/da.

profile *n* perfil *m*.

profit *n* ganancia *f*; provecho *m*; ventaja *f*; * *vi* aprovechar.

profitability *n* rentabilidad *f*.

profitable *adj* provechoso/sa, ventajoso/sa.

profiteering *n* explotación *f*.

profound *adj* profundo/da; **~ly** *adv* profundamente.

profuse *adj* profuso/sa, prodigo/ga; **~ly** *adv* profusamente.

program *n* programa *m*.

programme *n* programa *m*.

programmer *n* programador/a *m/f*.

programming *n* programación *f*.

progress *n* progreso *m*; curso *m*; * *vi* hacer progresos.

progression *n* progresión *f*; adelantamiento *m*.

progressive *adj* progresivo/va; **~ly** *adv* progresivamente.

prohibit *vt* prohibir, vedar; impedir.

prohibition *n* prohibición *f*.

project *vt* proyectar, trazar; * *n* proyecto *m*.

projectile *n* proyectil *m*.

projection *n* proyección *f*; estimación *f*.

projector *n* proyector *m*.

proletarian *adj* proletario/ria.

proletariat *n* proletariado *m*.

prolific *adj* prolífico/ca, fecundo/da.

prolix *adj* prolijo/ja, difuso/sa.

prologue *n* prólogo *m*.

prolong *vt* prolongar; diferir.

prom *n* baile de gala; concierto *m*.

promenade *n* paseo *m*.

prominence *n* prominencia *f*.

prominent *adj* prominente, saledizo/za.

promiscuous *adj* promiscuo/cua.

promise *n* promesa *f*; * *vt* prometer.

promising *adj* prometedor/a.

promontory *n* promontorio *m*.

promote *vt* promover.

promoter *n* promotor/a, promovedor/a *m/f*.

promotion *n* promoción *f*.

prompt *adj* pronto/ta; **~ly** *adv* prontamente; * *vt* sugerir, insinuar; apuntar (en el teatro).

prompter *n* apuntador/a *m/f*.

prone *adj* inclinado/da.

prong *n* diente *m*.

pronoun *n* pronombre *m*.

pronounce *vt* pronunciar; recitar.

pronounced *adj* marcado/da.

pronouncement *n* declaración *f*.

pronunciation *n* pronunciación *f*.

proof *n* prueba *f*; * *adj* impenetrable; de prueba.

prop *vt* sostener; * *n* apoyo, puntal *m*; sostén *m*.

propaganda *n* propaganda *f*.

propel *vt* impeler.

propeller *n* hélice *f*.

propensity *n* propensión, tendencia *f*.

proper *adj* propio/pia; conveniente; exacto/ta; bien parecido/da; **~ly** *adv* propiamente, justamente.

property *n* propiedad *f*.

prophecy *n* profecía *f*.

prophesy *vt* profetizar.

prophet *n* profeta *m*.

prophetic *adj* profético/ca.

proportion *n* proporción *f*; simetría *f*.

proportional *adj* proporcional.

proportionate *adj* proporcionado/da.

proposal *n* propuesta, proposición *f*; oferta *f*.

propose *vt* proponer.

proposition *n* proposición, propuesta *f*.

proprietor *n* propietario/ria *m/f*.

propriety *n* propiedad *f*.

pro rata *adv* de forma prorrateada.

prosaic *adj* prosaico/ca, en prosa.

prose *n* prosa *f*.

prosecute *vt* proseguir.

prosecution *n* prosecución *f*; acusación *f*.

prosecutor *n* fiscal *m/f*.

prospect *n* perspectiva *f*; esperanza *f*; * *vt* explorar; * *vi* buscar.

prospecting *n* prospección *f*.

prospective *adj* probable; futuro/ra.

prospector *n* explorador/a *m/f*.

prospectus *n* prospecto *m*.

prosper *vi* prosperar.

prosperity *n* prosperidad *f*.

prosperous *adj* próspero/ra, feliz.

prostitute *n* prostituta *f*.

prostitution *n* prostitución *f*.

prostrate *adj* postrado/da.

protagonist *n* protagonista *m*.

protect vt proteger; amparar.

protection n protección f.

protective adj protectorio/ria.

protector n protector/a, patrono/na m/f.

protégé(e) n protegido/da m/f.

protein n proteína f.

protest vi protestar; * n protesta f.

Protestant n protestante m/f.

protester n manifestante m/f.

protocol n protocolo m.

prototype n prototipo m.

protracted adj prolongado/da.

protrude vi sobresalir.

proud adj soberbio/bia, orgulloso/sa; ~ly adv soberbiamente.

prove vt probar, justificar; * vi resultar; salir (bien o mal).

proverb n proverbio m.

proverbial adj, ~ly adv proverbial(mente).

provide vt proveer; **to ~ for** mantener a; tener en cuenta.

provided conj: ~ that con tal que.

providence n providencia f.

province n provincia f; campo de acción m.

provincial adj provincial; * n provincial/a m/f.

provision n provisión f; precaución f.

provisional adj, ~ly adv provisional(mente).

proviso n estipulación f.

provocation n provocación f; apelación f.

provocative adj provocativo/va.

provoke vt provocar; apelar.

prow n (mar) proa f.

prowess n proeza, valentía f.

prowl vi rondar, vagar.

prowler n merodeador/a m/f.

proximity n proximidad f.

proxy n poder m; apoderado/da m/f.

prudence n prudencia f.

prudent adj prudente, circunspecto/ta; ~ly adv con juicio.

prudish adj gazmoño/ña, mojigato/ta.

prune vt podar; * n ciruela pasa f.

prussic acid n ácido prúsico m.

pry vi espiar, acechar; **to ~ open** vt abrir por fuerza.

psalm n salmo m.

pseudonym n seudónimo m.

psyche n psique f.

psychiatric adj psiquiátrico/ca.

psychiatrist n psiquiatra m/f.

psychiatry n psiquiatría f.

psychic adj psíquico/ca.

psychoanalysis n psicoanálisis m.

psychoanalyst n psicoanalista m/f.

psychological adj psicológico/ca.

psychologist n psicólogo/ga m/f.

psychology n psicología f.

puberty n pubertad f.

public adj público/ca; común; notorio/ria; ~ly adv publicamente; * n público m.

public address system n megafonía f.

publican n publicano m; tabernero/ra m/f.

publication n publicación f; edición f.

publicity n publicidad f.

publicize vt publicitar; hacer propaganda para.

public opinion n opinión pública f.

public school n instituto; colegio privado m.

publish vt publicar.

publisher n editorial f; editor/a m/f.

publishing n industria del libro f.

pucker vt arrugar, hacer pliegues.

pudding n pudín m; morcilla f.

puddle n charco m.

puerile adj pueril.

puff n soplo m; bocanada f; resoplido m; * vt chupar; * vi bufar; resoplar.

puff pastry n hojaldre m.

puffy adj hinchado/da, entumecido/da.

pull n tirar; coger; rasgar, desgarrar; **to ~ down** derribar; **to ~ in** parar; llegar a la estación; **to ~ off** cerrar; **to ~ out** vi irse; salir; * vt arrancar; **to ~ through** salir adelante; **to ~ up** vi parar; * vt arrancar; parar; * n tirón m; sacudida f.

pulley n polea, garrucha f.

pullover n jersey m.

pulp n pulpa f; pasta f.

pulpit n púlpito m.

pulsate vi pulsar, latir.

pulse n pulso m; legumbres fpl.

pulverize vt pulverizar.

pumice n piedra pómez f.

pummel vt aporrear.

pump n bomba f; (shoe) zapatilla f; * vt bombear; sondear; sonsacar.

pumpkin n calabaza f.

pun n juego de palabras m; * vi hacer juegos de palabras.

punch n puñetazo m; punzón m; taladro m; ponche m; * vt golpear; perforar.

punctual adj puntual, exacto/ta; **~ly** adv puntualmente.

punctuate vt puntuar.

punctuation n puntuación f.

pundit n experto/ta m/f.

pungent adj picante, acre, mordaz.

punish vt castigar.

punishment n castigo m; pena f.

punk n punk m/f; música punk f; rufián/fiana m/f.

punt n barco llano m.

puny adj joven, pequeño/ña; inferior.

pup n cachorro m; * vi parir (la perra).

pupil n alumno/na m/f; pupila f.

puppet n títere m, muñeco m.

puppy n perrito m.

purchase vt comprar; * n compra f; adquisición f.

purchaser n comprador/a m/f.

pure adj puro/ra; **~ly** adv puramente.

purée n puré m.

purge vt purgar.

purification n purificación f.

purifier n depuradora f.

purify vt purificar.

purist n purista m/f.

puritan n puritano/na m/f.

purity n pureza f.

purl n punto del revés m.

purple adj purpúreo/rea; * n púrpura f.

purport vi: **to ~ to** dar a entender que.

purpose n intención f; designio, proyecto m; **to the ~** al propósito; **to no ~** inútilmente; **on ~** a propósito.

purposeful adj resuelto/ta.

purr vi ronronear.

purse n bolsa f; cartera f.

purser n comisario m/f.

pursue vt perseguir; seguir, acosar.

pursuit n perseguimiento m; ocupación f.

purveyor n abastecedor m.

push vt empujar; estrechar, apretar; **to ~ aside** apartar; **to ~ off** (sl) largarse; **to ~ on** seguir adelante; * n impulso m; empujón m; esfuerzo m; asalto m.

pusher n traficante de drogas m/f.

put vt poner, colocar; proponer; imponer, obligar; **to ~ away** guardar; **to ~ away** hurriedly zampar; **to ~ down** poner en el suelo; sacrificar; apuntar; sofocar; **to ~ forward**

adelantar; **to ~ off** aplazar; desanimar; **to ~ on** ponerse; encender; presentar; ganar; echar; **to ~ out** apagar; extender; molestar; **to ~ up** alzar; aumentar; alojar.

putrid adj podrido/da.

putt n putt m; vt hacer un putt.

putty n masilla f.

puzzle n acertijo m; rompecabezas m inv ar.

puzzling adj extraño/ña.

pyjamas npl pijama m.

pylon n torre de alta tensión f.

pyramid n pirámide f.

python n pitón m.

Q

quack vi graznar; * n graznido m; (sl) curandero/ra m/f.

quadrangle n cuadrángulo m.

quadrant n cuadrante m.

quadrilateral adj cuadrilátero/ra.

quadruped n cuadrúpedo m.

quadruple adj cuádruplo.

quadruplet n cuatrillizo/za m/f.

quagmire n barrizal m, cenagal m.

quail n codorniz f.

quaint adj pulido/da; exquisito/ta.

quake vi temblar; tiritar.

Quaker n cuáquero/ra m/f.

qualification n calificación f; título m.

qualified adj capacitado/da; titulado/da.

qualify vt calificar; modificar; * vi clasificarse.

quality n calidad f.

qualm n escrúpulo m.

quandary n incertidumbre, duda f.

quantitative adj cuantitativo/va.

quantity n cantidad f.

quarantine n cuarentena f.

quarrel n riña, contienda f; * vi reñir, disputar.

quarrelsome adj pendenciero/ra.

quarry n cantera f.

quarter n cuarto m; cuarta parte f; ~ **of an hour** cuarto de hora; * vt cuartear.

quarterly adj trimestral; * adv trimestralmente.

quartermaster n (mil) comisario/ria m/f.

quartet n (mus) cuarteto m.

quartz n (min) cuarzo m.

quash vt fracasar; anular, abrogar.

quay n muelle m.

queasy adj nauseabundo/da.

queen n reina f; dama f.

queer adj extraño/ña; ridículo/la; * n (sl) maricón m.

quell vt calmar; sosegar.

quench vt apagar; extinguir.

query n cuestión, pregunta f; * vt preguntar.

quest n pesquisa, inquisición, busca f.

question n pregunta f; cuestión f; asunto m; duda f; * vt dudar de; interrogar.

questionable adj cuestionable, dudoso/sa.

questioner n interrogador/a m/f.

question mark n signo de interrogación m.

questionnaire n cuestionario m.

quibble vi buscar evasivas.

quick adj rápido/da; vivo/va; pronto/ta; ágil; **~ly** adv rápidamente.

quicken vt apresurar; * vi darse prisa.

quicksand n arenas movedizas f/pl.

quicksilver *n* azogue, mercurio *m*.

quick-witted *adj* agudo/da, perspicaz.

quiet *adj* callado/da; **~ly** *adv* tranquilamente.

quietness *n* tranquilidad *f*.

quinine *n* quinina *f*.

quintet *n* (*mus*) quinteto *m*.

quintuple *adj* quíntuplo.

quintuplet *n* quintillizo/za *m/f*.

quip *n* indirecta *f*; * *vt* echar pullas.

quirk *n* peculiaridad *f*.

quit *vt* dejar; desocupar; * *vi* renunciar; irse; * *adj* libre, descargado/da.

quite *adv* bastante; totalmente, enteramente, absolutamente.

quits *adv* ¡en paz!

quiver *vi* temblar.

quixotic *adj* quijotesco/ca.

quiz *n* concurso *m*; programa concurso *m*; * *vt* interrogar.

quizzical *adj* burlón/ona.

quota *n* cuota *f*.

quotation *n* citación, cita *f*.

quotation marks *npl* comillas *fpl*.

quote *vt* citar.

quotient *n* cociente *m*.

R

rabbi *n* rabino/na *m/f*.

rabbit *n* conejo *m*.

rabbit hutch *n* conejera *f*.

rabble *n* gentuza *f*.

rabid *adj* rabioso/sa; furioso/sa.

rabies *n* rabia *f*.

race *n* raza, casta *f*; carrera *f*; * *vt* hacer correr a; competir contra; acelerar; * *vi* correr; competir; latir rápidamente.

racehorse *n* caballo de carreras *m*.

racial *adj* racial.

raciness *n* vivacidad *f*.

racing *n* carreras *fpl*.

racist *adj*, *n* racista *m/f*.

rack *n* rejilla *f*; estante *m*; * *vt* atormentar; trasegar.

racket *n* ruido *m*; raqueta *f*.

rack-rent *n* alquiler abusivo *m*.

racy *adj* picante, vivo/va.

radiance *n* brillantez *f*, resplandor *m*.

radiant *adj* radiante, brillante.

radiate *vt*, *vi* radiar, irradiar.

radiation *n* radiación *f*.

radiator *n* radiador *m*.

radical *adj* radical; **~ly** *adv* radicalmente.

radicalism *n* radicalismo *m*.

radio *n* radio *f*.

radioactive *adj* radioactivo/va; ~ **fallout** lluvia radioactiva *f*.

radish *n* rábano *m*.

radius *n* radio *f*.

raffle *n* rifa *f* (juego); * *vt* rifar.

raft *n* balsa, almadía *f*.

rafter *n* par *m*; viga *f*.

rafting *n* rafting *m*.

rag *n* trapo, andrajo *m*.

ragamuffin *n* granuja, galopín/ina *m/f*.

rage *n* rabia *f*; furor *m*; * *vi* rabiar; encolerizarse.

ragged *adj* andrajoso/sa.

raging *adj* furioso/sa, rabioso/sa.

ragman, ~ picker *n* trapero *m*.

raid *n* incursión *f*; * *vt* invadir.

raider *n* invasor/a *m/f*.

rail *n* baranda, barandilla *f*; (*rail*) raíl, carril *m*; * *vt* cercar con barandillas.

raillery n burlas fpl.

railway n ferrocarril m.

raiment n vestido m.

rain n lluvia f; * vi llover.

rainbow n arco iris m.

rainwater n agua de lluvia f.

rainy adj lluvioso/sa.

raise vt levantar, alzar; fabricar, edificar; elevar.

raisin n pasa f.

rake n rastro, rastrillo m; libertino/na m/f; * vt rastrillar.

rakish adj libertino/na, disoluto/ta.

rally vt (mil) reunir; * vi reunirse.

ram n carnero, morueco m; ariete m; * vt chocar con.

ramble n divagar; salir de excursión a pie; * n excursión a pie, caminata f.

rambler n excursionista m/f.

ramification n ramificación f.

ramify vi ramificarse.

ramp n rampa f.

rampant adj exuberante.

rampart n terraplén m; (mil) muralla f.

ramrod n baqueta f; atacador m.

ramshackle adj en ruina.

ranch n hacienda, estancia f.

rancid adj rancio/cia.

rancour n rencor m.

random adj fortuito/ta, sin orden; at ~ al azar.

range vt colocar, ordenar; *vi vagar; * n clase f; orden m; hilera f; cordillera f; campo de tiro m; reja de cocina f.

ranger n guardabosques m invar.

rank adj exuberante; rancio/cia; fétido/da; * n fila, hilera, clase f.

rankle vi doler.

rankness n exuberancia f; olor o gusto rancio m.

ransack vt saquear, pillar.

ransom n rescate m.

rant vi vociferar.

rap vi dar un golpecito; * n golpecito m.

rapacious adj rapaz; ~ly adv con rapacidad.

rapacity n rapacidad f.

rape n violación f; estupro m; (bot) colza f; * vt violar.

rapid adj rápido/da; ~ly adv rápidamente.

rapidity n rapidez f.

rapier n espadín m.

rapist n violador m.

rapt adj arrebatado/da; absorto/ta.

rapture n rapto m; éxtasis m invar.

rapturous adj arrebatado/da.

rare adj raro/ra, extraordinario/ria; ~ly adv raramente.

rarity n raridad, rareza f.

rascal n pícaro/ra m/f.

rash adj precipitado/da, temerario/ria; ~ly adv temerariamente; * n salpullido m; erupción (cutánea) f.

rashness n temeridad f.

rasp n raspador m; * vt raspar, escofinar.

raspberry n frambuesa f; ~ bush frambueso m.

rat n rata f.

rate n tasa f, precio, valor m; grado m; * vt tasar, apreciar.

rather adv más bien; antes.

ratification n ratificación f.

ratify vt ratificar.

rating n tasación f; clasificación f; índice m.

ratio n razón f.

ration n ración f; (mil) víveres mpl.

rational adj racional; razonable; ~ly adv racionalmente.

rationality n racionalidad f.

rattan n (bot) rota f.
rattle vi golpear; traquetear; * vt sacudir; * n traqueteo m; sonajero m.
rattlesnake n serpiente de cascabel f.
ravage vt saquear, pillar; estragar; * n saqueo m.
rave vi delirar.
rave music n (fam) bakalao m.
raven n cuervo m.
ravenous adj, ~ly adv voraz(mente).
ravine n barranco m.
ravish vt encantar; raptar.
ravishing adj encantador/a.
raw adj crudo/da; puro/ra; novato/ta.
rawboned adj huesudo/da; magro/gra.
rawness n crudeza f; falta de experiencia f.
ray n rayo de luz m; raya f (pez).
raze vt arrasar.
razor n navaja f; máquina de afeitar f.
reach vt alcanzar; llegar hasta; * vi extenderse, llegar; alcanzar, penetrar; * n alcance m.
react vi reaccionar.
reaction n reacción f.
read vt leer; * vi estudiar.
readable adj legible.
reader n lector/a m/f.
readily adv pronto; de buena gana.
readiness n voluntad f, gana f; prontitud f.
reading n lectura f.
reading room n sala de lectura f.
readjust vt reajustar.
ready adj listo/ta, pronto/ta; inclinado/da; abonado/da; fácil.
real adj real, verdadero/ra; ~ly adv realmente.
reality n realidad f.
realization n realización f.
realize adv darse cuenta de; realizar.
realm n reino m.
ream n resma f.

reap vt segar.
reaper n segador/a m/f.
reappear vi reaparecer.
rear n parte trasera f; retaguardia f; zaga f; * vt levantar, alzar.
rearmament n rearme m.
reason n razon f; causa f; * vt, vi razonar.
reasonable adj razonable.
reasonableness n lo razonable.
reasonably adv razonablemente.
reasoning n razonamiento m.
reassure vt tranquilizar, alentar; (com) asegurar.
rebel n rebelde m/f; * vi rebelarse.
rebellion n rebelión f.
rebellious adj rebelde.
rebound vi rebotar.
rebuff n desaire m; * vt rechazar.
rebuild vt reedificar.
rebuke vt reprender; * n reprensión f.
rebut vi repercutir.
recalcitrant adj recalcitrante.
recall vt recordar; retirar; * n retirada f.
recant vt retractar, desdecirse.
recantation n retractación f.
recapitulate vt, vi recapitular.
recapitulation n recapitulación f.
recapture n recobra f.
recede vi retroceder.
receipt n recibo m; recepción f; ~s npl ingresos mpl.
receivable adj por cobrar.
receive vt recibir; aceptar, admitir.
recent adj reciente, nuevo/va; ~ly adv recientemente.
receptacle n receptáculo m.
reception n recepción f.
recess n descanso m; recreo m; hueco m.
recession n retirada f; (com) recesión f.

recipe n receta f.
recipient n recipiente m.
reciprocal adj recíproco/ca; **~ly** adv recíprocamente.
reciprocate vi reciprocar.
reciprocity n reciprocidad f.
recital n recital m.
recite vt recitar; referir, relatar.
reckless adj temerario/ria; **~ly** adv temerariamente.
reckon vt contar, computar; * vi calcular.
reckoning n cuenta f; cálculo m.
reclaim vt reformar; reclamar.
reclaimable adj reclamable.
recline vt (vi) reclinar(se); recostar(se).
recluse n recluso/sa m/f.
recognition n reconocimiento; recuerdo m.
recognize vt reconocer.
recoil vi recular.
recollect vt acordarse de; recordar.
recollection n recuerdo m.
recommence vt empezar de nuevo.
recommend vt recomendar.
recommendation n recomendación f.
recompense n recompensa f; * vt recompensar.
reconcilable adj reconciliable.
reconcile vt reconciliar.
reconciliation n reconciliación f.
recondite adj recóndito/ta, reservado/da.
reconnaissance n (mil) reconocimiento m.
reconnoitre vt (mil) reconocer.
reconsider vt reconsiderar.
reconstruct vt reedificar.
record vt registrar; grabar; * n registro, archivo m; disco; récord m; **~s** pl anales mpl.

recorder n registrador/a, archivero/ra m/f; (mus) flauta de pico f.
recount vt contar de nuevo; relatar.
recourse n recurso m; remedio m.
recover vt recobrar; recuperar; restablecer; * vi convalecer, restablecerse.
recoverable adj recuperable.
recovery n convalecencia f; recuperación f.
recreation n recreación f; recreo m.
recriminate vi recriminar.
recrimination n recriminación f.
recruit vt reclutar; * n (mil) recluta m/f.
recruiting n recluta f.
rectangle n rectángulo m.
rectangular adj rectangular.
rectification n rectificación f.
rectify vt rectificar.
rectilinear adj rectilíneo/nea.
rectitude n rectitud f.
rector n rector/a m/f.
recumbent adj recostado/da, reclinado/da.
recur vi repetirse.
recurrence n repetición f.
recurrent adj repetido/da.
recycle vt reciclar.
recycled adj reciclado/da.
red adj rojo/ja; tinto/ta; * n rojo m.
redden vt enrojecer; * vi ponerse colorado/da.
reddish adj rojizo/za.
redeem vt redimir, rescatar.
redeemable adj redimible.
redeemer n redentor/a m/f.
redemption n redención f.
redeploy vt reorganizar.
red-handed adj to catch somebody ~ pillar a alguien con las manos en la masa.
red-hot adj candente, ardiente.

red-letter day n dia señalado m.

redness n rojez, bermejura f.

redolent adj fragante, oloroso/sa.

redouble vt (vi) redoblar(se).

redress vt corregir; reformar; rectificar; * n reparación, compensación f.

red tape n (fig) trámites mpl.

reduce vt reducir; disminuir; rebajer.

reducible adj reducible.

reduction n reducción f; rebaja f.

redundancy n despido m.

redundant adj superfluo/lua.

reed n caña f.

reedy adj lleno de canas.

reef n (mar) rizo m; arrecife m.

reek n mal olor m; * vi humear; vahear.

reel n carrete m; bobina f; rollo m; * vi tambalear(se).

re-election n reelección f.

re-engage vt empeñar de nuevo.

re-enter vt volver a entrar.

re-establish vt restablecer, volver a establecer.

re-establishment n restablecimiento m; restauración f.

refectory n refectorio; comedor m.

refer vt, vi referir, remitir; referirse.

referee n árbitro/ra m/f.

reference n referencia, relación f.

refine vt refinar, purificar.

refinement n refinación f; refinadura f; cultura f.

refinery n refinería f.

refit vt reparar; (mar) reparar.

reflect vt, vi reflejar; reflexionar.

reflection n reflexión, meditación f.

reflector n reflector m; captafaros m invar.

reflex adj reflejo.

reform vt (vi) reformar(se).

reform, reformation n reformación f.

reformer n reformador/a m/f.

reformist n reformista m/f.

refract vt refractar.

refraction n refracción f.

refrain vi: to ~ from something abstenerse de algo.

refresh vt refrescar.

refreshment n refresco, refrigerio m.

refrigerator n nevera f; refrigerador m.

refuel vi repostar (combustible).

refuge n refugio, asilo m.

refugee n refugiado/da m/f.

refund vt devolver; * n reembolso m.

refurbish vt restaura, renovar.

refusal n negativa f.

refuse vt rehusar; * n basura f.

refuse collector n basurero m.

refute vt refutar.

regain vt recobrar, recuperar.

regal adj real.

regale vt regalar.

regalia n insignias fpl.

regard vt estimar; considerar; * n consideración f; respeto m.

regarding pr en cuanto a.

regardless adv a pesar de todo.

regatta n regata f.

regency n regencia f.

regenerate vt regenerar; * adj regenerado/da.

regeneration n regeneración f.

regent n regente m/f.

regime n régimen m.

regiment n regimiento m.

region n región f.

register n registro m; * vt registrar; ~ed letter n carta certificada f.

registrar n registrador/a m/f.

registration n registro m.

registry n registro m.

regressive adj regresivo/va.

regret n sentimiento m; remordimiento m; pensión f; * vt sentir.
regretful adj pesaroso/sa.
regular adj regular; ordinario/ria; ~ly adv regularmente; * n regular m.
regularity n regularidad f.
regulate vt regular, ordenar.
regulation n regulación f; arreglo m.
regulator n regulador m.
rehabilitate vt rehabilitar.
rehabilitation n rehabilitación f.
rehearsal n repetición f; ensayo m.
rehearse vt repetir; ensayar.
reign n reinado, reino m; * vi reinar; prevalecer.
reimburse vt reembolsar.
reimbursement n reembolso m.
rein n rienda f; * vt refrenar.
reindeer n reno m.
reinforce vt reforzar.
reinstate vt reintegrar.
reinsure vt (com) reasegurar.
reissue n reedición f.
reiterate vt reiterar.
reiteration n reiteración, repetición f.
reject vt rechazar.
rejection n rechazo m.
rejoice vt (vi) regocijar(se).
rejoicing n regocijo m.
relapse vi recaer; * n reincidencia f; recaída f.
relate vt, vi relatar, referirse.
related adj emparentado/da.
relation n relación f; pariente m.
relationship n parentesco m; relación f.
relative adj relativo/va; ~ly adv relativamente; * n pariente m/f.
relax vt, vi relajar; descansar.
relaxation n relajación f; descanso m; relax m.
relay n relevo m; * vt retransmitir.

release vt soltar, libertar; * n liberación f; descargo m.
relegate vt relegar.
relegation n relegación f, descenso m.
relent vi ablandarse.
relentless adj implacable.
relevant adj pertinente.
reliable adj fiable, de confianza.
reliance n confianza f.
relic n reliquia f.
relief n relieve m; alivio m.
relieve vt aliviar, consolar; socorrer.
religion n religión f.
religious adj religioso/sa; ~ly adv religiosamente.
relinquish vt abandonar, dejar.
relish n sabor m; gusto m; salsa f; * vt gustar de, agradar.
reluctance n repugnancia f.
reluctant adj reticente.
rely vi confiar en; contar con.
remain vi quedar, restar, permanecer, durar.
remainder n resto, residuo m.
remains npl restos, residuos mpl; sobras fpl.
remand vt: to ~ in custody mantener bajo prisión preventiva.
remark n observación, nota f; * vt notar, observar.
remarkable adj notable, interesante.
remarkably adv notablemente.
remarry vi volver a casarse.
remedial adj curativo/va.
remedy n remedio, recurso m; * vt remediar.
remember vt acordarse de; recordar.
remembrance n memoria f; recuerdo m.
remind vt recordar.
reminiscence n reminiscencia f.
remiss adj negligente.
remission n remisión f.

remit vt, vi remitir, perdonar; disminuir.

remittance n remesa f.

remnant n resto, residuo m.

remodel vt remodelar.

remonstrate vi protestar.

remorse n remordimiento m; compunción f.

remorseless adj implacable.

remote adj remoto/ta, lejano/na; ~ly adv remotamente, lejos.

remote control n mando a distancia m.

remoteness n alejamiento m; distancia f.

removable adj de quita y pon, de quitapón.

removal n remoción f; mudanza f.

remove vt quitar; * vi mudarse.

remunerate vt remunerar.

remuneration n remuneración f.

render vt devolver, restituir; traducir; rendir.

rendezvous n cita f; lugar de encuentro m.

renegade n renegado/da m/f.

renew vt renovar, restablecer.

renewal n renovación f.

rennet n cuajo m.

renounce vt renunciar.

renovate vt renovar.

renovation n renovación f.

renown n renombre m; celebridad f.

renowned adj célebre.

rent n renta f; arrendamiento m; alquiler m; * vt alquilar.

rental n alquiler m.

renunciation n renuncia f.

reopen vt reabrir.

reorganization n reorganización f.

reorganize vt reorganizar.

repair vt reparar; resarcir; * n reparación f.

reparable adj reparable.

reparation n reparación f.

repartee n réplica aguda o picante f.

repatriate vt repatriar.

repay vt devolver; pagar, restituir.

repayment n pago m.

repeal vt abrogar, revocar; * n revocación, anulación f.

repeat vt repetir.

repeatedly adv repetidamente.

repeater n reloj de repetición m.

repel vt repeler, rechazar.

repent vi arrepentirse.

repentance n arrepentimiento m.

repentant adj arrepentido/da.

repertory n repertorio m.

repetition n repetición, reiteración f.

replace vt reemplazar; reponer.

replant vt replantar.

replenish vt llenar, surtir.

replete adj repleto/ta, lleno/na.

reply n respuesta f; * vi responder.

report vt referir, contar; dar cuenta de; * n informe m; reportaje m; relación f.

reporter n reportero/ra m/f.

repose vt, vi reposar; * n reposo m.

repository n depósito m.

repossess vt reobrar.

reprehend vt reprender.

reprehensible adj reprensible.

represent vt representar.

representation n representación f.

representative adj representativo/va; * n representante m.

repress vt reprimir, domar.

repression n represión f.

repressive adj represivo/va.

reprieve vt suspender una ejecución; indultar; * n indulto m.

reprimand vt reprender, corregir; * n reprensión f; reprimenda f.

reprint vt reimprimir.

reprisal n represalia f.

reproach n improperio, oprobio m; * vt hacer reproches a.

reproachful adj ignominioso/sa; ~ly adv ignominiosamente.

reproduce vt reproducir.

reproduction n reproducción f.

reptile n reptil m.

republic n república f.

republican adj, n republicano/a m/f.

republicanism n republicanismo m.

repudiate vt repudiar.

repugnance n repugnancia f.

repugnant adj repugnante; ~ly adv con repugnancia.

repulse vt repulsar, desechar; * n repulsa f; rechazo m.

repulsion n repulsión, repulsa f.

repulsive adj repulsivo/va.

reputable adj honroso/sa.

reputation n reputación f.

repute vt reputar.

request n petición, súplica f; * vt rogar, suplicar.

request stop n parada a petición f.

require vt requerir, demandar.

requirement n requisito m; exigencia f.

requisite adj necesario/ria, indispensable; * n requisito m.

requisition n petición, demanda f.

requite vt recompensar.

rescind vt rescindir, abrogar.

rescue vt librar, rescatar; * n libramiento, recobro m.

research vt investigar; * n investigación f.

resemblance n semejanza f.

resemble vt asemejarse.

resent vt resentirse.

resentful adj resentido/da; vengativo/va; ~ly adv con resenti ento.

resentment n resentimiento m.

reservation n reserva f.

reserve vt reservar; * n reserva f.

reservedly adv con reserva.

reservoir n depósito m; pantano m.

reside vi residir, morar.

residence n residencia, morada f.

resident adj residente.

residuary adj sobrado/da; ~ legatee n (law) legatario/ria universal m/f.

residue n (law) residuo, resto m.

residuum n (chem) residuo m.

resign vt, vi resignar, renunciar, ceder; resignarse, rendirse.

resignation n resignación f; dimisión f.

resin n resina f.

resinous adj resinoso/sa.

resist vt resistir, oponerse.

resistance n resistencia f.

resolute adj resuelto/ta; ~ly adv resueltamente.

resolution n resolución f.

resolve vt, vr resolver(se); (fig) zanjar.

resonance n resonancia f.

resonant adj resonante.

resort vi recurrir, frecuentar; * n recurso m; resorte m.

resound vi resonar.

resource n recurso m; expediente m.

respect vt respecto m; respeto m; motivo m; ~s pl recuerdos mpl; * vt apreciar; respetar; venerar.

respectability n respetabilidad f.

respectable adj respetable; considerable; ~bly adv notablemente.

respectful adj respetuoso/sa; ~ly adv respetuosamente.

respecting prep con respecto a.

respective adj respectivo/va, relativo/va; ~ly adv respectivamente.

respirator n respirador m.

respiratory adj respiratorio/ria.

respite *n* suspensión *f*; respiro *m*; * *vt* suspender, diferir.
resplendence *n* resplandor, brillo *m*.
resplendent *adj* resplandeciente.
respond *vi* responder; corresponder.
respondent *n* (*law*) defensor/a *m*.
response *n* respuesta, réplica *f*.
responsibility *n* responsabilidad *f*.
responsible *adj* responsable.
responsive *adj* sensible.
rest *n* reposo *m*; sueño *m*; quietud *f*; (*mus*) pausa *f*; resto, residuo *m*; * *vt* descansar; apoyar; * *vi* dormir, reposar; descansarse.
restaurant *n* restaurante (económico) *m*.
resting place *n* última morada *f*.
restitution *n* restitución *f*.
restive *adj* inquieto/ta; obstinado/da.
restless *adj* insomne; inquieto/ta.
restoration *n* restauración *f*.
restorative *adj* restaurativo/va.
restore *vt* restaurar, restituir.
restrain *vt* restringir, restriñir.
restraint *n* refrenamiento, constreñimiento *m*.
restrict *vt* restringir, limitar.
restriction *n* restricción *f*.
restrictive *adj* restrictivo/va.
result *vi* resultar; * *n* resultado *m*.
resume *vt* resumir; empezar de nuevo.
resurrection *n* resurrección *f*.
resuscitate *vt* resucitar.
retail *vt* vender al por menor; * *n* venta por menor *f*.
retain *vt* retener, guardar.
retainer *n* adherente, partidario/ria *m/f*; ~s *pl* comitiva *f*; séquito *m*.
retake *vt* volver a tomar.
retaliate *vt* tomar represalias.
retaliation *n* represalias *fpl*.

retardation *n* retraso *m*.
retarded *adj* retrasado/da.
retch *vi* tener arcadas.
retention *n* retención *f*.
retentive *adj* retentivo/va.
reticence *n* reticencia *f*.
reticule *n* retículo *m*.
retina *n* retina *f*.
retire *vt* (*vi*) retirar(se); jubilar(se).
retired *adj* apartado/da, retirado/da; jubilado/da.
retirement *n* retiro *m*, jubilación *f*.
retouch *vt* retocar.
retrace *vt* volver a trazar.
retract *vt* retraer; retractar.
retrain *vt* reciclar.
retraining *n* reciclaje profesional *m*.
retreat *n* retirada *f*; * *vi* retirarse.
retribution *n* retribución, recompensa *f*.
retrievable *adj* recuperable; reparable.
retrieve *vt* recuperar, recobrar.
retriever *n* sabueso *m*.
retrograde *adj* retrógrado/da.
retrospect, retrospection *n* reflexión *f*.
retrospective *adj* retrospectivo/va.
return *vt* retribuir; restituir; devolver; * *n* retorno *m*; vuelta *f*; recompensa, rendimiento *m*; recaída *f*.
reunion *n* reunión *f*.
reunite *vt* (*vi*) reunir(se).
rev counter *n* cuentarrevoluciones *m invar*.
reveal *vt* revelar.
revel *vi* andar de juerga.
revelation *n* revelación *f*.
reveller *n* juerguista *m/f*.
revelry *n* juerga *f*.
revenge *vt* vengar; * *n* venganza *f*.
revengeful *adj* vengativo/va.

revenue *n* renta *f*; rédito *m*.

reverberate *vt*, *vi* reverberar; resonar, retumbar.

reverberation *n* rechazo *m*; reverberación *f*.

revere *vt* reverenciar, venerar.

reverence *n* reverencia *f*; * *vt* reverenciar.

reverend *adj* reverendo/da; venerable; * *n* padre *m*.

reverent, reverential *adj* reverencial, respetuoso/sa.

reversal *n* revocación *f*; cambio total *m*.

reverse *vt* trastrocar; abolir; poner en marcha atrás; * *n* vicisi tud *f*; contrario *m*; reverso *m* (de una moneda).

reversible *adj* revocable; reversible.

reversion *n* reversión *f*.

revert *vt*, *vi* trastrocar; volverse atrás.

review *vt* rever; (*mil*) revistar; * *n* revista *f*; reseña *f*.

reviewer *n* revisor/a *m/f*; crítico/ca *m/f*.

revile *vt* ultrajar; difamar.

revise *vt* rever; repasar.

reviser *n* revisor/a *m/f*.

revision *n* revisión *f*.

revisit *vt* volver a visitar.

revival *n* restauración *f*; restablecimiento *m*.

revive *vt* avivar; restablecer; * *vi* revivir.

revocation *n* revocación *f*.

revoke *vt* revocar, anular.

revolt *vi* rebelarse; * *n* rebelión *f*.

revolting *adj* asqueroso/sa.

revolution *n* revolución *f*.

revolutionary *adj*, *n* revolucionario/ria *m/f*.

revolve *vt* revolver; meditar; * *vi* girar.

revolver *n* revólver *m*.

revolving *adj* giratorio/ria.

revue *n* revista *f*.

revulsion *n* revulsión *f*.

reward *n* recompensa *f*; * *vt* recompensar.

rhapsody *n* rapsodia *f*.

rhetoric *n* retórica *f*.

rhetorical *adj* retórico/ca.

rheumatic *adj* reumático/ca.

rheumatism *n* reumatismo *m*.

rhinoceros *n* rinoceronte *m*.

rhomboid *n* romboide *m*.

rhombus *n* rombo *m*.

rhubarb *n* ruibarbo *m*.

rhyme *n* rima *f*; poema *m*; * *vi* rimar.

rhythm *n* ritmo *m*.

rhythmical *adj* rítmico/ca.

rib *n* costilla *f*.

ribald *adj* escabroso/sa.

ribbon *n* listón *m*; cinta *f*.

rice *n* arroz *m*.

rich *adj* rico/ca; opulento/ta; abundante; **~ly** *adv* ricamente.

riches *npl* riqueza *f*.

richness *n* riqueza *f*; abundancia *f*.

rickets *n* raquitismo *m*.

rickety *adj* raquítico/ca.

rid *vt* librar, desembarazar.

riddance *n*: **good ~!** ¡enhorabuena!

riddle *n* enigma *m*; criba *f*; * *vt* cribar.

ride *vi* cabalgar; andar en coche; * *n* paseo a caballo o en coche *m*.

rider *n* caballero/ra, jinete *m*, amazona *f*.

ridge *n* espinazo, lomo *m*; cumbre *f*; * *vt* formar lomos o surcos.

ridicule *n* ridiculez *f*; ridiculo *m*; * *vt* ridiculizar.

ridiculous *adj* ridículo/la; **~ly** *adv* ridiculamente.

riding *n* equitación *f*.

riding habit *n* traje de amazona *f*.

riding school n picadero m.

rife adj común, frecuente.

riffraff n desecho, desperdicio m.

rifle vt robar, pillar; estirar, rayar; * n rifle m.

rifleman n fusilero m.

rig vt ataviar; (mar) aparejar; n torre de perforación f; plataforma petrolera f.

rigging n (mar) aparejo m.

right adj derecho/cha, recto/ta; justo/ta; honesto/ta; ~! ¡bien!, ¡bueno!; ~ly adv rectamente, justamente; * n justicia f; razón f; derecho m; mano derecha f; * vt hacer justicia.

righteous adj justo/ta, honrado/da; ~ly adv justamente.

righteousness n equidad f; honradez f.

rigid adj rígido/da; austero/ra, severo/ra; yerto/ta; ~ly adv con rigidez.

rigidity n rigidez, austeridad f.

rigmarole n galimatías m.

rigorous adj riguroso/sa; ~ly adv rigorosamente.

rigour n rigor m; severidad f.

rim n margen m/f; orilla f.

rind n corteza f.

ring n círculo, cerco m; anillo m; campaneo m; * vt sonar; * vi retiñir, retumbar; **to ~ the bell** pulsar el timbre.

ringer n campanero/ra m/f.

ringleader n cabecilla m/f.

ringlet n anillejo m.

ring road n periférico m; carretera de circunvalación f.

ringworm n (med) tiña favosa f.

rink n (also ice ~) pista de hielo f.

rinse vt lavar, limpiar.

riot n tumulto, bullicio m; * vi amotinarse.

rioter n amotinado/da m/f.

riotous adj bullicioso/sa, sedicioso/sa; disoluto/ta; ~ly adv disolutamente.

rip vt rasgar, lacerar; descoser.

ripe adj maduro/ra, sazonado/da.

ripen vt, vi madurar.

ripeness n madurez f.

rip-off n (sl): **it's a ~!** ¡es una estafa!

ripple vi rizarse; * vt rizar; * n onda f, rizo m.

rise vi levantarse; nacer, salir; rebelarse; ascender; hincharse; elevarse; resucitar; * n levantamiento m; elevación f; subida f; salida (del sol) f; causa f.

rising n salida (del sol) f; fin (de una junta o sesión) m.

risk n riesgo, peligro m; * vt arriesgar.

risky adj peligroso/sa.

rissole n croqueta f.

rite n rito m.

ritual adj, n ritual m.

rival adj, n rival m/f; * vt competir, emular.

rivalry n rivalidad f.

river n río m.

riverside adj ribereño/ña.

rivet n remache m; * vt remachar, roblar.

rivulet n riachuelo m.

roach n rubio m.

road n camino m.

road sign n señal de trafico f.

roadstead n (mar) rada f.

roadworks npl obras fpl.

roam vt, vi corretear; vagar.

roan adj ruano/na.

roar vi rugir, aullar; bramar; * n rugido m; bramido, truendo m; mugido m.

roast vt asar; tostar.

roast beef n rosbif m.

rob vt robar, hurtar.

robber n ladrón/ona m/f.

robbery n robo m.

robe n manto m; toga f; * vt vestir de gala.

robin (redbreast) n petirrojo m.

robust adj robusto/ta.

robustness n robustez f.

rock n roca f; escollo m; rueca f; * vt mecer; arrullar; ape drear; * vi bambolear.

rock and roll n rocanrol m.

rock crystal n cuarzo m.

rocket n cohete m.

rocking chair n mecedora f.

rock salt n sal gema f.

rocky adj peñascoso/sa.

rod n varilla, verga, cana f.

rodent n roedor/a m/f.

roe n corzo m; hueva f.

roebuck n corzo m.

rogation n rogaciones fpl.

rogue n bribón/ona, pícaro/ra, villano/na m/f.

roguish adj pícaro/ra.

roll vt rodar; volver; arrollar; * vi rodar; girar; * n rodadura f; rollo m; lista f; catalogo m; bollo m; panecillo m.

roller n rodillo, cilindro m.

roller skates npl patines de rueda mpl.

rolling pin n rodillo de cocina m.

Roman Catholic adj, n católico/ca m/f (romano/na).

romance n romance m; ficción f; cuento m; fábula f.

romantic adj romántico/ca.

romp vi retozar.

roof n tejado m; paladar m; * vt techar.

roofing n techado, tejado m.

rook n grajo m; torre f (en el juego de ajedrez).

room n habitación, sala f; lugar, espacio m; aposento m.

roominess n espaciosidad, capacidad f.

roomy adj espacioso/sa.

roost n pértiga del gallinero f; * vi dormir en una pértiga.

root n raíz f; origen m; * vt, vi to ~ out desarraigar; arraigar.

rooted adj inveterado/da.

rope n cuerda f; cordel m; * vi hacer hebras.

rope maker n cordelero/ra m/f.

rosary n rosario m.

rose n rosa f.

rose bed n campo de rosales m.

rosebud n capullo de rosa m.

rosemary n (bot) romero m.

rose tree n rosal m.

rosette n roseta f.

rosé wine n vino rosado m.

rosewood n palo de rosa m.

rosiness n color rosado m.

rosy adj rosado/da.

rot vi pudrirse; * n putrefacción f.

rotate vt, vi girar.

rotation n rotación f.

rote n uso m; práctica f.

rotten adj podrido/da, corrompido/da.

rottenness n podredumbre, putrefacción f.

rotund adj rotundo/da, redondo/da, circular, esférico/ca.

rouble n rublo m.

rouge n arrebol, colorete m.

rough adj áspero/ra, tosco/ca; bronco/ca, bruto/ta, brusco/ca; tempestuoso/sa; ~-looking zarrapastroso/sa; ~-ly adv rudamente.

roughcast n mezcla gruesa f.

roughen vt poner áspero/ra.

roughness n aspereza f; rudeza, tosquedad f; tempestad f.

roulette n ruleta f.

round adj redondo/da; cabal; franco/ca, sincero/ra; * n círculo m; redondez f; vuelta f; giro m; escalón m; ronda f; andanada de canones f; descarga f; * adv alrededor; por todos lados; ~ly adv redondamente; francamente; * vt cercar, rodear; redondear.

roundabout adj amplio/lia, indirecto/ta, vago/ga; * n jubón m; glorieta f.

roundness n redondez f.

rouse vt despertar; excitar.

rout n derrota f; * vt derrotar.

route n ruta f; camino m.

routine adj rutinario/ria; * n rutina f; número m.

rove vi vagar, vaguear.

rover n vagabundo/da m/f; pirata m/f.

row n camorra f; rina f.

row n (line) hilera, fila f; * vt (mar) remar, bogar.

rowdy n alborotador/a, bullanguero/ra m/f.

rower n remero/ra m/f.

royal adj real; regio/gia; ~ly adv regiamente.

royalist n realista m/f.

royalty n realeza, dignidad real f; honorarios que paga el editor al autor por cada ejemplar vendido de su obra mpl; ~ ties npl regalías fpl.

rub vt estregar, fregar, frotar; raspar; * n frotamiento m; (fig) embarazo m; dificultad f.

rubber n caucho m, goma f; condón m.

rubber-band n goma, gomita f.

rubbish n basura f; tonterías fpl; escombro m; ruinas fpl.

rubric n rúbrica f.

ruby n rubí m.

rucksack n mochila f.

rudder n timón m.

ruddiness n tez encendida; rubicundez f.

ruddy adj colorado/da, rubio/bia.

rude adj rudo/da, brutal, rústico/ca, grosero/ra; tosco/ca; ~ly adv rudamente, groseramente.

rudeness n descortesía f; rudeza, insolencia f.

rudiment n rudimentos mpl.

rue vi compadecerse; * n (bot) ruda f.

rueful adj lamentable, triste.

ruffian n malhechor/a, bandolero/ra m/f; * adj brutal.

ruffle vt desordenar, desazonar; rizar.

rug n alfombra f.

rugby n rugby m.

rugged adj áspero/ra, tosco/ca; brutal; peludo/da.

ruin n ruina f; perdición f; escombros mpl; * vt arruinar; destruir.

ruinous adj ruinoso/sa.

rule n mando m; regla f; regularidad f; dominio m; * vt gobernar, reglar, arreglar, dirigir.

ruler n gobernador/a m/f; regla f.

rum n ron m.

rumble vi crujir, rugir.

ruminate vt rumiar.

rummage vt rebuscar.

rumour n rumor m; * vt rumorearse.

rump n ancas fpl.

run vt dirigir; organizar; llevar; pasar; **to ~ the risk** aventurar, arriesgar; * vi correr; fluir; manar; pasar rápidamente; proceder; ir; desteñirse; ser candidato/ta; * n corrida, carrera f; paseo m; curso m; serie f; moda f; ataque m.

runaway n fugitivo/va, desertor/a m/ f.

rung n escalón, peldaño m (de escalera de mano).

runner n corredor/a m/f; correo, mensajero/ra m/f.

running n carrera, corrida f; curso m.

runway n pista de aterrizaje f.

rupture n rotura f; hernia, quebradura f; * vt reventar, romper.

rural adj rural, campestre, rústico/ca.

ruse n astucia, maña f.

rush n junco m; ráfaga f; ímpetu m;

* vt apresurar; * vi abalanzarse, tirarse.

rusk n galleta f.

russet adj bermejo/ja.

rust n herrumbre f; * vi oxidarse.

rustic adj rústico/ca; * n patán/ana, rústico/ca m/f.

rustiness n herrumbre f.

rustle vi crujir, rechinar; * vt hacer crujir.

rustling n estruendo m; crujido m.

rusty adj oriniento/ta, mohoso/sa; oxidado/da.

rut n celo m; carril m.

ruthless adj cruel, insensible; ~ly adv inhumanamente.

rye n (bot) centeno m.

S

Sabbath n sábado m.

sable n cebellina f.

sabotage n sabotaje m.

sabre n sable m.

saccharin n sacarina f.

sachet n sobrecito m.

sack n saco m; * vt despedir; saquear.

sacrament n sacramento m; Eucaristía f.

sacramental adj sacramental.

sacred adj sagrado/da, sacro/cra; inviolable.

sacredness n santidad f.

sacrifice n sacrificio m; * vt, vi sacrificar.

sacrificial adj de sacrificio.

sacrilege n sacrilegio m.

sacrilegious adj sacrílego/ga.

sad adj triste, melanólico/ca; infausto/ra; obscuro/ra; ~ly adv tristemente.

sadden vt entristecer.

saddle n silla f; sillín m; * vt ensillar.

saddlebag n alforja f.

saddler n sillero m/f.

sadness n tristeza f.

safari n safari m.

safe adj seguro/ra; ileso/sa; fuera de peligro; de fiar; ~ly adv seguramente; ~ and sound sano y salvo; * n caja fuerte f.

safe-conduct n salvoconducto m.

safeguard n salvaguardia f; * vt proteger, defender.

safety n seguridad f; salvamento m.

safety belt n cinturón (de seguridad) m.

safety match n cerilla f.

safety pin n imperdible, seguro m.

saffron n azafrán m.

sage n (bot) salvia f; sabio/bia m/f; * adj sabio/bia; ~ly adv sabiamente.

Sagittarius n Sagitario m (signo del zodíaco).

sago n (bot) sagú m.

sail n vela f; * vt gobernar; * vi dar a la vela, navegar.

sailing n navegación f.

sailing boat n yate m.

sailor n marinero/ra m/f.

saint n santo/ta m/f.

sainted, saintly adj santo/ta.

sake n causa, razón f; **for God's ~** por amor de Dios.

salad n ensalada f.

salad bowl n ensaladera f.

salad dressing n aliño m.

salad oil n aceite para ensaladas m.

salamander n salamandra f.

salary n sueldo m.

sale n venta f; liquidación f.

saleable adj vendible.

salesman n vendedor m.

saleswoman n vendedora f.

salient adj saliente, saledizo/za.

saline adj salino/na.

saliva n saliva f.

sallow adj cetrino/na, pálido/da.

sally n (mil) salida, surtida f; * vi salir.

salmon n salmón m.

salmon trout n trucha salmonada f.

saloon n bar m.

salt n sal f; * vt salar.

salt cellar n salero m.

salting n saladura f.

saltpetre n salitre m.

saltworks npl salinas fpl.

salubrious adj salubre, saludable.

salubrity n salubridad f.

salutary adj salubre, salutífero/ra.

salutation n salutación f.

salute vt saludar; * n saludo m.

salvage n (mar) salvamento, rescate m.

salvation n salvación f.

salve n emplasto, ungüento m.

salver n salvilla, bandeja f.

salvo n salva, excusa f.

same adj mismo/ma, idéntico/ca.

sameness n identidad f.

sample n muestra f; ejemplo m; * vt probar.

sampler n muestra f; dechado, modelo m.

sanatorium n sanatorio m.

sanctify vt santificar.

sanctimonious adj santurrón/ona.

sanction n sanción f; * vt sancionar.

sanctity n santidad f.

sanctuary n santuario m; asilo m.

sand n arena f; * vt lijar.

sandal n sandalia f.

sandbag n (mil) saco de tierra m.

sandpit n arenal m.

sandstone n arenisca f.

sandwich n bocadillo, sandwich m.

sandy adj arenoso/sa.

sane adj sano/na.

sanguinary adj sanguinario/ria.

sanguine adj sanguíneo/nea.

sanitary towel n compresa f.

sanity n juicio sano, sentido común m.

sap n savia f; * vt minar.

sapient adj sabio/bia, cuerdo/da.

sapling n arbolito m.

sapper n (mil) zapador m.

sapphire n zafiro m.

sarcasm n sarcasmo m.

sarcastic adj sarcástico/ca; **~ally** adv sarcásticamente.

sarcophagus n sarcófago, sepulcro m.

sardine n sardina f.

sash n cingulo m, cinta f.

sash window n ventana o vidriera corrediza f.

Satan n Satanás m.

satanic(al) adj diabólico/ca.

satchel *n* mochila *f*.

satellite *n* satélite *m*.

satellite dish *n* antena parabólica *f*.

satiate, sate *vt* saciar, hartar.

satin *n* raso *m*; * *adj* de raso.

satire *n* satira *f*.

satiric(al) *adj* satírico/ca; ~ly *adv* satíricamente.

satirist *n* autor satírico *m*, autora satírica *f*.

satirize *vt* satirizar.

satisfaction *n* satisfacción *f*.

satisfactorily *adv* satisfactoriamente.

satisfactory *adj* satisfactorio/ria.

satisfy *vt* satisfacer; convencer.

saturate *vt* saturar.

Saturday *n* sábado *m*.

saturnine *adj* saturnino/na, melancólico/ca.

satyr *n* sátiro *m*.

sauce *n* salsa *f*; crema *f*; * *vt* condimentar.

saucepan *n* cazo *m*.

saucer *n* platillo *m*.

saucily *adv* desvergonzadamente.

sauciness *n* insolencia, impudencia *f*.

saucy *adj* insolente.

saunter *vi* callejear, corretear.

sausage *n* salchicha *f*.

savage *adj* salvaje, bárbaro/ra; ~ly *adv* bárbaramente; * *n* salvaje *m/f*.

savageness *n* salvajería, *f*; crueldad *f*.

savagery *n* crueldad *f*.

savanna(h) *n* sabana *f*.

save *vt* salvar; economizar; ahorrar; evitar; conservar; * *adv* salvo, excepto; * *n* parada *f*.

saveloy (sausage) *n* chorizo *m*.

saver *n* libertador/a *m/f*; ahorrador/a *m/f*.

saving *adj* frugal, económico/ca; * *prep* fuera de, excepto; * *n* salvamiento *m*; ~s *pl* ahorro *m*, economía *f*.

savings account *n* cuenta de ahorros *f*.

savings bank *n* caja de ahorros *f*.

Saviour *n* Salvador *m*.

savour *n* olor *m*; sabor *m*; * *vt* gustar, saborear.

savouriness *n* paladar; sabor *m*.

savoury *adj* sabroso/sa.

saw *n* sierra *f*; * *vt* serrar.

sawdust *n* serrín *m*.

sawfish *n* priste *m*.

sawmill *n* aserradero *m*.

sawyer *n* aserrador/a *m/f*.

saxophone *n* saxófono *m*.

say *vt* decir, hablar.

saying *n* dicho, proverbio *m*.

scab *n* roña *f*; roñoso *m*.

scabbard *n* vaina (de espada) *f*; cobertura *f*.

scabby *adj* sarnoso/sa.

scaffold *n* tablado *m*; cadalso *m*.

scaffolding *n* andamio *m*.

scald *vt* escaldar; * *n* escaldadura *f*.

scale *n* balanza *f*; escama *f*; escala *f*; gama *f*; * *vt*, *vi* escalar; descostrarse.

scallop *n* vieira *f*; festón *m*; * *vt* festonear.

scalp *n* cuero cabelludo *m*; * *vt* escalpar.

scamp *n* bribón/ona, ladrón/ona *m/f*.

scamper *vi* escapar, huir.

scampi *npl* gambas *fpl*.

scan *vt* escudriñar; registrar; escandir; escanear.

scandal *n* escándalo *m*; infamia *f*.

scandalize *vt* escandalizar.

scandalous *adj* escandaloso/sa; ~ly *adv* escandalosamente.

scanner *n* escáner *m*.

scant, scanty *adj* escaso/sa, parco/ca.

scantily adv escasamente, estrechamente.

scantiness n estrechez, escasez f.

scapegoat n chivo expiatorio m.

scar n cicatriz f; * vt dejar cicatriz en.

scarce adj raro/ra; **~ly** adv apenas.

scarcity n escasez f; raridad f.

scare vt espantar; * n susto m.

scarecrow n espantapájaros m invar.

scarf n bufanda f.

scarlet n escarlata f; * adj escarlata.

scarlet fever n escarlatina f.

scarp n escarpa f.

scat interj (sl) ¡zape!

scatter vt esparcir; disipar.

scavenger n basurero/ra m/f; carroñero/ra m/f.

scenario n argumento m; guión m; (fig) escenario m.

scene n escena f; panorama m; escándalo m; paisaje m.

scenery n vista f; decoración (de teatro) f.

scenic adj escénico/ca.

scent n olfato m; olor m; rastro m; * vt oler.

scent bottle n frasco de perfume m.

scentless adj sin olfato; inodoro/ra.

sceptic n escéptico/ca m/f.

sceptic(al) adj escéptico/ca.

scepticism n escepticismo f.

sceptre n cetro m.

schedule n horario m; programa m; lista f.

scheme n proyecto, plan m; esquema m; sistema m; modelo m; * vt proyectar; * vi intrigar.

schemer n proyectista, intrigante m/f.

schism n cisma m.

schismatic adj cismático/ca.

scholar n estudiante m/f; erudito/ta m/f, escolástico/ca m/f.

scholarship n ciencia f; erudición f.

scholastic adj escolástico/ca.

school n escuela f, colegio m; * vt enseñar.

schoolboy n alumno m.

schoolgirl n alumna f.

schooling n instrucción f.

schoolmaster n maestro de escuela m.

schoolmistress n maestra de niños o niñas f.

schoolteacher n maestro/tra m/f; profesor/a m/f.

schooner n (mar) goleta f.

sciatica n ciática f.

science n ciencia f.

scientific adj científico/ca; **~ally** adv científicamente.

scientist n científico/ca m/f.

scimitar n cimitarra f.

scintillate vi chispear, centellar.

scintillating adj brillante, ingenioso/sa.

scission n separación, partición f.

scissors npl tijeras fpl.

scoff vi mofarse, burlarse.

scold vt, vi regañar, reñir, refunfuñar.

scoop n cucharón m; pala f; exclusiva f; * vt cavar, socavar.

scooter n moto f; patinete m.

scope n objeto, intento, designio, blanco, espacio m; alcance m; libertad f.

scorch vt quemar; tostar; * vi quemarse, escorzar.

score n muesca, canalita f; consideración f; cuenta f; puntuación f; razón f; motivo m; veintena f; * vt ganar; señalar con una línea; * vi marcar.

scoreboard n marcador m.

scorn vt, vi despreciar; mofar; * n desdén, menosprecio m.

scornful adj desdeñoso/sa; **~ly** adv con desdén.

Scorpio n Escorpión m (signo del zodíaco).

scorpion n escorpión m.

scotch vt descartar.

Scotch n whisky escocés m.

scoundrel n pícaro/ra m/f.

scour vt fregar, estregar; limpiar; * vi corretear.

scourge n azote m; castigo m; * vt azotar, castigar.

scout n (mil) explorador/a m/f; espía m/f; * vi ir de reconocimiento.

scowl vi fruncir el ceño; * n ceño, semblante ceñudo m.

scragginess n flaqueza, aspereza f.

scraggy adj áspero/ra; macilento/ta.

scramble vi arrapar; trepar; disputar; * n disputa f; subida f.

scrap n migaja f; sobras fpl; pedacito m; riña f; chatarra f.

scrape vt, vi raer, raspar; arañar; tocar mal un instrumento; * n embarazo m; dificultad f.

scraper n rascador f.

scratch vt rascar, raspar; raer, garrapatear; * n rasguño m.

scrawl vt, vi garrapatear; * n garabatos mpl.

scream, screech vi chillar, dar alaridos; * n chillido, grito, alarido m.

screen n pantalla f; biombo m; mampara f; abanico de chimenea m; * vt abrigar, esconder; proyectar; cribar, cerner.

screenplay n guión m.

screw n tornillo m; * vt atornillar; forzar, apretar, estrechar.

screwdriver n destornillador m.

scribble vt escarabajear; * n escrito de poco mérito m.

scribe n escritor/a m/f; escriba m/f.

scrimmage n tumulto m.

script n guión m; letra f.

scriptural adj bíblico/ca.

Scripture n Sagrada Escritura f.

scroll n rollo (de papel o pergamino) m.

scrounger n mamón/ona m/f.

scrub vt restregar; anular; * n maleza f.

scruffy adj desaliñado/da.

scruple n escrúpulo m.

scrupulous adj escrupuloso/sa; **~ly** adv escrupulosamente.

scrutinize vt escudriñar, examinar.

scrutiny n escrutinio, examen m.

scuffle n quimera, riña f; * vi reñir, pelear.

scull n barquillo m.

scullery n fregadero m.

sculptor n escultor/a m/f.

sculpture n escultura f; * vt esculpir.

scum n espuma f; escoria f; canalla m/f.

scurrilous adj vil, bajo/ja; injurioso/sa; **~ly** adv injuriosamente.

scurvy n escorbuto m; * adj escorbútico/ca; vil, despreciable.

scuttle n carbonera f; * vt barrenar.

scythe n guadaña f.

sea n mar m/f; * adj de mar; **heavy ~** oleada f.

sea breeze n viento de mar m.

seacoast n costa marítima f.

sea fight n combate naval m.

seafood n mariscos mpl.

sea front n paseo marítimo m.

sea-green adj verdemar.

seagull n gaviota f.

sea horse n caballito de mar m.

seal n sello m; foca f; * vt sellar.

sealing wax n lacre m.

seam n costura f; * vt coser.

seaman n marinero m.

seamanship n pericia en la navegación m.

seamstress n costurera f.

seamy adj sórdido/da.

seaplane n hidroavión m.

seaport n puerto de mar m.

sear vt cauterizar.

search vt examinar; escudriñar; inquirir, tentar; investigar, buscar; * n pesquisa f; busca f; buscada f.

searchlight n reflector m.

seashore n ribera f, litoral m.

seasick adj mareado/da.

seasickness n mareo m.

seaside n orilla o ribera del mar f.

season n estación f; tiempo oportuno m; sazón f; * vt sazonar; imbuir.

seasonable adj oportuno/na, a propósito.

seasonably adv oportunamente.

seasoning n condimento m.

season ticket n abono m.

season ticket holder n abonado/da m/f.

seat n asiento m; silla f; escaño m; situación f; * vt situar; colocar; asentar.

seat belt n cinturón de seguridad m.

seaward adj del litoral; ~s adv hacia el mar.

seaweed n alga marina f.

seaworthy adj en condiciones de navegar.

secede vi apartarse, separarse.

secession n secesión f; separación f.

seclude vt apartar, excluir.

seclusion n separación f; exclusión f.

second adj segundo/da; ~(ly) adv en segundo lugar; * n defensor/a m/f; segundo m; (mus) segunda f; * vt ayudar; segundar.

secondary adj secundario/ria.

secondary school n centro de enseñanza secundaria m; escuela secundaria f.

secondhand adj de segunda mano.

secrecy n secreto m, confidencialidad f.

secret adj secreto/ta; * n secreto m; ~ly adv secretamente.

secretary n secretario/ria m/f.

secrete vt esconder; (med) secretar.

secretion n secreción f.

secretive adj misterioso/sa.

sect n secta f.

sectarian adj sectario/ria m/f.

section n sección f.

sector n sector m.

secular adj secular, seglar.

secularize vt secularizar.

secure adj seguro/ra; salvo/va; ~ly adv seguramente; * vt asegurar; salvar.

security n seguridad f; defensa f; confianza f; fianza f.

sedan, saloon n sedán m.

sedate adj sosegado/da, tranquilo/la; ~ly adv tranquilamente.

sedateness n tranquilidad f.

sedative n sedativo m.

sedentary adj sedentario/ria.

sedge n (bot) juncia f.

sediment n sedimento m; hez f; poso m.

sedition n sedición f; tumulto, alboroto, motín m; revuelta f.

seditious adj sedicioso/sa.

seduce vt seducir; engañar.

seducer n seductor/a m/f.

seduction n seducción f.

seductive adj seductor/a.

sedulous adj asiduo/dua; ~ly adv asiduamente.

see vt, vi ver, observar, descubrir; advertir; conocer, juzgar; comprender; ~! ¡mira!

seed n semilla, simiente f; * vi granar.
seedling n plantón m.
seedsman n tratante en semillas m.
seed time n sementera, siembra f.
seedy adj desaseado/da.
seeing conj: ~ that visto que, ya que.
seek vt, vi buscar; pretender.
seem vi parecer, semejarse.
seeming n apariencia f; ~ly adv al parecer.
seemliness n decencia f.
seemly adj decente, propio/pia.
seer n profeta m, profetisa f.
seesaw n vaivén m; * vi balancear.
seethe vi hervir, bullir.
segment n segmento m.
seize vt asir, agarrar; secuestrar (bienes o efectos).
seizure n captura f; secuestro m.
seldom adv raramente, rara vez.
select vt elegir, escoger; * adj selecto/ta, escogido/ta.
selection n selección f.
self n uno/na mismo/ma; **the ~** el yo; * pref auto-.
self-command n autocontrol m.
self-conceit n presunción f.
self-confident adj que tiene confianza en sí mismo/ma.
self-defence n defensa propia f.
self-denial n abnegación de sí mismo/ma f.
self-employed adj autónomo/ma.
self-evident adj obvio/via.
self-governing adj autónomo/ma.
self-interest n interés propio m.
selfish adj egoísta; ~ly adv interesadamente.
selfishness n egoísmo m.
self-medication n automedicación f.
self-pity n lástima de sí mismo/ma f.
self-portrait n autorretrato m.

self-possession n sangre fría, tranquilidad de ánimo f.
self-reliant adj independiente.
self-respect n amor propio m.
selfsame adj mismísimo/ma.
self-satisfied adj pagado/da de sí mismo/ma.
self-seeking adj egoísta.
self-service adj de autoservicio.
self-styled adj autoproclamado/da.
self-sufficient adj autosuficiente.
self-taught adj autodidacta.
self-willed adj obstinado/da.
sell vt, vi vender; traficar.
seller n vendedor/a m/f.
selling-off n privatización f.
Sellotape® n celo m.
semblance n semejanza, apariencia f.
semen n semen m.
semester n semestre m.
semicircle n semicírculo m.
semicircular adj semicircular.
semicolon n punto y coma m.
semiconductor n semiconductor m.
semi-final n semifinal f.
seminarist n seminarista m.
seminary n seminario m.
semitone n (mus) semitono m.
senate n senado m.
senator n senador/a m/f.
senatorial adj senatorio/ria.
send vt enviar, despachar, mandar; enviar; producir.
sender n remitente m/f.
senile adj senil.
senility n senectud f; vejez f.
senior n mayor m; * adj mayor; superior.
seniority n antigüedad, ancianidad f.
senna n (bot) sena f.
sensation n sensación f.
sense n sentido m; entendimiento m; razón f; juicio m; sentimiento m.

senseless adj insensible; insensato/ta; **~ly** adv insensatamente.

senselessness n tontería, insensatez f.

sensibility n sensibilidad f.

sensible adj sensato/ta; juicioso/sa.

sensibly adv sensatamente.

sensitive adj sensible.

sensual, sensuous adj, **~ly** adv sensual(mente).

sensuality n sensualidad f.

sentence n oración f; sentencia f; * vt sentenciar, condenar.

sententious adj sentencioso/sa; **~ly** adv sentenciosamente.

sentient adj sensitivo/va.

sentiment n sentimiento m; opinión f.

sentimental adj sentimental.

sentinel, sentry n centinela m.

sentry box n garita f.

separable adj separable.

separate vt (vi) separar(se); * adj separado/da; distinto/ta; **~ly** adv separadamente.

separation n separación f.

September n septiembre m.

septennial adj sieteñal.

septuagenarian n septuagenario/ria m/f.

sepulchre n sepulcro m.

sequel n continuación f; consecuencia f.

sequence n serie, continuación f.

sequester, sequestrate vt secuestrar.

sequestration n secuestro m.

seraglio n serallo m.

seraph n serafín m.

serenade n serenata f; * vt dar serenatas.

serene adj sereno/na; **~ly** adv serenamente.

serenity n serenidad f.

serf n siervo/va, esclavo/va m/f.

serge n sarga f.

sergeant n sargento/ta m/f; alguacil m/f.

serial adj consecutivo/va, en serie; * n serial m; telenovela f.

series n serie f.

serious adj serio/ria, grave; **~ly** adv seriamente.

sermon n sermón f; oración evangélica f.

serous adj seroso/sa.

serpent n serpiente, sierpe f.

serpentine adj serpentino/na; * n (chem) serpentina f.

serrated adj serrado/da.

serum n suero m.

servant n criado m; criada f.

servant girl n criada f.

serve vt, vi servir; asistir (a la mesa); hacer; cumplir; sacar; sacar por a propósito; **to ~ a warrant** ejecutar un auto de prisión.

service n servicio m; servidumbre, utilidad f; culto divino m; acomodo m; * vt mantener; reparar.

serviceable adj servible; oficioso/sa.

servile adj servil.

servitude n servidumbre, esclavitud f.

session n junta f; sesión f.

set vt poner, colocar, fijar; establecer, determinar; * vi ponerse (el sol o los astros); cuajarse; aplicarse; * n juego, conjunto m; servicio (de plata) m; conjunto o agregado de muchas cosas m; decorado m; set m; cuadrilla, bandada f; * adj puesto/ta, fijo/ja; listo/ta; decidido/da.

settee n sofá m.

setter n setter m.

setting n establecimiento m; marco m; montadura f; **~ of the sun** puesta del sol f.

settle vt colocar, fijar, afirmar; arreglar; calmar; * vi repo sarse; establecerse; sosegarse.

settlement n establecimiento m; domicilio m; contrato m; empleo m; poso m; colonia f.

settler n colono/na m/f.

set-to n riña f; combate m.

seven adj, n siete.

seventeen adj, n diecisiete.

seventeenth adj, n decimoséptimo/ma.

seventh adj, n séptimo/ma.

seventieth adj, n septuagésimo/ma.

seventy adj, n setenta.

sever vt, vi separar.

several adj, pn varios/as, algunos/nas.

severance n separación f.

severe adj severo/ra, riguroso/sa, áspero/ra, duro/ra; ~ly adv severamente.

severity n severidad f.

sew vt, vi coser.

sewer n alcantarilla f.

sewerage n alcantarillado m.

sewing machine n máquina de coser f.

sex n sexo m.

sexist adj, n sexista m/f.

sextant n sextante m.

sexton n sepulturero/ra m/f.

sexual adj sexual.

sexy adj sexy.

shabbily adv vilmente, mezquinamente.

shabbiness n miseria f.

shabby adj desharrapado/da, zarrapastroso/sa.

shackle vt poner grilletes; ~s npl grilletes mpl.

shade n sombra, oscuridad f; matiz m; sombrilla f; * vt dar sombra a; abrigar; proteger.

shadiness n sombraje m; umbría f.

shadow n sombra f; protección f.

shadowy adj umbroso/sa; oscuro/ra; quimérico/ca.

shady adj opaco/ca, oscuro/ra, sombrío/ría.

shaft n flecha, saeta f; fuste de columna m; pozo m; hueco m; rayo m.

shag n tabaco picado m; cormorán moñudo m.

shaggy adj lanoso/sa.

shake vt sacudir; agitar; **to ~ vigorously** zarandear; **to ~ hands** darse las manos; * vi vacilar; temblar; * n sacudida f; vibración f.

shaking n temblor m.

shaky adj titubeante.

shallow adj somero/ra, superficial; trivial.

shallowness n poca profundidad f; necedad f.

sham vt engañar; * n fingimiento m; impostura f; * adj fingido/da, disimulado/da.

shambles npl confusión f.

shame n vergüenza f; deshonra f; * vt avergonzar, deshonrar.

shamefaced adj vergonzoso/sa, pudoroso/sa.

shameful adj vergonzoso/sa; deshonroso/sa; ~ly adv ignominiosamente.

shameless adj desvergonzado/da; ~ly adv desvergonzadamente.

shamelessness n desvergüenza, impudencia f.

shammy, chamois n gamuza f.

shampoo vt lavar con champú; * n champú m.

shamrock n trébol m.

shank n caña f; asta (de ancla) f; cañón (de pipa) m.

shanty n chabola f.

hanty town n barrio de chabolas m.

shape vt, vi formar; proporcionar; concebir; * n forma, figura f; modelo m.

shapeless adj informe.

shapely adj bien hecho/cha.

share n parte, porción f; (com) acción f; reja del arado f; * vt, vi repartir; compartir.

sharer n partícipe m/f.

shark n tiburón m.

sharp adj agudo/da, aguzado/da; astuto/ta; perspicaz; penetrante; acre, mordaz, severo/ra, rígido/da; vivo/va, violento/ta; * n (mus) sostenido m; * adv en punto.

sharpen vt afilar, aguzar.

sharply adv con filo; severamente, agudamente; ingenios amente.

sharpness n agudeza f, sutileza, perspicacia f; acrimonia f.

shatter vt destrozar, estrellar; * vi hacerse pedazos.

shave vt afeitar, rasurar; * vi afeitarse, rasurarse; * n afeite m.

shaver n máquina de afeitar f.

shaving n rasurado m.

shaving brush n brocha de afeitar f.

shaving cream n crema de afeitar f.

shawl n chal m.

she pn ella.

sheaf n gavilla f; haz m.

shear vt atusar; tundir; ~s npl tijeras de podar fpl.

sheath n vaina f.

shed vt verter, derramar; esparcir; * n tejadillo m; cabaña f.

sheen n resplandor m.

sheep n oveja f.

sheepfold n redil m.

sheepish adj vergonzoso/sa; tímido/da.

sheepishness n timidez, cortedad de genio f.

sheep-run n dehesa f; carneril, pasto de ovejas m.

sheepskin n piel de carnero m; zamarra f; ~ **jacket** zamarra f.

sheer adj puro/ra, claro/ra, sin mezcla; escarpado/da; * adv verticalmente.

sheet n sábana f; lámina f; pliego de papel f; (mar) escota f.

sheet anchor n áncora mayor de un navío f.

sheeting n tela para sábanas f.

sheet iron n chapa de hierro batido f.

sheet lightning n relampagueamiento m.

shelf n anaquel m; (mar) arrecife m; escollera f; **on the** ~ desecho/cha.

shell n cáscara f; proyectil m; concha f; corteza f; * vt descas carar, descortezar; bombardear; * vi descascararse.

shellfish npl invarcrustáceo m; marisco m.

shelter n guardia f; amparo, abrigo m; asilo, refugio m; * vt guarecer, abrigar; acoger; * vi abrigarse.

shelve vt echar a un lado, arrinconar.

shelving n estantería f.

shepherd n pastor m.

shepherdess n pastora f.

sherbet n sorbete m.

sheriff n sheriff m/f.

sherry n jerez m.

shield n escudo m; patrocinio m; * vt defender.

shift vi cambiarse; moverse; * vt mudar, cambiar; transpor tar; * n cambio m; turno m.

shinbone n espinilla f.

shine vi lucir, brillar, resplandecer; * vt lustrar; * n brillo m.

shingle n guijarros mpl; ~s pl (med) herpes m invar.

shining adj resplandeciente; * n esplendor m.

shiny adj brillante, luciente.

ship n nave f; barco m; navío, buque m; * vt embarcar; transportar.

shipbuilding n construcción naval f.

shipmate n (mar) ayudante m/f.

shipment n cargamento m.

shipowner n naviero/ra m/f.

shipwreck n naufragio m.

shirt n camisa f.

shit excl (sl) ¡mierda!

shiver vi tiritar de frío.

shoal n banco m.

shock n choque m; descarga f; susto m; * vt asustar; ofender.

shock absorber n amortiguador m.

shoddy adj de pacotilla.

shoe n zapato m; herradura f; * vt calzar; herrar.

shoeblack n limpiabotas m invar.

shoe factory n zapatería f.

shoehorn n calzador m.

shoelace n cordón de zapato m.

shoemaker n zapatero/ra m/f.

shoemaking n zapatería f.

shoe shop n zapatería f.

shoestring n lazo de zapato m.

shoot vt tirar, arrojar, lanzar, disparar; * vi brotar, germinar; sobresalir; lanzarse; * n vástago m.

shooter n tirador m.

shooting n caza con escopeta f; tiroteo m.

shop n tienda f; taller m.

shopfront n escaparate m.

shopkeeper n tendero/ra m/f.

shoplifter n ladrón/ona de tiendas m/f.

shopper n comprador/a m/f.

shopping n compras fpl.

shopping centre n centro comercial m.

shopping mall n paseo m.

shore n costa, ribera, playa f.

short adj corto/ta, breve, sucinto/ta; conciso/sa; ~ly adv brevemente; pronto; en pocas palabras.

shortcoming n insuficiencia f; déficit m.

shorten vt acortar; abreviar.

shortness n cortedad f; brevedad f.

short-sighted adj miope, corto de vista.

short-sightedness n miopía f.

shortwave n onda corta f.

shot n tiro m; alcance m; perdigones mpl; tentativa f; toma f.

shotgun n escopeta f.

shoulder n hombro m; brazuelo m; * vt cargar al hombro.

shout vi gritar, aclamar; * vt gritar; * n aclamación f, grito m.

shouting n gritos mpl.

shove vt, vi empujar; impeler; * n empujón m.

shovel n pala f; * vt traspalar.

show vt mostrar; descubrir, manifestar; probar; ensenar, explicar; * vi parecer; * n espectaculo m; muestra f; exposición, parada f.

show business n el mundo del espectaculo m.

shower n nubada f; llovizna f; ducha f; (fig) abundancia f; * vi llover.

showery adj lluvioso/sa.

showjumping n hípica f.

showroom n sala de muestras f.

showy adj ostentoso/sa, suntuoso/sa.

shred n cacho, pedazo pequeño m; * vt hacer trizas.

shrew n mujer de mal genio f; musaraña f.

shrewd adj astuto/ta; maligno/gna; ~ly adv astutamente.

shrewdness n astucia f.

shriek vt, vi chillar; * n chillido m.

shrill adj agudo/da, penetrante.

shrillness n aspereza (del sonido o de la voz) f.

shrimp n camarón m; enano/na m/f, hombrecillo m.

shrine n relicario m.

shrink vi encogerse; angostarse, acortarse.

shrivel vi arrugarse, encogerse; * vt encoger.

shroud n cubierta f; mortaja f; * vt cubrir, defender; amortajar; proteger.

Shrove Tuesday n martes de carnaval m.

shrub n arbusto m.

shrubbery n plantío de arbustos m.

shrug vt encogerse de hombros; * n encogimiento de hombros m.

shudder vi estremecerse; * n temblor m.

shuffle vt desordenar; barajar.

shun vt huir, evitar.

shunt vt (rail) maniobrar.

shut vt cerrar, encerrar; vi cerrarse.

shutter n contraventana f.

shuttle n lanzadera f.

shuttlecock n volante, rehilete m.

shy adj tímido/da; reservado/da; vergonzoso/sa, contenido/da; ~ly adv tímidamente.

shyness n timidez f.

sibling n hermano/na m/f.

sibyl n sibila, profetisa f.

sick adj malo/la, enfermo/ma; disgustado/da.

sicken vt enfermar; * vi caer enfermo/ma.

sickle n hoz f.

sick leave n baja por enfermedad f.

sickliness n indisposición habitual f.

sickly adj enfermizo/za.

sickness n enfermedad f.

sick pay n subsidio por enfermedad m.

side n lado m; costado m; facción f; partido m; * adj lateral, oblicuo/cua; * vi unirse.

sideboard n aparador m; alacena f.

sidelight n luz lateral f.

sidelong adj lateral.

sideways adv de lado, al través.

siding n toma de partido f; (rail) aguja f.

sidle vi ir de lado.

siege n (mil) sitio m.

sieve n tamiz m; criba f; colador m; * vt cribar.

sift vt cerner; cribar; examinar; investigar.

sigh n suspirar, gemir; * n suspiro m.

sight n vista f; mira f; espectáculo m.

sightless adj ciego/ga.

sightly adj vistoso/sa, hermoso/sa.

sightseeing n excursionismo, turismo m.

sign n señal f, indicio m; letrero m; signo m; firma f; seña f; * vt firmar.

signal n señal f, aviso m; * adj insigne, señalado/da.

signalize vt señalar.

signal lamp n (rail) reflector de señales m.

signalman n (rail) guardavía m.

signature n firma f.

signet n sello m.

significance n importancia f.

significant adj significante.

signify vt significar.

signpost n indicador m.

silence n silencio m; * vt imponer silencio.

silent adj silencioso/sa; ~ly adv silenciosamente.

silex n sílex m.

silicon chip n chip de silicio m.

silk n seda f.

silken adj hecho/cha de seda; sedeño/ña.

silkiness n blandura, molicie f.

silkworm n gusano de seda m.

silky adj hecho/cha de seda; sedoso/sa.

sill n repisa f; umbral de puerta m.

silliness n simpleza, bobería, tontería, necedad f.

silly adj tonto/ta, imbécil; ñoño/ña.

silver n plata f; * adj de plata.

silversmith n platero/ra m/f.

silvery adj plateado/da.

similar adj similar; semejante; **~ly** adv del mismo modo.

similarity n semejanza f.

simile n símil m.

simmer vi hervir a fuego lento.

simony n simonía f.

simper vi sonreír; * n sonrisa f.

simple adj simple, puro/ra, sencillo/lla.

simpleton n simplón/ona, simplonazo/za m/f.

simplicity n sencillez f; simpleza f.

simplification n simplificación f.

simplify vt simplificar.

simply adv sencillamente; solo.

simulate vt simular, fingir.

simulation n simulación f.

simultaneous adj simultáneo/nea.

sin n pecado m; * vi pecar, faltar.

since adv desde, entonces, después; * prep desde; * conj desde que; ya que.

sincere adj sencillo/lla; sincero/ra; **~ly** adv sinceramente; **yours ~ly** le saluda atentamente.

sincerity n sinceridad f.

sinecure n sinecura f.

sinew n tendón m; nervio m.

sinewy adj nervioso/sa, robusto/ta.

sinful adj pecaminoso/sa, malvado/da; **~ly** adv malvadamente.

sinfulness n corrupción f.

sing vi, vt cantar; gorjear; (poet) celebrar.

singe vt chamuscar.

singer n cantante m/f.

singing n canto m.

single adj sencillo/lla, simple, solo/la; soltero/ra; * n billete sencillo m; sencillo m; * vt singularizar; separar.

singly adv separadamente.

singular adj singular, peculiar; * n singular m; **~ly** adv singularmente.

singularity n singularidad f.

sinister adj siniestro/tra, izquierdo/da; infeliz, funesto/ta.

sink vi hundirse; sumergirse; bajarse; arruinarse, decaer; * vt hundir, echar a lo hondo; destruir; * n fregadero m.

sinking fund n fondo de amortización m.

sinner n pecador/a m/f.

sinuosity n sinuosidad f.

sinuous adj sinuoso/sa.

sinus n seno m.

sip vt sorber; * n sorbo m.

siphon n sifón m.

sir n señor m.

sire n caballo padre m.

siren n sirena f.

sirloin n solomillo m.

sister n hermana f.

sisterhood n hermandad f.

sister-in-law n cuñada f.

sisterly adj de hermana.

sit vi sentarse; estar situado/da; * vt presentarse a.

sitcom n telecomedia f.

site n sitio m; situación f.

sit-in n ocupación f.
sitting n sesión, junta f; sentada f.
sitting room n sala de estar f.
situated adj situado/da.
situation n situación f.
six adj, n seis.
sixteen adj, n dieciséis.
sixteenth adj, n decimosexto/ta.
sixth adj, n sexto/ta.
sixtieth adj, n sexagésimo/ma.
sixty adj, n sesenta.
size n tamaño, talle m; calibre m; dimensión f; estatura f; condición f.
sizeable adj considerable.
skate n patín m; * vi patinar.
skateboard n monopatín m.
skating n patinaje m.
skating rink n pista de patinaje f.
skein n madeja f.
skeleton n esqueleto m.
skeleton key n llave maestra f.
sketch n esbozo m; esquicio m; * vt esquiciar, bosquejar.
skewer n aguja de lardear f; espetón m; * vt espetar.
ski n esquí m; * vi esquiar.
ski boot n bota de esquí f.
skid n patinazo m; * vi patinar.
skier n esquiador/a m/f.
skiing n esquí m.
skilful adj práctico/ca, diestro/tra; ~ly adv diestramente.
skilfulness n destreza f.
skill n destreza, arte, pericia f.
skilled adj práctico/ca, instruido/da.
skim vt espumar; tratar superficialmente.
skimmed milk n leche desnatada f.
skimmer n espumadera f.
skin n piel f; cutis m; * vt desollar.
skin diving n buceo m.
skinned adj desollado/da.
skinny adj flaco/ca, macilento/ta.

skip vi saltar, brincar; * vt pasar, omitir; * n salto, brinco m; cuba f.
ski pants npl pantalones de esquí mpl.
skipper n capitán/ana m/f.
skirmish n escaramuza f; * vi escaramuzar.
skirt n falda, orla f; * vt orillar.
skirting board n zócalo m.
skit n burla, zumba f.
skittish adj espantadizo/za, retozón/ona; terco/ca; inconstante; ~ly adv caprichosamente.
skittle n bolo m.
skulk vi escuchar, acechar.
skull n cráneo m.
skullcap n casquete m.
sky n cielo, firmamento m.
skylight n claraboya f.
skyrocket n cohete m.
skyscraper n rascacielos m invar.
slab n losa f.
slack adj flojo/ja, perezoso/sa, negligente, lento/ta.
slack(en) vt, vi aflojar; ablandar; entibiarse; decaer; relajar; aliviar.
slacker n zángano m.
slackness n flojedad, remisión f; descuido m.
slag n escoria f.
slam vt cerrar de golpe; * vi cerrarse de golpe.
slander vt calumniar, infamar; * n calumnia f.
slanderer n calumniador/a, maldiciente m/f.
slanderous adj calumnioso/sa; ~ly adv calumniosamente.
slang n argot m; jerigonza f.
slant vi pender oblicuamente; * n sesgo m; interpretación f.
slanting adj sesgado/da, oblicuo/cua.

slap n manotazo m; (on the face) bofetada f; * adv directamente; * vt golpear, dar una bofetada.

slash vt acuchillar; * n cuchillada f.

slate n pizarra f.

slater n pizarrero/ra m/f.

slating n techo de pizarras m.

slaughter n carnicería, matanza f; * vt matar atrozmente; hacer una matanza de.

slaughterer n matador/a, asesino/na m/f.

slaughterhouse n matadero m.

slave n esclavo/va m/f; * vi trabajar como esclavo/va.

slaver n baba f; * vi babosear.

slavery n esclavitud f.

slavish adj servil, humilde; ~ly adv servilmente.

slavishness n bajeza, servidumbre f.

slay vt matar, quitar la vida.

slayer n matador/a m/f.

sleazy adj de mala fama.

sledge, sleigh n trineo m.

sledgehammer n mazo m.

sleek adj liso/sa, brunido/da.

sleep vi dormir; * n sueño m.

sleeper n durmiente m.

sleepily adv con somnolencia o torpeza.

sleepiness n sueño m.

sleeping bag n saco m de dormir.

sleeping pill n somnífero m.

sleepless adj desvelado/da.

sleepwalking n sonambulismo m.

sleepy adj soñoliento/ta.

sleet n aguanieve f.

sleeve n manga f.

sleight n: ~ of hand escamoteo m.

slender adj delgado/da, débil, pequeño/ña, escaso/sa; ~ly adv delgadamente.

slenderness n delgadez f; tenuidad f; pequeñez f.

slice n rebanada f; espátula f; * vt rebanar.

slide vi resbalar, deslizarse; correr por encima del hielo; * n resbalón m; corredera f; diapositiva f; tobogán m.

sliding adj corredizo/za.

slight adj ligero/ra, leve, pequeño/ña; * n descuido m; * vt despreciar.

slightly adv ligeramente.

slightness n debilidad f; negligencia f.

slim adj delgado/da; * vi adelgazar.

slime n lodo m; substancia viscosa f.

sliminess n viscosidad f.

slimming n adelgazamiento m.

slimy adj viscoso/sa, pegajoso/sa.

sling n honda f; cabestrillo m; * vt tirar.

slink vi escaparse; esconderse.

slip vi resbalar; escapar, huirse; * vt deslizar; * n resbalón m; tropiezo m; escapada f; papelito m.

slipper n zapatilla f.

slippery adj resbaladizo/za.

slip road n vía de acceso f; rampa de acceso f.

slipshod adj descuidado/da.

slipway n grada f, gradas fpl.

slit vt rajar, hender; * n raja, hendedura f.

slobber n baba f.

sloe n endrina f.

slogan n eslogan, lema m.

sloop n (mar) balandro m.

slop n aguachirle f; lodazal m; ~s pl gachas fpl.

slope n cuesta f; sesgo m; declivio m; escarpa f; * vt sesgar.

sloping adj oblicuo/cua; en declive.

sloppy adj descuidado/da; desaliñado/da.

sloth n pereza f.

slouch vt, vi estar cabizbajo/ja; bambolearse pesadamente.

slovenliness n desaliño m; porquería f.

slovenly adj desaliñado/da, puerco/ca, sucio/cia.

slow adj tardío/día, lento/ta, torpe, perezoso/sa; **~ly** adv lentamente, despacio.

slowness n lentitud, tardanza, pesadez f.

slow worm n lución m.

slug n holgazán/ana m/f, zángano m; babosa f; ficha f; trago m.

sluggish adj perezoso/sa; lento/ta; **~ly** adv perezosamente.

sluggishness n pereza f.

sluice n compuerta f; * vt soltar la compuerta de.

slum n tugurio m; barrio bajo m.

slumber vi dormitar; * n sueño ligero m.

slump n depresión f.

slur vt ensuciar; calumniar; pronunciar mal; * n calumnia f.

slush n lodo, barro, cieno m.

slut n marrana f.

sly adj astuto/ta; **~ly** adv astutamente.

slyness n astucia, maña f.

smack n sabor, gusto m; beso fuerte (que se oye) m; chasquido de latigo m; * vi saber; besar con ruido; * vt golpear.

small adj pequeño/ña, menudo/da.

smallish adj algo pequeño/ña.

smallness n pequeñez f.

smallpox n viruelas fpl.

small talk n charla, prosa f.

smart adj elegante; listo/ta, ingenioso/sa; vivo/va; * vi escocer.

smartly adv agudamente, vivamente; elegantemente; inteligentemente.

smartness n agudeza, viveza, sutileza f.

smash vt romper, quebrantar; estrellar; batir; * vi hacerse pedazos; estrellarse; * n fracaso m; choque m.

smattering n conocimiento superficial m.

smear n (med) frotis m invar; * vt untar; difamar.

smell vt, vi oler; * n olfato m; olor m; hediondez f.

smelly adj maloliente.

smelt n espirenque de mar m; * vt fundir (el metal).

smelter n fundidor/a m/f.

smile vi sonreír; * n sonrisa f.

smirk vi sonreír.

smite vt herir; afligir.

smith n herrero/ra m/f.

smithy n herrería f.

smock n camisa de mujer f.

smoke n humo m; vapor m; * vt, vi ahumar; humear; fumar.

smoked herring, kipper n arenque ahumado m.

smokeless adj sin humo.

smoker n fumador/a m/f.

smoking: 'no ~' 'prohibido fumar'.

smoky adj humeante; humoso/sa.

smooth adj liso/sa, pulido/da, llano/na; suave; afable; * vt allanar; alisar; lisonjear.

smoothly adv llanamente; con blandura.

smoothness n lisura f; llanura f; suavidad f.

smother vt sofocar; suprimir.

smoulder vi arder debajo la ceniza.

smudge vt manchar; * n mancha f.

smug adj presumido/da.

smuggle vt pasar de contrabando.

smuggler n contrabandista m/f.

smuggling n contrabando m.

smut *n* tiznón *m*; suciedad *f*.

smuttiness *n* obscenidad *f*.

smutty *adj* tiznado/da; obsceno/na.

snack *n* bocado, bocadillo *m*, pinchito *m*.

snack bar *n* cafetería *f*.

snag *n* problema *m*.

snail *n* caracol *m*.

snake *n* serpiente, culebra *f*.

snaky *adj* serpentino/na.

snap *vt, vi* romper; agarrar; morder; insultar; to ~ one's fingers castañetear; * *n* estallido *m*; foto *f*.

snapdragon *n* (*bot*) boca de dragón *f*.

snap fastener *n* automático *m*.

snare *n* lazo *m*; trampa *f*.

snarl *vi* regañar, gruñir.

snatch *vt* arrebatar; agarrar; * *n* arrebatamiento; robo *m*; bocado *m*.

sneak *vi* arrastrar; * *n* soplón/ona *m/f*.

sneer *vi* hablar con desprecio.

sneeringly *adv* con desprecio.

sneeze *vi* estornudar.

sniff *vt* oler; * *vi* resollar con fuerza.

snigger *vi* reír disimuladamente.

snip *vt* tijeretear; * *n* tijeretada *f*, pedazo pequeño *m*; porción *f*.

snipe *n* agachadiza *f*; zopenco *m*.

sniper *n* francotirador/a *m/f*.

snivel *n* moquita *f*; * *vi* moquear.

sniveller *n* lloraduelos *m invar*.

snob *n* (e)snob *m/f*.

snobbish *adj* esnob.

snooze *n* sueño ligero *m*; * *vi* echar una siesta.

snore *vi* roncar.

snorkel *n* (tubo)respirador *m*.

snort *vi* resoplar.

snout *n* hocico *m*; morro *m*.

snow *n* nieve *f*; * *vi* nevar.

snowball *n* bola de nieve *f*.

snowdrop *n* (*bot*) campanilla blanca *f*.

snowman *n* muñeco de nieve *m*.

snowplough *n* quitanieves *m invar*.

snowy *adj* nevoso/sa; nevado/da.

snub *vt* reprender, regañar.

snub-nosed *adj* chato/ta; ñato/ta.

snuff *n* rapé *m*.

snuffbox *n* tabaquera *f*.

snuffle *vi* ganguear, hablar gangoso.

snug *adj* abrigado/da; conveniente, cómodo/da, agradable, grato/ta.

so *adv* así; de este modo; tan.

soak *vi, vt* remojarse; calarse; empapar, remojar.

so-and-so *n* zutano/na *m/f*.

soap *n* jabón *m*; * *vt* jabonar.

soap bubble *n* burbuja de jabón *f*.

soap opera *n* telenovela *f*.

soap powder *n* jabón en polvo *m*.

soapsuds *n* jabonaduras *fpl*.

soapy *adj* jabonoso/sa.

soar *vi* remontarse, sublimarse.

sob *n* sollozo *m*; * *vi* sollozar.

sober *adj* sobrio/ria; serio/ria; ~ly *adv* sobriamente; juiciosamente.

sobriety *n* sobriedad *f*; seriedad, sangre fría *f*.

soccer *n* fútbol *m*.

sociability *n* sociabilidad *f*.

sociable *adj* sociable, comunicativo/va.

sociably *adv* sociablemente.

social *adj* social, sociable; ~ly *adv* sociablemente.

socialism *n* socialismo *m*.

socialist *n* socialista *m/f*.

social work *n* asistencia social *f*.

social worker *n* asistente/ta social *m/f*.

society *n* sociedad *f*; compañía *f*.

sociologist *n* sociólogo/ga *m/f*.

sociology *n* sociología *f*.

sock *n* calcetín *m*; media *f*.

socket *n* enchufe *m*.

sod *n* césped *m*.

soda *n* sosa *f*; gaseosa *f*.

sofa *n* sofá *m*.

soft *adj* blando/da, suave; benigno/na, tierno/na; afeminado/da; mullido/da; ~ly *adv* suavemente; paso a paso.

soften *vt* ablandar, mitigar; enternecer.

soft-hearted *adj* compasivo/va.

softness *n* blandura, dulzura *f*.

soft-spoken *adj* de voz suave.

software *n* (*comput*) software *m*.

soil *vt* ensuciar, emporcar; * *n* mancha, porquería *f*; terreno *m*; tierra *f*.

sojourn *vi* residir, morar; * *n* morada *f*; residencia *f*.

solace *vt* solazar, consolar; * *n* consuelo *m*.

solar *adj* solar; ~ **energy** energía solar *f*.

solder *vt* soldar; * *n* soldadura *f*.

soldier *n* soldado/da *m/f*; militar *m*.

soldierly *adj* soldadesco/ca.

sole *n* planta (del pie) *f*; suela (del zapato) *f*; lenguado *m*; * *adj* único/ca, solo/la.

solecism *n* (*gr*) solecismo *m*.

solemn *adj*, ~ly *adv* solemne(mente).

solemnity *n* solemnidad *f*.

solemnize *vt* solemnizar.

solicit *vt* solicitar; implorar.

solicitation *n* solicitación *f*.

solicitor *n* representante, agente *m/f*.

solicitous *adj* solícito/ta, diligente; ~ly *adv* solícitamente.

solicitude *n* solicitud *f*.

solid *adj* sólido/da, compacto/ta; * *n* sólido *m*; ~ly *adv* sólidamente.

solidify *vt* solidificar.

solidity *n* solidez *f*.

soliloquy *n* soliloquio *m*.

solitaire *n* solitario *m*.

solitary *adj* solitario/ria, retirado/da; * *n* ermitaño/ña *m/f*.

solitude *n* soledad *f*; vida solitaria *f*.

solo *n* (*mus*) solo/la *m*.

solstice *n* solsticio *m*.

soluble *adj* soluble.

solution *n* solución *f*.

solve *vt* resolver.

solvency *n* solvencia *f*.

solvent *adj* solvente; *n* (*chem*) solvente *m*.

some *adj* algo de, un poco, algún, alguno, alguna, unos, pocos, ciertos.

somebody *n* alguien *m*.

somehow *adv* de algún modo.

someplace *adv* en alguna parte; a alguna parte.

something *n* alguna cosa, algo.

sometime *adv* algún día.

sometimes *adv* a veces.

somewhat *adv* algo; algún tanto, un poco.

somewhere *adv* en alguna parte; a alguna parte.

somnambulism *n* sonambulismo *m*.

somnambulist *n* sonámbulo/la *m/f*.

somnolence *n* somnolencia *f*.

somnolent *adj* somnoliento/ta.

son *n* hijo *m*.

sonata *n* (*mus*) sonata *f*.

song *n* canción *f*.

son-in-law *n* yerno *m*.

sonnet *n* soneto *m*.

sonorous *adj* sonoro/ra.

soon *adv* ya, pronto; as ~ as luego que.

sooner *adv* antes, más pronto.

soot *n* hollín *m*.

soothe *vt* adular; calmar.

soothsayer *n* adivino/na *m/f*.

sop n sopa f.

sophism n sofisma m.

sophist n sofista m/f.

sophistical adj sofístico/ca.

sophisticate vt sofisticar; falsificar.

sophisticated adj sofisticado/da.

sophistry n sofistería f.

soporific adj soporífero/ra.

sorcerer n hechicero m.

sorceress n hechicera f.

sorcery n hechizo, encanto m.

sordid adj sórdido/da, sucio/cia; asqueroso/sa.

sordidness n sordidez, suciedad f.

sore n llaga, úlcera f; * adj doloroso/sa, penoso/sa; resentido/da; ~ly adv penosamente.

sorrel n (bot) acedera f; * adj alazán rojo/ja.

sorrow n pesar m; tristeza f; * vi entristecerse.

sorrowful adj pesaroso/sa, afligido/da; ~ly adv con aflicción.

sorry adj triste, afligido/da; arrepentido/da; **I am** ~ lo siento.

sort n suerte f; género m; especie f; calidad f; manera f; * vt separar en distintas clases; escoger, elegir.

soul n alma f; esencia f; persona f.

sound adj sano/na; entero/ra; puro/ra; firme; ~ly adv sanamente, vigorosamente; * n sonido, ruido m; estrecho m; * vt sonar; tocar; celebrar; sondar; * vi sonar, resonar, parecer.

sounding board n diapasón m; sombrero de púlpito m.

sound effects npl efectos sonoros mpl.

soundings npl (mar) sondeo m; (mar) surgidero m.

soundness n sanidad f; fuerza, solidez f.

soundtrack n banda sonora f.

soup n sopa f.

sour adj agrio/ria, ácido/da; cortado/da; áspero/ra; ~ly adv agriamente; * vt, vi agriar, acedar; agriarse.

source n manantial m; principio m.

sourness n acedía, agrura f; acrimonia f.

souse n (sl) borracho/cha m/f; * vt escabechar; chapuzar.

souvenir n recuerdo m.

south n sur m; * adj del sur; * adv al sur.

southerly, southern adj del sur, meridional.

southward(s) adv hacia el sur.

southwester n (mar) viento de sudoeste m; sombrero grande de los marineros m.

sovereign adj, n soberano/na m/f.

sovereignty n soberanía f.

sow n puerca, marrana f.

sow vt sembrar; esparcir.

sowing-time n sementera, siembra f.

soy n soja f.

space n espacio m; intersticio m; * vt espaciar.

spacecraft n nave espacial f.

spaceman n astronauta m.

spacewoman n astronauta f.

spacious adj espacioso/sa, amplio/lia; ~ly adv con bastante espacio.

spaciousness n espaciosidad f.

spade n laya, azada f; pica f (en los naipes).

spaghetti n espaguetis mpl.

span n palmo m; envergadura f; * vt cruzar; abarcar.

spangle n lentejuela f; * vt adornar con lentejuelas.

spaniel n perro de aguas m.

Spanish adj, n español/a m/f.

Spanish America n Hispanoamérica f.

Spanish American *adj* hispano-americano/na; * *n* hispano-americano/na *m/f*.

Spanish light opera *n* zarzuela *f*.

spar *n* palo *m*; * *vi* entrenarse.

spare *vt*, *vi* ahorrar, economizar; perdonar; pasarse sin; vivir con economía; * *adj* de más; de reserva.

sparing *adj* escaso/sa, raro/ra, económico/ca; ~ly *adv* parcamente, frugalmente.

spark *n* chispa *f*.

sparkle *n* centella, chispa *f*; * *vi* chispear; espumar.

spark plug *n* bujía *f*.

sparrow *n* gorrión *m*.

sparrowhawk *n* gavilán *m*.

sparse *adj* delgado/da; tenue; ~ly *adv* tenuemente.

spasm *n* espasmo *m*.

spasmodic *adj* espasmódico/ca.

spatter *vt* salpicar, manchar.

spatula *n* espátula *f*.

spawn *n* freza *f*; * *vt*, *vi* desovar; engendrar.

spawning *n* freza *f*.

speak *vt*, *vi* hablar; decir; conversar; pronunciar.

speaker *n* altavoz; bafle *m*; orador/a *m/f*.

spear *n* lanza *f*; arpón *m*; * *vt* herir con lanza.

special *adj* especial, particular; ~ly *adv* especialmente.

speciality *n* especialidad *f*.

species *n* especie *f*.

specific *adj* específico/ca; * *n* específico *m*.

specifically *adv* específicamente.

specification *n* especificación *f*.

specify *vt* especificar.

specimen *n* muestra *f*; prueba *f*.

specious *adj* especioso/sa.

speck(le) *n* mácula, tacha *f*; * *vt* abigarrar, manchar.

spectacle *n* espectáculo *m*.

spectacles *npl* gafas *fpl*.

spectator *n* espectador/a *m/f*.

spectral *adj* espectral; ~ analysis *n* análisis espectral *m invar*.

spectre *n* espectro *m*.

speculate *vi* especular; reflexionar.

speculation *n* especulación *f*; especulativa *f*; meditación *f*.

speculative *adj* especulativo/va, teórico/ca.

speculum *n* espéculo *m*.

speech *n* habla *m*; discurso *m*; lenguaje *m*; conversación *f*.

speechify *vi* arengar.

speechless *adj* sin habla.

speed *n* prisa *f*; velocidad *f*; * *vt* apresurar; despachar; * *vi* darse prisa.

speedboat *n* lancha motora *f*.

speedily *adv* aceleradamente, deprisa.

speediness *n* celeridad, prontitud, precipitación *f*.

speed limit *n* límite de velocidad *m*, velocidad maxima *f*.

speedometer *n* velocímetro *m*.

speedway *n* pista de carreras *f*.

speedy *adj* veloz, pronto/ta, diligente.

spell *n* hechizo, encanto *m*; período *m*; * *vt*, *vi* escribir correctamente; deletrear; hechizar, encantar.

spelling *n* ortografía *f*.

spend *vt* gastar; pasar; disipar; consumir.

spendthrift *n* despilfarrador/a *m/f*.

spent *adj* agotado/da.

sperm *n* esperma *f*.

spermaceti *n* espermaceti *m*.

spew *vi* (*sl*) vomitar.

sphere *n* esfera *f*.

spherical adj esférico/ca; ~**ly** adv en forma esférica.

spice n especia f; * vt especiar.

spick-and-span adj aseado/da, (bien) arreglado/da.

spicy adj aromático/ca.

spider n araña f.

spigot n grifo m.

spike n espiga de grano f; espigón m; * vi clavar con espi gones.

spill vt derramar, verter; * vi derramarse.

spin vt hilar; alargar, prolongar; girar; * vi dar vueltas; * n vuelta f; paseo (en coche) m.

spinach n espinaca f.

spinal adj espinal.

spindle n huso m; quicio m.

spine n espinazo m, espina f.

spineless adj ñoño/ña.

spinet n (mus) espineta f.

spinner n hilador/a m/f; hilandero/ra m/f.

spinning top n trompa f.

spinning wheel n rueca f.

spin-off n derivado, producto secundario m.

spinster n soltera f.

spiral adj espiral; ~**ly** adv en figura de espiral.

spire n espira f; pirámide f; aguja f (de una torre).

spirit n aliento m; espíritu m; ánimo, valor m; brío m; humor m; fantasma m; * vt incitar, animar; **to** ~ **away** quitar secretamente.

spirited adj vivo/viva, brioso/sa; ~**ly** adv con espíritu.

spirit lamp n velón o quinque de alcohol m.

spiritless adj abatido/da, sin espíritu.

spiritual adj, ~**ly** adv espiritual(mente).

spiritualist n espiritista m/f.

spirituality n espiritualidad f.

spit n asador m; saliva f; * vt, vi espetar; escupir.

spite n rencor m, malevolencia f; **in** ~ **of** a pesar de, a despe cho; * vt dar pesar.

spiteful adj rencoroso/sa, malicioso/sa; ~**ly** adv malignamente, con tirria.

spitefulness n malicia f; rencor m.

spittle n saliva f; baba f, esputo m.

splash vt salpicar, enlodar; * vi chapotear; * n chapoteo m; mancha f.

spleen n bazo m; esplín m.

splendid adj espléndido/da, magnífico/ca; ~**ly** adv espléndidamente.

splendour n esplendor m; pompa f.

splice vt (mar) empalmar, empleitar.

splint n tablilla f.

splinter n cacho m; astilla f; brisna f; * vt (vi) hender(se).

split n hendedura f; división f; * vt hender, rajar; * vi hen derse.

splutter, sputter vi escupir con frecuencia; babosear; barbotar.

spoil vt despojar; arruinar; mimar.

spoiled adj pasado/da; cortado/da.

spoke n radio (de la rueda) m.

spokesman n portavoz m.

spokeswoman n portavoz f.

sponge n esponja f; * vt limpiar con esponja; * vi meterse de mogollón.

sponger n mogollón m.

sponginess n esponjosidad f.

spongy adj esponjoso/sa.

sponsor n patrocinador/a m/f; padrino m; madrina f.

sponsorship n patrocinio m.

spontaneity n espontaneidad, voluntariedad f.

spontaneous *adj* espontáneo/nea; **~ly** *adv* espontaneamente.

spool *n* carrete *m*; canilla, broca *f*.

spoon *n* cuchara *f*.

spoonful *n* cucharada *f*.

sporadic(al) *adj* esporádico/ca.

sport *n* deporte *m*; juego, retozo *m*; juguete, divertimiento, recreo, pasatiempo *m*.

sports car *n* coche deportivo *m*.

sports jacket *n* chaqueta deportiva *f*.

sportsman *n* deportista *m*.

sportswear *n* ropa de deporte *o* sport *f*.

sportswoman *n* deportista *f*.

spot *n* mancha *f*; borrón *m*; sitio, lugar *m*; grano *m*; * *vt* notar; manchar.

spotless *adj* limpio/pia, inmaculado/da.

spotlight *n* foco, reflector *m*.

spotted, spotty *adj* lleno/na de manchas; con granos.

spouse *n* esposo/a *m/f*.

spout *vi* borbotar; chorrear; * *vt* arrojar; vomitar; (*fig*) declamar; * *n* piton *m*, pico *m*.

sprain *adj* descoyuntar; * *n* dislocación *f*.

sprat *n* meleta, nuesa *f* (pez).

sprawl *vi* revolcarse.

spray *n* rociada *f*; espray *m*; ramita *f*; espuma de la mar *f*.

spread *vt* extender, desplegar; esparcir, divulgar; * *vi* extenderse, desplegarse; * *n* extensión, dilatación *f*.

spree *n* fiesta *f*; juerga *f*.

sprig *n* ramita *m*.

sprightliness *n* alegría, vivacidad *f*.

sprightly *adj* alegre, despierto/ta, vivaracho/cha.

spring *vi* brotar, arrojar; nacer, provenir; dimanar, originarse;

saltar, brincar; * *n* primavera *f*; elasticidad *f*; muelle, resorte *m*; salto *m*; manantial *m*.

springiness *n* elasticidad *f*.

spring onion *n* cebolleta *f*.

springtime *n* primavera *f*.

spring water *n* agua de fuente *f*.

springy *adj* elástico/ca; mullido/da.

sprinkle *vt* rociar.

sprinkling *n* rociadura *f*.

sprout *n* vástago, renuevo *m*; **~s** *npl* coles de Bruselas *fpl*; * *vi* brotar.

spruce *adj* pulido/da, gentil; **~ly** *adv* bellamente, lindamente; * *vr* vestirse con afectación.

spruceness *n* lindeza, hermosura *f*.

spur *n* espuela *f*; espolón (del gallo) *m*; estímulo *m*; * *vt* espolear; estimular.

spurious *adj* espurio/ria, falso/sa; contrahecho/cha; supuesto/ta; bastardo/da.

spurn *vt* despreciar.

spy *n* espía *m/f*; * *vt*, *vi* espiar.

squabble *vi* reñir, disputar; * *n* riña, disputa *f*.

squad *n* escuadra *f*; brigada *f*; equipo *m*.

squadron *n* (*mil*) escuadrón *m*.

squalid *adj* sucio/cia, puerco/ca.

squall *n* ráfaga *f*; chubasco *m*; * *vi* chillar.

squally *adj* borrascoso/sa.

squalor *n* porquería, suciedad *f*.

squander *vt* malgastar, disipar.

square *adj* cuadrado/da, cuadrángulo/la; exacto/ta; cabal; * *n* cuadrado *m*; plaza *f*; escuadra *f*; * *vt* cuadrar; ajustar, arreglar; * *vi* ajustarse.

squareness *n* cuadratura *f*.

squash *vt* aplastar; * *n* squash *m*.

squat *vi* agacharse; * *adj* agachado/da; rechoncho/cha.

squatter n ocupante ilegal m/f; (fam) okupa m/f.

squeak vi plañir, chillar; * n grito, plañido m.

squeal vi plañir, gritar.

squeamish adj fastidioso/sa; demasiado delicado/da.

squeeze vt apretar, comprimir; estrechar; * n presión f; apre ton m; restricción f.

squid n calamar m.

squint adj bizco/ca; * vi bizquear; * n estrabismo.

squirrel n ardilla f.

squirt vt jeringar; * n jeringa f; chorro m; pisaverde m.

stab vt apuñalar; * n puñalada f.

stability n estabilidad, solidez f.

stable n establo m; * vt poner en el establo; * adj estable.

stack n pila f; * vt hacinar.

staff n personal m, plantilla f; palo m; apoyo m.

stag n ciervo m.

stage n etapa f; escena f; tablado m; teatro m; parada f; escalón m.

stagger vi vacilar, titubear; estar incierto/ta; * vt asustar; esca lonar.

stagnant adj estancado/da.

stagnate vi estancarse.

stagnation n estancamiento m.

staid adj grave, serio/ria.

stain vt manchar; empañar la reputación de; * n mancha f; deshonra f.

stainless adj limpio/pia; inmaculado/da.

stair n escalón m; ~s pl escalera f.

staircase n escalera f.

stake n estaca f; apuesta f (en el juego); * vt estacar; apostar.

stale adj añejo/ja, viejo/ja, rancio/cia.

staleness n vejez f; rancidez f.

stalk vi andar con paso majestuoso;

* n tallo, pie, tronco m; troncho m (de ciertas hortalizas).

stall n pesebre m; puesto m; tabanco m; emplazamiento m; * vt parar; * vi pararse; buscar evasivas.

stallion n semental m; caballo entero m.

stalwart n partidario/ria leal m/f.

stamen n estambre m; fundamento m.

stamina n resistencia f.

stammer vi tartamudear; * n tartamudeo m.

stamp vt patear; estampar, imprimir; acuñar; andar con mucha pesadez; * vi patear; * n cuño m; sello m; impresión f; huella f; estampilla f; (dancing) zapatazo m.

stampede n estampida f.

stand vi estar de pie; ponerse de pie; sostenerse; permanecer; pararse, hacer alto, estar situado/da; hallarse; erizarse (el pelo); * vt poner; aguantar; sostener, defender; * n puesto, sitio m; posición, situación f; parada f; estado m (fijo); tribuna f; stand m.

standard n estandarte m; modelo m; precio ordinario m; norma f; * adj normal.

standing adj permanente, fijado/da, establecido/da; de pie; estancado/da; * n duración f; posición f; puesto m.

standstill n pausa f; alto m.

staple n grapa f; * adj básico/ca, establecido/da; * vt grapar.

star n estrella f; asterisco m.

starboard n estribor m.

starch n almidón m; * vt almidonar.

stare vi: to ~ at clavar la vista en; * n mirada fija f.

stark adj fuerte, áspero/ra; puro/ra; * adv del todo.

starling n estornino m.

starry adj estrellado/da.

start vi empezar; sobrecogerse, sobresaltarse; levantarse de repente; salir; * vt empezar; causar; fundar; poner en marcha; * n principio m; salida f; sobresalto m; ímpetu m; paso primero m.

starter n estárter m; juez de salida m.

starting point n punto de partida m.

startle vt sobresaltar.

startling adj alarmante.

starvation n hambre, inanición f.

starve vi pasar hambre.

state n estado m; condición f; estado (político); pompa, gran deza f; the S~s los Estados Unidos mpl; * vt afirmar; exponer.

stateliness n grandeza, pompa f.

stately adj augusto/ta, majestuoso/sa.

statement n afirmación, cuenta f.

statesman n estadista, político m.

statesmanship n política f.

static adj estático/ca; * n parásitos mpl.

station n estación f; emisora f; empleo, puesto m; situación f; condición f; (rail) estación; * vt apostar.

stationary adj estacionario/ria, fijo/ja.

stationer n papelero/ra m/f.

stationery n papelería f.

station wagon n ranchera f.

statistical adj estadístico/ca.

statistics npl estadística f.

statuary n estatuario/ria, escultor/a m/f.

statue n estatua f.

stature n estatura, talla f.

statute n estatuto m; reglamento m.

stay n estancia f; ~s npl corsé, justillo m; * vi quedarse, estarse; detenerse; esperarse; to ~ in quedarse en casa; to ~ on quedarse; to ~ up velar.

stead n lugar, sitio, paraje m.

steadfast adj firme, estable, sólido/da; ~ly adv firmemente, con constancia.

steadily adv firmemente; invariablemente.

steadiness n firmeza, estabilidad f.

steady adj firme, fijo/ja; * vt hacer firme.

steak n filete m; bistec m.

steal vt, vi robar.

stealth n hurto m; by ~ a hurtadillas.

stealthily adv furtivamente.

stealthy adj furtivo/va.

steam n vapor m; humo m; * vt cocer al vapor; * vi echar humo.

steam-engine n máquina de vapor f.

steamer n, steamboat n vapor, buque de vapor m.

steel n acero m; * adj de acero.

steelyard n romana f.

steep adj escarpado/da; excesivo/va; * vt empapar.

steeple n torre f; campanario m.

steeplechase n carrera de obstáculos f.

steepness n lo escarpado; lo abrupto.

steer n novillo m; * vt manejar, conducir; dirigir; gobernar; * vi conducir.

steering n dirección f.

steering wheel n volante m.

stellar adj estrellado/da.

stem n vástago, tallo m; estirpe f; pie m; cañón m; * vt cortar la corriente.

stench n hedor m.

stencil n cliché m.

stenographer n taquígrafo/fa m/f.

stenography n taquigrafía f.

step n paso, escalón m; huella f; * vi dar un paso; andar.

stepbrother n hermanastro m.

stepdaughter n hijastra f.

stepfather n padrastro m.

stepmother n madrastra f.

stepping stone n pasadera f.

stepsister n hermanastra f.

stepson n hijastro m.

stereo n estéreo m.

stereotype n estereotipo m; * vt estereotipar.

sterile adj estéril.

sterility n esterilidad f.

sterling adj esterlín/ina, genuino/na, verdadero/ra; * n libras esterlinas fpl.

stern adj austero/ra, rígido/da, severo/ra; * n (mar) popa f; ~ly adv austeramente.

stethoscope n (med) estetoscopio m.

stevedore n (mar) estibador m a m/f.

stew vt estofar; * n estufa, olla f.

steward n mayordomo m; (mar) despensero m.

stewardess n azafata f.

stewardship n mayordomía f.

stick n palo, palillo, bastón m; vara f; * vt pegar, hincar; aguantar; picar; * vi pegarse; detenerse; perseverar; dudar.

stickiness n viscosidad, gomosidad f.

sticking plaster n esparadrapo m.

stick-up n asalto, atraco m.

sticky adj viscoso/sa, tenaz.

stiff adj tieso/sa; duro/ra, torpe; rígido/da; yerto/ta; obstinado/da; ~ly adv obstinadamente.

stiffen vt atiesar, endurecer; * vi endurecerse.

stiff neck n tortícolis m.

stiffness n tesura, rigidez f; obstinación f.

stifle vt sofocar.

stifling adj bochornoso/sa.

stigma n estigma m.

stigmatize vt estigmatizar.

stile n portillo con escalones m (para pasar de un cercado a otro).

stiletto n estilete m; tacón de aguja m.

still vt aquietar, aplacar; destilar; * adj silencioso/sa, tranquilo/la; * n alámbique m; * adv todavía; hasta ahora; no obstante; aún así.

stillborn adj nacido/da muerto/ta.

stillness n calma, quietud f.

stilts npl zancos mpl.

stimulant n estimulante m.

stimulate vt estimular, aguijonear.

stimulation n estímulo m; estimulación f.

stimulus n estímulo m.

sting vt picar o morder (un insecto); * vi escocer; * n aguijón m; punzada, picadura, picada f; timo m.

stingily adv avaramente.

stinginess n tacañería, avaricia f.

stingy adj mezquino/na, tacaño/ña, avaro/ra.

stink vi heder; * n hedor m.

stint n tarea f.

stipulate vt estipular.

stipulation n estipulación f; condición f.

stir vt remover; agitar; incitar; * vi moverse; * n tumulto m; turbulencia f.

stirrup n estribo m.

stitch vt coser; * n punzada f; punto m.

stoat n armiño m.

stock n existencias fpl; ganado m; caldo m; estirpe f, linaje m; capital, principal m; fondo m; ~s pl acciones en los fondos públicos fpl; * vt proveer, abastecer.

stockade n prisión militar f.

stockbroker n agente de bolsa m/f.

stock exchange n bolsa f.
stockholder n accionista m/f.
stocking n media f.
stock market n bolsa f.
stoic n estoico/ca m/f.
stoical adj estoico/ca; **~ly** adv estoicamente.
stoicism n estoicismo m.
stole n estola f.
stomach n estómago m; apetito m; * vt aguantar.
stone n piedra f; pepita f; hueso de fruta m; * adj de piedra; * vt apedrear; deshuesar; empedrar; trabajar de albañil.
stone deaf adj sordo/da como una tapia.
stoning n apedreamiento m.
stony adj de piedra, pétreo/rea; duro/ra.
stool n banquillo, taburete m.
stoop vi encorvarse, inclinarse; bajarse; * n inclinación hacia abajo f.
stop vt detener, parar; tapar; * vi pararse, hacer alto; * n parada f; punto m; pausa f; obstáculo m.
stopover n parada; rescala f.
stoppage, stopping n obstrucción f; impedimiento m; (rail) alto m.
stopwatch n cronómetro m.
storage n almacenamiento m; almacenaje m.
store n abundancia f; provisión f; almacén m, tienda f; * vt surtir, proveer, abastecer.
storey n piso m (de una casa).
stork n cigüeña f.
storm n tempestad, borrasca f; asalto m; * vt tomar por asalto; * vi rabiar.
stormily adv violentamente.
stormy adj tempestuoso/sa; violento/ta.

story n historia f; chiste m.
stout adj robusto/ta, corpulento/ta, vigoroso/sa; terco/ca; * adv valientemente; obstinadamente.
stoutness n valor m; fuerza f; corpulencia f.
stove n cocina f; estufa f.
stow vt ordenar, colocar; (mar) estibar.
straggle vi rezagarse.
straggler n rezagado/da m/f.
straight adj derecho/cha; estrecho/cha; franco/ca; * adv directamente.
straightaway adv inmediatamente.
straighten vt enderezar.
straightforward adj derecho/cha; franco/ca; leal.
straightforwardness n derechura f, franqueza f.
strain vt colar, filtrar; apretar (a uno contra sí); forzar, violentar; * vi esforzarse; * n tensión f; retorcimiento m; raza f; linaje m; estilo m; sonido m; armonía f.
strainer n colador m, coladera f.
strait n estrecho m; aprieto, peligro m; penuria f.
strait-jacket n camisa de fuerza f.
strand n hebra f; costa, playa f.
strange adj raro/ra; extraño/ña; **~ly** adv extrañamente, extraordinariamente.
strangeness n rareza f, extrañeza f.
stranger n desconocido/da m/f; extranjero/ra m/f.
strangle vt estrangular.
strangulation n estrangulamiento m.
strap n correa, tira de cuero f; tirante de bota m; * vt atar con correa.
strapping adj abultado/da, corpulento/ta.
stratagem n estratagema f; astucia f.

strategic *adj* estratégico/ca.

strategy *n* estrategia *f*.

stratum *n* estrato *m*.

straw *n* paja *m*; pajita *f*.

strawberry *n* fresa *f*.

stray *vi* extraviarse; perder el camino; * *adj* extraviado/da; perdido/da.

streak *n* raya, lista *f*; vena *f*; * *vt* rayar.

stream *n* arroyo, río, torrente *m*; * *vi* correr.

streamer *n* serpentina *f*.

street *n* calle *f*.

strength *n* fuerza, robustez *f*; vigor *m*; fortaleza *f*.

strengthen *vt* fortificar; corroborar.

strenuous *adj* arduo/dua; ágil.

stress *n* presión *f*; estrés *m*; fuerza *f*; peso *m*; importancia *f*; acento *m*; * *vt* subrayar; acentuar.

stretch *vt*, *vi* extender, alargar; estirar; extenderse; esforzarse; * *n* extensión *f*; trecho *m*; estirón *m*.

stretcher *n* camilla *f*.

strew *vt* esparcir; sembrar.

strict *adj* estricto/ta, estrecho/cha; exacto/ta, riguroso/sa, severo/ra; **~ly** *adv* exactamente, con severidad.

strictness *n* exactitud *f*; severidad *f*, estrechez *f*.

stride *n* tranco *m*; zancada *f*; * *vi* atrancar.

strife *n* contienda, disputa *f*.

strike *vt*, *vi* golpear; herir; castigar; tocar; chocar; sonar; cesar de trabajar; * *n* ataque *m*; descubrimiento *m*; huelga *f*.

striker *n* huelguista *m/f*.

striking *adj* llamativo/va; notorio/ria; **~ly** *adv* sorprendentemente.

string *n* cordón *m*; hilo *m*; cuerda *f*;

hilera *f*; fibra *f*; * *vt* encordar; enhilar; estirar.

stringent *adj* astringente.

stringy *adj* fibroso/sa.

strip *vt* desnudar, despojar; * *vi* desnudarse; * *n* tira *f*; franja *f*; cinta *f*.

stripe *n* raya, lista *f*; azote *m*; * *vt* rayar.

strive *vi* esforzarse; empeñarse; disputar, contender; oponerse.

stroke *n* golpe *m*; toque (en la pintura) *m*; sonido (del reloj) *m*; plumada *f*; caricia *f*; apoplejía *f*; * *vt* acariciar.

stroll *n* paseo *m*; * *vi* dar un paseo.

strong *adj* fuerte, vigoroso/sa, robusto/ta; poderoso/sa; violento/ta; **~ly** *adv* fuertemente, con violencia.

strongbox *n* caja fuerte *f*.

stronghold *n* plaza fuerte *f*.

strophe *n* estrofa *f*.

structure *n* estructura *f*; edificio *m*.

struggle *vi* esforzarse; luchar; agitarse; * *n* lucha *f*.

strum *vt* (*mus*) rasguear.

strut *vi* pavonearse; * *n* contoneo *m*.

stub *n* talón *m*; colilla *f*; tronco *m*.

stubble *n* rastrojo *m*; cerda *f*.

stubborn *adj* obstinado/da, testarudo/da; **~ly** *adv* obstinadamente.

stubbornness *n* obstinación, pertinacia *f*.

stucco *n* estuco *m*.

stud *n* corchete *m*; taco *m*; cabelleriza *f*.

student *n* estudiante *m/f*; * *adj* estudiantil.

studio *n* estudio *m*.

studio flat *n* estudio *m*.

studious *adj* estudioso/sa; diligente; **~ly** *adv* estudiosamente, diligentemente.

study n estudio m; aplicación f; meditación profunda f; * vt estudiar; observar; * vi estudiar; aplicarse.

stuff n materia f; material m; estofa f; * vt henchir, llenar; disecar.

stuffing n relleno m.

stuffy adj cargado/da; de miras estrechas.

stumble vi tropezar; * n traspié, tropiezo m.

stumbling block n tropiezo m; escollo m.

stump n tronco m; tocón m; muñón m.

stun vt aturdir, ensordecer.

stunner n cosa estupenda f.

stunt n vuelo acrobático m; truco publicitario m; * vt no dejar crecer.

stuntman n especialista m.

stuntwoman n especialista f.

stupefy vt atontar, atolondrar.

stupendous adj estupendo/da, maravilloso/sa.

stupid adj estúpido/da; **very ~** zopenco/ca; **~ly** adv estúpidamente.

stupidity n estupidez f.

stupor n estupor m.

sturdily adv fuertemente.

sturdiness n fuerza, fortaleza f, obstinación f.

sturdy adj fuerte, tieso/sa, robusto/ta; bronco/ca, insolente.

sturgeon n esturión m.

stutter vi tartamudear.

sty n zahurda f; pocilga f.

stye(e) n orzuelo m.

style n estilo m; moda f; * vt titular; nombrar; estilizar.

stylish adj elegante, en buen estilo.

suave adj afable.

subdivide vt subdividir.

subdivision n subdivisión f.

subdue vt sojuzgar, sujetar; conquistar; mortificar.

subject adj sujeto/ta; sometido/da; * n sujeto m; súbdito/ta m/f; tema m; * vt sujetar; exponer.

subjection n sujeción f.

subjugate vt sojuzgar, subyugar.

subjugation n subyugación f.

subjunctive n subjuntivo m.

sublet vt subarrendar.

sublimate vt sublimar.

sublime adj sublime, excelso/sa; **~ly** adv de modo sublime; * n sublime m.

sublimity n sublimidad f.

submachine gun n metralleta f.

submarine adj submarino/na; * n submarino m.

submerge vt sumergir.

submersion n inmersión f; zambullida f.

submission n sumisión f.

submissive adj sumiso/sa, obsequioso/sa; **~ly** adv con sumisión.

submissiveness n obsequio m; sumisión f.

submit vt (vi) someter(se).

subordinate adj subordinado/da, inferior; * vt subordinar.

subordination n subordinación f.

subpoena n citación f; * vt citar.

subscribe vt, vi suscribir, certificar con su firma; consentir.

subscriber n suscriptor/a m/f.

subscription n suscripción f.

subsequent adj, **~ly** adv subsiguiente(mente).

subservient adj subordinado/da; servil.

subside vi sumergirse, irse a fondo.

subsidence n derrumbamiento m.

subsidiary adj subsidiario/ria.

subsidize vt subvencionar, dar subsidios.

subsidy n subvención f; subsidio, socorro m.

subsist vi subsistir; existir.

subsistence n existencia f; subsistencia f.

substance n substancia f; entidad f; esencia f.

substantial adj substancial; real, material; substancioso/sa; fuerte; ~ly adv substancialmente.

substantiate vt probar.

substantive n sustantivo m.

substitute vt sustituir; * n suplente m/f.

substitution n sustitución f.

substratum n sustrato m.

subterfuge n subterfugio m; evasión f.

subterranean adj subterráneo/nea.

subtitle n subtítulo m.

subtle adj sutil, astuto/ta.

subtlety n sutileza, astucia f.

subtly adv sutilmente.

subtract vt (math) sustraer.

suburb n zona residencial f.

suburban adj suburbano/na.

subversion n subversión f.

subversive adj subversivo/va.

subvert vt subvertir, destruir.

succeed vt, vi seguir; conseguir, lograr, tener éxito.

success n éxito m.

successful adj exitoso/sa; próspero/ra, dichoso/sa; ~ly adv con éxito; prósperamente.

succession n sucesión f; descendencia f; herencia f.

successive adj sucesivo/va; ~ly adv sucesivamente.

successor n sucesor/a m/f.

succinct adj sucinto/ta, compendioso/sa; ~ly adv con brevedad.

succulent adj suculento/ta, jugoso/sa.

succumb vi sucumbir.

such adj tal, semejante; ~ as tal como.

such and such a one n zutano/na y fulano m/f.

suck vt, vi chupar; mamar.

suckle vt amamantar.

suckling n mamantón/ona m/f.

suction n (med) succión f.

sudden adj repentino/na, no previsto/ta; ~ly adv de repente, súbitamente.

suddenness n precipitación f.

sue vt demandar.

suds npl jabonaduras fpl.

suede n ante m, gamuza f.

suet n sebo m.

suffer vt, vi sufrir, padecer; tolerar, permitir.

suffering n pena f; dolor m.

suffice vi bastar, ser suficiente.

sufficiency n suficiencia f; capacidad f.

sufficient adj suficiente; ~ly adv bastante.

suffocate vt asfixiar; sofocar; * vi asfixiarse.

suffocation n asfixia f.

suffrage n sufragio, voto m.

suffuse vt difundir, derramar.

sugar n azúcar m; * vt azucarar.

sugar beet n remolacha f.

sugar cane n caña de azúcar f.

sugar loaf n pan de azúcar m.

sugary adj azucarado/da.

suggest vt sugerir.

suggestion n sugestión f.

suicidal adj suicida.

suicide n suicidio m; suicida m/f.

suit n conjunto m; petición f; traje m; pleito m; surtido m; * vt convenir; sentar a; adaptar.

suitable adj conforme, conveniente.

suitably adv convenientemente.

suitcase n maleta, valija f.

suite n suite f; serie f; tren m, comitiva f.

suitor n suplicante m; amante, cortejo m; pleiteante m/f; galanteador m.

sulkiness n mal humor m.

sulky adj regañon, terco/ca.

sullen adj hosco/ca; intratable; ~ly adv de mal humor; tercamente.

sullenness n hosquedad f; obstinación, pertinacia, terquedad f.

sulphur n azufre m.

sulphurous adj sulfureo, azufroso/sa.

sultan n sultán m.

sultana n sultana f; pasa f.

sultry adj caluroso/sa; sofocante.

sum n suma f; total m.

summarily adv sumariamente.

summary adj sumario/ria; * n sumario m; resumen m.

summer n verano, estío m.

summerhouse n glorieta de jardín f.

summit n ápice m; cima f.

summon vt citar, requerir por auto de juez; convocar, convidar; (mil) intimar la rendición.

summons n citación f; requerimiento m.

sumptuous adj suntuoso/sa; ~ly adv suntuosamente.

sum up vt resumir; sumar; recopilar.

sun n sol m.

sunbathe vi tomar el sol.

sunburnt adj quemado/da por el sol.

Sunday n domingo m; * adj dominical; done or worn on ~ dominguero/ra.

Sunday driver n dominguero/ra m/f.

sundial n reloj de sol, cuadrante m.

sundry adj diversos/sas.

sunflower n girasol m.

sunglasses npl gafas de sol fpl.

sunless adj sin sol; sin luz.

sunlight n luz del sol f.

sunny adj soleado/da; brillante.

sunrise n salida del sol f; amanecer m.

sun roof n techo corredizo m.

sunset n puesta del sol f.

sunshade n quitasol m.

sunshine n solana f; claridad del sol f.

sunstroke n insolación f.

suntan n bronceado m.

suntan oil n aceite bronceador m.

super adj (fam) bárbaro/ra.

superannuated adj añejado/da; pensionado/da.

superannuation n pensión, jubilación f; retiro m.

superb adj magnífico/ca; ~ly adv magníficamente.

supercargo n (mar) sobrecargo m.

supercilious adj arrogante, altanero/ra; ~ly adv con altivez.

superficial adj, ~ly adv superficial(mente).

superfluity n superfluidad f.

superfluous adj superfluo/lua.

superhuman adj sobrehumano/na.

superintendent n superintendente m/f.

superior adj superior; * n superior/a m/f.

superiority n superioridad f.

superlative adj superlativo/va; * n superlativo m; ~ly adv superlativamente, en sumo grado.

supermarket n supermercado m.

supernatural adj sobrenatural.

supernumerary adj supernumerario/ria.

superpower n superpotencia f.

supersede vt sobreseer; sustituir; invalidar.

supersonic adj supersónico/ca.

superstition n superstición f.
superstitious adj supersticioso/sa;
~ly adv supersticiosamente.
superstructure n superestructura f.
supertanker n superpetrolero m.
supervene vi sobrevenir.
supervise vt supervisar, revistar.
supervision n supervisión f.
supervisor n supervisor/a m/f.
supine adj supino/na; negligente.
supper n cena f.
supplant vt suplantar.
supple adj flexible, manejable;
blando/da.
supplement n suplemento m.
supplementary adj adicional.
suppleness n flexibilidad f.
suppli(c)ant n suplicante m/f.
supplicate vt suplicar.
supplication n súplica, suplicación f.
supplier n proveedor/a m/f.
supply vt suministrar; suplir, completar; surtir; * n provisión f; sumi-
nistro m.
support vt sostener; soportar, asistir; * n apoyo m.
supportable adj soportable.
supporter n partidario/ria m/f;
aficionado/da m/f.
suppose vt, vi suponer.
supposition n suposición f.
suppress vt suprimir.
suppression n supresión f.
supremacy n supremacía f.
supreme adj supremo/ma; ~ly adv
supremamente.
surcharge vt sobrecargar; * n sobre-
tasa f.
sure¹ adj seguro/ra, cierto/ta; firme;
estable; to be ~ estar seguro/ra;
~ly adv ciertamente, seguramente, sin duda.
sure!² interj iya!

sureness n certeza, seguridad f.
surety n seguridad f; fiador m/f.
surf n (mar) resaca f.
surface n superficie f; * vt revestir;
* vi salir a la superficie.
surfboard n plancha de surf f.
surfeit n exceso m.
surge n ola, onda f; * vi avanzar en
tropel.
surgeon n cirujano/na m/f.
surgery n cirugía f.
surgical adj quirúrgico/ca.
surliness n mal humor m.
surly adj hosco/ca.
surmise vt sospechar; * n sospecha f.
surmount vt sobrepujar; (fig) zanjar.
surmountable adj superable.
surname n apellido, sobrenombre m.
surpass vt sobresalir, sobrepujar,
exceder, aventajar.
surpassing adj sobresaliente.
surplice n sobrepelliz f.
surplus n excedente m; sobrante m;
* adj sobrante.
surprise vt sorprender; * n sorpresa f.
surprising adj sorprendente.
surrender vt, vi rendir; ceder; rendirse; * n rendición f.
surreptitious adj subrepticio/cia;
~ly adv subrepticiamente.
surrogate vt subrogar; * n subro-
gado/da m/f.
surrogate mother n madre de alquiler f.
surround vt circundar, cercar, rodear.
surrounding area n inmediaciones
fpl.
survey vt inspeccionar, examinar;
apear; * n inspección f; apeo (de
tierras) m.
survive vi sobrevivir; * vt sobrevivir a.

survivor n superviviente m/f.

susceptibility n susceptibilidad f.

susceptible adj susceptible.

suspect vt, vi sospechar; * n sospechoso/sa m/f.

suspend vt suspender.

suspense n suspense m; detención f; incertidumbre f.

suspension n suspensión f.

suspension bridge n puente colgante m.

suspicion n sospecha f.

suspicious adj suspicaz; ~ly adv sospechosamente.

suspiciousness n suspicacia f.

sustain vt sostener, sustentar, mantener; apoyar; sufrir.

sustenance n sostenimiento, sustento m.

suture n sutura, costura f.

swab n algodón m; frotis m invar.

swaddle vt fajar.

swaddling-clothes npl pañales mpl.

swagger vi baladronear.

swallow n golondrina f; * vt tragar, engullir.

swamp n pantano m.

swampy adj pantanoso/sa.

swan n cisne m.

swap vt canjear; * n intercambio m.

swarm n enjambre m; gentío m; hormiguero m; * vi enjambrar; hormiguear de gente; abundar.

swarthy adj atezado/da.

swarthiness n tez morena f.

swashbuckling adj fanfarrón/ona.

swath n tranco m.

swathe vt fajar; * n faja f.

sway vt mover; * vi ladearse, inclinarse; * n balanceo m; poder, imperio, influjo m.

swear vt, vi jurar; hacer jurar; juramentar.

sweat n sudor m; * vi sudar; trabajar con fatiga.

sweater, sweatshirt n suéter m.

sweep vt, vi barrer; arrebatar; deshollinar; pasar o tocar ligeramente; oscilar; * n barredura f; vuelta f; giro m.

sweeping adj rápido/da; ~s pl barreduras fpl.

sweepstake n lotería f.

sweet adj dulce, grato/ta, gustoso/sa; suave; oloroso/sa; melodioso/sa; hermoso/sa; amable; * adv dulcemente, suavemente; * n dulce, caramelo m.

sweetbread n mellejas de ternera fpl.

sweeten vt endulzar; suavizar; aplacar; perfumar.

sweetener n edulcorante m.

sweetheart n novio/via m/f; querida f.

sweetmeats npl dulces secos mpl.

sweetness n dulzura, suavidad f.

swell vi hincharse; ensoberbecerse; embravecerse; * vt hinchar, inflar, agravar; * n marejada f; * adj (fam) estupendo/da, fenomenal.

swelling n hinchazón f; tumor m.

swelter vi ahogarse de calor.

swerve vi vagar; desviarse.

swift adj veloz, ligero/ra, rápido/da; * n vencejo m.

swiftly adv velozmente.

swiftness n velocidad, rapidez f.

swill vt beber en exceso; * n bazofia f.

swim vi nadar; abundar en; * vt pasar a nado; * n nadada f.

swimming n natación f.

swimming pool n piscina f.

swimsuit n traje de baño m.

swindle vt estafar.

swindler n estafador/a m/f.

swine n puerco, cochino m.

swing vi balancear, columpiarse;

vibrar; agitarse; * *vt* colum piar; balancear; girar; * *n* vibración *f*; balanceo *m*.

swinging *adj* (*fam*) alegre.

swinging door *n* puerta giratoria *f*.

swirl *n* remolino.

switch *n* varilla *f*; interruptor *m*; (*rail*) aguja *f*; * *vt* cambiar de; **to ~ off** apagar; parar; **to ~ on** encender, prender.

switchboard *n* centralita *f*.

swivel *vi* girar.

swoon *vi* desmayarse; * *n* desmayo, deliquio, pasmo *m*.

swoop *vi* calarse; * *n* calada; redada *f*; **in one ~** de un golpe.

sword *n* espada *f*.

swordfish *n* pez espada *f*.

swordsman *n* guerrero, espadachín *m*.

sycamore *n* sicomoro *m* (árbol).

sycophant *n* sicofante *m*.

syllabic *adj* silábico/ca.

syllable *n* sílaba *f*.

syllabus *n* programa de estudios *m*.

syllogism *n* silogismo *m*.

sylph *n* silfio *m*; sílfide *f*.

symbol *n* símbolo *m*.

symbolic(al) *adj* simbólico/ca.

symbolize *vt* simbolizar.

symmetrical *adj* simétrico/ca; **~ly** *adv* con simetría.

symmetry *n* simetría *f*.

sympathetic *adj* simpático/ca; **~ally** *adv* simpáticamente.

sympathize *vi* compadecerse.

sympathy *n* simpatía *f*.

symphony *n* sinfonía *f*.

symposium *n* simposio *m*.

symptom *n* síntoma *m*.

synagogue *n* sinagoga *f*.

synchronism *n* sincronismo *m*.

syndicate *n* sindicato *m*.

syndrome *n* síndrome *m*.

synod *n* sínodo *m*.

synonym *n* sinónimo *m*.

synonymous *adj* sinónimo/ma; **~ly** *adv* con sinonimia.

synopsis *n* sinopsis *f invar*; sumario *m*.

synoptic *adj* sinóptico/ca.

syntax *n* sintaxis *f*.

synthesis *n* síntesis *f invar*.

syringe *n* jeringa, lavativa *f*; * *vt* jeringar.

system *n* sistema *m*.

systematic *adj* sistemático/ca; **~ally** *adv* sistemáticamente.

systems analyst *n* analista de sistemas *m/f*.

T

tab *n* lengüeta *f*; etiqueta *f*.

tabernacle *n* tabernáculo *m*.

table *n* mesa *f*; tabla *f*; * *vt* someter a discusión; poner sobre la mesa; **~ d'hôte** menu *m*.

tablecloth *n* mantel *m*.

tablespoon *n* cuchara para comer *f*.

tablet *n* tableta *f*; pastilla *f*; comprimido *m*.

table tennis *n* ping-pong, tenis de mesa *m*.

taboo *adj* tabú; * *n* tabú *m*; * *vt* interdecir.

tabular *adj* tabular.

tacit *adj* tácito/ta; **~ly** *adv* tácitamente.

taciturn *adj* taciturno/na, callado/da.

tack *n* tachuela *f*; bordo *m*; * *vt* atar; pegar; * *vi* virar.

tackle *n* equipo *m*, aparejos *mpl*; placaje *m*; (*mar*) cordaje *m*, jarcia *f*.

tact *n* tacto *m*.

tactician *n* táctico/ca *m/f*.

tactics *npl* táctica *f*.

tadpole *n* renacuajo *m*.

taffeta *n* tafetán *m*.

tag *n* herrete *m*; * *vt* herretear.

tail *n* cola *f*; rabo *m*; * *vt* vigilar a.

tailgate *n* puerta trasera *f*.

tailor *n* sastre *m*.

tailoring *n* corte *m*.

tailor-made *adj* hecho/cha a la medida.

tailwind *n* viento de cola *m*.

taint *vt* tachar, manchar; viciar; * *n* mancha *f*.

tainted *adj* contaminado/da; manchado/da.

take *vt* tomar, coger, asir; recibir; aceptar; pillar; prender; admitir; entender; 'v *vt* prender el fuego; **to ~ apart** *vt* descoser; **to ~ away** quitar; llevar; **to ~ back** devolver; retractar; **to ~ down** derribar; apuntar; **to ~ in** entender, abarcar; acoger; **to ~ off** *vi* despegar; *vt* quitar; imitar; **to ~ on** aceptar; contratar; desafiar; **to ~ out** sacar; quitar; **to ~ to** encariñarse con; **to ~ up** acortar; ocupar; dedicarse a; * *n* toma *f*.

takeoff *n* despegue *m*.

takeover *n* absorción *f*; ~ **bid** opa *f*.

takings *npl* ingresos *mpl*.

talc *n* talco *m*.

talent *n* talento *m*; capacidad *f*.

talented *adj* con talento.

talisman *n* talismán *m*.

talk *vi* hablar, conversar; charlar; * *n* habla *f*; charla *f*; fama *f*.

talkative *adj* locuaz.

talk show *n* programa de entrevistas *m*.

tall *adj* alto/ta, elevado/da; robusto/ta.

tally *vi* corresponder.

talon *n* garra *f*.

tambourine *n* pandereta *f*.

tame *adj* amansado/da, domado/da, domesticado/da; **~ly** *adv* mansamente; bajamente; * *vt* domar, domesticar.

tameness *n* domesticidad *f*; sumisión *f*.

tamper *vi* tocar.

tampon *n* tampón *m*.

tan *vt* broncear; * *vi* broncearse, ponerse moreno/na; * *n* bronceado *m*.

tang *n* sabor fuerte *m*.

tangent *n* tangente *f*.

tangerine *n* mandarina *f*.

tangible *adj* tangible.

tangle *vt* enredar, embrollar.

tank *n* cisterna *f*; aljibe *m*.

tanker *n* petrolero *m*; camión cisterna *m*.

tanned *adj* bronceado/da.

tantalizing *adj* tentador/a.

tantamount *adj* equivalente.

tantrum *n* rabieta *f*.

tap *n* tocar ligeramente; utilizar; intervenir; zapatear; * *n* grifo *m*; palmada suave *f*; toque ligero *m*; llave *f*; espita *f*.

tape *n* cinta *f*; * *vt* grabar.

tape measure *n* metro *m*.

taper *n* cirio *m*.

tape recorder *n* grabadora *f*.

tapestry *n* tapiz *m*; tapicería *f*.

tar *n* brea *f*, alquitrán *m*.

target *n* blanco *m* (para tirar).

tariff *n* tarifa *f*.

Tarmac®, tarmac *n* asfalto *m*, alquitranado *m*.

tarnish *vt* deslustrar.

tarpaulin *n* lona *f* alquitranada.

tarragon *n* (*bot*) estragón *m*.

tart adj acedo/da, acre; * n tarta, torta f; (sl) zorra f.

tartan n tela escocesa f.

tartar n tártaro m.

task n tarea f.

tassel n borlita f.

taste n gusto m; sabor m; saboreo m; ensayo m; * vt, vi gustar; probar; experimentar; agradar; tener sabor.

tasteful adj sabroso/sa; **~ly** adv sabrosamente.

tasteless adj insípido/da, sin sabor.

tasty adj sabroso/sa.

tattoo n tatuaje m; * vt tatuar.

taunt vt mofar; ridiculizar; * n mofa, burla f.

Taurus n Tauro m (signo del zodíaco).

taut adj tieso/sa.

tautological adj tautológico/ca.

tautology n tautología f.

tawdry adj jarifo/fa, vistoso/sa, chabacano/na.

tax n impuesto m; contribución f; * vt gravar; poner a prueba.

taxable adj sujeto/ta a impuestos.

taxation n imposición de impuestos f.

tax collector n recaudador/a m/f de impuestos.

tax-free adj libre de impuestos.

taxi n taxi m; * vi rodar por la pista.

taxi driver n taxista m/f.

taxi rank n parada de taxis f.

tax payer n contribuyente m/f.

tax relief n desgravación fiscal f.

tax return n declaración de la renta f.

tea n té m.

teach vt enseñar, instruir; * vi enseñar.

teacher n profesor/a m/f; maestro/tra m/f.

teaching n enseñanza f.

teacup n taza de té f.

teak n teca f (árbol).

team n equipo m.

teamster n camionero/ra m/f.

teamwork n trabajo de equipo m.

teapot n tetera f.

tear vt despedazar, rasgar; **to ~ up** hacer trizas.

tear n lágrima f; gota f.

tearful adj lloroso/sa; **~ly** adv con lloro.

tear gas n gas lacrimógeno m.

tease vt tomar el pelo.

tea service, tea set n servicio para té m.

teasing adj zumbón/ona; * n zumba f.

teaspoon n cucharita f.

teat n ubre, teta f.

technical adj técnico/ca.

technicality n detalle técnico m.

technician n técnico/ca m

technique n técnica f.

technological adj tecnológico/ca.

technology n tecnología f.

teddy (bear) n osito de felpa m.

tedious adj tedioso/sa, fastidioso/sa; **~ly** adv fastidiosamente.

tedium n tedio, fastidio m.

tee n tee m.

teem vi rebosar de.

teenage adj juvenil; **~r** n adolescente m/f.

teens npl adolescencia f.

tee-shirt, T-shirt n camiseta f.

teeth n pl de **tooth**.

teethe vi echar los dientes.

teetotal adj abstemio/mia, sobrio/bria.

teetotaller n abstemio/mia m/f.

telegram n telegrama m.

telegraph n telégrafo m.

telegraphic adj telegráfico/ca.

telegraphy n telegrafía f.

telepathy n telepatía f.

telephone n teléfono m.

telephone banking n telebanca f.

telephone booth n cabina telefónica f.

elephone call n llamada telefónica f.

elephone directory n guía f telefónica.

elephone number n número de teléfono m.

telescope n telescopio m.

telescopic adj telescópico/ca.

televise vt televisar.

television n televisión f.

television news n telediario m.

television set n televisor m.

teleworker n teletrabajador/ra m/f.

teleworking n teletrabajo m.

telex n télex m; vt, vi enviar un télex.

tell vt decir; informar, contar.

teller n cajero/ra m/f.

telling adj contundente; revelador/a.

telltale adj indicador/a.

telly n (fam) tele f.

temper vt templar, moderar; * n mal genio m.

temperament n temperamento m.

temperance n templanza, moderación f.

temperate adj templado/da, moderado/da, sobrio/ria.

temperature n temperatura f.

tempest n tempestad f.

tempestuous adj tempestuoso/sa.

template n plantilla f.

temple n templo m; sien f.

temporarily adv temporalmente.

temporary adj temporal.

tempt vt tentar; provocar.

temptation n tentación f.

tempting adj tentador/a.

ten adj, n diez.

tenable adj defendible.

tenacious adj, ~ly adv tenaz(mente).

tenacity n tenacidad f; porfía f.

tenancy n tenencia f.

tenant n arrendatario/ria, inquilino/na m/f.

tend vt guardar, velar; * vi tener tendencia a.

tendency n tendencia f.

tender adj tierno/na, delicado/da; sensible; ~ly adv tiernamente; * n oferta f; * vt ofrecer; estimar.

tenderness n ternura f.

tendon n tendón m.

tendril n zarcillo m.

tenement n casa de pisos f.

tenet n dogma m; aserción f.

tennis n tenis m.

tennis court n cancha de tenis f.

tennis player n tenista m/f.

tennis racket n raqueta de tenis f.

tennis shoes npl zapatillas de tenis fpl.

tenor n (mus) tenor m; contenido m; substancia f.

tense adj tieso/sa, tenso/sa; * n (gr) tiempo m.

tension n tensión, tirantez f.

tent n tienda de campaña f.

tentacle n tentáculo m.

tentative adj de ensayo, de prueba; ~ly adv como prueba.

tenth adj, n décimo/ma.

tenuous adj tenue.

tenure n tenencia f.

tepid adj tibio/bia.

term n término m; dicción f; vocablo m; condición, estipulación f; * vt nombrar, llamar.

terminal adj mortal; * n terminal m; terminal f.

terminate vt terminar.

termination n terminación, conclusión f.

terminus n terminal f.

terrace n terraza f.

terrain n terreno m.

terrestrial adj terrestre, terreno/na.

terrible adj terrible.

terribly adv terriblemente.

terrier n terrier m.

terrific adj fantástico/ca; maravilloso/sa.

terrify vt aterrar, espantar.

territorial adj territorial.

territory n territorio, distrito m.

terror n terror m.

terrorism n terrorismo m.

terrorist n terrorista m/f.

terrorist attack n atentado m.

terrorize vt aterrorizar.

terse adj tajante.

test n examen m; prueba f; * vt probar; examinar.

testament n testamento m.

tester n ensayador/a m/f.

testicles npl testículos mpl.

testify vt testificar, atestiguar.

testimonial n atestación f.

testimony n testimonio m.

test pilot n piloto de pruebas m/f.

test tube n probeta f.

testy adj tétrico/ca.

tetanus n tétanos m invar.

tether vt atar.

text n texto m.

textbook n libro de texto m.

textiles npl textiles mpl.

textual adj textual.

texture n textura f; tejido m.

than adv que, de.

thank vt agradecer, dar las gracias a.

thankful adj grato/ta, agradecido/da; ~ly adv con gratitud.

thankfulness n gratitud f.

thankless adj ingrato/ta.

thanks npl gracias fpl.

Thanksgiving n día de acción de gracias m.

that pn aquel, aquello, aquella; que; este; * conj porque; para que; **so ~** de modo que.

thatch n techo de paja m; * vt techar con paja.

thaw n deshielo m; * vi deshelarse.

the art el, la, lo; los, las.

theatre n teatro m.

theatregoer n aficionado/da al teatro m/f.

theatrical adj teatral.

theft n robo m.

their pn su, suyo, suya; de ellos, de ellas; ~**s** el suyo, la suya, los suyos, las suyas; de ellos, de ellas.

them pn los, las, les; ellos, ellas.

theme n tema m.

themselves pn pl ellos mismos, ellas mismas; sí mismos; se.

then adv entonces, después; en tal caso; * conj en ese caso; * adv entonces; **now and ~** de vez en cuando.

theologian n teólogo/ga m/f.

theological adj teológico/ca.

theology n teología f.

theorem n teorema m.

theoretic(al) adj teórico/ca; ~**ly** adv teóricamente.

theorist n teórico/ca m/f.

theorize vt teorizar.

theory n teoría f.

therapeutics n terapéutica f.

therapist n terapeuta m/f.

therapy n terapia f.

there adv allí, allá.

thereabout(s) adv por ahí, acerca de.

thereafter adv después; según.

thereby adv así; de ese modo.

therefore adv por eso, por lo tanto.

thermal adj termal.

thermal printer n impresora térmica f.

thermometer n termómetro m.

thermostat n termostato m.

thesaurus n diccionario de sinónimos m.

these pn pl éstos; éstas; adj estos, estas.

thesis n tesis f invar.

they pn pl ellos, ellas.

thick adj espeso/sa, denso/sa; grueso/sa; torpe.

thicken vi espesar, condensar; condensarse.

thicket n espesura f.

thickness n espesor m.

thickset adj grueso/sa; rechoncho/cha.

thick-skinned adj duro/ra de pellejo.

thief n ladrón/ona m/f.

thigh n muslo m.

thimble n dedal m.

thin adj delgado/da, delicado/da, flaco/ca; claro/ra; * vt atenuar; adelgazar; aclarar.

thing n cosa f; objeto m; chisme m.

think vi pensar, imaginar, meditar, considerar; creer, juzgar; to ~ over reflexionar; to ~ up imaginar.

thinker n pensador/a m/f.

thinking n pensamiento m; juicio m; opinión f.

third adj tercero/ra; * n tercio m; ~ly adv en tercer lugar.

third rate adj mediocre.

thirst n sed f.

thirsty adj sediento/ta.

thirteen adj, n trece.

thirteenth adj, n decimotercero/ra.

thirtieth adj, n trigésimo/ma.

thirty adj, n treinta.

this adj este, esta; * pn éste, ésta, esto.

thistle n cardo m.

thorn n espino m; espina f.

thorny adj espinoso/sa; arduo/dua.

thorough adj entero/ra, perfecto/ta; ~ly adv enteramente, profundamente.

thoroughbred adj de sangre, de casta.

thoroughfare n paso, tránsito m.

those pn pl ésos; ésas; aquéllos, aquéllas; * adj esos, esas; aquellos, aquellas.

though conj aunque, no obstante; * adv sin embargo.

thought n pensamiento, juicio m; opinión f; cuidado m.

thoughtful adj pensativo/va.

thoughtless adj descuidado/da; insensato/ta; ~ly adv descuidadamente, sin reflexión.

thousand adj, n mil.

thousandth adj, n milésimo/ma.

thrash vt golpear; derrotar.

thread n hilo m; rosca f; * vt enhebrar.

threadbare adj raído/da, muy usado/da.

threat n amenaza f.

threaten vt amenazar.

three adj, n tres.

three-dimensional adj tridimensional.

three-monthly adj trimestral.

three-ply adj triple.

threshold n umbral m.

thrifty adj económico/ca.

thrill vt emocionar; * n emoción f.

thriller n película o novela de suspense f.

thrive vi prosperar; crecer.

throat n garganta f.

throb vi palpitar; vibrar; dar punzadas.

throne n trono m.

throng n tropel de gente m; * vt venir en tropel.

throttle n acelerador m; * vt estrangular.

through prep por; durante; mediante; * adj directo/ta; * adv completamente.

throughout prep por todo; * adv en todas partes.

throw vt echar, arrojar, tirar, lanzar; * n tiro m; golpe m; **to ~ away** tirar; **to ~ off** desechar; **to ~ out** tirar; **to ~ up** vomitar, devolver.

throwaway adj desechable.

thrush n tordo m (ave).

thrust vt empujar, introducir; * vr zamparse; * n empuje m.

thud n ruido sordo m; zarpazo m.

thug n gamberro/rra m/f.

thumb n pulgar m.

thump n golpe m; * vt, vi golpear.

thunder n trueno m; * vi tronar.

thunderbolt n rayo m.

thunderclap n trueno m.

thunderstorm n tormenta f.

thundery adj tormentoso/sa.

Thursday n jueves m invar.

thus adv así, de este modo.

thwart vt frustrar.

thyme n (bot) tomillo m.

thyroid n tiroides m invar.

tiara n tiara f.

tic n tic m.

tick n tictac m; palomita f; * vt marcar; **to ~ over** girar en marcha; ir tirando.

ticket n billete, boleto m; etiqueta f; tarjeta f.

ticket collector n (rail) revisor/a m/f.

ticket office n taquilla f, boletería f; despacho de boletos m.

tickle vt hacer cosquillas.

ticklish adj con cosquillas.

tidal adj (mar) de marea.

tidal wave n maremoto m.

tide n curso m; marea f.

tidy adj ordenado/da; arreglado/da; aseado/da.

tie vt anudar, atar; * vi empatar; **to ~ up** envolver; atar; amarrar; con-

cluir; * n atadura f; lazo m; corbata f; empate m.

tier n grada f; piso m.

tiger n tigre m.

tight adj tirante, tieso/sa, tenso/sa; cerrado/da; apretado/da; * adv con fuerza.

tighten vt apretar, estirar.

tightfisted adj tacaño/ña.

tightly adv muy fuerte.

tightrope n cuerda floja f.

tights npl medias fpl.

tigress n tigresa f.

tile n teja f; baldosa f; azulejo m; * vt tejar.

tiled adj embaldosado/da.

till n caja f; * vt cultivar, labrar.

tiller n cana del timón f.

tilt vt inclinar; * vi inclinarse.

timber n madera de construcción f; árboles mpl.

time n tiempo m; época f; hora f; momento m; (mus) compás m; **in ~ a tiempo**; **from ~ to ~** de vez en cuando; * vt medir el tiempo; cronometrar.

time bomb n bomba de relojería f.

time lag n desfase m.

timeless adj eterno/na.

timely adj oportuno/na.

time off n tiempo libre m.

timer n interruptor m; programador horario m.

time scale n escala de tiempo f.

time trial n contrarreloj f.

time zone n huso horario m.

timid adj tímido/da, temeroso/sa; **~ly** adv con timidez.

timidity n timidez f.

timing n cronometraje m; oportunidad f.

tin n estaño m; hojalata f.

tinder n yesca f.

tinfoil n papel de estaño m.

tinge n matiz m.

tingle vi zumbar; latir, punzar.

tingling n zumbido m; latido m.

tinker n calderero remendón m; gitano/na m/f.

tinkle vi tintinear.

tinplate n hojalata f.

tinsel n oropel m.

tint n tinte m; * vt teñir.

tinted adj teñido/da; ahumado/da.

tiny adj pequeño/ña, chico/ca.

tip¹ n punta, extremidad f.

tip² n propina f; consejo m; * vt dar una propina a.

tip³ vt inclinar; vaciar.

tip-off n advertencia f.

tipsy adj alegre.

tiptop adj excelente, perfecto/ta.

tirade n invectiva f.

tire vt cansar, fatigar; * vi cansarse; fastidiarse.

tireless adj incansable.

tiresome adj tedioso/sa, molesto/ta.

tiring adj cansado/da.

tissue n tejido m; pañuelo de papel m.

tissue paper n papel de seda m.

titbit n golosina f; pedazo m.

titillate vt estimular.

title n título m.

title deed n derecho de propiedad m.

title page n portada f.

titter vi reírse disimuladamente; * n risa disimulada f.

titular adj titular.

to prep a; para; por; de; hasta; con; que.

toad n sapo m.

toadstool n (bot) seta venenosa f.

toast n tostar; brindar; * n tostada f; brindis m.

toaster n tostadora f.

tobacco n tabaco m.

tobacconist n tabaquero/ra, estanquero/ra m/f.

tobacconist's (shop) n estanco m, tabaquería f.

tobacco pouch n petaca f.

toboggan n tobogán m.

today adv hoy.

toddler n niño/ña (que empieza a andar) m/f.

toddy n ponche m.

toe n dedo del pie m; punta f.

together adv juntamente, juntos; al mismo tiempo.

toil vi fatigarse, trabajar mucho; afanarse; * n trabajo m; fatiga f; afán m.

toilet n servicios mpl; sanitario m; * adj de aseo.

toilet bag n bolsa de aseo f.

toilet bowl n taza del retrete f.

toilet paper n papel higiénico m.

toiletries npl artículos de aseo mpl.

token n señal f; muestra f; recuerdo m; vale m; (games) ficha f.

tolerable adj soportable; pasable.

tolerance n tolerancia f.

tolerant adj tolerante.

tolerate vt tolerar.

toll n peaje m; número de víctimas m; * vi doblar.

tomato n tomate m.

tomb n tumba f; sepulcro m, sepultura f.

tomboy n muchachota f.

tombstone n piedra sepulcral f.

tomcat n gato m.

tomorrow adv mañana; * n mañana f.

ton n tonelada f.

tone n tono m; acento m; * vi armonizar; to ~ down suavizar.

tone-deaf adj sin oído musical.

tongs npl tenacillas fpl.

tongue n lengua f.

tongue-tied *adj* mudo/da.

tongue-twister *n* trabalenguas *m invar.*

tonic *n* (*med*) tónico *m*.

tonight *adv*, *n* esta tarde (*f*).

tonnage *n* tonelaje *m*.

tonsil *n* amígdala *f*; ~s *npl* agallas *fpl*.

tonsillitis *n* agalla *f*.

tonsure *n* tonsura *f*.

too *adv* demasiado; también.

tool *n* herramienta *f*; utensilio *m*.

tool box *n* caja de herramientas *f*.

toot *vi* tocar la bocina.

tooth *n* diente *m*.

toothache *n* dolor de muelas *m*.

toothbrush *n* cepillo de dientes *m*.

toothless *adj* desdentado/da.

toothpaste *n* pasta de dientes *f*.

toothpick *n* palillo *m*.

top *n* cima, cumbre *f*; último grado *m*; lo alto; superficie *f*; tapa *f*; cabeza *f*; * *adj* de arriba; primero/ra; * *vt* elevarse por encima; sobrepujar, exceder; to ~ off llenar.

topaz *n* topacio *m*.

top floor *n* último piso *m*.

top-heavy *adj* inestable.

topic *n* tema *m*; ~al *adj* actual.

topless *adj* topless.

top-level *adj* al más alto nivel.

topmost *adj* lo más alto.

topographic(al) *adj* topográfico/ca.

topography *n* topografía *f*.

topple *vt* derribar; * *vi* volcarse.

top-secret *adj* de alto secreto.

topsy-turvy *adv* al revés.

torch *n* antorcha *f*.

torment *vt* atormentar; * *n* tormento *m*.

tornado *n* tornado *m*.

torrent *n* torrente *m*.

torrid *adj* apasionado/da.

tortoise *n* tortuga *f*.

tortoiseshell *adj* de carey.

tortuous *adj* tortuoso/sa, sinuoso/sa

torture *n* tortura *f*; * *vt* torturar.

toss *vt* tirar, lanzar, arrojar; agitar, sacudir.

total *adj* total, entero/ra; ~ly *adv* totalmente.

totalitarian *adj* totalitario/ria.

totality *n* totalidad *f*.

totter *vi* vacilar.

touch *vt* tocar, palpar; to ~ on aludir a; to ~ up retocar; * *n* contacto *m*; tacto *m*; toque *m*; prueba *f*.

touch-and-go *adj* arriesgado/da.

touchdown *n* aterrizaje *m*; ensayo *m*.

touched *adj* conmovido/da; chiflado/da.

touching *adj* patético/ca, conmovedor/a.

touchstone *n* piedra de toque *f*.

touchwood *n* yesca *f*.

touchy *adj* quisquilloso/sa.

tough *adj* duro/ra; difícil; resistente, fuerte; * *n* gorila *m*.

toughen *vt* endurecer.

toupee *n* tupé *m*.

tour *n* viaje *m*; visita *f*; * *vt* visitar.

touring *n* viajes turísticos *mpl*.

tourism *n* turismo *m*; bicycle ~ cicloturismo; rural ~ turismo rural.

tourist *n* turista *m/f*.

tourist office *n* oficina de turismo *f*.

tournament *n* torneo *m*.

tow *vt* remolque *m*; * *vt* remolcar.

toward(s) *prep*, *adv* hacia, con dirección a; cerca de, respecto a.

towel *n* toalla *f*.

towelling *n* toalla *f*.

towel rack *n* toallero *m*.

tower *n* torre *f*.

towering *adj* imponente.

town *n* ciudad *f*.

own clerk n secretario/ria del ayuntamiento m/f.

own hall n ayuntamiento m.

owrope n cable de remolque m.

oy n juguete m.

oyshop n juguetería f.

race n huella, pisada f; * vt trazar, delinear; encontrar.

rack n vestigio m; huella f; camino m; vía f; pista f; canción f; * vt rastrear.

racksuit n chándal m.

ract n región, comarca f; serie f; tratado m.

raction n tracción f.

rade n comercio, tráfico m; negocio, trato m; ocupación f; * vi comerciar, traficar.

trade fair n feria de muestras f.

trademark n marca comercial f.

trade name n nombre comercial m.

trader n comerciante, traficante m.

tradesman n tendero m.

trade(s) union n sindicato m.

trade unionist n sindicalista m/f.

trading n comercio m; * adj comercial.

tradition n tradición f.

traditional adj tradicional.

traffic n tráfico m; tránsito m; * vi traficar, comerciar.

traffic jam n embotellamiento m.

trafficker n traficante, comerciante m/f.

traffic lights npl semáforo m.

tragedy n tragedia f.

tragic adj trágico/ca; ~ally adv trágicamente.

tragicomedy n tragicomedia f.

trail vt, vi rastrear; arrastrar; * n rastro m; pista f; cola f.

trailer n remolque m; avance m.

trainer n tráiler m.

train vt entrenar; amaestrar, enseñar, criar, adiestrar; disciplinar; vr ejercitarse; * n tren m; cola f; serie f; **high-speed ~** tren de alta velocidad m.

trained adj cualificado/da; amaestrado/da.

trainee n aprendiz/a m/f.

trainer n entrenador/a m/f.

trainers npl zapatillas de lona fpl.

training n entrenamiento m; formación f.

trait n rasgo m.

traitor n traidor/a m/f.

tram n tranvía f.

tramp n vagabundo/da m/f; (sl) puta f; * vi andar pesadamente; * vt pisotear.

trample vt pisotear.

trampoline n cama elástica f.

trance n rapto m; éxtasis m.

tranquil adj tranquilo/la.

tranquillize vt tranquilizar.

tranquillizer n tranquilizante m.

transact vt negociar.

transaction n transacción f; negociación f.

transatlantic adj transatlántico/ca.

transcend vt trascender, pasar; exceder.

transcription n transcripción f.

transfer vt transferir, trasladar; * n transferencia f; traspaso m; calcomanía f.

transform vt transformar.

transformation n transformación f.

transfusion n transfusión f.

transient adj pasajero/ra, transitorio/ria.

transit n tránsito m.

transition n tránsito m; transición f.

transitional adj de transición.

transitive adj transitivo/va.

translate vt traducir.

translation n traducción f.

translator n traductor/ra m/f.

transmission n transmisión f.

transmit vt transmitir.

transmitter n transmisor m; emisora f.

transparency n transparencia f.

transparent adj transparente, diáfano/na.

transpire vi resultar; ocurrir.

transplant vt trasplantar; * n trasplante m.

transport vt transportar; * n transporte m.

transportation n transporte m.

trap n trampa f; * vt atrapar, bloquear.

trap door n trampilla f; escotillón m.

trapeze n trapecio m.

trappings npl adornos mpl.

trash n basura f; tonterías fpl.

trash can n cubo de la basura m.

trashy adj vil, despreciable, de ningún valor.

travel vi viajar; * vt recorrer; * n viaje m.

travel agency n agencia de viajes f.

travel agent n agente de viajes m.

traveller n viajante, viajero/ra m/f.

traveller's cheque n cheque de viaje m.

travelling n viajes mpl.

travel-sickness n mareo m.

travesty n parodia f.

trawler n arrastrero m.

tray n bandeja f; cajón m.

treacherous adj traidor/a, perfido/da.

treachery n traición f.

tread vi pisar; pistoear; * n pisada f; ruido de pasos m; banda de rodadura f.

treason n traición f; high ~ alta tración f.

treasure n tesoro m; * vt atesorar.

treasurer n tesorero/ra m/f.

treat vt tratar; regalar; * n regalo m placer m.

treatise n tratado m.

treatment n trato m.

treaty n tratado m.

treble adj triple; * vt (vi) triplicar(se) * n (mus) tiple m.

treble clef n clave de sol f.

tree n árbol m.

trek n caminata f; expedición f.

trellis n enrejado m.

tremble vi temblar.

trembling n temor m; trino m.

tremendous adj tremendo/da; enorme; estupendo/da.

tremor n temblor m.

trench n foso m; (mil) trinchera f zanja f.

trend n tendencia f; curso m; moda f.

trendy adj de moda.

trepidation n inquietud f.

trespass vt transpasar, violar.

tress n trenza f; rizo de pelo m.

trestle n caballete de serrador m.

trial n proceso m; prueba f; ensayo m; desgracia f.

triangle n triángulo m.

triangular adj triangular.

tribal adj tribal.

tribe n tribu f; raza, casta f.

tribulation n tribulación f.

tribunal n tribunal m.

tributary adj, n tributario/ria m/f.

tribute n tributo m.

trice n momento, tris m.

trick n engaño, fraude m; burla f; baza f; zancadilla f; * vt engañar.

trickery n engaño m.

trickle vi gotear; * n reguero m.

tricky *adj* difícil; delicado/da.

tricycle *n* triciclo *m*.

trifle *n* bagatela, nineria *f*; * *vi* bobear; juguetear.

trifling *adj* frívolo/la, inútil.

trigger *n* gatillo *m*.

trigger off *vt* desencadenar.

trigonometry *n* trigonometría *f*.

trill *n* trino *m*; * *vi* trinar.

trillion *n* billón *m*.

trim *adj* aseado/da; en buen estado; arreglado/da; * *vt* arreglar; recortar; adornar.

trimester *n* trimestre *m*.

trimmings *npl* accesorios *mpl*.

Trinity *n* Trinidad *f*.

trinket *n* joya, alhaja *f*; adorno *m*.

trio *n* (mus) trío *m*.

trip *vt* hacer caer; * *vi* tropezar; resbalar; **to ~ up** *vi* caerse; *vt* hacer caer; * *n* resbalón *m*; viaje corto *m*; zancadilla *f*.

tripe *n* callos *mpl*; bobadas *fpl*.

triple *adj* triple; * *vt* triplicar.

triplets *npl* trillizos/zas *m/fpl*.

triplicate *n* triplicado *m*.

tripod *n* trípode *m*.

trite *adj* trivial; usado/da.

triumph *n* triunfo *m*; * *vi* triunfar.

triumphal *adj* triunfal.

triumphant *adj* triunfante; victorioso/sa; **~ly** *adv* en triunfo.

trivia *npl* trivialidades *fpl*.

trivial *adj* trivial, vulgar; **~ly** *adv* trivialmente.

triviality *n* trivialidad *f*.

trolley *n* carrito *m*.

trombone *n* trombón *m*.

troop *n* grupo *m*; **~s** *npl* tropas *fpl*.

trooper *n* soldado a caballo *m*.

trophy *n* trofeo *m*.

tropical *adj* trópico/ca.

trot *n* trote *m*; * *vi* trotar.

trouble *vt* afligir; molestar; * *n* problema *m*; disturbio *m*; inquietud *f*; aflicción, pena *f*.

troubled *adj* preocupado/da; agitado/da.

troublemaker *n* agitador/a *m/f*.

troubleshooter *n* conciliador/a *m/f*.

troublesome *adj* molesto/ta.

trough *n* abrevadero *m*; comedero *m*.

troupe *n* grupo *m*.

trousers *npl* bragas *fpl*; pantalones *mpl*.

trout *n* trucha *f*.

trowel *n* paleta *f*.

truce *n* tregua *f*.

truck *n* camión *m*; vagón *m*.

truck driver *n* camionero/ra *m/f*.

truculent *adj* truculento/ta, cruel.

trudge *vi* andar fatigosamente, andar con dificultad.

true *adj* verdadero/ra, cierto/ta; sincero/ra; exacto/ta.

truelove *n* amor verdadero *m*.

truffle *n* trufa *f*.

truly *adv* en verdad; sinceramente.

trump *n* triunfo (en el juego de naipes) *m*.

trumpet *n* trompeta *f*.

trunk *n* baúl, cofre *m*; trompa *f*.

truss *n* braguero *m*; * *vt* atar; espetar.

trust *n* confianza *f*; * *vt* tener confianza en; fideicomiso *m*; confiar algo a.

trusted *adj* de confianza.

trustee *n* fideicomisario/ria, curador/a *m/f*.

trustful *adj* fiel; confiado/da.

trustily *adv* fielmente.

trusting *adj* confiado/da.

trustworthy *adj* digno/na de confianza.

trusty *adj* fiel, leal; seguro/ra.

truth n verdad f; fidelidad f; realidad f; **in ~** en verdad.

truthful adj verídico/ca; veraz.

truthfulness n veracidad f.

try vt examinar, ensayar, probar, experimentar; tentar; intentar; juzgar; * vi probar; **to ~ on** probarse; **to ~ out** probar; * n tentativa f, ensayo m.

trying adj pesado/da; cansado/da.

tub n balde m, barreño m, cubo m; tina f.

tuba n tuba f.

tube n tubo, cañon, canuto m.

tuberculosis n tuberculosis f invar.

tubing n cañería f.

tuck n pliegue m; * vt poner.

Tuesday n martes m invar.

tuft n mechón m; manojo m.

tug vt remolcar; * n remolcador m.

tuition n matrícula f; enseñanza f.

tulip n tulipán m.

tumble n vi caer, hundirse; revolcarse; * vt revolver; volcar; * n caída f; vuelco m.

tumbledown adj destartalado/da.

tumbler n vaso m.

tummy n barriga f.

tumour n tumor m.

tumultuous adj tumultuoso/sa.

tuna n atún m.

tune n tono m; armonía f; aria f; * vt afinar; sintonizar.

tuneful adj armonioso/sa, acorde, melodioso/sa.

tuner n sintonizador/a m.

tunic n túnica f.

tuning fork n (mus) diapasón m.

tunnel n túnel m; * vt construir un tunel por.

turban n turbante m.

turbine n turbina f.

turbulence n turbulencia, confusión f.

turbulent adj turbulento/ta, tumultuoso/sa.

tureen n sopera f.

turf n césped m; * vt cubrir con césped.

turgid adj pesado/da.

turkey n pavo m.

turmoil n disturbio m; baraúnda f.

turn vi volver; cambiar; girar; dar vueltas; transformarse; **to ~ around** volverse; girar; **to ~ back** volverse; **to ~ down** rechazar; doblar; **to ~ in** acostarse; **to ~ off** vi desviarse; vt apagar; parar; **to ~ on** encender, prender; poner en marcha; **to ~ out** apagar; **to ~ over** vi volverse; vt volver; **to ~ up** vi llegar; aparecer; vt subir; * n vuelta f; giro m; rodeo m; turno m; vez f; inclinación f.

turncoat n desertor/a, renegado/da m/f.

turning n vuelta f.

turnip n nabo m.

turn-off n salida f.

turnout n concurrencia f.

turnover n facturación f.

turnpike n autopista de peaje f.

turnstile n torniquete m.

turntable n plato m.

turpentine n trementina f.

turquoise n turquesa f.

turret n torrecilla f, torreta f.

turtle n tortuga marina f.

turtledove n tórtola f.

tusk n colmillo m.

tussle n pelea f.

tutor n tutor/a m/f; profesor/a m/f; * vt enseñar, instruir.

tuxedo n smoking m.

twang n gangueo m; sonido agudo m.

tweezers npl tenacillas fpl.

twelfth adj, n duodécimo/ma.

twelve adj, n doce.

twentieth adj, n vigésimo/ma.

twenty adj, n veinte.

twice adv dos veces.

twig n ramita f; * vi caer en la cuenta.

twilight n crepúsculo m.

twin n gemelo/la m/f.

twine vi entrelazarse; caracolear; * n bramante m.

twinge vt punzar, pellizcar; * n dolor agudo o punzante m; punzada f.

twinkle vi centellear; parpadear.

twirl vt dar vueltas a; * vi piruetear; * n rotación f.

twist vt torcer, retorcer; entretejer; * vi serpentear; * n torsión f; vuelta f; doblez f.

twit n (sl) tonto/ta m/f.

twitch vi moverse nerviosamente; * n tirón; tic m.

twitter vi gorjear; * n gorjeo m.

two adj, n dos.

two-door adj de dos puertas.

two-faced adj falso/sa.

twofold adj doble, duplicado/da; * adv al doble.

two-seater n avión o coche de dos plazas m.

twosome n pareja f.

tycoon n magnate m.

type n tipo m; letra f; modelo m; * vt escribir a máquina.

typecast adj encasillado/da.

typeface n tipo m.

typescript n texto mecanografiado m.

typewriter n máquina de escribir f.

typewritten adj mecanografiado/da.

typical adj típico/ca.

tyrannical adj tiránico/ca.

tyranny n tiranía f; crueldad f.

tyrant n tirano/na m/f.

tyre n neumático m; llanta f.

tyre pressure n presión de los neumáticos f.

U

ubiquitous adj ubicuo/cua.

udder n ubre f.

ugh excl ¡puaj!

ugliness n fealdad f.

ugly adj feo, fea; peligroso/sa.

ulcer n úlcera f.

ulterior adj ulterior.

ultimate adj último/ma; ~ly adv al final; a fin de cuentas.

ultimatum n ultimátum m.

ultramarine n ultramar m; * adj ultramarino/na.

ultrasound n ultrasonido m.

ultrasound scan n ecografía f.

umbilical cord n cordón umbilical m.

umbrella n paraguas m invar.

umpire n árbitro/tra m/f.

umpteen adj enésimos/mas.

unable adj incapaz.

unaccompanied adj solo/la, sin acompañamiento.

unaccomplished adj incompleto/ta, no acabado/da.

unaccountable adj inexplicable, extraño/ña.

unaccountably adv extrañamente.

unaccustomed adj desacostumbrado/da, desusado/da.

unacknowledged adj desconocido/da; negado/da.

unacquainted adj desconocido/da; ignorado/da.

unadorned adj sin adorno.

unadulterated adj genuino/na, puro/ra; sin mezcla.

unaffected adj sincero/ra, sin afectación.

unaided adj sin ayuda.

unaltered adj invariado/da.

unambitious adj poco/ca ambicioso/sa.

unanimity n unanimidad f.

unanimous adj unánime; **~ly** adv unánimemente.

unanswerable adj incontrovertible, incontestable.

unanswered adj no contestado/da.

unapproachable adj inaccesible.

unarmed adj inerme, desarmado/da.

unassuming adj nada presuntuoso/sa, modesto/ta.

unattached adj independiente; disponible.

unattainable adj inasequible.

unattended adj sin atender.

unauthorized adj no autorizado/da.

unavoidable adj inevitable.

unavoidably adv inevitablemente.

unaware adj ignorante.

unawares adv inadvertidamente; de improviso.

unbalanced adj desequilibrado/da; trastornado/da.

unbearable adj insoportable.

unbecoming adj indecente, indecoroso/sa.

unbelievable adj increíble.

unbend vi relajarse; * vt enderezar.

unbiased adj imparcial.

unblemished adj sin mancha, sin tacha, irreprensible.

unborn adj no nacido/da.

unbreakable adj irrompible.

unbroken adj intacto/ta; indómito/ta; entero/ra; no batido/da.

unbutton vt desabotonar.

uncalled-for adj fuera de lugar.

uncanny adj extraordinario/ria.

unceasing adj sin cesar, continuo/nua

unceremonious adj brusco/ca.

uncertain adj incierto/ta, dudoso/sa.

uncertainty n incertidumbre f.

unchangeable adj inmutable.

unchanged adj no alterado/da.

unchanging adj inalterable, immutable.

uncharitable adj nada caritativo/va, duro/ra.

unchecked adj desenfrenado/da, incontrolado/da.

unchristian adj poco cristiano/na.

uncivil adj grosero/ra, descortés.

uncivilized adj tosco/ca, salvaje, incivilizado/da.

uncle n tío.

uncomfortable adj incómodo/da; molesto/ta.

uncomfortably adv incómodamente; inquietantemente.

uncommon adj raro/ra, extraordinario/ria.

uncompromising adj irreconciliable.

unconcerned adj indiferente.

unconditional adj sin condiciones, incondicional.

unconfined adj libre, ilimitado/da.

unconfirmed adj no confirmado/da.

unconnected adj inconexo/xa.

unconquerable adj invencible, insuperable.

unconscious adj inconsciente; **~ly** adv inconscientemente.

unconstrained adj libre, voluntario/ria.

uncontrollable adj incontrolable; desenfrenado/da.

unconventional adj poco convencional.

unconvincing adj no convincente.

uncork vt destapar.

uncorrected adj sin corregir, no corregido/a.

uncouth adj grosero/ra, zafio/fia.

uncover vt descubrir.

uncultivated adj inculto/ta.

uncut adj no cortado/da, entero/ra.

undamaged adj ileso/sa, libre de daño.

undaunted adj intrépido/da.

undecided adj indeciso/sa.

undefiled adj impoluto/ta, puro/ra.

undeniable adj innegable, incontestable; ~bly adv indubitablemente.

under prep debajo de; menos de; según; ~ adv debajo.

under-age adj menor de edad.

undercharge vt cobrar de menos.

underclothing n ropa íntima f.

undercoat n primera mano f.

undercover adj clandestino/na.

undercurrent n corriente subyacente f.

undercut vt vender más barato que.

underdeveloped adj subdesarrollado/da.

underdog n desvalido/da m/f.

underdone adj poco cocido/da.

underestimate vt subestimar.

undergo vt sufrir; sostener.

undergraduate n estudiante universitario/ria m/f.

underground n metro m; movimiento clandestino m.

undergrowth n soto m, maleza f.

underhand adv clandestinamente; * adj secreto/ta, clandestino/na.

underlie vi estar debajo.

underline vt subrayar.

undermine vt minar.

underneath adv debajo; * prep debajo de.

underpaid adj mal pagado/da.

underpants npl calzoncillos mpl.

underprivileged adj desvalido/da.

underrate vt menospreciar.

undersecretary n subsecretario/ria m/f.

underside n revés m.

understand vt entender, comprender.

understandable adj comprensible.

understanding n entendimiento m; inteligencia f; conocimiento m; correspondencia f; * adj comprensivo/va.

understatement n subestimación f; modestia f.

undertake vt, vi emprender.

undertaker n director de pompas fúnebres.

undertaking n empresa f; empeño m.

undervalue vt subestimar.

underwater adj submarino/na; * adv bajo el agua.

underwear n ropa íntima f.

underworld n hampa f.

underwrite vt suscribir; asegurar contra riesgos.

underwriter n asegurador/a m/f.

undeserved adj inmerecido/da; ~ly adv sin haberlo merecido.

undeserving adj indigno/na.

undesirable adj indeseable.

undetermined adj indeterminado/da, indeciso/sa.

undigested adj no digerido/da.

undiminished adj entero/ra, no disminuido/da.

undisciplined adj indisciplinado/da.

undisguised adj sin disfraz, cándido/da, sincero/ra.

undismayed adj intrépido/da.

undisputed adj incontestable.

undisturbed adj quieto/ta, tranquilo/la.

undivided adj indiviso/sa, entero/ra.

undo vt deshacer, destar, descoser.

undoing n ruina f.

undoubted adj indudable; ~ly adv indudablemente.

undress vi desnudarse.

undue adj indebido/da; injusto/ta.

undulating adj ondulante.

unduly adv indebidamente.

undying adj inmortal.

unearth vt desenterrar.

unearthly adj inverosímil.

uneasiness n inquietud f; zozobra f.

uneasy adj inquieto/ta, desasosegado/da; incomodo/da.

uneducated adj ignorante.

unemployed adj desempleado/da, parado/da; ~ person parado/da m/f.

unemployment n desempleo, paro m.

unending adj interminable.

unenlightened adj no iluminado/da.

unenviable adj poco envidiable.

unequal adj, ~ly adv desigual(mente).

unequalled adj incomparable.

unerring adj, ~ly adv infalible(mente).

uneven adj desigual; impar; ~ly adv desigualmente.

unexpected adj inesperado/da; inopinado/da; ~ly adv de repente; inopinadamente.

unexplored adj inexplorado/da, no descubierto/ta.

unfailing adj infalible, seguro/ra.

unfair adj falso/sa; injusto/ta; ~ly adv injustamente.

unfaithful adj infiel, pérfido/da.

unfaithfulness n infidelidad, perfidia f.

unfaltering adj firme, asegurado/da.

unfamiliar adj desacostumbrado/da, poco común.

unfashionable adj pasado/da de moda; ~bly adv contra la moda.

unfasten vt desatar, soltar, aflojar.

unfathomable adj insondable, impenetrable.

unfavourable adj desfavorable.

unfeeling adj insensible, duro/ra de corazón.

unfinished adj imperfecto/ta, no acabado/da.

unfit adj indispuesto/ta; incapaz.

unfold vt desplegar; revelar; * vi abrirse.

unforeseen adj imprevisto/ta.

unforgettable adj inolvidable.

unforgivable adj imperdonable.

unforgiving adj implacable.

unfortunate adj desafortunado/da, infeliz; ~ly adv por desgracia, infelizmente.

unfounded adj sin fundamento.

unfriendly adj antipático/ca.

unfruitful adj estéril; infructuoso/sa.

unfurnished adj sin muebles; desprovisto/ta.

ungainly adj desmañado/da.

ungentlemanly adj indigno/na de un hombre bien criado.

ungovernable adj indomable, ingobernable.

ungrateful adj ingrato/ta; desagradable; ~ly adv ingratamente.

ungrounded adj infundado/da.

unhappily adv infelizmente.

unhappiness n infelicidad f.

unhappy adj infeliz.

unharmed adj ileso/sa, sano/na y salvo/va.

unhealthy adj malsano/na; enfermizo/za.

unheard-of adj inaudito/ta, extraño/ña, sin ejemplo.

unheeding adj negligente; distraído/da.

unhitch vt (beasts) desaparejar.

unhook vt desenganchar; descolgar; desabrochar.

unhoped (for) adj inesperado/da.

unhurt adj ileso/sa.

unicorn n unicornio m.

uniform adj, ~ly adv uniforme(mente); * n uniforme m.

uniformity n uniformidad f.

unify vt unificar.

unimaginable adj inimaginable.

unimpaired adj no disminuido/da, no alterado/da.

unimportant adj poco importante.

uninformed adj desinformado/da.

uninhabitable adj inhabitable.

uninhabited adj inhabitado/da, desierto/ta.

uninjured adj ileso/sa, no dañado/da.

unintelligible adj ininteligible.

unintelligibly adv de modo ininteligible.

unintentional adj involuntario/ria, no intencionado/da.

uninterested adj desinteresado/da.

uninteresting adj poco interesante.

uninterrupted adj sin interrupción, continuo/nua.

uninvited adj no convidado/da.

union n unión f; sindicato m.

unionist n sindicalista m/f.

unique adj único/ca, uno/na, singular.

unison n unísono m.

unit n unidad f.

unitarian n unitario/ria m/f.

unite vt (vi) unir(se), juntarse; (fig) zurcir.

unitedly adv unidamente, de acuerdo.

United States (of America) npl Estados Unidos (de América) mpl.

unity n unidad, concordia, conformidad f.

universal adj, ~ly adv universal(mente).

universe n universo m.

university n universidad f.

unjust adj injusto/ta; ~ly adv injustamente.

unkempt adj despeinado/da; descuidado/da.

unkind adj poco amable; severo/ra.

unknowingly adv sin saberlo.

unknown adj incógnito/ta.

unlawful adj ilegal; ~ly adv ilegalmente.

unlawfulness n ilegalidad f.

unleash vt desencadenar.

unless conj a menos que, si no.

unlicensed adj sin licencia.

unlike, unlikely adj diferente; improbable; inverosímil.

unlikelihood n inverisimilitud f.

unlimited adj ilimitado/da.

unlisted adj que no viene en la guía.

unload vt descargar.

unlock vt abrir.

unluckily adv desafortunadamente.

unlucky adj desafortunado/da.

unmanageable adj inmanejable, intratable.

unmannered adj rudo/da, brutal, grosero/ra.

unmannerly adj malcriado/da, descortés.

unmarried adj soltero/ra.

unmask vt desenmascarar.

unmentionable adj que no se puede mencionar.

unmerited adj desmerecido/da.

unmindful adj olvidadizo/za, negligente.

unmistakable adj inconfundible; ~ly adv indudablemente.

unmitigated adj absoluto/ta.

unmoved adj inmoto, firme.

unnatural *adj* antinatural; perverso/sa; afectado/da.

unnecessary *adj* inútil, innecesario/ria.

unneighbourly *adj* poco atento/ta con sus vecinos; descortés.

unnoticed *adj* inadvertido/da.

unnumbered *adj* innumerable.

unobserved *adj* no observado/da.

unobtainable *adj* inconseguible; inexistente.

unobtrusive *adj* modesto/ta.

unoccupied *adj* desocupado/da.

unoffending *adj* sencillo/lla, inocente.

unofficial *adj* no oficial.

unorthodox *adj* heterodoxo/xa.

unpack *vt* desempacar; desenvolver.

unpaid *adj* no pagado/da.

unpalatable *adj* desabrido/da, desgradable.

unparalleled *adj* sin paralelo; sin par.

unpleasant *adj*, **~ly** *adv* desagradable(mente).

unpleasantness *n* desagrado *m*.

unplug *vt* desconectar.

unpolished *adj* que no está pulido/da; rudo/da, grosero/ra.

unpopular *adj* impopular.

unpractised *adj* inexperto/ta, no versado/da.

unprecedented *adj* sin precedentes.

unpredictable *adj* imprevisible.

unprejudiced *adj* imparcial.

unprepared *adj* no preparado/da.

unprofitable *adj* inútil, vano/na; poco lucrativo/va.

unprotected *adj* desvalido/da, sin protección.

unpublished *adj* no publicado/da; inédito/ta.

unpunished *adj* impune.

unqualified *adj* sin títulos; total.

unquestionable *adj* indubitable, indisputable; **~ly** *adv* sin duda, sin disputa.

unquestioned *adj* incontestable, no preguntado/da.

unravel *vt* desenredar.

unread *adj* no leído/da; ignorante.

unreal *adj* irreal.

unrealistic *adj* poco realista.

unreasonable *adj* poco razonable; disparatado/da.

unreasonably *adv* poco razonablemente; disparatadamente.

unrelated *adj* sin relación; inconexo/xa.

unrelenting *adj* implacable.

unreliable *adj* poco fiable.

unremitting *adj* constante, incansable.

unrepentant *adj* impenitente.

unreserved *adj* sin restricción; franco/ca; **~ly** *adv* abiertamente.

unrest *n* malestar *m*; disturbios *mpl*.

unrestrained *adj* desenfrenado/da; ilimitado/da.

unripe *adj* inmaduro/ra.

unrivalled *adj* sin rival, sin igual.

unroll *vt* desenrollar.

unruliness *n* turbulencia *f*; desenfreno *m*.

unruly *adj* desenfrenado/da.

unsafe *adj* inseguro/ra, peligroso/sa.

unsatisfactory *adj* insatisfactorio/ria.

unsavoury *adj* desabrido/da, insípido/da.

unscathed *adj* ileso/sa.

unscrew *vt* destornillar.

unscrupulous *adj* sin escrúpulos.

unseasonable *adj* intempestivo/va, fuera de propósito.

unseemly *adj* indecente.

unseen *adj* invisible.

unselfish *adj* desinteresado/da.

unsettle *vt* perturbar.

unsettled *adj* inquieto/ta; inestable; variable.

unshaken *adj* firme, estable.

unshaven *adj* sin afeitar.

unsightly *adj* desagradable a la vista, feo/a.

unskilful *adj* inhábil, poco mañoso/sa.

unskilled *adj* no cualificado/da.

unsociable *adj* insociable, intratable.

unspeakable *adj* inefable, indecible.

unstable *adj* instable, inconstante.

unsteadily *adv* ligeramente, inconstantemente.

unsteady *adj* inestable.

unstudied *adj* no estudiado/da; no premeditado/da.

unsuccessful *adj* infeliz, desafortunado/da; **~ly** *adv* sin éxito.

unsuitable *adj* inapropiado/da; inoportuno/na.

unsure *adj* inseguro/ra.

unsympathetic *adj* poco comprensivo/va.

untamed *adj* indomado/da.

untapped *adj* sin explotar.

untenable *adj* insostenible.

unthinkable *adj* inconcebible.

unthinking *adj* desatento/ta, irreflexivo/va.

untidiness *n* desaliño *m*.

untidy *adj* desordenado/da; sucio/cia.

untie *vt* desatar, deshacer, soltar, zafar.

until *prep* hasta; * *conj* hasta que.

untimely *adj* intempestivo/va.

untiring *adj* incansable.

untold *adj* nunca dicho/cha; indecible; incalculable.

untouched *adj* intacto/ta.

untoward *adj* impropio/pia; adverso/sa.

untried *adj* no ensayado/da *o* probado/da.

untroubled *adj* no perturbado/da, tranquilo/la.

untrue *adj* falso/sa.

untrustworthy *adj* indigno/na de confianza.

untruth *n* falsedad, mentira *f*.

unused *adj* sin usar, no usado/da.

unusual *adj* inusual, inusitado/da, raro/ra; **~ly** *adv* inusitadamente, raramente.

unveil *vt* quitar el velo, descubrir.

unwavering *adj* inquebrantable.

unwelcome *adj* desagradable, inoportuno/na.

unwell *adj* enfermizo/za, malo/la.

unwieldy *adj* pesado/da.

unwilling *adj* desinclinado/da; **~ly** *adv* de mala gana.

unwillingness *n* mala gana, repugnancia *f*.

unwind *vt* desenredar, desenmarañar; * *vi* relajarse.

unwise *adj* imprudente.

unwitting *adj* inconsciente.

unworkable *adj* poco práctico/ca.

unworthy *adj* indigno/na.

unwrap *vt* desenvolver.

unwritten *adj* no escrito/ta.

up *adv* arriba, en lo alto; levantado/da; * *prep* hacia; hasta.

upbraid *vt* zaherir.

upbringing *n* educación *f*.

update *vt* poner al día.

upheaval *n* agitación *f*.

uphill *adj* difícil, penoso/sa; * *adv* cuesta arriba.

uphold *vt* sos tener, apoyar.

upholstery *n* tapicería *f*.

upkeep *n* mantenimiento *m*.

uplift *vt* levantar.

upon *prep* sobre, encima.

upper *adj* superior; más elevado/da.
upper-class *adj* de la clase alta.
upper-hand *n* (*fig*) superioridad *f*.
uppermost *adj* más alto/ta, supremo/ma; **to be ~** predominar.
upright *adj* derecho/cha, perpendicular, recto/ta; puesto/ta en pie; honrado/da.
uprising *n* sublevación *f*.
uproar *n* tumulto, alboroto *m*.
uproot *vt* desarraigar.
upset *vt* trastornar; derramar, volcar; * *n* revés *m*; trastorno *m*; * *adj* molesto/ta; revuelto/ta.
upshot *n* remate *m*; fin *m*; conclusión *f*.
upside-down *adv* al revés.
upstairs *adv* arriba.
upstart *n* advenedizo/za *m/f*.
uptight *adj* nervioso/sa.
up-to-date *adj* al día.
upturn *n* mejora *f*.
upward *adj* ascendente; **~s** *adv* hacia arriba.
urban *adj* urbano/na.
urbane *adj* cortés.
urchin *n* golfillo/lla *m/f*.
urge *vt* animar; * *n* impulso *m*; deseo *m*.
urgency *n* urgencia *f*.
urgent *adj* urgente.
urinal *n* orinal *m*.

urinate *vi* orinar.
urine *n* orina *f*.
urn *n* urna *f*.
us *pn* nos; nosotros, nosotras.
usage *n* tratamiento *m*; uso *m*.
use *n* uso *m*; utilidad, práctica *f*; * *vt* usar, emplear.
used *adj* usado/da.
useful *adj*, **~ly** *adv* útil(mente).
usefulness *n* utilidad *f*.
useless *adj* inútil; **~ly** *adv* inútilmente.
uselessness *n* inutilidad *f*.
user-friendly *adj* fácil de utilizar.
usher *n* ujier *m/f*; acomodador/a *m/f*.
usherette *n* acomodadora *f*.
usual *adj* usual, común, normal; **~ly** *adv* normalmente.
usurer *n* usurero/ra *m/f*.
usurp *vt* usurpar.
usury *n* usura *f*.
utensil *n* utensilio *m*.
uterus *n* útero *m*.
utility *n* utilidad *f*.
utilize *vt* utilizar.
utmost *adj* extremo/ma, sumo/ma; último/ma.
utter *adj* total; todo; entero/ra; * *vt* proferir; expresar; publicar.
utterance *n* expresion *f*.
utterly *adv* enteramente, del todo.

V

vacancy *n* cuarto libre *m*, vacante *f*.
vacant *adj* vacío/cía; desocupado/da; vacante.
vacant lot *n* solar *m*.
vacate *vt* desocupar; dejar.
vacation *n* vacaciones *fpl*.
vaccinate *vt* vacunar.

vaccination *n* vacunación *f*.
vaccine *n* vacuna *f*.
vacuous *adj* vacío/cía, vacuo/cua.
vacuum *n* vacío *m*.
vacuum flask *n* termo *m*.
vagina *n* vagina *f*.
vagrant *n* vagabundo/da *m/f*.

vague *adj* vago/ga; **~ly** *adv* vagamente.

vain *adj* vano/na, inútil; vanidoso/sa.

valet *n* criado *m*.

valiant *adj* valiente, valeroso/sa.

valid *adj* válido/da.

valley *n* valle *m*.

valour *n* valor, aliento, brío, esfuerzo *m*.

valuable *adj* valioso/sa; **~s** *npl* objetos de valor *mpl*.

valuation *n* tasa, valuación *f*.

value *n* valor, precio *m*; * *vt* valuar; estimar, apreciar.

valued *adj* apreciado/da.

valve *n* válvula *f*.

vampire *n* vampiro *m*.

van *n* camioneta *f*.

vandal *n* gamberro/rra *m/f*.

vandalism *n* vandalismo *m*.

vandalize *vt* dañar.

vanguard *n* vanguardia *f*.

vanilla *n* vainilla *f*.

vanish *vi* desvanecerse, desaparecer.

vanity *n* vanidad *f*.

vanity case *n* neceser *m*.

vanquish *vt* vencer, conquistar.

vantage point *n* punto panorámico *m*.

vapour *n* vapor *m*; exhalación *f*.

variable *adj* variable; voluble.

variance *n* discordia, desavenencia *f*.

variation *n* variación *f*.

varicose vein *n* variz *f*.

varied *adj* variado/da.

variety *n* variedad *f*.

variety show *n* espectáculo de variedades *m*.

various *adj* vario/ria, diverso/sa, diferente.

varnish *n* barniz *m*; * *vt* barnizar.

vary *vt*, *vi* variar; cambiar.

vase *n* florero, jarrón *m*.

vast *adj* vasto/ta; inmenso/sa.

vat *n* tina *f*.

vault *n* bóveda *f*; cueva *f*; caverna *f*; * *vt* saltar.

veal *n* ternera *f*.

veer *vi* (*mar*) virar.

vegetable *adj* vegetal; * *n* vegetal *m*; **~s** *pl* verduras *fpl*.

vegetable garden *n* huerta *f*.

vegetarian *n* vegetariano/na *m/f*.

vegetate *vi* vegetar.

vegetation *n* vegetación *f*.

vehemence *n* vehemencia, violencia *f*.

vehement *adj* vehemente, violento/ta; **~ly** *adv* vehementemente.

vehicle *n* vehículo *m*; **all-terrain ~** todoterreno *m*.

veil *n* velo *m*; * *vt* encubrir, ocultar.

vein *n* vena *f*; cavidad *f*; inclinación del ingenio *f*.

velocity *n* velocidad *f*.

velvet *n* terciopelo *m*.

vending machine *n* máquina expendedora *f*.

vendor *n* vendedor/a *m/f*.

veneer *n* chapa *f*; barniz *m*.

venerable *adj* venerable.

venerate *vt* venerar, honrar.

veneration *n* veneración *f*.

venereal *adj* venéreo.

vengeance *n* venganza *f*.

venial *adj* venial.

venison *n* (carne de) venado *f*.

venom *n* veneno *m*.

venomous *adj* venenoso/sa; **~ly** *adv* venenosamente.

vent *n* respiradero *m*; salida *f*; * *vt* desahogar.

ventilate *vt* ventilar.

ventilation *n* ventilación *f*.

ventilator *n* ventilador *m*.

ventriloquist *n* ventrílocuo/cua *m/f*.

venture *n* empresa *f*; * *vi* aventurarse; * *vt* aventurar, arriesgar.

venue n lugar de reunión, local m.

veranda(h) n terraza f, porche m.

verb n (gr) verbo m.

verbal adj verbal, literal; **~ly** adv verbalmente.

verbatim adv literalmente.

verbose adj verboso/sa.

verdant adj verde.

verdict n (law) veredicto m; opinión f.

verification n verificación f.

verify vt verificar.

veritable adj verdadero/ra.

vermicelli npl fideos mpl.

vermin n bichos mpl.

vermouth n vermut m.

versatile adj versátil; polifacético/ca.

verse n verso m; versículo m.

versed adj versado/da.

version n versión f.

versus prep contra.

vertebra n vértebra f.

vertebral, vertebrate adj vertebral.

vertex n cenit, vértice m.

vertical adj, **~ly** adv vertical(mente).

vertigo n vértigo m.

verve n brío m.

very adj idéntico/ca, mismo/ma; * adv muy, mucho, sumamente.

vessel n vasija f; vaso m; barco m.

vest n camiseta f.

vestibule n vestíbulo m.

vestige n vestigio m.

vestment n vestido m; vestidura f.

vestry n sacristía f.

vet n veterinario/ria m/f.

veteran n, veterano/na m/f.

veterinary adj veterinario/ria.

veterinary surgeon n veterinario/ria m/f.

veto n veto m; * vt vetar.

vex vt molestar.

vexed adj molesto/ta; controvertido/da.

via prep por.

viaduct n viaducto m.

vial n ampolla f, vial m.

vibrate vi vibrar.

vibration n vibración f.

vicarious adj sustituto/ta.

vice n vicio m; culpa f; tornillo m.

vice-chairman n vice-presidente m.

vice-chancellor (of a university) n rector/ra m/f.

vice-chancellorship n rectorado m.

vice versa adv viceversa.

vicinity n vecindad, proximidad f; **immediate ~** inmediaciones fpl.

vicious adj vicioso/sa; **~ly** adv de manera viciosa.

victim n víctima f.

victimize vt victimizar.

victor n vencedor/a m/f.

victorious adj victorioso/sa.

victory n victoria f.

video n vídeo m.

video camera n videocámara f.

video cassette n videocasete m.

video game n videojuego m.

video tape n cinta de vídeo f.

vie vi competir.

view n vista f; perspectiva f; aspecto m; opinión f; paisaje m; * vt mirar, ver; examinar.

viewer n televidente m/f.

viewfinder n visor m.

viewpoint n punto de vista m.

vigil n vela f; vigilia f.

vigilance n vigilancia f.

vigilant adj vigilante, atento/ta.

vigorous adj vigoroso/sa; **~ly** adv vigorosamente.

vigour n vigor m; energía f.

vile adj vil, bajo/ja; asqueroso/sa.

vilify vt envilecer.

villa n chalet m; casa de campo f.

village n aldea f.

villager n aldeano/na m/f.

villain n malvado/da m/f.

vindicate vt vindicar, defender.

vindication n vindicación f; justificación f.

vindictive adj vengativo/va.

vine n vid f.

vinegar n vinagre m.

vineyard n viña f.

vintage n vendimia f.

vinyl n vinilo m.

viola n (mus) viola f.

violate vt violar.

violation n violación f.

violence n violencia f.

violent adj violento/ta; ~ly adv violentamente.

violet n (bot) violeta f.

violin n (mus) violín m.

violinist n violinista m/f.

violoncello, cello n (mus) violoncelo, violonchelo m.

VIP n vip m/f.

viper n víbora f.

virgin n virgen f; * adj virgen.

virginity n virginidad f.

Virgo n Virgo f (signo del zodiaco).

virile adj viril.

virility n virilidad f.

virtual adj, ~ly adv virtual(mente).

virtue n virtud f.

virtuous adj virtuoso/sa.

virulent adj virulento/ta.

virus n virus m invar.

visa n visado m, visa f.

vis-à-vis prep con respecto a.

viscous adj viscoso/sa, glutinoso/sa.

visibility n visibilidad f.

visible adj visible.

visibly adv visiblemente.

vision n visión f, visión f.

visit vt visitar; * n visita f.

visitation n visitación, visita f.

visiting hours npl horas de visita fpl.

visitor n visitante m/f; turista m/f.

visor n visera f.

vista n vista, perspectiva f.

visual adj visual.

visual aid n medio visual m.

visualize vt imaginarse.

vital adj vital; esencial; imprescindible; ~ly adv vitalmente; ~s npl partes vitales fpl.

vitality n vitalidad f.

vital statistics npl medidas vitales fpl.

vitamin n vitamina f.

vitiate vt viciar, corromper.

vivacious adj vivaz.

vivid adj vivo/va; gráfico/ca; intenso/sa; ~ly adv vivamente; gráficamente.

vivisection n vivisección f.

vixen n zorra f.

vocabulary n vocabulario m.

vocal adj vocal.

vocation n vocación f; oficio m; carrera, profesión f; ~al adj profesional.

vocative n vocativo m.

vociferous adj vocinglero/ra, clamoroso/sa.

vodka n vodka m.

vogue n moda f; boga f.

voice n voz f; * vt expresar.

void adj nulo * n vacío m.

volatile adj volátil; voluble.

volcanic adj volcánico/ca.

volcano n volcán m.

volition n voluntad f.

volley n descarga f; salva f; rociada f; volea f.

volleyball n voleibol m.

volt n voltio m.

voltage n voltaje m.

voluble adj locuaz.

volume n volumen m; libro m.

voluntarily adv voluntariamente.
voluntary adj voluntario/ria.
volunteer n voluntario/ria m/f; * vi ofrecerse voluntariamente.
voluptuous adj voluptuoso/sa.
vomit vt, vi vomitar; * n vómito m.
voracious adj, ~ly adv voraz(mente).
vortex n remolino, torbellino m.
vote n voto, sufragio m; votación f; * vt votar.
voter n votante m/f.

voting n votación f.
voucher n vale m.
vow n voto m; * vi jurar.
vowel n vocal f.
voyage n viaje m; travesía f.
vulgar adj vulgar, ordinario/ria; de mal gusto.
vulgarity n vulgaridad f, grosería f; mal gusto m.
vulnerable adj vulnerable.
vulture n buitre m.

W

wad n fajo m; bolita f.
waddle vi anadear.
wade vi vadear.
wafer n galleta f; oblea f.
waffle n gofre m.
waft vt hacer flotar; * vi flotar.
wag vt menear; * vi menearse.
wage n salario m.
wage earner n asalariado/da m/f.
wager n apuesta f; * vt apostar.
wages npl salario m.
waggish adj zumbón/ona.
waggle vt menear.
wagon n carro m; (rail) vagón m.
wail n lamento, gemido m; * vi gemir.
waist n cintura f.
waistline n talle m.
wait vi esperar; * n espera f; pausa f.
waiter n camarero m.
waiting list n lista de espera f.
waiting room n sala de espera f.
waive vt suspender.
wake vi despertarse; * vt despertar; * n vela f; (mar) estela f.
wakefulness n vela f.
waken vt (vi) despertar(se).
walk vt, vi pasear, ir; andar, caminar; * n paseo m; caminata f.

walker n paseante m/f.
walkie-talkie n walkie-talkie m.
walking n paseos mpl.
walking stick n bastón m.
walkout n huelga f.
walkover n (sl) pan comido m.
walkway n paseo m.
wall n pared f; muralla f; muro m.
walled adj amurallado/da.
wallet n cartera, billetera f.
wallflower n (bot) alhelí m.
wallow vi revolcarse.
wallpaper n papel pintado m.
walnut n nogal m; nuez f.
walrus n morsa f.
waltz n vals m invar.
wan adj pálido/da.
wand n varita mágica f.
wander vt, vi errar; vagar.
wane vi menguar.
want vt querer; necesitar; faltar; * n necesidad f; falta f.
wanting adj falto/ta, defectuoso/sa.
wanton adj lascivo/va; juguetón/ona.
war n guerra f.
ward n sala f; pupilo/la m/f.
wardrobe n guardarropa f, ropero m.
warehouse n almacén m.

warfare n guerra f.

warhead n ojiva f.

warily adv prudentemente.

wariness n cautela, prudencia f.

warm adj cálido/da; caliente; efusivo/va; * vt calentar; **to ~ up** vi calentarse; entrar en calor; acalorarse; vt calentar.

warm-hearted adj afectuoso/sa.

warmly adv con calor, ardientemente.

warmth n calor m.

warn vt avisar; advertir.

warning n aviso m.

warning light n luz de advertencia f.

warp vi torcerse; * vt torcer; pervertir.

warrant n orden judicial f; mandamiento judicial m.

warranty n garantía f.

warren n conejero f.

warrior n guerrero/ra, soldado/da m/f.

warship n barco de guerra m.

wart n verruga f.

wary adj cauto/ta, prudente.

wash vt lavar; bañar; * vi lavarse; * n lavado m; baño m.

washable adj lavable.

washbowl n lavabo m.

washcloth n manopla f.

washer n arandela f.

washing n ropa sucia f; colada f.

washing machine n lavadora f.

washing-up n fregado m.

wash out n (sl) fracaso m.

washroom n aseos mpl.

wasp n avispa f.

wastage n desgaste m; pérdida f.

waste vt malgastar; destruir, arruinar; perder; * vi gastarse; * n desperdicio m; destrucción f; despilfarro m; basura f; yermo m.

wasteful adj destructivo/va; pródigo/ga; **~ly** adv pródigamente.

wasteland n yermo m.

waste paper n papel usado m.

waste pipe n tubo de desagüe m.

watch n reloj m; centinela f; guardia f; * vt mirar; ver; vigilar; tener cuidado; * vi ver; montar guardia.

watchdog n perro guardián m.

watchful adj vigilante; **~ly** adv vigilantemente.

watchmaker n relojero/ra m/f.

watchman n sereno m; vigilante m.

watchtower n atalaya f; garita f.

watchword n santo y seña m.

water n agua f; * vt regar, humedecer, mojar; * vi hacerse agua.

water closet n váter m.

watercolour n acuarela f.

waterfall n cascada f.

water heater n calentador de agua m.

watering-can n regadera f.

water level n nivel del agua m.

water lily n ninfea f.

water line n línea de flotación f.

waterlogged adj anegado/da.

water main n cañería del agua f.

watermark n filigrana f.

water melon n sandía f.

watershed n momento crítico m.

watertight adj impermeable.

waterworks npl depuradora de agua f.

watery adj aguado/da; desvaído/da; lloroso/sa.

watt n vatio m.

wave n ola, onda f; oleada f; señal f; * vi agitar la mano; ondear; * vt agitar.

wavelength n longitud de onda f.

waver vi vacilar, balancear.

wavering adj inconstante.

wavy adj ondulado/da.

wax n cera f; * vt encerar; * vi crecer.

wax paper n papel de cera m.

waxworks n museo de cera m.

way n camino m; vía f; ruta f; modo m; recorrido m; **to give** ~ ceder.

waylay vt salir al paso.

wayward adj caprichoso/sa.

we pn nosotros, nosotras.

weak adj, **~ly** adv débil(mente).

weaken vt debilitar.

weakling n enclenque m/f.

weakness n debilidad f; punto débil m.

weal, wheal n roncha f.

wealth n riqueza f; bienes mpl.

wealthy adj rico/ca.

wean vt destetar.

weapon n arma f.

wear vt gastar, consumir; usar, llevar; * vi consumirse; **to** ~ **away** vt gastar; vi desgastarse; **to** ~ **down** vt gastar; agotar; **to** ~ **off** pasar; **to** ~ **out** desgastar; agotar; * n uso m; desgaste m.

weariness n cansancio m; fatiga f; enfado m.

wearisome adj tedioso/sa.

weary adj cansado/da, fatigado/da; tedioso/sa.

weasel n comadreja f.

weather n tiempo m; **to** ~ **out** vt aguantar, sufrir, superar.

weather-beaten adj curtido/da.

weather cock n gallo de campanario m; veleta f.

weather forecast n boletín meteorológico m.

weave vt tejer; trenzar; (fig) zurcir.

weaving n tejido m.

web n telaraña f; membrana f; red f.

wed vt (vi) casar(se).

wedding n boda f; nupcias fpl; casamiento m.

wedding day n día de la boda m.

wedding dress n traje de novia m.

wedding present n regalo de boda m.

wedding ring n alianza f.

wedge n cuña f; * vt acuñar; apretar.

wedlock n matrimonio m.

Wednesday n miércoles m invar.

wee adj pequeñito/ta.

weed n mala hierba f; * vt escardar.

weedkiller n herbicida m.

weedy adj lleno/na de malas hierbas.

week n semana f; **tomorrow** ~ mañana en una semana; **yesterday** ~ ayer hace ocho días.

weekday n día laborable m.

weekend n fin de semana m.

weekly adj semanal; * adv semanalmente, por semana.

weep vt, vi llorar; lamentar.

weeping willow n sauce llorón f.

weigh vt, vi pesar.

weight n peso m.

weightily adv pesadamente.

weightlifter n levantador/a de pesas m/f.

weighty adj ponderoso/sa; importante.

welcome adj bienvenido/da; ~! ¡bienvenido!; * n bienvenida f; * vt dar la bienvenida a.

weld vt soldar; * n soldadura f.

welfare n prosperidad f; bienestar m; subsidio de paro m.

welfare state n estado del bienestar m.

well n fuente f; manantial m; pozo m; * adj bueno/na, sano/na; * adv bien, felizmente; favorablemente; suficientemente; convenientemente; as ~ as así como, además de, lo mismo que.

well-behaved adj bien educado/da.

wellbeing n felicidad, prosperidad f.

well-bred adj bien criado/da, bien educado/da.

well-built adj fornido/da.

well-deserved adj merecido/da.

well-dressed adj bien vestido/da.

well-known adj conocido/da.

well-mannered adj educado/da.

well-meaning adj bien intencionado/da.

well-off adj acomodado/da.

well-to-do adj acomodado/da.

well-wisher n partidario/ria m/f.

wench n mozuela, cantonera f.

west n oeste, occidente m; * adj occidental; * adv hacia el oeste.

westerly, western adj occidental.

westward adv hacia el oeste.

wet adj húmedo/da, mojado/da; * n humedad f; * vt mojar, hume decer.

wet-nurse n ama de leche f.

whack vt aporrear; * n golpe m.

whale n ballena f.

wharf n muelle m.

what pn que, ¿qué?, el que, la que, lo que; * adj ¿qué?; * excl ¡cómo!

whatever pn cualquier, cualquiera cosa que, lo que sea.

wheat n trigo m.

wheedle vt halagar, engañar con lisonjas, sonsacar.

wheedler n zalamero/ra m/f.

wheel n rueda f; volante m; timón m; * vt (hacer) rodar; volver, girar; * vi rodar.

wheelbarrow n carretilla f.

wheelchair n silla de ruedas f.

wheel clamp n cepo m.

wheeze vi jadear.

when adv ¿cuándo?; mientras que; * conj cuando.

whenever adv cuando; cada vez que.

where adv ¿dónde?; * conj donde;

any~ en cualquier parte; **every~** en todas partes.

whereabout(s) adv ¿dónde?

whereas conj mientras que; pues que, ya que.

whereby pn por lo cual, con lo cual.

whereupon conj con lo cual.

wherever adv dondequiera que.

wherewithal npl recursos mpl.

whet vt excitar.

whether conj si.

which pn qué; lo que; el que, el cual; cuál; * adj ¿qué?; cuyo.

whiff n bocanada de humo f.

while n rato m; vez f; * conj durante; mientras; aunque.

whim n antojo, capricho m.

whimper vi sollozar, gemir.

whimsical adj caprichoso/sa, fantástico/ca.

whine vi llorar, lamentar; * n quejido, lamento m.

whinny vi relinchar.

whip n azote m; látigo m; * vt azotar; batir.

whipped cream n nata montada f.

whirl vt, vi girar; hacer girar; mover(se) rápidamente.

whirlpool n remolino m.

whirlpool bath n hidromasaje m.

whirlwind n torbellino m.

whisky n whisky m.

whisper vi cuchichear; susurrar.

whispering n cuchicheo m; susurro m.

whistle vi silbar; * n silbido m.

white adj blanco/ca, pálido/da; cano/na; puro/ra; * n color blanco m; clara del huevo f.

white elephant n maula f.

white-hot adj incandescente.

white lie n mentirijilla f.

whiten vt, vi blanquear; emblanquecerse.

whiteness n blancura f; palidez f.

whitewash n enlucimiento m; * vt encalar; jalbegar.

whiting n pescadilla f.

whitish adj blanquecino/na.

who pn ¿quién?, que.

whoever pn quienquiera, cualquiera.

whole adj todo/da, total; sano/na, entero/ra; * n total m; conjunto m.

wholehearted adj sincero/ra.

wholemeal adj integral.

wholesale n venta al por mayor f.

wholesome adj sano/na, saludable.

wholly adv enteramente.

whom pn ¿quién?; que.

whooping cough n tos ferina f.

whore n puta f; (fam) zorra f.

why n ¿por qué?; * conj por qué; * excl ¡hombre!

wick n mecha f.

wicked adj malvado/da, perverso/sa; ~ly adv malamente.

wickedness n perversidad, malignidad f.

wicker n mimbre m; * adj tejido/da de mimbre.

wide adj ancho/cha, vasto/ta; grande; ~ly adv muy; far and ~ por todos lados.

wide-awake adj despierto/ta.

widen vt ensanchar, extender.

wide open adj de par en par.

widespread adj extendido/da.

widow n viuda f.

widower n viudo m.

width n anchura f.

wield vt manejar, empuñar.

wife n esposa f; mujer f.

wig n peluca f; tupé m.

wiggle vt menear; * vi menearse.

wild adj silvestre, feroz; desierto/ta; descabellado/da; salvaje.

wilderness n desierto m; yermo m.

wild life n fauna f.

wildly adv violentamente; locamente; desatinadamente.

wilful adj deliberado/da; testarudo/da.

wilfulness n obstinación f.

wiliness n fraude, engaño m.

will n voluntad f; testamento m; * vt querer, desear.

willing adj inclinado/da, dispuesto/ta; ~ly adv de buena gana.

willingness n buena voluntad, buena gana f.

willow n sauce m (árbol).

willpower n fuerza de voluntad f.

wilt vi marchitarse.

wily adj astuto/ta.

win vt ganar, conquistar; alcanzar; lograr.

wince vi encogerse, estremecerse.

winch n torno m.

wind n viento m; aliento m; flatulencia f.

wind vt enrollar; envolver; dar cuerda a; * vi serpentear.

windfall n golpe de suerte m.

wind farm n parque eólico m.

winding adj tortuoso/sa.

windmill n molino de viento m.

window n ventana f.

window box n jardinera de ventana f.

window cleaner n limpiacristales m invar.

window ledge n repisa f.

windowpane n cristal m.

windowsill n repisa f.

windpipe n tráquea f.

windscreen n parabrisas m invar.

windscreen washer n lavaparabrisas m invar.

windscreen wiper n limpiaparabrisas m invar.

windsurfer n windsurfista m/f.

windsurfing n windsurf m.

wind turbine n aerogenerador m.

windy adj de mucho viento.

wine n vino m.

wine cellar n bodega f.

wine glass n copa de vino f.

wine list n carta de vinos f.

wine merchant n vinatero/ra m/f.

wine-tasting n degustación de vinos f.

wing n ala f.

winged adj alado/da.

winger n extremo m.

wink vi guiñar; * n pestañeo m; guiño m.

winner n ganador/a m/f; vencedor/a m/f.

winning post n meta f.

winter n invierno m; * vi invernar.

winter sports npl deportes de invierno mpl.

wintry adj invernal.

wipe vt limpiar; borrar.

wire n alambre m; telegrama m; * vt instalar el alambrado en; conectar.

wiring n alambrado m.

wiry adj delgado/da y fuerte.

wisdom n sabiduría, prudencia f.

wisdom teeth npl muelas del juicio fpl.

wise adj sabio/bia, docto/ta, juicioso/sa, prudente.

wisecrack n broma f.

wish vt querer, desear, anhelar; * n anhelo, deseo m.

wishful adj deseoso/sa.

wisp n mechón m; voluta f.

wistful adj pensativo/va, atento/ta.

wit n entendimiento, ingenio m.

witch n bruja, hechicera f.

witchcraft n brujería f; sortilegio m.

with prep con; por, de, a.

withdraw vt quitar; privar; retirar; * vi retirarse, apartarse.

withdrawal n retirada f.

withdrawn adj reservado/da.

wither vi marchitarse, secarse.

withhold vt detener, impedir, retener.

within prep dentro de, adentro; * adv interiormente; en casa.

without prep sin.

withstand vt resistir.

witless adj necio/cia, tonto/ta, falto/ta de ingenio.

witness n testimonio m; testgo m/f; * vt atestiguar, testificar.

witness stand n estrado de los testigos m.

witticism n ocurrencia f.

wittily adv ingeniosamente.

wittingly adv adrede, de propósito.

witty adj ingenioso/sa, agudo/da, chistoso/sa.

wizard n brujo, hechicero m.

wobble vi tambalearse.

woe n dolor m; miseria f.

woeful adj triste, funesto/ta; **~ly** adv tristemente.

wolf n lobo m; **she ~** loba f.

woman n mujer f.

womanish adj mujeril.

womanly adj mujeril, mujeriego/ga.

womb n útero m.

women's lib n la liberación de la mujer f.

wonder n milagro m; maravilla f; asombro m; * vi maravil larse; preguntarse si.

wonderful adj maravilloso/sa; **~ly** adv maravillosamente.

wondrous adj maravilloso/sa.

won't abrev de **will not**.

wont n uso m; costumbre f.

woo vt cortejar.

wood n bosque m; selva f; madera f; leña f.

wood alcohol n alcohol metílico m.

wood carving n tallado en madera m.

woodcut n estampa de madera f.

woodcutter n leñador/a m/f; grabador en láminas de madera, xilógrafo m/f.

wooded adj arbolado/da.

wooden adj de madera.

wood engraver n xilógrafo m.

wooden shoe n zueco m.

woodland n arbolado m.

woodlouse n cochinilla f.

woodman n cazador m; guardabosque m.

woodpecker n pájaro carpintero m.

woodwind n intrumento de viento de madera m.

woodwork n carpintería f.

woodworm n carcoma f.

wool n lana f.

woollen adj de lana.

woollens npl géneros de lana mpl.

woolly adj lanudo/da, lanoso/sa.

word n palabra f; noticia f; * vt expresar; componer en escri tura.

wordiness n verbosidad f.

wording n redacción f.

word processing n tratamiento de textos m.

word processor n procesador de textos m.

wordy adj verboso/sa.

work vi trabajar; obrar; estar en movimiento o en acción; fermentar; * vt trabajar, labrar; fabricar, manufacturar; to ~ out vi salir bien; * vt resolver; * n trabajo m; fábrica f; obra f; empleo m.

workable adj práctico/ca.

workaholic n trabajador obsesivo m, trabajadora obsesiva f.

worker n trabajador/a m/f; obrero/ra m/f.

workforce n mano de obra f.

working-class adj obrero/ra, de clase trabajadora.

workman n labrador m.

workmanship n manufactura f; destreza del artífice f.

workmate n compañero/ra de trabajo m/f.

workshop n taller, obrador m.

world n mundo m; * adj del mundo; mundial.

worldliness n mundanería f.

worldly adj mundano/na, terreno/na.

worldwide adj mundial.

worm n gusano m; (of a screw) rosca de tornillo f.

worn-out adj gastado/da; rendido/da.

worried adj preocupado/da.

worry vt preocupar; * n preocupación f; pensión f.

worrying adj inquietante.

worse adj, adv peor; ~ and ~ cada vez peor; * n lo peor.

worship n culto m; adoración f; your ~ su señoría; * vt adorar, venerar.

worst adj el/la peor; * adv peor; * n lo peor m.

worth n valor, precio m; mérito m.

worthily adv dignamente, convenientemente.

worthless adj sin valor; inútil.

worthwhile adj que vale la pena; valioso/sa.

worthy adj digno/na; respetable; honesto/ta.

would-be adj aspirante.

wound n herida, llaga f; * vt herir, llagar.

wrangle vi reñir; * n riña f.

wrap vt envolver.

wrath n ira, rabia, cólera f.

wreath n corona, guirnalda f.

wreck n naufragio m; ruina f; destrucción f; navío naufragado m; * vt naufragar; arruinar.

wreckage n restos mpl; escombros mpl.

wren n chochín m.

wrench vt arrancar; dislocar; torcer; * n llave inglesa f; tirón m.

wrest vt arrancar, arrebatar.

wrestle vi luchar; disputar.

wrestling n lucha f.

wretched adj infeliz, miserable.

wriggle vi menearse, agitarse.

wring vt torcer; arrancar; estrujar.

wrinkle n arruga f; * vt arrugar; * vi arrugarse.

wrist n muñeca f.

wristband n puño de camisa m.

wristwatch n reloj de pulsera m.

writ n escrito m; escritura f; orden f.

write vt escribir; componer; to ~ down apuntar; to ~ off borrar; desechar; to ~ up redactar.

write-off n pérdida total f.

writer n escritor/a, m/f; autor/a m/f.

writhe vi retorcerse.

writing n escritura f; letra f; obras fpl; escrito m.

writing desk n escritorio m.

writing paper n papel para escribir m.

wrong n injuria f; injusticia f; perjuicio m; error m; * adj malo/la; injusto/ta; equivocado/da, inoportuno/na; falso/sa; * adv mal, equivocadamente; * vt agraviar, injuriar.

wrongful adj injusto/ta.

wrongly adv injustamente.

wry adj irónico/ca.

X

xenophobia n xenofobia f.

Xmas n Navidad f.

X-ray n radiografía f.

xylographer n xilógrafo m.

xylophone n xilófano m.

Y

yacht n yate m.

yachting n vela f.

Yankee n yanqui m/f.

yard n corral m; yarda f.

yardstick n criterio m.

yarn n estambre m; hilo de lino m.

yawn vi bostezar; * n bostezo m.

yawning adj muy abierto/ta.

yeah adv sí.

year n año m.

yearbook n anuario m.

yearling n añal m.

yearly adj anual; * adv anualmente, todos los años.

yearn vi añorar.

yearning n añoranza f.

yeast n levadura f.

yell vi aullar; * n aullido m.

yellow adj amarillo/lla; * n amarillo m.

yellowish adj amarillento/ta.

yelp vi latir, gañir; * n aullido m.

yes adv sí; * n sí m.

yesterday adv ayer; * n ayer m.

yet conj sin embargo; pero; * adv todavía.

yew n tejo m.

yield vt dar, producir; rendir; * vi rendirse; ceder el paso; * n producción f; cosecha f; rendimiento m.

yoga n yoga m.

yoghurt n yogur m.

yoke n yugo m; (of oxen) yunta f.

yolk n yema (de huevo) f.

yonder adv allá.

you pn vosotros/tras, tú, usted, ustedes.

young adj joven, mozo/za; ~**er** adj menor.

youngster n jovencito/ta m/f; joven m/f.

your(s) pn tuyo, tuya, vuestro, vuestra, suyo, suya.

yourself pn tú mismo, tú misma, usted mismo, usted misma.

yourselves pn pl vosotros mismos, vosotras mismas, ustedes mismos, ustedes mismas.

youth n juventud, adolescencia f; jo ven m/f.

youthful adj juvenil.

youthfulness n juventud f.

yuppie adj, n yupi m/f.

Z

zany adj estrafalario/ria.

zap vt borrar.

zeal n celo m; ardor m.

zealous adj celoso/sa.

zebra n cebra f.

zenith n cénit m.

zero n zero, cero m.

zest n ánimo m.

zigzag n zigzag m; * adj zigzag; * vi zigzaguear.

zinc n zinc m.

zip n cremallera f; cierre m.

zodiac n zodíaco m.

zone n banda, faja f; zona f.

zoo n zoo, zoológico m.

zoological adj zoológico/ca.

zoologist n zóologo/ga m/f.

zoology n zoología f.

zoom vi zumbar.

zoom lens n zoom m.

Verbs

Verbos Irregulares en Ingles

Infinitivo	Pretérito	Participio de pasado
arise	arose	arisen
awake	awoke	awaked, awoken
be [I am, you/we/they are, he/she/it is, gerundio being]		
	was, were	been
bear	bore	borne
beat	beat	beaten
become	became	become
begin	began	begun
behold	beheld	beheld
bend	bent	bent
beseech	besought, beseeched	besought, beseeched
beset	beset	beset
bet	bet, betted	bet, betted
bid	bade, bid	bade, bid, bidden
bite	bit	bitten
bleed	bled	bled
bless	blessed	blessed, blest
blow	blew	blown
break	broke	broken
breed	bred	bred
bring	brought	brought
build	built	built
burn	burnt, burned	burnt, burned
burst	burst	burst
buy	bought	bought
can	could	(been able)
cast	cast	cast
catch	caught	caught
choose	chose	chosen
cling	clung	clung
come	came	come
cost	cost	cost
creep	crept	crept
cut	cut	cut
deal	dealt	dealt
dig	dug	dug
do [he/she/it does]	did	done

Infinitivo	Pretérito	Participio de pasado
draw	drew	drawn
dream	dreamed, dreamt	dreamed, dreamt
drink	drank	drunk
drive	drove	driven
dwell	dwelt, dwelled	dwelt, dwelled
eat	ate	eaten
fall	fell	fallen
feed	fed	fed
feel	felt	felt
fight	fought	fought
find	found	found
flee	fled	fled
fling	flung	flung
fly [he/she/it flies]	flew	flown
forbid	forbade	forbidden
forecast	forecast	forecast
forget	forgot	forgotten
forgive	forgave	forgiven
forsake	forsook	forsaken
forsee	foresaw	foreseen
freeze	froze	frozen
get	got	got, gotten
give	gave	given
go [he/she/it goes]	went	gone
grind	ground	ground
grow	grew	grown
hang	hung, hanged	hung, hanged
have [I/you/we/they have, he/she/it has, *gerundio* having]	had	had
hear	heard	heard
hide	hid	hidden
hit	hit	hit
hold	held	held
hurt	hurt	hurt
keep	kept	kept
kneel	knelt, kneeled	knelt, kneeled
know	knew	known
lay	laid	laid
lead	led	led
lean	leant, leaned	leant, leaned

Infinitivo	*Pretérito*	*Participio de pasado*
leap	leapt, leaped	leapt, leaped
learn	learnt, learned	learnt, learned
leave	left	left
lend	lent	lent
let	let	let
lie [*gerundio* lying]	lay	lain
light	lighted, lit	lighted, lit
lose	lost	lost
make	made	made
may	might	–
mean	meant	meant
meet	met	met
mistake	mistook	mistaken
mow	mowed	mowed, mown
must	(had to)	(had to)
overcome	overcame	overcome
pay	paid	paid
put	put	put
quit	quit, quitted	quit, quitted
read	read	read
rid	rid	rid
ride	rode	ridden
ring	rang	rung
rise	rose	risen
run	ran	run
saw	sawed	sawn
say	said	said
see	saw	seen
seek	sought	sought
sell	sold	sold
send	sent	sent
set	set	set
sew	sewed	sewn
shake	shook	shaken
shall	should	–
shear	sheared	sheared, shorn
shed	shed	shed
shine	shone	shone
shoot	shot	shot
show	showed	shown, showed

Infinitivo	*Pretérito*	*Participio de pasado*
shrink	shrank	shrunk
shut	shut	shut
sing	sang	sung
sink	sank	sunk
sit	sat	sat
slay	slew	slain
sleep	slept	slept
slide	slid	slid
sling	slung	slung
smell	smelt, smelled	smelt, smelled
sow	sowed	sown, sowed
speak	spoke	spoken
speed	sped, speeded	sped, speeded
spell	spelt, spelled	spelt, spelled
spend	spent	spent
spill	spilt, spilled	spilt, spilled
spin	spun	spun
spit	spat	spat
split	split	split
spoil	spoilt, spoiled	spoilt, spoiled
spread	spread	spread
spring	sprang	sprung
stand	stood	stood
steal	stole	stolen
stick	stuck	stuck
sting	stung	stung
stink	stank	stunk
stride	strode	stridden
strike	struck	struck
strive	strove	striven
swear	swore	sworn
sweep	swept	swept
swell	swelled	swelled, swollen
swim	swam	swum
swing	swung	swung
take	took	taken
teach	taught	taught
tear	tore	torn
tell	told	told
think	thought	thought

Infinitivo	*Pretérito*	*Participio de pasado*
throw	threw	thrown
thrust	thrust	thrust
tread	trod	trodden
understand	understood	understood
upset	upset	upset
wake	woke	woken
wear	wore	worn
weave	wove, weaved	woven, weaved
wed	wed, wedded	wed, wedded
weep	wept	wept
win	won	won
wind	wound	wound
withdraw	withdrew	withdrawn
withhold	withheld	withheld
withstand	withstood	withstood
wring	wrung	wrung
write	wrote	written

Spanish Verbs

Regular

	comprar *to buy*	temer *to fear*	partir *to divide*
Gerund	comprando	temiendo	partiendo
Part participle	comprado	temido	partido
Present indicative	compro	temo	parto
	compras	temes	partes
	compra	teme	parte
	compramos	tememos	partimos
	compráis	teméis	partís
	compran	temen	parten
Imperfect indicative	compraba	temía	partía
	comprabas	temías	partías
	compraba	temía	partía
	comprábamos	temíamos	partíamos
	comprabais	temíais	partíais
	compraban	temían	partían
Past absolute *(or preterit)*	compré	temí	partí
	compraste	temiste	partiste
	compró	temió	partió
	compramos	temimos	partimos
	comprasteis	temisteis	partisteis
	compraron	temieron	partieron
Future	compraré	temeré	partiré
	comprarás	temerás	partirás
	comprará	temerá	partirá
	compraremos	temeremos	partiremos
	compraréis	temeréis	partiréis
	comprarán	temerán	partirán

Conditional	compraría	temería	partiría
	comprarías	temerías	partirías
	compraría	temería	partiría
	compraríamos	temeríamos	partiríamos
	compraríais	temeríais	partiríais
	comprarían	temerían	partirían
Imperative	compra	teme	parte
	compre	tema	parta
	compremos	temamos	partamos
	comprad	temed	partid
	compren	teman	partan
Present subjunctive	compre	tema	parta
	compres	temas	partas
	compre	tema	parta
	compreemos	temamos	partamos
	compreéis	temáis	partáis
	compren	teman	partan
Imperfect subjunctive	comprara	temiera	partiera
	ase	iese	iese
	compraras	temieras	partieras
	ases	ieses	ieses
	comprara	temiera	partiera
	ase	iese	iese
	compráramos	temiéramos	partiéramos
	ásemos	iésemos	iésemos
	comprarais	temierais	partierais
	aseis	ieseis	ieseis
	compraran	temieran	partieran
	asen	iesen	iesen

Auxiliary Verbs

Infinitive	haber	ser	tener	estar
	to have	*to be*	*to have*	*to be*
Gerund	habiendo	siendo	teniendo	estando
Part participle	habido	sido	tenido	estado
Present indicative	he	soy	tengo	estoy
	has	eres	tienes	estás
	ha	es	tiene	está
	hemos	somos	tenemos	estamos
	habéis	sois	tenéis	estáis
	han	son	tienen	están
Imperfect indicative	había	era	tenía	estaba
	habías	eras	tenías	estabas
	había	era	tenía	estaba
	habíamos	éramos	teníamos	estábamos
	habíais	erais	teníais	estabais
	habían	eran	tenían	estaban
Past absolute	hube	fui	tuve	estuve
(or preterit)	hubiste	fuiste	tuviste	estuviste
	hubo	fue	tuvo	estuvo
	hubimos	fuimos	tuvimos	estuvimos
	hubisteis	fuisteis	tuvisteis	estuvisteis
	hubieron	fueron	tuvieron	estuvieron
Future	habré	seré	tendré	estaré
	habrás	serás	tendrás	estarás
	habrá	será	tendrá	estará
	habremos	seremos	tendremos	estaremos
	habréis	seréis	tendréis	estaréis
	habrán	serán	tendrán	estarán

Conditional	habría	sería	tendría	estaría
	habrías	serías	tendrías	estarías
	habría	sería	tendría	estaría
	habríamos	seríamos	tendríamos	estaríamos
	habríais	seríais	tendríais	estaríais
	habrían	serían	tendrían	estarían

Imperative	–	sé(tu)	ten(tu)	está(tu)

Present subjunctive	haya	sea	tenga	esté
	hayas	seas	tengas	estés
	haya	sea	tenga	esté
	hayamos	seamos	tengamos	estémos
	hayáis	seáis	tengáis	estéis
	hayan	sean	tengan	estén

Imperfect subjunctive	hubiera	fuera	tuviera	estuviera
	iese	ese	iese	iese
	hubieras	fueras	tuvieras	estuvieras
	ieses	eses	ieses	ieses
	hubiera	fuera	tuviera	estuviera
	iese	ese	iese	iese
	hubiéramos	fuéramos	tuviéramos	estuviéramos
	iésemos	ésemos	iésemos	iésemos
	hubierais	fuerais	tuvierais	estuvierais
	ieseis	eseis	ieseis	ieseis
	hubieran	fueran	tuvieran	estuvieran
	iesen	esen	iesen	iesen